THE DIRECTORY OF
British Engine Sheds
and Principal Locomotive Servicing Points: 1
Southern England, the Midlands, East Anglia and Wales

Roger Griffiths & Paul Smith

Ex-LMS 0-6-0 locomotives Nos 43754 and 58071 at **Tewkesbury** shed (SO8932.1/1A) on August 20th, 1955.
WA Potter

OPC

Oxford Publishing Co

CONTENTS

Artwork and Design by **Paul Smith**

All shed maps reproduced by kind permission
of
The Syndics of Cambridge University

Upper front cover: **Penzance** shed is seen about 1961, with No.5003 *Lulworth Castle*, an unidentified Class 4500 2-6-2T and, representing the New Order No.D858 *Valorous*. This 1914 Churchward design shed closed to steam a year later but continued servicing diesels for several more years.
Collection: Brian Arman

Lower front and back covers: The LSWR shed at **Salisbury** was re-roofed by the Southern Region in 1954 with a standard corrugated iron louvre pitched style over each track.   *Ivo peters*

Back cover, top: The **East Moors** 6TS shed (ST1975.2/1A) of the Marquis of Bute Railways – later Cardiff Railway – origins was rarely photographed. This brick and timber structure was opened in 1881 to replace the 1862 MofBR shed (ST1875.2/1A) at Tyndall Street. East Moors closed in March 1926 as part of a GWR rationalization scheme and is shown here some four years prior to closure.   *Author's Collection*

Back cover, centre left: Opened in 1882 by the Lynn & Fakenham Railway, the works and shed at **Melton Constable** became the main centre for the Midland & Great Northern Railway.
H Garrett Collection

Back cover, centre right: The former Plymouth, Devonport & South Western Junction Railway's shed at **Callington** is seen here about 1963, with 2-6-2T No. 41206 the solitary resident.
Collection: Brian Arman

Ex-GWR Class 5100 2-6-2T No.4117 about to run round its train at **Moretonhampstead** on February 28th, 1959, two days before the official closure of the branch to passenger traffic. In the background can be seen the engine shed (SX7585.1/1A) which despite closure in 1947 remained in use for locomotive servicing and still stood in 1998, in use as a garage for a commercial transport company.
T. Nicholls

First published 1999

ISBN 0 86093 542 6

Published by Oxford Publishing Co

an imprint of Ian Allan Publishing Ltd, Terminal House, Shepperton, Surrey TW17 8AS.

Printed by Ian Allan Printing Ltd, Riverdene Business Park, Hersham, Surrey KT12 4RG.

Code: 9910/A2

THE DIRECTORY OF •
BRITISH ENGINE SHEDS
AND PRINCIPAL LOCOMOTIVE SERVICING POINTS

VOLUME ONE
PREFACE

1825

1968

This work is the result of over thirty years of interest in steam locomotive sheds. Those wonderfully atmospheric places are, alas, no longer with us in Britain, save for the railway preservation groups that have tried to recapture that unique, totally sensory, experience with a few achieving some measure of success. *The Directory of British Engine Sheds* is an attempt at recording the existence and passage of something that was once intrinsic to life in almost every one of the country's cities and towns - in fact to almost every conurbation of any size.

The authors' involvement with locomotive depots, as they were also known, began in the heady days of British Railways in the 1950s and 1960s whilst taking part in those marathon "shed bashes" that were so much part of the scene. It was while travelling the length and breadth of the British Isles that many other buildings were noted, which had at one time patently been employed as engine sheds, but were no longer serving such a purpose - or so it seemed! Being intensely curious and usually outrageous with the laws of trespass, entrance was gained to many of those old sheds, to twice be rewarded by the spectre of engines. Alas those particular locomotives days were done, as they had been withdrawn and stored pending the final journey to oblivion.

But the appetite was whetted and with the dwindling number of steam locomotives to be seen, interest in the old sheds began to increase. The authors' first purchase of the *Ian Allan Locoshed Book*, in the early summer of 1954 was a revelation. The engine sheds of the six regions of British Railways were listed at the front of the book and totalled some 660 locations, at which the 18,000 or so locomotives were housed. With the end of steam, the "project" more or less came about without conscious thought *(had we known what we were letting ourselves in for, we may have taken up a different hobby!)*. We set ourselves the task of identifying every engine shed used by the passenger carrying railways of England, Wales, Scotland and the Isle of Wight, between the years of 1825 and 1968. In addition, and being gluttons for punishment, we began the equally absorbing task of obtaining an illustration of some kind and maps of as many of these sheds as possible.

Thus, for more than a quarter of a century now, it has been our pleasant experience to come into contact with innumerable individuals, societies and British Railways offices and also to be involved with Britain's matchless libraries, records offices and museums. We would particularly like to place on record our thanks to Shirley Smith for her assistance and wholehearted endeavours in researching

the maps on our many treks to Cambridge University Map Library. These sources have invariably been generous with their time and effort on our behalf and it is only with their aid that we have today reached a total of over 2200 engine shed locations. Here it should be said that included in the list are the sheds of passenger carrying narrow gauge lines and Light Railways and also a considerable number of sites that, as far as is known, never had an engine shed building as such. Those "Stabling Points", as they are termed, are included where it is known that locomotives were allocated there, if perhaps only on a weekly basis and/or where the footplatemen booked on and off duty.

With such a vast amount of research, going back over the sometimes incomplete records of 143 years, errors are bound to have occurred. These are the authors' own and we would greatly appreciate any help, comments and corrections from readers via the publishers. All letters will be answered as quickly as possible. Finally for like-minded enthusiasts, indeed for anyone who wishes to find out more about engine sheds, the authors can strongly recommend membership of *The Engine Shed Society* and study of the society's quarterly magazine *Link*. For details of membership please contact the publishers.

Roger Griffiths, Cotham, Bristol
Paul Smith, Kings Heath, Birmingham

DOVER PRIORY (TR3141.1/1A) 1888

BASIC BUILDING DESIGN

Contemporary engravings reveal that in the early days engine sheds were often built in a decorative style in keeping with the architecture employed at the railway stations, no doubt reflecting the pride with which the companies viewed the technical marvels which were housed within them. Pictorial records of these buildings are scarce but it is quite obvious that as the railways quickly grew they became more functional and the designs of all sheds were eventually based on one of three different configurations;

STRAIGHT SHED; As the name implies the building was straight (or in very rare instances slightly curved) and covered one or a multiple of tracks. It was either dead ended or the lines passed right through the shed, or a combination of both.

ROUNDHOUSE; In early days the loco was detached from the tender and "stabled" around the turntable on short spurs. In general the buildings were circular in shape with a conical (qv) self supporting roof. As the turntables and spurs became longer in order to accommodate larger engines square buildings with multi-pitched roofs were proven to be more suitable. *Barrow Hill*, a classic example of a Midland Railway square roundhouse, has been preserved.

SEMI-ROUNDHOUSE; Although popular on the continent, this style of design with a semi-circular building housing tracks radiating from an outside turntable was not utilized to a great extent in Britain. *Nine Elms* and *Kings Cross* were famous examples of this sort of building on the grand scale whilst *St. Blazey* has been preserved, albeit as industrial units.

The other major characteristic of the building was the design of the roof and to assist the reader an illustrated summary of the basic designs which are recorded in this directory are shown:

PITCHED

As would be expected this basic design was the most popular type of roof construction, both in single and multiple forms and almost without exception a gable end was employed, generally in the medium used to build the walls.

The ITS shed at **Abingdon** (SU5097.1/1A) is a typical example of this style of construction in a single pitch. In this instance the roof has the luxury of a raised vent along the apex.

B Matthews Collection

HIPPED

Of all the railway companies, the L&NWR in particular adopted this design as the standard method of roof construction at their larger depots. Odd examples turned up on other lines, such as *Annfield Plain (NZ1651.1/1A)* on the NER but they were almost all exclusively to be found within the LMS system.

The L&NWR employed this particular design to a greater extent than any other company, more often in multiples such as the vast sheds at Crewe and the more modest structures such as seen here at **Craven Arms** (SO4383.1/1C) in 1957. *RS Carpenter*

NORTHLIGHT PATTERN

This design could be found throughout Britain, varying from 2TS engine sheds to the very largest. They were usually constructed in multiple pitches with one face in slate and the other, facing north, in glass. At some locations, the disposition of the building was sometimes west-east but in both instances the objective was to give a good working light without glare from the sun. The roof was generally built with the pitches at right angles to the sides but in some instances, notably at *Stewarts Lane (TQ2976.1/1C)* the shed was rebuilt with a transverse northlight pattern roof. *(Some depots were built with a sawtooth style of roof which, in view of the similarity of design have been described in this book as having northlight pattern roofs.)*

Abergavenny (L&NWR) shed (SO2914.1/1A & 2A), viewed here in 1935, was a typical example of its utilization on larger buildings. *Author's Collection*

DUTCH BARN

A simple curved roof in the style, as the name would imply, of a barn. Not a common design and all, as far as we know, constructed in corrugated iron. Generally employed as a single span, a double version of a bizarre style was used at *Fackenham West (TF9129.1/1A)* and the only example found to date of a transverse structure was that at *Bournemouth Central (SZ0992.1/1A)*.

The second shed at **Whitland** (SN1916.1/1B) was originally built in timber with a corrugated iron roof and as such was one of the very few examples of this style to be found on the GWR network.
Author's Collection

LEAN-TO

Used mainly as a simple extension to existing facilities, as at *Slough (SU9780.2/2A)*. Instances of the shed itself being of a lean-to structure are not common. *Trawsfynydd (SH7135.1/1A)* is the only known example, certainly amongst those depots surviving into BR days.

Slough shed (SU9780.2/1B) on September 25th, 1963 with the lean-to extension (SU9780.2/2A) in view on the left of the building.
WT Stubbs Collection

CONICAL

Employed in the construction of the first generation of roundhouses, the smaller examples would have been almost self supporting but larger roofs were supported by props. A preserved example, although no longer in railway use is found at *Camden (TQ2884.1/1B)*.

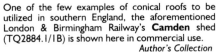

One of the few examples of conical roofs to be utilized in southern England, the aforementioned London & Birmingham Railway's **Camden** shed (TQ2884.1/1B) is shown here in commercial use.
Author's Collection

FLAT

This design was most commonly employed by British Railways during the construction of the last generation of steam sheds. Those built in the 1950s took into account that dieselization was imminent and embraced the designs of the new generation of depots under the assumption that they would house and maintain the new locomotives. They were usually constructed in concrete with glazed panels to maximize natural light.

Ipswich shed (TM1643.1/2C) was totally rebuilt in 1954 and was typical of the style of depot that BR were building during the transition stage from steam to diesel.
NE Preedy

LOUVRE

This was an LMS design and featured a series of shallow pitches supported on cross beams. Many of the depots rebuilt in BR days adopted this style, one of the features of which was a brick screen at each end. Both the SR and LMS had distinctive designs for these screens. The SR version, which was also utilized on the Southern Region during BR days, had diagonal corners (as at *Templecombe ST7022.2/1C*) whilst the LMS utilized a plain brick wall on top of a long concrete lintel (as at *Camden TQ2884.2/1B*).

An elevated view of the **Stratford** *"Jubilee"* shed (TQ3884.2/1E) showing the shallow pitched roof and LMS-style brick screen typical of this form of construction.
Author's Collection

TANK SHED

The basic design of these consisted of a 1TS building surmounted by a water tank and they were not usually considered as sheds in themselves but as locomotive servicing areas offering covered accommodation to both locomotives and crews as required. However some sheds proper were constructed with this configuration, GWR structures at *Bath (ST7464.1/1A)* and *Glyn Neath (SN8605.1/1A)* and an LNWR 2TS depot at *Market Harborough (SP7487.1/1A)* being better known examples.

Glyn Neath shed is shown here in its final form with the single pitched extension (SN8605.2/1A) having been built at the eastern end of the tank shed (SN8605.1/1A) in 1937.   *Authors Collection*

ACKNOWLEDGEMENTS

Amongst the individuals who have given invaluable assistance in the accumulation of information for this volume, may we thank:
Chris Bush, Sid Nash, Ray Smith, Philip Stuart, Maurice Newman, Maurice Wilson, Eric Hannan,   John Watling, Allan Somerfield, Graham Kenworthy, Harold James, Barry Kitts, Eddie Lyons, PJ Fry, Lawrence Waters, John Hooper, Paul Davidson at Barnstaple Library, David Lee of the Southwold Railway Society and John Williams.

We would particularly like to thank Tony Rawlings, Anne Taylor, Karen Amies and Karen Murkin at Cambridge University Map Library.

And, sadly no longer with us, we acknowledge the help and/or photographic artistry of Peter Winding, Ron Dyer, HC Casserley and the doyen shed fan of them all, WA (Bill) Camwell. It was a privilege and pleasure to have known each of them.

PLEASE NOTE

Since preparing the pages for this volume, and mainly due to the researches of *Ray Smith*, much additional information has come to light. Some of it has been assimilated into the main body of this book but where this has proved to be impossible it has been incorporated into the **Addenda** on Page xiii.

*Please note that any additional sites are indicated on the County maps by means of ** and do not appear in the Index.*

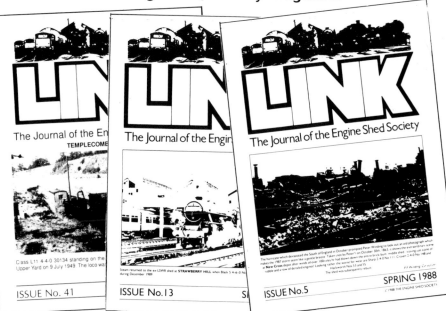

NOTES ON THE USE OF THIS BOOK

THE INDEXING SYSTEM

With any listing that is "fluid", with changes and amendments likely at any time, it is helpful that a system able to embrace them is employed. Alphabetical and numerical sequences were considered and discarded but one based on locations was found to possess the greatest flexibility.

Using the National Grid and dividing the country into 1km squares enables each site and building to be allocated a unique index number. The method of creating this number is demonstrated here;

Example: **BUSHBURY**

a) The OS square in which it is found - SJ9101

b) The general site area - *On the east side of the line, at Bushbury Junction, north of Wolverhampton High Level Station - SJ9101.1*

(Other sites within the OS square would be numbered 2,3,4 and so on)

c) The foundations of the shed building - SJ9101.1/1

(Other foundations on the site would be numbered 2,3,4 and so on)

d) The building on those foundations is given a letter, yielding a unique index number for the shed - SJ9101.1/1A

Shed extensions may, depending upon circumstances, be considered either as an additional building appended to the original (and thus given its own "foundations" number) or simply as a rebuilt building and given a new "building" letter. An anomoly in this area is where a new building has been appended, which under normal conditions would justify the allocation of a "foundations" number, and then both the "new" and "original" buildings are demolished and replaced by another building which embraces both foundations. In this instance all are considered to be on one set of foundations and allocated "building" letters

Although the letter part of the code is generally in chronological order (as the building is modified or re-roofed subsequent letters B,C etc are applied) it is not hard and fast. The situation could easily arise in which earlier buildings or rebuilds on the foundations are subsequently discovered and these would simply be allocated further letters in the sequence as they come to light. Once a code number is established then this remains unchanged.

There are, of course, situations where the details regarding a shed are very obscure, particularly with early depots and temporary sheds and these, in some instances, are given "holding codes". In locations of intense railway development the general site code of "0"; *"In the vicinity of ..."* is given. This counters the problem that one of these sheds may have occupied the same site as later buildings in which case it would have been allocated one of the specific site codes. The "holding code" is thus given until research confirms the true site.

Similarly, in other locations where the exact site is not known but it is the only known shed in the area it is quite conceivable to allocate a "final" code, eg. 1: *"In the vicinity of ..."*, with the true site possibly being clarified at a later date.

Anomalies occur with this system where the grid line passes through the, shed site. *Shrewsbury Coleham* is a case in point but the basic rules, as detailed above, are still applied although the general site is given a "twin" coding (eg Coleham SJ4911.1 & SJ5011.1). In other instances the grid line passes through the shed itself (*Belle Vue* actually has two) and it is purely arbitrary as to which square the site is allocated.

MAPS AND DESCRIPTIVE ANALYSIS

As the simplest and most understandable method of dividing up the areas the country has been split into counties.

Preceding each county section is a map showing the location of each site within that county. Conurbations are dealt with similarly but Greater London with, in some areas, a great concentration of shed sites has been further sub-divided into 10km National Grid squares.

Although it is preferable it has not been possible to arrange each site in alphabetical order within each section. In order to accommodate all the sites within an economically viable set of books a "best-fit" approach has had to be undertaken in order to save space. For this reason the Index at the end of this volume should be consulted.

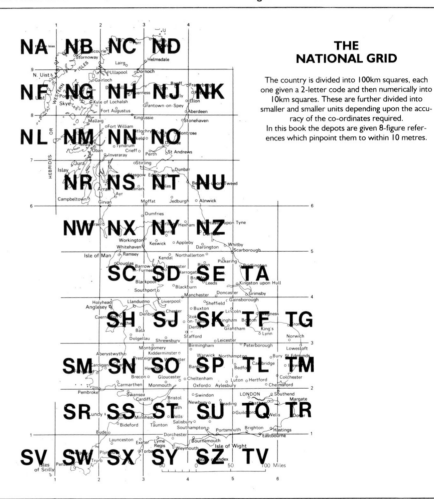

THE NATIONAL GRID

The country is divided into 100km squares, each one given a 2-letter code and then numerically into 10km squares. These are further divided into smaller and smaller units depending upon the accuracy of the co-ordinates required.
In this book the depots are given 8-figure references which pinpoint them to within 10 metres.

There are a considerable number of instances where shed sites have not appeared on OS maps. As discussed previously the very early depots pre-dated the first surveys but there are numerous examples of 20th century sites not being mapped either. These are typically those that were opened in the early years of the century and closed prior to 1960, or only existed for a short period of time and were located in rural areas which did not require frequent surveys. In these instances track, as well as buildings, may be superimposed as a general guide to the layout.

Furthermore other rural areas were not drawn up to 25in scale and only 6in maps are available (eg. *Hawes Junction, Rosedale*). These have been enlarged to 17.5in:1mile

The basic information given for each shed is;
The code (*qv*), site location with National Grid reference to 8 figures, originating company, opening and closing dates, description of building(s) and facilities available.

Each shed with a known site is accompanied by a map. These are based upon the Ordnance Survey 25in series and are reproduced at a scale of 17.5in:1mile. Where possible the map is contemporary to the sheds existence, otherwise the site is superimposed upon it. Unfortunately the reproduction quality on some of the extracts is not as high as we would like but has nonetheless been included as too invaluable to omit.

Excessive use of abbreviations and footnotes has been avoided as it is felt that this destroys the flow of the narrative and hinders the assimilation of information. Although it is assumed that the reader is well aware of the abbreviations of the major companies a short appendix has been added whilst those initials of the more obscure companies are expanded upon in the general information on each depot. It is only necessary, therefore, to acquaint the reader with the terms "TS" which is shorthand for track straighthouse and "RH" for roundhouse.

THE DIRECTORY OF
• BRITISH ENGINE SHEDS •
AND PRINCIPAL LOCOMOTIVE SERVICING POINTS

Track Diagrams are scaled at 17.5in/mile

0 FEET   500

VOLUME ONE
SOUTHERN ENGLAND, THE MIDLANDS,
EAST ANGLIA & WALES

Opened by the 3ft 6in gauge East Cornwall Mineral Railway in 1872, the shed stood at the summit of the Calstock Incline. The ECMR was taken over by the Plymouth, Devonport & South Western Junction Railway in 1894 with the new owners converting the line to standard gauge in 1908.

Calstock Shed (SX4269.1/1A) closed at that time but continued to stand for many years after, it is seen here in about 1930, complete with remains of a water tank support. *H Garrett Collection*

(See Page 10)

This view of an S&DJR 0-4-4T traversing the east to north side of the triangle at **Wimborne Junction** offers a rare glimpse of the two sheds sited there from about 1863. One building was of one road (SZ0198.1/1A), the other of two (SZ0198.1/2A), but the actual date(s) of opening are not yet clear. Both buildings were removed in 1909, to be replaced by a building utilizing the tracks and pits of the first 2TS structure. Wimborne Junction's third shed (SZ0198.1/2B) not yet clearly depicted in any known photograph, closed in 1923.

Author's Collection

(See Page 17)

A superbly atmospheric c1890 picture of the Lynton-Minehead stagecoach leads the eye to a side view of **Minehead**'s engine shed (SS9746.1/1A), which readers will recall had originally stood at Watchet from 1862 to 1874 *(as ST0743.1/1A)*. This particular scene is valuable in that it shows the original square water tank, which would later be replaced by one of the familiar GWR conical-topped "parachute" tanks. *Cty Garath Bewes*

(See Page 22)

A GWR broad gauge branch line reached **Radstock** in 1854, with the stone-built shed being provided at the then terminus. Seen here in the 1930s (as ST6954.1/1B), the building was extended around 1866 and served until closure in 1929. Afterwards the shed served as part of the wagon works (seen at rear) until that too closed in 1988.

In 1999 the engine shed housed a tank engine imported from Poland, as the nucleus of an attempt by local enthusiasts to preserve at least part of the line from Frome as a tourist attraction.   *J Peden*

(See Page 23)

The West Somerset Mineral Railway had a chequered career, opening in 1857, closing in 1898, only to re-open again in 1907 and finally close in 1910.

The stone building at **Watchet** (ST0643.1/1A) visible behind the GWR 2-4-0 (decorated with the flag of Australia it is said, because the engine was trialling a new braking system of Australian design), doubtless dated from 1857, with possible later additions in wood and stone. The shed stood for many years after closure, at the foot of an incline leading up into the Brendon Hills.

H Garrett Collection

(See Page 24)

The West Somerset Railway between 1862 and 1874 terminated at **Watchet**. This 1870 picture shows Watchet's broad gauge wooden engine shed (ST0743.1/1A), four years before it was dismantled and re-erected at the new terminus at Minehead (as ST9746.1/1A).   *Bernard Matthews*

(See Page 24)

Two sheds were provided at **Ascot**. The first (SU9268.1/1A) stood by the station between 1856 and 1889, being replaced by a second building (SU9168.1/1A) beside the line to Aldershot. That timber building served until closure in 1937 but remained standing for many years afterwards. This picture dates from June 25th, 1969, just three months before demolition.   *Ray Ruffell*

(See Page 38)

GWR trains had been serving **Chippenham** for about 17 years before an engine shed was provided for the town. That 3TS stone and timber broad gauge building (ST9274.1/1A) would thereafter serve until closure in 1964 and subsequent removal. It is seen here about two years prior to closure and in 1999 the shed floor and filled-in pits could still be discerned.   *Terry Nicholls*

(See Page 43)

When opened by the Sittingbourne & Sheerness Railway in 1860, **Sheerness Dockyard** shed was of one road (TQ9174.1/1A). Lengthening and addition of a second road was effected around 1885, the depot *(as TQ9174.1/1B)* thereafter serving until 1915. However, as an emergency measure, it was reopened for a year during 1922/23, with final removal in 1930. This somewhat imperfect view dates from around 1905.   *Bernard Matthews*

(See Page 66)

The East Kent Light Railway opened in 1912 and provided itself with a fairly basic 2TS shed and facilities (TR2548.1/1A) at **Shepherds Well** to house the motley collection of second-hand locomotives. Some of those engines are seen in this view of the shed, dating from around 1930. Closure came in 1948.   *Ian Allan Library*

(See Page 67)

When the Southern Railway closed the 3TS 1851 shed (TQ8109.1/1A) at **Hastings** in 1929 to accommodate station enlargements, facilities had to be maintained for local pilot and visiting locomotives. This was achieved by siting an engine servicing and stabling point (TQ8109.2/F1) near the eastern portal of Bo Peep Tunnel.

The facility's turntable, coal stage and one water point are seen here a few years after opening. They served until dieselization of (most) of the remaining steam-worked services brought about closure in 1957.   *Author's Collection*

(See Page 73)

The Metropolitan Railway, and its successor the London Transport Executive, provided themselves with four engine sheds at **Neasden** over the years from 1880. The last shed (TQ2085.1/2A) dated from 1937 and is seen here on October 4th, 1958 with L50, L45 and L53 visible with the whole scene being backdropped by the "Met's" Neasden Power Station, now long-gone. In contrast the engine shed still stood in 1998 serving, it is believed, as an engineering building.   *HC Casserley*

(See Page 91)

There were several sheds provided at the Metropolitan Railway's station at **Edgware Road**, between 1863 and the end of steam on the "underground" in 1905. Nevertheless, at least two buildings remained in use until about 1925, when the station was greatly re-developed. This blemished, but priceless picture dates from the opening day in 1863 and partly shows one of the timber sheds (TQ2781.1/1A) situated at Edgware Road at that time. *Bernard Matthews*

(See Page 90)

Under the auspices of an LNER/Metropolitan Railway Joint agreement, the LNER, and later BR, worked Metropolitan/LTE services north of Rickmansworth to Aylesbury. This entailed the provision of a locomotive stabling and servicing facility (TL0594.1/F1) comprising of a coal stage and sidings with pits and sited just north of **Rickmansworth** Station. Steam locomotives were "sub-shedded" from Neasden depot; ex-GCR 4-6-2T Nos 5807 and 5808 being in residence on April 7th, 1947. *HC Casserley*

(See Page 105)

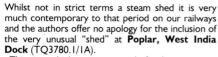

Whilst not in strict terms a steam shed it is very much contemporary to that period on our railways and the authors offer no apology for the inclusion of the very unusual "shed" at **Poplar, West India Dock** (TQ3780.1/1A).

This site, which was composed of a short spur under the platform that supported the sidings alongside of the West India Dock (GE) Station, housed one of the ex-MR battery electric locomotives No.BEL1.

It is not known if, prior to their introduction, steam locomotives were housed here, but it is felt that we would be failing if such an interesting piece of railway history was omitted on a "technicality". *Author's Collection*

(See Page 98)

Contemporary plans of GWR's **Bristol Temple Meads Station**, at opening in 1841, show that the three centre terminating roads of the station were designated as an engine shed (ST5972.1/1A). A traverser gave access from the two platform roads, there were ash drops between the rails, venting into the cellars below the station and, finally, a large water tank formed the roof over the lines at this point. Such facilities may perhaps be more accurately described as an engine stabling/servicing point, serving until a date that has not yet been discovered.

This 1965 view shows the former Bristol terminus and the centre roads, then holding nothing more than a few vans.   *Bill Potter*

(See Page 115)

Sited in the shadow of Brunel's Clifton Suspension Bridge, crossing Bristol's Avon Gorge, was the southern terminus of the Bristol Port & Pier Railway at **Clifton (Hotwells)**, which opened in 1865. An engine shed (ST5673.1/1A) was provided at the terminus and this is just visible above the rake of carriages, with a turntable ouside of the shed entrance.

This building had the misfortune to burn down on March 27th, 1873, never to be replaced. Although undated this view, from the top of the Avon Gorge, must therefore have been taken at some time between 1865 and the shed's demise eight years later.   *Author's Collection*

(See Page 116)

Despite its position beside one of Britain's busiest stations, for 95 years from 1840, the Midland shed at **Rugby** is surprisingly shy when it comes to pictures, this was perhaps due to the high wall which separated the depot from the station.

Comprised of 2TS (SP5076.1/2A) and 4TS (SP5076.1/1A) buildings, the MR depot was progressively run down from 1902 and ended its days in 1935 as an engineering plant before demolition. This portrait of MR 0-6-0 No.3106 dates from the early 20th Century and shows the 4TS building's roof and a shearlegs, with all else concealed behind that frustrating wall!

Author's Collection

(See Page 154)

Opened in 1882 by the Lynn & Fakenham Railway, the works and shed at **Melton Constable** became the main centre for the Eastern & Midlands Railway, later the Midland & Great Northern Joint. This delightful picture from the 1920s shows the works at left, some items of rolling stock, a twin water tank and, in the distance, the 3TS timber built L&F engine shed (TG0433.1/1A).

In 1951 this building had the misfortune to more or less fall down, leaving British Railways to pick up the bill for replacement. This was done by way of a brick and concrete 3TS structure (TG0433.1/1B) on the same site, which served for only eight years before the M&GN closed. Such a modern building was bound to survive, and still stood in 1999, utilized as a warehouse.   *H Garrett Collection*

(See Page 130)

Familiar to most people, the Midland & Great Northern Joint Railway had a complex origin, which was reflected in the history of engine sheds at the **Yarmouth Beach** terminus.

First was the 1877-1880 depot (TG5208.0/1A) of the Great Yarmouth & Stalham Light Railway which was replaced by the 2TS shed (TG5208.1/1A) of the Yarmouth & North Norfolk Railway, which became the Eastern & Midlands Railway and, eventually, the M&GNR. The last-named provided a new 4TS shed (TG5208.1/2A) in 1903 and this is seen here in a picture taken on October 24th, 1936. The second "Dutch roof" section of the building was utilized for light repairs, and both bays had lost their roofs by the time that closure came in February 1959.
WA Camwell

(See Page 135)

The 3ft 0in gauge Southwold Railway opened in 1879, providing itself with a 1TS engine shed at Halesworth (TM3877.1/1A) and another at the terminus at **Southwold**.

The latter shed (TM5076.1/1A)) is depicted here in a picture dating from about 1920, some nine years before the Southwold Railway was closed.
Author's Collection

(See Page 138)

CORNWALL

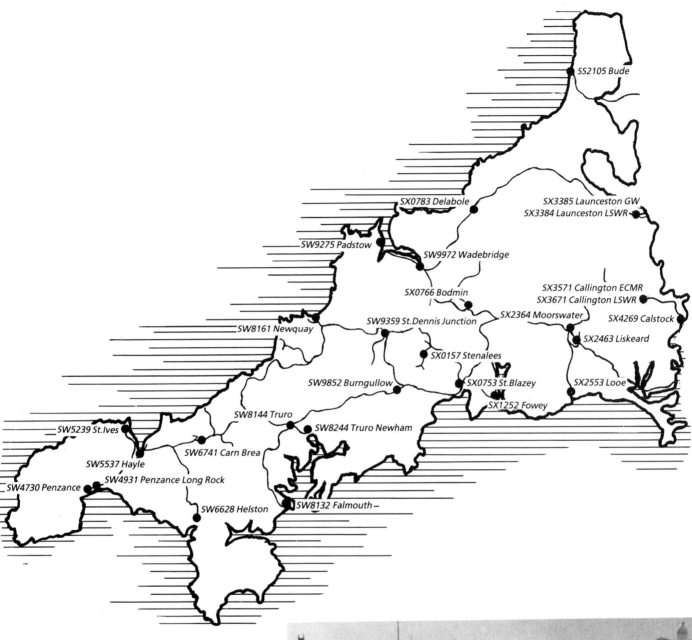

SS2105 Bude

SX3385 Launceston GW
SX3384 Launceston LSWR

SX0783 Delabole

SW9275 Padstow
SW9972 Wadebridge

SX3571 Callington ECMR
SX3671 Callington LSWR

SX0766 Bodmin

SX2364 Moorswater
SX4269 Calstock

SW8161 Newquay
SW9359 St.Dennis Junction

SX2463 Liskeard

SX0157 Stenalees

SW9852 Burngullow
SX0753 St.Blazey
SX2553 Looe

SW8144 Truro
SX1252 Fowey

SW8244 Truro Newham

SW5239 St.Ives

SW6741 Carn Brea

SW5537 Hayle
SW4931 Penzance Long Rock

SW4730 Penzance

SW6628 Helston
SW8132 Falmouth

A c1870 picture of the station at **Penzance** in-
cludes, in the middle distance, the only known
glimpse of the West Cornwall Railway's single road
engine shed (SW4730.1/1A) opened in March 1852.
The WCR was standard gauge, but after association
with the GWR, that railway's broad gauge (BG) ar-
rived in Penzance in November 1866. At that time
a shed for BG engines (SW4730.2/1A) was added
to the east of the station.

Both of these early sheds were replaced in 1876
by a larger 2TS GWR structure (SW4730.2/2A)
which was itself superseded in 1919 by the 4TS
building (SW4931.1/1A) which lasted into BR days.

Despite being taken out of locomotive use as
early as 1876 the WCR's standard gauge shed depicted here remained in use as a goods shed for
many years after; the date of its final demise being
unrecorded.   *Author's Collection.*

BODMIN

Site SX0766.1; On the west side of the line, at the south end of Bodmin General Station.
Bodmin (GWR) SX0766.1/1A
A stone built 1TS dead ended shed with a pitched slate roof, located at SX07356628 and opened on May 27th, 1887. The facilities included a water tower and coal stage sited outside the shed entrance. It was closed by BR in April 1962 and was leased by the GWS (SW Group) for a short period as a preserved rolling stock depot. It was subsequently relinquished back to BR and later demolished. The site is now part of the *Bodmin and Wenford Railway Preservation Group* premises and there are long term plans to rebuild the shed.

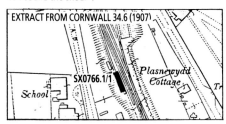

BUDE

Site SS2105.1; On the west side of the line, at the south end of Bude Station.
Bude (L&SWR) SS2105.1/1A
A brick built 1TS through road shed with pitched roof, located at SS21050575 and opened on August 10th, 1898. The facilities included a 50ft turntable at the rear of the building with a coal stage and water tank on the approach road. The depot was closed by BR in September 1964.

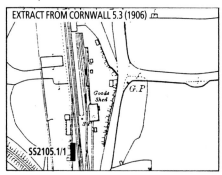

BURNGULLOW

Site SW9852.1; On the north side of Burngullow Station.
Burngullow (N&WCR) SW9852.1/1A
A stone built 1TS dead ended shed with gable style slated roof, located at SW98115238 and opened in July 1869 by the Newquay and West Cornwall Railway. It was absorbed as part of the GWR on July 1st, 1896, closed in March 1906 and finally demolished in 1929.

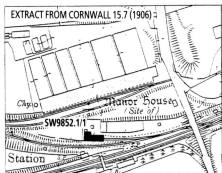

CALLINGTON

Site SX3571.1; On the north side of Callington Station yard.

Callington (ECMR) SX3571.1/1A
A 1TS through road shed, opened on May 7th, 1872 by the 3ft 6in gauge East Cornwall Mineral Railway and located at SX35987147. It is believed to have been constructed of corrugated iron sheets on a timber frame supported by a dwarf brick wall with a corrugated iron pitched roof.

The line was bought by the Plymouth Devonport & South Western Junction Railway in 1894 and converted to standard gauge in 1908 when the shed was replaced by ...
Site SX3671.1; On the north side of the line, at the east end of Callington Station.
Callington (PDSWJR) SX3671.1/1A
A 2TS dead ended shed, of similar construction to its predecessor (SX3571.1/1A) but sited further eastwards at SX36087148. The entrance to the shed faced west and a coaling stage was provided alongside the approach road.

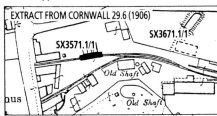

In 1924 the layout of the station and shed yards was altered and the shed was 'turned around', access to the depot now being gained from the east end ...
Callington (SR) SX3671.1/1B
A water column was sited adjacent to the shed doors with coaling effected from wagons.

In 1935/36 the length of the shed was reduced and a new, higher pitched, gable roof installed ...
Callington (SR) SX3671.1/1C
The shed yard now incorporated a coaling stage and it was in this final condition that the depot was closed in September 1964 by BR and demolished.

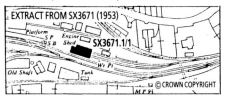

CALSTOCK

Site SX4269.1; On the east side of the line, at the top of Calstock Incline, about 1 mile north west of Calstock.
Calstock (ECMR) SX4269.1/1A
A stone built 1TS dead ended shed with a gable style slated roof, it was located at SX42566955 and opened on May 7th, 1872 by the 3ft 6in gauge East Cornwall Mineral Railway. The facilities included a large substantially built water tower. The line was absorbed by the Plymouth Devonport and South Western Junction Railway in 1894 with the shed closing in 1908.

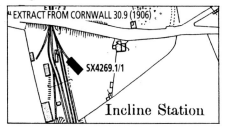

DELABOLE

Site SX0783.1; On the east side of Delabole Station.
Delabole (LSWR) SX0783.1/1A
A corrugated iron 1TS through road shed it was located at SX07248379 and opened on October 18th, 1893. A 50ft turntable was provided at the entrance to the depot and a small coaling stage was sited alongside the approach road. Delabole was a temporary terminus whilst the branch was being constructed through to Wadebridge and, following the opening of the shed (SW9972.2/1A) there on June 1st, 1895, Delabole Shed became redundant. It may have remained open for a short while servicing local traffic but did not last beyond 1900 when it was sold and removed.

CARN BREA

Site SW6741.1; North of the line, east of Carnbrea Station.
Carn Brea (Hayle Railway) SW6741.1/1A
A stone and timber built 2TS dead ended shed with a twin gable style roof, it was located at SW67544111 and opened in 1838. It formed part of the Hayle Railway's main depot and workshop and adjoined a small wagon shop. It was taken over by the West Cornwall Railway in 1846 and absorbed by the GWR in 1876.

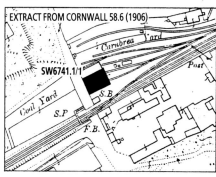

Following the takeover by the GWR it probably underwent rebuilding or conversion ...
Carn Brea (Hayle Railway) SW6741.1/1B
Improvements carried out in December 1896 included the installation of a Smithy, Sand Furnace and a Water Tank with a coaling stage. It may have continued as the westerly repair depot until the opening of Truro Shed (SW8144.2/1A) in 1900, not finally closing until August 1917.

FALMOUTH

Site SW8132.1; South of the line, at the west end of Falmouth Station.
Falmouth (Cornwall Railway)[SW8132.1/1A]
A stone built 2TS dead ended shed with a slated gable style roof, it was located at SW81533213 and opened on August 24th, 1863. The facilities included a coaling stage and 23ft turntable.

In 1897 the shed and yard were remodelled ...
Falmouth (GWR)[SW8132.1/1B]
The back end of the shed was removed and rebuilt with one road passing through and accessing to a 55ft turntable. A water tank was built adjacent to the approach road and the old turntable removed. The shed closed on September 21st, 1925 but was used as a servicing facility in this condition until it was demolished at the end of 1932.

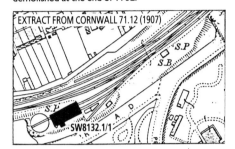

A servicing point was then established ...
Falmouth (SR)[SW8132.1/F1]
The water tank and an engine pit was retained for some years, the precise date at which closure came has not, so far, been discovered but it lasted into BR days and may well have lingered on until the end of steam in that area.

LAUNCESTON

Site SX3385.1; South of the line, at the east end of Launceston (GW) Station.
Launceston (L&SDR)[SX3385.1/1A]
A stone built 1TS dead ended shed with a slated gable style roof, it was located at SX33248501 and was opened by the Launceston & South Devon Railway on June 1st, 1865.

The shed was extended in 1899 ...
Launceston (GWR)[SX3385.1/1B]
The facilities included a turntable in the yard with a water tower outside of the shed entrance. The turntable appeared to go out of use in 1961, engines thereafter utilizing the one at the adjacent ex-SR depot (SX3384.1/1A). The depot was officially closed on December 13th, 1962, but it remained in use until September 1964.

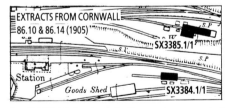

Site SX3384.1; South of the line, at the east end of Launceston (LSWR) Station.
Launceston (LSWR)[SX3384.1/1A]
A corrugated iron 1TS through road shed with a corrugated iron gable style roof, it was located at SX33218497 and opened on July 21st, 1886. It appears that it was originally planned to only be a temporary shed, in the same way as Delabole (SX0783.1/1A), but events proved otherwise and it lasted into BR days. During its existence a turntable was installed at the rear of the shed and a coal stage added at the entrance. With the ex-GWR shed (SX3385.1/1B) nearby it fell into disuse during the mid-50's and quickly became derelict, the turntable, however, was in use until 1963.

HAYLE

Site SW5537.1; On the north side of Hayle Station.
Hayle (WCR)[SW5537.1/1A]
A stone built 1TS dead ended shed with a slated gable style roof, it was located at SW55963735. The depot was possibly of West Cornwall Railway origin but was in existence by 1879 at the latest. It was out of use by 1896 but did not officially close until 1906. Demolition did not occur immediately and it could well have survived into BR days.

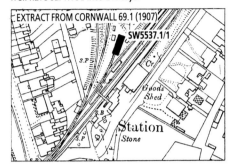

LISKEARD

Site SX2463.1; South of the line, at the east end of Liskeard (GW) Station.
Liskeard (Cornwall Railway)[SX2463.1/1A]
A stone built 1TS dead ended shed with a slated gable style roof, it was located at SX24866362 and opened in May 1859. Access to the shed was gained via a 23ft 6in turntable, but this was removed in June 1909. The shed ceased to have a locomotive allocation after October 10th, 1912 and remained open to service engines until totally closed in 1918.

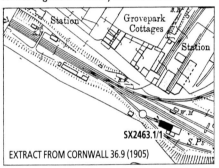

MOORSWATER

Site SX2364.1; On the west side of a goods spur, about 0.5 miles north of Coombe Junction Halt.
Moorswater (L&C)[SX2364.1/1A]
A wooden built 2TS dead ended shed with gable style roof, originally erected by the lines contractor, J. Murphy, it was opened by the Liskeard & Caradon Railway on December 27th, 1860*. The shed was located at SX23626427, but did not remain in use for locomotive purposes for too long, being closed in March 1862 and thereafter being utilized as a carriage shed as part of the Locomotive and Wagon Works of the L&L.

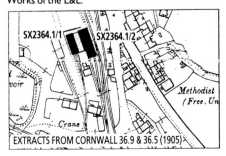

HELSTON

Site SW6628.1; West of the line, at the north end of Helston Station.
Helston (Helston Railway)[SW6628.1/1A]
A stone built 1TS dead ended shed with a slated gable style roof, it was located at SW66152816 and opened on May 9th, 1887. The facilities included a water tower and coaling stage outside of the shed entrance. It was absorbed into the GWR in 1898 and was closed by BR in December 1963.

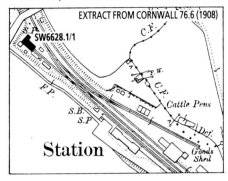

LOOE

Site SX2553.1; At the south end of Looe Station.
Looe (L&LR)[SX2553.1/1A]
A corrugated iron 1TS through road shed with a corrugated iron gable style roof, it was located at SX25435383 and opened by the Liskeard and Looe Railway in November 1901. It was not utilized for long as authorization for demolition of the shed was given on August 7th, 1919, closure probably coming a year or so earlier.

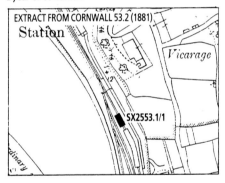

Replaced in 1862 on an adjacent site by ...
Moorswater (L&L)[SX2364.1/2A]
A stone built 2TS dead ended shed with a slated gable style roof, it was located at SX23646427 and opened by the Liskeard & Looe Railway in March 1862*. This building formed part of the Locomotive & Wagon Works of the L&L and it had a stone built water tower and coaling platform outside of the shed entrance. The depot was closed by BR on September 11th, 1961.

*The L&C opened as a goods only line on November 28th, 1844 using horse power, but passengers were unofficially carried from 1860 to 1896. On December 27th, 1860 the Looe line was opened by the L&L Union Canal Company with the contractor, J. Murphy, using steam locomotives. This arrangement lasted until March 1862 when the L&C took over and introduced their own engines.
The L&L was leased by the L&C on January 29th, 1878 with L&L commencing a passenger service on September 11th, 1879. The L&C was leased by the L&L on May 8th, 1901 but was absorbed by the GWR on July 1st, 1909. The L&L remained independent until grouping and became part of the GWR.*

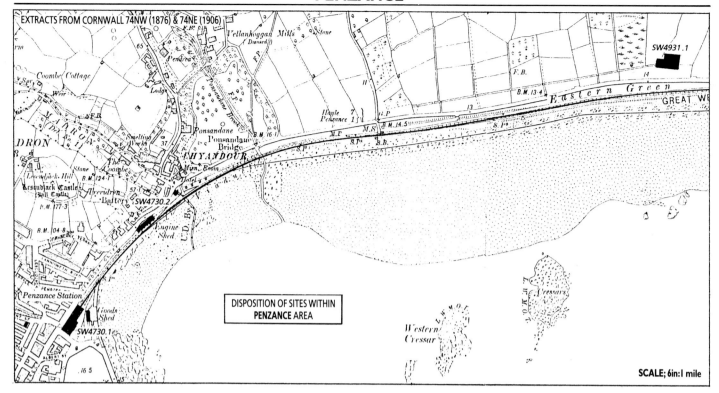

EXTRACTS FROM CORNWALL 74NW (1876) & 74NE (1906)

DISPOSITION OF SITES WITHIN
PENZANCE AREA

SCALE; 6in:1 mile

Site SW4730.1; On the east side of Penzance Station.
Penzance (WCR)^{SW4730.1/1A}
A wooden built 1TS dead ended shed with a slated gable style roof, it was located at SW47633064 and probably opened by the West Cornwall Railway in March 1852. The WCR was absorbed by the GWR in 1876 when the shed was considered as too small for requirements and was closed in the same year. It would appear that the building saw further alternative use becoming incorporated into the goods shed.

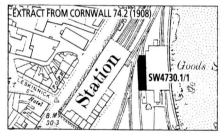

EXTRACT FROM CORNWALL 74.2 (1908)

SW4730.1/1

Site SW4730.2; On the west side of the line, north of Penzance Station.
Penzance (WCR)^{SW4730.2/1A}
A wooden built 2TS dead ended shed with a slated hipped gable style roof, it was located at SW47913098 and opened by the West Cornwall Railway in 1866* as their broad gauge shed. Following absorption by the GWR it was also closed in 1876, and was then utilized as the coaling plant for the replacement depot (SW4730.2/2A).

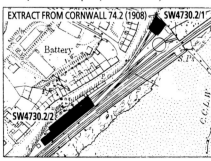

EXTRACT FROM CORNWALL 74.2 (1908) — SW4730.2/1

SW4730.2/2

Replaced in 1876 by ...
Penzance (GWR)^{SW4730.2/2A}
A stone built 2TS dead ended shed with slated gable style roof. It was located at SW47813090 and was opened by the GWR in 1876. The facilities included a 40ft turntable, sand furnace, water tank and coal plant *(qv)*. The restricted nature of the site precluded any expansion and traffic requirements enforced its closure in June 1914.

*Broad gauge goods traffic commenced on November 11th, 1866 with the passenger service first reaching Penzance on March 3rd, 1867.

Replaced in 1914 by ...
Site SW4931.1; On the north side of the line, about 1.25 miles east of Penzance Station.
Long Rock (GWR)^{SW4931.1/1A}
A brick built 4TS dead ended shed with slated twin gable style roof. It was located on a much larger site at SW49323130 and opened by the GWR in June 1914. It was a standard Churchward shed with all facilities and was sufficiently large enough to last out to the end of steam without any further alterations. The depot was closed by BR on September 10th, 1962 but it was then utilized for diesel locomotive servicing until 1976, being demolished a year later.

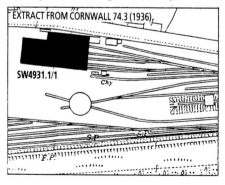

EXTRACT FROM CORNWALL 74.3 (1936)

SW4931.1/1

NEWQUAY

Site SW8161.1; On the west side of the line at the south end of Newquay Station.
Newquay (CMR)^{SW8161.1/1A}
A stone built 1TS dead ended shed with a slated gable style roof, it was located at SW81626164 and opened by the Cornwall Mineral Railway on June 1st, 1874. It was closed and demolished in 1904.

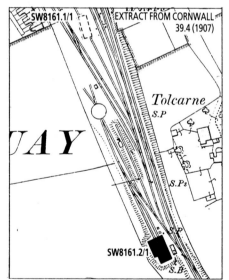

EXTRACT FROM CORNWALL 39.4 (1907)

SW8161.1/1

SW8161.2/1

Replaced in 1905 by ...
Site SW8161.2; On the west side of the line, south of Newquay Station.
Newquay (GWR)^{SW8161.2/1A}
A brick built 2TS open ended shed with a slated gable style roof, it was located further south at SW81686144 and opened by the GWR on May 1st, 1905. The facilities included a 45ft turntable, water tower and coaling stage. It was officialy closed on September 22nd, 1930 but may have been retained for servicing engines for another three years. Demolition was authorized in August 1936.

PADSTOW

Site SW9275.1; On the east side of Padstow Station.
Padstow (LSWR)^{SW9275.1/F1}

Site SW9275.1; On the east side of Padstow Station.
Padstow (LSWR)^SW9275.1/F1

A servicing area opened by the LSWR in 1900 and consisting of a 50ft turntable, located at SW92137506, and sidings.

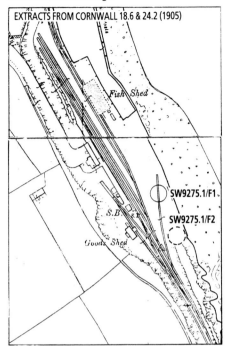

EXTRACTS FROM CORNWALL 18.6 & 24.2 (1905)

Rebuilding work in 1933 necessitated the re-siting of the turntable slightly further south ...
Padstow (SR)^SW9275.1/F2

The turntable and siding was relocated at SW92157502, to allow the construction of an improved access to the new quay. After the war the introduction of Bulleid Pacifics required the turntable to be enlarged to 65ft. It is reasonable to assume that the facility fell out of use at some stage in the early 60's.

ST.DENNIS JUNCTION

Site SW9359.1; On the south side of the line, just west of St.Dennis Junction.
St.Dennis Junction (GWR)^SW9359.1/F1

A servicing area located at SW93275996 and consisting of a water tower, coaling stage, engine pit and siding. Opening and closing dates are not known.

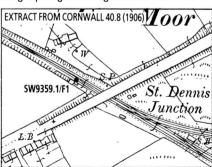

EXTRACT FROM CORNWALL 40.8 (1906)

ST.BLAZEY

Site SX0753.1; On the west side of the line, south of St.Blazey Station.
St.Blazey (CMR)^SX0753.1/1A

A brick built 9-track semi-roundhouse with slated single gable style roofs over each stall, it was located at SX07335374 and opened by the Cornwall Mineral Railway on June 1st, 1874. It remained more or less unaltered for its entire existence, the turntable was replaced by a vacuum assisted type and the GWR, which absorbed the company in July 1896, built a standard coal stage. The depot was closed to steam in April 1962 after which it serviced diesel locomotives until April 25th, 1987, when they were transferred to the adjacent 3TS building (SX0753.1/2A). After closure a preservation order was sought and granted and it became a listed building, being utilized as industrial units, with the turntable remaining *in situ* and fully operational in the yard.

St.Blazey (CMR)^SX0753.1/2A

A brick built 3TS through road shed with a slated single gable style roof, it was located at the north end of the shed yard, at SX07335386 and opened by the Cornwall Mineral Railway. The precise opening and closing dates of this building are unknown but research would suggest that 1877 and 1896, respectively, would approximate to the position. What is known, however, is that the building was then converted into workshops and was utilized, in one form or another, until it re-assumed its role as an engine shed, this time to diesel traction, on April 25th, 1987.

FOWEY

Site SX1252.1 : On the south side of the line, at the east end of Fowey Station.
Fowey (CMR)^SX1252.1/1A

A 1TS dead ended shed, it was located at SX12705229 and was opened by the Cornwall Mineral Railway at some time prior to 1874. Details of the facilities and closure date are not known but it was converted to a goods shed and remained standing until at least 1912.

EXTRACT FROM CORNWALL 52.5 (1906)

ST.IVES

Site SW5239.1; On the west side of the line, south of St.Ives Station.
St.Ives (GWR)^SW5239.1/1A

A stone built 1TS dead ended shed with a slated gable style roof, it was located at SW52063997 and was opened by the GWR on June 1st, 1877. The facilities included a water tank and coaling stage. It was closed by BR in September 1961 and demolished.

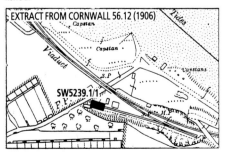

EXTRACT FROM CORNWALL 56.12 (1906)

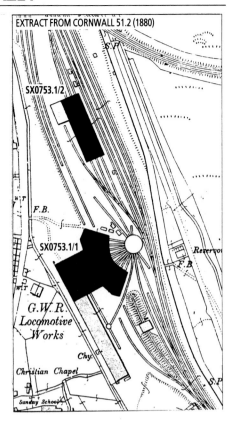

EXTRACT FROM CORNWALL 51.2 (1880)

STENALEES

Site SX0157.1; On the east side of the Gunheath Branch, south of Goonbarrow Junction.
Stenalees (N&CJ)^SX0157.1/1A

A corrugated iron 1TS dead ended shed with a corrugated iron gable style roof, it was located at SX01555739 and opened by the Newquay and Cornwall Junction Railway in October 1869. The facilities included a water tank surmounting a coaling stage. The railway was taken over by the Cornwall Mineral Railway on July 21st, 1873 and absorbed into the GWR on July 1st, 1896. It was rapidly closed under the new ownership, in October 1896, but found a new lease of life when it was removed in March 1897, being re-erected at Brixham (as SX9256.1/1B).

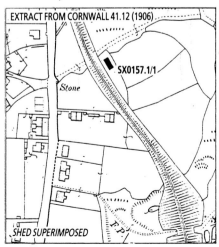

EXTRACT FROM CORNWALL 41.12 (1906)

SHED SUPERIMPOSED

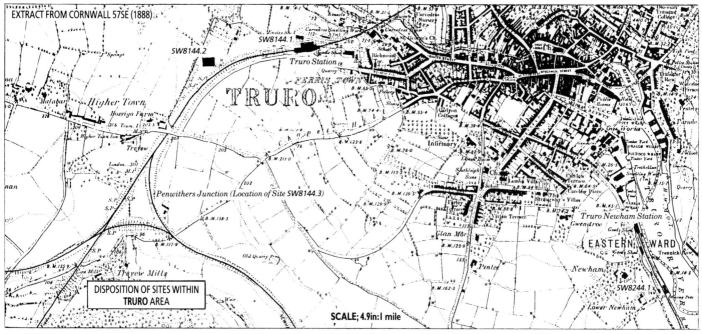

EXTRACT FROM CORNWALL 57SE (1888)

DISPOSITION OF SITES WITHIN **TRURO** AREA

SCALE; 4.9in:1 mile

Site SW8144.1; On the north side of Truro Station.
Truro (Cornwall Railway)^{SW8144.1/1A}
A wooden built 2TS dead ended shed with a slated gable style roof, it was located at SW81734498 and was opened by the Cornwall Railway on May 4th, 1859. The facilities included a 23ft 6in turntable, and a coaling stage and water tank sited outside of the entrance to the shed. The railway was absorbed by the GWR on July 1st, 1889 and the shed was closed in May 1900, demolished and replaced by sidings..

Replaced in 1900 by ...
Site SW8144.2; On the north side of the line, at the west end of Truro Station.
Truro (GWR)^{SW8144.2/1A}
A stone built 3TS dead ended shed with a northlight pattern roof, it was located further west than its predecessor (SW8144.1/1A) at SW81394492, at the west end of the station yard. The shed was opened by the GWR in May 1900, included all facilities, and formed part of a larger building, also housing a wagon repair shop. It remained virtually unaltered, except for the provision of slightly more extended cover over the three tracks, until closure came in November 1965. It was later demolished.

Site SW8244.1; On the west side of the line, south of Truro Newham Station.
Newham (WCR)^{SW8244.1/1A}
A wooden built 1TS dead ended shed with a gable style roof, it was located at SW82994405 and opened by the West Cornwall Railway on April 16th, 1855*. No turntable was provided but a coal stage and water tower was sited outside of the shed entrance.

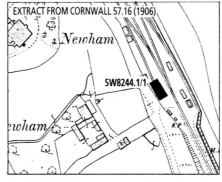

EXTRACT FROM CORNWALL 57.16 (1906)

Site SW8144.3; In the vicinity of Penwithers Junction, west of Truro Station.
Penwithers (WCR)^{SW8144.3/1A}
Some sort of facility was opened here by the West Cornwall Railway*, its approximate position being SW810444.

*The West Cornwall Railway opened its line into Newham on April 16th, 1855 with a new link line to Truro (Cornwall Railway) Station being established at Penwithers Junction on May 11th, 1859. The sequence of events between the two facilities is not clear. Newham probably opened on April 16th, 1855, and could have closed upon the establishment of a facility at Penwithers Junction when the link opened on May 11th, 1859. Or it could have remained open longer with the Penwithers Junction facility opening later. Either way very little information surrounding these events is available at the moment.

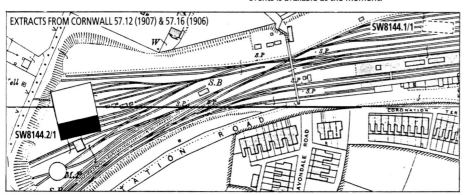

EXTRACTS FROM CORNWALL 57.12 (1907) & 57.16 (1906)

WADEBRIDGE

Site SW9972.1; On the west side of the line, at the north end of Wadebridge Station.
Wadebridge (B&WR)^{SW9972.1/1A}
A stone built 1TS dead ended shed with a slated gable style roof, it was located at SW99067233 and opened by the Bodmin & Wadebridge Railway on July 4th, 1834. The depot was part of the main works for the railway and was constructed alongside the carriage shed, with a stone built water tank at the entrance to the engine shed. The line was absorbed by the LSWR in 1846, but the shed remained open until June 1st, 1895. It remained standing for over 128 years until demolition took place in 1962.

Replaced in 1895 by ...
Site SW9972.2; On the east side of Wadebridge Station.
Wadebridge (LSWR)^{SW9972.2/1A}
A wooden built 2TS shed with one through road and a slated gable style roof, it was located at SW99177225 and was opened by the LSWR on June 1st, 1895. The facilities included a 50ft turntable, coaling stage and water tank.

In 1906 the shed was altered to accommodate steam railcars ...
Wadebridge (LSWR)^{SW9972.2/1B}
The building was extended at its eastern end, in the existing style, with both tracks now passing through the shed, at the same time the shed yard was extensively re-modelled to allow better access to the depot. The railcars lasted at the depot until 1919.

In 1949 the shed was refurbished ...
Wadebridge (LSWR)^{SW9972.2/1C}
A new roof, including gable ends, of corrugated asbestos sheeting, was installed and the walls were renewed as required. The shed was closed by BR in October 1964 and subsequently demolished.

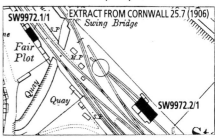

EXTRACT FROM CORNWALL 25.7 (1906)

DORSET

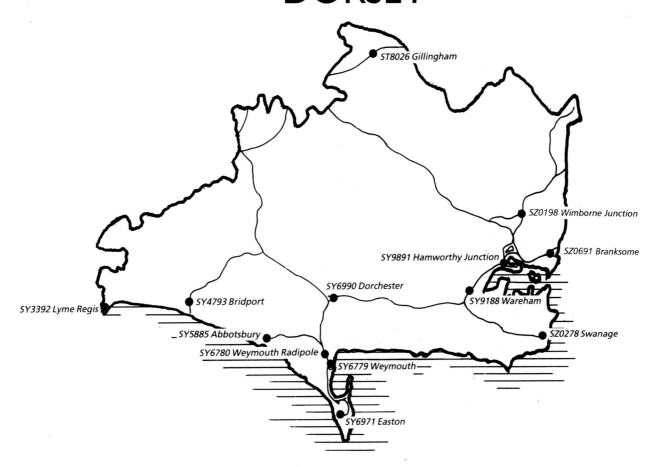

ST8026 Gillingham

SZ0198 Wimborne Junction

SY9891 Hamworthy Junction

SZ0691 Branksome

SY6990 Dorchester

SY9188 Wareham

SY3392 Lyme Regis

SY4793 Bridport

SZ0278 Swanage

SY5885 Abbotsbury

SY6780 Weymouth Radipole

SY6779 Weymouth

SY6971 Easton

ABBOTSBURY

Site SY5885.1; On the south side of the line, east of Abbotsbury Station.

Abbotsbury (Abbotsbury Railway)[SY5885.1/1A]
A stone built 1TS dead ended shed with gable style slated roof, it was located at SY58498530 and opened on November 9th, 1885. The facilities included a coaling platform and stone built water tower located at the entrance to the shed. The line was absorbed by the GWR in 1896 and the shed was closed in the same year. It was only partially demolished and parts of the walls remained standing until at least 1992.

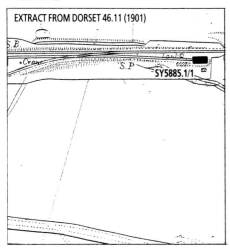

EXTRACT FROM DORSET 46.11 (1901)

SY5885.1/1

BRANKSOME

Site SZ0691.1; In the fork of the Bournemouth West to Branksome and Central lines, east of Branksome Station.

Branksome (S&DJR)[SZ0691.1/1A]
A wooden framed, corrugated iron 2TS shed with one through road and pitched roof, it was located at SZ06259193 and built by the L&SWR for the Somerset & Dorset Joint Railway in 1895. The facilities included a water tower, turntable and a coaling stage, the latter falling out of use in LMS days as locomotives carried enough fuel for the return trip. The shed was temporarily closed by the LMS as a wartime economy measure.

Following re-opening it was refurbished ...
Branksome (LMS)[SZ0691.1/1B]
Sometime later, possibly in BR days, the corrugated iron was replaced by asbestos sheeting and the turntable was removed. The shed was closed by BR on August 2nd, 1965 and subsequently demolished.

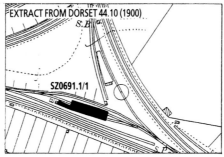

EXTRACT FROM DORSET 44.10 (1900)

SZ0691.1/1

BRIDPORT

Site SY4793.1; On the east side of Bridport Station.

Bridport (Bridport Railway)[SY4793.1/1A]
A stone built 1TS dead ended shed with a slated gable style roof, it was located at SY47389337 and opened on November 12th, 1857. The facilities included a water tower and coal stage located at the entrance to the shed. The line was leased to the GWR in 1882 and absorbed by them on July 1st, 1901. The shed remained virtually unaltered until closure by BR on June 15th, 1959. It was demolished shortly afterwards.

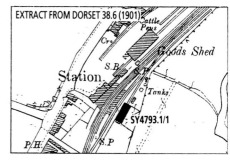

EXTRACT FROM DORSET 38.6 (1901)

SY4793.1/1

DORCHESTER

Site SY6990.1; On the south side of the line, at the east end of Dorchester (LSWR) Station.

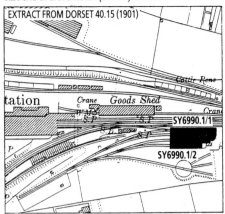

EXTRACT FROM DORSET 40.15 (1901)

Dorchester (S&DR)[SY6990.1/1A]
A brick built 2TS dead ended shed with a pitched slated roof, located at SY69379006 and opened on June 1st, 1847 by the Southampton and Dorchester Railway. The line was worked by the L&SWR.

In 1875 the shed was enlarged ...
Dorchester (L&SWR)[SY6990.1/2A]
A wooden built 2TS dead ended shed, constructed on dwarf brick walls and with a pitched roof was built adjacent to the south side of the original building, at SY69379005. The facilities, by now, included a large coal stage and turntable sited at the west end of the yard. Some time later the turntable was replaced by one of 50ft diameter, sited on the south side of the shed.

The shed was re-roofed ...
Dorchester (SR)[SY6990.1/2B]
At some time after 1931 the wooden gable and roof was replaced by corrugated asbestos sheeting. By the time that closure came, by BR on June 17th, 1957, the wooden section had fallen into disrepair and had been removed. The brick section was demolished on closure.

LYME REGIS

Site SY3392.1; On the east side of the line, at the north end of Lyme Regis Station.
Lyme Regis (A&LRR)[SY3392.1/1A]
A timber built 1TS dead ended shed with a pitched roof, it was located at SY33279278 and opened by the Axminster & Lyme Regis Railway on August 24th, 1903. The line did not remain independent for long, being absorbed by the L&SWR in 1907 with the little shed not lasting much longer either, being destroyed by a fire on December 28th, 1912.

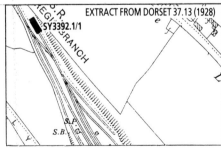

EXTRACT FROM DORSET 37.13 (1928)

Replaced in 1913 by ...
Lyme Regis (L&SWR)[SY3392.1/1B]
A 1TS dead ended shed, built on the same site and of an asbestos clad, wooden framed construction with an asbestos pitched roof. The facilities included a water column and small coal stage built adjacent to the shed entrance. The shed was closed by BR on November 27th, 1965.

HAMWORTHY JUNCTION

Site SY9891.1; In the fork of the Dorchester and Hamworthy (Goods) lines, south of Hamworthy Junction Station.
Hamworthy Junction (L&SWR)[SY9891.1/1A]
A brick built 1TS dead ended shed with a slated pitched roof, it was located at SY98609157 and opened in 1847. The only facility provided was a small coal stage built adjacent to a siding on the east side of the shed.

Prior to 1900 the layout was remodelled ...
Hamworthy Junction (L&SWR)[SY9891.1/1B]
The shed was modified to a through building and the coaling siding was extended to form a run-round loop. At the same time the coal stage was enlarged. The shed was closed by BR in May 1954 and converted for use as a store. It has since been demolished.

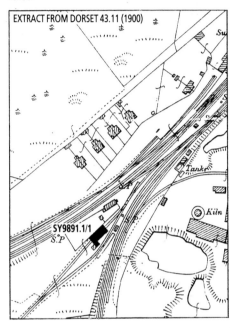

EXTRACT FROM DORSET 43.11 (1900)

GILLINGHAM

Site ST8026.1; On the south side of the line, at the west end of Gillingham Station.
Gillingham (S&YR)[ST8026.1/1A]
A stone built 2TS dead ended shed with a slated gable style roof, it was located at ST80932606. The shed was opened on May 2nd, 1859 by the Salisbury & Yeovil Railway, with the line being worked by the L&SWR. Neither the facilities available, or its closure date are known, but the tracks were still *in situ* in 1901, and it is known that the building remained in existence for some time afterwards, in private use.

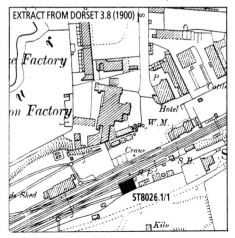

EXTRACT FROM DORSET 3.8 (1900)

EASTON

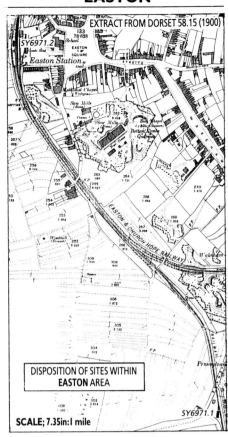

EXTRACT FROM DORSET 58.15 (1900)

DISPOSITION OF SITES WITHIN
EASTON AREA

SCALE; 7.35in:1 mile

Site SY6971.1; On the west side of a spur line, about 1100 yards south of Easton Station.
Easton (E&CHR)[SY6971.1/1A]
A 1TS dead ended shed, located at SY69507100 and opened by the Easton & Church Hope Railway on October 1st, 1900. No details are known of its construction, but it was probably built of timber or corrugated iron as it was destroyed by a fire in 1904.

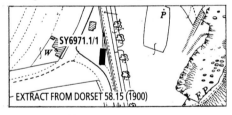

EXTRACT FROM DORSET 58.15 (1900)

Replaced in 1904 by ...
Site SY6971.2; On the west side of Easton Station.
Easton (GWR/LSWR)[SY6971.2/1A]
A stone built 1TS dead ended shed with a gable style slated roof, it was located at SY69027183 and opened in 1904. The only facility supplied was a conical water tower located at the entrance to the depot. The line was run jointly by the GWR and L&SWR from the commencement of passenger working in 1902, but by 1925 the status of the shed had been reduced to that of a servicing point. The facility was closed by BR, at the cessation of passenger services, on March 3rd, 1952.

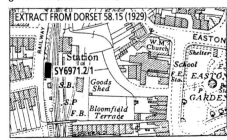

EXTRACT FROM DORSET 58.15 (1929)

SWANAGE

Site SZ0278.1; On the north side of the line, at the west end of Swanage Station.
Swanage (L&SWR)^{SZ0278.1/1A}
A stone built 1TS through road shed with a slated pitched roof, it was located at SZ02637893 and opened on May 20th, 1885. The facilities included a 50ft turntable, coaling stage and water tank, all sited on the shed approach road. Apart from minor rebuilding to the entrance, removing the original arched doorway and replacing it with a single lintel after a collision with an M7 tank engine, the shed was unaltered until its closure by BR in September 1966. The shed remained standing and was re-opened in May 1985 by the *Swanage Railway Society*.

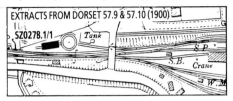

EXTRACTS FROM DORSET 57.9 & 57.10 (1900)

WAREHAM

Site SY9188.1; On the north side of the line, west of Wareham Station.
Wareham (S&DR)^{SY9188.1/1A}
A wooden built 1TS dead ended shed with a pitched roof, it was located at SY91918812 and opened by the Southampton & Dorchester Railway in June 1847 as an Engineers Department depot. It was closed and demolished in 1886 to make way for the re-siting of Wareham Station.

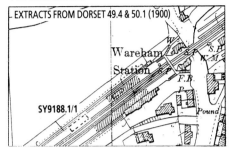

EXTRACTS FROM DORSET 49.4 & 50.1 (1900)

WIMBORNE JUNCTION

Site SZ0198.1; In the fork of the Templecombe and Poole lines, south of Wimborne Station.
Wimborne Junction (S&D/L&SWR)^{SZ0198.1/1A}
A 1TS dead ended shed, located at SZ01869875 and opened in 1863, it was joint-owned by the Somerset & Dorset and London & South Western Railways and probably made of timber. The facilities included a turntable, sited outside of the shed entrance, water tank and coal stage. It was demolished in 1909.

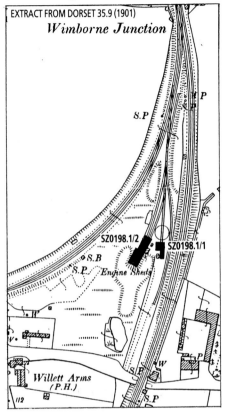

EXTRACT FROM DORSET 35.9 (1901)
Wimborne Junction

Sometime prior to 1909, a second shed was erected alongside ...
Wimborne Junction (S&D/L&SWR)^{SZ0198.1/2A}
This was a larger 2TS dead ended shed, again probably built in timber, located at SZ01849874. It is not known when this building was erected but additional coaling stage and water tank facilities were provided. In 1886 the provision of a new link line further south deprived the shed of much of its passenger work and by 1909 the decision was taken to rationalize the decrepit buildings and the shed was demolished.

Replaced in 1909 by ...
Wimborne Junction (S&DJR/L&SWR)^{SZ0198.1/2B}
A wooden built 2TS dead ended shed with a single pitched roof and built on the site of the previous 2-road establishment (SZ0198.1/2A). With the decline in traffic continuing it was closed upon grouping, in January 1923, although the turntable saw some use until at least 1931.

WEYMOUTH

Site SY6779.1; On the east side of Weymouth Station.
Weymouth (L&SWR)^{SY6779.1/1A}
A timber built 2TS dead ended shed with a pitched slated roof, it was located at SY67877977 and opened on January 20th, 1857. The facilities included a water tank and coaling stage, outside the entrance to the shed, and a turntable which was shared with the GWR establishment (qv). After the GWR transferred their operations to Radipole (SY6780.1/1A) in 1885 the L&SWR locomotives were turned there. Expansion of the station forced the closure and removal of the shed in January 1939, after which the SR locomotives were serviced and stabled as required at the GWR Radipole shed.

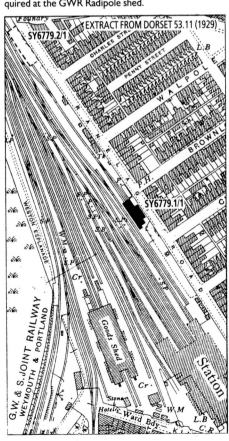

EXTRACT FROM DORSET 53.11 (1929)

Site SY6779.2; On the east side of the line, at the north end of Weymouth Station.
Weymouth (GWR)^{SY6779.2/1A}
A timber built 2TS dead ended shed with a single pitched roof, it was located at SY67777994 and opened on January 20th, 1857. The facilities included a coal stage and a dual-gauged turntable of which it shared use with the adjacent LSWR shed (SY6779.1/1A). With a substantial growth in traffic ensuing, and no room for expansion of the facilities, it was closed in June 1885 and demolished.

Replaced in 1885 by ...
Site SY6780.1; On the east side of the line, north of Weymouth Station.

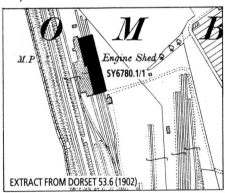

EXTRACT FROM DORSET 53.6 (1902)

Radipole (GWR)^{SY6780.1/1A}
A brick built 3TS through road shed, with a north-light pattern slated and glazed roof, it was located at SY67518070 and opened in June 1885. Its facilities included a water tank, repair shop, coaling plant and a 45ft turntable, which was replaced by a 65ft unit and re-sited in 1925.

In 1930 the shed was refurbished ...
Radipole (GWR)^{SY6780.1/1B}
The roof was replaced by a single pitched slated roof, the coaling stage was enlarged and re-sited and the crane in the repair shop was up-graded. The shed was closed by BR on July 9th, 1967, but was used to service diesel locomotives until October 1970. It was demolished in the following year.

SOMERSET

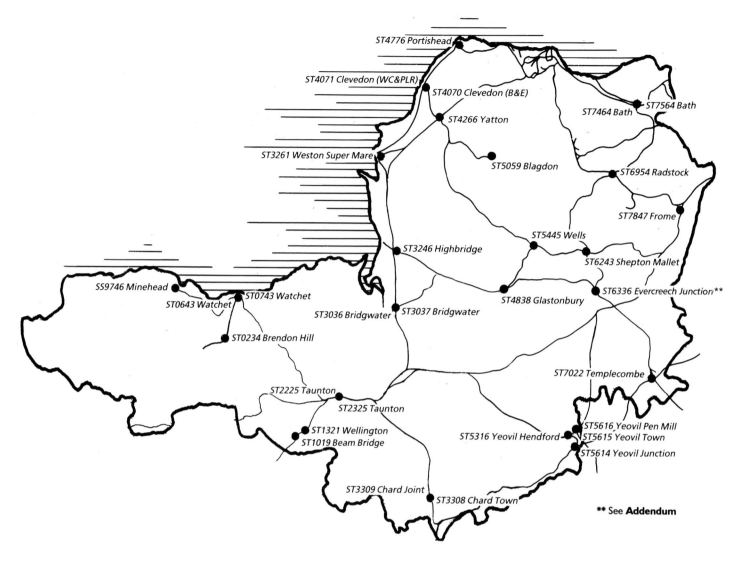

ST4776 Portishead
ST4071 Clevedon (WC&PLR)
ST4070 Clevedon (B&E)
ST7464 Bath
ST7564 Bath
ST4266 Yatton
ST5059 Blagdon
ST6954 Radstock
ST3261 Weston Super Mare
ST7847 Frome
ST5445 Wells
ST3246 Highbridge
ST6243 Shepton Mallet
SS9746 Minehead
ST4838 Glastonbury
ST6336 Evercreech Junction**
ST0743 Watchet
ST0643 Watchet
ST3036 Bridgwater
ST3037 Bridgwater
ST0234 Brendon Hill
ST7022 Templecombe
ST2225 Taunton
ST2325 Taunton
ST5616 Yeovil Pen Mill
ST5316 Yeovil Hendford
ST5615 Yeovil Town
ST1321 Wellington
ST5614 Yeovil Junction
ST1019 Beam Bridge
ST3309 Chard Joint
ST3308 Chard Town
** See **Addendum**

The rural idyll of **Blagdon**'s branch terminus is seen here on August 22nd, 1938. The line, which opened in December 1901 as the Wrington Vale Light Railway, was worked from the outset by the GWR. A single road wooden shed (ST5059.1/1A) was provided for the branch engine, but this structure was badly damaged by fire during the night of October 13/14th, 1912. The GWR did not repair the building but maintained a stabling point (ST5059.1/F1) with a set of men in lodgings in the village.

When not in use, usually at the weekends, the branch locomotive (for example, 0-4-2T No.518 in March 1914) was protected by a tarpaulin! The wooden lean-to seen at the left marks the site of the engine shed; indeed that may have formed part of the original structure. The stabling point closed, with the end of passenger services, in May 1924.
WA Camwell

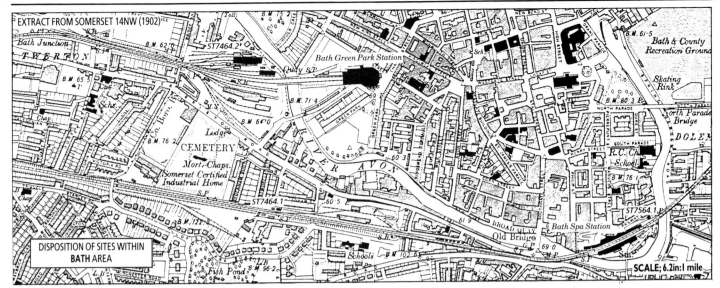

EXTRACT FROM SOMERSET 14NW (1902)

DISPOSITION OF SITES WITHIN **BATH** AREA

SCALE; 6.2in:1 mile

Site ST7564.1; On the north side of the line, at the east end of Bath (GW) Station.
Bath (GWR)[ST7564.1/1A]
A 1TS dead ended shed, probably built in timber, it was located at ST75366441 and opened on August 31st, 1840. A 35ft turntable was sited outside of the entrance to the building and apart from that, few details are known. It was closed in November 1880 and demolished to make way for station enlargement.

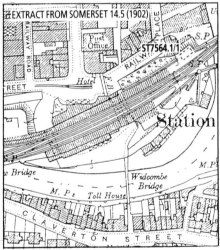

EXTRACT FROM SOMERSET 14.5 (1902)

ST7564.1/1

Station

Replaced in 1880 by ...
Site ST7464.1; In a goods yard, on the north side of the line, west of Bath (GW) Station.

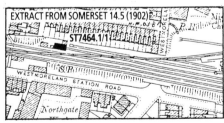

EXTRACT FROM SOMERSET 14.5 (1902)

ST7464.1/1

Bath Spa (GWR)[ST7464.1/1A]
A brick built 1TS through road shed with a water tank, mounted on cast iron columns, forming the roof. It was located at ST74446443 and opened in November 1880. It was closed by BR in February 1961.

Site ST7464.2; On the north side of the line, west of Bath Green Park Station.
Bath Green Park (MR)[ST7464.2/1A]
A stone built 2TS dead ended shed with a slated gable style roof, it was located at ST74306479 and was opened on August 4th, 1869 by the Midland Railway. The facilities included a water tank and turntable, which were shared with the S&DJR shed (ST7464.2/2). In later years the building was mainly used for repairs until the depot was closed by BR on March 7th, 1966.

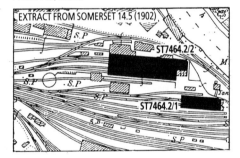

EXTRACT FROM SOMERSET 14.5 (1902)

ST7464.2/2

ST7464.2/1

Bath Green Park (S&DJR)[ST7464.2/2A]
A wooden built 2TS dead ended shed with a gable style roof, it was sited on the north side of the yard at ST74246483 and opened on July 20th, 1874.

The shed was enlarged in 1878 ...
Bath Green Park (S&DJR)[ST7464.2/2B]
A wooden built 2TS dead ended shed with a gable style roof was erected along the south side of the existing building, forming an *offset* 4TS shed. Construction of the enlarged depot involved the removal and installation of a 46ft turntable to a point further west.

The shed was enlarged again, in 1884 ...
Bath Green Park (S&DJR)[ST7464.2/2C]
The original building was extended by 100ft, and the extension by 56ft, eliminating the *offset* aspect of the entrance to the shed and resorting to a more orthodox structure. At the same time the shed yard was relaid out and enlarged coaling facilities provided. Apart from the provision of a larger 60ft turntable, and resultant alterations to the depot layout in 1935 the shed remained more or less unaltered until closure came, by BR, on March 7th, 1966.

A Sunday in the late 1930s finds 0-6-0PT No.3731 and 2-6-2T No.4573 resting outside **Bath (GWR)** shed (ST7464.1/1A). This fairly basic, and no doubt cost-effective, design utilized an elevated water tank with brick or wooden walls between the support columns and was deployed at a few locations by the GWR between 1879 and 1881.
WA Camwell cty WT Stubbs

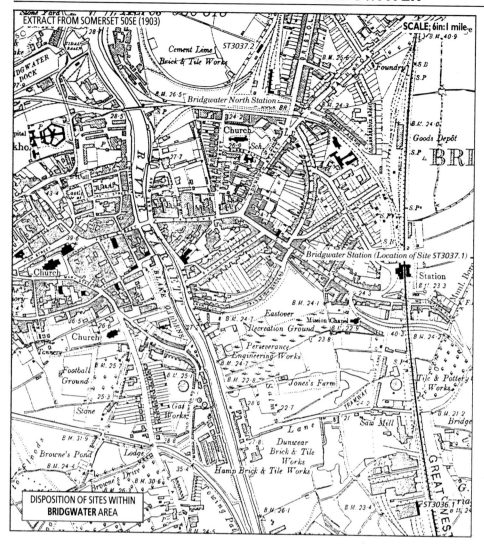

EXTRACT FROM SOMERSET 50SE (1903)

SCALE; 6in:1 mile

DISPOSITION OF SITES WITHIN BRIDGWATER AREA

Site ST3037.1; In the vicinity of Bridgwater Station.
Bridgwater (B&E)^{ST3037.1/1A}
A timber built 2TS shed with a gable style slated roof, it was approximately located at ST308370 and was opened by the Bristol & Exeter Railway on June 14th, 1841. The shed was only of a temporary nature, servicing locomotives whilst the line was being built onwards to Taunton. Following completion of the extension, in June 1842, the shed was removed to Taunton and re-erected (as ST2225.1/1A).

Site ST3036.1; On the west side of the line, south of Bridgwater (GW) Station.
Bridgwater (GWR)^{ST3036.1/1A}
An unusual 1TS through road shed, converted from the last bay of a brick built, northlight pattern roofed, Carriage Workshop, it was located at ST30843631 and was opened in 1893.

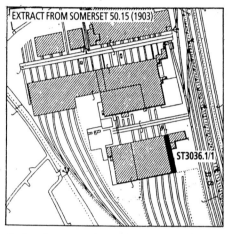

EXTRACT FROM SOMERSET 50.15 (1903)

ST3036.1/1

During the running-down of the carriage works it was partially rebuilt ...
Bridgwater (GWR)^{ST3036.1/1B}
Following the demolition of adjacent bays, probably in the 1930s, the shed was reconstructed with a single pitch, corrugated asbestos roof. It remained in this condition until closed by BR in July 1960. It remained standing and was in private use until at least 1994.

BLAGDON

Site ST5059.1; On the east side of Blagdon Station.
Blagdon (WVLR)^{ST5059.1/1A}
A timber built 1TS through road shed, it was located at ST50355974 and was opened by the Wrington Vale Light Railway on December 4th, 1901. It was destroyed by a fire on October 14th, 1912.

A servicing point was then established ...
Blagdon (WVLR)^{ST5059.1/F1}
Locomotives utilized the shed pit and siding, being covered with a tarpaulin sheet whilst stabled at weekends, until closed by the GWR in March 1924.

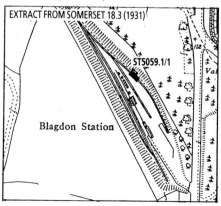

EXTRACT FROM SOMERSET 18.3 (1931)

ST5059.1/1

Blagdon Station

BEAM BRIDGE

Site ST1019.1; In the vicinity of Beam Bridge Station.
Beam Bridge (B&E)^{ST1019.1/1A}
A temporary shed, probably built in timber and approximately located at ST10771934 was opened here on May 1st, 1843 by the Bristol & Exeter Railway and closed on May 1st, 1844 following extension of the line through to Exeter.

EVERCREECH JUNCTION

Site ST6336.1; On the east side of the line, north of Evercreech Junction Station.
Evercreech Junction (SDR)^{ST6336.1/1A}
A 1TS dead ended shed, it was located at ST63783674 and was opened by the Somerset & Dorset Railway at some time prior to 1884. The facilities included a turntable. Although the depot was closed in c1900 locomotives continued to utilize the facilities until the turntable was re-sited in the fork of the junction, north of the station.

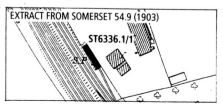

EXTRACT FROM SOMERSET 54.9 (1903)

ST6336.1/1

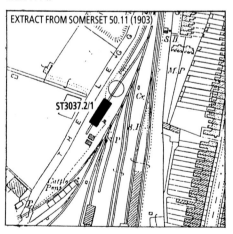

EXTRACT FROM SOMERSET 50.11 (1903)

ST3037.2/1

Site ST3037.2; On the west side of the line, at the north end of Bridgwater North Station.
Bridgwater North (Bridgwater)^{ST3037.2/1A}
A brick built 1TS through road shed with gable style slated roof, it was located at ST30383759 and was opened by the Bridgwater Railway in July 1890. The facilities included a 50ft turntable sited outside of the entrance to the shed, and a coaling stage. The line was worked by the Somerset & Dorset Joint Railway and it was they who closed the shed in about 1920 and let it out to a commercial concern. The turntable, however, remained in regular use until early BR days.

CHARD

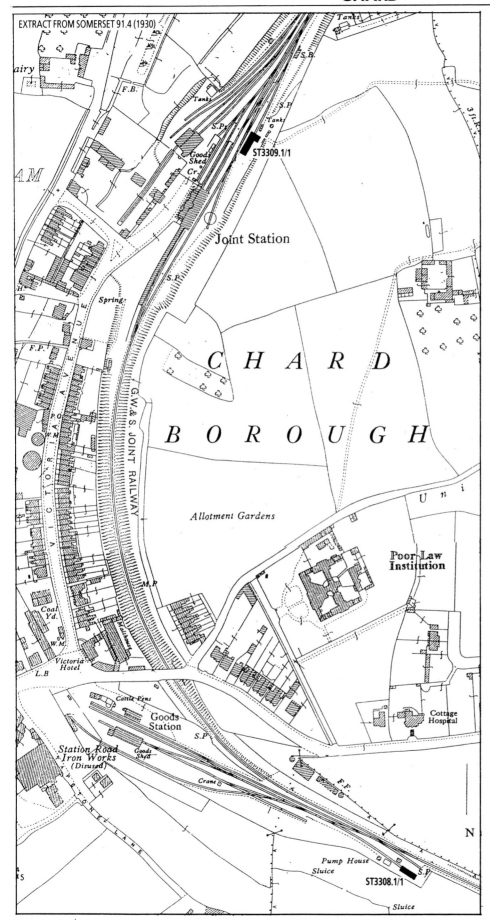

EXTRACT FROM SOMERSET 91.4 (1930)

Site ST3308.1; On the west side of the line, south of Chard Joint Station.

Chard Town (L&SWR)^{ST3308.1/1A}

A 1TS open ended shed of a corrugated clad, wooden framed construction with a corrugated iron dutch barn type roof. It was located at ST33160859 and opened on May 8th, 1863. The only facility provided was a small coaling stage sited outside of the shed entrance, but locomotives were able to utilize the turntable at Chard Joint shed (ST3309.1/1A). The depot closed on December 31st, 1916 and remained in a derelict state until demolished in December 1929.

Site ST3309.1; On the east side of Chard Joint Station.

Chard Joint (B&E)^{ST3309.1/1A}

A brick built 1TS dead ended shed with a slated gable style roof, located at ST33010927 and opened by the Bristol & Exeter Railway on September 11th, 1866. The facilities included a water tank, coaling stage and a 43ft 3in mixed gauge turntable for joint use with the L&SWR shed (ST3308.1/1A). The line was absorbed by the GWR in 1876 and the shed was closed by them on July 14th, 1924.

CLEVEDON

Site ST4070.1; On the west side of the line, at the south end of Clevedon Station.

Clevedon (B&E)^{ST4070.1/1A}

A 1TS dead ended shed, located at ST40787095 and opened by the Bristol & Exeter Railway on July 28th, 1847. The construction details are not known, but it was believed to have been built in stone with a slated gable style roof, with the only facility being a 35ft turntable. The line was absorbed by the GWR in 1876 and the shed was closed in May 1879 to make way for station enlargements. It was proposed to dismantle the shed and re-erect it at Yatton (as ST4266.1/1A), but it is not certain that this was expedited.

Site ST4071.1; On the east side of Clevedon (WC&PLR) Station.

Clevedon (WC&PLR)^{ST4071.1/1A}

A timber built 2TS dead ended shed, located at ST40747100 and opened by the Weston, Clevedon & Portishead Light Railway on December 1st, 1897. It was closed on May 18th, 1940.

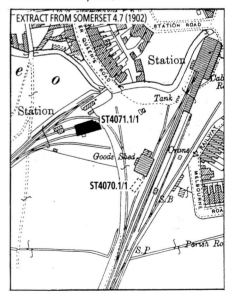

EXTRACT FROM SOMERSET 4.7 (1902)

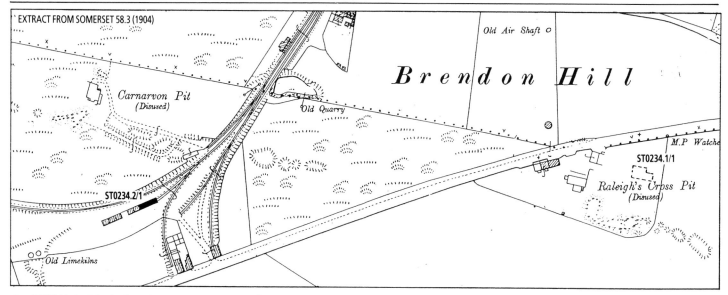

EXTRACT FROM SOMERSET 58.3 (1904)

Site ST0234.1; At Raleighs Cross Pit, on a short spur from the east side of the line, at the top of Comberow Incline.

Brendon Hill (WSMR)[ST0234.1/1A]

A ITS dead ended shed, located at ST02593422 and opened by the West Somerset Mineral Railway on commencement of the public goods service on September 28th, 1859. Few details are known about this depot, except that it fell out of use prior to 1880 and was thereafter utilized as a Carpenters Shop until the pit closed, probably in the 1890s.

Replaced, prior to 1880, by ...

Site ST0234.2; On the south side of the line, west of the top of Comberow Incline.

Brendon Hill (WSMR)[ST0234.2/1A]

A ITS dead ended shed, located at ST02113419 and opened by the West Somerset Mineral Railway. Neither details of the construction of the building, or facilities are available, but it is known that the shed was initially closed on November 7th, 1898. The line had been leased by the Ebbw Vale Company from June 24th, 1859 and it was they that re-opened the line and the shed on July 4th, 1907. Mine working was finally abandoned in 1910 when the line and shed were closed, with the track being lifted in 1917.

FROME

Site ST7847.1; On the west side of the line, at the south end of Frome Station.

Frome (GWR)[ST7847.1/1A]

A ITS dead ended shed, it was located at ST78414745 and opened in March 1854. Little is known of this building, or its facilities but it is believed to have closed in 1890.

Replaced on the same site by ...

Frome (GWR)[ST7847.1/1B]

A timber built ITS dead ended shed with a slated gable style roof, it was opened in 1890 and closed by BR in September 1963.

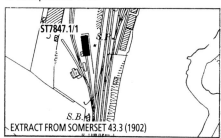

EXTRACT FROM SOMERSET 43.3 (1902)

GLASTONBURY

Site ST4838.1; In the vicinity of Glastonbury (SCR) Station.

Glastonbury (SCR)[ST4838.1/1A]

Some sort of facility was opened here by the Somerset Central Railway on August 24th, 1854, and closed in 1859.

HIGHBRIDGE

Site ST3246.1; Within the Highbridge Works complex, on the south side of the line, east of Highbridge (S&DJR) Station.

Highbridge (S&DJR)[ST3246.1/1A]

A brick built 2TS through road shed with a slated gable style roof, it was located at ST32594670 and was opened, along with the works, in 1862 by the Somerset & Dorset Joint Railway. Facilities included a 50ft turntable and coaling crane, with all other requirements being incorporated within the works area. Although the works itself closed in 1930 the shed continued in regular use, basically unaltered until closure came, by BR on May 11th, 1959.

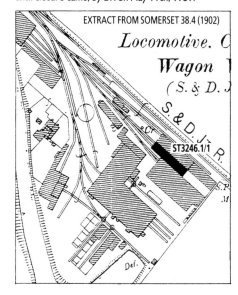

EXTRACT FROM SOMERSET 38.4 (1902)

MINEHEAD

Site SS9746.1; On the south side of Minehead Station.

Minehead (Minehead)[SS9746.1/1A]

A wooden built ITS dead ended shed with a slated gable style roof, it was located at SS97434630 and was opened by the Minehead Railway on July 16th, 1874. The building had originally stood at Watchet (as ST0743.1/1A) and at some stage, possibly on re-erection at Minehead, the entrance to the depot had been modified from an archway to a straight lintel type opening. The facilities included a water tank and turntable. The line was worked initially by the Bristol & Exeter Railway, and subsequently the GWR, with the depot lasting into BR days, closing on November 3rd, 1956.

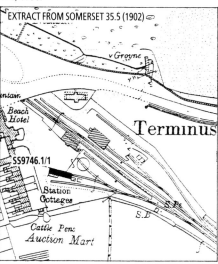

EXTRACT FROM SOMERSET 35.5 (1902)

RADSTOCK

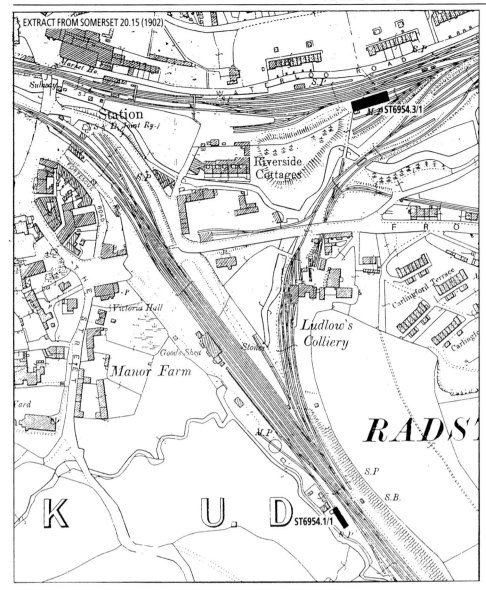

EXTRACT FROM SOMERSET 20.15 (1902)

Site ST6954.1; On the west side of the line, south of Radstock (GWR) Station.

Radstock (GWR)ST6954.1/1A

A stone built 1TS dead ended shed with a slated gable style roof, it was located at ST69165455 and opened on November 14th, 1854. The facilities included a water tank, with a coal stage and 41ft 6in turntable installed in 1896.

Following enlargement of the adjacent Wagon Works, the layout of the shed was re-arranged ...

Radstock (GWR)ST6954.1/1B

Probably in the early 1900s, the building was converted to a through road type to facilitate additional access to the works. The shed was closed in 1929 and became part of the Wagon Works itself, being utilized in its new role until June 1988. In 1991 it was secured for preservation by the *Somerset & Avon Railway.*

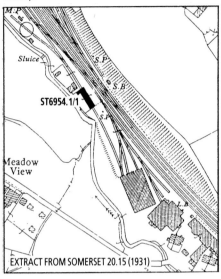

EXTRACT FROM SOMERSET 20.15 (1931)

Site ST6954.2; In the vicinity of Radstock North Station.

Radstock (SDR)ST6954.2/1A

Some sort of facility was established here after the line was opened by the Somerset & Dorset Railway on July 20th, 1874 and lasted until the construction of Radstock Shed (ST6954.3/1A) in 1888.

Site ST6954.3; On the south side of the line, east of Radstock North Station.

Radstock (S&DJR)ST6954.3/1A

A stone built 2TS dead ended shed with a slated gable style roof it was located at ST69195494 and was opened by the Somerset & Dorset Joint Railway in 1888. The facilities included a coaling crane and water column. The depot, famous for its collection of odd assortments of locomotives over the years, was closed by BR on March 7th, 1966. It was not demolished immediately but was occupied for a while by the *S&D Trust* until they relocated, after which the site was cleared and redeveloped.

PORTISHEAD

Site ST4776.1; On the east side of Portishead Station.

Portishead (B&PPR)ST4776.1/1A

A brick built 1TS through road shed with a slated gable style roof, it was located at ST47177698 and was opened by the Bristol & Portishead Pier Railway in April 1867. The facilities included a coaling shed, water tank and a turntable, originally sited at the north end of the shed, but later removed further north onto a short spur. The line was worked by the Bristol & Exeter Railway, and following absorption by the GWR in 1876, the shed went out of use, probably in about 1896. The disposition of the shed site meant that the depot access line was utilized daily to facilitate locomotive movements to and from the turntable and as a run-around line. The building had a new lease of life in 1915 when it was handed over to the Goods Department, although it is difficult to see what they were able to do with it with locomotives passing through it at regular intervals. Despite all this the shed remained standing until at least 1956.

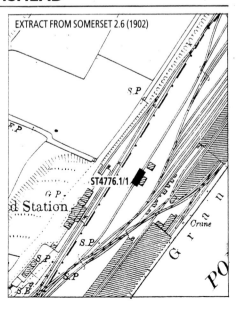

EXTRACT FROM SOMERSET 2.6 (1902)

SHEPTON MALLET

Site ST6243.1; In the vicinity of Shepton Mallet (ESR) Station.

Shepton Mallet (ESR)ST6243.1/1A

An engine shed was opened here by the East Somerset Railway on November 9th, 1858. It was closed on March 1st, 1862 and converted into a Goods Shed. No further details are currently available.

TAUNTON

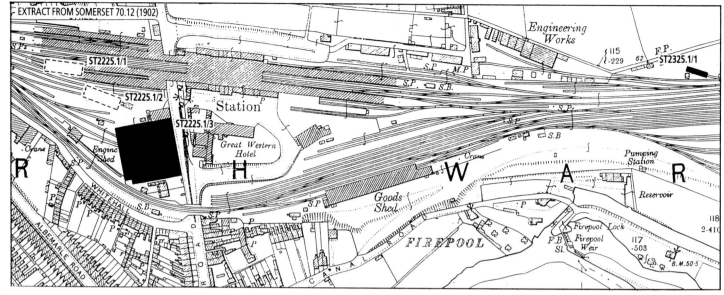

EXTRACT FROM SOMERSET 70.12 (1902)

Site ST2225.1; On the south side of the line, at the west end of Taunton Station.

Taunton (B&E)ST2225.1/1A
A timber built 2TS through road shed with a slated gable style roof, it was located at ST22582547 and opened by the Bristol & Exeter Railway on July 1st, 1842. The building had previously been used, as a temporary measure, at Bridgwater (as ST3037.1/1A) and amongst the facilities provided were a coke store, water tank and 22ft turntable. The shed closed in 1860, to make way for track widening and station enlargements, and it is believed that it was re-sited a second time.

The shed was re-located, or a new one constructed ...
Taunton (B&E)ST2225.1/2A
A timber built 2TS through road shed with a slated gable style roof, it was located at ST22632543 and opened by the Bristol & Exeter Railway in 1860. The facilities included a small coal plant and a 40ft turntable. The line was absorbed by the GWR in 1876 and the shed was closed in April 1896.

Replaced on an adjacent site by ...
Taunton (GWR)ST2225.1/3A
A brick built square roundhouse with a northlight pattern roof, it was located at ST22662537 and was opened by the GWR in 1896. It possessed all major facilities with a repair shop being added in 1932. The shed was closed by BR in October 1964.

Site ST2325.1; On the north side of the line, east of Taunton Station.

Engineers Siding (GWR)ST2325.1/F1
Some sort of basic facility was installed here, incorporating a siding for locomotive use at ST23202545. No further details are known.

Replaced, prior to 1902 by ...
Engineers Siding (GWR)ST2325.1/1A
A 1TS dead ended shed, probably built in timber. No further details are known.

Probably rebuilt at an unknown date ...
Engineers Siding (GWR)ST2325.1/1B
A concrete built 1TS dead ended shed. It lasted into BR days as a permanent way diesel depot, housing PWM652 for a number of years. No further details are known.

WATCHET

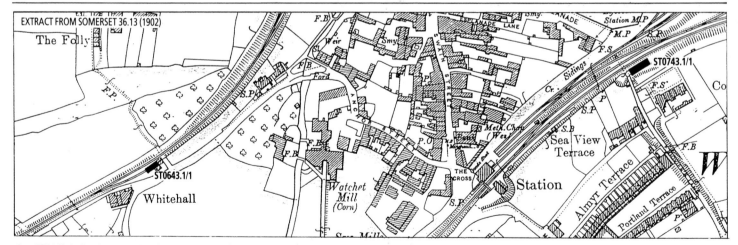

EXTRACT FROM SOMERSET 36.13 (1902)

Site ST0643.1; On the east side of the line, south of Watchet (WSMR) Station.

Watchet (WSMR)ST0643.1/1A
A 1TS dead ended shed, it was located at ST06824324 and was opened by the West Somerset Mineral Railway in April 1857. The shed was closed on November 7th, 1898 only to re-open for a short period from July 4th, 1907 to 1910*.

*See Brendon Hill (ST0234.2/1) for more details on the ownership of the line and its working arrangements.

Site ST0743.1; On the south side of the line, east of Watchet (WSR) Station.

Watchet (WSR)ST0743.1/1A
A timber built 1TS dead ended shed with slated gable style roof, it was located at ST07304332 and opened by the West Somerset Railway on March 31st, 1862. The facilities included a water tank and 37ft 8ins turntable. The line was worked by the Bristol & Exeter Railway from the outset and it was they that closed the shed in July 1874, upon completion of the branch to Minehead, removing the building and turntable and re-siting them at the terminus (as SS9746.1/1A).

Site ST7022.1; On the north side of the line, west of Templecombe Upper Station.

Templecombe Upper (L&SWR)^{ST7022.1/1A}
A timber built 1TS dead ended shed with a slated gable style roof, it was located at ST70102229 and was opened by the London & South Western Railway in 1870. The facilities included a coal stage and water tank sited outside of the shed entrance. During 1935 the building was destroyed, its demise is not recorded but it was probably as the result of a fire or severe weather conditions.

A servicing point was then established ...

Templecombe Upper (SR)^{ST7022.1/F1}
Locomotives then utilized the engine shed pit, water tank and coal stage from 1935 until 1942 when a small expansion of the facilities was authorized.

The servicing point was remodelled in 1942 ...

Templecombe Upper (SR)^{ST7022.1/F2}
The original engine shed road was extended to form a long head shunt, with the facilities, the engine pit, coaling stage and water column being re-sited on the adjacent track at ST70092228. Following nationalisation, and the availability of the adjacent Templecombe Shed (ST7022.2/1) for engine servicing the necessity for this facility diminished, but it is believed to have seen sporadic use until about 1955. The sidings were lifted by 1963.

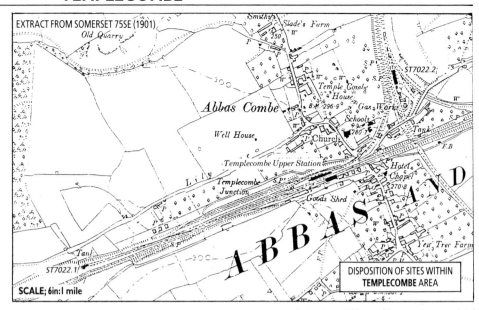

EXTRACT FROM SOMERSET 75SE (1901)

DISPOSITION OF SITES WITHIN
TEMPLECOMBE AREA

SCALE; 6in:1 mile

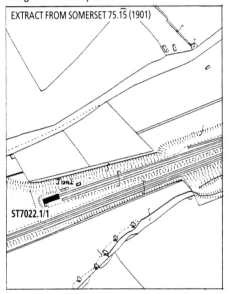

EXTRACT FROM SOMERSET 75.15 (1901)

ST7022.1/1

Site ST7022.2; On the east side of the Wincanton to Henstridge line, north of the point where it passes under the Waterloo to Exeter line.

Templecombe (SDR)^{ST7022.2/1A}
A timber built 1TS shed, located at ST70202283 and opened by the Somerset & Dorset Railway on August 31st, 1863. The facilities included a 30ft turntable. By 1877 the shed had become too small for operational requirements and was closed.

Replaced, on the same site, by ...

Templecombe (S&DJR)^{ST7022.2/1B}
A timber built 2TS dead ended shed with a slated gable style roof, it was opened in 1877 and the facilities included the original 30ft turntable and a coaling crane. The turntable was later re-sited and enlarged to 50ft. By 1948, after years of neglect, the shed had fallen into complete disrepair and the decision was taken to rebuild it.

The shed was rebuilt in 1951 ...

Templecombe (BR,SR)^{ST7022.2/1C}
A brick built 2TS dead ended shed with an asbestos pitched roof and SR-style brick gable end and screen. The depot closed on March 7th, 1966, but was not demolished immediately and was later sold into private ownership, being utilized as a workshop until at least 1994.

EXTRACT FROM SOMERSET 75.16 (1901)

ST7022.2/1

A portrait of Ex-LMS Class 3F 0-6-0 No.43436 also provides a good view of the engine shed erected at **Templecombe** in 1951/2 (ST7022.2/1C) as a replacement for the, by then, decrepit 2TS wooden structure (ST7022.2/1B) opened by the S&DJR in 1877.

The standard British Railways depot construction materials of brick and concrete with steel framed asbestos roofs served so well that after the shed closed, along with most of the much lamented S&D, in March 1966 it found further commercial use and still stood in 1997.   *Author's Collection*

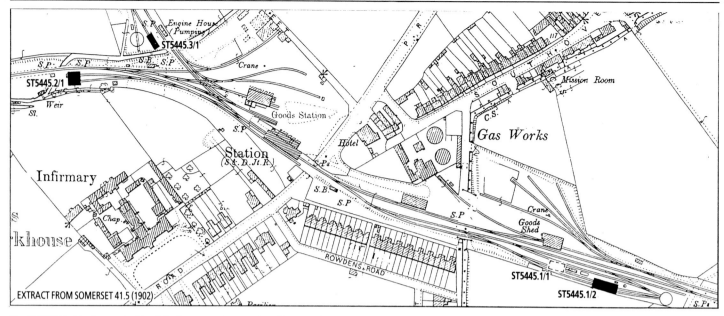

EXTRACT FROM SOMERSET 41.5 (1902)

Site ST5445.1; On the south side of the line, east of Wells Priory Road Station.

Wells (ESR)[ST5445.1/1A]

A 1TS through road shed, located at ST54764510 and opened by the East Somerset Railway on March 1st, 1862. The facilities included a water tank, coaling platform and 40ft turntable. Following the transfer of locomotives in 1876 from the closed Tucker Street Shed (ST5445.3/1A) it was found to be too small and was closed in September 1879 by the GWR.

Replaced, on an adjacent site, by ...

Wells (GWR)[ST5445.1/2A]

A brick built 2TS through road shed with a slated northlight pattern roof, it was located a few yards east of its predecessor at ST54814508 and was opened by the GWR in 1879. The facilities included a water tank and coaling platform sited adjacently to the shed entrance and a turntable at the rear of the building. At some stage the turntable was re-sited at a new location west of the shed. The depot was closed by BR on September 9th, 1963.

Site ST5445.2; On the south side of the Glastonbury line, west of Wells Priory Road Station.

Priory Road (SCR)[ST5445.2/1A]

A stone built 2TS through road shed with a gable style roof over each road, it was located at ST54294528 and was opened by the Somerset Central Railway on March 15th, 1859. The line was initially worked by the Bristol & Exeter until the SCR amalgamated with the Dorset Central Railway in 1861, becoming part of the Somerset & Dorset network. The shed had the unique feature of an internal water wheel used for pumping water from a stream for locomotive use. In 1901 the northern-most track through the shed was extended to form a wagon siding.

The shed was re-roofed ...

Priory Road (LMS)[ST5445.2/1B]

At some point, probably in the late 1930s, the roof over part of the northernmost track was replaced by a flat one, with a raised smoke vent. The shed was closed by the LMS in 1947, but it remained open at least as a stabling point for a few more years until the branch closed on October 29th, 1951.

Site ST5445.3; On the west side of the line, south of Wells Tucker Street Station.

Tucker Street (B&E)[ST5445.3/1A]

A 1TS dead ended shed, located at ST54374532 and opened by the Bristol & Exeter Railway on April 5th, 1870. The facilities included a 40ft turntable. The line was absorbed by the GWR in 1876 with the shed closing more or less immediately, the locomotives transferring to the nearby ex-East Somerset Shed (ST5445.1/1A).

YATTON

Site ST4266.1; On the north side of the Clevedon line, at the west end of Yatton Station.

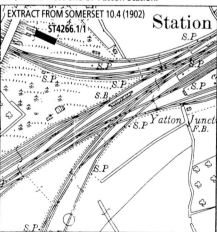

EXTRACT FROM SOMERSET 10.4 (1902)

Yatton (GWR)[ST4266.1/1A]

A stone built 1TS dead ended shed with a slated pitched roof and timber gable, it was located at ST42276606 and was opened by the GWR in 1879. There is some conjecture that the building materials for the depot were obtained from the closed Clevedon Shed (ST4070.1/1A). The shed was closed by BR in August 1960.

There may have been a previous shed at this site, but research to date has failed to confirm this.

WESTON SUPER MARE

Site ST3261.1; In the goods yard, on the north side of Weston Super Mare Station.

Weston Super Mare (B&E)[ST3261.1/1A]

A 1TS shed, it was located at ST32356120 and was opened by the Bristol & Exeter Railway on April 1st, 1851. The depot was closed in 1861.

Replaced, on the same site, by ...

Weston Super Mare (B&E)[ST3261.1/1B]

A stone built 1TS through road shed with a slated single pitch roof, it was opened by the Bristol & Exeter Railway in 1861. The facilities included a turntable in the shed yard, but this was re-sited further eastwards as a result of the building of Locking Road Station, adjacent to the north side of the shed. The line was leased to the GWR on June 1st, 1876 and then absorbed by them on August 1st, 1876. The shed was closed by BR in August 1960.

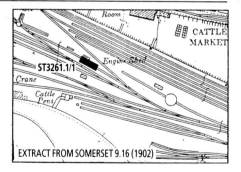

EXTRACT FROM SOMERSET 9.16 (1902)

WELLINGTON

Site ST1321.1; In the vicinity of Wellington Station.

Wellington (B&E)[ST1321.1/1A]

A 1TS shed was opened here by the Bristol & Exeter Railway in May 1845 and was probably closed in 1860 on the opening of a new shed at Taunton (ST2225.1/2A).

DRAWN FROM SOMERSET 83SW & 90NW (1904)

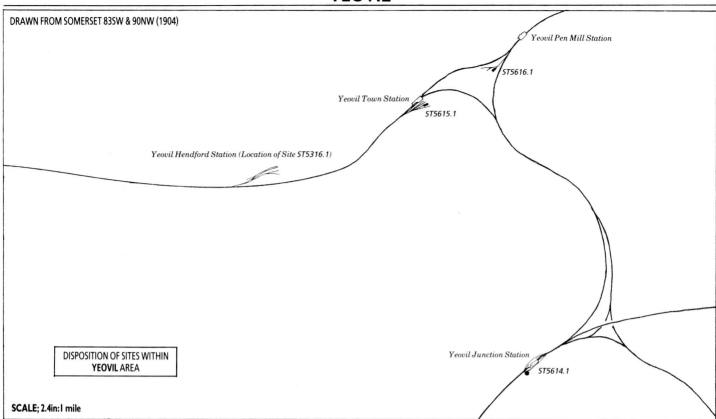

Yeovil Pen Mill Station

ST5616.1

Yeovil Town Station

ST5615.1

Yeovil Hendford Station (Location of Site ST5316.1)

Yeovil Junction Station

ST5614.1

DISPOSITION OF SITES WITHIN
YEOVIL AREA

SCALE; 2.4in:1 mile

Site ST5616.1; In the fork of the Weymouth and Yeovil Town lines, at the south end of Yeovil Pen Mill Station.
Pen Mill (GWR)[ST5616.1/1A]
A timber built 2TS dead ended shed with a slated gable style roof, it was located at ST56811609 and was opened on September 1st, 1856. The facilities included a coal stage surmounted by a water tank, and a turntable.

The shed was extended in 1877 ...
Pen Mill (GWR)[ST5616.1/2A]
A 1TS dead ended extension was built on the west side of the shed at ST56791608 but in later years it was mainly utilized for repairs. The shed was closed by BR on January 5th, 1959, its remaining locomotives transferring to the nearby Yeovil Town Shed (ST5615.1).

EXTRACT FROM SOMERSET 83.14 (1901)

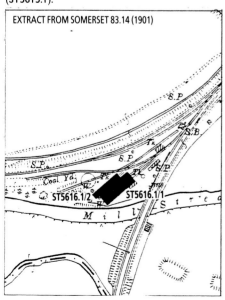

ST5616.1/2   ST5616.1/1

Site ST5615.1; On the south side of Yeovil Town Station.
Yeovil Town (E&YR)[ST5615.1/1A]
A brick built 3TS dead ended shed with a slated style gable roof, it was located at ST56301585 and was opened by the Exeter & Yeovil Railway on July 19th, 1860. It was equipped with all facilities, including a turntable which was removed in 1917.

The shed was refurbished ...
Yeovil Town (SR)[ST5615.1/1B]
In about 1947 the roof was replaced with asbestos sheeting and the doorways were widened slightly to improve clearances. At a later date the water tank, originally positioned in the shed roof was replaced by a larger capacity unit sited above the stores. The depot was closed by BR in June 1965.

EXTRACT FROM SOMERSET 83.14 (1901)

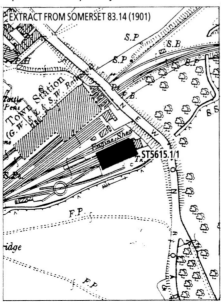

ST5615.1/1

Site ST5614.1; On the south side of the line, at the west end of Yeovil Junction Station.
Yeovil Junction (E&YR)[ST5614.1/F1]
A servicing area was opened here by the Exeter & Yeovil Railway in October 1860. The facility, consisting of a turntable (enlarged to 70ft in BR days), water tower, coaling stage and engine pit, was located at ST56971401 and remained operational until the end of steam in the area, in around 1966.

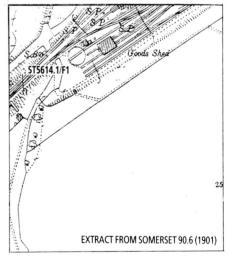

ST5614.1/F1   Goods Shed

EXTRACT FROM SOMERSET 90.6 (1901)

There may have been a shed here, prior to the establishment of the servicing area, but, at the moment, no details are known and its existence remains unconfirmed.

Site ST5316.1; In the vicinity of Yeovil Hendford Station.
Hendford (B&E)[ST5316.1/1A]
A shed was opened here by the Bristol & Exeter Railway on October 1st, 1853 and closed in 1857. No further details are available.

DEVON

SS7148 Lynton

SS5146 Ilfracombe

SS5533 Pilton Yard
SS5632 Barnstaple
SS5532 Barnstaple Junction

SS4630 Appledore

SS4526 Bideford (NDR&D)

SS4527 Bideford (BWH&A)

SS4719 Torrington

ST0716 Burlescombe

ST0311 Tiverton Junction

ST1314 Hemyock

SS3403 Holsworthy

SY2998 Axminster

SX8399 Crediton

SX9397 Stoke Canon

SX9193 Exeter
SX9293 Exeter Queen St.

SX9393 Exmouth Junction

SY2590 Seaton (S&
SY2589 Seaton (SR)

SX5994 Okehampton

SY1288 Sidmouth

SX5692 Meldon Quarry

SX7585 Moretonhampstead

SX8483 Ashton

SY0582 Budleigh Salterton

SY0081 Exmouth

SX4873 Tavistock

SX9473 Teignmouth

SX5873 Princetown

SX8671 Newton Abbot

SX7569 Ashburton

SX9064 Torquay Torre

SX8959 Goodrington Sands

SX7960 Totnes

SX8956 Churston

SX9256 Brixham

SX4654 Devonport
SX4754 Millbay
SX4654 Plymouth Dock

SX5055 Laira

SX4854 Friary
SX4954 Friary

SX8851 Kingswear

SX7344 Kingsbridge

APPLEDORE

Site SS4630.1; At the end of the line, at the south end of Appledore Station.

Appledore (BWH&AR)^SS4630.1/1A

A ITS dead ended shed, it was located at SS46363072 and opened by the Bideford, Westward Ho! & Appledore Railway on May 1st, 1908. It is believed to have been of wooden construction and the facilities included a water tower and coaling stage sited outside the shed entrance. The shed was only open for a brief period, closing in 1910.

EXTRACT FROM DEVON 12.11 (1903)
SS4630.1/1

Please Note; The construction and dismantling dates of this line precludes its inclusion in a complete form in OS maps. The shed site has been superimposed.

ASHBURTON

Site SX7569.1; On the east side of the line, at the south end of Ashburton Station.

Ashburton (BT&SDR)^SX7569.1/1A

A stone built ITS dead ended shed with a gable style slated roof, located at SX75666956 and opened on May 1st, 1872 by the Buckfastleigh, Totnes and South Devon Railway. The facilities included a water tower and coaling stage sited on the shed approach road. It was absorbed as part of the GWR in 1897 and was closed by BR in November 1958. The shed was sold for private use and was still in existence in 1994.

EXTRACT FROM DEVON 114.3 (1904)
SX7569.1/1

ASHTON

Site SX8483.1; On the east side of the line, at the south end of Ashton Station.

Ashton (Teign Valley Railway)^SX8483.1/1A

A brick built ITS through road shed with a gable style slated roof, located at SX84458398 and opened on October 9th, 1882. The facilities included a coal stage and water tower, sited at the southern end of the building. The depot is believed to have closed in about 1908, but it is known to have still been standing over fifty years later

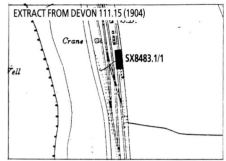
EXTRACT FROM DEVON 111.15 (1904)
SX8483.1/1

AXMINSTER

Site SY2998.1; On the east side of the line, at the south end of Axminster Station.

Axminster (L&SWR)^SY2998.1/1A

A ITS through road shed it was located at SY29189804 and was opened on July 19th, 1860. It is believed to have been constructed in corrugated iron and had a coal stage at the southern end of the building. The shed went out of use by 1896 and was demolished between 1900 and 1903.

Replaced in 1903 by ...
Site SY2998.2; On the west side of Axminster Station.

Axminster (L&SWR)^SY2998.2/F1

Following the opening of the Lyme Regis branch in 1903 a small servicing point, located at SY29249821, was established. This consisted of a coaling stage, built alongside the water tower, and a water column and probably lasted until the line was dieselized in 1963.

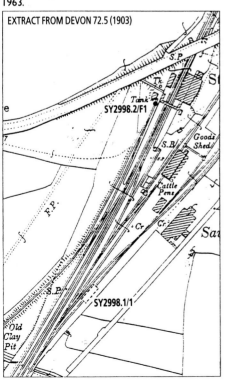
EXTRACT FROM DEVON 72.5 (1903)
SY2998.2/F1
SY2998.1/1

BIDEFORD

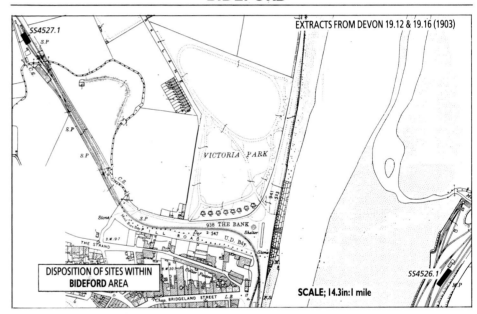
EXTRACTS FROM DEVON 19.12 & 19.16 (1903)
VICTORIA PARK
DISPOSITION OF SITES WITHIN BIDEFORD AREA
SS4527.1
SS4526.1
SCALE; 14.3in:1 mile

Site SS4526.1; On the west side of the line, at the north end of Bideford Cross Parks Goods Station.

Bideford (NDR&DR)^SS4526.1/1A

A ITS dead ended shed with a gable style slated roof, located at SS45842683 and opened by the North Devon Railway & Dock Company on August 1st, 1854. The facilities included a turntable. The line was worked by the Bristol & Exeter Railway from July 28th, 1855 until 1861 when a contractor, Thomas Brassey, took over. It was absorbed by the L&SWR on January 1st, 1865. The shed probably went out of use sometime shortly after 1872 when the line was extended to Torrington and a small depot (SS4719.1/1A) was established there. The building found further use as part of the goods depot, being utilized as a store at some point, and was still standing until at least 1960.

EXTRACT FROM DEVON 19.16 (1903)
SS4526.1/1

Site SS4527.1; On the west side of the line, north of The Quay terminus.

Bideford (BWH&A)^SS4527.1/1A

A brick built 2TS shed with one through road and a timber and corrugated iron pitched roof, located at SS45142725 and opened by the Bideford, Westward Ho! & Appledore Railway on May 20th, 1901. The facilities included a coaling stage and water column. The line only enjoyed a short existence, closing on March 27th, 1917, but the shed building found many more years of use under private ownership and was still standing in 1995.

EXTRACT FROM DEVON 19.12 (1903)
SS4527.1/1

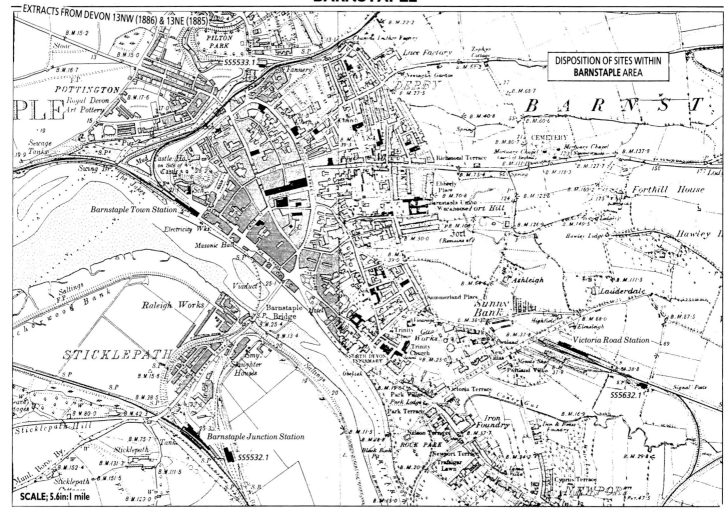

EXTRACTS FROM DEVON 13NW (1886) & 13NE (1885)

DISPOSITION OF SITES WITHIN **BARNSTAPLE** AREA

SCALE; 5.6in:1 mile

Site SS5632.1; On the south side of the line, at the east end of Barnstaple Victoria Road Station.
Barnstaple (D&SR)^{SS5632.1/1A}
A timber built 2TS dead ended shed with a gable style slated roof, located at SS56933264 and opened by the Devon & Somerset Railway on November 1st, 1873. The facilities included a water tower, coal stage and turntable. It was absorbed by the GWR in 1901 and closed by BR in January 1951 being subsequently demolished.

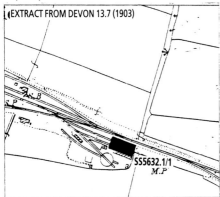

EXTRACT FROM DEVON 13.7 (1903)

SS5632.1/1
M.P

Site SS5532.1; On the east side of Barnstaple Junction Station.
Barnstaple Junction (NDR&DC)^{SS5532.1/1A}
A shed opened by the North Devon Railway & Dock Company on August 1st, 1854. Documentary evidence is inconclusive about this depot but it is assumed to be the 1TS stone and timber building located at SS55663246. The shed was closed in 1863.

Replaced by ...
Barnstaple Junction (L&SWR)^{SS5532.1/2A}
A timber built 2TS through road shed with a slated gable style roof, located at SS55643247 and opened in 1863. This building was erected alongside its assumed predecessor (SS5532.1/1A) utilizing the former shed as a stores and workshop. Other facilities included a turntable, coaling stage and water column. *(From the appearance of the building it could have been constructed in two phases, the northernmost portion being slightly narrower and having a lower roof. However, with no documentary evidence to confirm the building of an extension at a later date it is assumed to have all been built at the same time.)*

At some point, prior to 1947 it was re-roofed...
Barnstaple Junction (SR)^{SS5532.1/2B}
The roof was replaced with corrugated iron. By the time that the shed was closed by BR in September 1964 the building was virtually roofless and derelict. Demolition followed shortly afterwards.

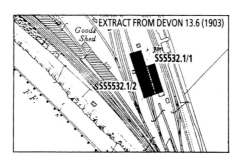

EXTRACT FROM DEVON 13.6 (1903)

Goods Shed

SS5532.1/1

SS5532.1/2

Site SS5533.1; On the west side of the line, north of Barnstaple Town Station.
Pilton Yard (L&BR)^{SS5533.1/1A}
A corrugated iron 1ft 11½in gauge 2TS shed with one through line, extending into an adjoining workshop, located at SS55783364 and opened by the Lynton & Barnstaple Railway on May 16th, 1898. It formed part of the railway's main depot with a carriage and wagon shed built alongside and a coal stage, water column and 30ft turntable in the yard.

At some stage the shed was rebuilt ...
Pilton Yard (L&BR)^{SS5533.1/1B}
The corrugated iron was replaced by timber and the pitched roof was reclad with tiles, remaining in this state until the line was closed by the SR on September 30th, 1935. Whilst the turntable was sold to the Romney Hythe & Dymchurch Railway, most of the buildings at Pilton Yard, including the shed, were sold for private use. The shed building was destroyed by a fire on September 8th, 1992.

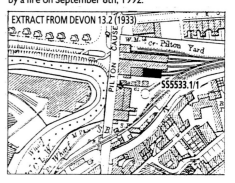

EXTRACT FROM DEVON 13.2 (1933)

Pilton Yard

SS5533.1/1

BRIXHAM

Site SX9256.1; On the west side of the line, at the south end of Brixham Station.
Brixham (T&BR)[SX9256.1/1A]
A timber built ITS dead ended shed with a slated gable style roof, located at SX92395632 and opened by the Torbay & Brixham Railway on February 28th, 1868. In August 1890 a small coal stage was built by the shed entrance. The line was initially worked by the South Devon Railway but was absorbed in 1893 by the GWR who demolished the shed in 1896.

Replaced on the same site in 1897 by ...
Brixham (GWR)[SX9256.1/1B]
A corrugated iron ITS dead ended shed, surmounted on a dwarf brick wall and with a corrugated iron gable style roof. The building had originally stood at Stenalees (as SX0157.1/1A) and had been removed in March 1897. Upon re-erection at Brixham a small extension was added to the rear of the shed. The depot was closed on July 22nd, 1929.

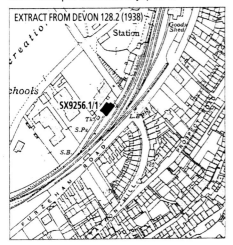
EXTRACT FROM DEVON 128.2 (1938)
SX9256.1/1

EXMOUTH

Site SY0081.1; On the east side of Exmouth Station.
Exmouth (E&E)[SY0081.1/1A]
A timber built ITS dead ended shed with a slated gable style roof, it was located at SY00048115 and opened by the Exeter & Exmouth Railway on July 1st, 1861. The facilities included a turntable and *two* water tanks sited outside of the shed entrance. The line was absorbed by the L&SWR in 1866 and the building lasted until 1927 when it was demolished.

Replaced in 1927 by ...
Exmouth (SR)[SY0081.1/1B]
A concrete built ITS dead ended shed with a felt and tar pitched roof it occupied the same site as its predecessor (SY0081.1/1A). The turntable and water tanks were removed, with a new tank being incorporated in the roof at the rear of the building.

At some stage it was re-roofed ...
Exmouth (SR)[SY0081.1/1C]
Either prior to nationalization or in early BR days the roof was replaced with corrugated asbestos. It lasted in this condition until closed by BR on November 8th, 1963. It was subsequently demolished, the site being utilized in a new road scheme.

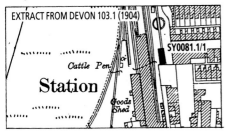
EXTRACT FROM DEVON 103.1 (1904)
SY0081.1/1

BUDLEIGH SALTERTON

Site SY0582.1; On the west side of the line, at the north end of Budleigh Salterton Station.
Budleigh Salterton (BSR)[SY0582.1/1A]
A timber built ITS dead ended shed, it was located at SY05988267 and opened by the Budleigh Salterton Railway on May 15th, 1897. The facilities included a coaling stage and water tank sited outside of the entrance to the shed. The line was worked from the outset by the L&SWR and the shed was closed on June 1st, 1903 following the opening of the line through to Exmouth. It was demolished by 1925.

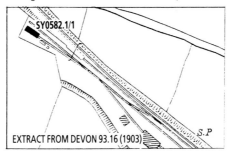
SY0582.1/1
EXTRACT FROM DEVON 93.16 (1903)

CREDITON

Site SX8399.1; On the north side of the line, at the west end of Crediton Station.
Crediton (EC&BR)[SX8399.1/1A]
A ITS dead ended shed, probably constructed in timber, located at SX83959951 and opened by the Exeter, Crediton & Barnstaple Railway on May 12th, 1851. Little is known about this depot, other than that it was destroyed by fire on August 20th, 1862 just after the L&SWR had taken over the lease of the line.

Replaced on the same site by ...
Crediton (L&SWR)[SX8399.1/1B]
A timber built ITS dead ended shed opened by the L&SWR in about 1864. The facilities included a small turntable, with three stub sidings radiating from it, sited outside of the shed entrance. The shed went out of use, probably in about 1872.

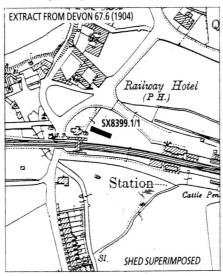
EXTRACT FROM DEVON 67.6 (1904)
SX8399.1/1
SHED SUPERIMPOSED

CHURSTON

Site SX8956.1; In the vicinity of Churston Station.
Churston (D&TR)[SX8956.1/F1]
Some form of servicing area, incorporating a turntable and siding was opened here on March 4th, 1861 by the Dartmouth & Torbay Railway. The line was worked from the outset by the South Devon Railway, the facility closing on August 16th, 1864.

BURLESCOMBE

Site ST0716.1; On the north side of the line, at the west end of Burlescombe Station.
Burlescombe (B&ER)[ST0716.1/1A]
A timber built 3ft 0in gauge ITS dead ended shed with a slated gable style roof, it was located at ST07231696 and opened by the Bristol & Exeter Railway (Westleigh Mineral Railway) in January 1875. It was specifically built to house the Quarry locomotives and was closed in October 1898 when the line was rebuilt to standard gauge.

EXTRACT FROM DEVON 35.12 (1903)
ST0716.1/1
SHED SUPERIMPOSED

HEMYOCK

Site ST1314.1; On the north side of the line, at the west end of Hemyock Station.
Hemyock (CVLR)[ST1314.1/1A]
A timber built ITS dead ended shed with a slated gable style roof, it was located at ST13761402 and opened by the Culm Valley Light Railway on May 29th, 1876. The facilities included a coal stage and water tank sited outside of the shed entrance. The line was absorbed by the GWR in 1880 and the shed was closed by them as an economy measure on October 21st, 1929.

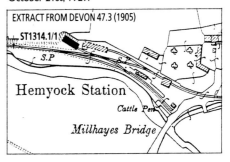
EXTRACT FROM DEVON 47.3 (1905)
ST1314.1/1
Hemyock Station
Millhayes Bridge

HOLSWORTHY

Site SS3403.1; On the north side of the line, at the east end of Holsworthy Station.
Holsworthy (L&SWR)[SS3403.1/1A]
A timber built ITS dead ended shed with a slated gable style roof, it was located at SS34370358 and opened on January 20th, 1879. The facilities included a 42ft turntable and coaling stage sited outside of the shed entrance. Although it was probably *officially* closed after the depot at Bude (SS2105.1/1A) had opened in 1898, it was nevertheless utilized to service locomotives for a number of years after. The turntable was removed in 1915 and it is believed the shed ceased to function in 1917, subsequently being used as a store. It was finally demolished by the SR sometime after the grouping.

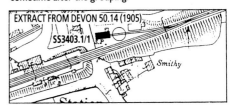
EXTRACT FROM DEVON 50.14 (1905)
SS3403.1/1
Smithy

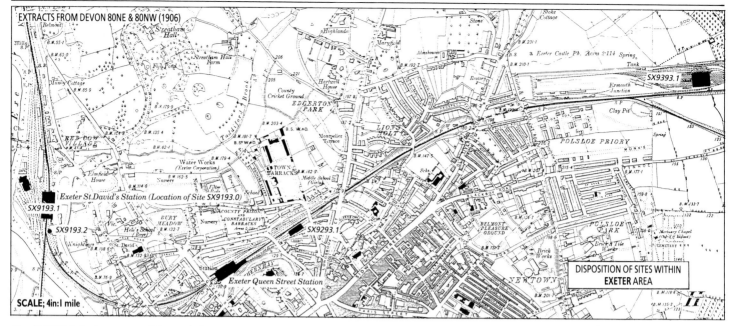

EXTRACTS FROM DEVON 80NE & 80NW (1906)

Exeter St.David's Station (Location of Site SX9193.0)

SX9193.1

SX9193.2

SX9293.1

Exeter Queen Street Station

SCALE; 4in:1 mile

DISPOSITION OF SITES WITHIN
EXETER AREA

Site SX9193.0; In the vicinity of Exeter St.David's Station.

Exeter (B&E)[SX9193.0/1A]
A temporary 1TS shed, probably constructed in timber and opened by the Bristol & Exeter Railway on May 1st, 1844. It was closed in 1851.

Site SX9193.1; On the west side of Exeter St.David's Station.

Exeter (B&E)[SX9193.1/1A]
A 3TS dead ended shed located at SX91159318 and opened by the Bristol & Exeter Railway in 1851. It was probably constructed in timber with a gable style slated roof and had a coal stage sited outside of the shed entrance. It was closed in 1864 and demolished to make way for station enlargements.

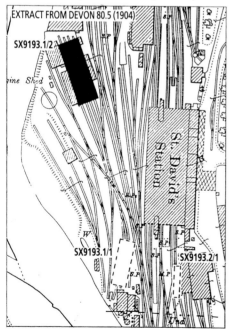

EXTRACT FROM DEVON 80.5 (1904)

SX9193.1/2

St. David's Station

SX9193.1/1   SX9193.2/1

Replaced in 1864 by ...

Exeter (B&E)[SX9193.1/2A]
A brick built 4TS through road shed with a glazed and tiled northlight pattern roof, it was located slightly further north than its predecessor (SX9193.1/1A) at SX91069338 and was opened by the Bristol & Exeter Railway in 1864.

The shed was extended in 1894...

Exeter (GWR)[SX9193.1/2B]
The building was extended by 60ft and improvements to the yard and facilities, including a coal stage with ramp, were expedited. A large turntable was sited in the shed yard. By the time that the depot was closed to steam on October 14th, 1963 the roof had been removed and the shell of the building was subsequently utilized as a diesel stabling point. A small 1TS diesel depot (SX9193.1/2C) was constructed on part of the shed site in 1980.

Site SX9193.2; On the east side of the line, at the south end of Exeter St.David's Station.

Exeter (SDR)[SX9193.2/1A]
A 1TS dead ended shed, located at SX91099320 and opened by the South Devon Railway in July 1846. It was probably built in stone with a gable style slated roof. Little more is known of this depot and it most probably closed in 1864 to facilitate station enlargement.

Site SX9293.1; On the south side of the line, at the east end of Exeter Queen Street Station.

Queen Street (E&YR)[SX9293.1/1A]
A brick built 3TS through road shed with a gable style slated roof, it was located at SX92229318 and was opened by the Exeter & Yeovil Railway on July 19th, 1860. The facilities included a water tank, coal stage and a 42ft turntable. The line was absorbed by the L&SWR in 1866 and the shed was closed in 1887, following the opening of Exmouth Junction depot (SX9393.1/1A).

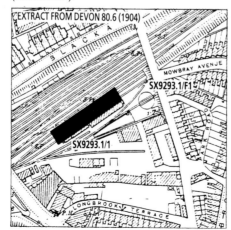

EXTRACT FROM DEVON 80.6 (1904)

SX9293.1/F1

SX9293.1/1

A servicing point was then established ...

Queen Street (L&SWR)[SX9293.1/F1]
In 1887 the turntable, located at SX92289320, was replaced by a 50ft unit and this. along with the coaling stage were utilized as a locomotive servicing and stabling area. The shed building was still retained and used until about 1900 when it was demolished and the site used as carriage sidings. The service point continued in use until the early 1930s.

In this 1902 elevated picture **Exeter (GWR)** shed (SX9193.1/2B) provides a backdrop to a superb collection of period GWR locomotive power. This 4TS northlight structure was actually opened by the Bristol & Exeter Railway in 1864 as its third engine shed in the city, following the earlier buildings of 1844 (SX9193.0/1A) and 1851 (SX9193.1/1A).

The B&ER was absorbed by the GWR in 1876 and eighteen years later the new owners extended the building to the form depicted here. Although the shed closed to steam in October 1963 and was demolished sections of the walls remained into the 1990s as part of the diesel servicing point.

B Matthews

Continued ...

EXTRACT FROM DEVON 80.3 (1905)

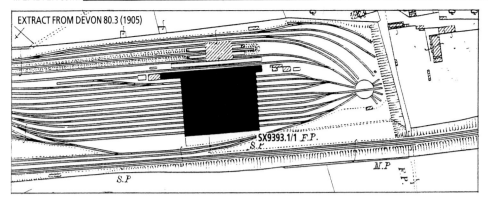

SX9393.1/1 F.P.

Site SX9393.1; On the north side of the line, about 1¼ miles east of Exeter Queen Street Station, at Exmouth Junction.

Exmouth Junction (L&SWR)SX9393.1/1A

A large 11TS through road shed, it was constructed in corrugated iron supported by a metal framework and surmounted by four large gables, again in corrugated iron but with glazed gable ends. It was located at SX93909378 and opened on November 3rd,

1887. The depot enjoyed all the facilities of a main shed; raised coal stage, water tank, repair shop, ash removal system and a 55ft turntable at the rear of the depot from which all the shed roads radiated. The choice of principal building material undoubtedly led to the early demise of the shed, as the structure slowly deteriorated and by 1920 the decision to replace it was made, the shed finally closing during 1927.

During 1926/27 a new depot was constructed at the rear of the shed ...

Exmouth Junction (SR)SX9393.1/2A

A ferro-concrete 12TS dead ended shed with a concrete and asphalt eastlight pattern roof, it was located at the eastern end of the yard at SX93999380. The facilities included a repair bay, mechanical coaling plant, water tower and an electrically operated 65ft turntable. The depot was closed to steam in June 1965 and totally closed in March 1967. The shed was subsequently demolished.

EXTRACTS FROM SX9393 (1962) & SX9493 (1951)

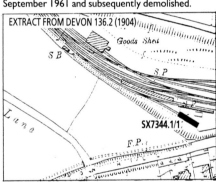

SX9393.1/2

ILFRACOMBE

Site SS5146.1; On the east side of Ilfracombe Station.

Ilfracombe (B&IR)SS5146.1/1A

A timber built 1TS dead ended shed with a slated gable style roof, it was located at SS51454679 and opened by the Barnstaple & Ilfracombe Railway on July 24th, 1874. The facilities included a 40ft turntable sited outside of the shed entrance. The shed was demolished in 1928 to make way for station improvements.

Replaced in 1928 by ...
Site SS5146.2; On the east side of the line, south of Ilfracombe Station.

Ilfracombe (SR)SS5146.2/1A

A concrete built 1TS through road shed with a corrugated asbestos gable style roof, it was located some distance south from its predecessor (SS5146.1/1A) at SS51444644. The facilities included a 65ft turntable, water tank, coal stage and ash handling equipment. The shed was closed by BR during 1964.

EXTRACT FROM SS5146 (1962)

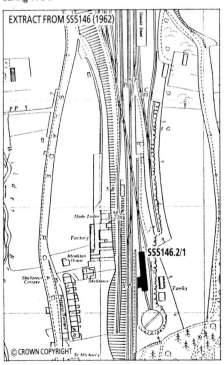

SS5146.2/1

EXTRACT FROM DEVON 4.4 (1904) F.P.

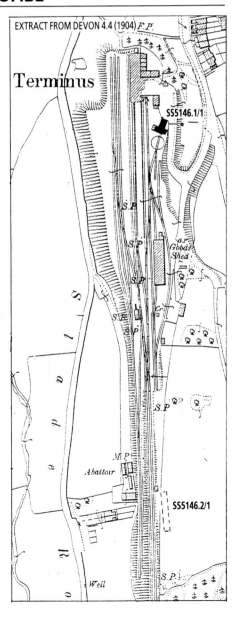

Terminus

SS5146.1/1

SS5146.2/1

KINGSBRIDGE

Site SX7344.1; On the south side of Kingsbridge Station.

Kingsbridge (GWR)SX7344.1/1A

A stone built 1TS dead ended shed with a slated gable style roof, it was located at SX73174405 and opened on December 19th, 1893. The facilities included a water tower and coaling stage sited on the shed approach road. The depot was closed by BR in September 1961 and subsequently demolished.

EXTRACT FROM DEVON 136.2 (1904)

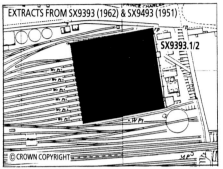

SX7344.1/1

KINGSWEAR

Site SX8851.1; On the south side of the line, at the east end of Kingswear Station.

Kingswear (D&TR)SX8851.1/1A

A timber built 1TS dead ended shed with a slated gable style roof, it was located at SX88355115 and was opened by the Dartmouth & Torbay Railway on August 16th, 1864. The facilities included a water tank and 23ft 5in turntable (enlarged to 55ft 8in in 1900) sited outside of the shed entrance. The line was operated by the South Devon Railway and was absorbed by the GWR on August 1st, 1878. The shed was closed on July 14th, 1924 and demolished in 1931.

EXTRACT FROM DEVON 128.13 (1904)

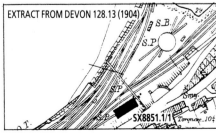

SX8851.1/1

LYNTON

Site SS7148.1; On the west side of the line, at the south end of Lynton & Lynmouth Station.

Lynton (L&BR)^{SS7148.1/1A}
A stone built 1ft 11½in gauge 1TS dead ended shed with a corrugated iron pitched roof, it was located at SS71864871 and opened by the Lynton & Barnstaple Railway on May 16th, 1898. The facilities included a coaling stage on the approach road, with a water column sited adjacently at the platform end.

Sometime after 1904 the track layout was altered...
Lynton (L&BR)^{SS7148.1/1B}
Access was altered from the southern end to the north, the building now remodelled as a through road shed with the coaling stage remaining *in situ* on a short siding. The shed remained in this condition until it was closed by the SR on September 30th, 1935.

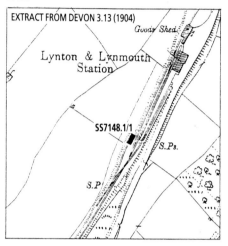

MELDON QUARRY

Site SX5692.1; At the south end of Meldon Quarry sidings, on the east side of the line.

Meldon Quarry (SR)^{SX5692.1/1A}
A wooden framed 1TS dead ended shed clad in corrugated iron with a corrugated iron gable style roof, it was located at SX56699258 and opened in March 1927. The depot was built to house the Departmental locomotive allocated to shunt the quarry sidings and by early post war years had deteriorated to the point that a replacement was required.

Replaced, on the same site by ...
Meldon Quarry (BR)^{SX5692.1/1B}
A concrete built 1TS dead ended shed with a flat concrete roof opened by the Southern Region in about 1950. Steam locomotives ceased to be used at the quarry in about 1966 and the depot was still in use in 1995, housing a Class 08 diesel shunter.

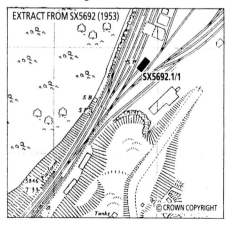

OKEHAMPTON

Site SX5994.1; On the north side of the line, at the east end of Okehampton Station.

Okehampton (L&SWR)^{SX5994.1/F1}
A siding and 42ft turntable, located at SX59359446, were installed, possibly in 1879 to facilitate the arrival of three Class 46 4-6-0T locomotives allocated there from new.

In 1894 a shed was built ...
Okehampton (L&SWR)^{SX5994.1/1A}
A timber built 1TS dead ended shed with a slated gable style roof, it was located at SX59409446 and opened in 1894. The turntable was enlarged to 50ft during the following year.

In 1914 the building was enlarged ...
Okehampton (L&SWR)^{SX5994.1/1B}
The shed was extended at the eastern end, nearly doubling in size and it remained in this condition until destroyed by a fire on June 7th, 1920.

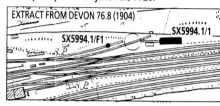

Replaced on the same site by ...
Okehampton (L&SWR)^{SX5994.1/1C}
A concrete built 1TS dead ended shed with a corrugated asbestos gable style roof, it opened during 1920 and a small coaling stage was provided outside of the shed entrance.

During 1943 further modifications were made ...
Okehampton (SR)^{SX5994.1/1D}
A new 70ft turntable was laid down alongside the station and the shed yard was increased in size and refurbished with new pits and water columns. The gable ends of the shed were replaced by corrugated asbestos sheeting and new smoke vents installed. The shed was closed by BR in 1964.

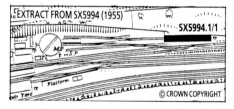

MORETONHAMPSTEAD

Site SX7585.1; On the south side of the line, at the east end of Moretonhampstead Station.

Moretonhampstead (M&SDR)^{SX7585.1/1A}
A stone built 1TS dead ended shed with a slated gable style roof, it was located at SX75838564 and opened by the Moretonhampstead & South Devon Railway on July 4th, 1866. The facilities included a coal stage and water tank on the shed approach road. The line was absorbed by the South Devon Railway in 1872 and by the GWR four years later. The shed was closed in November 1947, but was used as a stabling point into BR days. The shed was still standing in 1995, in use as a garage for a transport company.

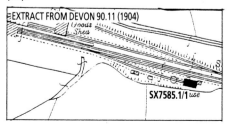

NEWTON ABBOT

Site SX8671.1; On the east side of the line, north of Newton Abbot Station.

Newton Abbot (SDR)^{SX8671.1/1A}
A 2TS dead ended shed, probably built in timber with a slated roof, it was located at SX86807143 and opened by the South Devon Railway on December 30th, 1846*. The facilities included a small turntable and coal stage. The shed was closed in November 1893.

Replaced by ...
Site SX8671.2; On the east side of Newton Abbot Station.

Newton Abbot (GWR)^{SX8671.2/1A}
A stone built 6TS dead ended shed with a slated and glazed northlight pattern roof, it was located at SX86857121 and was opened in November 1893. The building was attached to a locomotive factory and possessed all facilities. The shed was closed to steam on April 1st, 1962, with a new purpose built diesel depot (SX8671.2/2A) being constructed almost immediately on the west side of the original building. The steam shed, roofless by the mid-1970s, was then utilized for stabling diesel locomotives until the diesel depot itself was closed in the 1980s. The buildings were still standing, in a derelict condition, until at least 1993.

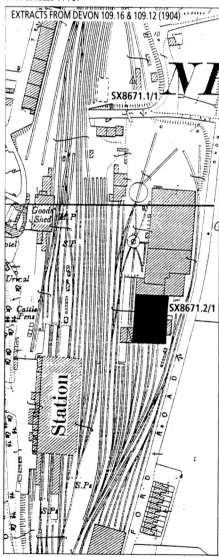

Initially there may have been a temporary shed (SX8671.0/1A) located at the south end of Newton Abbot Station. This would have opened on December 30th, 1846 with its successor (SX8671.1/1A) opening about a year later.

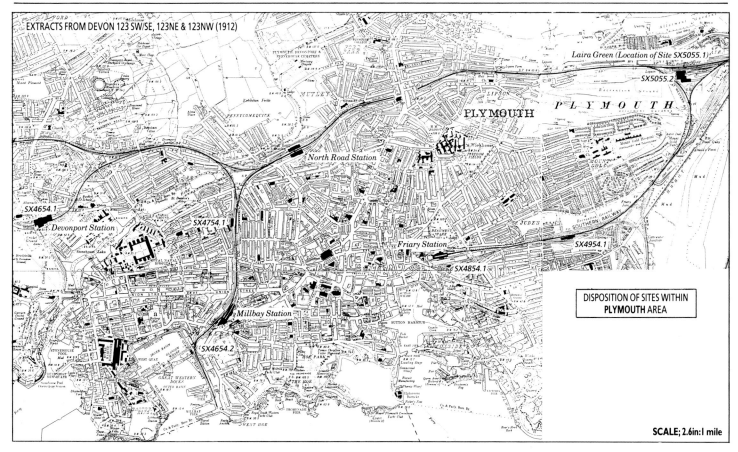

EXTRACTS FROM DEVON 123 SW/SE, 123NE & 123NW (1912)

DISPOSITION OF SITES WITHIN **PLYMOUTH** AREA

SCALE; 2.6in:1 mile

Site SX5055.1; In the vicinity of Laira Halt Station.
Laira Green (SDR)^{SX5055.1/F1}
Some sort of facility would have been required here as on May 5th, 1848 this location became the temporary terminus of the South Devon Railway. It would have lasted until April 1849 when the line was extended to Millbay.

Site SX5055.2; On the south side of Laira Halt Station.
Laira (GWR)^{SX5055.2/1A}
A brick built 1RH with a slated and glazed eastlight pattern roof, it was located at SX50265573 and was opened in 1901. The depot possessed all facilities, including a raised coaling stage in the yard.

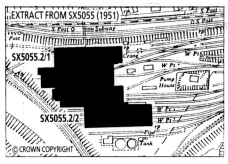

EXTRACT FROM SX5055 (1951)
SX5055.2/1
SX5055.2/2
© CROWN COPYRIGHT

It was enlarged in 1931 ...
Laira (GWR)^{SX5055.2/2A}
An asbestos built 4TS through road shed with an asbestos gable style roof, it was built along the southern wall of SX5055.2/1A in 1931 and was located at SX50295569. The shed was closed in April 1964 and replaced by a purpose built diesel depot (SX5055.2/3A) which had been opened in December 1961 and was located at the east end of the yard at SX50455555. The shed buildings and yard were thereafter used for stabling diesel locomotives and rolling stock.

Site SX4654.2; On the west side of the docks branch, about 200 yards south of Millbay Station.
Plymouth Dock (SDR)^{SX4654.2/1A}
A stone built 1TS dead ended shed with a slated gable style roof, it was located at SX46965405 and opened by the South Devon Railway in about 1869.

It was enlarged ...
Plymouth Dock (GWR)^{SX4654.2/1B}
The building was extended about 10ft at some time around about 1903. The facilities included a water tower on the approach road. The depot lasted into BR days, probably not closing until 1955 when it was taken over by the port authority and was still in use, as a workshop, in 1998.

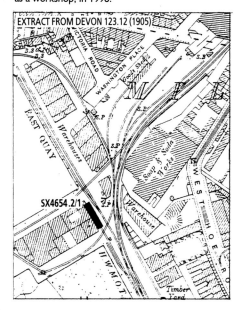

EXTRACT FROM DEVON 123.12 (1905)
SX4654.2/1

Site SX4654.1; On the north side of Plymouth Devonport Station.
Devonport (L&SWR)^{SX4654.1/1A}
A stone built 2TS dead ended shed with a slated gable style roof, it was located at SX46035494 and was opened on May 17th, 1876. The facilities included a 40ft turntable, onto which both tracks converged, a coal stage and water tank. The shed was regarded as being too small and on the opening of Friary depot (SX4854.1/1A) in 1891 it declined in use, lingering on until final closure in 1908. It was let for private use and remained standing at least until the station closed completely on January 4th, 1971.

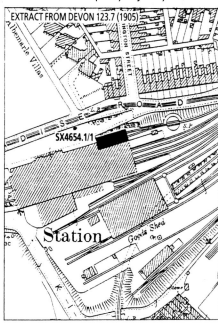

EXTRACT FROM DEVON 123.7 (1905)
SX4654.1/1
Station

Continued ...

Site SX4854.1; On the south side of Plymouth Friary Station.

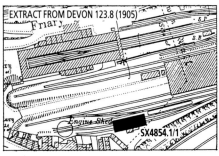

EXTRACT FROM DEVON 123.8 (1905)

Friary (L&SWR)SX4854.1/1A

A stone built 2TS through road shed with a slated gable style roof, it was located at SX48665456 and was opened on July 1st, 1891. The facilities included a coal stage, water column and a 50ft turntable. Like its predecessor at Devonport (SX4654.2/1A) the whole layout was very cramped and altogether too small for the job. It closed when a new Friary shed (SX4954.1/1A) was opened in 1908 and was utilized, for a while, as part of the Goods Department.

Replaced by ...
Site SX4954.1; On the south side of the line, east of Plymouth Friary Station.
Friary (L&SWR)SX4954.1/1A
A brick built 3TS through road shed with a slated pitched roof and glazed gable ends, it was located at SX49485471 and was opened in 1908. The shed possessed all facilities including a raised coal stage and 50ft turntable.

It was later re-roofed ...
Friary (BR)SX4954.1/1B
The roof and gable ends were replaced by corrugated asbestos sheeting, probably by the Southern Region just after nationalization. The shed was closed on May 6th, 1963 and subsequently demolished.

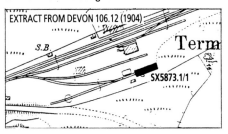

EXTRACT FROM DEVON 124.5 (1912)

Site SX4754.1; On the west side of the line, north of Plymouth Millbay Station.
Millbay (SDR)SX4754.1/1A
A stone built 2TS through road shed with a slated gable style roof, it was located at SX47225484 and was opened in 1849, or shortly after, by the South Devon Railway.

It was probably extended ...
Millbay (SDR)SX4754.1/1B
At some point prior to 1899 a wooden built extension was probably added at the southern end.

Millbay (GWR)SX4754.1/2A
A timber built shed with a slated gable style roof, it was located at SX47255485 and is believed to have originally been 3TS. The opening date is not known but it is assumed to have been built after 1849 upon amalgamation of the GWR and South Devon Railway.

The track layout was re-arranged ...
Millbay (SDR)SX4754.1/2B
At some point it is assumed that the shed was rebuilt as a 4TS shed with one through road.

The facilities included a turntable (44ft 10in after 1884), coal plant and lifting shop. The depot was closed by the GWR in 1924, but had to remain open temporarily until 1931 when additional accommodation (SX5055.2/2A) had been made available at Laira shed.

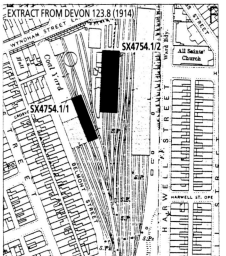

EXTRACT FROM DEVON 123.8 (1914)

SEATON

Site SY2590.1; On the east side of Seaton Station.
Seaton (S&BR)SY2590.1/1A
A timber built 1TS dead ended shed with a slated gable style roof, it was located at SY25179007 and was opened by the Seaton & Beer Railway on March 16th, 1868. The facilities included a water tank and coal stage. The line was absorbed by the L&SWR in 1885 and although the depot was, by now, considered inadequate it was not dispensed with until 1937 when it was demolished to accommodate a new track layout.

Replaced by ...
Site SY2589.1; On the east side of Seaton Station, at the southern end.
Seaton (SR)SY2589.1/1A
A concrete built 1TS dead ended shed with a corrugated asbestos gable style roof, it was located at SY25178999 and opened in 1937 as part of the station remodelling plan. The new facilities included a coaling stage and water tank. The shed was closed by BR on November 14th, 1963 and demolished.

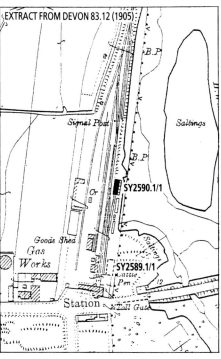

EXTRACT FROM DEVON 83.12 (1905)

PRINCETOWN

Site SX5873.1; On the south side of Princetown Station.
Princetown (Princetown)SX5873.1/1A
A rendered stone built 1TS dead ended shed with a slated gable style roof, incorporating a water tank over the shed entrance. The building was located at SX58697340 and was opened by the Princetown Railway on August 11th, 1883. The facilities included a turntable and coal stage. The line was worked from the outset by the GWR, being absorbed by them just prior to grouping, and the shed was closed by BR on March 11th, 1956. The building stood derelict for some time before being demolished.

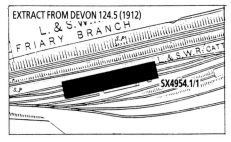

EXTRACT FROM DEVON 106.12 (1904)

SIDMOUTH

Site SY1288.1; On the west side of Sidmouth Station.
Sidmouth (L&SWR)SY1288.1/1A
A timber built 1TS dead ended shed with a slated gable style roof, it was located at SY12098860 and was opened on July 6th, 1874. The facilities included a 42ft turntable, sited outside of the shed entrance, coal stage and water column. The shed was destroyed by a fire on January 7th, 1900.

Replaced on the same site by ...
Sidmouth (L&SWR)SY1288.1/1B
A brick built 1TS dead ended shed with a slated gable style roof, it was opened in 1900, utilizing the facilities of its predecessor (SY1288.1/1A). The depot gradually went out of use, the turntable was removed in the 1920s and locomotives ceased using the building, coaling and watering on the shed road only. It was totally dispensed with in the mid-30s, but the building was let to a commercial concern and a short section of the northern end was still standing, in private use, early in 1995.

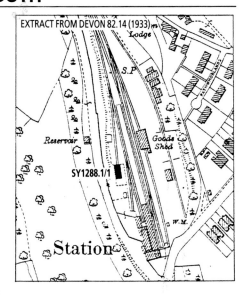

EXTRACT FROM DEVON 82.14 (1933)

STOKE CANON

Site SX9397.1; *On the east side of the Taunton line, north of Stoke Canon Junction Station.*
Stoke Canon (B&E)^{SX9397.1/1A}
A 1TS through road shed with a gable style roof, it was located at SX93599785 and opened by the Bristol & Exeter Railway in 1860. No further details are known except that it was closed in 1879 and was then later utilized as a goods shed from 1894.

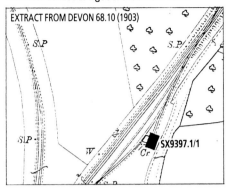

TIVERTON JUNCTION

Site ST0311.1; *On the west side of the Exeter line, at the south end of Tiverton Junction Station.*
Tiverton Junction (B&E)^{ST0311.1/1A}
A brick built 1TS dead ended shed with a slated gable style roof, it was located at ST03151125 and opened by the Bristol & Exeter Railway on June 12th, 1848. The facilities included a 34ft 6in turntable and coal stage on the shed approach road. The line was absorbed by the GWR in 1876 who removed the turntable in May 1908. The shed was closed in 1932.

Replaced by ...
Tiverton Junction (GWR)^{ST0311.1/2A}
A steel framed brick built 1TS dead ended shed with a corrugated iron gable style roof, it was located on an adjacent site at ST03121127 and was opened in 1932. The facilities included a coal stage and water column sited outside of the shed entrance. The depot was closed by BR in October 1964.

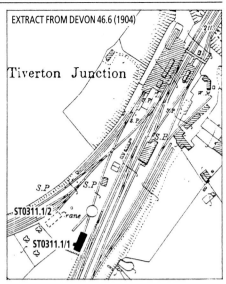

TAVISTOCK

Site SX4873.1; *On the west side of the line, at the south end of Tavistock Station.*
Tavistock (SD&TR)^{SX4873.1/1A}
A timber built 1TS through road shed with a slated gable style roof, it was located at SX48067398 and opened by the South Devon & Tavistock Railway on June 22nd, 1859. The facilities included a 23ft 7in turntable at the rear of the shed. The line was worked by the South Devon Railway and was absorbed by them in 1865. The new owners closed the shed in July of the same year due to the dilapidated state of the building and the opening of the line to Launceston and the establishment of a new depot (SX3385.1/1A) there. The shed was demolished in about 1900.

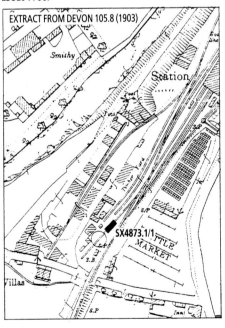

TEIGNMOUTH

Site SX9473.1; *In the vicinity of Teignmouth Station.*
Teignmouth (SDR)^{SX9473.1/1A}
Some form of temporary facility, including a small shed, was opened here by the South Devon Railway on May 30th, 1846. It was closed on March 19th, 1847.

TORQUAY TORRE

Site SX9064.1; *On the east side of the line, at the south end of Torre Station.*
Torquay Torre (SDR)^{SX9064.1/F1}
A small facility including a siding and turntable, located at SX90416479, was opened by the South Devon Railway in 1848. It was closed in 1864 but the turntable saw further use until 1868, and probably until 1883 when it was removed as part of the station rebuilding plan.

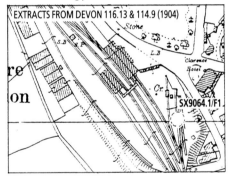

TOTNES

Site SX7960.1; *On the east side of the line, south of Totnes Station.*
Totnes (SDR)^{SX7960.1/1A}
A timber built 2TS dead ended shed with a slated gable style roof, it was located at SX79966072 and was opened by the South Devon Railway on July 20th, 1847. The facilities included a coal platform, sited inside the building, a water tank and a 34ft 5in turntable. The shed was closed in 1904 and subsequently demolished.

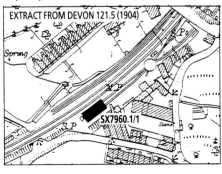

TORRINGTON

Site SS4719.1; *On the west side of Torrington Station.*
Torrington (L&SWR)^{SS4719.1/1A}
A timber built 1TS dead ended shed with a slated gable style roof, it was located at SS47971981 and was opened on July 18th, 1872. The facilities included a 42ft turntable sited outside of the shed entrance and a coal stage and water tank. In 1925 the yard was slightly rearranged and the turntable was removed. The shed was closed by BR on November 2nd, 1959.

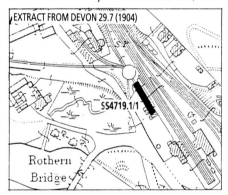

GOODRINGTON SANDS

Site SX8959.1; *On the west side of the line, south of Goodrington Sands Halt.*
Goodrington Sands (BR)^{SX8959.1/F1}
A servicing area consisting of a turntable, located at SX89175918, and siding was opened here by the Western Region in 1957. The facility was closed in c1964.

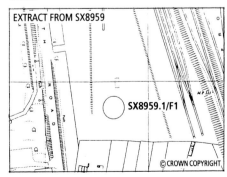

BERKSHIRE

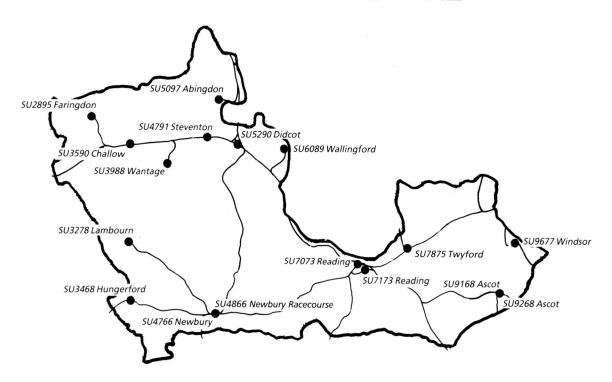

SU2895 Faringdon
SU5097 Abingdon
SU4791 Steventon
SU5290 Didcot
SU3590 Challow
SU3988 Wantage
SU6089 Wallingford
SU3278 Lambourn
SU9677 Windsor
SU7073 Reading
SU7875 Twyford
SU7173 Reading
SU9168 Ascot
SU3468 Hungerford
SU9268 Ascot
SU4866 Newbury Racecourse
SU4766 Newbury

ABINGDON

Site SU5097.1; On the south side of the line, at the east end of Abingdon Station.
Abingdon (Abingdon)^{SU5097.1/1A}
A brick built ITS dead ended shed with a slated gable style roof, it was located at SU50069733 and was opened by the Abingdon Railway on June 2nd, 1856. The facilities included a coal stage, sited outside of the shed entrance, and a water tank. The line was absorbed by the GWR in 1904 and the shed was closed by BR on March 20th, 1954. The building was subsequently demolished.

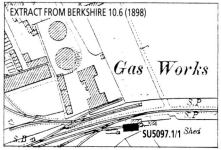

EXTRACT FROM BERKSHIRE 10.6 (1898)

Gas Works

SU5097.1/1 *Shed*

CHALLOW

Site SU3590.1; In the vicinity of Challow Station.
Faringdon Rd, Challow (GWR)^{SU3590.1/1A}
A temporary shed was opened here on June 20th, 1840. It was accidently demolished by the locomotive *Fire King* on October 25th in the same year, engines thereafter being serviced in the open until some time in 1841 when the facility was no longer required.

ASCOT

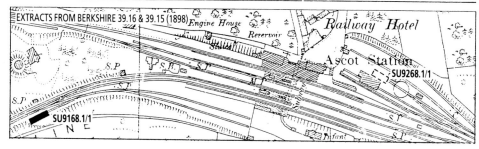

EXTRACTS FROM BERKSHIRE 39.16 & 39.15 (1898)

Engine House

Railway Hotel

Ascot Station

SU9268.1/1

SU9168.1/1

Site SU9268.1; On the north side of Ascot Station.
Ascot (SW&WJR)^{SU9268.1/1A}
A ITS dead ended shed, located at SU92256831 and opened by the Staines, Woking & Wokingham Junction Railway on June 4th, 1856. No details of construction or facilities are known except that there was a 50ft turntable sited outside of the shed entrance. The line was absorbed by the L&SWR in 1878 and the depot closed in 1889. The building was demolished and replaced by a goods shed, but the turntable was retained for further use.

Replaced by ...
Site SU9168.1; On the south side of the Aldershot line, at the west end of Ascot Station.
Ascot (L&SWR)^{SU9168.1/1A}
A timber built ITS dead ended shed with a slated gable style roof, it was located at SU91936827 and was opened in 1889. The facilities included a coal stage. The shed closed in 1937 but was not demolished until September 1969.

HUNGERFORD

Site SU3468.1; On the north side of the line, at the east end of Hungerford Station.
Hungerford (B&HR)^{SU3468.1/1A}
A 2TS shed with one through road, it was located at SU34206848 and opened by the Berks & Hants Railway on December 21st, 1847. No details of its construction are known, but the facilities included a coal stage and turntable. The shed was closed in November 1862 following the extension of the line to Devizes.

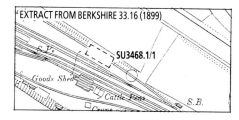

EXTRACT FROM BERKSHIRE 33.16 (1899)

SU3468.1/1

Goods Shed

Cattle Pens

DIDCOT

Site SU5290.1; In the fork of Didcot East Curve and the main line, on the north side of Didcot Station.
Didcot (GWR)$^{SU5290.1/1A}$
A 2TS shed, it was located at SU52529059 and was opened on June 12th, 1844. No further details are known.

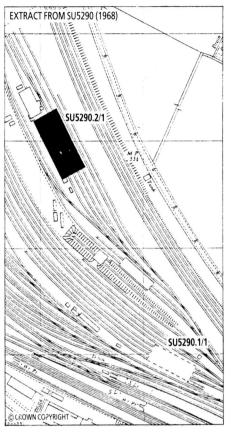

EXTRACT FROM SU5290 (1968)

SU5290.2/1

SU5290.1/1

© CROWN COPYRIGHT

In 1857 it was enlarged or rebuilt ...
Didcot (GWR)$^{SU5290.1/1B}$
A brick built 3TS dead ended shed with a slated gable style roof, it was located on the same site as its predecessor (SU5290.1/1A) and was opened in July 1857. The facilities included a water tank and small coal stage, the latter being replaced by a larger raised type at a later date. It was closed in June 1932.

Replaced by ...
Didcot (GWR)$^{SU5290.2/1A}$
A brick and corrugated asbestos built 4TS shed, with 3 through roads and a metal sheeted gable style roof. It was located slightly north of the previous site, at SU52429080 and was opened in June 1932, being built under the Loans and Guarantees Act (1929). It possessed all facilities and was closed by BR on April 5th, 1965. It was taken over by the Great Western Society and is now the *Didcot Railway Centre*, housing a large collection of preserved rolling stock.

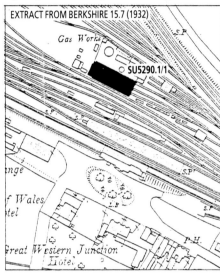

EXTRACT FROM BERKSHIRE 15.7 (1932)

Gas Works

SU5290.1/1

STEVENTON

Site SU4791.1; In the vicinity of Steventon Station.
Steventon (GWR)$^{SU4791.1/1A}$
A temporary shed was opened here on June 1st 1840. It was closed during 1841.

TWYFORD

Site SU7875.1; In the vicinity of Twyford Station.
Twyford (GWR)$^{SU7875.1/F1}$
A temporary facility comprised of locomotive sidings opened here on July 1st, 1839. It closed on March 30th, 1840.

LAMBOURN

Site SU3278.1; At the west end of Lambourn Station.
Lambourn (LVR)$^{SU3278.1/1A}$
A corrugated iron 1TS dead ended shed with a corrugated iron gable style roof, it was located at SU32737858 and was opened by the Lambourn Valley Railway on April 2nd, 1898. The facilities included a coal stage and water tower. The line was absorbed by the GWR in 1905.

The shed was enlarged ...
Lambourn (GWR)$^{SU3278.1/1B}$
At some stage the building was extended, probably to accommodate a railmotor. The shed was closed in 1937 and demolished in 1940.

A servicing point was then established ...
Lambourn (GWR)$^{SU3278.1/F1}$
The engine pit and siding was utilized from 1937 until the branch line was closed on January 4th, 1960.

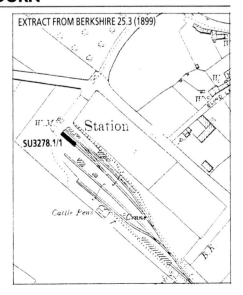

EXTRACT FROM BERKSHIRE 25.3 (1899)

Station

SU3278.1/1

Cattle Pens

FARINGDON

Site SU2895.1; On the south side of Faringdon Station.
Faringdon (Faringdon)$^{SU2895.1/1A}$
A stone built 1TS dead ended shed with a slated gable style roof, it was located at SU28779511 and was opened by the Faringdon Railway on June 1st, 1864. The facilities included a water tank and coal stage sited near the shed entrance. The line was absorbed by the GWR in 1886 and the depot was closed by BR in December 1951. The building was let for private use and remained standing until at least the mid-1970s. It has since been demolished.

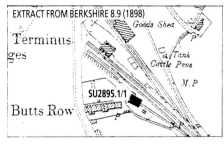

EXTRACT FROM BERKSHIRE 8.9 (1898)

Terminus
Butts Row
Goods Shed
Tank
Cattle Pens
M.P
SU2895.1/1

NEWBURY

Site SU4866.1; On the south side of the line, at the east end of Newbury Racecourse Station.
Newbury Racecourse (GWR)$^{SU4866.1/F1}$
A servicing area consisting of a turntable, located at SU48606684 and siding, it was opened in 1907. The facility was closed by BR in March 1960.

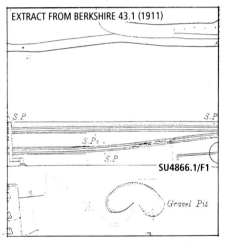

EXTRACT FROM BERKSHIRE 43.1 (1911)

S.P

SU4866.1/F1

Gravel Pit

Site SU4766.1; On the north side of the line, at the west end of Newbury Station.
Newbury (GWR)$^{SU4766.1/F1}$
A basic servicing facility, consisting of an engine pit, coal stack and water tank was provided here, possibly from 1898. It was located at SU47106673 and was adjacent to the Lambourn bay platform. It probably went out of use when the Lambourn branch was closed on January 4th, 1960.

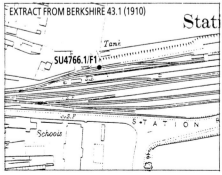

EXTRACT FROM BERKSHIRE 43.1 (1910)

Stat

Tank

SU4766.1/F1

STATION

Schools

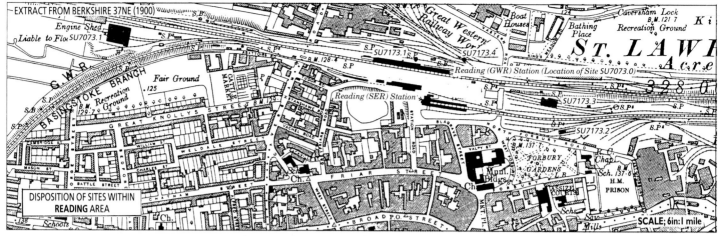

EXTRACT FROM BERKSHIRE 37NE (1900)

DISPOSITION OF SITES WITHIN
READING AREA

SCALE; 6in:1 mile

Site SU7173.0; In the vicinity of Reading (GWR) Station.

Reading (GWR)^SU7173.0/1A

A temporary shed was opened here on March 30th, 1840 and was closed in July 1841.

Replaced by ...
Site SU7173.1; On the north side of Reading (GWR) Station.

Reading (GWR)^SU7173.1/1A

A timber built 2TS through road shed with a slated gable style roof and flat roof extensions at each end, it was located at SU71477389 and was opened in July 1841. Details of its facilities are not known. It was closed in about 1876.

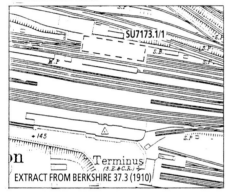

EXTRACT FROM BERKSHIRE 37.3 (1910)

Replaced by ...
Site SU7073.1; In the fork of the Bristol and Basing-stoke lines, west of Reading (GWR) Station.

Reading (GWR)^SU7073.1/1A

A brick built 1RH with a slated gable style roof of three bays, it was located at SU70697394 and was opened in about 1876. It possessed all major facilities, with the iron built coal stage being rebuilt and re-sited in 1900. A 65ft turntable was installed in the shed yard by 1925.

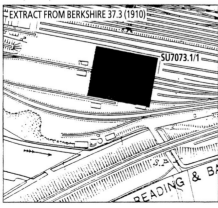

EXTRACT FROM BERKSHIRE 37.3 (1910)

The shed was rebuilt in 1930 ...
Reading (GWR)^SU7073.1/1B

The building was converted to a 9TS shed with three through roads, and glazed gables. The shed was closed on January 4th, 1965 and a purpose built diesel depot (SU7073.1/3A) was constructed at the western end of the shed site.

Reading Railmotor Shed (GWR)^SU7073.1/2A

A corrugated iron 1TS through road shed it was sited at the rear of the main shed building at SU70637393. Its opening and closure dates are not known.

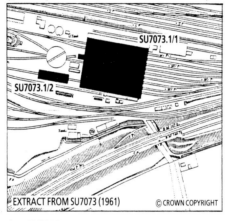

EXTRACT FROM SU7073 (1961)   © CROWN COPYRIGHT

Site SU7173.4; At the east end of Reading Signal Works yard.

Reading Signal Works (GWR)^SU7173.4/F1

A stand siding was provided for the works shunter. This was located at SU71657388 and was sited under the bridge carrying the access line to the works. The precise opening and closing dates are not known, but after dieselization the locomotive then stood at SU7173.4/F2, adjacent to the level crossing a few yards east at SU71757387.

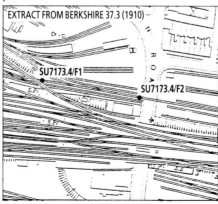

EXTRACT FROM BERKSHIRE 37.3 (1910)

Site SU7173.2; On the south side of the line, at the east end of Reading (SE&CR) Station.

Reading (RR&GR)^SU7173.2/F1

A locomotive facility consisting of a 45ft turntable, located at SU71897369, and sidings was opened by the Reading, Reigate & Guildford Railway on July 4th, 1849. The line was absorbed by the South Eastern Railway in 1852, the facility closing in the same year.

Replaced by ...
Reading (SER)^SU7173.2/1A

A brick and stone built 2TS through road shed with a slated gable style roof it was located at SU71947370 and was opened by the South Eastern Railway in 1852. It was constructed on the sidings of SU7173.1/F1 and utilized the existing turntable. Other facilities included a water tank. The shed was closed in 1875 becoming part of the goods depot, and subsequently was used for warehousing, lasting until demolition in the 1970s.

Replaced by ...
Site SU7173.3; On the north side of the line, at the east end of Reading (SE&CR) Station.

Reading (SER)^SU7173.3/1A

A brick built 3TS through road shed with a slated gable style roof it was located at SU71887378 and was opened by the South Eastern Railway in 1875. The facilities included a turntable, enlarged to 65ft in SR days, coal stage and water tank.

The shed was re-roofed ...
Reading (BR)^SU7173.3/1B

At some time in the 1950s the gable ends were rebuilt by the Southern Region and the roof re-clad in corrugated asbestos sheeting. By this time the depot was considered to be no more than a stabling point but lasted until January 1965 when it was completely closed. The building has since been de-molished.

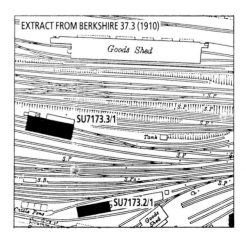

EXTRACT FROM BERKSHIRE 37.3 (1910)

Goods Shed

WALLINGFORD

Site SU6089.1; On the west side of Wallingford Station.
Wallingford (W&WR)^{SU6089.1/1A}

A 1TS dead ended shed, probably built in timber, it was located at SU60228956 and was opened by the Wallingford & Watlington Railway on July 2nd, 1866. Further details with regard to its construction and facilities are not known. The line was absorbed by the GWR in 1872 and the shed was closed in 1890.

Replaced, on the same site, by ...
Wallingford (GWR)^{SU6089.1/1B}

A brick built 1TS dead ended shed with a slated gable style roof, it was opened by the GWR in 1890. The facilities included a coal stage, sited outside of the shed entrance, and a water tower. The depot was closed by BR in February 1956 but stood, in private use, until the mid-1960s at least.

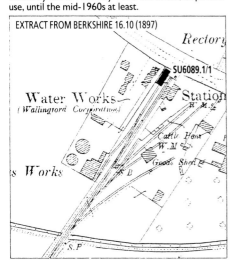
EXTRACT FROM BERKSHIRE 16.10 (1897)

WANTAGE

Site SU3988.1; On the west side of the line, at the north end of Wantage Station.
Wantage (Wantage Tramway)^{SU3988.1/1A}

A timber built 1TS through road shed with a slated gable style roof and located at SU39848807. An unusual feature was that due to the cramped layout the shed road was also the access line to the local gas works.

Site SU3988.2; On the east side of the line, at the north end of Wantage Station.
Wantage (Wantage Tramway)^{SU3988.2/1A}

A 1TS dead ended shed, probably built in timber with a slated gable style roof and located at SU39818803.

The depot opened on October 1st, 1875 and the facilities included a workshop. The last passenger train ran in 1925, but the line and sheds were not closed until January 29th, 1946.

EXTRACT FROM BERKSHIRE 14.14 (1898)

WINDSOR

Site SU9677.1; On the west side of the line, at the north end of Windsor Station.
Windsor (L&SWR)^{SU9677.1/1A}

A 1TS shed, located at SU96897738 and opened on October 1st, 1849. Details of the construction and facilities are not known. It was closed prior to 1868.

Replaced, on the same site, by ...
Windsor (L&SWR)^{SU9677.1/1B}

A brick built 2TS dead ended shed with a slated gable style roof, it was opened prior to 1868. The facilities included a turntable and coal stage, both originally located near to the shed entrance but later rebuilt at the north end of the yard, and a water tank. The shed was closed by the SR in 1940 and was subsequently demolished.

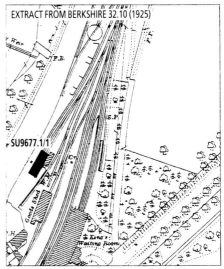
EXTRACT FROM BERKSHIRE 32.10 (1925)

From the earliest days, the opening of a railway line was almost invariably the excuse for some form of celebration, something which continued well after railways had become quite commonplace, as depicted here in this picture of **Lambourn** taken on April 2nd, 1898. The Lambourn Valley Railway was built through local investment, but worked by the GWR from the outset - in usual keeping with such arrangements therefore, it may be seen that the locomotive and coach, water tank and engine shed (SU3278.1/1A) were somewhat rudimentary.

The GWR fully absorbed the line in 1905, closed the shed in 1937 and demolished it three years later but established a servicing area (SU3278.1/F1) on the site. This arrangement lasted until closure of the line (north of Welford Park) on January 2nd, 1960. *Author's Collection.*

WILTSHIRE

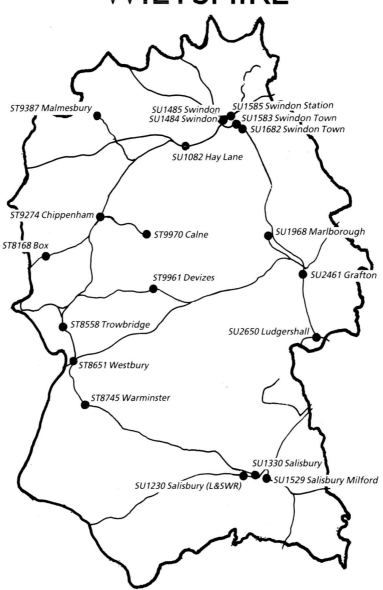

ST9387 Malmesbury

SU1485 Swindon
SU1484 Swindon
SU1585 Swindon Station
SU1583 Swindon Town
SU1682 Swindon Town

SU1082 Hay Lane

ST9274 Chippenham

ST9970 Calne

SU1968 Marlborough

ST8168 Box

ST9961 Devizes

SU2461 Grafton

ST8558 Trowbridge

SU2650 Ludgershall

ST8651 Westbury

ST8745 Warminster

SU1330 Salisbury
SU1230 Salisbury (L&SWR)
SU1529 Salisbury Milford

BOX

Site ST8168.1; On the north side of the line, at the west end of Box Station.
Box (GWR)ST8168.1/F1
A locomotive servicing facility was provided here from 1841 until 1845 when the shed (ST8161.1/1A) was erected either on the site or very adjacent to it.

Replaced by ...
Box (GWR)ST8168.1/1A
A timber built 1TS through road shed with a slated gable style roof, it was located at ST81406869 and was opened in 1845. The facilities included a water tank sited outside of the shed entrance. The depot was closed on February 24th, 1919.

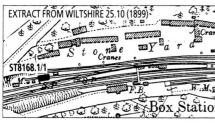

EXTRACT FROM WILTSHIRE 25.10 (1899)

ST8168.1/1

Box Station

CALNE

Site ST9970.1; On the north side of the line, at the west end of Calne Station.
Calne (Calne)ST9970.1/1A
A stone built 1TS dead ended shed with a slated gable style roof, it was located at ST99437067 and was opened by the Calne Railway on November 13th, 1863. The facilities included a water tank. The line was absorbed by the GWR in 1892 and, with Chippenham shed (ST9274.1/1A) being at the other end of the branch, the depot was no longer required and was probably closed in the same year. The building was demolished in March 1906.

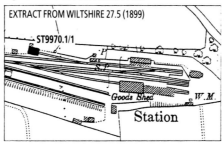

EXTRACT FROM WILTSHIRE 27.5 (1899)

ST9970.1/1

Goods Shed

Station

CHIPPENHAM

Site ST9274.1; On the west side of the line, north of Chippenham Station.
Chippenham (GWR)ST9274.1/1A
A stone built 3TS dead ended shed with a slated gable style roof, it was located at ST92587412 and was opened in 1858*. The facilities included a turntable and coal stage, the latter being replaced by a covered coaling platform in 1938. The shed was closed on March 2nd, 1964 and was subsequently demolished.

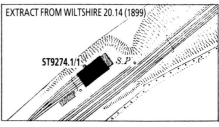

EXTRACT FROM WILTSHIRE 20.14 (1899)

ST9274.1/1

A broad gauge shed may have existed on this site previously to ST9274.1/1A, with the later building either being a replacement or a partial rebuild.

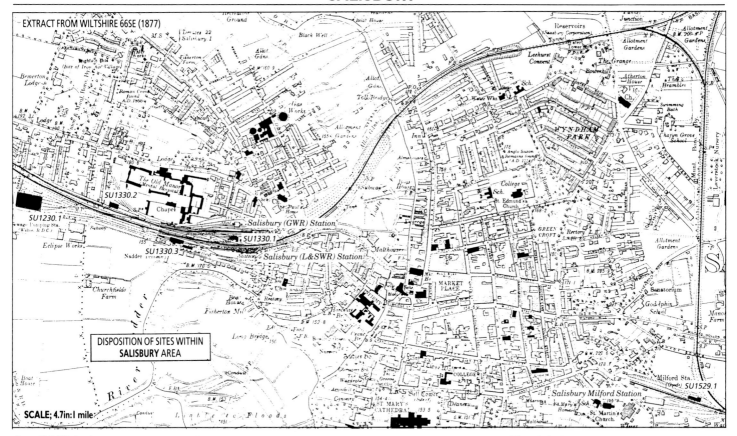

EXTRACT FROM WILTSHIRE 66SE (1877)

DISPOSITION OF SITES WITHIN **SALISBURY** AREA

SCALE; 4.7in:1 mile

Site SU1330.1; On the south side of Salisbury (GWR) Station.
Salisbury (GWR)[SU1330.1/1A]
A stone built 2TS dead ended shed with a slated gable style roof, it was located at SU13693018 and was opened in April 1858. The facilities included a coal stage and turntable. The shed was closed in 1899.

Replaced by ...
Site SU1330.2; On the north side of the line, west of Salisbury (GWR) Station.
Salisbury (GWR)[SU1330.2/1A]
A brick built 3TS dead ended shed with a glazed and slated northlight pattern roof, it was located at SU13213029 and was opened in 1899. The facilities included a raised coal stage, water tower and a turntable. The shed was closed by BR in November 1950 and was subsequently demolished.

Site SU1529.1; On the north side of the line, at the east end of Milford Station.
Salisbury Milford (L&SWR)[SU1529.1/1A]
A brick built 2TS through road shed with a slated hipped roof, it was located at SU15342963 and was opened on January 27th, 1847. The facilities included a water tank and 25ft turntable. The depot was closed in July 1859 following the opening of Fisherton Station and engine shed (SU1330.3/1A). Milford Station was converted to a Goods Depot and the shed was utilized as a goods shed at least until 1934. The building was demolished in 1968.

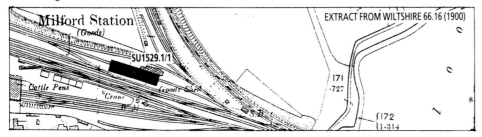

Milford Station (Goods)

SU1529.1/1

Cattle Pens

EXTRACT FROM WILTSHIRE 66.16 (1900)

Replaced by ...
Site SU1330.3; On the south side of the line, at the west end of Fisherton Station.
Salisbury Fisherton (L&SWR)[SU1330.3/1A]
A brick built 3TS dead ended shed with a slated gable style roof, it was located at SU13453016 and opened in July 1859. The facilities included a coal stage and 45ft turntable, both located at the west end of the yard, and a water tower.

The shed was extended in 1870 ...
Salisbury Fisherton (L&SWR)[SU1330.3/1B]
The building was lengthened by 40ft and the northernmost track made into a through road.

Further major modifications were made ...
Salisbury Fisherton (L&SWR)[SU1330.3/1C]
During the late 1870s the centre road was extended through the building, the coal stage was lengthened to 160ft and the turntable was enlarged to 50ft.

In 1885 an additional shed was built ...
Salisbury Fisherton (L&SWR)[SU1330.3/2A]
A timber built 3TS through road shed with a corrugated iron gable style roof, it was located just to the east of the original shed (SU1330.3/1) at SU13503014 and made use of all the existing facilities.

The whole depot was closed on January 12th, 1901 to make way for station enlargement and improvements, the locomotives transferring to ...
Site SU1230.1; On the south side of the line, west of Fisherton Station.

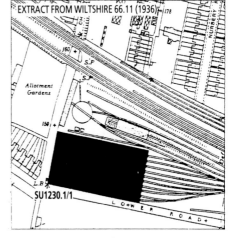

EXTRACT FROM WILTSHIRE 66.11 (1936)

SU1230.1/1

Salisbury (L&SWR)[SU1230.1/1A]
A brick built 10TS dead ended shed with 5 pitched slated roofs and glazed gable ends, it was located at SU12893030 and was opened on January 12th, 1901. The depot possessed all major facilities, including a 55ft turntable which was enlarged to 65ft after 1912.

The shed was re-roofed in 1954 ...
Salisbury (BR)[SU1230.1/1B]
The building was partially re-roofed by the Southern Region, with a standard corrugated iron louvre pitched style over each track. Unusually this was not expedited along the complete length of the shed, only the front portion being replaced. The depot was closed at the end of steam locomotion on the Southern Region, on July 9th, 1967 and stood derelict for some years before being demolished.

Continued ...

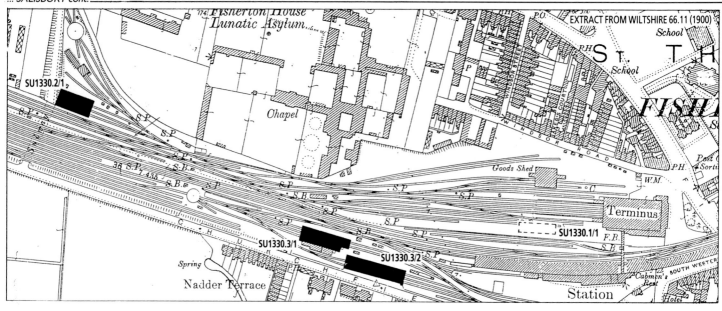

EXTRACT FROM WILTSHIRE 66.11 (1900)

DEVIZES

Site ST9961.1; On the south side of the line, at the west end of Devizes Station.

Devizes (GWR)^ST9961.1/1A

A 1TS through road shed, probably built in stone with a slated gable style roof, it was located at ST99936147 and was opened in April 1857. The facilities included a turntable sited outside of the shed entrance. The shed was closed in about 1875 and may have seen further sporadic use for a while as a stabling point.

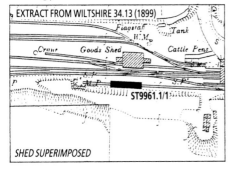

EXTRACT FROM WILTSHIRE 34.13 (1899)

ST9961.1/1

SHED SUPERIMPOSED

MALMESBURY

Site ST9387.1; On the east side of Malmesbury Station.

Malmesbury (Malmesbury)^ST9387.1/1A

A stone built 1TS through road shed with wooden gables and a slated roof, it was located at ST93198771 and was opened by the Malmesbury Railway on December 17th, 1877. The facilities included a water tank and coal stage sited outside of the shed entrance. The line was absorbed by the GWR in 1880 and the shed was closed by BR on September 10th, 1951. The building was still standing, in private use, in 1997.

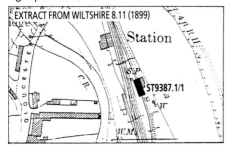

EXTRACT FROM WILTSHIRE 8.11 (1899)

ST9387.1/1

GRAFTON

Site SU2461.1; In the vicinity of Grafton & Burbage Station.

Grafton (SM&AR)^SU2461.1

A temporary shed was opened here by the Swindon, Marlborough & Grafton Railway on May 2nd, 1882. It was closed on February 5th, 1883.

HAY LANE

Site SU1082.1; In the vicinity of Hay Lane Station.

Hay Lane (GWR)^SU1082.1/F1

A temporary facility, approximately located at SU10908243, was opened here on December 17th, 1840. It was closed in 1842 upon opening of the shed at Swindon (SU1484.1/1A).

LUDGERSHALL

Site SU2650.1; In the fork of the Grafton and Tidworth lines, west of Ludgershall Station.

Ludgershall (WD)^SU2650.1/1A

A timber built 2TS dead ended shed with a slated gable style roof, it was located at SU26045087 and was opened by the War Department in 1903. The facilities included a water tank, coal stage and 55ft turntable. The depot was utilized by the Midland & South Western Junction Railway solely for traffic to the nearby Tidworth Military Camp. The line was absorbed by the GWR in 1923 and the shed was closed in July 1925, being demolished shortly afterwards.

A servicing point was established ...
Ludgershall (GWR)^SU2650.1/F1

The existing turntable and engine shed pits were subsequently utilized for a while, the precise date when the facility was totally dispensed with is not known.

MARLBOROUGH

Site SU1968.1; On the east side of Marlborough (GWR) Station.

Marlborough (Marlborough)^SU1968.1/1A

A stone built 1TS dead ended shed with a slated gable style roof, it was located at SU19306863 and was opened by the Marlborough Railway on April 14th, 1864. The facilities included a water tank and coal stage.

The shed was extended in 1899 ...
Marlborough (GWR)^SU1968.1/1B

A small timber built extension with a slated roof was added at the northern end. The shed was due to close in April 1929 but this was deferred until July 1933, the building being later demolished.

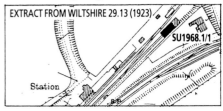

EXTRACT FROM WILTSHIRE 29.13 (1923)

SU1968.1/1

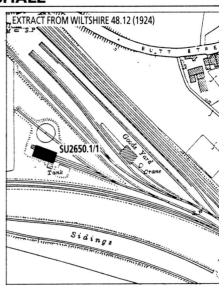

EXTRACT FROM WILTSHIRE 48.12 (1924)

SU2650.1/1

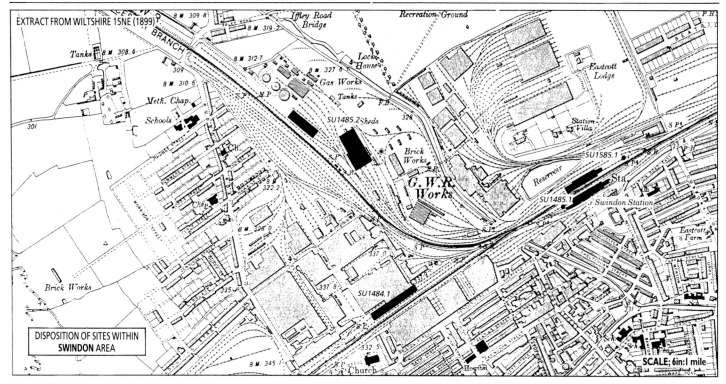

EXTRACT FROM WILTSHIRE 15NE (1899)

DISPOSITION OF SITES WITHIN SWINDON AREA

SCALE: 6in:1 mile

Site SU1484.1; On the north side of the Bristol line, west of Swindon Station.

Swindon (GWR)[SU1484.1/1A]

A timber built 4TS through road shed with a slated twin gable style roof*, it was located at SU14178475 and was opened in 1842. The facilities included 30ft and 40ft turntables and a coke/coal plant. By about 1871 it would appear that only the two southernmost tracks were in use as a running shed, the other two lines being used for locomotives awaiting entry to the adjacent works. In May 1892 the whole building was given over to works use and it remained in use until 1930 when it was demolished.

An official photograph of the building, taken in 1929, shows that the northernmost roof was hipped. Whether this was the original condition, or the result of a re-roofing is not clear.

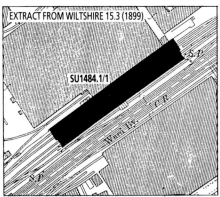

EXTRACT FROM WILTSHIRE 15.3 (1899)

SU1484.1/1

Site SU1485.2; On the east side of the Gloucester line, west of Swindon Station.

Swindon (GWR)[SU1485.2/1A]

A brick built 9TS dead ended shed with three slated pitched roofs, it was located at SU14308527 and was opened in 1871.

In 1892 the shed was enlarged ...

Swindon (GWR)[SU1485.2/2A]

A brick built 1RH with three slated pitched roofs, it was located at SU14288532 and adjoined the first building (SU1485.2/1A) at its northern end.

In 1908 the shed was enlarged again ...

Swindon (GWR)[SU1485.2/3A]

A brick built 1RH with a slated multi-gable style roof, it was located at SU14348530 and adjoined the first building (SU1485.2/1A) on its eastern side.

The depot possessed all major facilities and was closed by BR in October 1964. The entire site was later demolished.

Swindon Stock Shed (GWR)[SU1485.2/4A]

A brick built 6TS dead ended shed with a slated and glazed northlight pattern roof, it was located at SU14158535 and was opened by the GWR in c1882. It was closed by BR in October 1964.

Site SU1485.1; At the west end of Swindon Station.

Swindon Station (GWR)[SU1485.1/1A]

A stone built 1TS through road shed with a slated gable style roof, it was located at SU14888515 but the date of opening is not known. The facilities included a coal stage and water tank. The depot was closed in the 1890s.

Site SU1585.1; At the east end of Swindon Station.

Swindon Station (GWR)[SU1585.1/1A]

A stone built 1TS through road shed with a slated gable style roof, it was located at SU15048527 but the date of opening is not known. The facilities included a coal stage and water tank. The depot was closed in the 1890s.

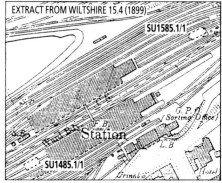

EXTRACT FROM WILTSHIRE 15.4 (1899)

SU1585.1/1

SU1585.1/1

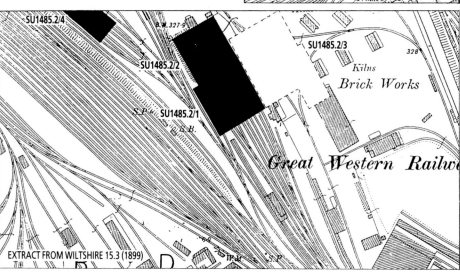

SU1485.2/4

SU1485.2/2

SU1485.2/1

SU1485.2/3

Kilns
Brick Works

Great Western Railwa

EXTRACT FROM WILTSHIRE 15.3 (1899)

Continued ...

Site SU1583.1; On the west side of the line, at the south end of Swindon Town Station.

Swindon Town (SM&AR)^{SU1583.1/1A}SU1583.1/1A

A timber built 2TS dead ended shed with a corrugated iron gable style roof, it was located at SU15828333 and was opened by the Swindon, Marlborough & Andover Railway in February 1881. The facilities included a 40ft turntable. The shed was closed in 1905 and subsequently demolished, but the turntable was retained for further use.

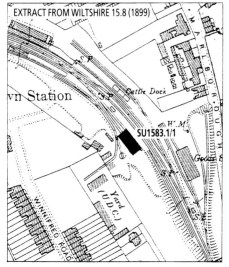

EXTRACT FROM WILTSHIRE 15.8 (1899)

SU1583.1/1

Replaced in 1905 by ...
Site SU1682.1; On the east side of the line, south of Swindon Town Station.

Swindon Town (M&SWJR)^{SU1682.1/1A}SU1682.1/1A

A brick built 2TS dead ended shed with a slated gable style roof, it was located at SU16088294 and was opened by the Midland & South Western Junction Railway. The facilities included a coal stage, sited outside of the shed entrance, with the turntable at the original shed site (SU1583.1/1A) being utilized. The depot was closed by the GWR on January 21st, 1924 but remained standing until at least 1961. It has since been demolished.

EXTRACT FROM WILTSHIRE 15.12 (1923)

SU1682.1/1

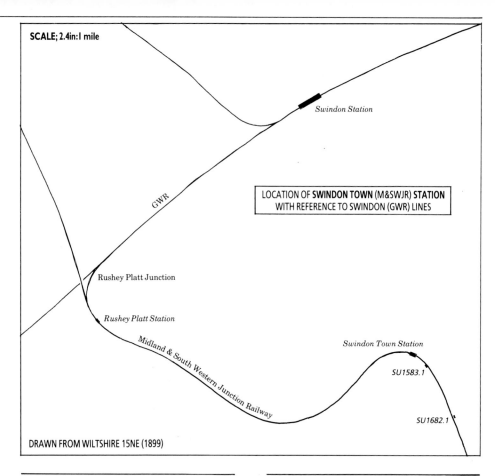

SCALE; 2.4in:1 mile

Swindon Station

GWR

LOCATION OF **SWINDON TOWN** (M&SWJR) STATION WITH REFERENCE TO SWINDON (GWR) LINES

Rushey Platt Junction

Rushey Platt Station

Swindon Town Station

SU1583.1

Midland & South Western Junction Railway

SU1682.1

DRAWN FROM WILTSHIRE 15NE (1899)

WARMINSTER

Site ST8745.1; In the vicinity of Warminster Station.
Warminster (GWR)^{ST8745.1/1A}ST8745.1/1A
A 1TS shed was opened here probably on September 9th, 1851. An official drawing details its construction as wooden with a tiled gable style roof. Details of the facilities are unknown and it is assumed to have closed when the line was extended through to Salisbury on June 30th, 1856*.

It is more likely to have closed earlier, in March 1854, with the building being relocated at Frome as ST7847.1/1A.

TROWBRIDGE

Site ST8558.1; On the west side of the line, north of Trowbridge Station.
Trowbridge (GWR)^{ST8558.1/1A}ST8558.1/1A
A brick built 3TS dead ended shed with a glazed gable and slated single pitched roof, it was located at ST85025840 and was opened in 1875. The facilities included a water tank, coal stage and, sited at the south end of the yard, a 45ft turntable. The depot was closed on June 2nd, 1923 and the buildings were converted to use as a carriage shed and small wagon works.

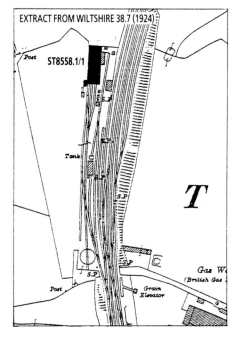

EXTRACT FROM WILTSHIRE 38.7 (1924)

ST8558.1/1

T

WESTBURY

Site ST8651.1; On the west side of the line, at the south end of Westbury Station.
Westbury (WS&WR)^{ST8651.1/1A}ST8651.1/1A
A shed was opened here by the Wilts, Somerset & Weymouth Railway on September 5th, 1848. Details of its construction, facilities or precise location are not available. The line was absorbed by the GWR on March 14th, 1850 and the shed was closed in 1862.

Site ST8651.2; On the east side of the line, south of Westbury Station.
Westbury (GWR)^{ST8651.2/1A}ST8651.2/1A
A brick built 4TS through road shed with a slated twin gabled roof, it was located at ST86015152 and was opened in February 1915. The depot possessed all major facilities and was closed by BR in September 1965.

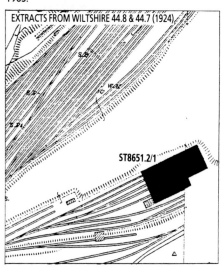

EXTRACTS FROM WILTSHIRE 44.8 & 44.7 (1924)

ST8651.2/1

HAMPSHIRE

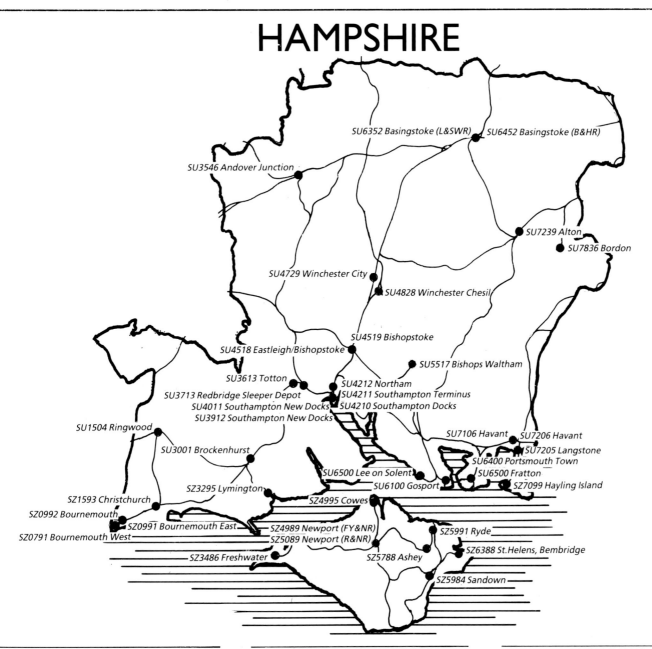

SU6352 Basingstoke (L&SWR)
SU6452 Basingstoke (B&HR)
SU3546 Andover Junction
SU7239 Alton
SU7836 Bordon
SU4729 Winchester City
SU4828 Winchester Chesil
SU4519 Bishopstoke
SU4518 Eastleigh/Bishopstoke
SU5517 Bishops Waltham
SU3613 Totton
SU4212 Northam
SU3713 Redbridge Sleeper Depot
SU4211 Southampton Terminus
SU4011 Southampton New Docks
SU4210 Southampton Docks
SU3912 Southampton New Docks
SU1504 Ringwood
SU7106 Havant
SU7206 Havant
SU3001 Brockenhurst
SU7205 Langstone
SU6400 Portsmouth Town
SU6500 Lee on Solent
SU6500 Fratton
SZ3295 Lymington
SU6100 Gosport
SZ7099 Hayling Island
SZ1593 Christchurch
SZ4995 Cowes
SZ0992 Bournemouth
SZ0991 Bournemouth East
SZ4989 Newport (FY&NR)
SZ5991 Ryde
SZ0791 Bournemouth West
SZ5089 Newport (R&NR)
SZ3486 Freshwater
SZ6388 St.Helens, Bembridge
SZ5788 Ashey
SZ5984 Sandown

ALTON

Site SU7239.1; On the east side of the line, at the north end of Alton Station.
Alton (L&SWR)[SU7239.1/1A]
A ITS dead ended shed, probably built in brick and with a slated gable style roof, it was located at SU72463981 and was opened on July 28th, 1852. The facilities included a water column and 35ft turntable. The building was closed in 1903 and mostly removed to make way for station enlargements. The water tank and shed offices, complete with the former side wall of the shed, were retained for further utilization for some years afterwards and were still extant in 1947.

EXTRACT FROM HAMPSHIRE 35.7 (1895)

BISHOPS WALTHAM

Site SU5517.1; At the north end of Bishops Waltham Station.
Bishops Waltham (BWR)[SU5517.1/1A]
A timber built ITS through road shed, it was located at SU55091763 and was opened by the Bishops Waltham Railway in 1866. The facilities included a water tank and coal stage. The line was worked from the outset by the L&SWR and the depot was closed by the SR on January 2nd, 1933.

A servicing point was then established ...
Bishops Waltham (SR)[SU5517.1/F1]
The shed was demolished with locomotives thereafter being serviced and stabled in the open alongside the water tank. The depot was finally closed by BR during 1958.

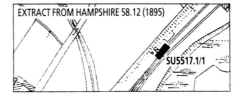

EXTRACT FROM HAMPSHIRE 58.12 (1895)

BORDON

Site SU7836.1; On the west side of the line, at the north end of Bordon Station.
Bordon (L&SWR)[SU7836.1/1A]
A corrugated iron ITS dead ended shed with a pitched corrugated iron roof, it was located at SU78403646 and was opened on December 11th, 1905. The facilities included a coal stage, sited outside of the shed entrance, and water column.

The shed was extended ...
Bordon (L&SWR)[SU7836.1/1B]
Prior to 1910 a short corrugated iron extension was added. The depot was little used and by post war days had become totally dilapidated. The shed was closed by BR in 1950 but it was not finally demolished until 1957.

EXTRACT FROM HAMPSHIRE 36.14 (1910)

BASINGSTOKE

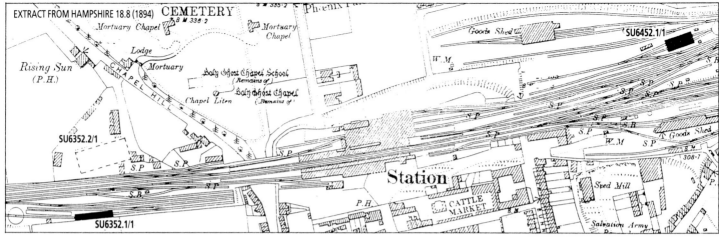

EXTRACT FROM HAMPSHIRE 18.8 (1894)

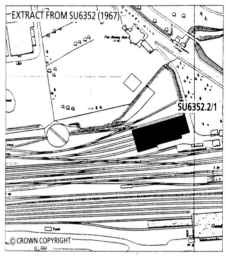

EXTRACT FROM SU6352 (1967)
© CROWN COPYRIGHT

Site SU6452.1; On the north side of the line, at the east end of Basingstoke Station.

Basingstoke (B&H)^{SU6452.1/1A}
A timber and brick built 2TS through road shed with a slated hipped roof, it was located at SU64035267 and was opened by the Berks & Hants Railway in 1850*. The facilities initially included a coal stage and turntable sited outside of the shed entrance. A water tower was built and the turntable removed at some time before 1930. The shed was closed by BR in November 1950 and was demolished to make way for sidings.

*Facilities to service locomotives were in place from November 1st, 1848 and the depot may not have opened until c1856.

Site SU6352.1; On the south side of the line, at the west end of Basingstoke Station.

Basingstoke (L&SWR)^{SU6352.1/1A}
A brick built 1TS through road shed with a slated gable style roof, it was located at SU63475249 and was opened on June 10th, 1839. The facilities included a coaling stage and turntable. The shed was closed in 1905 to make way for station enlargements.

Replaced by ...
Site SU6352.2; On the north side of the line, at the west end of Basingstoke Station.

Basingstoke (L&SWR)^{SU6352.2/1A}
A brick built 3TS dead ended shed with a slated roof and glazed gables it was located at SU63475255 and was opened in about 1905. The facilities included a water tank, double coal stage and 55ft turntable, enlarged to 70ft in c1942. The shed was closed by BR in March 1963, but remained in use as a servicing point until the end of steam on the Southern Region, on July 9th, 1967. The building was demolished in 1969.

ANDOVER JUNCTION

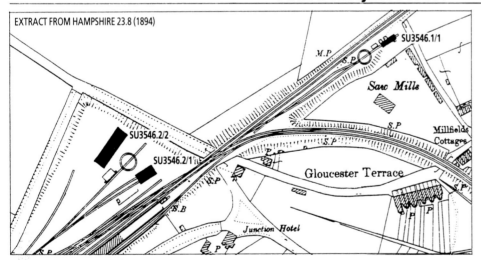

EXTRACT FROM HAMPSHIRE 23.8 (1894)

Andover Junction (SM&AR)^{SU3546.2/1A}
A timber built 2TS dead ended shed with a slated gable style roof, it was located at SU35644604 and was opened by the Swindon, Marlborough & Andover Railway on May 1st, 1882. The facilities included a coal stage, improved and re-sited in the 1930s, water column and a 50ft turntable which was shared with the L&SWR depot (SU3546.2/2A) after it opened in 1904. The site was rented from the L&SWR and the SM&AR was incorporated in the Midland & South Western Junction Railway in 1884. The shed was closed in about 1958 and was subsequently demolished.

Despite their proximity BR regarded these two sheds, and their facilities, as separate depots and allocated them to the Southern and Western Regions respectively: SU3546.2/2A as a sub-shed of Eastleigh and SU3546.2/1A as a sub-shed of Swindon.

Site SU3546.1; In the fork of the Basingstoke and Southampton lines, east of Andover Junction Station.

Andover Junction (L&SWR)^{SU3546.1/1A}
A 1TS dead ended shed, it was located at SU35874617 and was opened on July 3rd, 1854. Details of its construction are not known, but the facilities included a water tank, coal stage and turntable. The shed was damaged on June 30th, 1856 when the boiler of 2-2-2 locomotive No.107 Gem exploded. The shed was destroyed by a fire in 1899.

Replaced in 1904 by ...
Site SU3546.2; On the west side of the line, at the north end of Andover Junction Station.

Andover Junction (L&SWR)^{SU3546.2/2A}
A corrugated iron 2TS dead ended shed with a corrugated iron gable style roof, it was located at SU35604606. The facilities included a coal stage, water column and use of a 50ft turntable belonging to the neighbouring SM&AR shed (SU3546.2/1A) alongside. The depot was closed by BR in June 1962 and was later demolished.

Site SU4519.1; *In the fork of the Romsey and Winchester lines, at the north end of Eastleigh & Bishopstoke Station.*

Bishopstoke (L&SWR)^{SU4519.1/1A}

A 1TS through road shed, it was located at SU45781933 and probably opened at the same time as the line, on June 12th, 1839. Details of its construction and facilities are not known but it is assumed to have remained in use until Eastleigh shed (SU4518.3/1A) opened on January 1st, 1903. It was subsequently demolished.

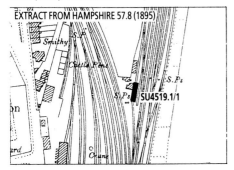

EXTRACT FROM HAMPSHIRE 57.8 (1895)

Site SU4518.1; *On the east side of the line, at the south end of Eastleigh & Bishopstoke Station.*

Bishopstoke (L&SWR)^{SU4518.1/1A}

A 2TS through road shed, it was located at SU45731880 and probably opened at the same time as the Gosport line, on November 29th, 1841. Details of its construction are not known but the facilities originally included a turntable which was later removed to accommodate track widening. The closure date is not known but it is assumed to have remained in use until the opening of Eastleigh shed (SU4518.3/1A) on January 1st, 1903. The building was demolished by 1908.

Site SU4518.2; *In the fork of the Southampton and Gosport lines, south of Eastleigh & Bishopstoke Station.*

Bishopstoke (L&SWR)^{SU4518.2/1A}

A 2TS through road shed, it was located at SU45681861 and was opened in c1891. Details of its construction are not known but the facilities included a coal stage and turntable. The shed only enjoyed a short existence, being closed in c1899 and demolished to allow construction of the access line to the new Eastleigh shed (SU4518.3/1A) a short distance to the south.

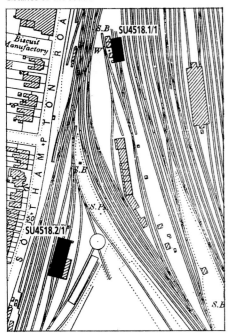

Site SU4518.3; *On the east side of the Southampton line, south of Eastleigh & Bishopstoke Station.*

Eastleigh (L&SWR)^{SU4518.3/1A}

A brick built 15TS through road shed with 5 slated and glazed roofs and glazed gable ends. It was located at SU45641809 and opened on January 1st, 1903. The depot was supplied with all facilities, including a 55ft turntable and coaling ramp.

The shed was re-roofed ...

Eastleigh (BR)^{SU4518.3/1B}

Shortly after nationalization the shed roof and gable ends were re-clad in corrugated asbestos sheeting. The depot lasted until the end of steam locomotion on the Southern Region, closing on July 9th, 1967. The building was demolished and a diesel depot established on the site.

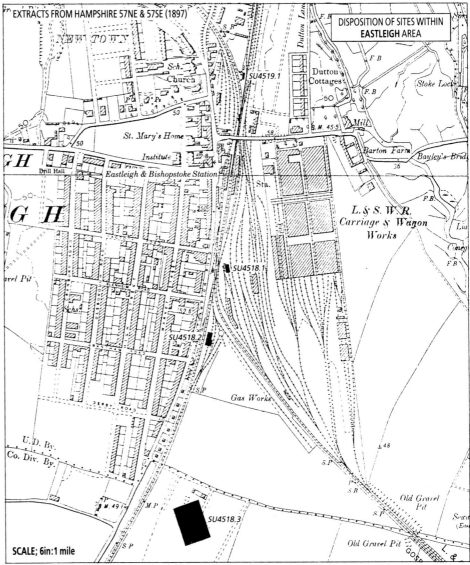

EXTRACTS FROM HAMPSHIRE 57NE & 57SE (1897)

DISPOSITION OF SITES WITHIN **EASTLEIGH** AREA

SCALE; 6in:1 mile

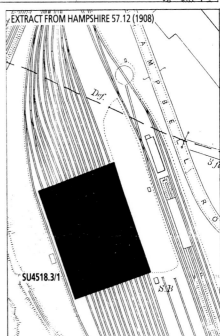

EXTRACT FROM HAMPSHIRE 57.12 (1908)

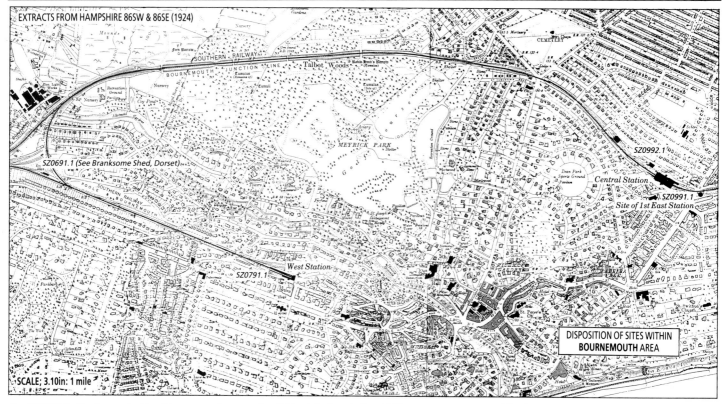

EXTRACTS FROM HAMPSHIRE 86SW & 86SE (1924)

SZ0691.1 (See Branksome Shed, Dorset)

West Station
SZ0791.1

SZ0992.1

Central Station

SZ0991.1
Site of 1st East Station

DISPOSITION OF SITES WITHIN
BOURNEMOUTH AREA

SCALE; 3.10in: 1 mile

Site SZ0991.1; On the south side of Bournemouth East Station.

Bournemouth East (RC&BR)^{SZ0991.1/1A}
A 1TS shed, it was located at SZ09909190 and was opened by the Ringwood, Christchurch & Bournemouth Railway on March 14th, 1870. Details of its construction and facilities are not known but the line was absorbed by the L&SWR on January 1st, 1874. The depot was closed on July 20th, 1883 upon the opening of a new station and shed (SZ0992.1/1A) sited a few yards to the west of the original terminus.

Replaced by ...
Site SZ0992.1; On the north side of the line, at the west end of Bournemouth Central Station.*

Bournemouth Central (L&SWR)^{SZ0992.1/1A}
A brick and corrugated iron 3TS dead ended shed with an unusual transverse twin dutch barn roof, it was located at SZ09609205 and was opened on July 20th, 1883. The facilities included a coal stage and 50ft turntable sited outside of the shed and from which all the tracks radiated. The shed was closed in 1921.

*Originally Bournemouth East Station it was renamed Bournemouth Central on May 1st, 1899.

An additional shed was built in 1888 ...
Bournemouth Central (L&SWR)^{SZ0992.1/2A}
A brick built 4TS dead ended shed with a twin slated gable style roof, it was sited at the west end of the yard at SZ09409219 and was opened on March 6th, 1888. The facilities included a coal stage, with the turntable of the original shed (SZ0992.1/1A) being utilized.

In 1921 some alterations were made ...
Bournemouth Central (L&SWR)^{SZ0992.1/2B}
Following closure of the original shed (SZ0992.1/1A) three of the shed roads were extended through the back of the shed, no doubt to increase capacity.

Major alterations were made in 1936 ...
Bournemouth Central (SR)^{SZ0992.1/2C}
A brick built extension, with northlight pattern tiled and glazed roof was added at the rear, doubling the length of the shed. At the same time the original turntable was replaced by a 65ft unit, the old coal platform was demolished and replaced by an electric crane, and the yard layout was remodelled and additional pits provided. A water softener was installed in 1938.

The shed was re-roofed by BR.
Bournemouth Central (BR)^{SZ0992.1/2D}
The original section of the shed was re-roofed by the Southern Region, in about 1956, in the standard asbestos louvre pitched style over each track. The shed was closed on July 9th, 1967 and demolished. Part of the walls were retained as a boundary for the station car park which then was located on the shed site.

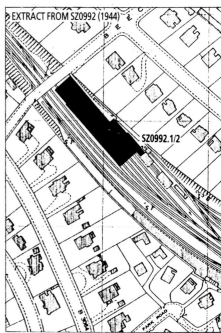

EXTRACT FROM SZ0992 (1944)

SZ0992.1/2

Ex-SR Battle of Britain Class 4-6-2 No.34074 *46 Squadron*, and ex-SR King Arthur Class N15 4-6-0 No.30740 *Merlin* are seen standing in the shed yard at **Bournemouth** (SZ0992.1/2C) at some time in 1950. The depot would be completely re-roofed in steel and asbestos some two years later and survive until the end of steam on the Southern Region in July 1967.

As an aside, those readers old enough to remember early 1956 British television may recall a programme called *"Saturday Night Out"*, one airing of which showed the just-withdrawn *Merlin* being wrecked, in a demonstration from the *Longmoor Military Railway*. True to her (his?) thoroughbred though *Merlin* underwent this indignity and stoically remained upright and blowing-off to the end!
H Garrett Collection.

Site SZ0791.1; On the south side of Bournemouth West Station.

Bournemouth West (L&SWR)^{SZ0791.1/1A}
A brick built 1TS shed, it was opened on June 15th, 1874. The precise location, and details of its facilities are not known. It was closed in 1895.

Cont ...

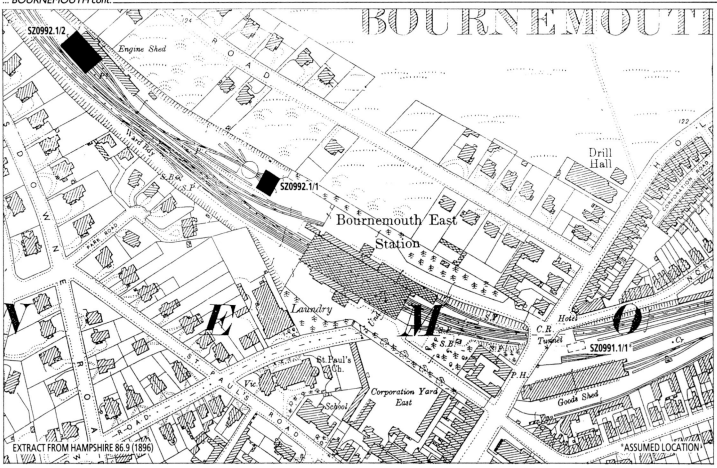

EXTRACT FROM HAMPSHIRE 86.9 (1896)

*ASSUMED LOCATION

LANGSTONE

Site SU7205.1; On the east side of the line, about 800 yards north of Langstone Station.

Langstone (HIR)^SU7205.1/1A

A temporary ITS shed, it was located at SU72060568 and was opened by the Hayling Island Railway on January 12th, 1865. It was assumed to have been built in timber and it is known that it was sited adjacent to a stream to facilitate water supply to the locomotives. The shed closed when the branch line was completed to the Hayling Island terminus and the depot SZ7099.1/1A was opened on July 16th, 1867.

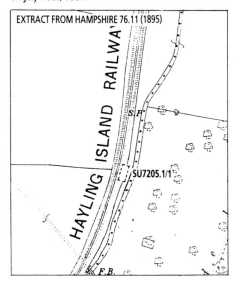

EXTRACT FROM HAMPSHIRE 76.11 (1895)

CHRISTCHURCH

Site SZ1593.1; On the east side of the Ringwood line, at the north end of Christchurch Station.

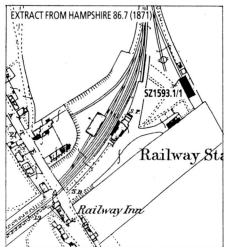

EXTRACT FROM HAMPSHIRE 86.7 (1871)

Christchurch (RC&BR)^SZ1593.1/1A

A ITS dead ended shed, it was located at SZ15549343 and was opened by the Ringwood, Christchurch & Bournemouth Railway on November 13th, 1862. Details of its construction are not known but the facilities included a water tank and coal stage sited outside of the shed entrance, and a 20ft turntable. The line was worked from the outset by the L&SWR and absorbed by them on January 1st, 1874. The date of closure is not known but the shed was demolished to make way for the Brockenhurst line which opened on March 5th, 1888.

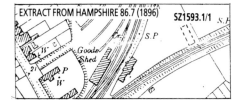

EXTRACT FROM HAMPSHIRE 86.7 (1896)

BROCKENHURST

Site SU3001.1; On the east side of the line, at the south end of Brockenhurst Station.

Brockenhurst (L&SWR)^SU3001.1/F1

A servicing area consisting of a turntable, latterly 50ft, located at SU30010172, and siding was opened in 1889. It lasted into BR days and probably until the end of steam on the Lymington branch on April 3rd, 1967.

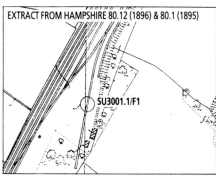

EXTRACT FROM HAMPSHIRE 80.12 (1896) & 80.1 (1895)

PORTSMOUTH

DISPOSITION OF SITES WITHIN PORTSMOUTH AREA

SCALE; 6in:1 mile

Site SU6400.1; On the north side of the line, at the east end of Portsmouth Town Station..

Portsmouth Town (LB&SCR/L&SWR)$^{SU6400.1/1A}$
A 4TS shed, it was located at SU64530022 and was opened on June 14th, 1847. Details of its construction are not known but the facilities included a turntable. The shed was closed in 1891 and demolished, the site being utilized for sidings with the turntable being retained for further use.

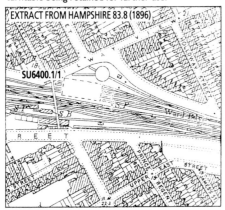

EXTRACT FROM HAMPSHIRE 83.8 (1896)

SU6400.1/1

Replaced by ...
Site SU6500.1; In the fork of the Southsea and Co-sham lines, at the east end of Fratton Station.

Fratton (LB&SCR/L&SWR)$^{SU6500.1/1A}$
A brick built square roundhouse with a transverse slated and glazed twin pitched roof, it was located at SU65750003 and was opened in 1891. It possessed all major facilities, including two coal stages, one for each company.

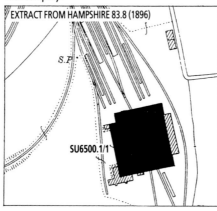

EXTRACT FROM HAMPSHIRE 83.8 (1896)

S.P.

SU6500.1/1

It was re-roofed ...
Fratton (BR)$^{SU6500.1/1B}$
As a result of wartime damage the shed was re-roofed by the Southern Region in 1948 with corrugated asbestos sheeting. Although the depot was closed on November 2nd, 1959 locomotives were still serviced and stabled at the shed until the end of steam operation in the area in 1967. The buildings were demolished in 1969.

HAYLING ISLAND

Site SZ7099.1; On the west side of the line, at the north end of Hayling Island Station.

Hayling Island (HIR)$^{SZ7099.1/1A}$
A timber built 1TS dead ended shed it was located at SZ70939986 and was opened by the Hayling Island Railway on July 16th, 1867. The building had originally stood at Petworth in Sussex (as SU9619.1/1A), being removed to here after closure. The facilities included a coal stage. The shed was closed in 1894.

A servicing point was then established ...
Site SZ7099.2; On the east side of Hayling Island Station.

Hayling Island (HIR)$^{SZ7099.2/F1}$
A servicing area consisting of a coal stage, located at SZ70949984, and a siding was opened in 1894. This was utilized until the branch line was closed by BR on November 4th, 1963.

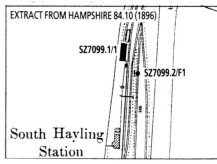

EXTRACT FROM HAMPSHIRE 84.10 (1896)

SZ7099.1/1

SZ7099.2/F1

South Hayling Station

LEE ON SOLENT

Site SU5600.1; On the west side of Lee on Solent Station.

Lee on Solent (LSLR)$^{SU5600.1/F1}$
A servicing area consisting of a coal stage and water column was opened by the Lee on Solent Light Railway on May 12th, 1894. The precise location is not known, but it is reasonable to assume that it was sited at about SU56280039. The facility probably lasted until the line was closed by the SR on September 30th, 1935.

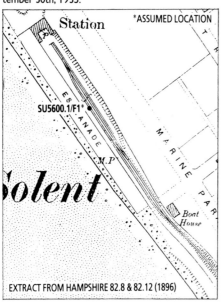

Station

*ASSUMED LOCATION

SU5600.1/F1*

Solent

EXTRACT FROM HAMPSHIRE 82.8 & 82.12 (1896)

LYMINGTON

Site SZ3295.1; On the east side of the line, at the north end of Lymington Station.

Lymington (Lymington)$^{SZ3295.1/1A}$
A brick built 1TS through road shed with a pitched slated roof, it was located at SZ32729590 and was opened on July 12th, 1858. The facilities included a water tower. The line was absorbed by the L&SWR in 1878.

The layout was rearranged ...
Lymington (L&SWR)$^{SZ3295.1/1B}$
The approach to the shed was originally from the north, but this was reversed in 1884, probably in connection with the opening of the short extension of the line to Lymington Pier. At the same time a new coal stage was provided at the south end of the building. The shed was closed by BR on April 3rd, 1967.

EXTRACT FROM HAMPSHIRE 88.3 (1896)

SZ3295.1/1

Engine House

Station

REDBRIDGE

Site SU3713.1; In Redbridge Permanent Way Works, on the south side of Redbridge Station.

Redbridge Sleeper Depot (L&SWR)$^{SU3713.1/1A}$
A stone built 1TS dead ended shed with a pitched slated roof, it was located at SU37151354 and was opened in 1884. As with similar departmental sheds none of the usual facilities were provided. The depot closed to steam in about 1967 when the duties were taken over by a diesel shunter. The final date of closure is not known, but the works were still in use in 1989. They have since been closed.

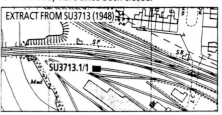

EXTRACT FROM SU3713 (1948)

SU3713.1/1

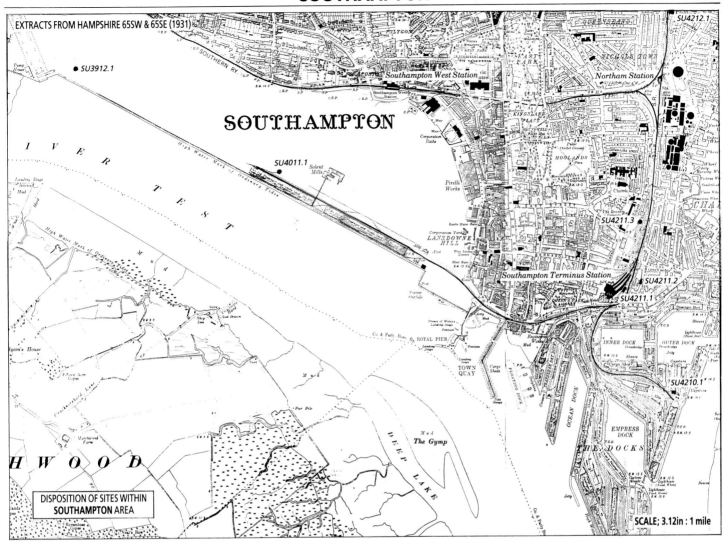

EXTRACTS FROM HAMPSHIRE 65SW & 65SE (1931)

SOUTHAMPTON

DISPOSITION OF SITES WITHIN
SOUTHAMPTON AREA

SCALE; 3.12in : 1 mile

Site SU4212.1; On the east side of the line, north of Northam Station.
Northam (L&SWR)^{SU4212.1/1A}
A brick built 14TS shed with one through road and a transverse pitched slated roof, it was located at SU42891260 and was opened in October 1840. The facilities included a water tank, coal stage and turntable. The shed was closed in January 1903.

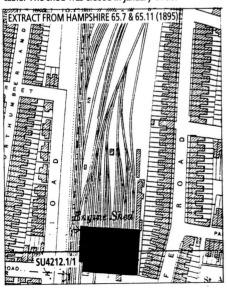

EXTRACT FROM HAMPSHIRE 65.7 & 65.11 (1895)

Engine Shed

SU4212.1/1

Site SU4210.1; In Southampton Docks.
Southampton Docks (SDR)^{SU4210.1/1A}
A brick built 1TS dead ended shed converted from stables, it was located at SU42921054 and was opened by the Southampton Docks Railway in October 1865. The shed was closed in February 1879.

Replaced on the same site by ...
Southampton Docks (SDR)^{SU4210.1/1B}
A brick built 2TS dead ended shed with a slated gable style roof and timber gable ends, it was opened in February 1879. The docks were taken over by the L&SWR in 1892.

At some stage, probably in the 1930s the shed was enlarged ...
Southampton Docks (SR)^{SU4210.1/1C}
A third, through road was added at the northern side and the shed was re-roofed with a tiled northlight pattern roof.

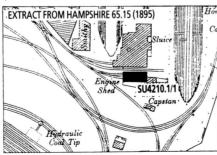

EXTRACT FROM HAMPSHIRE 65.15 (1895)

Sluice

Engine
Shed   SU4210.1/1
Capstan

Hydraulic
Coal Tip

The shed was re-built ...
Southampton Docks (BR)^{SU4210.1/1D}
The shed was reconstructed in 1955 by the Southern Region with a flat roof and small brick screen and was closed to steam in 1963. Diesel locomotion took over until January 1966 when it was officially closed, but engines continued to visit from time to time until July 1967. The depot was subsequently demolished.

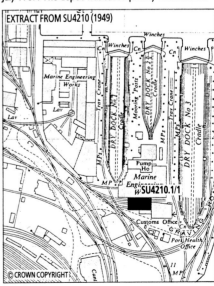

EXTRACT FROM SU4210 (1949)

Winches   Winches
Winches

Marine Engineering
Works

DRY DOCK No.1
DRY DOCK No.2
DRY DOCK No.3

Pump
Ho
Marine
Engineering   SU4210.1/1

Customs Office
Port Health
Office

© CROWN COPYRIGHT

Cont ...

Site SU4211.1; On the east side of Southampton Terminus Station.

Southampton Terminus (L&SWR)[SU4211.1/1A]

A 2TS dead ended shed it was located at SU42621108 and was opened on June 10th, 1839. It was a combined 'Engine & Carriage Shed', but details of its construction and facilities are not known. The closure date is not known, but it was probably connected with track widening through to the docks in the late 1840s.

Replaced by ...
Site SU4211.2; On the east side of the line, at the north end of Southampton Terminus Station.

Southampton Terminus (L&SWR)[SU4211.2/1A]

A 1TS dead ended shed, it is believed to have been built adjacently to the east side of the Goods Shed, at SU42731114. No further details are known except that it was closed in 1895.

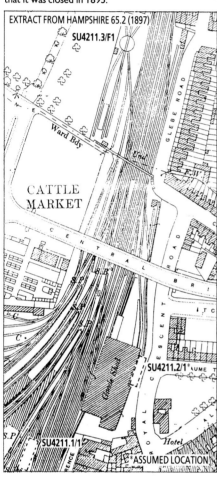

EXTRACT FROM HAMPSHIRE 65.2 (1897)
SU4211.3/F1
CATTLE MARKET
SU4211.2/1
SU4211.1/1
© CROWN COPYRIGHT

Replaced by ...
Site SU4211.3; On the west side of the line, north of Southampton Terminus Station.

Southampton Terminus (L&SWR)[SU4211.3/F1]

A servicing area consisting of a 50ft turntable, coal stage, sidings and water columns, it was located at SU42711147 and was opened in 1895. The turntable was enlarged to 70ft during the 1940s and the depot was officially closed by BR on September 5th, 1966 although it probably saw further use until the end of steam in the area in 1967.

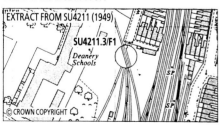

EXTRACT FROM SU4211 (1949)
SU4211.3/F1
Deanery Schools
© CROWN COPYRIGHT

Site SU4011.1; In the middle of Southampton New Docks.

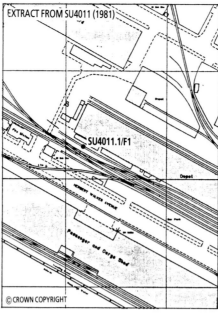

EXTRACT FROM SU4011 (1981)
SU4011.1/F1

Southampton New Docks (SR)[SU4011.1/F1]

A servicing area consisting of engine pits and water columns, it was located at SU40731172 and was opened in 1933. The depot went out of use in about 1966.

Site SU3912.1; At the west end of Southampton New Docks.

Southampton New Docks (SR)[SU3912.1/F1]

A servicing area consisting of a 65ft turntable, sidings, coal stage and water column, it was located at SU39611232 and was opened in 1933. The turntable was enlarged to 70ft by BR in 1949 and the depot went out of use in about 1966. The turntable was sold and removed to the *Great Western Society* at Didcot.

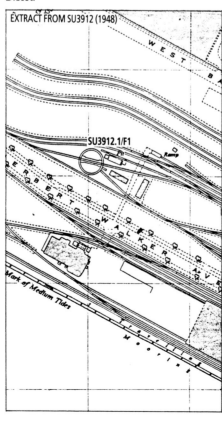

EXTRACT FROM SU3912 (1948)
SU3912.1/F1

GOSPORT

Site SU6100.1; On the south side of the line, at the west end of Gosport Station.

Gosport (L&SWR)[SU6100.1/1A]

A brick built 2TS dead ended shed with a gable style slated roof, it was located at SU61060015 and was opened on February 7th, 1842. The facilities included a coal stage and water tank, the locomotives turning on the adjacent triangular junction. The building was badly damaged during the blitz in 1941.

Replaced on the same site by ...

Gosport (SR)[SU6100.1/1B]

A corrugated asbestos 1TS dead ended shed with a pitched corrugated asbestos roof, it covered the southernmost track and was opened in 1942. The shed was closed by BR on the cessation of passenger services, on June 8th, 1953 and was demolished.

A servicing point was then established ...

Gosport (BR)[SU6100.1/1]

A siding was retained until about 1962 when the facility was finally dispensed with.

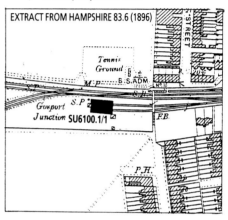

EXTRACT FROM HAMPSHIRE 83.6 (1896)
Tennis Ground
B.S.ADM
Gosport Junction SU6100.1/1

HAVANT

Site SU7106.1; On the south side of Havant Station.

Havant (LB&SCR)[SU7106.1/F1]

A servicing point consisting of a coal stage and siding, it was located at SU71890656.

Site SU7206.1; In the fork of the Hayling Island and Chichester lines, at the east end of Havant Station.

Havant (LB&SCR)[SU7206.1/F1]

A servicing point consisting of a coal stage and siding, it was located at SU72030656.

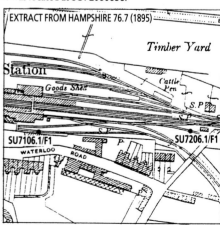

EXTRACT FROM HAMPSHIRE 76.7 (1895)
Timber Yard
Station
Goods Shed
Cattle Pen
SU7106.1/F1
SU7206.1/F1
WATERLOO ROAD

It is assumed that these two locations were opened in c1865 to service locomotives on the Hayling Island Branch, although one of them may have opened later as an emergency wartime measure. They remained in use into BR days and probably until closure of the line on November 4th, 1963.

RINGWOOD

Site SU1504.1; On the north side of the line, at the east end of Ringwood Station.
Ringwood (RC&BR)^{SU1504.1/1A}
A 1TS through road shed, it was located at SU15540468 and was opened by the Ringwood, Christchurch & Bournemouth Railway on November 13th, 1862. Details of the construction and facilities or its closure date are not known.

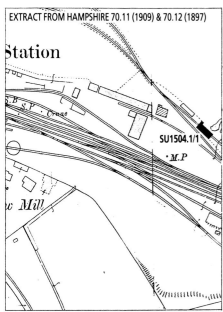
EXTRACT FROM HAMPSHIRE 70.11 (1909) & 70.12 (1897)

TOTTON

Site SU3613.1; On the south side of the line, at the west end of Totton Station.
Totton (L&SWR)^{SU3613.1/1A}
A 1TS dead ended shed, it was located at SU36241319 and was opened in c1851. No further details are known.

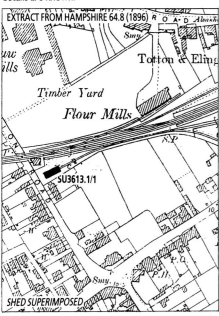
EXTRACT FROM HAMPSHIRE 64.8 (1896)
SHED SUPERIMPOSED

WINCHESTER

DISPOSITION OF SITES WITHIN
WINCHESTER AREA

EXTRACT FROM HAMPSHIRE 41SW (1931)

Site SU4828.1; On the east side of the line, south of Winchester Cheesehill Station.

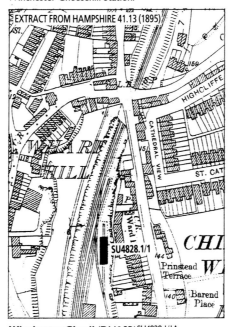
EXTRACT FROM HAMPSHIRE 41.13 (1895)

Winchester Chesil (DN&SR)^{SU4828.1/1A}
A stone and brick built 1TS through road shed with a slated gable style roof and timber gables, it was located at SU48672881 and was opened by the Didcot, Newbury & Southampton Railway on May 4th, 1885. The facilities included a coal stage, sited outside of the shed entrance, turntable and water tank. The shed was closed by BR in July 1953.

Site SU4729.1; In the goods yard on the west side of Winchester City Station.
Winchester City (L&SWR)^{SU4729.1/F1}
A servicing point consisting of a coal stage, it was located at SU47692997 and was opened in c1920.

A shed was erected in 1928 ...
Winchester City (SR)^{SU4729.1/1A}
A corrugated iron 1TS through road shed with a pitched corrugated iron roof was built adjacently to the coal stage at SU47692998. It was closed by BR, to steam in October 1963 and totally by 1969.

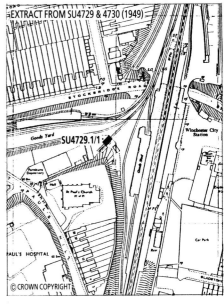
EXTRACT FROM SU4729 & 4730 (1949)
© CROWN COPYRIGHT

ASHEY

Site SZ5788.1; In the vicinity of Ashey Station.
Ashey (R&NR)^{SZ5788.1/1A}
A temporary 1TS shed was opened by the Ryde & Newport Railway during the construction of the line in 1873. It was probably built in timber and was approximately located at SZ57808884. The shed was closed on December 20th, 1875.

SANDOWN

Site SZ5984.1; In the vicinity of Sandown Station.
Sandown (IOWR)^{SZ5984.1/F1}
A servicing area consisting of a pit and siding was opened here by the Isle of Wight Railway on February 1st, 1875. No further details are known.

COWES

Site SZ4995.1; On the south side of the line, at the west end of Cowes Station.
Cowes (C&NR)^{SZ4995.1/1A}
A timber built 1TS dead ended shed with a pitched slated roof, it was located at SZ49489603 and was opened by the Cowes & Newport Railway on June 16th, 1862. Details of its facilities are not known. The line was absorbed by the Isle of Wight Central Railway on July 1st, 1887 and the shed was closed in 1892 and demolished to make way for station enlargements.

EXTRACT FROM HAMPSHIRE 90.2 (1862)
SZ4995.1/1

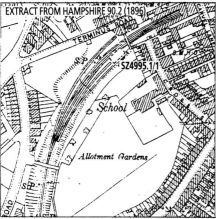
EXTRACT FROM HAMPSHIRE 90.2 (1896)
SZ4995.1/1

FRESHWATER

Site SZ3486.1; On the south side of the line, at the east end of Freshwater Station.
Freshwater (FY&NR)^{SZ3486.1/1A}
A 1TS dead ended shed, it was located at SZ34458699 and was opened by the Freshwater, Yarmouth & Newport Railway on September 10th, 1888. Details of its construction and facilities are not known, but it was destroyed by a fire in 1890.

Replaced on the same site by ...
Freshwater (FY&NR)^{SZ3486.1/1B}
A timber built 1TS dead ended shed with a pitched slated roof, it was opened in 1890. The facilities included a water tank. The shed was closed by the SR on August 1st, 1923.

Freshwater (FY&NR)^{SZ3486.1/2A}
A timber built 1TS dead ended shed with a pitched slated roof, it was located alongside SZ3486.1/1B at SZ34458698 and was opened in 1908. It was built to house the petrol railcar and was closed by the SR on August 1st, 1923.

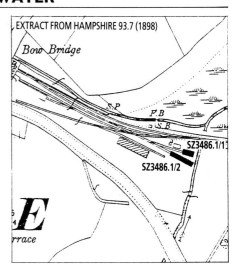
EXTRACT FROM HAMPSHIRE 93.7 (1898)
Bow Bridge
SZ3486.1/1
SZ3486.1/2

NEWPORT

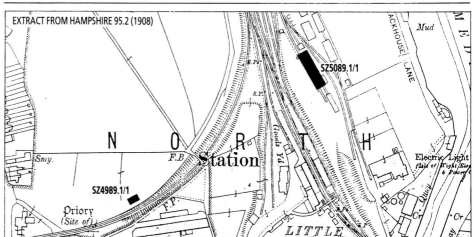
EXTRACT FROM HAMPSHIRE 95.2 (1908)
SZ5089.1/1
SZ4989.1/1

Site SZ4989.1; On the north side of the Freshwater line, west of Newport Station.
Newport (FY&NR)^{SZ4989.1/1A}
A timber built 1TS dead ended shed with a pitched roof, it was located at SZ49878947 and was opened by the Freshwater, Yarmouth & Newport Railway on July 1st, 1913. The facilities included a coal stage sited outside of the shed entrance. The depot was closed by the SR on August 1st, 1923.

Site SZ5089.1; On the east side of the line, at the north end of Newport Station.
Newport (R&NR)^{SZ5089.1/1A}
A corrugated iron 2TS shed with one through road and a pitched corrugated iron roof, it was located at SZ50038959 and was opened by the Ryde & Newport Railway on December 20th, 1875. The facilities included a water tank and, installed at a later date, a coal stage. The line was absorbed by the Isle of Wight Central Railway on July 1st, 1887 and the shed was closed by BR on November 4th, 1957.

ST.HELENS

Site SZ6388.1; On the north side of the line, at the east end of St.Helens Station.
St.Helens (Bembridge) (IOWR)^{SZ6388.1/1A}
A brick built 1TS dead ended shed with a corrugated iron gable style roof and timber gables, it was located at SZ63118867 and was opened by the Isle of Wight Railway on May 27th, 1882. The facilities included a coal stage, sited outside of the shed entrance, and a water tank. The shed was closed in 1921 but was not demolished until BR days, having served as a private workshop.

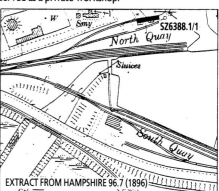
SZ6388.1/1
North Quay
EXTRACT FROM HAMPSHIRE 96.7 (1896)

RYDE

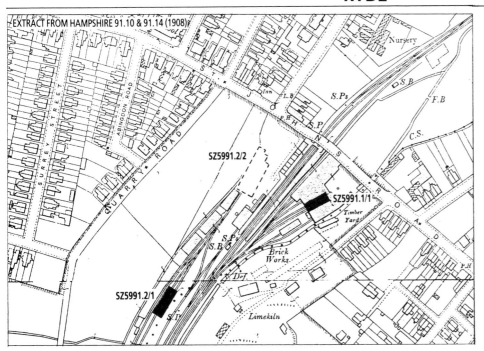

EXTRACT FROM HAMPSHIRE 91.10 & 91.14 (1908)

Replaced by ...
Ryde (SR)^{SZ5992.2/2A}
A corrugated asbestos 2TS dead ended shed with a corrugated asbestos transverse pitched roof, it was sited at the north end of the yard at SZ59589196 and was opened in 1930. The facilities included water columns and a coal stage. The shed was closed by BR on December 31st, 1966 and demolished.

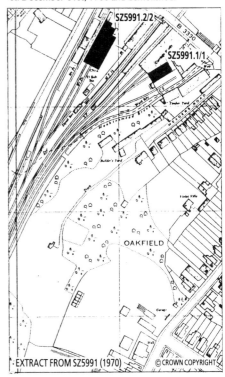

EXTRACT FROM SZ5991 (1970)   © CROWN COPYRIGHT

Site SZ5991.1; On the east side of Ryde St.John's Road Station.
Ryde (IOWR)^{SZ5991.1/1A}
A brick built 2TS dead ended shed with a gable style slated roof, it was located at SZ59649193 and was opened by the Isle of Wight Railway on August 23rd, 1864. It was closed in 1874 and absorbed as part of the works. The shed building was still standing in 1995, the works having being utilized as an emu depot from the end of steam on the island on December 31st, 1966.

Replaced by ...
Site SZ5991.2; On the west side of Ryde St.John's Road Station.
Ryde (IOWR)^{SZ5991.2/1A}
A corrugated iron 2TS through road shed with a corrugated iron dutch barn roof, it was located at SZ59509184 and was opened by the Isle of Wight Railway in 1874. The facilities included a covered coaling stage. The shed was closed by the SR in 1930 and demolished.

Ryde's third engine shed (SZ5991.2/2A) is seen here just after opening in 1930. Using standard materials of concrete blocks, steel and asbestos sheeting the Southern Railway erected this shed as a replacement of an 1874 Isle of Wight Railway 2TS building (SZ5991.2/1A), which itself had succeeded the original 1864 shed (SZ5991.1/1A).

The third depot remained in use until the end of steam on New Year's Eve 1966 and was subsequently demolished. However, the very first shed still stood on 1998 as part of Ryde's railway workshops complex.
H Garrett Collection

KENT

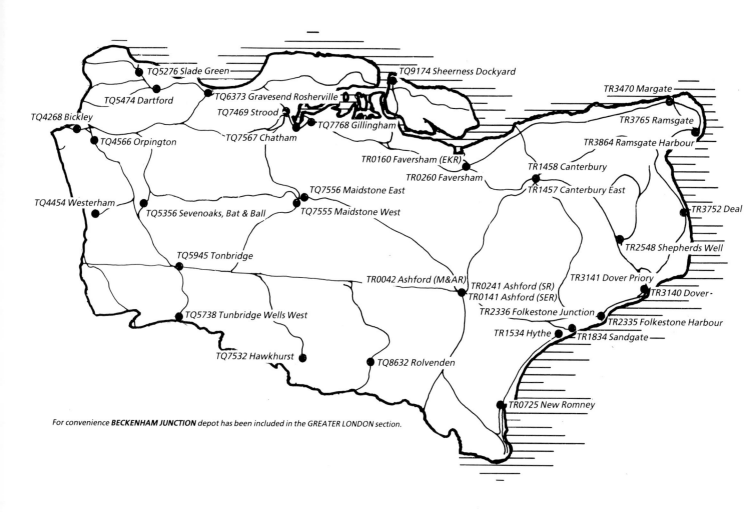

TQ5276 Slade Green
TQ5474 Dartford
TQ4268 Bickley
TQ4566 Orpington
TQ6373 Gravesend Rosherville
TQ7469 Strood
TQ7768 Gillingham
TQ7567 Chatham
TQ9174 Sheerness Dockyard
TR3470 Margate
TR3765 Ramsgate
TR3864 Ramsgate Harbour
TR0160 Faversham (EKR)
TR0260 Faversham
TR1458 Canterbury
TR1457 Canterbury East
TR3752 Deal
TQ7556 Maidstone East
TQ4454 Westerham
TQ5356 Sevenoaks, Bat & Ball
TQ7555 Maidstone West
TR2548 Shepherds Well
TQ5945 Tonbridge
TR0042 Ashford (M&AR)
TR0241 Ashford (SR)
TR0141 Ashford (SER)
TR3141 Dover Priory
TR3140 Dover
TQ5738 Tunbridge Wells West
TR2336 Folkestone Junction
TR2335 Folkestone Harbour
TR1534 Hythe
TR1834 Sandgate
TQ7532 Hawkhurst
TQ8632 Rolvenden
TR0725 New Romney

For convenience **BECKENHAM JUNCTION** depot has been included in the GREATER LONDON section.

PADDOCK WOOD

Site TQ6645.1; In the vicinity of Paddock Wood Station.
Paddock Wood (SER)^TQ6645.1/F1
It is believed that some sidings were utilized for locomotive servicing. No details are known.

SANDGATE

Site TR1834.1; On the south side of the line, at the east end of Sandgate Station.
Sandgate (SER)^TR1834.1/1A
A brick built 1TS dead ended shed with a slated gable style roof, it was located at TQ18983498 and was opened on October 9th, 1874. The facilities included a water tank. The depot was closed on December 31st, 1921.

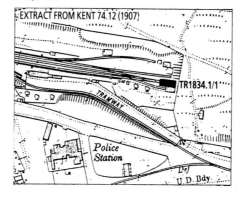

EXTRACT FROM KENT 74.12 (1907)

TR1834.1/1

SEVENOAKS

Site TQ5356.1; On the east side of the line, at the south end of Sevenoaks Bat & Ball Station.
Sevenoaks Bat & Ball (Sevenoaks)^TQ5356.1/1A
A timber built 1TS dead ended shed with a slated pitched roof, it was located at TQ53045675 and was opened by the Sevenoaks Railway on June 2nd, 1862. The facilities included a 45ft turntable and water tank. The line was absorbed by the LC&DR on June 30th, 1879 and the shed was closed by the SR in 1935. It was demolished in 1936.

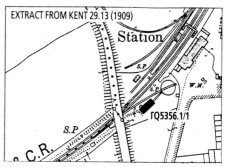

EXTRACT FROM KENT 29.13 (1909)

Station

TQ5356.1/1

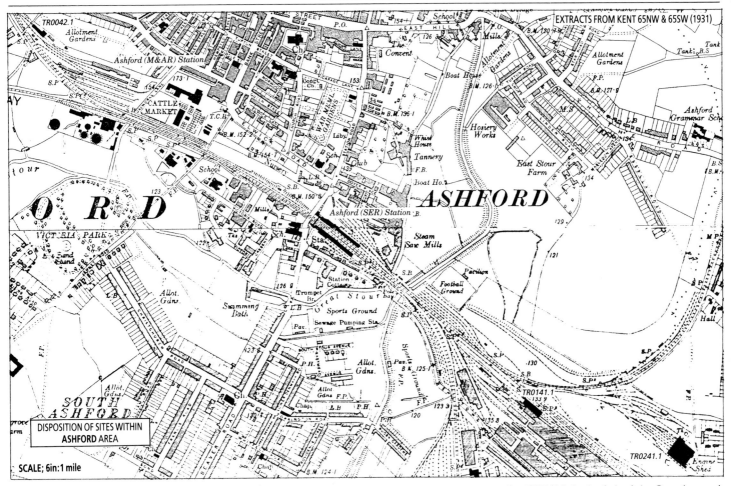

EXTRACTS FROM KENT 65NW & 65SW (1931)

DISPOSITION OF SITES WITHIN
ASHFORD AREA

SCALE: 6in:1 mile

Site TR0042.1; On the north side of the line, at the west end of Ashford (M&AR) Station.

Ashford (M&AR)^{TR0042.1/1A}

A brick built 2TS through road shed with a slated pitched roof, it was located at TR00294275 and was opened by the Maidstone & Ashford Railway in 1894. The facilities included a water tank, coal stage and turntable. The depot enjoyed only a brief existence as an engine shed, closing on January 1st, 1899 on the cessation of passenger working into the station. It was converted into a goods shed and survived until 1971 when it was demolished by BR.

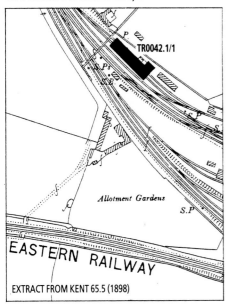

EXTRACT FROM KENT 65.5 (1898)

Site TR0141.1; On the north side of Ashford Works, on the south side of the line, east of Ashford (SER) Station.

Ashford (SER)^{TR0141.1/1A}

A brick built 4TS through road shed with a single slated pitched roof, it was located at TR01744176 and was opened by the South Eastern Railway on December 1st, 1842. The facilities included a water tank, coal stage and turntable. The shed was closed, following the construction of a new Ashford shed (TR0241.1/1A) in 1931 and demolished.

A servicing point was then established ...

Ashford Works (SR)^{TR0141.1/F1}

The engine pits, turntable and coal stage were utilized for servicing and stabling the works shunters, from 1931 until the end of steam locomotion in 1967.

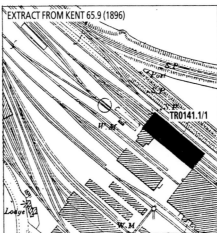

EXTRACT FROM KENT 65.9 (1896)

Site TR0241.1; In the fork of the Canterbury and Folkestone lines, east of Ashford (SER) Station.

Ashford (SR)^{TR0241.1/1A}

A concrete built 10TS shed with two through roads and a northlight pattern roof, it was located at TR02164163 and was opened in 1931. The shed possessed all facilities and was closed to steam by BR in June 1962. Diesel locomotives were serviced at the shed until 1968 when the building was taken over in an abortive preservation attempt by the *Ashford Steam Centre*. It was gradually demolished so that by 1995 only a small part was still standing.

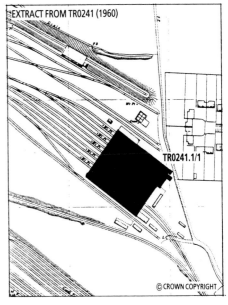

EXTRACT FROM TR0241 (1960)

© CROWN COPYRIGHT

BICKLEY

Site TQ4268.1; On the north side of the line, at the west end of Bickley Station.

Bickley (LC&DR)[TQ4268.1/1A]
A ITS dead ended shed, believed to have been built in brick, it was located at TQ42036874 and was opened by the London Chatham & Dover Railway in c1858. The facilities included a water column and a 44ft turntable sited on the other side of the line. The shed was closed in 1901 and demolished.

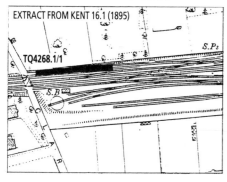

EXTRACT FROM KENT 16.1 (1895)

CHATHAM

Site TQ7567.1; On the north side of Chatham Station.

Chatham (EKR)[TQ7567.1/F1]
A servicing point consisting of a turntable and sidings, it was located at TQ75576763 and was opened by the East Kent Railway, probably on January 25th, 1858 when the line was completed. The closure date is not known but it lasted into BR days and probably until the end of steam in the area in c1960.

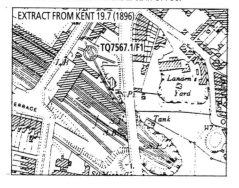

EXTRACT FROM KENT 19.7 (1896)

DARTFORD

Site TQ5474.1; On the south side of Dartford Station.

Dartford (SECR)[TQ5474.1/F1]
A servicing point consisting of a turntable, coal stage and sidings, it was located at TQ54327436. No further details are known.

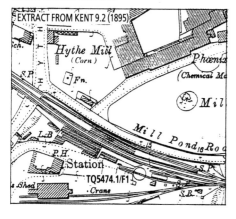

EXTRACT FROM KENT 9.2 (1895)

CANTERBURY

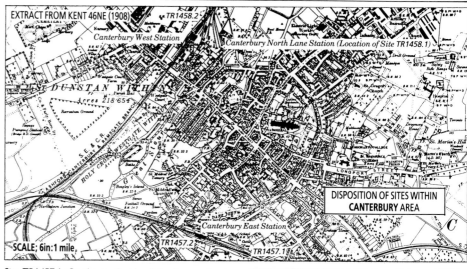

EXTRACT FROM KENT 46NE (1908)

DISPOSITION OF SITES WITHIN **CANTERBURY** AREA

SCALE: 6in:1 mile

Site TR1457.1; On the south side of the line, at the east end of Canterbury East Station.

Canterbury East (LC&DR)[TR1457.1/1A]
A ITS dead ended shed, it was located at TR14905718 and was opened, it is believed, in c1860. No further details are known and it is assumed to have closed in 1899.

Site TR1457.2; On the south side of Canterbury East Station.

Canterbury East (LC&DR)[TR1457.2/1A]
A 3TS through road shed, it was located at TR14635726 and was opened on July 9th, 1860. The precise details regarding this depot are not available, but it is believed to have closed on July 22nd, 1861 on the opening of Dover Priory shed (TR3141.1/1A), and was thereafter used for engine storage and light repairs. When this practice ceased is not known, but the building had been reduced to a ITS by 1896.

Site TR1458.1; In the vicinity of Canterbury North Lane Station.

Canterbury North Lane (C&W)[TR1458.1/1A]
A ITS shed, it was opened by the Canterbury & Whitstable Railway in 1830 and was closed in 1846. No further details are known.

Site TR1458.2; On the west side of the line, at the north end of Canterbury West Station.

Canterbury West (SER)[TR1458.2/1A]
A brick built ITS dead ended shed with a slated pitched roof, it was located at TR14635853 and was opened on April 6th, 1846. The facilities included a water tank and a turntable.

The shed was rebuilt ...

Canterbury West (SER)[TR1458.2/1B]
At some stage the shed was rebuilt to a through road type and the turntable was removed. The depot was closed by BR in March 1955 and was subsequently demolished.

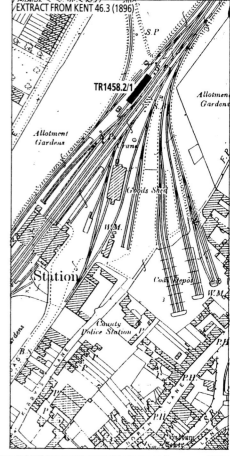

EXTRACT FROM KENT 46.3 (1896)

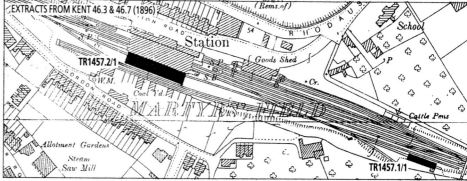

EXTRACTS FROM KENT 46.3 & 46.7 (1896)

60

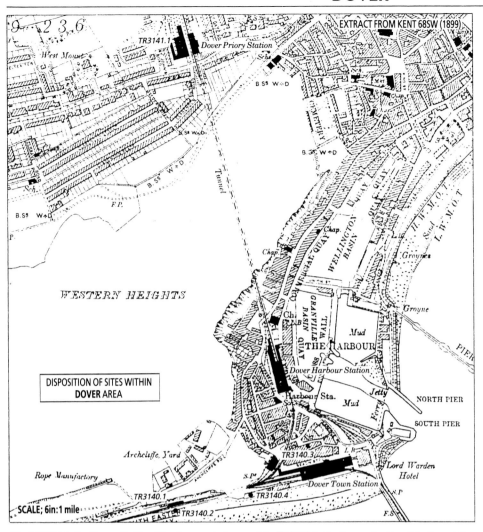

DISPOSITION OF SITES WITHIN DOVER AREA

SCALE; 6in:1 mile

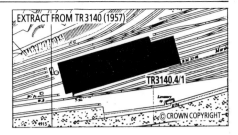

EXTRACT FROM TR 3140 (1957)

© CROWN COPYRIGHT

Site TR3141.1; On the west side of Dover Priory Station.

Dover Priory (LC&DR)[TR3141.1/1A]
A brick built 4TS dead ended shed with a slated twin gable style roof, it was located at TR31324145 and was opened on July 22nd, 1861. The facilities included a coal stage, water tank and a turntable, replaced by a 50ft unit in c1900. The shed was closed in 1932 subsequent to the opening of Dover Marine shed (TR3140.4/1A) in 1928 and was demolished.

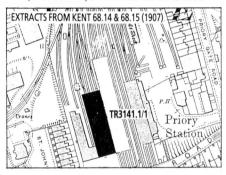

EXTRACTS FROM KENT 68.14 & 68.15 (1907)

Site TR3140.1; On the north side of the line, west of Dover Town Station.

Dover Town (SER)[TR3140.1/1A]
A brick built 1TS dead ended shed with a slated pitched roof, it was located at TR31354018 and was opened on February 7th, 1844. The facilities included a turntable. The shed probably closed at the same time as Dover Town Station on October 14th, 1914.

Site TR3140.2; On the south side of the line, west of Dover Town Station.

Dover Town (SER)[TR3140.2/1A]
Very little is known of this 1TS shed. It was located at TR31364017 and it is assumed to have opened at the same time, February 14th, 1844, as Dover Town shed (TR3140.1/1A), on the opposite side of the line. No further details are known except that it had been removed by 1862.

Site TR3140.3; On the north side of the line, at the west end of Dover Town Station.

Dover Town (SER)[TR3140.3/1A]
A brick built 4TS dead ended shed with twin slated hipped roofs, it was located at TR31644030. The opening and closing dates are not known but it was in existence by 1862 and probably closed at the same time as Dover Town Station on October 14th, 1914.

Site TR3140.4; On the south side of the line, at the west end of Dover Town Station.

Dover Marine (SR)[TR3140.4/1A]
A concrete built 5TS shed with one through road and an eastlight pattern roof, it was located at TR31554020 and was opened in 1928. The depot possessed all facilities, including a 65ft turntable and a water softener. The shed was closed by BR on June 12th, 1961 and was subsequently demolished.

DEAL

Site TR3752.1; On the west side of the line, at the north end of Deal Station.

Deal (SER)[TR3752.1/1A]
A brick built 2TS dead ended shed, it was located at TR37325280 and was opened on July 1st, 1847.

It was enlarged in 1881 ...
Deal (SER)[TR3752.1/1B]
A third road was added and the building was surmounted by a slated single pitched roof. It was officially re-opened on June 15th and the facilities included a 50ft turntable, water tower and coal stage. The shed was closed by the SR in September 1930, but found further use in the CME and goods departments until the 1960s. It was subsequently demolished and the site turned over to housing.

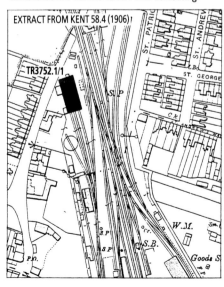

EXTRACT FROM KENT 58.4 (1906)

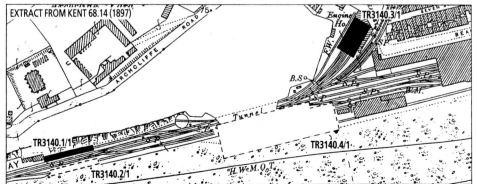

EXTRACT FROM KENT 68.14 (1897)

FAVERSHAM

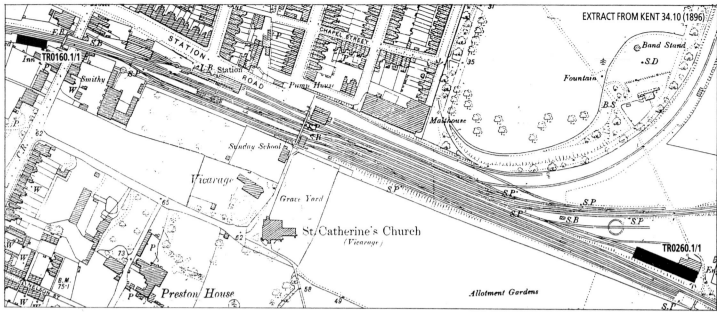

Site TR0160.1; On the south side of the line at the west end of Faversham Station.

Faversham (EKR)^{TR0160.1/1A}
A 2TS dead ended shed, it was located at TR01446093 and was opened by the East Kent Railway on January 25th, 1858. No further details of its construction or facilities are known. The EKR became the London, Chatham & Dover Railway on August 1st, 1859 and the shed was closed in 1895.

Site TR0260.1; In the fork of the Margate and Canterbury lines, east of Faversham Station.

Faversham (LC&DR)^{TR0260.1/1A}
A brick built 2TS dead ended shed with a slated pitched roof, it was located at TR02066075 and was opened in 1860. The facilities included a turntable and coal stage.

The shed was re-roofed in 1935...

Faversham (SR)^{TR0260.1/1B}
The building was re-roofed in corrugated asbestos sheeting. It was closed by BR in June 1959 and demolished.

Adjoined by ...

Faversham (LC&DR)^{TR0260.1/2A}
A brick built 2TS dead ended shed with a slated hipped roof, it was located at TR02056077 and was opened in 1900. It adjoined the northern wall of TR0260.1/1A and the facilities were improved by the installation of a larger 50ft turntable.

The shed was re-roofed in 1951 ...

Faversham (BR)^{TR0260.1/2B}
The shed was rebuilt with an asbestos pitched roof and Southern Region-style brick gable end and screen. The shed was closed in June 1959 but was used for a while for the stabling and fuelling of diesel locomotives. After closure a preservation order was granted to the *Faversham Society* and the shed remains standing, although by 1995 no use was being made of it.

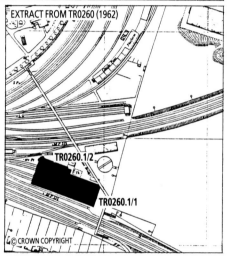

GILLINGHAM

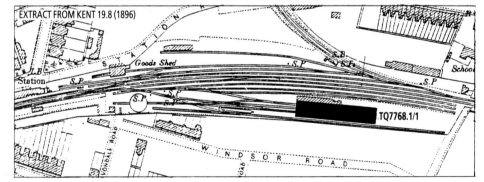

Site TQ7768.1; On the south side of the line, at the east end of Gillingham Station.

Gillingham* (LC&DR)^{TQ7768.1/1A}
A brick built 3TS dead ended shed with a slated pitched roof, it was located at TQ77956842 and was opened by the London, Chatham & Dover Railway in 1885. The facilities included a water tank, coal stage and a 50ft turntable.

**The depot was originally known as New Brompton.*

Some modifications were made ...

Gillingham (SECR)^{TQ7768.1/1B}
At some time after 1896, the two southernmost tracks were extended through the back of the shed.

The shed was re-roofed ...

Gillingham (SR)^{TQ7768.1/1C}
The shed was re-roofed in 1931 and at a later stage a sheltered coal stage was provided. The depot was closed by BR on June 13th, 1960 and was subsequently demolished.

GRAVESEND

Site TQ6373.1; On the west side of the line, south of Gravesend Rosherville Station.

Rosherville* (LC&DR)^{TQ6373.1/1A}
A 2TS dead ended shed, probably built in brick, with a pitched roof, it was located at TQ63427377 and was opened on May 10th, 1886. The facilities included a coal stage, with a 50ft turntable available about ½ mile away at West Street. These circumstances were apparently brought about to effect a lower rateable value on the shed building, which was sited in a different local authority area to the turntable. The shed was closed by the SR in 1923.

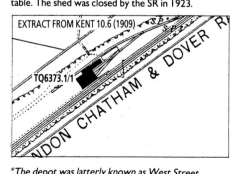

**The depot was latterly known as West Street.*

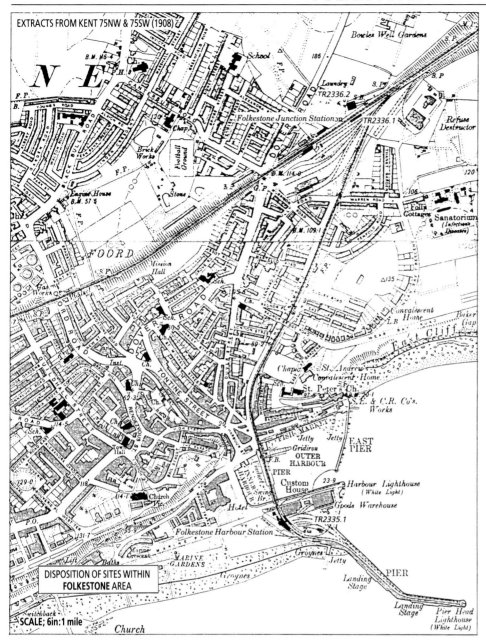

EXTRACTS FROM KENT 75NW & 75SW (1908)

DISPOSITION OF SITES WITHIN
FOLKESTONE AREA

SCALE; 6in:1 mile

Site TR2336.1; On the south side of the line, at the east end of Folkestone Junction Station.
Folkestone Junction (SER)^{TR2336.1/1A}
A brick built 1TS dead ended shed with a slated gable style roof, it was located at TR23533693.

Adjoined by ...
Folkestone Junction (SER)^{TR2336.1/2A}
A brick built 1TS dead ended shed with a slated gable style roof, it abutted to the east end of TR2336.1/1A and was located at TR23563696.

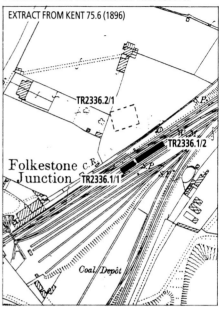

EXTRACT FROM KENT 75.6 (1896)

Folkestone Junction

Coal Depôt

The buildings were opened on December 18th, 1843 and the facilities included a water column. The depot was closed in 1900.

Replaced by ...
Site TR2336.2; On the north side of the line, at the east end of Folkestone Junction Station.

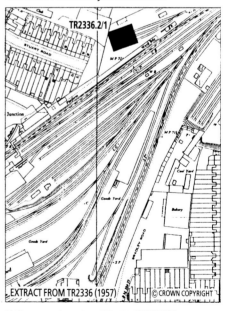

EXTRACT FROM TR2336 (1957)   © CROWN COPYRIGHT

Folkestone Junction (SE&CR)^{TR2336.2/1A}
A brick built 3TS dead ended shed with a single gable style slated roof, it was located at TR23533697 and was opened in 1900. The facilities included a coal stage, water tank and, after 1917, a 65ft turntable. The shed was closed by BR on June 12th, 1961. It was used for stabling diesel locomotives for a short while, but was subsequently demolished.

Site TR2335.1; In Folkestone Harbour goods yard.
Folkestone Harbour (SER)^{TR2335.1/1A}
A 1TS dead ended shed, it was located at TR23383580 and was opened in 1881. No further details are known, except that it was closed in 1899.

Replaced by ...
Folkestone Harbour (SER)^{TR2335.1/2A}
A 1TS through road shed, it was located at TR23473579 and was opened in 1899. No further details are known, except that it was closed in c1910.

Replaced by ...
Folkestone Harbour (SER)^{TR2335.1/3A}
A brick built 1TS dead ended shed with a slated gable style roof, it was located at TR23413579 and was opened in c1910. No details of its facilities are known. The shed was closed in 1919 but it saw further use, probably by the goods department, and still remained standing into BR days. It was demolished in c1960.

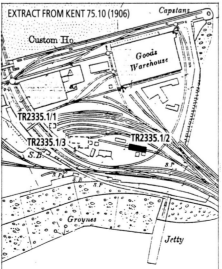

EXTRACT FROM KENT 75.10 (1906)

Custom Ho

Goods Warehouse

MAIDSTONE

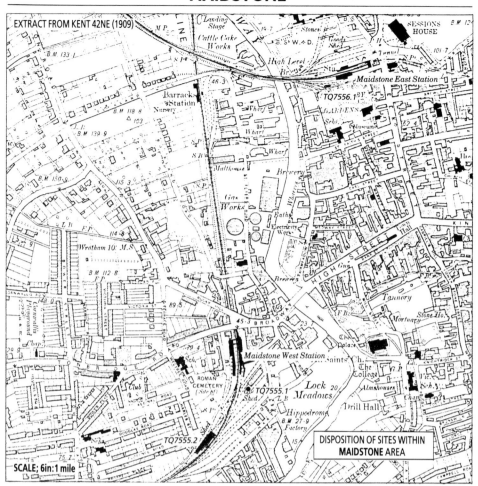

EXTRACT FROM KENT 42NE (1909)

SCALE; 6in:1 mile

DISPOSITION OF SITES WITHIN
MAIDSTONE AREA

Site TQ7556.1; On the south side of Maidstone East Station.

Maidstone East (SM&TR)[TQ7556.1/1A]
A brick built 1TS through road shed with a slated pitched roof, it was located at TQ75825613 and was opened by the Sevenoaks, Maidstone & Tunbridge Railway on June 1st, 1874. The facilities included a water tank, coal stage and, sited outside of the shed entrance, a 45ft turntable. The line was absorbed by the LC&DR on June 30th, 1879 and the shed was closed by the SR in 1933 and subsequently demolished.

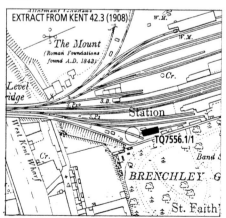

EXTRACT FROM KENT 42.3 (1908)

Site TQ7555.1; On the east side of the line, at the south end of Maidstone West Station.

Maidstone West (SER)[TQ7555.1/1A]
A timber built 1TS shed, it was located at TQ75625525 and was opened on September 25th, 1844. No further details are known, except that it was closed on June 18th, 1856.

Replaced by ...
Site TQ7555.2; On the west side of the line, at the south end of Maidstone West Station.

Maidstone West (SER)[TQ7555.2/1A]
A brick built 3TS dead ended shed with a slated gable style roof and wooden gable. The facilities included a water tank, coal stage and 45ft turntable. The shed was closed by the SR in 1933.

A servicing point was then established ...
Maidstone West (SR)[TQ7555.2/F1]
The shed building was demolished, but the remaining facilities were utilized as a servicing area until the line was electrified in 1939.

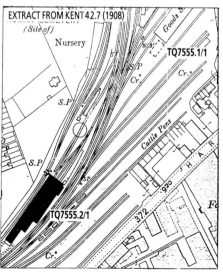

EXTRACT FROM KENT 42.7 (1908)

HAWKHURST

Site TQ7532.1; On the west side of the line, at the north end of Hawkhurst Station.

Hawkhurst (C&PWR)[TQ7532.1/1A]
A brick built 2TS dead ended shed with a slated gable style roof, it was located at TQ75583235 and was opened by the Cranbrook & Paddock Wood Railway on September 4th, 1893. The facilities included a coal stage and water tank. The line was absorbed by the SE&CR in 1900 and although the shed was closed by the SR in 1931 it was used for servicing until the branch closed on June 11th, 1961. The shed was still standing, in private use, until at least 1995.

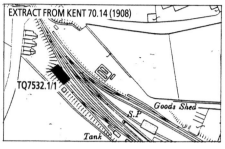

EXTRACT FROM KENT 70.14 (1908)

HYTHE

Site TR1534.1; On the south side of the line, at the west end of Hythe (RH&DR) Station.

Hythe (RH&DR)[TR1534.1/1A]
A concrete block built 1ft 3in gauge 2TS dead ended shed with a tiled gable style roof, it was located at TR15223465 and was opened by the Romney Hythe and Dymchurch Railway on July 27th, 1927. The facilities included a turntable and water tank. It was still in use in 1995.

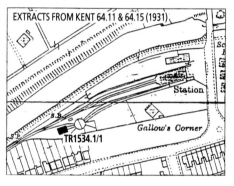

EXTRACTS FROM KENT 64.11 & 64.15 (1931)

NEW ROMNEY

Site TR0725.1; On the east side of the line, at the north end of New Romney Station.

New Romney (RH&DR)[TR0725.1/1A]
A brick and timber built 1ft 3in gauge 3TS dead ended shed with a tiled gable style roof, it was located at TR07522501 and was opened by the Romney Hythe & Dymchurch Railway on July 27th, 1927. The facilities included a turntable. It was still in use in 1995.

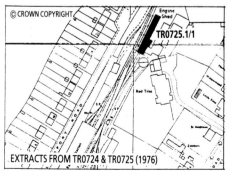

EXTRACTS FROM TR0724 & TR0725 (1976)

RAMSGATE

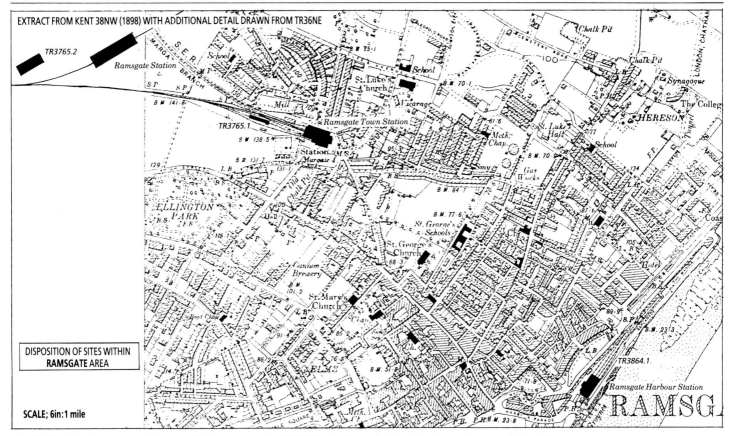

DISPOSITION OF SITES WITHIN **RAMSGATE** AREA

SCALE; 6in:1 mile

Site TR3864.1; In the vicinity of Ramsgate Harbour Station.

Site TR3765.1; On the south side of the line, at the west end of Ramsgate Town Station.

Replaced by ...
Site TR3765.2; On the north side of the line, at the west end of Ramsgate Station.

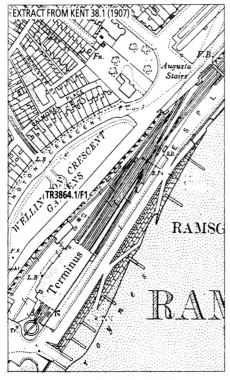

EXTRACT FROM KENT 38.1 (1907)

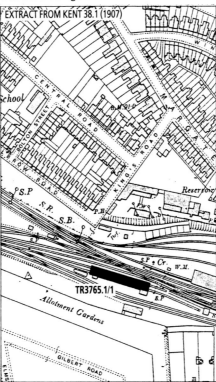

EXTRACT FROM KENT 38.1 (1907)

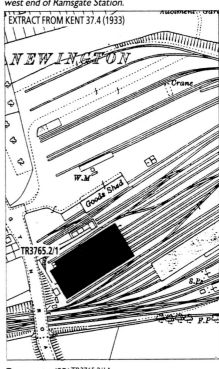

EXTRACT FROM KENT 37.4 (1933)

Ramsgate Harbour (F&HBR)^{TR3864.1/F1}
A servicing area consisting of water tank, sidings and, located at TR38656406, a turntable, it was opened by the Faversham & Herne Bay Railway on October 5th, 1863. The line was absorbed by the LC&DR in 1871 and the depot was closed by the SR on July 2nd, 1926.

Ramsgate Town (SER)^{TR3765.1/1A}
A brick built 2TS through road shed with a slated gable style roof, it was located at TR37696556 and was opened on April 13th, 1846. The facilities included a water column and coal stage. The depot was closed by the SR on July 2nd, 1926.

Ramsgate (SR)^{TR3765.2/1A}
A concrete built 6TS dead ended shed with an east-light pattern roof, it was located at TR37056569 and was opened in September 1930. The depot possessed all facilities, including a 65ft turntable. The depot was closed to steam by BR in June 1959 and the building was converted for emu use. The shed was still in service in 1995.

MARGATE

Site TR3470.1; On the north side of Margate West Station.
Margate West (LC&DR)^{TR3470.1/1A}
A brick built 3TS dead ended shed with a slated hipped roof, it was located at TR34697059 and was opened in 1865. The facilities included a coal stage and a 60ft turntable from which the shed roads radiated. The shed was closed by the SR in 1930 and demolished to make way for a parcels depot.

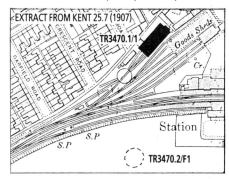

Replaced by ...
Site TR3470.2; On the south side of Margate West Station.
Margate (SR)^{TR3470.2/F1}
A servicing area consisting of a turntable, located at TR34687047, coal stage, water tank and sidings was established in 1933. The depot was closed to steam by BR in June 1961, thereafter being utilized for the stabling of emus.

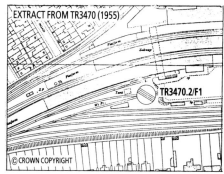

ORPINGTON

Site TQ4566.1; On the east side of the line, at the north end of Orpington Station.
Orpington (SE&CR)^{TQ4566.1/1A}
A brick built 2TS shed with a slated gable style roof, it was located at TQ45456606 and was opened in 1901. The facilities included a water tank, coal stage and 55ft turntable. The shed was closed by the SR in 1926, following the electrification of the line. The shed was not demolished but was converted for use by a service department and was still standing in 1995.

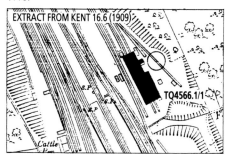

ROLVENDEN

Site TQ8632.1; On the west side of Rolvenden Station.
Rolvenden (RVR)^{TQ8632.1/1A}
A timber built 2TS dead ended shed with a dutch barn style roof, it was located at TQ86463278 and was opened by the Rother Valley Railway on March 29th, 1900. The facilities included a water tank. In 1904 the line was re-named as the Kent & East Sussex Railway.

The shed was rebuilt ...
Rolvenden (K&ESR)^{TQ8632.1/1B}
A brick and timber built 2TS dead ended shed with a slated gable style roof and corrugated iron gable. It is not known when construction took place, but it lasted until closure by BR on January 4th, 1954 and was subsequently demolished.

Rolvenden Railcar Shed (K&ESR)^{TQ8632.1/2A}
A 1TS dead ended shed, it was located at TQ86503273 and was opened in 1905. No further details are known.

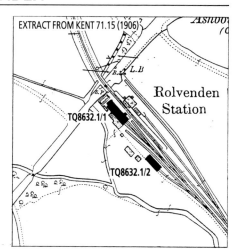

Rolvenden site became part of the *Kent & East Sussex Railway*, a preserved line running from Robertsbridge to Tenterden.

SLADE GREEN

Site TQ5276.1; At Crayford Creek Junction, on the east side of the Teddington line, south of Slade Green Station.
Slade Green* (SE&CR)^{TQ5276.1/1A}
A brick built 8TS through road shed with a north-light pattern roof and concrete screen, it was located at TQ52507623 and was opened in 1901. It possessed all major facilities including 50ft turntables sited at each end from which most of the shed roads radiated. The depot was closed to steam by the SR in 1926, the building being converted to an emu inspection shed and was still in use in 1995.

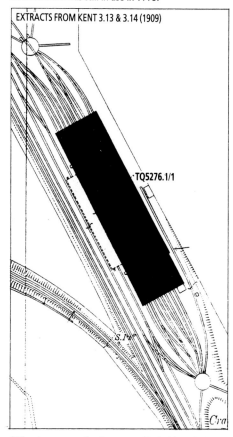

*The depot was also known as Erith, Whitehall and Slades Green.

SHEERNESS

Site TQ9174.1; On the east side of the line, at the south end of Sheerness Dockyard Station.
Sheerness Dockyard (S&SR)^{TQ9174.1/1A}
A brick built 1TS dead ended shed with a slated pitched roof, it was located at TQ91167465 and was opened by the Sittingbourne & Sheerness Railway on July 19th, 1860. The line was absorbed by the LC&DR in 1866.

The shed was enlarged in 1884/5 ...
Sheerness Dockyard (LC&DR)^{TQ9174.1/1B}
The original shed was extended and an additional one road section was added. The facilities included a turntable and coal stage. The shed was closed in 1915, possibly as the result of structural damage received when the battleship *HMS Bulwark* blew up at her moorings nearby on November 26th, 1914, an event which cost 729 lives and devastated large areas of Sheerness. Despite this the building was still standing in December 1922, when it was re-opened as a temporary measure due to the failure of the Kings Ferry Bridge, cutting off Sheerness from the rest of the railway system. It was finally closed by the SR in 1923.

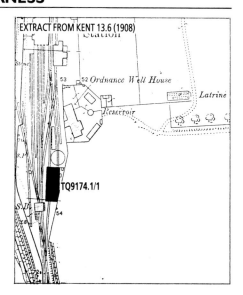

SHEPHERDS WELL

Site TR2548.1; On the west side of the line, at the north end of Shepherds Well (EKLR) Station.

Shepherds Well (EKLR)^{TR2548.1/1A}
A timber built 2TS dead ended shed with a gable style roof, it was located at TR25854844 and was opened by the East Kent Light Railway in 1912. The facilities included a water column. The shed was closed by BR on October 30th, 1948.

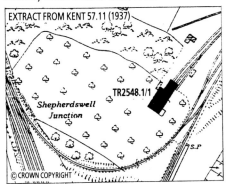

STROOD

Site TQ7469.1; On the west side of the line at the north end of Strood Junction Station.

Strood (G&RR)^{TQ7469.1/1A}
A brick built 1TS shed, it was located at TQ74076964 and was opened by the Gravesend & Rochester Railway, it is believed, on February 10th, 1845. No more details are known and it is assumed to have closed on June 18th, 1856.

Replaced on the same site by ...
Strood (SER)^{TQ7469.1/1B}
A brick built 2TS dead ended shed with a slated gable style roof it was opened in 1856. The facilities included a water tank, coal stage and 40ft turntable. The shed was closed by the SR in 1939 and the building was converted to a goods shed, lasting until 1970 when it was demolished.

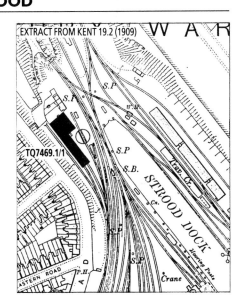

TONBRIDGE

Site TQ5945.1; In the fork of the Ashford and Tunbridge Wells lines, east of Tonbridge Station.

Tonbridge (SER)^{TQ5945.1/1A}
A brick built 3TS dead ended shed with a slated gable style roof, it was located at TQ59124595 and was opened on May 26th, 1842.

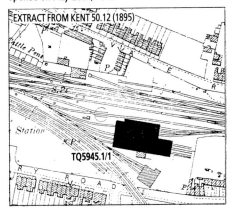

Prior to 1880 it was enlarged...
Tonbridge (SER)^{TQ5945.1/1B}
The building was lengthened, with one track extended through the back wall, and a new brick built 3TS through road section, with a slated gable style roof added to the southern side. The facilities included a coal stage, water columns and a 42ft turntable, repositioned and enlarged to 55ft by the SR.

The shed was re-roofed in 1952 ...
Tonbridge (BR)^{TQ5945.1/1C}
The shed was rebuilt by the Southern Region with a twin asbestos pitched roof and SR-style brick gable ends. It was closed to steam on June 17th, 1962 though steam locomotives continued to visit until January 1965. During this period, and after, diesels also stabled at the shed, and although the buildings were later demolished the site remained in use as a stabling point until the 1970s.

WESTERHAM

Site TQ4454.1; On the east side of the line, at the north end of Westerham Station.

Westerham (WVR)^{TQ4454.1/1A}
A timber built 1TS through road shed with a slated pitched roof, it was located at TQ44935452 and was opened by the Westerham Valley Railway on July 7th, 1881. The facilities included a water tank. The line was absorbed by the SER in 1881 and the shed was closed by the SR in 1926.

A servicing point was then established ...
Westerham (SR)^{TQ4454.1/F1}
Locomotives stabled on the shed site and utilized the water and coaling facilities until BR days and probably until closure of the line on October 30th, 1961.

TUNBRIDGE WELLS

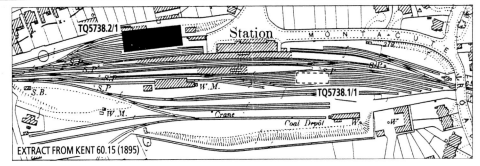

Site TQ5738.1; On the south side of Tunbridge Wells West Station.

Tunbridge Wells West (EGG&TWR)^{TQ5738.1/1A}
A 2TS shed with one through road, it was located at TQ57943844 and was opened by the East Grinstead, Groombridge & Tunbridge Wells Railway (LB&SCR) on October 1st, 1866. The facilities included a 52ft turntable. It was closed in 1890.

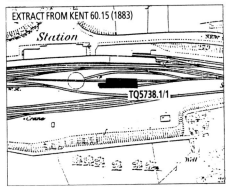

Replaced by ...
Site TQ5738.2; On the north side of Tunbridge Wells West Station.
Tunbridge Wells West (LB&SCR)^{TQ5738.2/1A}
A brick built 4TS dead ended shed with a slated twin gable roof, it was located at TQ57773847 and was opened in 1890. The facilities included a water tank and 46ft turntable.

The shed was re-roofed in 1955 ...
Tunbridge Wells West (BR)^{TQ5738.2/1B}
The shed was rebuilt by the Southern Region with a standard asbestos and steel louvre pitched style roof over each track. The depot was closed by BR on September 9th, 1963 but was retained to house a BR Emergency Control Train. After the building was abandoned it was acquired by the *Tunbridge Wells & Eridge Rail Preservation Society* and the shed was still standing in 1997.

SUSSEX

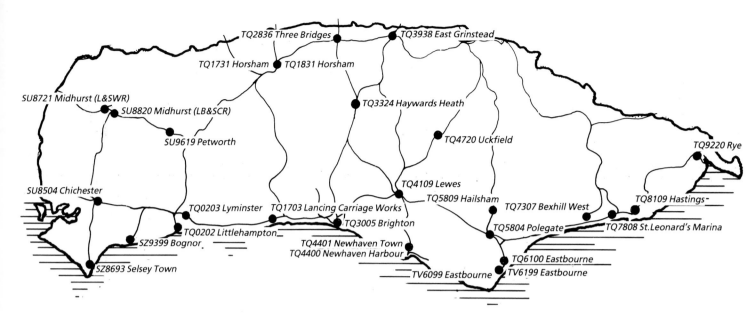

TQ2836 Three Bridges
TQ3938 East Grinstead
TQ1731 Horsham
TQ1831 Horsham
SU8721 Midhurst (L&SWR)
TQ3324 Haywards Heath
SU8820 Midhurst (LB&SCR)
SU9619 Petworth
TQ4720 Uckfield
TQ9220 Rye
SU8504 Chichester
TQ4109 Lewes
TQ0203 Lyminster
TQ1703 Lancing Carriage Works
TQ5809 Hailsham
TQ7307 Bexhill West
TQ8109 Hastings
TQ0202 Littlehampton
TQ3005 Brighton
TQ5804 Polegate
TQ7808 St.Leonard's Marina
SZ9399 Bognor
TQ4401 Newhaven Town
TQ4400 Newhaven Harbour
SZ8693 Selsey Town
TQ6100 Eastbourne
TV6099 Eastbourne
TV6199 Eastbourne

BEXHILL

Site TQ7307.1; On the west side of Bexhill West Station.

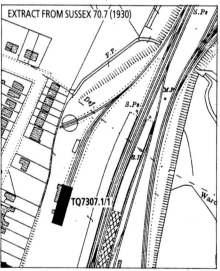

EXTRACT FROM SUSSEX 70.7 (1930)

TQ7307.1/1

Bexhill West (CS&BR)^{TQ7307.1/1A}
A brick built 2TS dead ended shed with a slated and glazed northlight pattern roof, it was located at TQ73530759 and was opened by the Crowhurst, Sidley & Bexhill Railway on June 1st, 1902. The facilities included a coal stage, water tank and 55ft turntable. The line was worked from the outset by the SE&CR and the shed was closed by the SR in 1936. It found further use as a store for redundant locomotives before being sold off for private use. It was still standing in 1995 being utilized as a council depot.

BOGNOR

Site SZ9399.1; On the east side of the line, at the north end of Bognor Station.

Bognor (LB&SCR)^{SZ9399.1/1A}
A timber built 2TS dead ended shed, it was located at SZ93539972 and was opened on June 1st, 1864. The facilities included a turntable, from which the shed roads radiated. The depot was closed in 1903.

Replaced by ...

Bognor (LB&SCR)^{SZ9399.1/2A}
A brick built 2TS through road shed with a slated transverse pitched roof, it was located on an adjacent site at SZ93959965 and was opened in 1903. The facilities included a water tank, coal stage and 55ft turntable sited outside of the northern end to the building. The shed was closed by BR in 1953 and, although the shed was demolished in 1956, the site remained in use for servicing visiting engines until 1965.

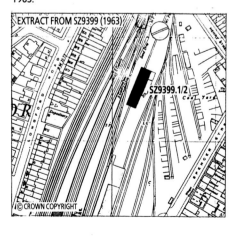

EXTRACT FROM SZ9399 (1963)

SZ9399.1/2

© CROWN COPYRIGHT

EXTRACT FROM SUSSEX 74.6 (1896)

SZ9399.1/1

SZ9399.1/2

UCKFIELD

Site TQ4720.1; In the vicinity of Uckfield Station.
Uckfield (LB&SCR)^{TQ4720.1/1A}
A 1TS shed for two engines, approximately located at TQ472209, was opened here on October 18th, 1858 and closed on August 3rd, 1868. No further details are known.

BRIGHTON

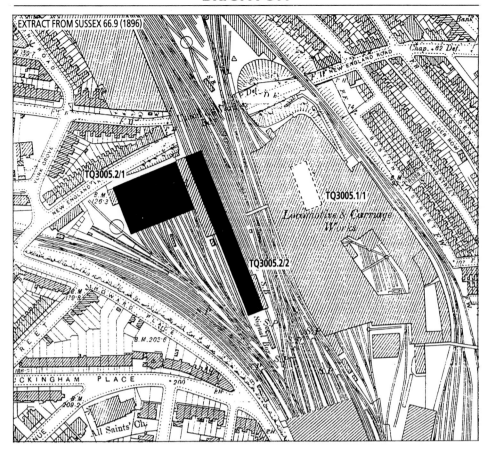

EXTRACT FROM SUSSEX 66.9 (1896)

HAILSHAM

Site TQ5809.1. On the east side of Hailsham Station
Hailsham (LB&SCR)$^{TQ5809.1/1A}$
A brick built 1TS dead ended shed with a slated hipped roof, it was located at TQ58960919 and was opened in 1858. Details of its facilities are not known. The depot was closed in 1880 and subsequently demolished, although one retaining wall remained *in situ* until closure of the station itself on September 9th, 1968.

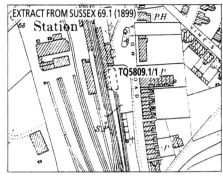

EXTRACT FROM SUSSEX 69.1 (1899)

HAYWARDS HEATH

Site TQ3324.1; On the east side of Haywards Heath Station.
Haywards Heath (LB&SCR)$^{TQ3324.1/1A}$
A brick built 2TS dead ended shed with a slated gable style roof, it was located at TQ33032450 and was opened on October 1st, 1847. The facilities included a water tank, coal stage and turntable. It closed in c1872 and was converted for use as a goods shed.

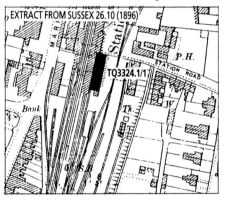

EXTRACT FROM SUSSEX 26.10 (1896)

Site TQ3005.0; In the vicinity of Brighton Station.
Brighton (L&B)$^{TQ3005.0/1A}$
A small shed was opened here by the London & Brighton Railway on May 12th, 1840. It was probably a 1TS building, sited by the Shoreham line, north west of the station. No confirmed details are available except that it was closed in 1861.

Site TQ3005.1; On the east side of the London line, north of Brighton Station.
Brighton (L&B)$^{TQ3005.1/1A}$
A brick built 4TS through road shed with a slated gable style roof, it was located at TQ30960532 and was opened by the London & Brighton Railway on September 21st, 1841. The facilities included two turntables and a large coal stage and water tank. The depot was closed by the LB&SCR in 1861 and absorbed into the Brighton Works complex.

Site TQ3005.2; In the fork of the London and Shoreham lines, at the north end of Brighton Station.
Brighton (LB&SCR)$^{TQ3005.2/1A}$
A brick built 16TS dead ended shed with a slated multi-pitched roof, it was located at TQ30810529 and was opened in 1861. The facilities included a large water tank, coal stage and a 40ft turntable, which was enlarged to 60ft in 1909.

The shed was rebuilt in 1938 ...
Brighton (SR)$^{TQ3005.2/1B}$
The shed was reduced to 10 roads and the roof was replaced by an asbestos clad northlight pattern roof. The depot was closed by BR on June 15th, 1961 and demolished in 1966.

Brighton (LB&SCR)$^{TQ3005.2/2A}$
A brick built 3TS dead ended shed with a slated transverse pitched roof, it was located on the east side of the site at TQ30880529. It was originally constructed as a four-road carriage shed, with a slated twin pitched roof and was rebuilt in 1912 following the removal of the Carriage & Wagon Department to Lancing Works. The building was then utilized as the Brighton Works stock shed and later it was absorbed into the adjacent running shed. It was closed by the SR in c1933 and converted to a workshop for use by the Road Motor Engineers Department. It was demolished in 1966.

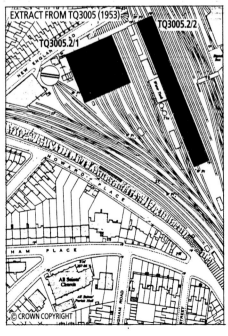

EXTRACT FROM TQ3005 (1953)

© CROWN COPYRIGHT

CHICHESTER

Site SU8504.1; On the south side of Chichester Station.
Chichester (LB&SCR)$^{SU8504.1/1A}$
A 2TS dead ended shed, it was located at SU85800429 and was opened on June 8th, 1846. The facilities included a coal stage and turntable. The shed was closed in c1870.

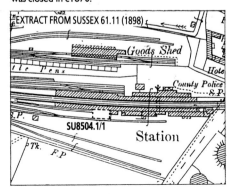

EXTRACT FROM SUSSEX 61.11 (1898)

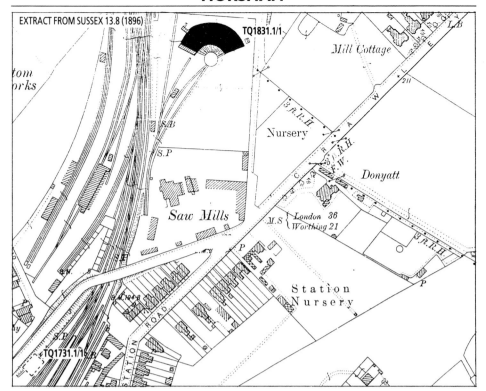

EXTRACT FROM SUSSEX 13.8 (1896)

TQ1831.1/1

Mill Cottage

Nursery

Donyatt

Saw Mills

London 36
Worthing 21

Station
Nursery

TQ1731.1/1

Site TQ1731.1; On the west side of the line, at the north end of Horsham Station.
Horsham (LB&SCR)^{TQ1731.1/1A}
A timber built 3TS dead ended shed, it was located at TQ17903104 and was opened on February 14th, 1848. The facilities included a turntable from which the shed roads radiated. The depot was closed in 1896.

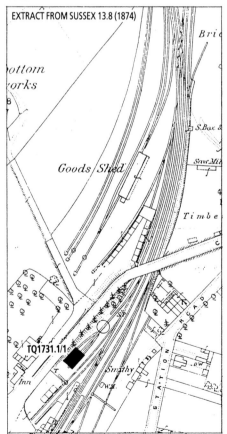

EXTRACT FROM SUSSEX 13.8 (1874)

Bri

ottom
orks

Goods Shed

Saw Mi

Timbe

S.Box &

TQ1731.1/1

Inn

Smithy

Replaced by ...
Site TQ1831.1; On the east side of the line, north of Horsham Station.
Horsham (LB&SCR)^{TQ1831.1/1A}
A brick built 10-stall semi-roundhouse with a continuous slated pitched roof, it was located at TQ18063133 and was opened in 1896. The facilities included a water tank, coal stage and 46ft turntable.

The shed was enlarged in 1901 ...
Horsham (LB&SCR)^{TQ1831.1/1B}
A further 8 stalls were added on the east side of the shed. The depot was closed to steam by BR on July 18th, 1959 and totally in June 1964. The shed was subsequently demolished.

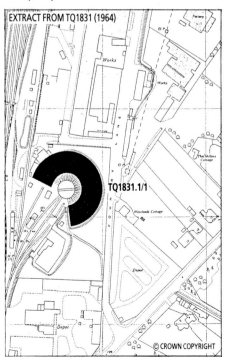

EXTRACT FROM TQ1831 (1964)

TQ1831.1/1

© CROWN COPYRIGHT

Site TQ4109.1; On the east side of Lewes Station.

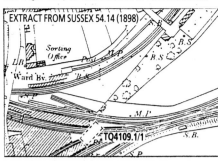

EXTRACT FROM SUSSEX 54.14 (1898)

Sorting
Office

Post

Ward By.

TQ4109.1/1

S.B.

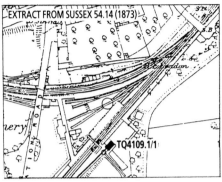

EXTRACT FROM SUSSEX 54.14 (1873)

TQ4109.1/1

Lewes (LB&SCR)^{TQ4109.1/1A}
A brick built 2TS dead ended shed with a slated gable style roof, it was located at TQ41680983 and was opened in 1853. Details of the facilities are not known, but a 35ft turntable and water tank were sited in the fork of Wivesfield and Brighton lines nearby. The depot was closed in 1870 and the building was converted for use as a goods shed. It was demolished in 1889 as part of extensive rebuilding of the station.

LITTLEHAMPTON

Site TQ0202.1; On the north side of Littlehampton Station.
Littlehampton (LB&SCR)^{TQ0202.1/1A}
A brick built 2TS dead ended shed with a slated hipped roof, it was located at TQ02540220 and was opened on August 17th, 1863. The facilities included a water tank and a 42ft turntable. The depot was closed in 1937 and converted for use as a store. It was still standing in 1995, being utilized as a BR train crew depot.

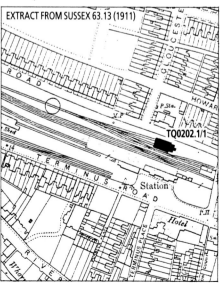

EXTRACT FROM SUSSEX 63.13 (1911)

GLOUCESTE

ROAD

HOWAR

P.Sta.

Shed

TQ0202.1/1

TERMINUS

ROAD

Station

Hotel

RIVE

EAST GRINSTEAD

Site TQ3938.1; On the south side of East Grinstead (EGR) Station, east of the High Level Station.

East Grinstead (EGR)[TQ3938.1/1A]
A 1TS dead ended shed, it was located at TQ39133827 and was opened by the East Grinstead Railway on July 9th, 1855. Details of its construction are not known but its facilities included a water tank. The line was absorbed by the LB&SCR in 1858 and the depot was closed in c1896.

A servicing point was then established ...

East Grinstead (LB&SCR)[TQ3938.1/F1]
Although the shed building was demolished in c1906 locomotives continued to utilize the water tank and engine pit. It is not known when it went out of use.

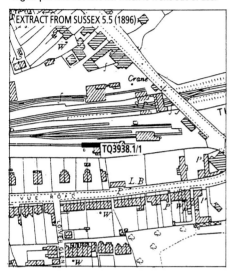

EXTRACT FROM SUSSEX 5.5 (1896)

TQ3938.1/1

POLEGATE

Site TQ5804.1; In the fork of the Hailsham and Eastbourne lines, at the east end of Polegate Junction Station.

Polegate (LB&SCR)[TQ5804.1/1A]
A brick built 1TS dead ended shed with a water tank incorporated in the roof, it was located at TQ58420483 and probably opened in c1860. The facilities included a 36ft turntable sited outside of the shed entrance.

The shed was rebuilt in 1881 ...

Polegate (LB&SCR)[TQ5804.1/1B]
The shed was reduced in length to accommodate the re-aligning of the Hailsham branch into the new Polegate Junction Station which was re-sited to the east. It is not known when the depot closed but the building was retained, no doubt for its water tank, until BR days. It has since been demolished.

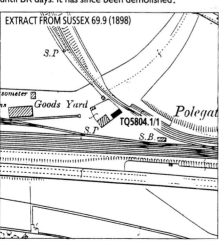

EXTRACT FROM SUSSEX 69.9 (1898)

TQ5804.1/1

EASTBOURNE

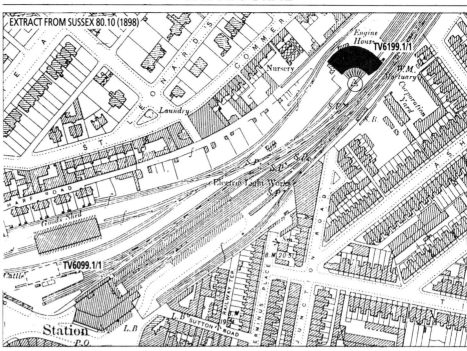

EXTRACT FROM SUSSEX 80.10 (1898)

TV6199.1/1

TV6099.1/1

EXTRACTS FROM SUSSEX 80.6 & 80.10 (1898)

TQ6100.1

DISPOSITION OF SITES WITHIN EASTBOURNE AREA

SCALE; 7in:1 mile

TV6199.1

TV6099.1

Eastbourne Station

Site TV6099.1; In the goods yard on the north side of Eastbourne Station.

Eastbourne (LB&SCR)[TV6099.1/1A]
A 2TS dead ended shed, it was located at TV60899915 and was opened on May 14th, 1849. Details of its construction are not known, but its facilities included a coke/coal stage. It was closed in 1876.

Replaced by ...
Site TV6199.1; On the north side of the line, at the east end of Eastbourne Station.

Eastbourne (LB&SCR)[TV6199.1/1A]
A brick built 8-track semi-roundhouse with a slated continuous transverse pitched roof, it was located at TV61199935. The facilities included a turntable and, later, a coaling crane. The depot was closed in 1912 and demolished, with the turntable being retained for use until 1935.

Replaced by ...
Site TQ6100.1; On the west side of the line, north of Eastbourne Station.

Eastbourne (LB&SCR)[TQ6100.1/1A]
A brick built 7TS through road shed with a slated transverse pitched roof, it was located at TQ61200035 and was opened in 1911. The facilities included a water tank, coal stage and, sited at the north end of the yard, a 60ft turntable. The depot was closed by BR in 1952 but it continued to service visiting locomotives and was also utilized as a store for condemned engines awaiting scrapping at Ashford Works. It was abandoned in 1968 and demolished a year later.

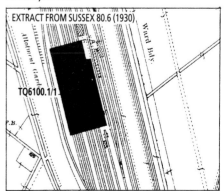

EXTRACT FROM SUSSEX 80.6 (1930)

TQ6100.1/1

MIDHURST

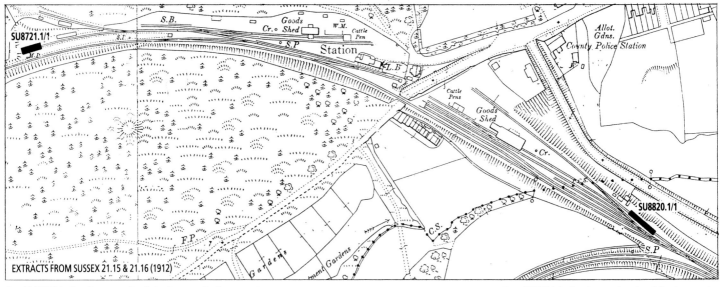

EXTRACTS FROM SUSSEX 21.15 & 21.16 (1912)

Site SU8820.1; On the east side of the line, north of Midhurst (LB&SCR) Station.

Midhurst (M&MJR)[SU8820.1/1A]

A timber built 1TS through road shed with a pitched roof, it was located at SU88152096 and was opened by the Mid-Sussex and Midhurst Junction Railway on October 15th, 1866. The facilities included a water tank and coal stage, sited outside of the shed entrance, and a turntable. The line was absorbed by the LB&SCR in June 1874. By 1907 the shed had become very dilapidated and it was demolished.

Replaced on the same site by ...

Midhurst (LB&SCR)[SU8820.1/1B]

A timber built 1TS through road shed with a slated pitched roof, it was opened in 1907. The facilities were retained from the original shed but by this time the turntable had been removed. The depot was closed by the SR in 1923.

Site SU8721.1; On the north side of the line, at the west end of Midhurst (L&SWR) Station.

Midhurst (L&SWR)[SU8721.1/1A]

A brick built 1TS dead ended shed with a slated pitched roof incorporating a water tank over the entrance, it was located at SU87542112 and was opened on September 1st, 1864. The facilities included a coal stage and, sited outside of the shed entrance, a 45ft turntable which was removed prior to 1912. The depot was closed by the SR in 1937.

LANCING

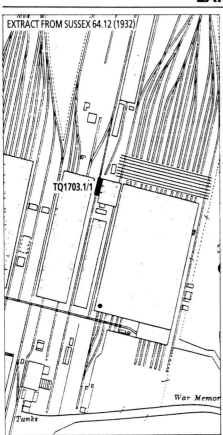

EXTRACT FROM SUSSEX 64.12 (1932)

(The unique petrol locomotive No. 499 was housed in the south western corner of the Carriage Shop at TQ17690373.)

Site TQ1703.1; In Lancing Carriage Works, on the south side of the Lancing to Worthing line.

Lancing Carriage Works (SR)[TQ1703.1/1A]

A corrugated iron 1TS through road shed with a corrugated iron pitched roof, it was located at TQ17680385 and was opened in June 1929.

At some stage it was rebuilt ...

Lancing Carriage Works (BR)[TQ1703.1/1B]

A corrugated asbestos and steel framed 1TS through road shed with a corrugated asbestos roof, it was probably constructed in early BR days. The shed was closed at the same time as the Works, on June 28th, 1965.

RYE

Site TQ9220.1; At the west end of Rye (R&CT) Station.

Rye (R&CT)[TQ9220.1/1A]

A 1TS 3ft 0in gauge dead ended shed, probably built in timber, with a pitched roof, it was located at TQ92532063 and was opened by the Rye & Camber Tramway on July 13th, 1895. It was effectively closed in 1925 when its only steam locomotive was replaced by a small petrol engined unit. The line was commandeered by the War Department in 1939 and never re-opened, being totally closed in 1946.

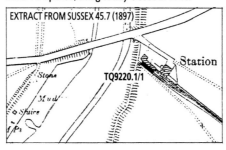

EXTRACT FROM SUSSEX 45.7 (1897)

LYMINSTER

Site TQ0203.1; On the south side of Lyminster Station.

Lyminster (B&CR)[TQ0203.1/1A]

A brick built 2TS dead ended shed with a slated hipped roof, it was located at TQ02840385 and was opened by the Brighton & Chichester Railway on March 16th, 1846. Details of its facilities are not known. The depot was closed upon the opening of Littlehampton shed (TQ0202.1/1A) on August 17th, 1863, and it was converted for private use. It survived into BR days but has since been demolished.

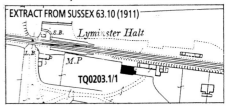

EXTRACT FROM SUSSEX 63.10 (1911)

PETWORTH

Site SU9719.1; In the vicinity of Petworth Station.

Petworth (MSR)[SU9719.1/1A]

A timber built 1TS shed, it was approximately located at TQ970191 and was opened by the Mid-Sussex Railway on October 10th, 1859. The line was absorbed by the LB&SCR in 1864 and no further details are known, except that it was closed on October 15th, 1866 and removed to Hayling Island and re-erected as SZ7099.1/1A.

HASTINGS

Site TQ8109.1; On the north side of Hastings Station.

Hastings (SER)[TQ8109.1/1A]
A brick built 3TS shed with one through road and a slated gable style roof, it was located at TQ81420969 and was opened on February 13th, 1851. The facilities included a 45ft turntable, sited on the middle shed road, water tank and coal stage. The depot was closed by the SR in 1929 to facilitate station enlargements.

Replaced by ...
Site TQ8109.2; On the north side of the line, at the west end of Hastings Station.

Hastings (SR)[TQ8109.2/F1]
A servicing area consisting of a 55ft turntable, located at TQ81150962, coal stage and water column was opened in 1929. It was closed by BR in 1957.

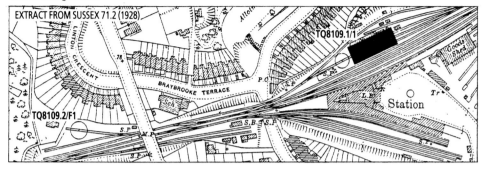

EXTRACT FROM SUSSEX 71.2 (1928)

ST.LEONARD'S

Site TQ7808.0; In the vicinity of West St.Leonard's Station.

St.Leonard's Marina (LB&SCR)[TQ7808.0/F1]
Some form of facility was probably established here in November 1846 when LB&SCR locomotives were first allocated here.

Replaced by ...
Site TQ7808.1; On the north side of West St.Leonard's Station.

St.Leonard's Marina (LB&SCR)[TQ7808.1/1A]
A brick built 2TS dead ended shed with a slated gable style roof, it was located at TQ78750893 and was opened in c1872 . The facilities included a water tank and a turntable which was later re-sited and enlarged to 50ft. By 1898 the shed had become inadequate.

Replaced on the same site by ...
St.Leonard's West Marina (LB&SCR)[TQ7808.1/1B]
A brick built 4TS shed with 3 through roads and a slated and glazed northlight pattern roof, it was opened in 1898. Additional facilities included a coal stage.

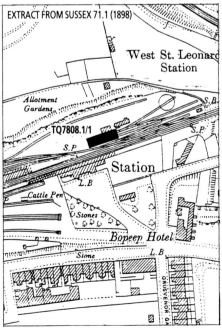

EXTRACT FROM SUSSEX 71.1 (1898)

The shed was re-roofed in 1949 ...
St.Leonard's West Marina (BR)[TQ7808.1/1C]
The shed was re-built by the Southern Region with a steel and asbestos pitched roof over each track and an SR-style brick gable end and screen. It was closed in June 1958 but visiting locomotives continued to be serviced in the yard and the building was utilized to stable diesel locomotives until the mid-1960s. The shed was subsequently demolished.

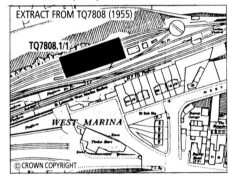

EXTRACT FROM TQ7808 (1955)

© CROWN COPYRIGHT

SELSEY

Site SZ8693.1; On the north side of Selsey Town Station.
Selsey Town (HM&ST)[SZ8693.1/1A]
A timber built 2TS dead ended shed with a gable style roof, it was located at SZ86069367 and was opened by the Hundred of Manhood & Selsey Tramway on August 27th, 1897. The depot was closed. along with the line, on January 19th, 1935.

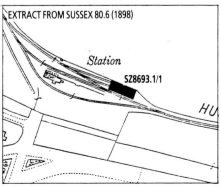

EXTRACT FROM SUSSEX 80.6 (1898)

NEWHAVEN

Site TQ4400.1; On the east side of Newhaven Harbour Station.

Newhaven Harbour (LB&SCR)[TQ4400.1/1A]
A brick built 2TS dead ended shed, it was located at TQ44950097 and was opened on December 8th, 1847. The facilities included a 35ft turntable. The depot was closed in 1887 and demolished.

Replaced by ...
Site TQ4401.1; On the west side of Newhaven Town Station.

Newhaven Town (LB&SCR)[TQ4401.1/1A]
A corrugated iron 4TS dead ended shed with twin corrugated iron pitched roofs, it was located at TQ44820143 and was opened in 1887. The facilities included a coal stage, water column and a turntable, enlarged to 60ft in 1917.

The shed was re-roofed ...
Newhaven Town (SR)[TQ4401.1/1B]
A corrugated asbestos roof, with corrugated asbestos gables was installed either by the SR or BR prior to 1950. The depot was closed on September 9th, 1963 and converted for private use. It was still standing in 1995.

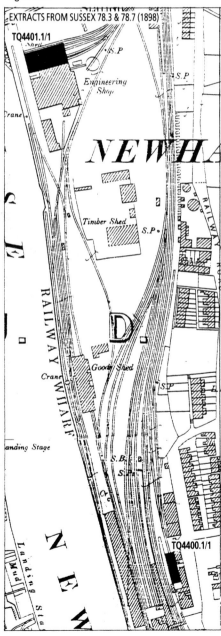

EXTRACTS FROM SUSSEX 78.3 & 78.7 (1898)

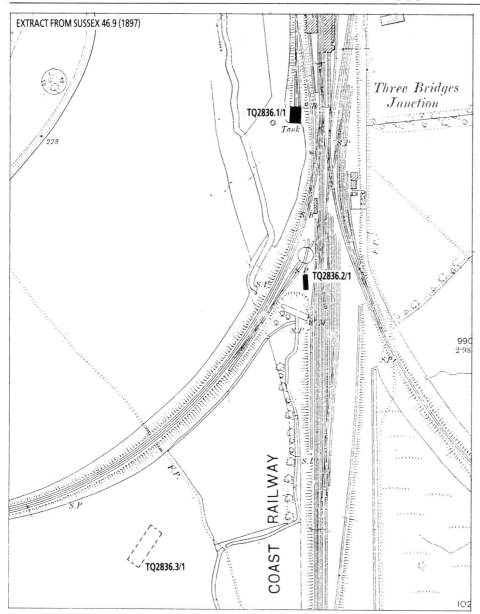

EXTRACT FROM SUSSEX 46.9 (1897)

Three Bridges Junction

TQ2836.1/1
Tank

TQ2836.2/1

COAST RAILWAY

TQ2836.3/1

Site TQ2836.1; On the west side of the line, at the south end of Three Bridges Junction Station.

Three Bridges (LB&SCR)[TQ2836.1/1A]
A brick built 2TS dead ended shed with a slated gable style roof, it was located at TQ28793682 and was opened in July 1848. The facilities included a coal stage, water tank and 45ft turntable but, because of the cramped nature of the site, these were located south of the shed, in the fork of the Horsham and Brighton lines. The depot was closed in 1909 to accommodate station enlargements.

Replaced by ...
Site TQ2836.2; In the fork of the Horsham and Brighton lines, south of Three Bridges Junction Station.

Three Bridges (LB&SCR)[TQ2836.2/1A]
A temporary shed was established in 1909 at the site of the facilities for TQ2836.1/1A, utilizing the brick built 1TS tank shed, turntable and coal stage until the new depot (TQ2836.3/1A) was completed in 1911.

Replaced by ...
Site TQ2836.3; On the east side of the Horsham line, south of Three Bridges Junction Station.

Three Bridges (LB&SCR)[TQ2836.3/1A]
A brick built 3TS through road shed with a slated northlight pattern roof, it was located at TQ28653642 and was opened in 1911. The facilities included a water tank, coal stage and 60ft turntable. The depot was closed by BR in June 1964 but was not demolished immediately, being utilized as a diesel stabling point and wagon repair shop until c1974. The site has since been cleared.

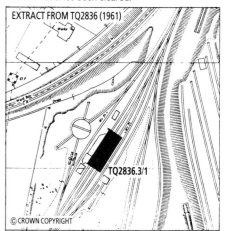

EXTRACT FROM TQ2836 (1961)

TQ2836.3/1

© CROWN COPYRIGHT

The 1911 LB&SCR shed (TQ2836.3/1A) at **Three Bridges** is here seen on June 4th, 1959 with Standard Class 4 2-6-4T No.80011 simmering besides the 1930s concrete yard buildings. This replaced a temporary (1909-1911) depot (TQ2836.2/1A) sited near the station which had bridged the gap following closure of the 1855 shed (TQ2836.1/1A) at the station. Closed to locomotive use in June 1964, the 1911 building saw further use as a wagon shop prior to final demolition in 1974.   *K Fairey*

SURREY

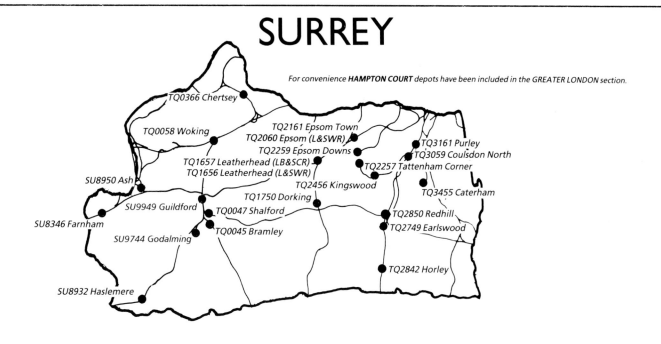

For convenience **HAMPTON COURT** depots have been included in the GREATER LONDON section.

TQ0366 Chertsey
TQ0058 Woking
TQ2161 Epsom Town
TQ2060 Epsom (L&SWR)
TQ2259 Epsom Downs
TQ3161 Purley
TQ3059 Coulsdon North
TQ1657 Leatherhead (LB&SCR)
TQ1656 Leatherhead (L&SWR)
TQ2257 Tattenham Corner
SU8950 Ash
TQ2456 Kingswood
TQ3455 Caterham
SU9949 Guildford
TQ1750 Dorking
SU8346 Farnham
TQ0047 Shalford
TQ2850 Redhill
TQ0045 Bramley
TQ2749 Earlswood
SU9744 Godalming
TQ2842 Horley
SU8932 Haslemere

ASH

Site SU8950.1; On the south side of Ash Station.
Ash (L&SWR/SER)[SU8950.1/1A]
A brick built 2TS through road shed with a slated gable style roof, it was located at SU89955082 and was opened in 1856. The building was utilized both as an engine shed and as a goods shed, one track being allocated to each.

The shed was rebuilt in 1905 ...
Ash (L&SWR/SER)[SU8950.1/1B]
The goods side was removed and the building was remodelled as a 1TS through road shed with a slated gable style roof. The facilities included a water column. The depot was closed by the SR in 1946, but locomotives continued to utilize the yard into BR days. The building was converted to private use and was still standing in 1995.

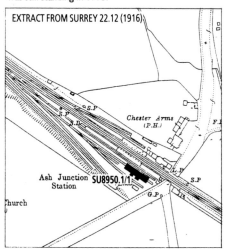

CATERHAM

Site TQ3455.1; At the north end of Caterham Station.
Caterham (Caterham)[TQ3455.1/1A]
A brick built 1TS dead ended shed with a slated gable style roof, it was located at TQ34095550 and was opened by the Caterham Railway in 1856. The depot was closed in 1877 and the building was converted into a goods shed.

After closure locomotives were still being allocated to Caterham, suggesting the construction of a replacement shed. However the OS maps of 1870 and 1895 show only the original building TQ3455.1/1A and it is probable that the locomotives were stabled in the open on the east side of the station at TQ34135547. This facility (TQ3455.2/F1) was closed in 1898 with the opening of Purley shed (TQ3161.1/1A).

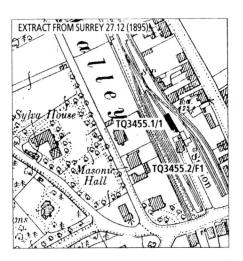

BRAMLEY

Site TQ0045.1 On the east side of the line, at the north end of Bramley Station;.
Bramley (LB&SCR)[TQ0045.1/1A]
A 1TS through road shed, it was located at TQ00894527 and was opened on October 2nd, 1865. It was destroyed during a storm in 1882. No further details are known.

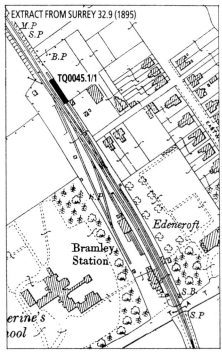

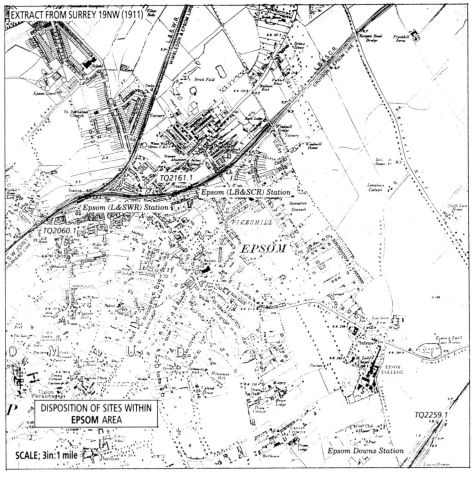

EXTRACT FROM SURREY 19NW (1911)

DISPOSITION OF SITES WITHIN
EPSOM AREA

SCALE; 3in:1 mile

CHERTSEY

Site TQ0366.1; On the south side of the line, east of Chertsey Station.
Chertsey (L&SWR)^{TQ0366.1/1A}
A brick built 2TS dead ended shed with a slated gable style roof, it was located at TQ03986623 and was opened in 1848.

At some stage the shed was rebuilt ...
Chertsey (L&SWR)^{TQ0366.1/1B}
The shed was made open-ended, the entrance arches were reconstructed and new wooden gables provided, along with a pitched slated roof. When this was done is not clear but the facilities by now included a water tank and coal stage. At a later date, one of the tracks was extended through the shed. The depot was closed by the SR in January 1937.

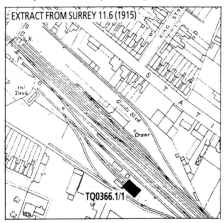

EXTRACT FROM SURREY 11.6 (1915)

TQ0366.1/1

Site TQ2161.0; In the vicinity of Epsom Town Station.
Epsom Town (LB&SCR)^{TQ2161.0/F1}
Some form of facility was provided here from May 10th, 1847 until September 1851. No further details are known.

Replaced by ...
Site TQ2161.1; On the north side of Epsom Town Station.
Epsom Town (LB&SCR)^{TQ2161.1/1A}
A brick built 2TS dead ended shed with a slated gable style roof, it was located at TQ21326101 and was opened in September 1851. The facilities included a 40ft turntable and water tank.

The shed entrance was rebuilt in 1913 ...
Epsom Town (LB&SCR)^{TQ2161.1/1B}
The two single doors were replaced by a larger single entrance. The depot was closed by the SR on March 3rd, 1929 and converted for use as a goods shed. It was demolished in the mid-1930s.

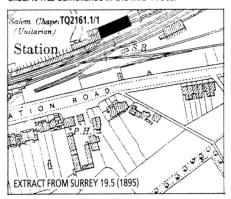

Salem Chapel TQ2161.1/1
(Unitarian)
Station

EXTRACT FROM SURREY 19.5 (1895)

Site TQ2259.1; On the east side of the line, at the north end of Epsom Downs Station.
Epsom Downs (B&EDR)^{TQ2259.1/1A}
A 2TS dead ended shed, it was located at TQ22885978 and was opened by the Banstead & Epsom Downs Railway on May 22nd, 1865. Details of the construction are not known but the facilities included a 40ft turntable. It is believed that the depot was never used as the line was absorbed by the LB&SCR from the outset and they provided a locomotive from West Croydon shed (TQ3266.1/1A).

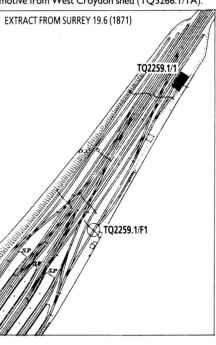

EXTRACT FROM SURREY 19.6 (1871)

TQ2259.1/1

TQ2259.1/F1

A servicing point was established ...
Epsom Downs (LB&SCR)^{TQ2259.1/F1}
The turntable, located at TQ22745964, and sidings were utilized as a servicing point. It is logical to assume that this facility was used from May 22nd, 1865 in preference to the shed, probably not being dispensed with until SR days.

Site TQ2060.1; On the north side of the line, west of Epsom (L&SWR) Station.
Epsom (L&SWR)^{TQ2060.1/F1}
A servicing area consisting of a turntable, located at TQ20426076 and sidings was established here. No further details are known.

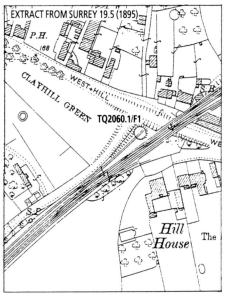

EXTRACT FROM SURREY 19.5 (1895)

P.H.

CLAYHILL GREEN

WEST HILL

TQ2060.1/F1

Hill House

COULSDON

Site TQ3059.1; At the south end of Coulsdon North Station.
Coulsdon North* (LB&SCR)^{TQ3059.1/1A}
A brick built 2TS dead ended shed with a slated transverse pitched roof, it was located at TQ30035950 and was opened in 1900. The facilities included a coal stage, water tank and a turntable, sited in the adjacent goods yard. A water softener was provided in 1911. The depot was closed by the SR in June 1929 and whilst most of the shed building was demolished the offices and rear wall were retained, these finally being dispensed with in 1986.

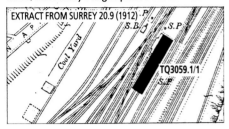

* The depot was originally known as Stoats Nest.

DORKING

Site TQ1750.1; On the west side of Dorking Station.
Dorking (LB&SCR)^{TQ1750.1/1A}
A timber built 2TS dead ended shed with a gable style roof, it was located at TQ17055041 and was opened on March 4th, 1867. The facilities included a turntable and water column. The building was destroyed during a storm in 1922.

A servicing point was then established ...
Dorking (LB&SCR)^{TQ1750.1/F1}
The original facilities, including the engine pits on the shed site, were utilized with locomotives stabling on adjacent sidings until the facility was closed when the line was electrified on March 3rd, 1929.

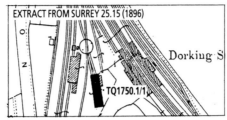

FARNHAM

Site SU8346.1; On the north side of the line, west of Farnham Station.
Farnham (L&SWR)^{SU8346.1/1A}
A 1TS dead ended shed, it was located at SU83904615 and was opened on October 8th, 1849. Details of its construction and facilities are not known, but it is assumed to have been a Civil Engineer's Departmental shed to serve a nearby ballast siding. It was probably closed in c1890.

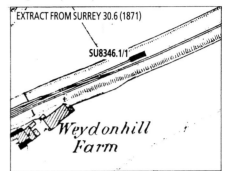

GUILDFORD

Site SU9949.1; On the west side of Guildford Station
Guildford (L&SWR)^{SU9949.1/1A}
A brick built 2TS through road shed with a pitched slated roof, it was located at SU99584967 and was opened on May 5th, 1845. The facilities included a turntable. The depot was closed in 1887 and demolished to accommodate station enlargements.

Replaced by ...
Site SU9949.2; On the west side of the line, south of Guildford Station.
Guildford (L&SWR)^{SU9949.2/1A}
A brick built 13-track semi-roundhouse with a slated continuous pitched roof, it was located at SU99674940 and was opened in 1887. The facilities included a 50ft turntable, water tank and, on the site of its predecessor (SU9949.1/1A), a coal stage.

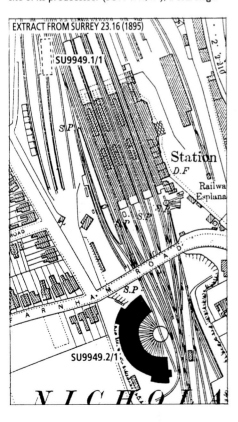

The shed was enlarged in 1897 ...
Guildford (L&SWR)^{SU9949.2/1B}
A brick built 7TS shed with one through road and a slated multi-transverse pitched roof was added to the south side of the building.

The shed was re-roofed in 1953 ...
Guildford (BR)^{SU9949.2/1C}
The shed was rebuilt by the Southern Region with a steel and corrugated asbestos pitched roof over each track. The depot closed on July 7th, 1967 and was subsequently demolished.

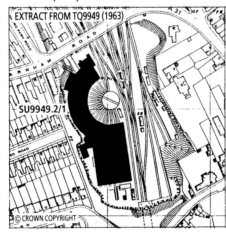

SHALFORD

Site TQ0047.1; In the vicinity of Shalford Station.
Shalford (SER)^{TQ0047.1/F1}
Some sort of facility was provided here in pre-1900 days. No further details are known. The approximate location was TQ002471.

EARLSWOOD

Site TQ2749.1; In the goods yard on the west side of the line, north of Earlswood Station.
Earlswood (LB&SCR)^{TQ2749.1/F1}
Some sort of basic facility was in existence here. No precise details are known, but it is assumed that a siding was given over to stable the pilot locomotive. The opening and closure dates are not known and the approximate location was TQ278497.

GODALMING

Site SU9744.1; On the west side of the line, at the north end of Godalming (Old) Station.
Godalming (L&SWR)^{SU9744.1/1A}
A 1TS through road shed, located at SU97374465 and opened on October 15th, 1849. Details of its construction and facilities are not known. The depot closed on January 24th, 1859.

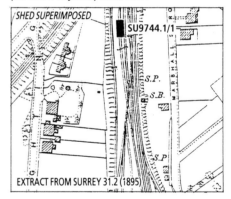

HASLEMERE

Site SU8932.1; On the south side of the line, at the west end of Haslemere Station.
Haslemere (L&SWR)^{SU8932.1/1A}
A 1TS dead ended shed, probably built in brick, it was located at SU89743292 and was opened on January 24th, 1859. The facilities included a coal stage. The depot only saw sporadic use, being utilized to house a banking locomotive during busy periods. The closure date is not known.

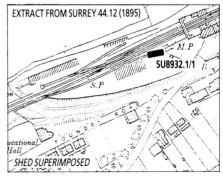

REDHILL

Site TQ2850.1; In the fork of the Brighton and Tonbridge lines, south of Redhill Station.

Redhill (SER)^{TQ2850.1/1A}

A brick built 3TS through road shed with a slated gable style roof, it was located at TQ28055014 and was opened in May 1853. The facilities originally included a turntable and coal stage, both sited some distance away near the station. Some time later a 45ft turntable was installed in the shed yard, this being replaced by the SR in 1928 with a 65ft turntable on a new site. At the same time a ramped coaling stage was also constructed.

The shed was re-roofed in 1950 ...

Redhill (BR)^{TQ2850.1/1B}

The shed was rebuilt by the Southern Region with a corrugated asbestos pitched roof over each track, a corrugated asbestos gable at the south end and an SR-type brick gable end and screen at the north. The depot was closed on January 4th, 1965 but remained open for visiting locomotives until June of that year. A diesel stabling point was established at the site with the shed buildings, apart from the offices, eventually being demolished.

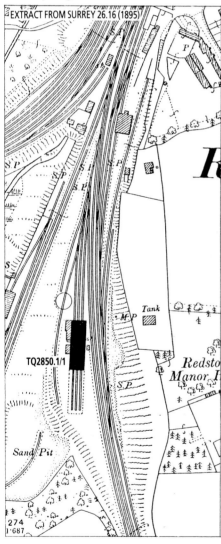

EXTRACT FROM SURREY 26.16 (1895)

TATTENHAM CORNER

Site TQ2257.1; On the east side of the line, at the south end of Tattenham Corner Station.

Tattenham Corner (SER)^{TQ2257.1/F1}

A servicing area consisting of a turntable, located at TQ22725787, and a siding was provided here from June 4th, 1900. No further details are known.

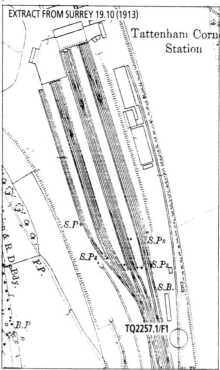

EXTRACT FROM SURREY 19.10 (1913)

WOKING

Site TQ0058.1; On the south side of the line, at the east end of Woking Station.

Woking (L&SWR)^{TQ0058.1/1A}

A brick built 1TS through road shed with a slated hipped roof, it was located at TQ00835881 and was opened in 1838. The facilities included a 50ft turntable. The depot was closed in 1897 but visiting engines continued to be serviced there for a few years afterwards. The building had been demolished by 1914.

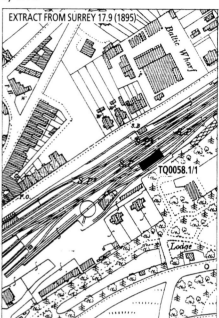

EXTRACT FROM SURREY 17.9 (1895)

The shed (TQ2850.1/1A) at the busy junction of **Redhill** is depicted here in 1935. The original roof of 1853 still serves and so, surprisingly, do the shed doors which were perennial victims of over-zealous shunting through all of locomotive history!

The depot received a new roof in 1950 (as TQ2850.1/1B) and closed to steam in 1965. Today, the tracks are used as an occasional stabling point for locomotives and civil engineeering vehicles.

H Garrett Collection

KINGSWOOD

Site TQ2456.1; In the vicinity of Kingswood Station.

Kingswood (CVR)^{TQ2456.1/F1}

A temporary facility was opened here by the Chipstead Valley Railway on November 2nd, 1897. It was approximately located at TQ248566 and was closed in 1898. No further details are known.

HORLEY

Site TQ2842.1; On the west side of Horley Station.

Horley (L&BR)^{TQ2842.1/1A}

A brick built 3TS dead ended shed with a slated gable style roof, it was located at TQ28654297 and was opened by the London & Brighton Railway on July 12th, 1841. It was built as the main workshops of the railway, with a 4TS carriage shed along the eastern side, as well as a running shed and as such possessed all major facilities. In 1847 it was decided to base the main works at Brighton and use Horley as a stock shed and store for condemned locomotives. It probably ceased to function as an engine shed in 1861 but continued to receive redundant engines until 1903. At this point the carriage shed was demolished to allow quadrupling of the main line, and the depot was converted to use as a goods shed. The building was still standing, in private use, in 1995.

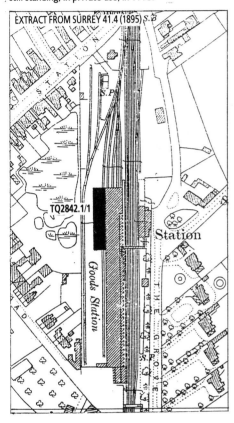

EXTRACT FROM SURREY 41.4 (1895)

TQ2842.1/1

PURLEY

Site TQ3161.1; In the fork of the Brighton and Reedham lines, south of Purley Station.

Purley (SER)^{TQ3161.1/1A}

A brick built 3TS through road shed with a slated and glazed northlight pattern roof, it was located at TQ31236115 and was opened in 1898. The facilities included a coal stage, water tank and a 50ft turntable. The depot was closed by the SR in 1928 and converted to private use. The building was still standing in 1995, being utilized by BR as a repository for legal archives.

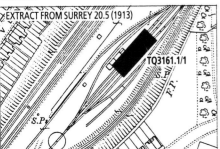

EXTRACT FROM SURREY 20.5 (1913)

TQ3161.1/1

LEATHERHEAD

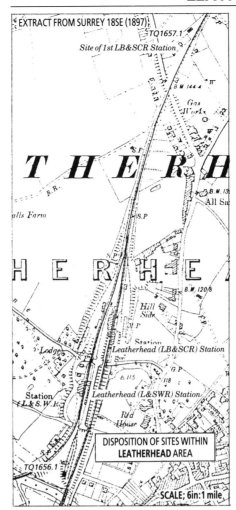

EXTRACT FROM SURREY 18SE (1897)

TQ1657.1

Site of 1st LB&SCR Station

DISPOSITION OF SITES WITHIN **LEATHERHEAD** AREA

TQ1656.1

SCALE: 6in:1 mile

Site TQ1657.1; On the west side of the line, north of Leatherhead (LB&SCR No.2) Station.

Leatherhead (LB&SCR)^{TQ1657.1/1A}

A brick built 1TS shed with a slated hipped roof, it was located at TQ16535769 and was opened on August 8th, 1859. Details of the facilities are not known. The depot was closed in 1874 and converted to private use, being utilized as a chapel, school and then a motor car repairers. The building was not demolished until the late 1980s.

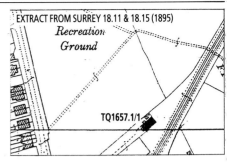

EXTRACT FROM SURREY 18.11 & 18.15 (1895)

Recreation Ground

TQ1657.1/1

Site TQ1656.1; On the west side of the line, at the south end of Leatherhead (L&SWR) Station.

Leatherhead (L&SWR)^{TQ1656.1/1A}

A 1TS dead ended shed, it was located at TQ16185647 and was opened on February 1st, 1859. The facilities included a water tank and a turntable sited outside of the shed entrance. The depot was closed in 1904.

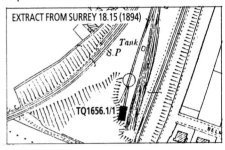

EXTRACT FROM SURREY 18.15 (1894)

Tank

TQ1656.1/1

Replaced on the same site by ...

Leatherhead (L&SWR)^{TQ1656.1/1B}

A corrugated iron built 2TS dead ended shed with a corrugated iron gable style roof, it was opened in 1904. The turntable was enlarged to 55ft. The depot was closed by the SR on July 9th, 1927.

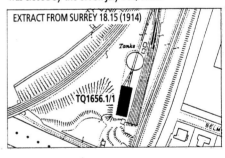

EXTRACT FROM SURREY 18.15 (1914)

Tanks

TQ1656.1/1

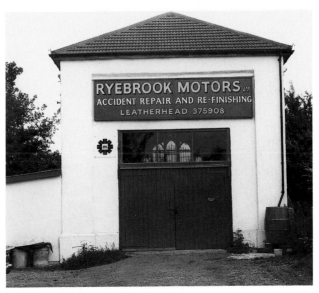

The LBSCR shed at **Leatherhead** (TQ1657.1/1A) in use as a car repair shop in August 1986. It has since been demolished. *Author.*

GREATER LONDON

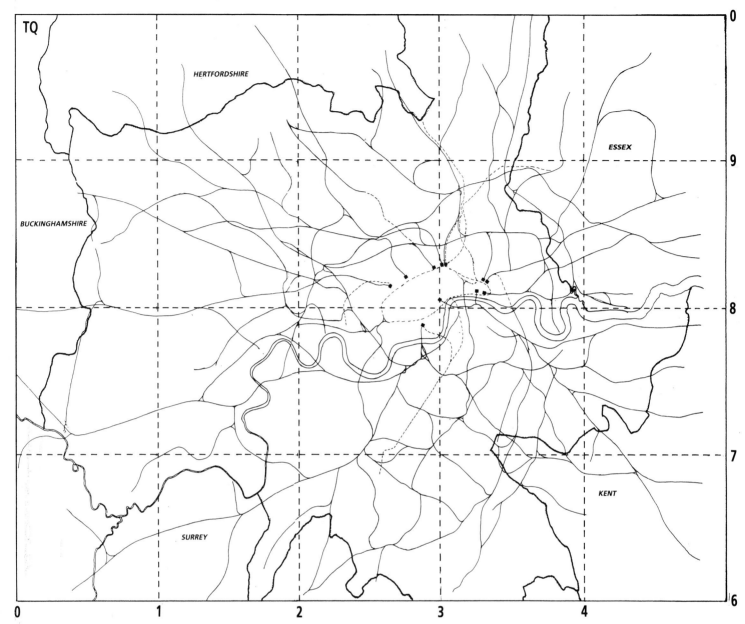

TQ

HERTFORDSHIRE

ESSEX

BUCKINGHAMSHIRE

KENT

SURREY

GREATER LONDON

This area is split into National Grid 10km squares as shown in the above diagram. For the purposes of this section **TQ06, TQ09, TQ26, TQ29, TQ46** and **TQ49** have been omitted as having no depots within the Greater London area.

Hampton Court *(Surrey)* depots have been included in **TQ16**
Beckenham *(Kent)* has been included in **TQ36**
Chingford *(Essex)* has been included in **TQ39**
Goodmayes & Ilford *(Essex)* depots have been included in **TQ48.**

A flawed, but priceless photograph from the 1860s shows the only known view of what, for the time, was a surprisingly large building (TQ3782.1/1A) for housing and repairing the North London Railway's locomotive fleet at **Bow**. The date of the construction is unclear but it was probably soon after the NLR's opening in June 1850.   *Author's Collection*

TQ07

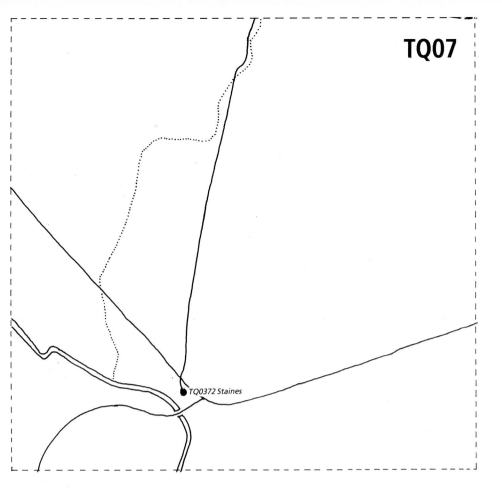

TQ0372 Staines

TQ08

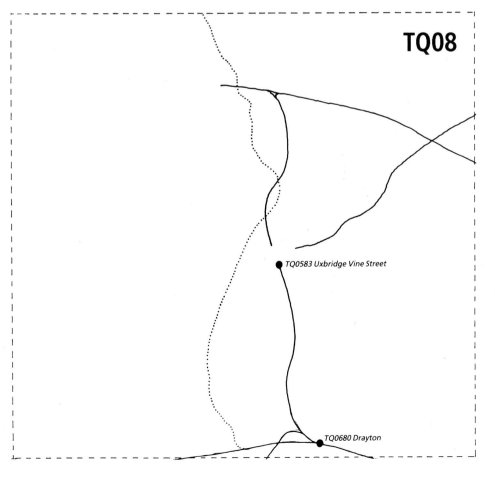

TQ0583 Uxbridge Vine Street

TQ0680 Drayton

STAINES

Site TQ0372.1; On the west side of the line, at the north end of Staines Station.

Staines (S&WDR) TQ0372.1/1A

A timber built ITS through road shed with a slated gable style roof, it was located at TQ03307201 and was opened by the Staines & West Drayton Railway on November 2nd, 1885. The facilities included a water tank. The line was worked by the GWR prior to absorption in 1900. The depot was closed by BR in June 1952 and was subsequently demolished.

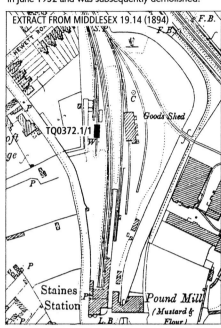

DRAYTON

Site TQ0680.1; On the north side of the line, east of West Drayton Station.

Drayton (GWR) TQ0680.1/1A

A temporary shed, probably built in timber, it was opened in 1837 and closed on June 4th, 1838. The exact site is not known but it was very approximately located at TQ065800. No further details are available.

UXBRIDGE

Site TQ0583.1; On the east side of Uxbridge Vine St. Station.

Uxbridge Vine Street (GWR) TQ0583.1/1A

A brick built ITS dead ended shed with a slated gable style roof, it was located at TQ05588389 and was opened on December 8th, 1856. The facilities included a 20ft turntable and a coal stage with water tank over. The depot was closed in December 1897 and demolished.

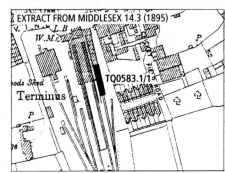

TQ16

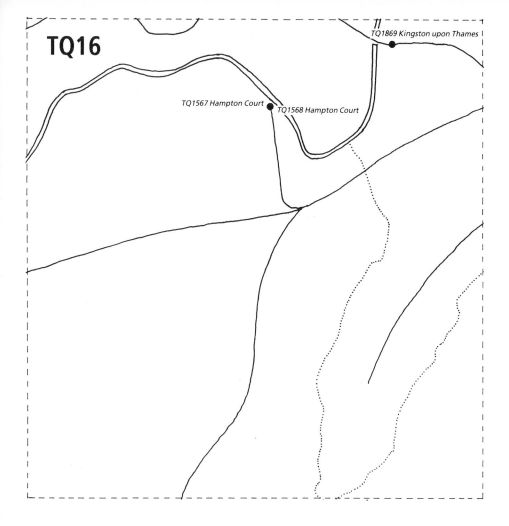

TQ1869 Kingston upon Thames

TQ1567 Hampton Court — TQ1568 Hampton Court

HAMPTON COURT

Site TQ1568.1; On the east side of Hampton Court Station.

Hampton Court (L&SWR) TQ1568.1/1A

A brick built 1TS dead ended shed with a tiled gable style pitched roof, it was located at TQ15416831 and was opened on February 1st, 1849. Details of the facilities are not known. The depot was closed in 1894 and the building was converted into a goods shed, lasting into BR days until it was demolished.

Replaced by ...

Site TQ1567.1; On the west side of the line, south of Hampton Court Station.

Hampton Court (L&SWR) TQ1567.1/1A

A brick built 2TS dead ended shed with a tiled gable style roof, it was located at TQ15446789 and was opened in 1894. The facilities included a coal stage and turntable. The depot was closed on June 18th, 1916 and the building utilized for other purposes, not being demolished until the 1960s.

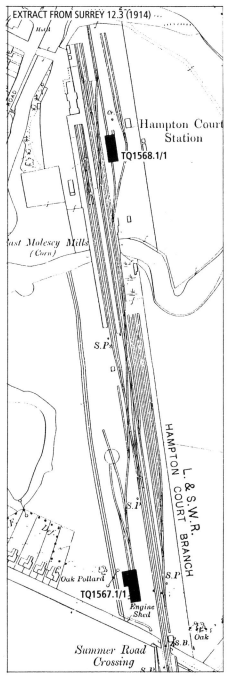

EXTRACT FROM SURREY 12.3 (1914) ...

Hampton Court Station

TQ1568.1/1

East Molesey Mills (Corn)

L. & S.W.R. HAMPTON COURT BRANCH

Oak Pollard

TQ1567.1/1

Engine Shed

Summer Road Crossing

KINGSTON UPON THAMES

Site TQ1869.1; On the north side of Kingston upon Thames Station.

Kingston upon Thames (L&SWR) TQ1869.1/1A

A brick built 2TS through road shed with a slated gable style roof incorporating a water tank over the entrance, it was located at TQ18156963 and was opened on July 1st, 1863. The facilities also included a turntable and coal stage. The depot was closed in 1907 and was utilized by the goods department. The building was demolished in 1995, having served as a garage in its latter years.

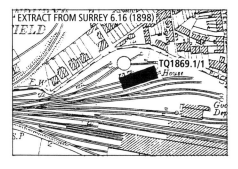

EXTRACT FROM SURREY 6.16 (1898)

TQ1869.1/1

An integral part of the MS&LR/GCR's London Extension was a standard design of engine shed based upon the 12TS building (SK4374.1/1A) put up at Staveley in 1892. This building design, yard layout etc., was utilized in two 4TS and two 6TS instances with one of the latter **Neasden** (TQ2184.1/1A) seen here in 1913.

The building of the Empire Exhibition and Stadium at Wembley in 1924 led to Neasden becoming probably the most cosmopolitan engine shed in Britain, when it was often host to locomotives of the Big Four and several regions of BR, right up until closure in June 1962. *H Garrett Collection*

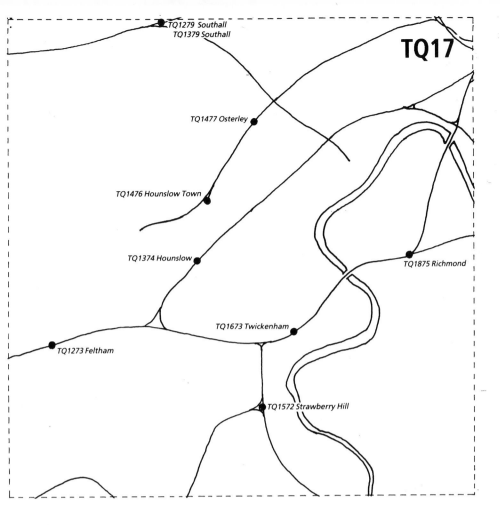

TQ17

TQ1279 Southall
TQ1379 Southall

TQ1477 Osterley

TQ1476 Hounslow Town

TQ1374 Hounslow

TQ1875 Richmond

TQ1673 Twickenham

TQ1273 Feltham

TQ1572 Strawberry Hill

The District Railway had two sheds at **Lillie Bridge** with opening dates of 1872 (TQ2578.1/1A) and 1902 (TQ2478.1/1A). The latter, a 2TS timber building was replaced by this shed (TQ2478.1/2A), probably by the London Transport Executive which was formed in 1933.

The brick, steel and asbestos built structure is seen here in June 1946 with 0-6-0T No.L31, a battery electric locomotive and a Victorian steam crane in view. The shed saw out the days of steam in 1971 and still stood in 1997, in use as a workshop.
AG Ellis

RICHMOND

Site TQ1875.1; On the south side of Richmond Station.
Richmond (Richmond) TQ1875.1/1A
A shed, located at TQ18217514, was opened here by the Richmond Railway on July 27th, 1846. It was possibly a 1TS building with the facilities *"limited and inconvenient"*. The line was worked from the outset by the L&SWR and they removed an *"engine house, turntable and tank to Twickenham"* (as TQ1673.0/1A) in 1850. No further details are known.

Site TQ1875.2; On the north side of the line, at the east end of Richmond Station.
Richmond (L&SWR) TQ1875.2/F1
A servicing area consisting of a turntable, located at TQ18287523, coal stage and engine pit, it was opened in 1850. No further details are known.

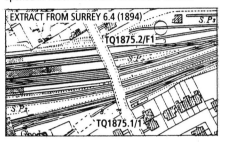
EXTRACT FROM SURREY 6.4 (1894)
TQ1875.2/F1
TQ1875.1/1

TWICKENHAM

Site TQ1673.0; In the vicinity of Twickenham Junction Station.
Twickenham (L&SWR) TQ1673.0/1A
An *"engine house"*, probably a 1TS building formerly TQ1875.1/1A, turntable and water tank were moved here from Richmond in cJune 1850. No further details are known except that it was closed on June 1st, 1863.

Replaced by ...
Site TQ1673.1; On the north side of Twickenham Junction Station.
Twickenham (L&SWR) TQ1673.1/1A
A brick built 2TS dead ended shed with a tiled gable style roof incorporating a water tank at the front, it was located at TQ16017353 and was opened on July 1st, 1863. The facilities also included a coal stage and turntable, sited at the west end of the yard. The depot was closed in 1897 and all except the section supporting the water tank was demolished.

EXTRACT FROM SURREY 6.7 (1894)
TQ1673.1/1
Twickenham

OSTERLEY

Site TQ1477.1; At the east end of Osterley Park & Spring Grove Station.
Osterley (H&MR) TQ1477.1/F1
A servicing area consisting of an engine pit and siding, it was located at TQ14977737 and was opened by the Hounslow & Metropolitan Railway on July 21st, 1884. The facility was dispensed with on June 13th, 1905.

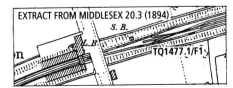
EXTRACT FROM MIDDLESEX 20.3 (1894)
TQ1477.1/F1

SOUTHALL

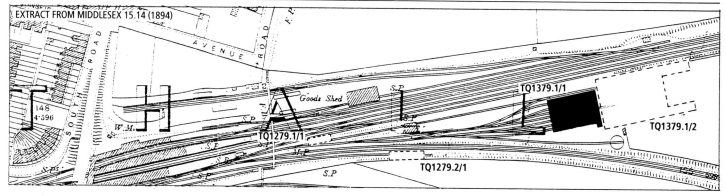

EXTRACT FROM MIDDLESEX 15.14 (1894)

Site TQ1279.1; On the south side of the Paddington line, at the east end of Southall Station.
Southall (GW&B) TQ1279.1/1A
A 1TS dead ended shed, it was located at TQ12847984 and was probably built in brick with a gable style slated roof. It was opened by the GW & Brentford Railway in July 1859 and the facilities included a 40ft turntable sited outside of the shed entrance. The depot was closed in 1884.

Replaced by ...
Site TQ1379.1; In the fork of the Paddington and Brentford lines, east of Southall Station.
Southall (GWR) TQ1379.1/1A
A brick built 6TS dead ended shed with a slated and glazed northlight pattern roof, it was located at TQ13097988 and was opened in 1884. The facilities included a turntable, coal stage and water tank.

It was modified in 1922 ...
Southall (GWR) TQ1379.1/1B
The back wall was removed and an engine yard established at the rear of the shed.

The shed was re-roofed ...
Southall (GWR) TQ1379.1/1C
As the result of war damage a low pitched single gable roof was installed in 1943. The building was demolished in 1953.

Replaced by ...
Southall (BR) TQ1379.1/2A
A brick built 8TS through road shed with a corrugated sheet and glazed transverse pitched roof, it was built by the Western Region in 1953 at the rear of its predecessor (TQ1379.1/1), being located at TQ13157989. The facilities included a coal stage, water tank and turntable. The shed was closed to steam on January 3rd, 1966, and a diesel depot was established at the site. After total closure it was taken over by a railway preservation group and the building was still standing in 1996.

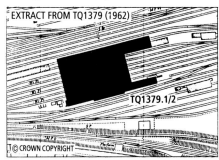

EXTRACT FROM TQ1379 (1962)
TQ1379.1/2
© CROWN COPYRIGHT

Site TQ1279.2; On the south side of the Brentford Branch east of Southall Station.
Southall Railmotor Shed (GWR) TQ1279.2/1A
A corrugated iron 1TS through road shed with a shallow dutch barn roof, it was located at TQ12937983 and was opened in 1904. The shed was closed by BR in 1953 but was not demolished immediately, being utilized for dmu stabling until 1960.

HOUNSLOW

Site TQ1374.1; On the south side of the line, at the west end of Hounslow & Whitton Station.
Hounslow (L&SWR) TQ1374.1/F1
A servicing area consisting of a turntable, located at TQ13807484, and siding, it was opened on February 1st, 1850. The closure date is not known, but the turntable was removed prior to 1894.

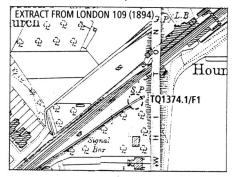

EXTRACT FROM LONDON 109 (1894)
TQ1374.1/F1

Site TQ1476.1; On the east side of the line, north of Hounslow Town Station.
Hounslow Town (Hounslow&Met) TQ1476.1/F1
A servicing area consisting of a coal stage and engine pit, it was located at TQ14407629 and was opened by the Hounslow & Metropolitan Railway on May 1st, 1883. The facility was dispensed with on March 31st, 1886.

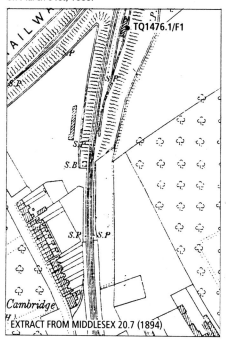

TQ1476.1/F1

Cambridge
EXTRACT FROM MIDDLESEX 20.7 (1894)

STRAWBERRY HILL

Site TQ1572.1; In the triangle of lines, south of Strawberry Hill Station.
Strawberry Hill *(L&SWR) TQ1572.1/1A
A brick built 6TS dead ended shed with a slated triple pitched roof with glazed gable ends, it was located at TQ15447200 and was opened in 1897. The facilities included a turntable, coal stage and water tank.

The shed was enlarged ...
Strawberry Hill (L&SWR) TQ1572.1/1B
A brick built 3TS dead ended extension with a slated pitched roof and glazed gable ends was added to the western side of the shed in 1907. At the same time the turntable was enlarged to 50ft. The depot was closed to steam by the SR in 1923 and converted to an emu maintenance shed. It was still operational in 1996.

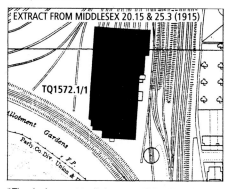

EXTRACT FROM MIDDLESEX 20.15 & 25.3 (1915)
TQ1572.1/1

*The shed was originally known as Fulwell Junction

FELTHAM

Site TQ1273.1; On the south side of the line, east of Feltham Station.
Feltham (L&SWR) TQ1273.1/1A
A concrete built 6TS through road shed with a northlight pattern roof, it was located at TQ12307362 and was opened in 1922. The depot had use of all facilities including a 65ft turntable, mechanical coaling plant and a 2TS repair shop. The shed was closed by BR on July 9th, 1967 and was subsequently demolished.

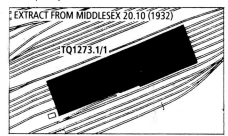

EXTRACT FROM MIDDLESEX 20.10 (1932)
TQ1273.1/1

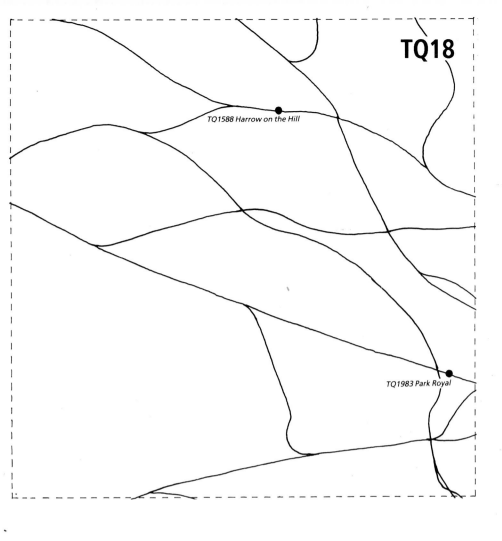

TQ18

TQ1588 Harrow on the Hill

TQ1983 Park Royal

HARROW ON THE HILL

Site TQ1588.1; On the north side of the line, at the west end of Harrow on the Hill Station.

Harrow on the Hill (K&HR) TQ1588.1/1A

A timber built 2TS dead ended shed, it was located at TQ15218806 and was opened by the Kingsbury & Harrow Railway on August 2nd, 1880. The facilities included a coal stage. The line was worked by the Metropolitan Railway and they closed the shed in 1883, the building being removed and re-erected at Neasden as TQ2185.1/1A.

A servicing point was then established ...
Harrow on the Hill (Met) TQ1588.1/F1

Locomotives utilized the sidings and coal stage until it was closed in 1925.

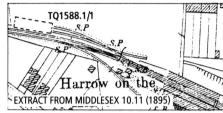

EXTRACT FROM MIDDLESEX 10.11 (1895)

PARK ROYAL

Site TQ1983.1; In the goods yard on the north side of Park Royal Station.

Park Royal (GWR) TQ1983.1/F1

A servicing point consisting of a water tank and siding, it was located at TQ19598300 and was opened during the 1920s. The facility was closed by BR in c1964.

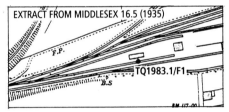

EXTRACT FROM MIDDLESEX 16.5 (1935)

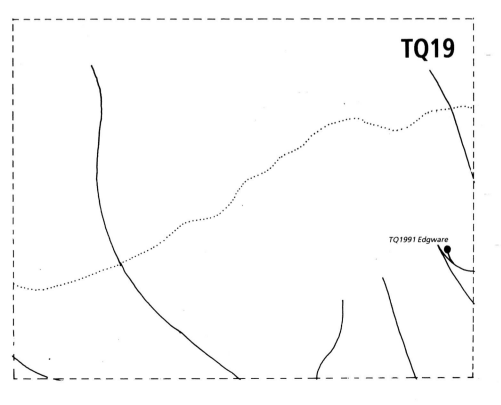

TQ19

TQ1991 Edgware

EDGWARE

Site TQ1991.1; On the north side of Edgware Station.
Edgware (EH&LR) TQ1991.1/1A

A brick built 1TS shed with a glazed gable style roof, it was located at TQ19069197 and was opened by the Edgware, Highgate & London Railway on August 27th, 1867. The facilities included a turntable, sited outside of the shed entrance, and a coal stage with water tank over. The line was worked by the GNR and they closed the depot in July 1878. The building was destroyed in a blizzard in about 1885.

Replaced by ...
Edgware (GNR) TQ1991.1/F1

The turntable was removed and a servicing area was established on the shed site utilizing the engine pit, coal stage and water tower. The facility lasted until the end of steam on the branch in BR days.

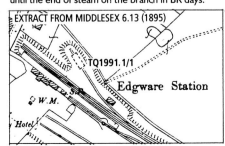

EXTRACT FROM MIDDLESEX 6.13 (1895)

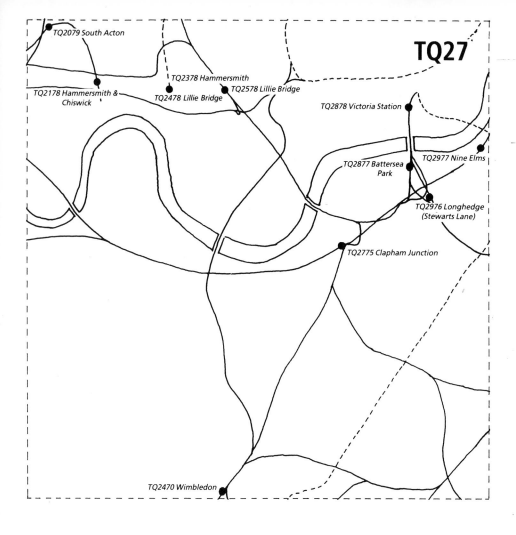

TQ27

- TQ2079 South Acton
- TQ2378 Hammersmith
- TQ2178 Hammersmith & Chiswick
- TQ2478 Lillie Bridge
- TQ2578 Lillie Bridge
- TQ2878 Victoria Station
- TQ2977 Nine Elms
- TQ2877 Battersea Park
- TQ2976 Longhedge (Stewarts Lane)
- TQ2775 Clapham Junction
- TQ2470 Wimbledon

HAMMERSMITH

Site TQ2378.1; On the east side of Hammersmith Station.

Hammersmith (H&CR) TQ2378.1/1A

A brick built 2TS dead ended shed with a slated gable style roof, it was located at TQ23157871 and was opened by the Hammersmith & City Railway on June 13th, 1864. The facilities included a coal stage. The line was worked by the GWR and they closed the depot on November 5th, 1906.

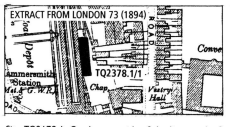

Site TQ2178.1; On the west side of the line, north of Hammersmith & Chiswick Station.

Hammersmith & Chiswick (N&SWJR) TQ2178.1/1A

A timber built 1TS dead ended shed, it was located at TQ21707838 and was opened by the North & South West Junction Railway on May 1st, 1857. No further details are known except that it was closed in 1880 and demolished.

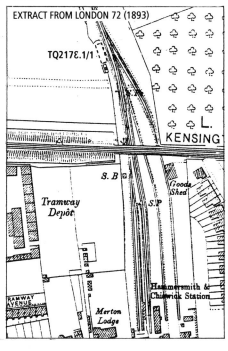

SOUTH ACTON

Site TQ2079.1; On the south side of the Hammersmith branch, east of South Acton Station.

South Acton (NLR) TQ2079.1/1A

A brick built 2TS through road shed with a slated gable style roof, it was located at TQ20617982 and was opened by the North London Railway in 1880. Details of the facilities are not known. The depot was closed by the MR in 1916 and remained standing until it was destroyed in a storm on December 8th, 1954.

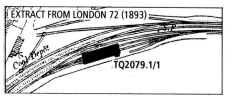

LILLIE BRIDGE

Site TQ2478.1 & TQ2578.1; In Lillie Bridge Works, on the west side of the line, north of West Brompton Station.

Lillie Bridge (District) TQ2578.1/1A

A 4TS through road shed, probably built in brick and with a slated gable style roof, it was located at TQ25037826 and was opened in 1872 by the District Railway. Details of the facilities are not known. The shed was closed in 1902 and demolished to make way for a 6TS electric car shed.

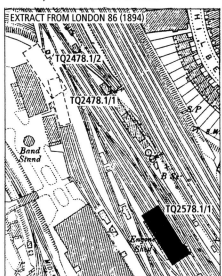

Replaced by ...

Lillie Bridge (District) TQ2478.1/1A

A timber built 2TS dead ended shed with a corrugated iron pitched roof and gables, it was located at TQ24947837 and was opened in 1902. The facilities included a coal stage. The shed was closed at some time after 1931.

Replaced, after 1931, by ...

Lillie Bridge (LT) TQ2478.1/2A

A 2TS dead ended shed with a corrugated asbestos pitched gable style roof, it was located at TQ24927841. The facilities included a coal stage and water column. The depot was closed to steam in c1962 and the building was utilized in another capacity. It was still standing in 1996.

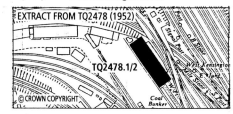

WIMBLEDON

Site TQ2470.1; In Wimbledon Engineering Works, on the east side of the line, south of Wimbledon Station.
Wimbledon Engineers Depot (L&SWR) TQ2470.1/1A
A brick built 2TS through road shed with a slated gable style roof, it was located at TQ24587034 and was opened in 1857. Details of the facilities are not known. It was utilized to service the engineers locomotive fleet until it was disbanded on May 31st, 1888 following which the building was absorbed into the works. It remained in existence until the 1960s.

Site TQ2470.2; On the east side of the line, south of Wimbledon Station.
Wimbledon (SR) TQ2470.2/F1
A servicing area consisting of a water tank and sidings, it was located at TQ24397014. The opening date is not known and it was closed by BR in the 1960s.

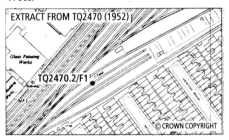

CLAPHAM JUNCTION

Site TQ2775.1; On the west side of Clapham Junction Station.
Clapham Junction (L&SWR) TQ2775.1/1A
A 2TS through road shed, it was located at TQ27097544. No further details are known except that it had been removed by 1893.

LONGHEDGE

Site TQ2976.1; In a maze of lines between Wandsworth Road and Battersea Park Stations.
Longhedge (LCDR) TQ2976.1/1A
A brick built semi-roundhouse shed with a continuous pitched slated roof, it was located at TQ29057662 and was opened in February 1862. It was sited adjacently to the locomotive works and possessed all facilities. It was closed in 1881 and demolished.

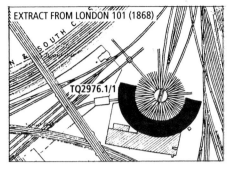

Replaced, on the same site, by ...
Stewarts Lane (LCDR) TQ2976.1/1B
A brick built 16TS dead ended shed with a slated transverse multi-pitched roof, it was opened in 1881. The facilities included a turntable, ramped coaling stage and water tank.

It was re-roofed ...
Stewarts Lane (SR) TQ2976.1/1C
A corrugated asbestos transverse northlight pattern roof was installed in 1934. At the same time the turntable was re-sited and the facilities were improved. The depot was closed to steam by BR in September 1963 and given over to diesel and electric locomotive servicing.

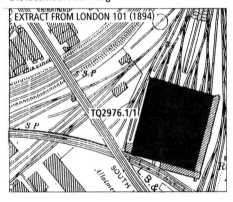

VICTORIA STATION

Site TQ2878.1; On the east side of the line, at the south end of Victoria Station.
Victoria Station (LB&SCR) TQ2878.1/F1
A servicing area consisting of a turntable, located at TQ28797870, engine pits and sidings, it was opened on October 1st, 1860. No further details are known.

Site TQ2878.2; On the west side of the line, at the south end of Victoria Station.
Victoria Station (LCDR/GWR/SER) TQ2878.2/F1
A servicing area consisting of a turntable, located at TQ28737871, engine pits and sidings, it was opened on October 1st, 1860. No further details are known.

It was re-sited ...
Victoria Station (LCDR/GWR/SER) TQ2878.2/F2
At some stage the servicing facility was moved and the turntable was enlarged. It was dispensed with by BR at the end of steam.

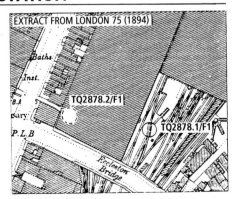

NB. A number of coal stages were sited throughout the station area, their precise locations, opening and closure dates not known.

BATTERSEA PARK

Site TQ2877.1; On the west side of the line, south of Battersea Park Goods Station.
Battersea Park (WEofL&CPR) TQ2877.1/1A
A brick built 3TS shed with one through road and a slated pitched roof, it was located at TQ28857725 and was opened by the West End of London & Crystal Palace Railway on March 29th, 1858. The facilities included a turntable. The line was absorbed by the LB&SCR in 1859 and the depot was closed in 1877 and demolished.

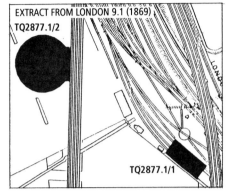

Battersea Park (LB&SCR) TQ2877.1/2A
A brick built circular 1RH shed with a slated continuous pitched roof, it was located at TQ28717733 and was opened in 1869. The facilities included a water tank.

Adjoined by ...
Battersea Park (LB&SCR) TQ2877.1/3A
A brick built 1RH shed with a slated roof, it was of an unusual "triangular" shape and was located at TQ28777731. It was opened in 1870.

Adjoined by ...
Battersea Park (LB&SCR) TQ2877.1/4A
A brick built circular 1RH shed with a slated continuous pitched roof, it was located at TQ28707728 and was opened in 1889.

The depot was closed by the SR on July 15th, 1934. The buildings were then utilized as a road transport depot until they were demolished in 1986.

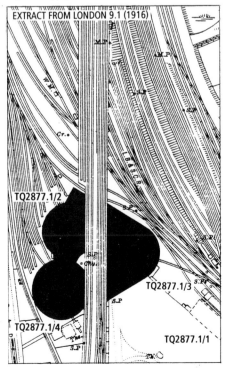

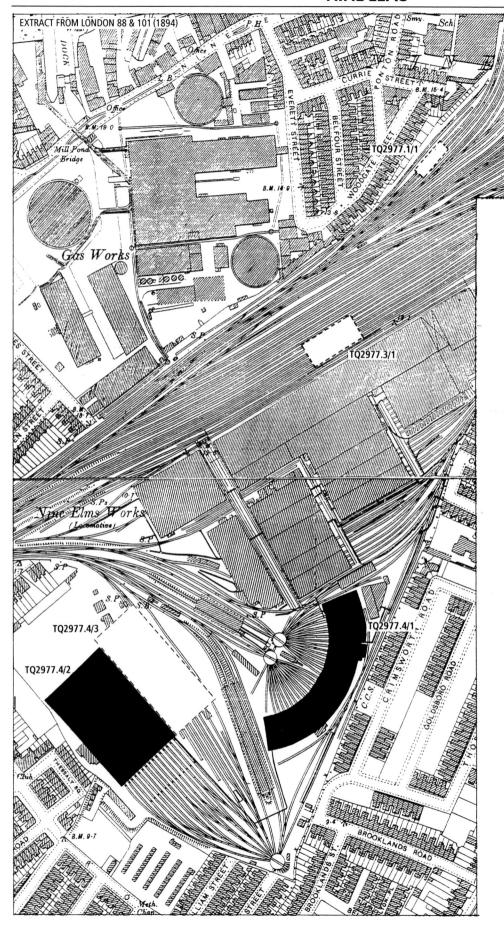

EXTRACT FROM LONDON 88 & 101 (1894)

Site TQ2977.1; On the north side of the line, at the west end of Nine Elms Goods Depot.

Nine Elms (L&SR) TQ2977.1/1A

A brick built 3TS shed*, located at TQ29827752 and opened by the London & Southampton Railway on May 21st, 1838. No further details are known except that it was closed in 1865 and subsequently demolished.

*According to Wishaw, this may have been a 4TS shed.

Site TQ2977.2; On the south side of the line, at the west end of Nine Elms Goods Depot.

Nine Elms (L&SWR) TQ2977.2/1A

A brick built 6TS shed, it was located at TQ29977763 and was opened in 1849. No further details are known except that it was closed in 1865 and demolished.

Replaced by ...
Site TQ2977.3; On the south side of the line, between Vauxhall and Queens Road Stations.

Nine Elms (L&SWR) TQ2977.3/1A

A brick built 7TS through road shed, it was located at TQ29747735 and was opened in 1865. An unusual feature was that access was gained via turntables sited at both ends. It was closed in 1876 and demolished.

Replaced by ...
Site TQ2977.4; On a spur on the south side of the line between Vauxhall and Queens Road Stations.

Nine Elms (L&SWR) TQ2977.4/1A

A brick built semi-roundhouse shed with a slated continuous pitched roof, it was located at TQ29717704 and was opened in 1876. It was unique in this country in that access was gained from two turntables. Other facilities included a ramped coal stage and water tank. The building was closed and demolished in 1909.

Nine Elms (L&SWR) TQ2977.4/2A

A brick built 15TS dead ended shed with five slated and glazed gable style pitched roofs, it was located at TQ29497701 and was opened in 1885. The facilities included a turntable, from which all the access roads radiated, coal stage and water tank. The building became known as the "Old Shed".

The shed was modified ...
Nine Elms (SR) TQ2977.4/2B

The building was badly damaged during WW2 and as a result it was rebuilt to a reduced length with a corrugated asbestos roof.

Adjoined by ...
Nine Elms (L&SWR) TQ2977.4/3A

A brick built 10TS dead ended shed with a transverse slated multi-pitched roof, it was located at TQ29557706 and was opened in 1910. The building was known as the "New Shed".

The depot was closed by BR on July 9th, 1967 and demolished to be replaced by a fruit and vegetable market.

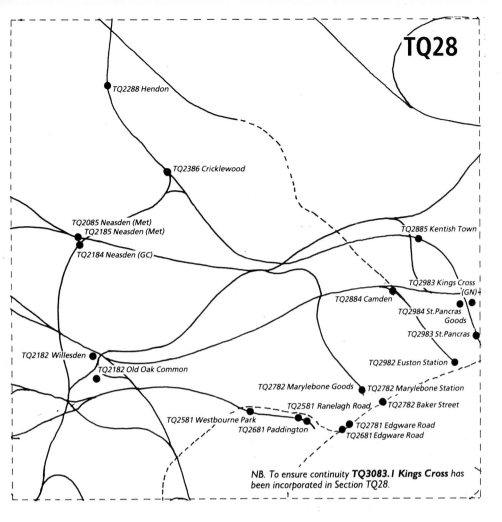

TQ28

TQ2288 Hendon

TQ2386 Cricklewood

TQ2085 Neasden (Met)
TQ2185 Neasden (Met)
TQ2184 Neasden (GC)

TQ2885 Kentish Town

TQ2983 Kings Cross (GN)
TQ2884 Camden
TQ2984 St.Pancras Goods
TQ2983 St.Pancras

TQ2982 Euston Station

TQ2182 Willesden
TQ2182 Old Oak Common

TQ2782 Marylebone Goods TQ2782 Marylebone Station

TQ2581 Ranelagh Road TQ2782 Baker Street
TQ2581 Westbourne Park TQ2781 Edgware Road
TQ2681 Paddington TQ2681 Edgware Road

NB. To ensure continuity **TQ3083.1 Kings Cross** has been incorporated in Section TQ28.

BAKER STREET

Site TQ2782.1; On the east side of the line, at the north end of Baker Street Station.
Baker Street (Met & St. Johns Wood) TQ2782.1/F1
A servicing area consisting of a coal stage and engine pit, it was located at TQ27918213 and was opened on April 13th, 1868. The line was worked from the outset by the Metropolitan Railway and was absorbed by them in 1882. The facility was closed on July 1st, 1905.

Site TQ2782.2; On the west side of the line, at the north end of Baker Street Station.
Baker Street (Met & St. Johns Wood) TQ2782.2/F1
A servicing area consisting of a coal stage and engine pit, it was located at TQ27918209 and was opened on April 13th, 1868. The line was worked from the outset by the Metropolitan Railway and was absorbed by them in 1882. The facility was closed on July 1st, 1905.

PADDINGTON

Site TQ2681.1; On the north side of the line, at the west end of Paddington Station.
Paddington (GWR) TQ2681.1/1A
A timber built polygonal 1RH shed with a conical slated roof and a 4TS extension with a slated gable style pitched roof, it was located at TQ26188158 and was opened on June 4th, 1838. The facilities included a 35ft turntable and repair shop. The depot was closed in March 1855 and demolished to make way for station enlargements.

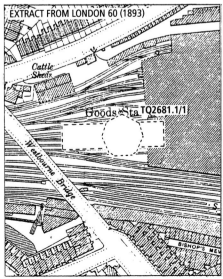

ST.PANCRAS

Site TQ2983.2; On the east side of the line, at the north end of St.Pancras Station.
St.Pancras (MR) TQ2983.2/F1
A servicing area consisting of a turntable, located at TQ29998323, water tank and sidings, it was opened on October 1st, 1868. The facility was closed to steam by BR in c1966 and a diesel servicing point established on the site.

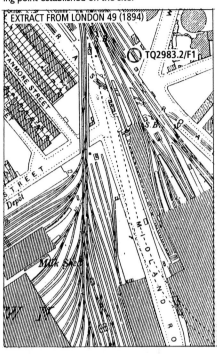

Site TQ2984.1; In St.Pancras Goods Depot, on the west side of the line, north of St.Pancras Station.
St.Pancras Goods (MR) TQ2984.1/F1
A servicing area consisting of a turntable, located at TQ29728404, and a siding. No further details are known.

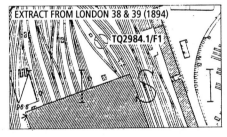

HENDON

Site TQ2288.1; On the east side of the line, north of Hendon Station.
Hendon (MR) TQ2288.1/1A
A brick built 1TS dead ended shed with a slated gable style roof, it was located at TQ22108875 and was opened in 1870. The facilities included a turntable and coaling crane. The shed was closed in 1882 but remained standing until 1965 when it was demolished to make way for the M1 Motorway.

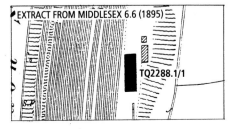

OLD OAK COMMON

Site TQ2182.1; On the north side of the junction of the Reading and High Wycombe lines, about 2 miles west of Westbourne Park Station.

Old Oak Common (GWR) TQ2182.1/1A

A brick built 4RH shed with a multi-pitched slated and glazed roof, it was located at TQ21708235 and was opened on March 17th, 1906. The depot possessed all facilities including a repair shop and large ramped coaling stage. Demolition of the buildings commenced in March 1964 and the depot was closed to steam by BR on March 22nd, 1965. A diesel depot was established on the site, this utilized the repair shop (TQ2182.1/1B), located at TQ21808237, with a new brick built 3TS diesel shed (TQ2182.1/1C) being sited on the southern turntable at TQ21758233. The western turntable and stalls were also retained as a stabling area.

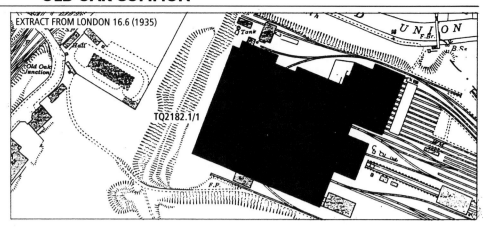

EXTRACT FROM LONDON 16.6 (1935)

TQ2182.1/1

KINGS CROSS

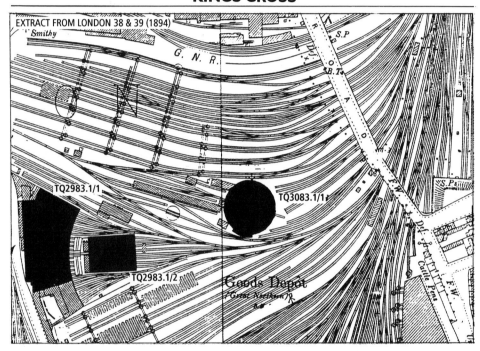

EXTRACT FROM LONDON 38 & 39 (1894)

TQ2983.1/1

TQ3083.1/1

TQ2983.1/2

Site TQ2983.1 & TQ3083.1; In Kings Cross Goods Depot, on the west side of the line, north of Kings Cross Station.

Kings Cross (GNR) TQ2983.1/1A

A brick built 25 track "crescent" shed with a longitudinal gable style slated pitched roof, it was located at TQ29888385 and was opened in 1851. The building was unique in that all the tracks radiated from a single line, rather than a turntable as in the case of a semi-roundhouse. The facilities included a 40ft turntable, coke/coal stage and fitting shop.

It was modified in 1862 ...

Kings Cross (GNR) TQ2983.1/1B

The building was partially converted to a carriage shed (8 tracks) with the remainder in use for locomotive repairs.

Part of the building was re-opened ...

Kings Cross (LNER) TQ2983.1/1C

The carriage shed portion, located at TQ29888389 was re-instated as a 7 track engine shed (known as the "Met Shed") in 1931.

The shed was re-roofed ...

Kings Cross (BR) TQ2983.1/1D

The shed was rebuilt in 1949 by the Eastern Region with an asbestos roof.

Kings Cross (GNR) TQ2983.1/2A

A brick built 8TS shed with one through road and a slated four-pitched transverse roof, it was located at TQ29958385 and was opened in 1862.

The building was modified ...

Kings Cross (LNER) TQ2983.1/2B

In 1931 the shed was converted to an 8TS through road structure with all the tracks leading into the repair shops behind it.

The shed was re-roofed ...

Kings Cross (BR) TQ2983.1/2C

The shed was rebuilt by the Eastern Region in 1949 with a flat asbestos roof.

The depot was closed by BR on June 17th, 1963 and demolished.

Kings Cross (MR) TQ3083.1/1A

A brick built polygonal 1RH shed with a slated circular gable roof over the stalls and a conical roof over the turntable, it was located at TQ30088390 and was opened in 1859. The building was built by the GNR and taken over by them in September 1868 and was initially used by them for carriage and wagon repairs. It saw further use as an engine shed prior to closure by the LNER in 1931 when it was demolished and replaced by sidings.

EDGWARE ROAD

Site TQ2781.1; On the north side of the line, at the east end of Edgware Road Station.

Edgware Road (Met) TQ2781.1/1A

A timber built 2TS dead ended shed, it was located at TQ27268175 and was opened on January 1st, 1863. Details of the facilities are not known.

Replaced, on the same site, by ...

Edgware Road (Met) TQ2781.1/1B

A brick built 2TS dead ended shed. The opening date is not known but it was closed in 1880.

Site TQ2781.2; On the south side of the line, at the east end of Edgware Road Station.

Edgware Road (Met) TQ2781.2/1A

A brick built 2TS dead ended shed, it was located at TQ27288172 and was opened on January 1st, 1863. Details of the facilities are not known. The shed was closed in 1880.

Edgware Road (Met) TQ2781.2/2A

A brick built 2TS dead ended shed, it was located at TQ27368177 and was converted from a carriage works. The opening date is not known but it was closed in 1880.

The three buildings were all demolished prior to 1916.

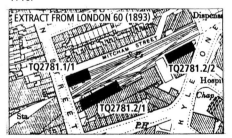

EXTRACT FROM LONDON 60 (1893)

TQ2781.1/1

TQ2781.2/2

TQ2781.2/1

Site TQ2681.3; On the south side of the line at Praed Street Junction, about 500 yards west of Edgware Road Station.

Praed Street Junction (Met) TQ2681.3/1A

A brick built 2TS dead ended shed, it was located at TQ26988141 and was opened on January 1st, 1863. Details of the facilities are not known. The depot was closed in 1880.

TQ2681.3/1

EXTRACT FROM LONDON 60 (1893)

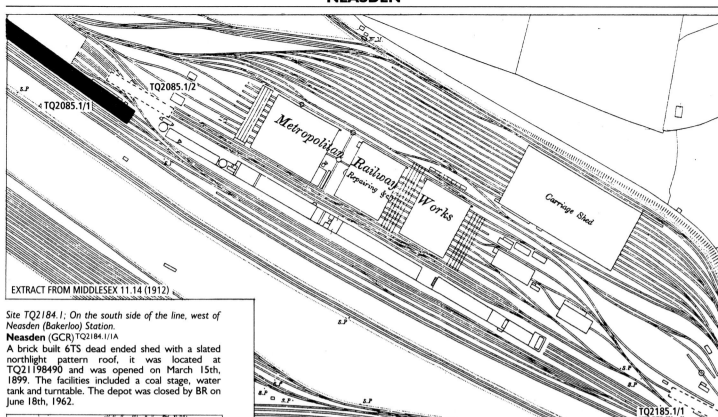

EXTRACT FROM MIDDLESEX 11.14 (1912)

Site TQ2184.1; On the south side of the line, west of Neasden (Bakerloo) Station.

Neasden (GCR) TQ2184.1/1A

A brick built 6TS dead ended shed with a slated northlight pattern roof, it was located at TQ21198490 and was opened on March 15th, 1899. The facilities included a coal stage, water tank and turntable. The depot was closed by BR on June 18th, 1962.

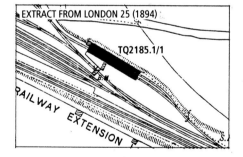

Site TQ2085.1 & TQ2185.1; In Neasden Works on the north side of the line, west of Neasden Station.

Neasden (Met) TQ2185.1/1A

A timber built 2TS shed with one through road, it was located at TQ21068555 and was opened in 1883. The building had been removed from Harrow on the Hill (as TQ1588.1/1A). Details of the facilities are not known. It was closed in 1898.

EXTRACT FROM LONDON 25 (1894)

Replaced by ...

Neasden (Met) TQ2085.1/3A

A 1RH shed, it was opened in 1898 and it is believed that it was approximately located at TQ20508590. No further details are known except that it was closed and demolished in 1909.

Replaced by ...

Neasden (Met) TQ2085.1/1A

A corrugated iron 3TS through road shed with a pitched roof, it was located at TQ20448584 and was converted from a carriage wash shed in 1909. Details of the facilities are not known. The depot was closed by London Transport in 1936.

Replaced by ...

Neasden (LT) TQ2085.1/2A

A brick built 2TS through road shed, it was located at TQ20518581 and was opened in 1937. Details of the facilities are not known. The depot was closed on June 6th, 1971 with the building finding alternative use and was still standing in 1996.

MARYLEBONE

Site TQ2782.3; In the goods yard on the west side of the line, north of Marylebone Station.

Marylebone Goods (GCR) TQ2782.3/1A

A 1TS dead ended shed, it was located at TQ27068239 and was opened in 1897. It was probably built in brick with a slated pitched roof. No further details are known.

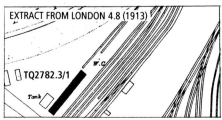

EXTRACT FROM LONDON 4.8 (1913)

Site TQ2782.4: On the east side of the line, north of Marylebone Station.

Marylebone Station (GCR) TQ2782.4/F1

A servicing area consisting of a turntable, located at TQ27308210, coal stage and sidings, it opened in 1897.

The facility was improved ...

Marylebone Station (LNER) TQ2782.4/F2

A mechanical coaler was installed in 1937. The facility was closed by BR in1966 although the turntable was retained *in situ* until the 1980s.

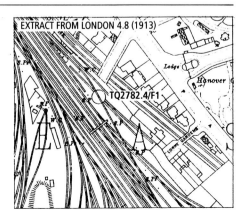

EXTRACT FROM LONDON 4.8 (1913)

Site TQ2885.1; On the east side of the line, north of Kentish Town Station.

Kentish Town No.1 (MR) TQ2885.1/1A

A brick built 1RH shed with a slated multi-pitched roof, it was located at TQ28618537 and was opened on September 8th, 1867. The facilities included a coal shed, water tank and fitting shop. The building was demolished in 1898 to make way for track alterations.

Adjoined by ...

Kentish Town No.2 (MR) TQ2885.1/2A

A brick built 1RH shed with a slated multi-pitched roof, it was located at TQ28628543 and was opened on September 8th, 1867.

The building was modified in 1898 ...

Kentish Town No.2 (MR) TQ2885.1/2B

The south eastern corner of the building was removed to allow track reorganization and, following the removal of TQ2885.1/1A, it became known as No.1 shed.

The shed was re-roofed ...

Kentish Town No.1 (BR) TQ2885.1/2C

At some stage the shed was re-roofed in steel and glass by the London Midland Region.

Adjoined by ...

Kentish Town No.2 (MR) TQ2885.1/3A

A brick built 1RH shed with a slated multi-pitched roof, it was located at TQ28618550 and was opened in 1899.

The shed was re-roofed ...

Kentish Town No.2 (BR) TQ2885.1/3B

At some stage the shed was re-roofed in steel and glass by the London Midland Region.

Adjoined by ...

Kentish Town No.3 (MR) TQ2885.1/4A

A brick built 1RH shed with a slated multi-pitched roof, it was located at TQ28598556 and was opened in 1899.

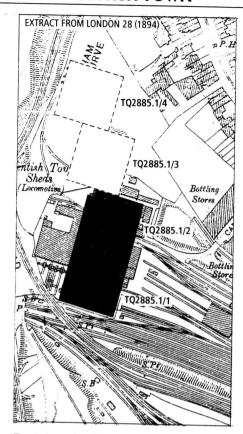

EXTRACT FROM LONDON 28 (1894)

The shed was re-roofed ...

Kentish Town No.3 (BR) TQ2885.1/4B

At some stage the shed was re-roofed in steel and glass by the London Midland Region.

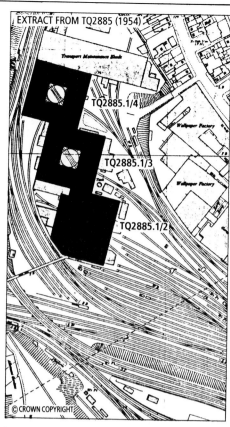

EXTRACT FROM TQ2885 (1954)

The depot was closed by BR in April 1963. The buildings were not demolished but were leased out for private use and were still standing in 1996.

CRICKLEWOOD

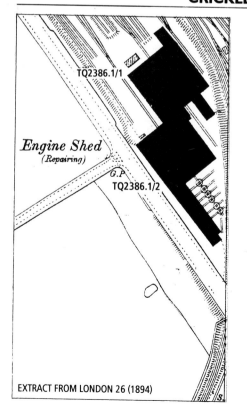

Engine Shed
(Repairing)

TQ2386.1/1

G.P.

TQ2386.1/2

EXTRACT FROM LONDON 26 (1894)

Site TQ2386.1; On the west side of the line, north of Cricklewood Station.

Cricklewood No.1* (MR) TQ2386.1/1A

A brick built square roundhouse with a slated triple pitched roof, it was located at TQ23258665 and was opened in 1882. The facilities included a ramped coaling stage and water tank.

The shed was re-roofed in 1949 ...

Cricklewood No.1 (BR) TQ2386.1/1B

The shed was rebuilt by the London Midland Region with a flat concrete and steel roof.

Adjoined by ...

Cricklewood No.2* (MR) TQ2386.2/1A

A brick built square roundhouse with a triple pitched roof, it was located at TQ23258658 and was opened in 1893. The facilities were improved with a larger coal stage and a fitting shop. By 1948 the building was roofless.

The shed was re-roofed in 1949 ...

Cricklewood No.1 (BR) TQ2386.2/1B

The shed was rebuilt by the London Midland Region with a flat concrete and steel roof.

The depot was closed by BR on December 14th, 1964 and was used for a few years as a diesel stabling point. The buildings were subsequently demolished.

*The shed was originally known as Childs Hill

RANELAGH ROAD

Site TQ2581.2; On the south side of Royal Oak Station.

Ranelagh Road (GWR) TQ2581.2/F1

A servicing area consisting of a turntable, located at TQ25828150, water tank and sidings. It was opened at some time after 1893 and closed to steam in c1965. The area was remodelled to incorporate sidings only and a diesel servicing point was established. It went out of use in about 1976.

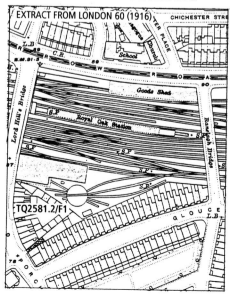

EXTRACT FROM LONDON 60 (1916)

TQ2581.2/F1

CAMDEN

Site TQ2884.1; On the north side of the line, at the east end of Chalk Farm Station.

Camden (L&BR) TQ2884.1/1A

A stone built shed, it was located at TQ28268432 and was opened by the London & Birmingham Railway on June 20th, 1837. Details of its construction are not known but it could have been a traverser-type shed or even a roundhouse. The depot was closed in 1847.

Replaced, on the same site by ...

Camden (L&BR) TQ2884.1/1B

A brick built circular roundhouse with a slated conical roof, it was opened in 1847 and was known as the *"Luggage Engine House"*. Details of the facilities are not known. The shed was closed in 1871 and leased out for use as a gin store. The building is now listed and in use as an arts centre.

Site TQ2884.2; On the south side of the line at the east end of Chalk Farm Station.

Camden (L&BR) TQ2884.2/1A

A brick built 5TS through road shed with a slated gable style roof, it was located at TQ28208416 and was opened in 1847. It was known as the *"Passenger Engine House"* and the facilities included a 35ft turntable (later enlarged to 40ft), coke/coal shed, water tank and fitting shop. An additional turntable and mechanical coaling stage were installed by the L&NWR by 1920.

The shed was rebuilt in 1932 ...

Camden (LMS) TQ2884.2/1B

The shed was enlarged to 7TS and the building was re-roofed with an LMS louvre-style roof and brick screen. At the same time a 70ft turntable was installed. The depot was closed to steam by BR on September 9th, 1963 and totally on January 3rd, 1966. It was subsequently demolished and replaced with sidings.

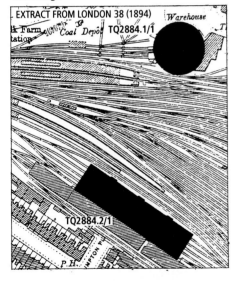

EUSTON STATION

Site TQ2982.1; On the west side of Euston Station.

Euston Station (L&NWR) TQ2982.1/F1

A servicing facility consisting of a turntable and sidings, it was located at TQ29318285. The opening and closing dates are not known.

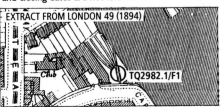

WESTBOURNE PARK

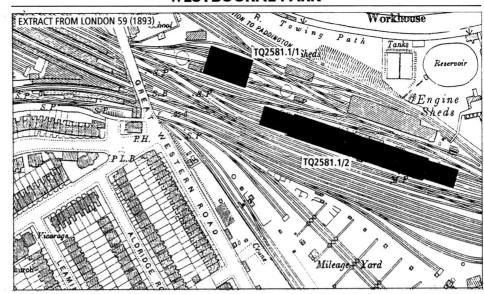

Site TQ2581.1; On the north side of the line, east of Westbourne Park Station.

Westbourne Park (GWR) TQ2581.1/1A

A brick built 4TS through road shed with a slated gable style roof, it was located at TQ25108173 and was opened in March 1855. The facilities included a turntable.

Westbourne Park (GWR) TQ2581.1/2A

A brick built 3TS dead ended shed with a slated gable style roof, it was located at TQ25038178 and was opened in 1862. The additional facilities included a coal stage and repair shop.

It was enlarged in 1873 ...

Westbourne Park (GWR) TQ2581.1/2B

A brick built 3TS extension with a slated gable style roof was added on the northern side of the shed.

The depot was closed and demolished in March 1906 upon the opening of Old Oak Common (TQ2182.1/1), the site later being utilized for a goods depot.

WILLESDEN

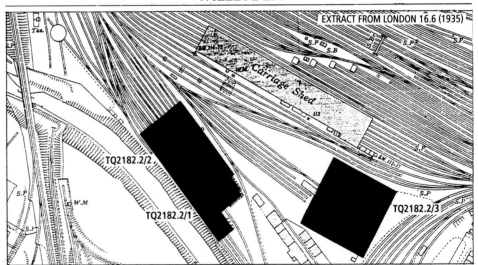

Site TQ2182.2; On the south side of the line, west of Willesden Junction Station.

Willesden (L&NWR) TQ2182.2/1A

A brick built 12TS dead ended shed with a slated triple hipped roof, it was located at TQ21288292 and was opened in 1873. The facilities included a coal stage, turntable and water tank.

It was enlarged in 1898 ...

Willesden (L&NWR) TQ2182.2/2A

A brick built 12TS through road shed with a north-light pattern roof, it was located at TQ21258297 and was added at the western end. Due to the deteriorating state of the roof this portion of the shed was demolished in 1939, leaving the original building (TQ2182.1/1A) *in situ*.

Willesden (LMS) TQ2182.2/3A

A brick built square roundhouse with a slated and glazed multi-pitched roof, it was located at TQ21438289 and was opened in October 1929.

The depot was closed by BR on August 27th, 1965 and demolished, the site being utilized as a Freightliner terminal.

TQ36

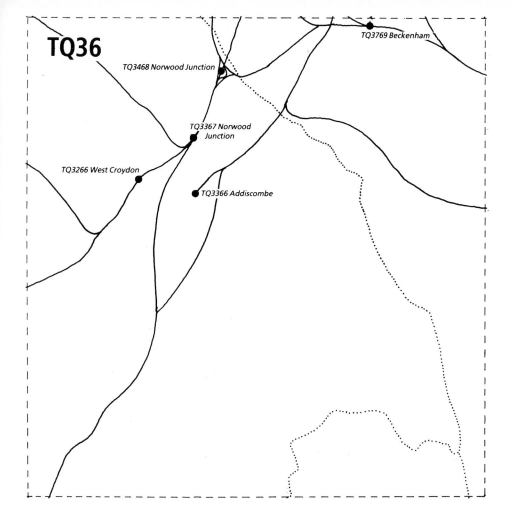

NORWOOD JUNCTION

Site TQ3367.2; On the east side of the line, south of Norwood Junction Station.

Norwood Junction (LB&SCR) [TQ3367.2/1A]
A 1TS dead ended shed, it was located at TQ33976792 and was opened prior to 1868. No further details are known except that the facilities included a turntable and the depot was closed prior to 1911.

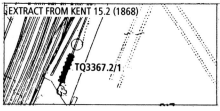

EXTRACT FROM KENT 15.2 (1868)
TQ3367.2/1

Replaced by ...
Site TQ3367.1; In Norwood Junction Yard, south of Norwood Junction Station.

Norwood Junction Yard (LB&SCR) [TQ3367.1/F1]
A servicing area consisting of a coal stage and siding, it was approximately located at TQ33705760. The opening date is not known but it was closed by the SR on the opening of Norwood Junction shed (TQ3468.1/1A) in 1935.

Replaced by ...
Site TQ3468.1: On the east side of the line, north of Norwood Junction Station.

Norwood Junction (SR) [TQ3468.1/1A]
A concrete built 6TS dead ended shed with a corrugated asbestos northlight pattern roof, it was located at TQ34346897 and was opened in 1935. The facilities included a 65ft turntable, water tank and ramped coal stage. The depot was closed by BR on June 5th, 1964 and subsequently demolished.

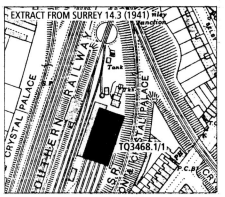

EXTRACT FROM SURREY 14.3 (1941)
TQ3468.1/1

BECKENHAM

Site TQ3769.1; On the north side of the line, at the west end of Beckenham Station.

Beckenham (SER) [TQ3769.1/1A]
A 1TS dead ended shed, it was located at TQ37306990 and was opened on May 3rd, 1858. Details of its construction and facilities are not known. The depot was closed in 1864 and demolished to make way for station enlargements when it became known as Beckenham Junction.

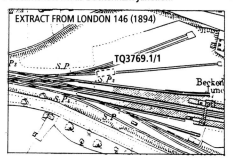

EXTRACT FROM LONDON 146 (1894)
TQ3769.1/1

ADDISCOMBE

Site TQ3366.1; At Addiscombe Station.
Addiscombe (SER) [TQ3366.1/F1]
A servicing area consisting of a turntable, located at TQ33626625, and coal stage, it was opened on April 1st, 1864. No further details are known.

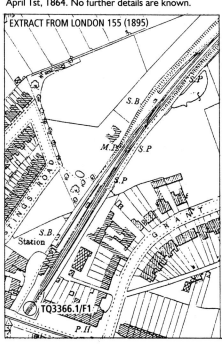

EXTRACT FROM LONDON 155 (1895)
TQ3366.1/F1

WEST CROYDON

Site TQ3266.1; On the west side of the line, at the north end of West Croydon Station.
West Croydon (L&CR) [TQ3266.1/1A]
A brick built 2TS dead ended shed with a slated gable style roof, it was located at TQ32186623 and was opened by the London & Croydon Railway on June 5th, 1839. The facilities included a coal stage, turntable and water column.

It was extended ...
West Croydon (LB&SCR) [TQ3266.1/1B]
The building was lengthened in c1865. The depot was closed by the SR in 1935 and was subsequently demolished.

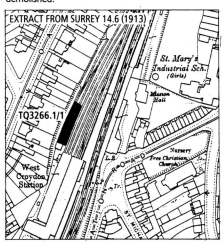

EXTRACT FROM SURREY 14.6 (1913)
TQ3266.1/1

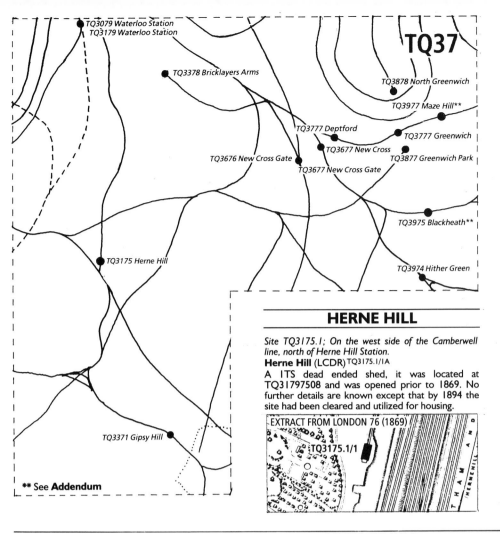

TQ37

- TQ3079 Waterloo Station
- TQ3179 Waterloo Station
- TQ3378 Bricklayers Arms
- TQ3878 North Greenwich
- TQ3977 Maze Hill**
- TQ3777 Deptford
- TQ3777 Greenwich
- TQ3677 New Cross
- TQ3676 New Cross Gate
- TQ3877 Greenwich Park
- TQ3677 New Cross Gate
- TQ3975 Blackheath**
- TQ3175 Herne Hill
- TQ3974 Hither Green
- TQ3371 Gipsy Hill

** See **Addendum**

WATERLOO STATION

Site TQ3079.1; In Waterloo Station.
Waterloo Station (L&SWR) TQ3079.1/1A
A stone built 2TS through road shed with a slated gable style roof, it was located at TQ30997981 and was opened on July 11th, 1848. Details of the facilities are not known. The depot was closed in c1900 as part of the station rebuilding.

Waterloo Station (L&SWR) TQ3079.1/F1
A servicing area consisting of a turntable, located at TQ30907985, and sidings it was opened in 1871. The facility was closed by BR in 1967.

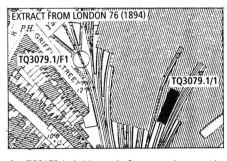

EXTRACT FROM LONDON 76 (1894)

TQ3079.1/F1

TQ3079.1/1

Site TQ3179.1; At Necropolis Station on the east side of the line, south of Waterloo Station.
Waterloo Station (L&SWR) TQ3179.1/F1
A servicing area consisting of a turntable, located at TQ31007943, and sidings it was opened in 1900. The facility was closed at some stage by the SR.

EXTRACT FROM LONDON 5.14 (1912)

TQ3179.1/F1

HERNE HILL

Site TQ3175.1; On the west side of the Camberwell line, north of Herne Hill Station.
Herne Hill (LCDR) TQ3175.1/1A
A 1TS dead ended shed, it was located at TQ31797508 and was opened prior to 1869. No further details are known except that by 1894 the site had been cleared and utilized for housing.

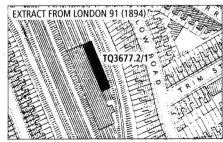

EXTRACT FROM LONDON 76 (1869)

TQ3175.1/1

NEW CROSS

Site TQ3676 & TQ3677.1; On the west side of New Cross Gate Station.
New Cross Gate (L&CR) TQ3677.1/1A
A brick built octagonal roundhouse with a slated roof, it was located at TQ36127702 and was opened by the London & Croydon Railway on June 1st, 1839. Details of the facilities are not known. Although the building was destroyed by a fire on October 14th, 1844 the turntable and spurs were later incorporated into a repair shop.

Replaced by ...
New Cross Gate (LB&SCR) TQ3677.1/2A
A brick built 3TS dead ended shed with a slated gable style roof, it was located at TQ36157701 and was opened in 1845. The building was known as the *"Croydon Shed"*. By the time it was closed the structure was derelict.

New Cross Gate (LB&SCR) TQ3677.1/3A
A brick built 3TS dead ended shed with a slated gable style roof, it was located at TQ36117713 and was opened in 1848. The building was known as the *"Middle Shed"* and it was destroyed in a gale in October 1863.

It was rebuilt ...
New Cross Gate (LB&SCR) TQ3677.1/3B
The building was totally rebuilt in 1863/4 to its original specification.

New Cross Gate (LB&SCR) TQ3676.1/1A
A brick built roundhouse with a slated conical roof, it was located at TQ36147696 and was opened in 1869. The building was known as the *"Rooter Shed"*

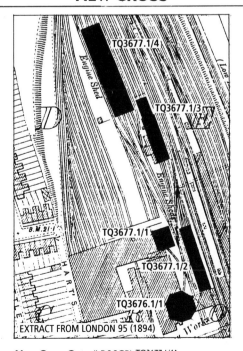

TQ3677.1/4

Engine Shed

TQ3677.1/3

Engine Shed

B.M.2/1

TQ3677.1/1

TQ3677.1/2

TQ3676.1/1

HART'S

EXTRACT FROM LONDON 95 (1894)

New Cross Gate (LB&SCR) TQ3677.1/4A
A brick built 4TS through road shed with a slated gable style roof, it was located at TQ36077719 and was opened in 1882. The building was known as the *"New Shed"*.

It was rebuilt ...
New Cross Gate (LB&SCR) TQ3677.1/4B
At some stage prior to 1929 it was rebuilt with a twin slated gable style roof.

The depot accumulated all facilities and was closed as a running shed by the SR in June 1947. It lasted into BR days as an Engine Repair Depot and was finally closed on May 23rd, 1949 afterwhich it was utilized for storing locomotives until 1951. The whole site was demolished and replaced by emu sidings.

Site TQ3677.2; On the east side of the line, north of New Cross Station.
New Cross (Met) TQ3677.2/1A
A brick built 2TS through road building, it was part of a combined locomotive and carriage shed and was located at TQ36577755. It was opened on October 6th, 1884 and closed on December 2nd, 1906. No further details are known except that the building was then converted for alternative use and was still standing in 1996.

EXTRACT FROM LONDON 91 (1894)

TQ3677.2/1

BRICKLAYERS ARMS

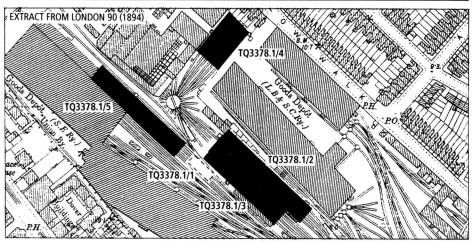

EXTRACT FROM LONDON 90 (1894)

TQ3378.1/4
TQ3378.1/5
TQ3378.1/2
TQ3378.1/1
TQ3378.1/3

Site TQ3378.1; In Bricklayers Arms Goods Depot, at the end of Bricklayers Arms branch.
Bricklayers Arms (SER) TQ3378.1/1A
A brick built 2TS shed with a slated pitched roof, it was located at TQ33447873 and was opened on May 1st, 1844. Details of the facilities are not known. It was closed in 1869 and demolished.

Bricklayers Arms (SER) TQ3378.1/2A
A brick built 4TS through road shed with a twin slated gable style roof, it was located at TQ33507872 and was opened in 1847.

The shed was re-roofed ...
Bricklayers Arms (SR) TQ3378.1/2B
A corrugated asbestos northlight pattern roof was installed in 1937.

Adjoined by ...
Bricklayers Arms (SER) TQ3378.1/3A
A brick built 4TS shed with one through road and a slated twin gable style roof, it was built along the south wall of the existing shed (TQ3378.1/2). It was located at TQ33487870 and was opened in 1865. The combined building became known as the "Old Shed" in 1869.

The shed was re-roofed ...
Bricklayers Arms (BR) TQ3378.1/3B
The building was re-roofed by the Southern Region in 1952 with a standard corrugated asbestos louvre pitched style over each track.

Bricklayers Arms (SER) TQ3378.1/4A
A brick built 6TS dead ended shed with a slated twin gable style roof, it was located at TQ33457885 and was opened in 1869. It became known as the "New Shed".

The shed was modified ...
Bricklayers Arms (SR) TQ3378.1/4B
The building was reduced to a 4TS structure in 1938. It became roofless as a result of bomb damage during the war and was utilized for storing locomotives.

Bricklayers Arms (SECR) TQ3378.1/5A
A brick built 4TS dead ended shed, it was located at TQ33367879 and was converted from a carriage shed in 1902. It was known as "St.Patricks Shed".

The shed was re-roofed ...
Bricklayers Arms (SR) TQ3378.1/5B
A northlight pattern roof was installed in 1937.

The facilities included a turntable, coaling plant, water tank and repair shop. The depot was closed by BR on June 17th, 1962.

NORTH GREENWICH

Site TQ3878.1; On the east side of North Greenwich Station.
North Greenwich (MER) TQ3878.1/1A
A brick built 1TS dead ended shed with a slated gable style roof, it was located at TQ38337831 and was opened by the Millwall Extension Railway on July 29th, 1872. Details of the facilities are not known. The line was worked by the GER and the depot was closed by the LNER in 1926.

TQ3878.1/1

EXTRACT FROM LONDON 10.1 (1916)

GREENWICH

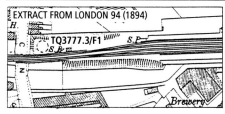

EXTRACT FROM LONDON 94 (1894)

TQ3777.3/F1

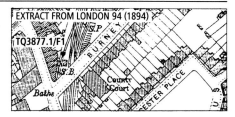

EXTRACT FROM LONDON 94 (1894)

TQ3877.1/F1

Site TQ3777.3; On the north side of the line, at the west end of Greenwich Station.
Greenwich (SER) TQ3777.3/F1
A servicing area consisting of a turntable, approximately located at TQ37787733, and siding. No further details are known.

Site TQ3877.1; On the west side of the line, at the south end of Greenwich Park Station.
Greenwich Park (LCDR) TQ3877.1/F1
A servicing area consisting of a siding, it was located at TQ38287736 and was opened on October 1st, 1888. The facility was closed on January 1st, 1917.

DEPTFORD

Site TQ3777.1; In the vicinity of Deptford Station, at a lower level than the main line.
Deptford (L&GR) TQ3777.1/1A
An engine shed, and workshops, were established under the arches of the viaduct. They were opened by the London & Greenwich Railway on February 8th, 1836. Access to the depot, which was approximately located at TQ37157737 and had coke and water facilities, was via an incline. It was closed in 1839.

Replaced by ...
Site TQ3777.2; On the south side of the line, at the west end of Deptford Station.
Deptford (L&GR) TQ3777.2/1A
A brick built 1TS dead ended shed with a slated pitched roof, it was located at TQ37157738 and was opened in 1839. An unusual feature was that a signal box straddled the entrance. The facilities included a coke/coal stage and water tank.

Deptford (L&GR) TQ3777.2/2A
A brick built 3TS dead ended shed, it was converted from a works building sited at the west end of the shed yard and opened in 1864. It was located at TQ37097741 and shared the facilities of TQ3777.2/1.

The depot was closed in 1903 and both buildings were later demolished.

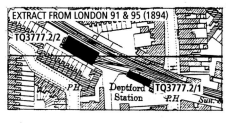

EXTRACT FROM LONDON 91 & 95 (1894)

TQ3777.2/2
Deptford TQ3777.2/1
Station

HITHER GREEN

Site TQ3974.1; On the east side of the line, at the south end of Hither Green Station.
Hither Green (SR) TQ3974.1/1A
A concrete built 6TS dead ended shed with a corrugated asbestos northlight pattern roof, it was located at TQ39227423 and was opened on September 10th, 1933. The facilities included a ramped coaling stage, 65ft turntable and water tank. The depot was closed to steam by BR in October 1961 and was utilized for servicing diesel locomotives. It was still operational in 1996.

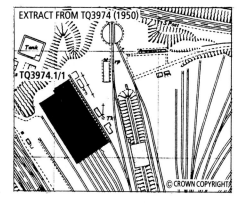

EXTRACT FROM TQ3974 (1950)

Tank

TQ3974.1/1

© CROWN COPYRIGHT

GIPSY HILL

Site TQ3371.1; On the south side of the line, at the west end of Gipsy Hill Station.
Gipsy Hill (LB&SCR) TQ3371.1/F1
A servicing point consisting of a turntable, approximately located at TQ33057133, and siding. No further details are known.

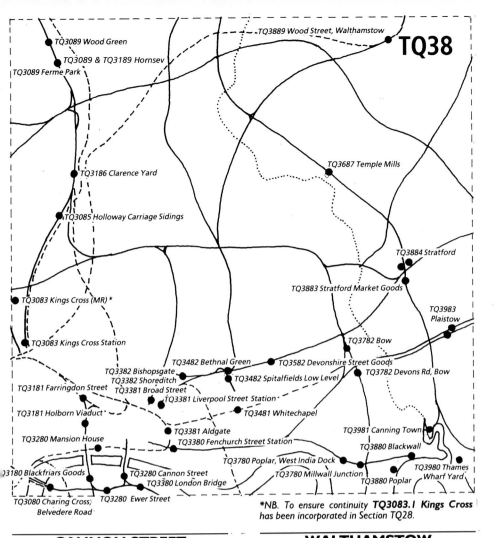

TQ3889 Wood Street, Walthamstow

TQ38

TQ3089 Wood Green

TQ3089 & TQ3189 Hornsey

TQ3089 Ferme Park

TQ3186 Clarence Yard

TQ3687 Temple Mills

TQ3085 Holloway Carriage Sidings

TQ3884 Stratford

TQ3883 Stratford Market Goods

TQ3983 Plaistow

TQ3083 Kings Cross (MR) *

TQ3782 Bow

TQ3083 Kings Cross Station

TQ3482 Bethnal Green

TQ3582 Devonshire Street Goods

TQ3382 Bishopsgate

TQ3782 Devons Rd, Bow

TQ3382 Shoreditch

TQ3482 Spitalfields Low Level

TQ3181 Farringdon Street

TQ3381 Broad Street

TQ3381 Liverpool Street Station

TQ3181 Holborn Viaduct

TQ3481 Whitechapel

TQ3280 Mansion House

TQ3381 Aldgate

TQ3981 Canning Town

TQ3380 Fenchurch Street Station

TQ3880 Blackwall

3180 Blackfriars Goods

TQ3780 Poplar, West India Dock

TQ3980 Thames Wharf Yard

TQ3280 Cannon Street

TQ3780 Millwall Junction

TQ3380 London Bridge

TQ3880 Poplar

TQ3080 Charing Cross, Belvedere Road

TQ3280 Ewer Street

*NB. To ensure continuity **TQ3083.1 Kings Cross** has been incorporated in Section TQ28.

CANNON STREET

Site TQ3280.2; On the east side of the line at the south end of the river bridge, south of Cannon Street Station.
Cannon Street (SER) TQ3280.2/1A
A brick built 5TS dead ended shed with a transverse multi-pitched roof, it was located at TQ32538037 and was opened on September 1st, 1866. The facilities included a turntable, from which access to the shed was gained, coal stage and water column. The depot was closed by the SR in 1924 and partially demolished, the remainder being incorporated into a building housing an electricity sub-station.

Site TQ3280.3; On the west side of the line at the south end of the river bridge, south of Cannon Street Station.
Cannon Street (SER) TQ3280.3/F1
A servicing area consisting of a turntable, located at TQ32488037, water column and coal stage. The turntable was removed at an unknown date and the facility was closed by BR in the 1960s.

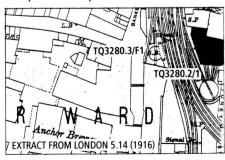

EXTRACT FROM LONDON 5.14 (1916)

TQ3280.3/F1

TQ3280.2/1

WALTHAMSTOW

Site TQ3889.1; On the west side of the line, north of Wood Street Station.
Wood Street, Walthamstow (GER) TQ3889.1/1A
A brick built 2TS through road shed with a slated gable style roof, it was located at TQ38608964 and was opened in 1879. The facilities included a coal stage.

The shed was extended in 1898 ...
Wood Street, Walthamstow (GER) TQ3889.1/1B
The building was extended at the southern end, doubling its length.

The building was modified ...
Wood Street, Walthamstow (LNER) TQ3889.1/1C
At some stage the brick gable ends and arched entrances were replaced with a single lintel and wooden gable. The roof was probably refurbished at the same time. The depot was closed by BR in 1960 and demolished.

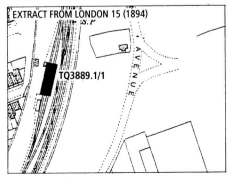

EXTRACT FROM LONDON 15 (1894)

TQ3889.1/1

BOW

Site TQ3782.1; In the fork of the Poplar and Bromley Junction lines, at Bow Junction.
Bow (NLR) TQ3782.1/1A
A brick built 6TS dead ended shed with a transverse multi-pitched slate and glass roof, it was located at TQ37448277 and was opened by the North London Railway at some time after 1850. Details of the facilities are not known. It was closed in 1882 and incorporated into the works, being utilized until BR days when the whole site was demolished.

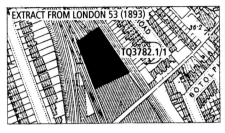

EXTRACT FROM LONDON 53 (1893)

TQ3782.1/1

Replaced by ...
Site TQ3782.2; On the east side of the Poplar line, south of Bow Station.
Devons Road No.1 (NLR) TQ3782.2/1A
A brick built 10TS dead ended shed with a north-light pattern roof, it was located at TQ37808200 and was opened by the North London Railway in 1882. The facilities included a coal stage, water tank and turntable.

The shed was rebuilt in 1946 ...
Devons Road No.1 (LMS) TQ3782.2/1B
A louvre style roof was installed and the accommodation reduced to 9TS. The depot was closed to steam by BR on August 25th, 1958 and became the first shed on the system to exclusively house diesel locomotives. It was totally closed on February 10th, 1964 and was subsequently demolished.

Devons Road No.2 (NLR) TQ3782.2/2A
A brick built 10TS dead ended shed with a north-light pattern roof, it was located at TQ37858202 and was opened by the North London Railway in 1882. The building was demolished by the LMS in 1935 and the site given over to sidings.

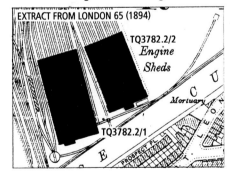

EXTRACT FROM LONDON 65 (1894)

TQ3782.2/2 *Engine Sheds*

TQ3782.2/1

HOLLOWAY

Site TQ3085.1; On the west side of the line, south of Holloway Station.
Holloway Carriage Sidings (GNR) TQ3085.1/F1
A servicing area consisting of a turntable, located at TQ30648530, sidings and engine pits, it was opened in 1885. The closure date is not known.

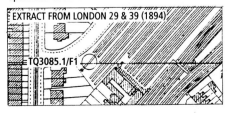

EXTRACT FROM LONDON 29 & 39 (1894)

TQ3085.1/F1

BROAD ST & LIVERPOOL ST

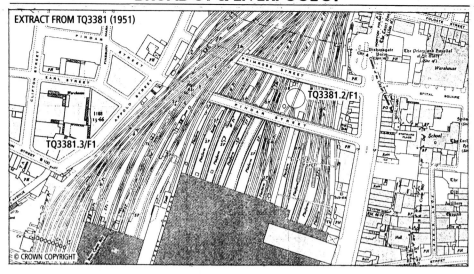

EXTRACT FROM TQ3381 (1951)

TQ3381.3/F1

TQ3381.2/F1

© CROWN COPYRIGHT

Site TQ3381.3; In the vicinity of Broad Street Station.
Broad Street (LNWR/NLR) TQ3381.3/F1
A number of coaling stages, water tanks and engine sidings were opened by the L&NWR and North London Railway on November 1st, 1865. It is not possible to define each of the numerous sites which were relocated several times during their existence but the approximate position of these was TQ331818. The surviving facilities were closed by BR at the end of steam on the line.

Site TQ3381.2; In Liverpool Street Station.
Liverpool Street (GE) TQ3381.2/F1
A number of coal stages, water columns and engine pits were provided from the opening of the station on February 2nd, 1874. A turntable was also provided and this was located at TQ33088188. Over the years the facilities were moved as station improvements were made. The servicing areas became redundant on September 9th, 1962 and a diesel stabling point was established in the bay platform at TQ33288182.

PLAISTOW

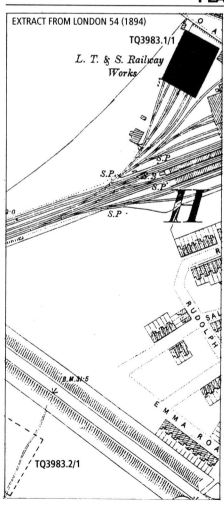

EXTRACT FROM LONDON 54 (1894)

TQ3983.1/1

L. T. & S. Railway Works

TQ3983.2/1

Site TQ3983.1; On the north side of Plaistow Station.
Plaistow (LT&SR) TQ3983.1/1A
A brick built 6TS dead ended shed with a slated gable style triple pitched roof, it was located at TQ39928335 and was opened in 1896. The facilities included a coal stage. The depot was closed in 1911 and it was absorbed as part of the adjacent works.

Replaced by ...
Site TQ3983.2; On the south side of the line, west of Plaistow Station.
Plaistow (LT&SR) TQ3983.2/1A
A brick built 8TS dead ended shed with a slated four-pitched gable style roof, it was located at TQ39748301 and was opened in 1911. The facilities included a ramped coal stage with water tank over and a turntable. The depot was closed by BR on November 2nd, 1959 and was subsequently demolished.

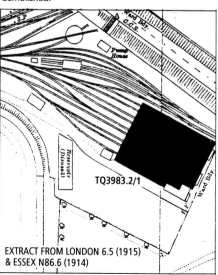

TQ3983.2/1

EXTRACT FROM LONDON 6.5 (1915)
& ESSEX N86.6 (1914)

POPLAR

Site TQ3880.2; On the north side of Poplar (MR) Goods Station.
Poplar (MR) TQ3880.2/1A
A timber built 1TS dead ended shed, it was opened in March 1890 and is believed to have been located at TQ38608062. No further details are known.

POPLAR EAST WARD

TQ3880.2/1

EXTRACT FROM ESSEX N86.13 (1916)

Site TQ3780.1; At the west end of Poplar (MR) Coal Depot.
Poplar, West India Dock (MR) TQ3780.1/1A
An unusual 1TS depot consisting of a track running between a set of brick arches supporting the sidings adjacent to West India Dock (GER) Station. It was located at TQ37288069 and housed a Battery Electric shunting locomotive. No further details are known except that during BR days it housed BEL1 (formerly MR No.1550) and was probably dispensed with upon the withdrawal of the locomotive.

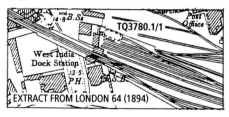

TQ3780.1/1

West India Dock Station

EXTRACT FROM LONDON 64 (1894)

MILLWALL JUNCTION

Site TQ3780.2; On the south side of the line, at the west end of Millwall Junction Station.
Millwall Junction (GER) TQ3780.2/1A
A brick built 3TS through road building with a slated gable style roof, it was located at TQ37908062. It had originally been constructed as a goods shed by the GNR and was purchased by the Great Eastern Railway in 1871 for conversion to an engine and carriage shed. The two southernmost bays formed the loco shed and the facilities included a coal stage and water column. The depot was closed by the LNER in May 1926 and the building then reverted back to goods use. It has since been demolished.

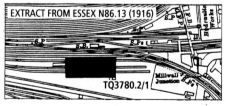

EXTRACT FROM ESSEX N86.13 (1916)

TQ3780.2/1

Millwall Junction

FENCHURCH ST. STATION

Site TQ3380.2; On the north side of the line, east of Fenchurch Street Station.
Fenchurch Street Station (GER) TQ3380.2/F1
A servicing point consisting of a turntable, located at TQ33658086, and siding. The opening and closure dates are not known.

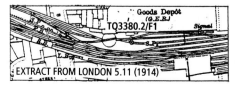

Goods Depot (G.E.R.)

TQ3380.2/F1

EXTRACT FROM LONDON 5.11 (1914)

BISHOPSGATE

Site TQ3382.2; In Bishopsgate Goods Station.
Bishopsgate* (ECR)^{TQ3382.2/F1}
Some sort of facility was established here by the Eastern Counties Railway on July 1st, 1840. No further details are known.

Replaced by ...
Bishopsgate (GER)^{TQ3382.2/1A}
A ITS through road shed, probably constructed in brick with a slated gable style roof, was opened here at an unknown date. It was located at TQ33748222 and was closed by BR in 1965. No further details are known.

Site TQ3382.1; In the vicinity of Shoreditch (N&ER) Station.
Shoreditch (N&ER)^{TQ3382.1/F1}
A servicing area consisting of a coal stage and engine pit, it was opened by the Northern & Eastern Railway on July 1st, 1840. No further details are known

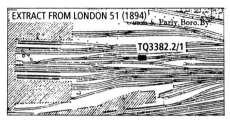
EXTRACT FROM LONDON 51 (1894)
TQ3382.2/1

*Known as Shoreditch until July 27th, 1846

DEVONSHIRE ST. GOODS

Site TQ3582.1; On the south side of the line, at the east end of Devonshire Street Station.
Devonshire Street Goods (GER)^{TQ3582.1/F1}
A servicing facility consisting of a coal stage, it was located at TQ35598262 and was opened in 1888. It was dispensed with by BR in 1956 when the duties were taken over by diesel shunters.

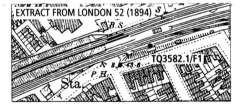
EXTRACT FROM LONDON 52 (1894)
TQ3582.1/F1

CHARING CROSS

Site TQ3080.1; On the south side of the line, at the east end of Hungerford Bridge.
Belvedere Road (SER)^{TQ3080.1/1A}
A brick built ITS through road tank shed, it was located at TQ30768015 and was opened on January 11th, 1864. The facilities also included a coal stage, sited outside of the shed entrance, and a turntable. At an unknown date the shed was demolished.

A servicing point was then established ...
Belvedere Road (SER)^{TQ3080.1/F1}
It is believed that the turntable, coal stage and siding were then utilized for a short while. The facility was removed prior to 1894 to accommodate track widening.

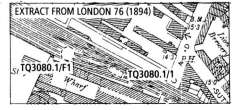
EXTRACT FROM LONDON 76 (1894)
TQ3080.1/F1   TQ3080.1/1

ALDGATE

Site TQ3381.1; On the west side of the line at the north end of Aldgate (Met) Station.
Aldgate (Met)^{TQ3381.1/1A}
A ITS dead ended shed, probably built in brick with a slated gable style roof, it was located at TQ33558132 and was opened on November 18th, 1876. The facilities included a coal stage and water column. The building was closed and demolished in 1880.

Replaced by ...
Aldgate (Met)^{TQ3381.1/F1}
A servicing point consisting of an engine pit, coal stage and water columns was established on the same site. The facility was closed on November 5th,1905.

EXTRACT FROM LONDON 5.11 (1914)
TQ3381.1/1

CANNING TOWN

Site TQ3981.1; On the south side of the Blackwall Pepper Warehouse branch, west of Canning Town Station.
Canning Town (GER)^{TQ3981.1/F1}
A servicing area consisting of a coal stage, engine pit and water column, it was located at TQ39178132. The opening and closing dates are not known but the facility was utilized into BR days.

EXTRACT FROM ESSEX N86.9 (1916)
TQ3981.1/F1

EWER STREET

Site TQ3280.4; On the north side of the Blackfriars line, west of London Bridge Station.
Ewer Street (SECR)^{TQ3280.4/F1}
A servicing area consisting of a turntable, located at TQ32028011, coal stage and water tank, it was opened in 1899. The facility was closed by BR in 1961.

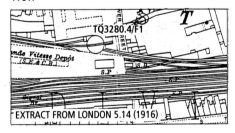
TQ3280.4/F1
EXTRACT FROM LONDON 5.14 (1916)

MANSION HOUSE

Site TQ3280.1; In the vicinity of Mansion House Station.
Mansion House (District)^{TQ3280.1/F1}
An underground servicing facility consisting of a coal stage and water tank, it was approximately located at TQ32308095 and was opened by the District Railway on July 3rd, 1871. The facility was probably dispensed with on October 6th, 1884 when the Circle Line was completed.

BLACKWALL

Site TQ3380.1; On the south side of the line, west of Blackwall Station.
Blackwall (London & Blackwall)^{TQ3380.1/1A}
A ITS through road shed, probably built in brick with a slated gable style roof, it was located at TQ38568067 and was opened in 1849 by the London & Blackwall Railway. Details of the facilities are not known. The depot was closed by the GER in 1872 and demolished.

Replaced by ...
Blackwall (GER)^{TQ3380.1/F1}
A servicing area consisting of an engine pit and siding was established, possibly on the same site, in 1872. The facility was dispensed with by the LNER in 1926.

EXTRACT FROM LONDON 65 (1894)
TQ3880.1/1

BLACKFRIARS

Site TQ3180.1; On the west side of the line, south of Blackfriars Goods Station.
Blackfriars Goods (SER)^{TQ3180.1/F1}
A servicing area consisting of a turntable, located at TQ31728029, and coal stage, it was opened on June 1st, 1864. The facility was originally provided for the station when it was a passenger terminus and continued to be utilized when it was turned over to goods use. The closure date is not known.

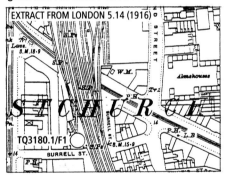
EXTRACT FROM LONDON 5.14 (1916)
TQ3180.1/F1

FARRINGDON STREET

Site TQ3181.1; On the west side of the line, at the north end of Farringdon Street Station.
Farringdon Street (GWR/Met)^{TQ3181.1/1A}
A brick built ITS dead ended shed, probably with a slated gable style roof, it was located at TQ31568190 and was opened on January 10th, 1863. The facilities included a 45ft turntable sited outside of the shed entrance. The depot was closed in 1865 and demolished to make way for the line to Moorgate.

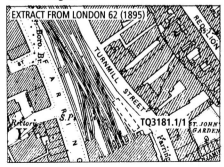
EXTRACT FROM LONDON 62 (1895)
TQ3181.1/1

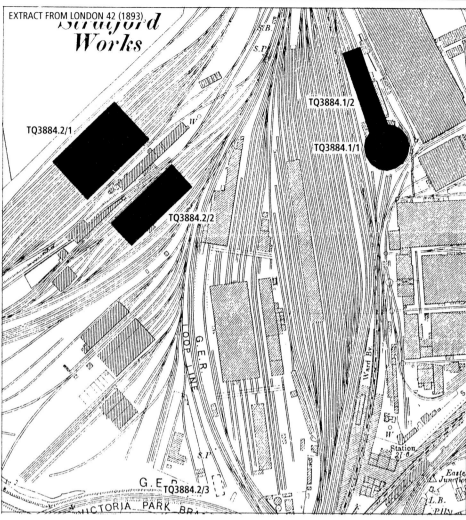

EXTRACT FROM LONDON 42 (1893)

Stratford Works

TQ3884.2/1

TQ3884.1/2

TQ3884.1/1

TQ3884.2/2

TQ3884.2/3

G.E.R. LOOP LINE

G.E.R.

VICTORIA PARK BRA

Site TQ3884.1; On the east side of the Cambridge line, north of Stratford Station.

Stratford (N&ER) TQ3884.1/1A

A brick built polygonal 1RH shed with a slated conical roof, it was located at TQ38588484 and was opened by the Northern & Eastern Railway in 1840. It was adjacent to the works complex and had use of all facilities.

It may have been extended ...

Stratford (N&ER) TQ3884.1/2A

A brick built 4TS structure was added on the northern side of the roundhouse (TQ3884.1/1) with two of the tracks linking the two buildings. It was located at TQ38568490 and was opened prior to 1867. The precise function of the building is not known but it is assumed that at some stage it formed some part of the running shed.

The depot was closed in 1887 and absorbed into the adjacent works.

Site TQ3884.2; On the west side of the Cambridge line, north of Stratford Station.

Stratford (GER) TQ3884.2/2A

A brick built 6TS through road shed with a slated twin gable style roof, it was located at TQ38348478 and was opened in 1871. It was known as the "New Shed" and the facilities included a coal stage, water tank and turntable.

Stratford (GER) TQ3884.2/1A

A brick built 12TS through road shed with a slated and glazed northlight pattern roof, it was located at TQ38278480 and was opened in 1887. It was known as the "Jubilee Shed" and was sited just north of the "New Shed".

After 1895 it was extended ...

Stratford (GER) TQ3884.2/1B

The building was extended at its south western end by 150ft.

It was re-roofed ...

Stratford (LNER) TQ3884.2/1C

At some stage it was rebuilt with a transverse multi-pitched roof.

It was re-roofed again ...

Stratford (BR) TQ3884.2/1D

The depot was rebuilt in 1949 by the Eastern Region with a louvre style roof and brick screen.

The building was reduced in size ...

Stratford (BR) TQ3884.2/1E

To accommodate a new diesel maintenance shed the northern part of the building was demolished in c1960 reducing it to a 6TS shed.

The shed was closed to steam by BR in September 1962 and a large diesel depot established on the site. The Jubilee Shed (TQ3884.2/1) was subsequently demolished but the New Shed (TQ3884.2/2) was used to store part of BRs collection of preserved steam locomotives prior to their dispersal.

Stratford Departmental Shed (GER) TQ3884.2/3A

A corrugated iron 2TS dead ended shed with a slated gable style pitched roof, it was located at TQ38418451 and was brought into use at some time after 1900. It housed the works locos and they used the facilities at the main depot. The depot was closed by BR upon the withdrawal of Service Locomotive No.33 in December 1963, but was not demolished until the 1980s.

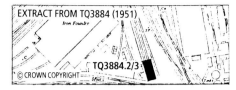

EXTRACT FROM TQ3884 (1951)

Iron Foundry

TQ3884.2/3

© CROWN COPYRIGHT

Site TQ3883.1; On the west side of the line, at the south end of Stratford Market Goods Depot.

Stratford Market Goods (GER) TQ3883.1/F1

A servicing area consisting of a water column, engine pit and siding, it was located at TQ39018335 and was opened in c1900. No further details are known.

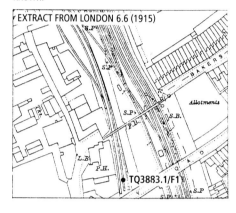

EXTRACT FROM LONDON 6.6 (1915)

Allotments

TQ3883.1/F1

SPITALFIELDS

Site TQ3482.1; In the fork of the Spitalfields Coal depot branch and the main line, west of Bethnal Green Station.

Bethnal Green (GER) TQ3482.1/1A

A brick built 1TS dead ended shed with a slated gable style roof, it was located at TQ34488226 and was opened in 1866. The facilities included a coal stage and water column sited outside of the shed entrance. The depot was closed by BR in 1960 and was subsequently demolished.

EXTRACT FROM LONDON 51 (1894)

West Junction

TQ3482.1/1

Site TQ3482.2; On the east side of the line, north of Whitechapel (Low Level) Station.

Spitalfields Low Level* (ELR) TQ3482.2/F1

A servicing area consisting of a coal stage, engine pit and water column, it was located at TQ34518208 and was opened by the East London Railway at some time after 1894. The facility was closed by BR in 1951.

TQ3482.2/F1

EXTRACT FROM LONDON 5.11 (1914)

*Also known as Whitechapel Sidings

KINGS CROSS STATION

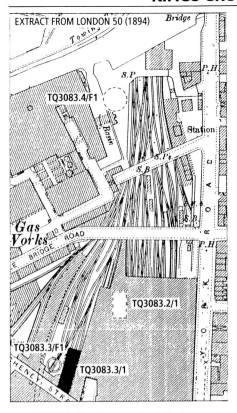

Site TQ3083.2; On the west side of the line, at the north end of Kings Cross Station.
Kings Cross Station (GNR) TQ3083.2/1A
A brick built 3TS dead ended shed with a slated gable style roof, it was converted from a carriage shed in 1862 and was located at TQ30248323. The facilities included a 42ft turntable and coal stage. The depot was closed in 1873 and demolished to accommodate station enlargements.

Replaced by ...
Site TQ3083.3; On the west side of Kings Cross Station.
Kings Cross Station (GNR) TQ3083.3/1A
A brick built 3TS dead ended shed with a slated gable style roof, it was located at TQ30208317 and was opened in 1873. The facilities included a coal stage, turntable and water tank. The depot was closed in 1893 and demolished.

A servicing point was then established ...
Kings Cross Station (GNR) TQ3083.3/F1
The turntable and coal stage with some sidings were retained as a facility until it was closed by the LNER in 1924 to accommodate further station enlargements.

WOOD GREEN

Site TQ3089.2; On the west side of the line, north of Hornsey Station.
Wood Green (GNR) TQ3089.2/1A
A brick built 2TS dead ended shed with a slated gable style roof, it was located at TQ30688985 and was opened in 1866. The facilities included a coal stage and water tank. The depot was closed in 1899 and demolished.

Replaced by ...
Site TQ3083.4; On the west side of the line, north of Kings Cross Station.
Kings Cross Station (LNER) TQ3083.4/F1
A servicing area consisting of a turntable, located at TQ30238343, water columns and coal stage (later replaced with a small mechanical coaling plant), it was opened in 1924. The facility was closed by BR in 1965 and remodelled as a diesel stabling point with fuel tanks and inspection shed (TQ3083.4/1A) established on the site. It was totally closed in 1980 and subsequently demolished.

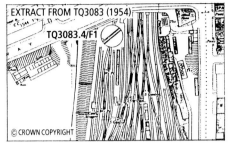

© CROWN COPYRIGHT

HOLBORN VIADUCT

Site TQ3181.1; On the east side of Holborn Viaduct Station.
Holborn Viaduct (LC&DR) TQ3181.1/1A
A brick built 1TS dead ended tankshed, it was located at TQ31698128 and was opened on March 2nd, 1874. The closure date is not known but the building remained standing, virtually intact, until it was demolished in the late 1980s.

CLARENCE YARD

Site TQ3186.1; On the west side of the line, south of Finsbury Park Station.
Clarence Yard (GNR) TQ3186.1/F1
A servicing area consisting of a coal stage and siding, it was located at TQ31128606 and was opened in about 1890. It was closed by BR in c1952.

TEMPLE MILLS

Site TQ3687.1; On the west side of the line, at the north end of Temple Mills Marshalling Yard.
Temple Mills (GER) TQ3687.1/F1
A servicing area consisting of a turntable, located at TQ36768657, coal stage, water tank, engine pit and siding, it was opened in 1883. The facility was closed by BR in 1967.

FERME PARK & HORNSEY

Site TQ3089.3; On the east side of Hornsey Station.
Hornsey (GNR) TQ3089.3/1A
A 2TS dead ended shed, located at TQ30928924 and opened in August 1850. No further details are known except that it probably closed in 1866, upon the opening of Wood Green shed (TQ3089.2/1A) and was later demolished to make way for track widening.

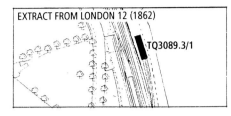

Site TQ3089.1; On the west side of the line, at the south end of Hornsey Station.
Ferme Park (GNR) TQ3089.1/F1
A servicing point consisting of a turntable, located at TQ30938907, siding and coal stage, it was opened in 1891. The turntable was removed in 1929 but the facility remained in use for some years afterwards.

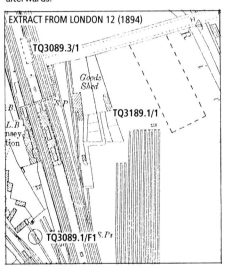

Site TQ3189.1; On the east side of Hornsey Station.
Hornsey (GNR) TQ3189.1/1A
A brick built 8TS dead ended shed with a slated northlight pattern roof, it was located at TQ31058922 and was opened in 1899. The facilities included a 52ft turntable, water tank and a ramped coal stage.

The shed was re-roofed ...
Hornsey (BR) TQ3189.1/1B
The shed was rebuilt in 1955 by the Eastern Region with an asbestos transverse multi-pitched style roof. The depot was closed to steam in July 1961 and was utilized as a diesel depot until c1971. The building was still standing in 1996, in use as part of Hornsey emu depot.

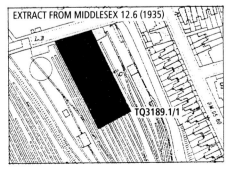

LONDON BRIDGE

Site TQ3380.1; At the east end of London Bridge Station.

London Bridge (LB&SCR) [TQ3380.1/F1]
A servicing area consisting of a turntable, located at TQ33178003, coal stage and sidings, it was opened on August 13th, 1866. The closure date is not known.

WHITECHAPEL

Site TQ3481.1; On the north side of the line, at the west end of Whitechapel (MetDist) Station.

Whitechapel (MetDist) [TQ3481.1/1A]
A 1TS dead ended shed, it was located at TQ34518180 and was opened by the Metropolitan District Railway in 1882. Details of its construction and facilities are not known. The depot was closed on June 2nd, 1902 upon the extension of the line eastwards.

THAMES WHARF YARD

Site TQ3980.1; In Thames Wharf Yard, south of the line, east of Canning Town Station.

Thames Wharf Yard (GER) [TQ3980.1/F1]
A servicing area consisting of a water column and coaling stage, it was located at TQ39908050. No further details are known.

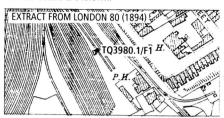

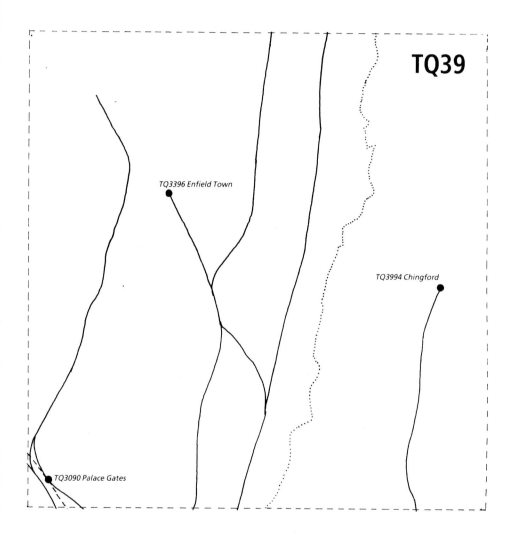

PALACE GATES

Site TQ3090.1; On the east side of the line, at the north end of Palace Gates Station.

Palace Gates (GER) [TQ3090.1/1A]
A brick built 2TS dead ended shed with a slated gable style roof, it was located at TQ30179093 and was opened on October 7th, 1878. The facilities included a water tank, coal stage and turntable. The depot was closed by BR in 1954 and was subsequently demolished. The site was later incorporated into the shed yard of Bounds Green HST depot.

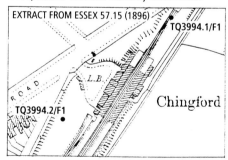

CHINGFORD

Site TQ3994.1; At the north end of Chingford Station.

Chingford (GER) [TQ3994.1/F1]
A servicing area consisting of an engine pit and sidings, it was located at TQ39259468. It was opened in September 1878 and closed by BR in c1960.

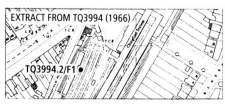

Site TQ3994.2; On the west side of Chingford Station.

Chingford (GER*) [TQ3994.2/F1]
A servicing area consisting of engine pits, sidings and water columns, it was located at TQ39169459. The opening date is not known but it was closed by BR in c1960.

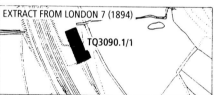

*It may have possibly been opened during LNER days

ENFIELD

Site TQ3396.1; On the west side of Enfield Town Station.

Enfield (ECR) [TQ3396.1/1A]
A 1TS shed, probably built in brick, it was located at TQ33059645 and was opened by the Eastern Counties Railway on March 1st, 1849. No further details are known except that it was closed in 1866.

Replaced, on the same site, by ...

Enfield Town (GER) [TQ3396.1/1B]
A brick built 1TS through road shed with a slated gable style roof, it was opened in 1869. The facilities included a turntable and water columns. The depot was closed by BR on November 30th, 1960.

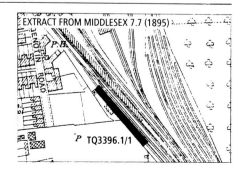

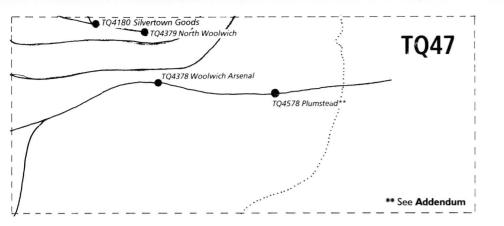

TQ47

** See **Addendum**

NORTH WOOLWICH

Site TQ4379.1; On the south side of the line, at the west end of North Woolwich Station.
North Woolwich (NWR) [TQ4379.1/F1]
A servicing area consisting of a water tank, coal stage and turntable, it was located at TQ43127988 and was opened on June 14th, 1867. The closure date is not known.

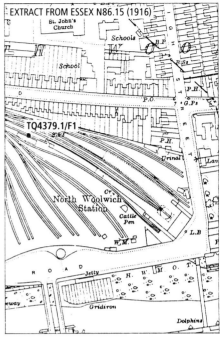

SILVERTOWN GOODS

Site TQ4279.1; On the north side of the goods branch, at the west end of Silvertown Station.
Silvertown Goods Yard (GER) [TQ4279.1/F1]
A servicing area consisting of water column and stand siding, it was located at TQ41858011. The opening date is not known but it was closed by BR on June 18th, 1951.

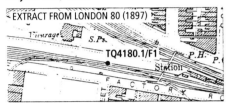

WOOLWICH ARSENAL

Site TQ4378.1; On the south side of the line, east of Woolwich Arsenal Station.
Woolwich Arsenal (SER) [TQ4378.1/1A]
A curved brick built 2TS dead ended shed with a slated gable style pitched roof, it was located at TQ43847878 and was opened in the 1840s. The facilities included a turntable and coal stage. The depot was closed in 1899 and subsequently demolished.

GOODMAYES

Site TQ4687.1; On the north side of the line, east of Goodmayes Station.
Goodmayes (GER) [TQ4687.1/F1]
A servicing area consisting of a turntable, located at TQ46818744, engine pit and coal stage. The opening and closing dates are not known.

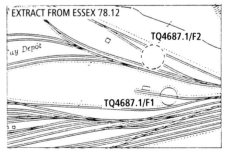

It was re-sited ...
Goodmayes (LNER) [TQ4687.1/F2]
A servicing area consisting of a turntable, located at TQ46798747, coal stage and water columns. It was re-located to accommodate the extension of the sidings into a marshalling yard. The opening and closing dates are not known.

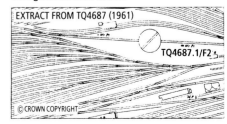

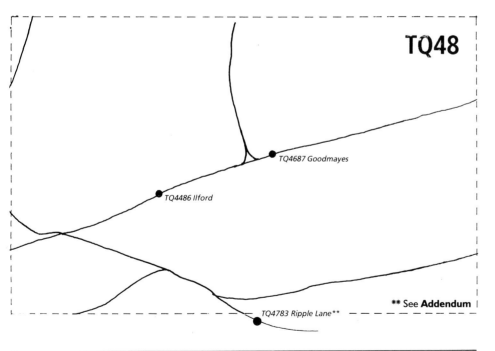

TQ48

** See **Addendum**

ILFORD

Site TQ4486.1; On the north side of the line, west of Seven Kings Station.
Ilford (GER) [TQ4486.1/1A]
A brick built 3TS dead ended shed with a northlight pattern roof, it was located at TQ44508695 and was opened in 1901. The facilities included a coal stage and water tank. The depot was closed by the LNER in May 1939 and demolished.

HERTFORDSHIRE

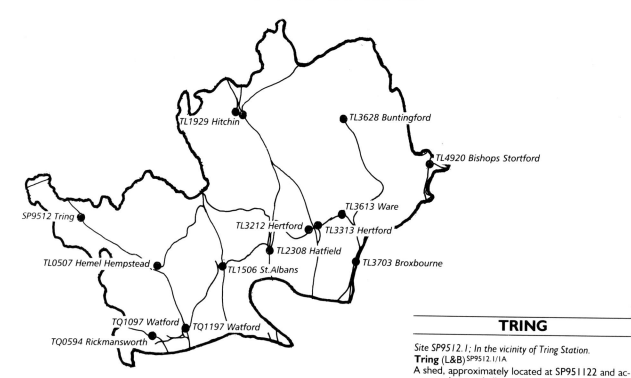

TL1929 Hitchin
TL3628 Buntingford
TL4920 Bishops Stortford
TL3613 Ware
SP9512 Tring
TL3212 Hertford
TL3313 Hertford
TL2308 Hatfield
TL0507 Hemel Hempstead
TL1506 St.Albans
TL3703 Broxbourne
TQ1097 Watford
TQ1197 Watford
TQ0594 Rickmansworth

TRING

Site SP9512.1; In the vicinity of Tring Station.
Tring (L&B) SP9512.1/1A
A shed, approximately located at SP951122 and ac-
commodating a ballast engine was opened here by
the London & Birmingham Railway on October
16th, 1837. No further details are known.

BISHOPS STORTFORD

Site TL4920.1; On the west side of Bishops Stortford Station.
Bishops Stortford (N&E) TL4920.1/1A
A timber built 2TS dead ended shed, it was probably
located at TL49052089 and was opened by the
Northern & Eastern Railway on May 16th, 1842. The
facilities included a coal stage and small turntable.
The depot was closed in 1845 and demolished to
accommodate an access line to the gasworks.

Replaced by ...
Site TL4920.2; On the east side of Bishops Stortford
Station.
Bishops Stortford (ECR) TL4920.2/F1
A servicing point consisting of a turntable, located at
TL49172094, siding and coal stage was opened by
the Eastern Counties Railway in 1845. The depot
was closed by BR on November 21st, 1960.

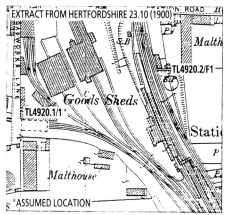

*Locomotives also stabled in the north bay of the
station and the goods yard during busy periods.*

BUNTINGFORD

Site TL3628.1; On the east side of the line, at the
south end of Buntingford Station.
Buntingford (WH&BR) TL3628.1/F1
A servicing point consisting of a coal stage, engine pit
and water tank, it was located at TL36462875 and
was opened by the Ware, Hadham & Buntingford
Railway on July 3rd, 1863. The line was worked by
the GE and absorbed by them on September 1st,
1868. The depot was closed by BR on June 15th,
1959.

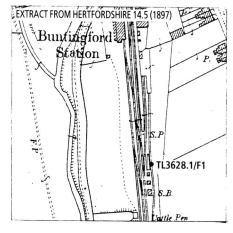

BROXBOURNE

Site TL3703.1; In the vicinity of Broxbourne Station.
Broxbourne (ECR) TL3703.1/1A
A 2TS shed was opened here by the Eastern Counties Railway in 1845. A turntable was located outside
of the shed entrance but further details of its construction and closure date are not known.

HATFIELD

Site TL2308.1; On the west side of Hatfield Station.
Hatfield (GN) TL2308.1/1A
A brick built 2TS dead ended shed with a gable style
slated roof, located at TL23180876 and opened in
1854. The facilities included a water tank, coke/coal
stage and, installed in 1860, a 40ft turntable.

The track layout was re-arranged in c1900 ...
Hatfield (GN) TL2308.1/1B
The westernmost track was extended through the
back of the shed creating a through road.

The shed was re-roofed in c1923 ...
Hatfield (LNER) TL2308.1/1C
The roof was raised by 2ft and a new brick screen
constructed. The depot was closed by BR on January
2nd, 1961.

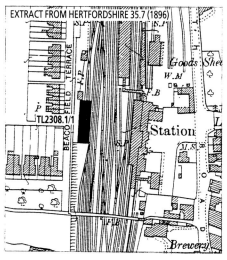

HERTFORD

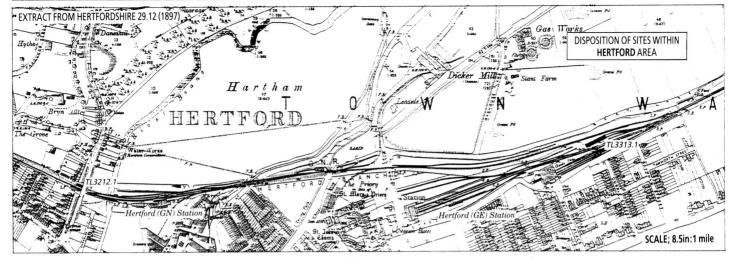

EXTRACT FROM HERTFORDSHIRE 29.12 (1897)

DISPOSITION OF SITES WITHIN **HERTFORD** AREA

SCALE; 8.5in:1 mile

Site TL3212.1; On the north side of the line, at the west end of Hertford (GN) Station.

Hertford (H&WJR)^{TL3212.1/1A}
A dead ended 1TS shed it was unusual in that it utilized a brick built road overbridge with a timber built extension on the western side. It was located at TL32321296 and was opened by the Hertford & Welwyn Junction Railway in 1860. Details of its facilities are not known. The line was worked from the outset by the GNR and it was absorbed by them on September 1st, 1868. The depot was closed in 1890.

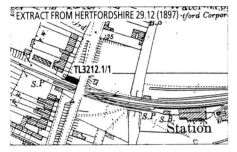

EXTRACT FROM HERTFORDSHIRE 29.12 (1897) ·tford Corpor

(A proposal was made in 1874 to construct a replacement 1TS shed in the goods yard. It would have been located at TL32401295 as TL3212.2/1A but as no further record has been found it is assumed that it was not built.)

Site TL3313.0; In the vicinity of Hertford (N&E) Station.

Hertford (N&E)^{TL3313.0/1A}
A 1TS shed was opened here on October 31st, 1843 by the Northern & Eastern Railway. It was closed in c1866.

Site TL3313.1; On the north side of the line, east of Hertford East Station.

Hertford East (GE)^{TL3313.1/1A}
A brick built 2TS dead ended shed with a slated gable style roof, it was located at TL33341307 and was opened in c1858. The facilities included a water tower and 42ft turntable sited outside of the shed entrance.

It was enlarged in 1891 ...
Hertford East (GE)^{TL3313.1/1B}
The shed was extended by 45ft at its eastern end. At the same time the turntable was replaced and re-sited at the western end of the building and a new coal stage and water cranes were installed.

The roof was partially destroyed by a fire in 1901 ...
Hertford East (GE)^{TL3313.1/1C}
A new roof was installed to replace the damaged portion.

The shed was rebuilt in 1955 ...
Hertford East (BR)^{TL3313.1/1D}
The roof was replaced by the Eastern Region with a flat corrugated asbestos style with a brick screen and the northernmost line was extended through the back of the shed, necessitating the removal of the turntable. The depot was closed on November 21st, 1960 and was subsequently demolished

EXTRACT FROM HERTFORDSHIRE 29.12 (1897)

HEMEL HEMPSTEAD

Site TL0507.1; On the west side of Hemel Hempstead Station.

Hemel Hempstead (MR)^{TL0507.1/1A}
A timber built 1TS dead ended shed, it was located at TL05850743 and was opened on July 16th, 1877. The facilities included a water tank and, sited on the shed approach road, a turntable. The depot was closed in 1910 and subsequently demolished.

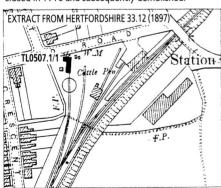

EXTRACT FROM HERTFORDSHIRE 33.12 (1897)

RICKMANSWORTH

Site TL0594.1; On the south side of the line, west of Rickmansworth (LNER/Met) Station.

Rickmansworth (LNER/Met)^{TL0594.1/F1}
A servicing point consisting of coal stage, engine pits and sidings, it was located at TL05579464 and was opened on January 5th, 1925. It was closed by BR on September 9th, 1961.

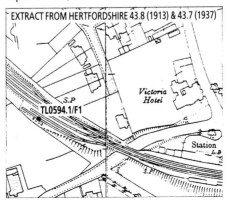

EXTRACT FROM HERTFORDSHIRE 43.8 (1913) & 43.7 (1937)

WARE

Site TL3613.1; In the goods yard on the north side of the line, at the east end of Ware Station.

Ware (LNER)^{TL3613.1/F1}
A short siding, located at TL36121397, was utilized as a stabling point for a petrol shunter from 1930. The locomotive was replaced in BR days by a diesel shunter and this was utilized until the depot was closed on January 3rd, 1966.

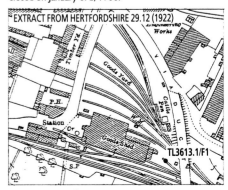

EXTRACT FROM HERTFORDSHIRE 29.12 (1922)

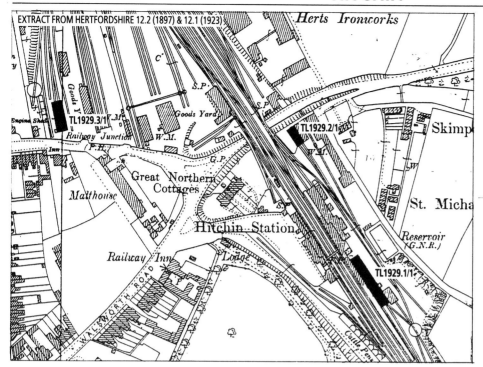

EXTRACT FROM HERTFORDSHIRE 12.2 (1897) & 12.1 (1923)

Site TL1929.2; On the east side of the line, at the north end of Hitchin (GN) Station.
Hitchin (GN)^{TL1929.2/1A}
A timber built 2TS dead ended shed with a slated gable style roof, it was located at TL19432983. It is not certain whether the building was at any time used for locomotive purposes. No further details are known.

Site TL1929.3; In Hitchin (MR) goods yard, on the west side of the GN main line.
Hitchin (MR)^{TL1929.3/0A}
A shed was opened here on May 8th, 1857. No further details are known except that after closure in 1860 it was let out for private use.

Replaced by ...
Hitchin (MR)^{TL1929.3/1A}
A brick built 2TS dead ended shed with a slated gable style roof, it was located at TL19192984 and was opened in 1860. The northern end of the shed was damaged in a storm on December 11th, 1891.

The shed was repaired ...
Hitchin (MR)^{TL1929.3/1B}
The building was re-opened in 1892 and the facilities included a 42ft turntable, installed two years later. The depot was closed prior to grouping but the turntable was still utilized as late as 1960. The shed buildings were still standing until at least 1980.

Site TL1929.1; On the east side of Hitchin (GN) Station.
Hitchin (GN)^{TL1929.1/1A}
A brick built 2TS dead ended shed with a slated gable style roof, it was located at TL19512969 and was opened on August 7th, 1850. The facilities included a coke/coal stage, water tank and a 40ft turntable installed in the following year.

The shed was enlarged in 1865 ...
Hitchin (GN)^{TL1929.1/1B}
A brick built 160ft extension was provided at the southern end of the building. At a later date the turntable was re-sited and enlarged to 60ft. The depot was closed by BR in June 1961 and was subsequently demolished with the turntable finding further use at *The Buckinghamshire Railway Centre.*

WATFORD cont ...

Replaced by ...
Site TQ1097.1; On the east side of the Bletchley line, at the north end of Watford Junction Station.
Watford (L&NWR)^{TQ1097.1/1A}
A brick built 3TS dead ended shed with a slated hipped roof, it was located at TQ10929752 and was opened in 1872. The facilities included the turntable of its predecessor (TQ1197.1/1A).

The shed was re-roofed in 1937 ...
Watford (LMS)^{TQ1097.1/1B}
A new roof was installed utilizing a slated pitch over each track with a single gable end.

The shed was enlarged in 1890 ...
Watford (L&NWR)^{TQ1097.1/2A}
A brick built 3TS dead ended shed with a slated hipped roof was added along the western wall. It was located at TQ10919752 and new facilities installed at this time included a coal stage and water tank.

The depot was closed by BR on March 29th, 1965.

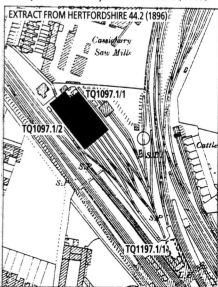

EXTRACT FROM HERTFORDSHIRE 44.2 (1896)

ST.ALBANS

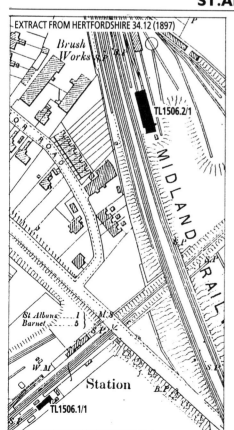

EXTRACT FROM HERTFORDSHIRE 34.12 (1897)

Site TL1506.1; On the south side of the line, at the west end of St.Albans (GN) Station.
St.Albans (H&SR)^{TL1506.1/1A}
A brick built 1TS dead ended shed with a slated gable style roof, it was located at TL15520642 and was opened by the Hatfield & St.Albans Railway on October 16th, 1865. The facilities included a coal stage, water tank and 40ft turntable. The line was worked by the GN and absorbed by them on November 1st, 1883. The depot was closed in 1876 and converted for use, initially as stables but subsequently as a store and remained in existence until it was demolished in 1996.

Site TL1506.2; On the east side of the line, south of St.Albans (MR) Station.
St.Albans (MR)^{TL1506.2/1A}
A brick built 2TS dead ended shed with a slated gable style roof, it was located at TL15600670 and was opened in 1868. The facilities included a coal stage, water tank and 42ft turntable. The depot was closed by BR on January 11th, 1960 and was subsequently demolished.

WATFORD

Site TQ1197.1; In the fork of the St.Albans and Bletchley lines, at the north end of Watford Junction Station.
Watford (L&NWR)^{TQ1197.1/1A}
A 1TS through road shed, it was located at TQ11019740 and was opened in 1856. The facilities included a 40ft turntable sited at the northern end of the shed yard. The depot was closed in 1872 and demolished to make way for station enlargements.

OXFORDSHIRE

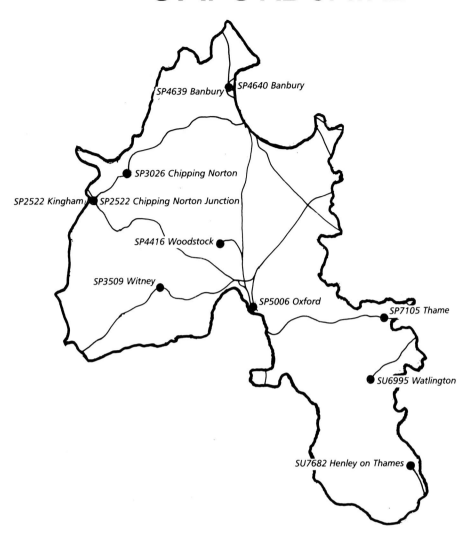

SP4639 Banbury • SP4640 Banbury

SP3026 Chipping Norton

SP2522 Kingham • SP2522 Chipping Norton Junction

SP4416 Woodstock

SP3509 Witney

SP5006 Oxford

SP7105 Thame

SU6995 Watlington

SU7682 Henley on Thames

CHIPPING NORTON

Site SP3026.1; On the east side of the goods yard, at the south end of Chipping Norton Station.

Chipping Norton (OW&WR)^{SP3026.1/1A}
A stone and brick built ITS through road shed with a slated gable style roof, it was located at SP30762688 and was opened by the Oxford, Worcester & Wolverhampton Railway on August 30th, 1855. The facilities included a coal stage and water tank sited outside of the shed entrance. The line was absorbed by the GWR in 1863 and the depot was closed in July 1922.

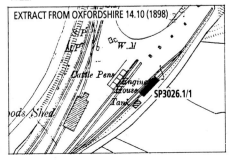

CHIPPING NORTON JUNCTION

Site SP2522.1; In the fork of the Banbury and Honey-bourne lines, north of Chipping Norton Junction Station.

Chipping Norton Junction (GWR)^{SP2522.1/1A}
A timber built ITS dead ended shed with a water tank surmounted on cast iron columns forming the roof, it was located at SP25622286 and was opened in 1881. The facilities included a coal stage and turntable sited outside of the shed entrance. The depot was closed in 1906 and demolished.

Replaced by ...

Kingham (GWR)^{SP2522.1/2A}
A brick built ITS dead ended shed with a slated gable style roof, it was located slightly north of its predecessor at SP25622296 and was opened in 1913. The facilities included a coal stage, water tank and, later removed, a turntable sited outside of the shed entrance. The depot was closed by BR in December 1962 and was later demolished.

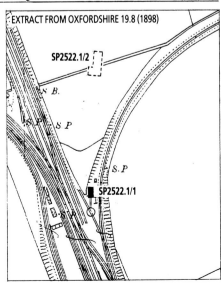

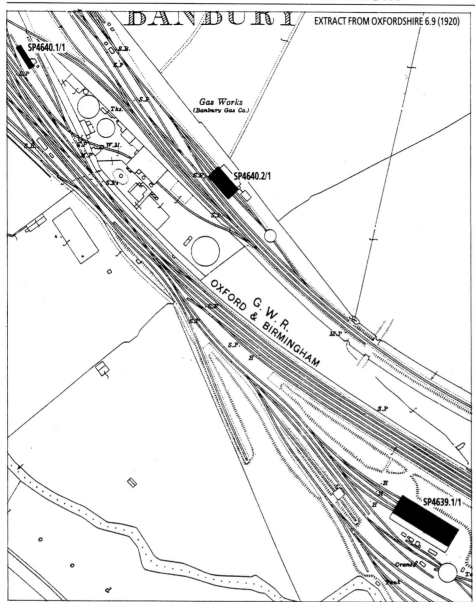

EXTRACT FROM OXFORDSHIRE 6.9 (1920)

Site SP4640.0; In the vicinity of Banbury (GW) Station.
Banbury (GWR)^{SP4640.0/1A}
A temporary shed was opened here on September 2nd, 1850. It was closed in October 1852. No further details are available.

Site SP4640.1; On the east side of the line, south of Banbury (GW) Station.
Banbury (GWR)^{SP4640.1/1A}
A brick built ITS through road shed with a slated gable style roof, it was located at SP46324031 and was opened in 1889. The facilities included a coal stage and 45ft turntable sited outside of the shed entrance. The depot was closed on August 24th, 1908 but it remained standing until at least 1960. It has since been demolished.

Replaced by ...
Site SP4639.1; On the west side of the line, south of Banbury (GW) Station.
Banbury (GWR)^{SP4639.1/1A}
A brick built 4TS shed with one through road and a twin slated gable style roof, it was located at SP46703988 and was opened on October 6th, 1908. The depot possessed all major facilities and remained basically unaltered until it was closed by BR on October 3rd, 1966. The building was subsequently demolished.

Site SP4640.2; On the east side of the line, south of Banbury Merton St. Station.
Banbury (Buckinghamshire)^{SP4640.2/1A}
A timber built 3TS shed with two through roads and a gable style roof, it was located at SP46524039 and was opened by the Buckinghamshire Railway on May 1st, 1850. The facilities included a coal stage and, installed in 1917, a turntable. The depot was closed on April 11th, 1932 and was demolished.

A servicing point was then established ...
Banbury (LMS)^{SP4640.2/F1}
Locomotives utilized the turntable, located at SP46424032, and a siding. The depot was closed by BR in December 1960.

HENLEY ON THAMES

Site SU7682.1; On the east side of Henley on Thames Station.
Henley on Thames (GWR)^{SU7682.1/1A}
A timber built ITS dead ended shed with a slated gable style roof, it was located at SU76368232 and was opened on June 1st, 1857. The facilities included a coal stage, water tank and a turntable which was re-sited in the shed yard at a later date. The depot was closed by BR in December 1958 and converted for private use. It has since been demolished.

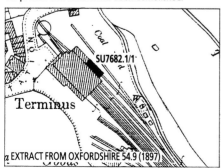

EXTRACT FROM OXFORDSHIRE 54.9 (1897)

THAME

Site SP7105.1; On the south side of Thame Station.
Thame (WR)^{SP7105.1/1A}
A timber built ITS shed with a slated gable style roof, it adjoined the train shed and was located at SP71270520. It was opened on August 1st, 1862 by the Wycombe Railway and probably closed when the line was extended to Oxford on October 2nd, 1864. No further details are known.

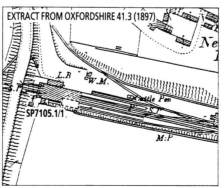

EXTRACT FROM OXFORDSHIRE 41.3 (1897)

WITNEY

Site SP3509.1; At the north end of Witney (Terminus) Station.
Witney (Witney)^{SP3509.1/1A}
A ITS dead ended shed, probably built in stone, it was located at SP35700917 and was opened by the Witney Railway on November 14th, 1861. Details of the facilities are not known. The depot was closed upon the opening of the shed at Fairford (SP1600.1/1A) on January 15th, 1873. The building found further use as a store until it was demolished in November 1905.

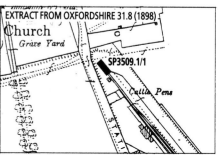

EXTRACT FROM OXFORDSHIRE 31.8 (1898)

OXFORD

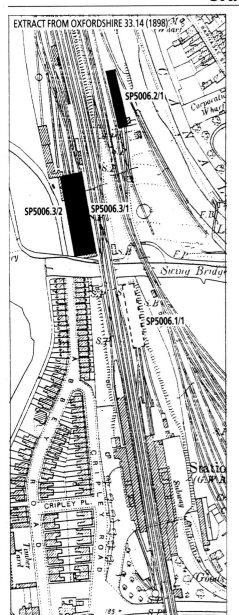

EXTRACT FROM OXFORDSHIRE 33.14 (1898)

Site SP5006.1; On the east side of the line, at the north end of Oxford (GWR) Station.

Oxford (GWR)^{SP5006.1/1A}

A 2TS dead ended shed, probably built in timber with a slated roof, it was located at SP50430655 and was opened in July 1850. Apart from the provision of a 25ft turntable, details of the facilities are not known. The depot was closed in 1872 and converted to a carriage shed. It was demolished in 1879 to accommodate station enlargements.

Site SP5006.2; On the east side of the line, north of Rewley Road Station.

Oxford (Buckinghamshire)^{SP5006.2/1A}

A corrugated iron 3TS shed it was located at SP50420673 and was opened by the Buckinghamshire Railway on May 20th, 1851. The facilities included a turntable. The line was worked by the L&NWR and the depot was blown down on October 14th, 1877.

The shed was re-built ...

Oxford (L&NWR)^{SP5006.2/1B}

The shed was rebuilt in corrugated iron but this proved to provide only a temporary solution and the depot was closed in 1882.

Replaced, on the same site, by ...

Rewley Road (L&NWR)^{SP5006.2/1C}

A brick built 2TS dead ended shed with a slated northlight pattern roof, it was opened in 1882. The facilities included a water tank and turntable. The depot was closed by BR on December 3rd, 1950 and was later demolished.

Site SP5006.3; On the west side of the line, north of Oxford (GWR) Station.

Oxford (OW&WR)^{SP5006.3/1A}

A timber built 1TS shed dead ended shed with a slated gable style roof, it was located at SP50390663 and was opened by the Oxford, Worcester & Wolverhampton Railway on April 1st, 1854. The line was absorbed by the West Midland Railway on July 1st, 1860.

The shed was enlarged in 1862...

Oxford (WMR)^{SP5006.3/2A}

A timber built 3TS dead ended shed with a slated gable style roof, it was constructed by the West Midland Railway on the west side of SP5006.3/1A being located at SP50380663. The facilities included a coal stage, water tank and turntable. The line was absorbed by the GWR in 1863 and the depot was closed by BR on January 3rd, 1966. The buildings were subsequently demolished and a diesel fuelling point established on the site.

Seen in August 1954 **Oxford (Rewley Road)** ex-L&NWR shed (SP5006.2/1C) had been closed for nearly four years. This building had been erected in c1882 to replace a 3TS shed (SP5006.2/1A) opened in May 1851 by the Buckinghamshire Railway.
It was subsequently demolished at an unknown date. *Author's Collection*

WATLINGTON

Site SU6995.1; On the east side of the line, at the north end of Watlington Station.

Watlington (W&PRR)^{SU6995.1/1A}

A timber built 1TS dead ended shed with a slated gable style roof, it was located at SU69619517 and was opened by the Watlington & Princes Risborough Railway on August 15th, 1872. The facilities included a water tower. The line was absorbed by the GWR on July 1st, 1883 and the shed was destroyed by a fire in 1906.

A servicing point was then established ...

Watlington (GWR)^{SU6995.1/F1}

Locomotives were stabled and serviced on the shed site. The depot was closed by BR on July 1st, 1957.

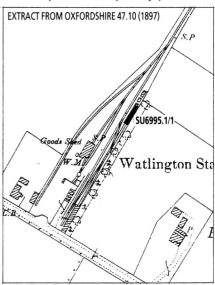

EXTRACT FROM OXFORDSHIRE 47.10 (1897)

WOODSTOCK

Site SP4416.1; On the south side of the line, at the east end of Woodstock Station.

Woodstock (Woodstock)^{SP4416.1/1A}

A corrugated iron 1TS dead ended shed with a corrugated iron gable style roof, it was located at SP44841676 and was opened by the Woodstock Railway on May 19th, 1890. The facilities included a coal stage and water tank. The line was absorbed by the GWR in 1890. The building was dismantled in March 1899 to accommodate station improvements.

The shed was re-erected ...

Woodstock (GWR)^{SP4416.1/2A}

The depot was moved slightly to the east at SP44851676, to allow the shed access line to enter the building from the east. At the same time the building was reduced in length from 70ft to 46ft 9in and the coal stage was dispensed with. The depot was closed on June 17th, 1927.

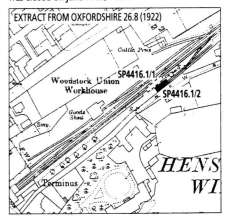

EXTRACT FROM OXFORDSHIRE 26.8 (1922)

GLOUCESTERSHIRE

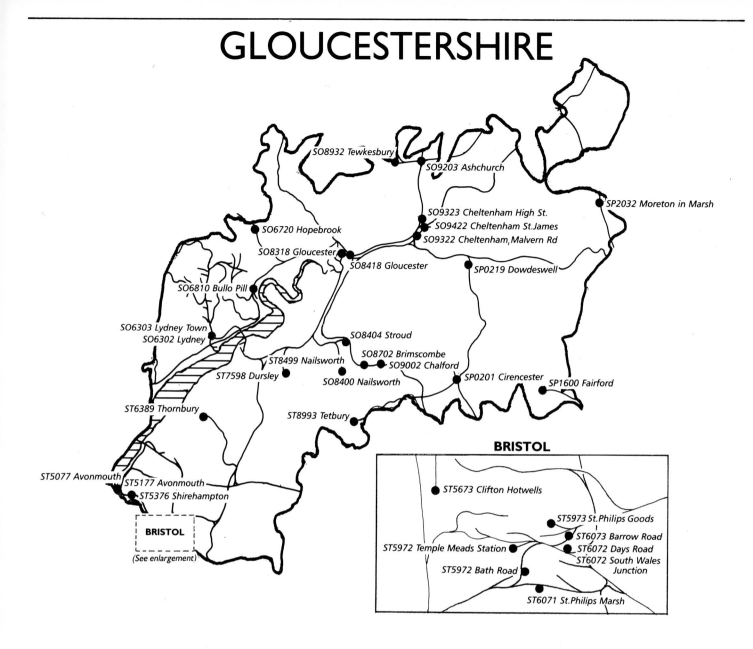

BRISTOL

ASHCHURCH

Site SO9203.1; On the east side of the line, on the east side of Ashchurch Station.

Ashchurch (MR)^{SO9203.1/1A}
A corrugated iron ITS through road shed, it was located at SO92670343 and was opened in 1863. The facilities included a coal stage and a turntable. The depot was closed by the LMS in 1923*.

EXTRACT FROM GLOUCESTERSHIRE 12.11 (1923)
SO9203.1/1

The original building may have been removed prior to 1900 and a servicing area SO9203.1/F1 established in its place. The OS map for 1901 does not show one on the site whereas the map for 1923 reveals that a shelter had been constructed at the coal stage and it is reasonable to assume that the locomotives were serviced and stabled here.

BRIMSCOMBE

Site SO8702.1; On the north side of the line, at the east end of Brimscombe Station.

Brimscombe (GWR)^{SO8702.1/1A}
A brick built ITS dead ended shed with a slated gable style roof, it was located at SO87870221 and was opened in 1845. The facilities included a water tank and coal stage sited outside of the shed entrance.

The shed was extended ...
Brimscombe (GWR)^{SO8702.1/1B}
At some stage a 20ft extension, built in stone and surmounted by a new water tank was constructed. The depot was closed by BR on October 28th, 1963 and partially demolished, the northern wall being retained as a boundary to the railway line.

EXTRACT FROM GLOUCESTERSHIRE 49.8 & 50.5 (1901)
SO8702.1/1

BULLO PILL

Site SO6810.1; On the west side of the Newport line, north of the junction with the Forest of Dean branch.

Bullo Pill (SWR)^{SO6810.1/1A}
A brick built ITS through road shed with a slated gable style roof and timber gables, it was located at SO68851056 and was opened by the South Wales Railway in August 1854. The facilities included a coal stage and water tank. The depot was considered to be a GW shed and it was they who closed it on March 21st, 1931.

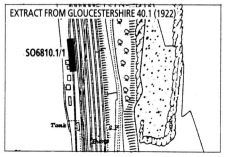

EXTRACT FROM GLOUCESTERSHIRE 40.1 (1922)
SO6810.1/1

AVONMOUTH

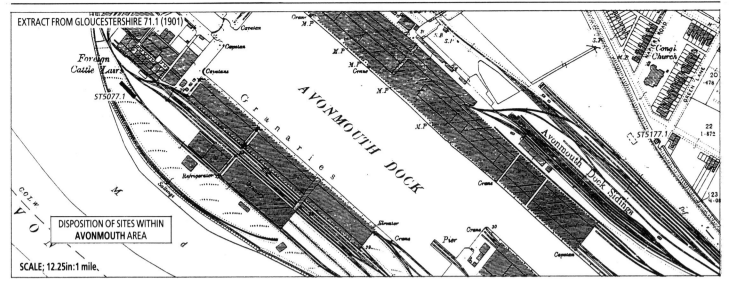

DISPOSITION OF SITES WITHIN
AVONMOUTH AREA

SCALE; 12.25in:1 mile.

Site ST5077.1; On the west side of Avonmouth Dock.

Avonmouth (BP&PR)^{ST5077.1/1A}
A 1TS dead ended shed, it is was opened by the Bristol Port & Pier Railway on March 6th, 1865. It is believed that it was the building located at ST50937799. Details of its construction and facilities are not known. The line was absorbed by the GWR/MR on September 1st, 1890 and the depot was closed in 1901.

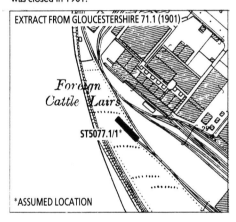

Replaced in 1905 by ...
Site ST5177.1; On the west side of the line, at the south end of Avonmouth Docks Station.

Avonmouth (GWR/MR)^{ST5177.1/1A}
A timber built 1TS dead ended shed with a gable style slated roof, it was located at ST51657795 and was opened on January 1st, 1905. The facilities included a coal stage, sited outside of the shed entrance, and a 60ft turntable from which access was gained to the building. The depot was closed in 1924.

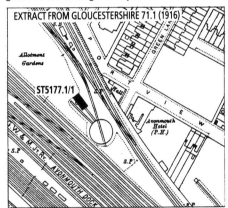

DURSLEY

Site ST7598.1; On the east side of the line, north of Dursley Station.

Dursley (D&MJR)^{ST7598.1/1A}
A brick built 1TS dead ended shed with a slated gable style roof, it was located at ST75639882 and was opened by the Dursley & Midland Junction Railway on August 26th, 1856. Unusually, the building had been in existence for a considerable period of time prior to opening and had been purchased from the contractors of the line and converted to locomotive use. The facilities included a water tank and coal stage. The line was worked by the MR and was absorbed by them on January 1st, 1861. Apart from modifications to the doorway the shed remained unaltered until it was closed by BR on September 10th, 1962 and demolished.

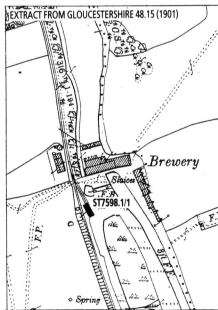

CHALFORD

Site SO9002.1; On the north side of the line, west of Chalford Station.

Chalford (GWR)^{SO9002.1/F1}
A corrugated iron 1TS dead ended shed, it was located at SO90100245 and was opened in 1903. The facilities included a coal stage and water tank. The building was dismantled in 1935.

A servicing point was then established ...

Chalford (GWR)^{SO9002.1/F1}
The engine pit and siding were utilized until the depot was closed by BR on May 19th, 1951.

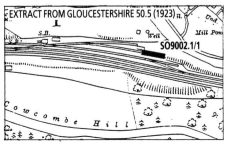

FAIRFORD

Site SP1600.1; At the end of the branch line, west of Fairford Station.

Fairford (EGR)^{SP1600.1/1A}
A timber built 1TS dead ended shed with a slated gable style roof, it was located at SP16290081 and was opened by the East Gloucestershire Railway on January 15th, 1873. The facilities included a water tower, coal stage and turntable. The line was absorbed by the GWR in 1890 and the depot was closed by BR on June 18th, 1962 and was subsequently demolished.

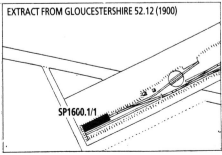

DOWDESWELL

Site SP0219.1; In the vicinity of Andoversford & Dowdeswell Station.

Dowdeswell (M&SWJR)^{SP0219.1/1A}
A temporary shed, it was opened by the Midland & South Western Junction Railway in 1890 and closed by them in 1893. No more details are available.

CIRENCESTER

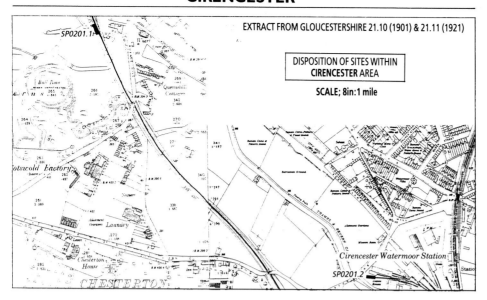

EXTRACT FROM GLOUCESTERSHIRE 21.10 (1901) & 21.11 (1921)

DISPOSITION OF SITES WITHIN
CIRENCESTER AREA

SCALE; 8in:1 mile

Site SP0201.1; On the west side of the line, at the south end of Cirencester Town Station.
Cirencester Town (C&GWRU)$^{SP0201.1/1A}$
A ITS shed, it was opened by the Cirencester and Great Western Railway Union on May 31st, 1841. No details of its construction or facilities are available and it is assumed to have been located at SP02120154. The depot was closed by the GWR in 1872.

Replaced in 1872 on the same site by ...
Cirencester Town (GWR)$^{SP0201.1/1B}$
A timber built ITS dead ended shed with a slated gable style roof. The facilities included a water tank and coal stage. The depot was closed by BR in April 1964 and was subsequently demolished.

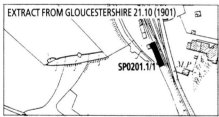

EXTRACT FROM GLOUCESTERSHIRE 21.10 (1901)

SP0201.1/1

Site SP0201.2; On the east side of Cirencester Watermoor Station.
Cirencester Watermoor (M&SWJR)$^{SP0201.2/1A}$
A timber built ITS dead ended shed with a corrugated iron gable style roof, it was located at SP02730101 and was opened by the Midland & South Western Junction Railway in 1895. Details of its facilities are not known. The depot was closed by the GWR in March 1924 and was demolished.

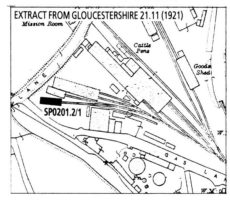

EXTRACT FROM GLOUCESTERSHIRE 21.11 (1921)

SP0201.2/1

TEWKESBURY

Site SO8932.1; On the north side of the Quay branch line, west of Tewkesbury (MR) Station.
Tewkesbury (B'ham&G)$^{SO8932.1/1A}$
A brick built ITS dead ended shed with a slated gable style roof, it was located at SO89543298 and was opened by the Birmingham & Gloucester Railway on July 21st, 1840. The facilities included a water column and coal stage. The line was absorbed by the MR in 1846 and the depot was closed by BR on September 7th, 1962. The building was subsequently demolished, the site being utilized for housing.

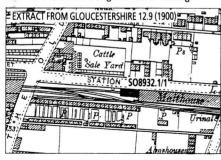

EXTRACT FROM GLOUCESTERSHIRE 12.9 (1900)

SO8932.1/1

THORNBURY

Site ST6389.1; On the south side of the line, at the east end of Thornbury Station.
Thornbury (MR)$^{ST6389.1/1A}$
A timber built ITS through road shed with a slated gable style roof, it was located at ST63908962 and was opened on September 2nd, 1872. The facilities included a water tank and a turntable sited in the adjacent goods yard. The depot was closed by the LMS on June 19th, 1944 and was converted for private use. It has since been demolished.

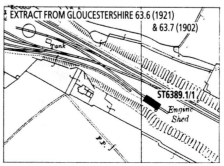

EXTRACT FROM GLOUCESTERSHIRE 63.6 (1921)
& 63.7 (1902)

ST6389.1/1

NAILSWORTH

Site ST8499.1;. On the west side of the line, at the south end of Nailsworth Station
Nailsworth (S&NR)$^{ST8499.1/1A}$
A ITS through road shed, it was located at ST84959996 and was opened by the Stonehouse & Nailsworth Railway on February 1st, 1867. No further details of its construction or facilities are known. The line was absorbed by the MR in 1868 and the depot was closed in 1895, being demolished shortly afterwards.

A servicing area was then established ...
Site SO8400.1; On the east side of the line, at the north end of Nailsworth Station.
Nailsworth (MR)$^{SO8400.1/F1}$
A servicing area consisting of a turntable, located at SO84830012, water tank and coal stage was opened in 1895. The depot was closed by BR in c1963

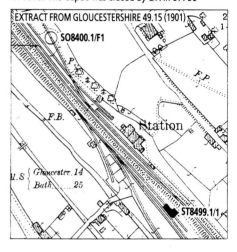

EXTRACT FROM GLOUCESTERSHIRE 49.15 (1901)

SO8400.1/F1

ST8499.1/1

SHIREHAMPTON

Site ST5376.1; On the south side of the line, at the east end of Shirehampton Station.
Shirehampton (BP&PR)$^{ST5376.1/1A}$
A timber built ITS dead ended shed with a gable style slated roof, it was located at ST53117637 and was opened by the Bristol Port & Pier Railway in 1875. The facilities included a water tank. The line was absorbed by the GWR/MR on September 1st, 1890. The building was destroyed by a fire on February 13th, 1900.

A servicing point was then established ...
Shirehampton (GWR/MR)$^{ST5376.1/F1}$
Locomotives then stabled on the shed site until a new depot was opened at Avonmouth (ST5177.1/1A) in 1905.

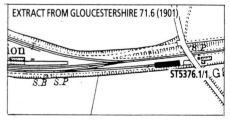

EXTRACT FROM GLOUCESTERSHIRE 71.6 (1901)

ST5376.1/1

HOPEBROOK

Site SO6720.1; In the vicinity of Hopesbrook Tunnel.
Hopebrook* (HR&GR)$^{SO6720.1/1A}$
A temporary shed, it was opened by the Hereford, Ross & Gloucester Railway on July 11th, 1853 and closed by them on June 1st, 1855. The location of the shed was approximately SO677209.

The location was actually called Hopesbrook.

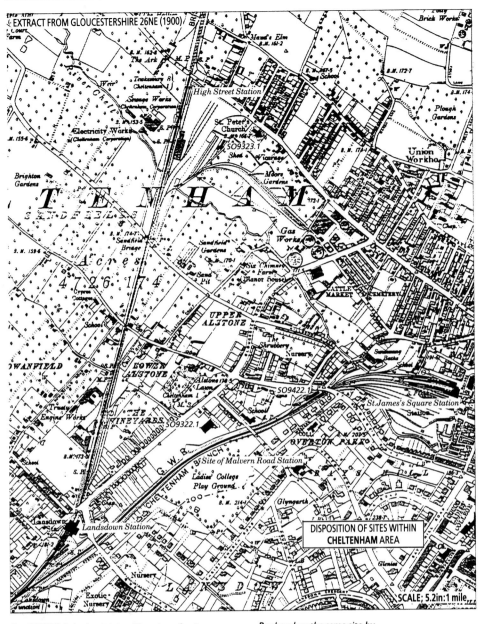

EXTRACT FROM GLOUCESTERSHIRE 26NE (1900)

DISPOSITION OF SITES WITHIN CHELTENHAM AREA

SCALE; 5.2in:1 mile

Site SO9322.0; In the vicinity of Lansdown Station.
Cheltenham (B'ham & G)^{SO9322.0/1A}
A shed was opened here on June 24th, 1840 by the Birmingham & Gloucester Railway. No further details are known.

Site SO9323.1; On the east side of Cheltenham High St. Station.
High Street (M&SWJR)^{SO9323.1/1A}
A timber built 1TS dead ended shed with a slated gable style roof, it was located at SO93742333 and was opened by the Midland & South Western Junction Railway in 1893. The facilities included a coal stage and water tank. The depot was closed in 1911.

EXTRACT FROM GLOUCESTERSHIRE 26.3 (1901)
St. Peter's Church
SO9323.1/1

Replaced on the same site by ...
High Street (M&SWJR)^{SO9323.1/1B}
A brick built 3TS through road shed with a slated gable style roof, it was opened by the Midland & South Western Junction Railway in 1911. The depot was closed by the GWR on December 28th, 1935 but it found further use as a warehouse. The building was still standing, in private use, in 1993.

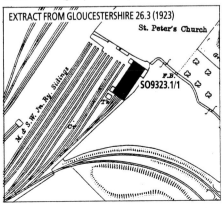

EXTRACT FROM GLOUCESTERSHIRE 26.3 (1923)
St. Peter's Church
SO9323.1/1

Site SO9422.1; On the north side of the line, at the west end of Cheltenham St.James Station.
St.James (GWR)^{SO9422.1/1A}
A timber built 2TS dead ended shed with a slated gable style roof with hipped ends, it was located at SO94062252 and was opened in October 1847. The facilities included a coal stage and 40ft turntable. The depot was closed in 1906 and dismantled to accommodate a junction for the new line to Honeybourne.

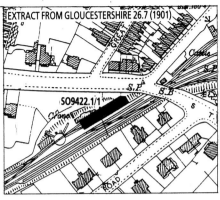

EXTRACT FROM GLOUCESTERSHIRE 26.7 (1901)
SO9422.1/1

Replaced by ...
Site SO9322.1; On the north side of the line, at the east end of Cheltenham Malvern Road Station.
Malvern Road (GWR)^{SO9322.1/1A}
A brick built 2TS dead ended shed with a slated gable style roof, it was located at SO93692241 and was opened in 1907. The facilities included a ramped coal stage and water tank.

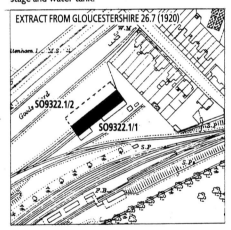

EXTRACT FROM GLOUCESTERSHIRE 26.7 (1920)
SO9322.1/2
SO9322.1/1

In 1943 the shed was enlarged ...
Malvern Road (GWR)^{SO9322.1/2A}
A corrugated asbestos built 2TS dead ended shed with a gable style corrugated asbestos roof was built adjacent to the north side of the original building at SO93682242. The depot was closed by BR in October 1963 and let out for private use. The original portion was demolished but the later building (SO9322.1/2A) was still in use in 1995

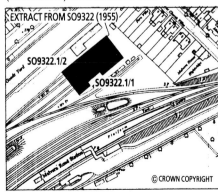

EXTRACT FROM SO9322 (1955)
SO9322.1/2
SO9322.1/1
© CROWN COPYRIGHT

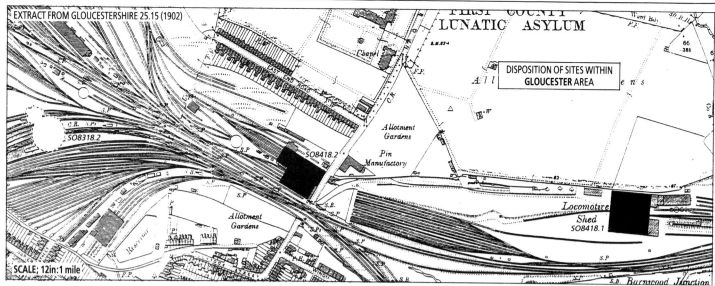

EXTRACT FROM GLOUCESTERSHIRE 25.15 (1902)

SCALE: 12in:1 mile

Site SO8318.1; *In the vicinity of Gloucester (B'ham&G) Terminus Station.*

Gloucester (B'ham&G)^SO8318.1/1A

A 2TS shed, it was opened by the Birmingham & Gloucester Railway on June 24th, 1840. No details of its construction or facilities are available. The line was absorbed by the MR on May 7th, 1845 and the depot was closed in c1852.

Adjoined by ...

Gloucester (B'ham&G)^SO8318.1/2A

A 1TS shed, it was opened by the Birmingham & Gloucester Railway on June 24th, 1840. No details of its construction or facilities are available. The line was absorbed by the MR on May 7th, 1845 and the depot was closed in c1852.

Site SO8318.0; *In the vicinity of Gloucester (GWR) Station.*

Gloucester (B&G)^SO8318.0/1A

A 1TS shed, it was opened by the Bristol & Glocester Railway on May 8th, 1844. No details of its construction or facilities are available. The line was leased to the MR and was then absorbed by them on August 3rd, 1846. The depot was closed in 1854.

Gloucester (C&GWRUR)^SO8318.0/2A

A 1TS shed it was opened by the Cheltenham & GWR Union Railway on July 8th, 1844. No details of its construction or facilities are known except that a turntable was provided and it was located between this shed and the B&G shed (SO8318.0/1A). The depot was closed in 1854.

Site SO8318.2; *In the fork of the Bristol and Gloucester (MR) Station lines, at the east end of Gloucester (MR) Station.*

Gloucester (MR)^SO8318.2/1A

A circular roundhouse, it was located at SO3881833 and was opened on July 8th, 1850. The facilities included a coaling stage, water tank and an exterior 50ft turntable. The depot was closed in 1895 and demolished to make way for a new station.

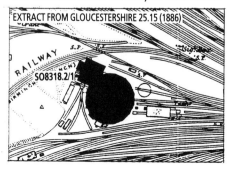

EXTRACT FROM GLOUCESTERSHIRE 25.15 (1886)

SO8318.2/1

Replaced by ...

Site SO8418.1; *On the north side of Barnwood Junction, east of Gloucester Station.*

Barnwood (MR)^SO8418.1/1A

A brick built roundhouse with three gable style slated pitched roofs, it was located at SO84701823 and was opened in 1895. It possessed all major facilities, including a four road fitting shop added later. The depot was closed by BR on May 4th, 1964.

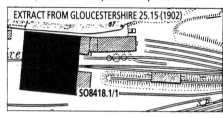

EXTRACT FROM GLOUCESTERSHIRE 25.15 (1902)

SO8418.1/1

Site SO8418.2; *On the north side of the line, east of Gloucester Station.*

Horton Road (SWR)^SO8418.2/1A

A 2TS dead ended shed, it was probably built in timber and it was located at SO84241826 and opened by the South Wales Railway on September 19th, 1851.

Replaced on the same site in 1854 by ...

Horton Road (GWR)^SO8418.2/1B

A brick built 4TS dead ended shed with a slated single gable style roof.

It was enlarged again in 1872 ...

Horton Road (GWR)^SO8418.2/2A

A brick built 6TS dead ended shed with a twin gable style slated roof was built adjacent to the north side of the original building at SO84241829. The depot possessed all major facilities and these were improved in 1921 by the provision of a ramped coaling stage and a track layout re-organization. The shed was closed to steam by BR on January 1st, 1966 and although most of the buildings were demolished it saw continued use as a diesel depot until well into the 1990s.

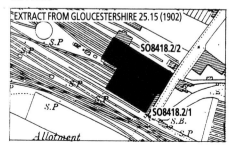

EXTRACT FROM GLOUCESTERSHIRE 25.15 (1902)

SO8418.2/2

SO8418.2/1

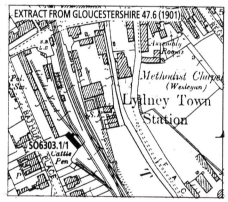

LYDNEY

Site SO6303.1; *On the west side of the line, at the south end of Lydney Town Station.*

Lydney Town (MR)^SO6303.1/1A

A 1TS dead ended shed, it was located at SO63350308. No further details are available.

EXTRACT FROM GLOUCESTERSHIRE 47.6 (1901)

SO6303.1/1

Site SO6302.1; *On the west side of the line, at the north end of Lydney Junction Station.*

Lydney (S&WR)^SO6302.1/1A

A stone built 3TS dead ended shed with a slated pitched roof and timber gables, it was located at SO63280216 and was opened by the Severn & Wye Railway in 1868. As it formed part of the main works of the railway it enjoyed the use of all facilities. The depot was closed by BR on March 2nd, 1964 and was subsequently demolished.

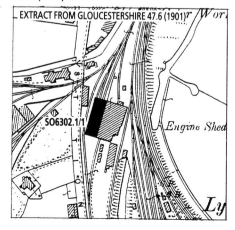

EXTRACT FROM GLOUCESTERSHIRE 47.6 (1901)

SO6302.1/1

EXTRACT FROM GLOUCESTERSHIRE 76.1 (1912)

ST5972.2/1

ST5972.2/2

ST6071.1/1

Site ST5972.2; On the east side of the line, at the south end of Bristol Temple Meads Station.

Bath Road (B&E)^ST5972.2/1A
A stone built 6TS dead ended shed with a twin slated gable style roof, it was located at ST59937208 and was opened by the Bristol & Exeter Railway in 1850.

It was enlarged in 1859 ...
Bath Road (B&E)^ST5972.2/1B
The building was extended by 54ft 4ins. The line was absorbed by the GWR in 1876.

Bath Road (GWR)^ST5972.2/2A
A stone built 2RH shed with a twin slated gable style roof, it was located at ST59897201 and was opened in 1877, being converted from the former B&E works.

The depot possessed all major facilities including two outside turntables and a ramped coal stage.

It was progressively demolished from 1933 onwards and was replaced by ...
Bath Road (GWR)^ST5972.2/2B
A brick built 10TS dead ended shed with five slated gable style roof bays, it was built on the site of the 2RH (ST5972.2/2A) and opened in 1934. The shed was closed to steam by BR on September 12th, 1960 and the buildings were demolished, being replaced by a purpose-built diesel depot.

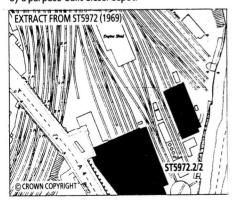

EXTRACT FROM ST5972 (1969)

ST5972.2/2

© CROWN COPYRIGHT

Site ST6071.1; On the south side of the Bristol relief line, east of Pyle Hill Junction.

St.Philips Marsh (GWR)^ST6071.1/1A
A brick built 2RH shed with six slated gable style roof bays, it was located at ST60307196 and was opened in July 1910. The shed possessed all major facilities. The depot was closed by BR on June 17th, 1964 and was demolished.

Site ST5673.1; At the south end of Clifton Hotwells Station.

Clifton Hotwells (BP&PR)^ST5673.1/1A
A 1TS dead ended shed, probably built in timber, it was located at ST56517316 and was opened by the Bristol Port & Pier Railway on March 6th, 1865. The facilities included a turntable, sited outside of the shed entrance, and a water tank. The building was destroyed by a fire on March 27th, 1873.

A servicing point was then established ...
Clifton Hotwells (BP&PR)^ST5673.1/F1
Locomotives stabled on the shed site until a new depot was opened at Shirehampton (ST5376.1/1A) in 1875.

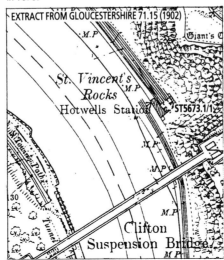

EXTRACT FROM GLOUCESTERSHIRE 71.15 (1902)

St. Vincent's Rocks
Hotwells Station

ST5673.1/1

Clifton Suspension Bridge

Site ST5972.1; At the west end of Bristol Temple Meads (Terminus) Station.

Temple Meads (GWR)^ST5972.1/1A
A 3TS shed it was located between the station platforms at ST59637244 and was opened on August 31st, 1840. The roof of the depot was part of the train shed, with a water tank incorporated in the station buildings. Access to the depot was gained via a traverser from either of the two outside platform roads. The facilities also included ash drops between the rails, being serviced by wagons standing in the stations lower level. The closure date is not known.

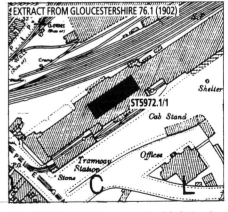

EXTRACT FROM GLOUCESTERSHIRE 76.1 (1902)

ST5972.1/1

Site ST5973.1; On the north side of St.Philips Station.

St.Philips Station (MR)^ST5973.1/F1
A servicing area consisting of a turntable, located at ST59977315, and siding. Details of the facilities and opening and closure dates are not known.

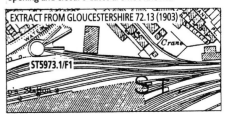

EXTRACT FROM GLOUCESTERSHIRE 72.13 (1903)

ST5973.1/F1

Continued ...

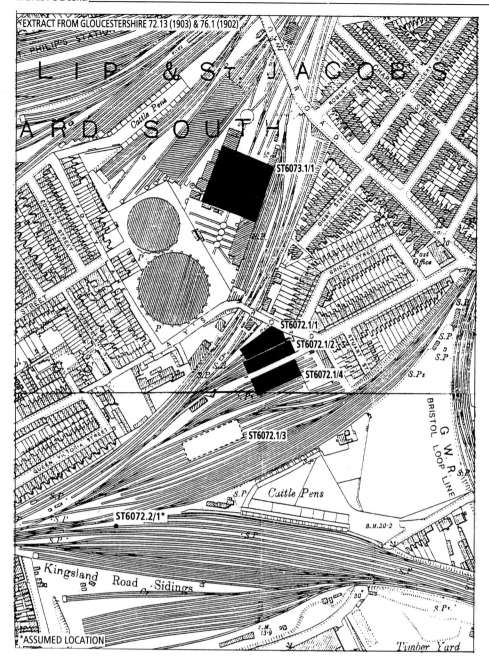

EXTRACT FROM GLOUCESTERSHIRE 72.13 (1903) & 76.1 (1902)

Site ST6072.1; In the fork of the Gloucester and Filton lines at South Wales Junction, east of Bristol Temple Meads Station.

Days Road (B&G)^{ST6072.1/1A}
A stone built 2TS dead ended shed with a slated gable style roof it was located at ST60477287 and was opened by the Bristol & Gloucester Railway on July 8th, 1844.

Adjoined by ...

Days Road (B&G)^{ST6072.1/2A}
A stone built 3TS dead ended shed with a slated gable style roof it was located at ST60477285 and was opened by the Bristol & Gloucester Railway on July 8th, 1844.

The facilities included a coal stage and 40ft turntable. The line was initially worked by the GWR and then leased to the MR on July 1st, 1845. It was absorbed by them on August 3rd, 1846 and the depot was closed and converted to a wagon works in 1873. The buildings were still standing in 1995 with ST6072.1/2A having been refurbished and re-opened as Barton Hill Diesel Depot for RES Class 47 locomotives.

South Wales Junction (GWR)^{ST6072.1/3A}
A stone built 3TS through road shed with a slated gable style roof, it was located at ST60427277 and was opened on August 31st, 1840. The facilities included a 40ft turntable. The depot was closed in 1876 and demolished to make way for additional sidings.

South Wales Junction (GWR)^{ST6072.1/4A}
A brick built 4TS through road shed with a slated gable style roof it was located at ST60487284 and was opened in 1872. It served as an engine shed only for a brief period, being closed and converted to a wagon works in 1877. It was still standing in 1995, in use as part of Barton Hill Diesel Depot.

Site ST6073.1; On the west side of the Fishponds line, north of Bristol Temple Meads Station.

Barrow Road (MR)^{ST6073.1/1A}
A brick built square roundhouse with three gable style slated pitched roofs, it was located at ST60447302 and was opened in 1873. It possessed all major facilities, with improvements being made to the coal and ash plants by the LMS in 1938. The depot was closed on November 20th, 1965 and later demolished.

Site ST6072.2: On the north side of the Bath line, east of Bristol Temple Meads Station.

Bristol (GWR)^{ST6072.2/1A}
A shed, approximately located at ST60387270, was opened here at some stage prior to 1840. No further details are known.

TETBURY

Site ST8993.1; On the east side of the line, at the north end of Tetbury Station.

Tetbury (GWR)^{ST8993.1/1A}
A brick built 1TS dead ended shed with a slated gable style roof incorporating a water tank surmounting the rear of the building. It was located at ST89349316 and was opened on December 2nd, 1889. The facilities included a coal stage sited outside of the shed entrance. The depot was closed by BR in April 1964 and subsequently demolished.

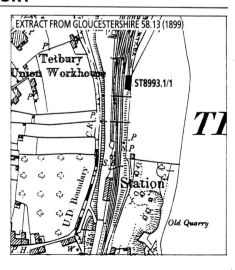

EXTRACT FROM GLOUCESTERSHIRE 58.13 (1899)

STROUD

Site SO8404.1; In the vicinity of Stroud (MR) Station.

Stroud (MR)^{SO8404.1/1A}
Some sort of facility, approximately located at SO849049, was opened here on November 16th, 1885. No further details are available, except that it was closed in c1900.

MORETON IN MARSH

Site SP2032.1; In the vicinity of Moreton in Marsh Station.

Moreton in Marsh (GWR)^{SP2032.1/F1}
A servicing area, approximately located at SP207326, was established here. No further details are available.

BUCKINGHAMSHIRE

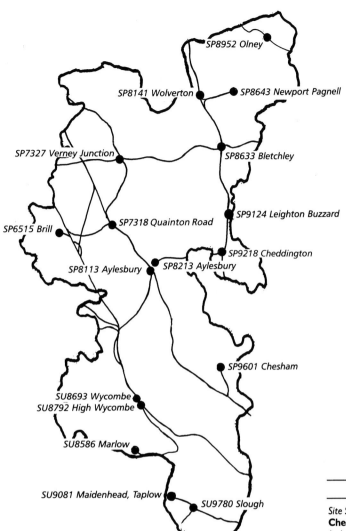

SP8952 Olney

SP8141 Wolverton   SP8643 Newport Pagnell

SP7327 Verney Junction   SP8633 Bletchley

SP9124 Leighton Buzzard

SP6515 Brill   SP7318 Quainton Road

SP9218 Cheddington

SP8113 Aylesbury   SP8213 Aylesbury

SP9601 Chesham

SU8693 Wycombe
SU8792 High Wycombe

SU8586 Marlow

SU9081 Maidenhead, Taplow   SU9780 Slough

CHEDDINGTON

Site SP9218.1; In the vicinity of Cheddington Station.
Cheddington (L&B)^{SP9218.1/1A}

A shed, probably 1TS and approximately located at SP922184 was opened here on April 9th, 1838 by the London & Birmingham Railway. No further details are known.

CHESHAM

Site SP9601.1; On the east side of Chesham Station.
Chesham (Met)^{SP9601.1/F1}
A servicing point consisting of a turntable, located at SP96110168, water tank, coal stage and engine pit, it was opened by the Metropolitan Railway on July 8th, 1889. An unusual feature was that the engine pit was situated at SP96050151 on the running line at the south end of the station. The depot was closed by BR on September 12th, 1960.

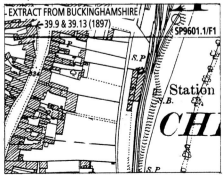

EXTRACT FROM BUCKINGHAMSHIRE
39.9 & 39.13 (1897)   SP9601.1/F1

Station

MARLOW

Site SU8586.1; On the north side of the line, at the east end of Marlow Station.
Marlow (GMR)^{SU8586.1/1A}
A brick built 1TS dead ended shed with a slated gable style roof, it was located at SU85658655 and was opened by the Great Marlow Railway on June 28th, 1873. The facilities included a water tank and coal stage sited outside of the shed entrance. The line was worked from the outset by the GWR and was absorbed by them in 1897. The shed was closed by BR in July 1962 and subsequently demolished.

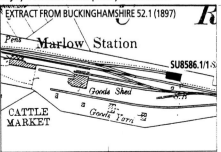

EXTRACT FROM BUCKINGHAMSHIRE 52.1 (1897)

Pens   Marlow Station   SU8586.1/1S

CATTLE   Goods Shed
MARKET   Goods Yard

NEWPORT PAGNELL

Site SP8643.1; On the south side of the line, at the west end of Newport Pagnell Station.
Newport Pagnell (L&NWR)^{SP8643.1/1A}
A corrugated iron and timber built 1TS dead ended shed with a slated gable style roof, it was located at SP86964350 and was opened on September 2nd, 1867. The facilities included a coal stage. The shed was closed by BR on June 15th, 1955.

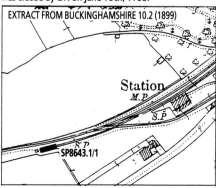

EXTRACT FROM BUCKINGHAMSHIRE 10.2 (1899)

Station
M.P.

SP8643.1/1

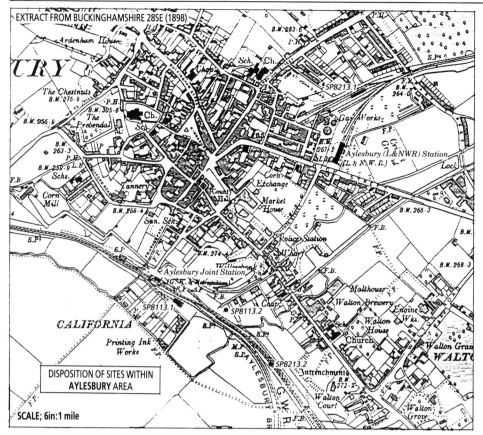

EXTRACT FROM BUCKINGHAMSHIRE 28SE (1898)

DISPOSITION OF SITES WITHIN
AYLESBURY AREA

SCALE; 6in:1 mile

Site SP8113.1; On the south side of the line, at the east end of Aylesbury Joint Station.
Aylesbury (Wycombe)[SP8113.1/1A]
A 1TS shed, it was located at SP81841340 and was opened by the Wycombe Railway on October 1st, 1863. The line was worked by the GWR. No further details are known.

The shed was enlarged in 1871 ...
Aylesbury (GWR)[SP8113.1/1B]
The shed was rebuilt to a 2TS building. No further details are known.

The shed was rebuilt in 1893 ...
Aylesbury (GWR)[SP8113.1/1C]
A 2TS dead ended shed with a slated northlight pattern roof. The facilities included a coal stage, water tank and a turntable. The turntable was later removed and the glazed portion of the roof replaced with corrugated sheeting. The depot was closed by BR on June 16th, 1962 and subsequently demolished.

Site SP8213.2; On the west side of the Amersham line, south of Aylesbury Joint Station.
Aylesbury (Met)[SP8213.2/F1]
A servicing area consisting of a coal stage, siding and engine pit, it was probably located at SP82121321 and was opened by the Metropolitan Railway on September 1st, 1892. No further details are known except that it is assumed to have been removed as a result of track widening.

Replaced by ...
Site SP8113.2; On the east side of the line, at the south end of Aylesbury Joint Station.
Aylesbury (Met)[SP8113.2/F1]
A servicing area consisting of a siding, it was located at SP81981339. It probably closed in c1960.

Site SP8213.1; On the west side of the line, at the north end of Aylesbury High Street Station.
Aylesbury (L&B)[SP8213.1/1A]
A 1TS shed, it was probably located at SP82361399 and was opened by the London & Birmingham Railway on June 10th, 1839. The depot was closed by the L&NWR in 1857. No further details are known.

Replaced, on the same site, by ...
Aylesbury (L&NWR)[SP8213.1/1B]
A brick built 1TS through road shed with a slated gable style roof incorporating a water tank, it was opened in 1857.

The shed was reduced in size in 1947 ...
Aylesbury (LMS)[SP8213.1/1C]
The building was reduced in length to about half its original size and the arched entrance replaced with a lintel. The depot was closed by BR on January 31st, 1953 and subsequently demolished.

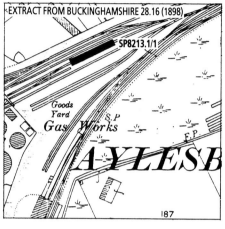

EXTRACT FROM BUCKINGHAMSHIRE 28.16 (1898)

BLETCHLEY

Site SP8633.1; On the west side of the line, at the north end of Bletchley Station.
Bletchley (L&NWR)[SP8633.1/1A]
A timber built 3TS shed with a corrugated iron roof, it was located at SP86793383 and was opened in 1851. The facilities included a coke/coal stage and water tank. The building was blown down in a gale in 1872.

Replaced on the same site by ...
Bletchley (L&NWR)[SP8633.1/1B]
A brick built 6TS dead ended shed with a slated twin gable style roof, it was opened in 1873. The facilities included a coal stage, surmounted by a water tank and a 42ft turntable, later enlarged to 50ft.

The shed was re-roofed in 1954 ...
Bletchley (BR)[SP8633.1/1C]
The roof was replaced with a BR style louvre roof and brick screen. The depot was closed on July 15th, 1965 and subsequently demolished.

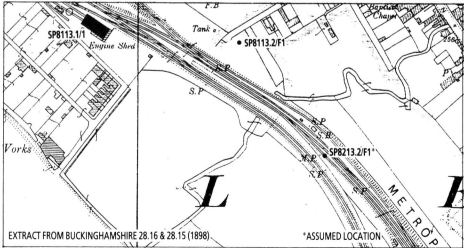

EXTRACT FROM BUCKINGHAMSHIRE 28.16 & 28.15 (1898)   *ASSUMED LOCATION

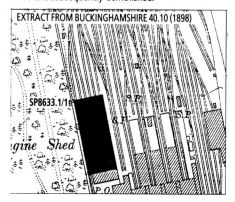

EXTRACT FROM BUCKINGHAMSHIRE 40.10 (1898)

BRILL

Site SP6515.1; On the north side of the line, at the east end of Brill Station.
Brill (DofBR)^{SP6515.1/1A}

Brill (DofBR)^SP6515.1/1A

A timber built 1TS dead ended shed with a slated gable style roof, it was located at SP65731533 and was opened by the Duke of Buckingham's Railway on April 1st, 1871. Details of its facilities and closure date are not known but the building found further use as a permanent way store.

Replaced by ...
Brill (Met)^SP6515.1/2A
A timber built 2TS dead ended shed with a slated gable style roof, it was located at SP65761534 and was opened by the Metropolitan Railway at some point prior to 1898. The facilities included a water tank. The shed was closed by London Transport on December 1st, 1935.

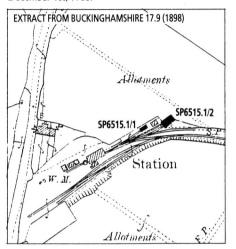
EXTRACT FROM BUCKINGHAMSHIRE 17.9 (1898)

SLOUGH

Site SU9780.1; On the south side of the line, at the west end of Slough Station.
Slough (GWR)^SU9780.1/1A
A 1TS dead ended shed, probably built in timber with a gable style slated roof, it was located at SU97628022 and was opened in November 1840. The facilities included a 25ft turntable, water tank and coke/coal stage. The shed was closed in 1868 and demolished to make way for track re-modelling.

Replaced by ...
Site SU9780.2; On the south side of the Windsor branch west of Slough Station.
Slough (GWR)^SU9780.2/1A
A brick built 4TS shed, converted from a goods shed, with 3 through roads and a twin slated gable style roof with timber gables, it was located at SU97468018 and was opened in 1868. The facilities included a turntable, water tank and a coal stage.

The shed was re-roofed ...
Slough (GWR)^SU9780.2/1B
At some stage, probably in late GWR or early BR days, the gables were rebuilt in brick and the roof was replaced with corrugated asbestos.

Adjoined by ...
Slough Diesel Railcar (GWR)^SU9780.2/2A
A corrugated iron 1TS through road shed with a corrugated iron lean-to style roof, it was built adjacently to the north wall of SU9780.2/1A and was opened in 1935. Although initially constructed to accommodate diesel railcars it was later utilized for steam locomotives.

The shed was closed by BR on June 1st, 1964 and subsequently demolished.

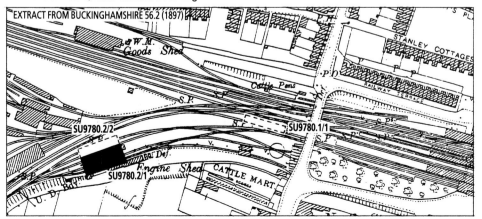
EXTRACT FROM BUCKINGHAMSHIRE 56.2 (1897)

LEIGHTON BUZZARD

Site SP9124.1; On the east side of the line, at the south end of Leighton Buzzard Station.
Leighton Buzzard (L&NWR)^SP9124.1/1A
A brick built 2TS through road shed with a slated gable style roof, it was located at SP91082485 and was opened in 1859. There were no major facilities.

The shed was re-roofed in 1957 ...
Leighton Buzzard (BR)^SP9124.1/1B
The roof was replaced and the shed entrances rebuilt by the London Midland Region with corrugated asbestos. The shed was closed on November 5th, 1962 and subsequently demolished.

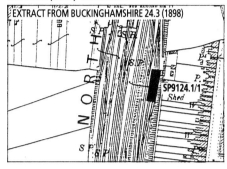
EXTRACT FROM BUCKINGHAMSHIRE 24.3 (1898)

MAIDENHEAD

Site SU9081.1; In the vicinity of Maidenhead Taplow (Temporary) Station.
Taplow (GWR)^SU9081.1/1A
A temporary shed, it was sited at the railhead terminus adjacent to the east bank of the River Thames approximately located at SU903811, and was opened on June 4th, 1838. The shed was closed on March 30th, 1840. No further details are known.

OLNEY

Site SP8952.1; On the east side of Olney Station.
Olney (MR)^SP8952.1/1A
A 1TS dead ended shed, it was located at SP89225205 and was opened in 1892. Details of its construction are not known but the facilities included a 50ft turntable and water tank. The shed was closed in 1928 but locomotives continued to utilize the site until BR days.

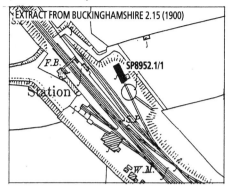
EXTRACT FROM BUCKINGHAMSHIRE 2.15 (1900)

QUAINTON ROAD

Site SP7318.1; On the south side of the line, at the east end of Quainton Road Station.
Quainton Road (GC/Met)^SP7318.1/F1
A servicing area consisting of a coal stage and engine pit, it was located at SP73991888. No further details are known.

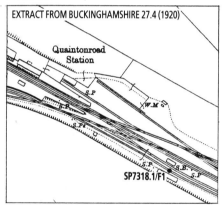
EXTRACT FROM BUCKINGHAMSHIRE 27.4 (1920)

VERNEY JUNCTION

Site SP7327.1; On the south side of the line, at the east end of Verney Junction Station.
Verney Junction (A&BR)^SP7327.1/F1
A servicing area consisting of a turntable, probably located at SP73822743, coal stage and engine pit was opened by the Aylesbury & Buckinghamshire Railway either in May 1851 or September 1868. It was closed in 1891 when the Metropolitan Railway was opened through to Baker Street.

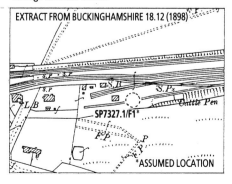
EXTRACT FROM BUCKINGHAMSHIRE 18.12 (1898)
*ASSUMED LOCATION

WOLVERTON

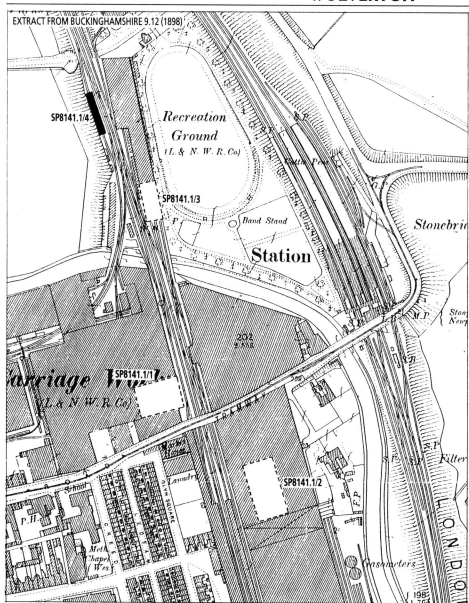

EXTRACT FROM BUCKINGHAMSHIRE 9.12 (1898)

Site SP8141.1; Within Wolverton Works.
Wolverton (L&B)^{SP8141.1/1A}
A stone built shed, it was located at SP81884131 and was opened by the London & Birmingham Railway on September 17th, 1838. Little is known of this depot except that the track was laid out in the form of stalls, probably radiating from turnplates at the east end of the building. The shed was closed in 1856 and incorporated into the works as an Erecting Shop.

Replaced by ...
Wolverton (L&NWR)^{SP8141.2/1A}
A 6TS dead ended shed, it was located at SP81994123 and was opened in 1856. Details of its construction are not known. From 1859 the building was known as the 'Reserve Locomotive Shed' and the facilities included a turntable. The closure date is not known but by 1898 the whole site had been absorbed into the works complex.

Wolverton (L&NWR)^{SP8141.3/1A}
A brick built 4TS dead ended shed with a tiled gable style roof, it was located at SP81884150 and was opened in 1859. No further details are known except that it was closed in 1874 and the building was incorporated into the works.

Wolverton Works (L&NWR)^{SP8141.4/1A}
A timber built 1TS through road shed with a slated gable style roof, it was located at SP81824159 and was opened in 1874. The facilities included a coal stage, sited outside of the shed entrance. The shed was utilized by the works shunters and lasted into BR days finally housing Class 08 shunters. By 1990 it had been demolished.

The original main line passed through the works, with the sheds dispersed around it. Following the deviation of the main line in 1882 the works expanded absorbing all the shed sites.

HIGH WYCOMBE

Site SU8792.1; On the south side of the line, at the east end of High Wycombe Station.
High Wycombe (GC/GWR)^{SU8792.1/F1}
A servicing area consisting of a siding. The date it was established is not known but locomotives were serviced until BR days probably not closing until c1965.

Site SU8693.1; On the north side of Wycombe Station.
Wycombe (Wycombe)^{SU8693.1/1A}
A brick built 1TS through road shed with a slated gable style roof it adjoined the train shed and was located at SU86859306. It was opened by the Wycombe Railway on August 1st, 1854. The facilities are not known. The shed was closed in August 1870 and incorporated, along with the station, into a goods shed. The building was still standing in 1994, in use as a garage.

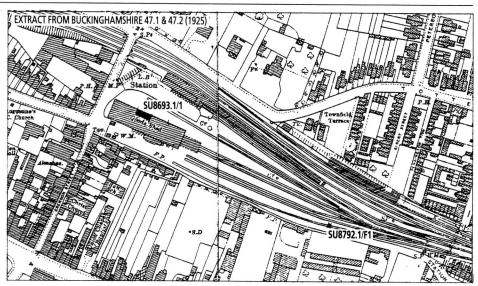

EXTRACT FROM BUCKINGHAMSHIRE 47.1 & 47.2 (1925)

BEDFORDSHIRE

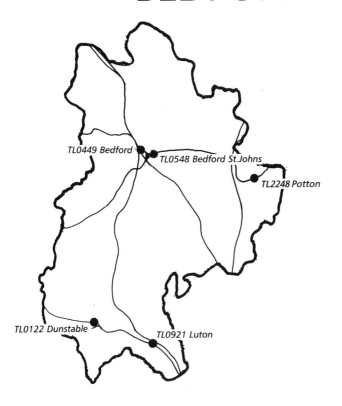

TL0449 Bedford
TL0548 Bedford St.Johns
TL2248 Potton
TL0122 Dunstable
TL0921 Luton

POTTON

Site TL2248.1; On the south side of Potton (S&PR) Station.

Potton (S&PR) TL2248.1/1A

A brick built 1TS dead ended shed with a slated gable style roof, it was located at TL22024898 and was opened by the Sandy & Potton Railway on June 23rd, 1857. Details of the facilities are not known. The line became part of the Bedford & Cambridge Railway on July 7th, 1862 and was worked by the L&NWR, being absorbed by them in 1865. The closure date is not known but the shed was leased out for private use and was still standing in 1995.

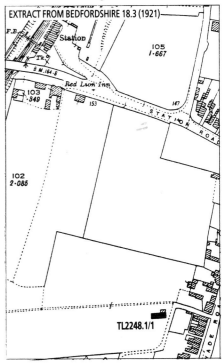

EXTRACT FROM BEDFORDSHIRE 18.3 (1921)

TL2248.1/1

DUNSTABLE

Site TL0122.1; On the north side of Dunstable North Station.

Dunstable (GNR) TL0122.1/F1

A servicing area consisting of a turntable, located at TL01102262, and siding was established here. The opening and closing dates are not known but the turntable was still in use in BR days.

Site TL0122.2; In the vicinity of Dunstable (L&NWR) Station.

Dunstable (L&NWR) TL0122.2/1A

A 1TS shed, it was probably built in timber and was approximately located at TL011226. No further details are known.

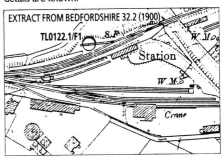

EXTRACT FROM BEDFORDSHIRE 32.2 (1900)

TL0122.1/F1

LUTON

Site TL0921.2; On the north side of the line, at the west end of Luton (GN) Station.

Luton (LD&WJR) TL0921.2/1A

A 1TS dead ended shed, probably constructed in timber, it was located at TL09142159 and was opened by the Luton, Dunstable & Welwyn Junction Railway on May 3rd, 1858. The facilities included a 40ft turntable. The line was absorbed by the GNR on June 12th, 1861 and the depot was probably closed in the same year.

Replaced in c1861 by ...

Luton (GNR) TL0921.2/2A

A brick built 1TS dead ended shed with a tiled pitched roof incorporating a water tank, it was sited slightly west of its predecessor (TL0921.2/1A) at TL09082160. Additional facilities included a coke-/coal stage.

The shed was extended ...

Luton (GNR) TL0921.2/2B

At some stage a 20ft pitched roof extension was built at the western end. The depot was closed c1901, the eastern portion of the building was demolished and the track continued through the rear wall to gain access to the yard at the rear. It was then utilized as a store until October 1970 when it was demolished and the whole site was given over to car parking.

Site TL0921.0; In the vicinity of Luton (MR) Station.

Luton (MR) TL0921.0/1A

Some sort of shed was provided here, probably from c1868. No further details are available.

Replaced by ...

Site TL0921.1; On the south side of the line, at the west end of Luton (MR) Station.

Luton (MR) TL0921.1/F1

A servicing point consisting of a turntable, located at TL09152162, and a siding was established here. No further details are available.

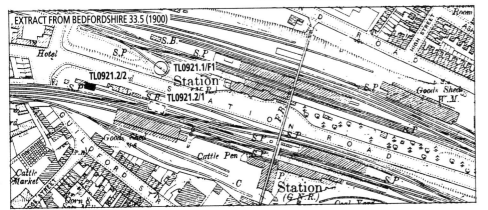

EXTRACT FROM BEDFORDSHIRE 33.5 (1900)

TL0921.2/2
TL0921.1/F1
TL0921.2/1

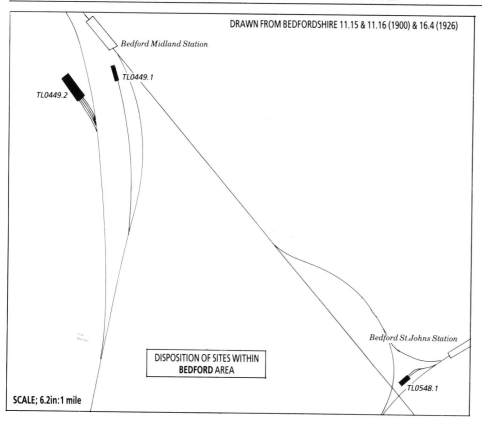

DRAWN FROM BEDFORDSHIRE 11.15 & 11.16 (1900) & 16.4 (1926)

Bedford Midland Station

TL0449.1

TL0449.2

Bedford St.Johns Station

TL0548.1

DISPOSITION OF SITES WITHIN
BEDFORD AREA

SCALE; 6.2in:1 mile

Site TL0449.1; On the west side of the Hitchin line, south of Bedford (MR) Station.
Bedford (MR)^{TL0449.1/1A}
A brick built 2TS dead ended shed with a slated gable style roof, it was located at TL04304950 and was opened in 1868. The facilities included a water crane and a 42ft turntable, later enlarged to 46ft. The depot was closed in 1886, but saw further use as a PW depot until well into BR days. The building was reduced in length and was still standing in 1990.

Replaced by ...
Site TL0449.2; On the west side of the avoiding line, south of Bedford (MR) Station.
Bedford (MR)^{TL0449.2/1A}
A brick built 4TS dead ended shed with a slated northlight pattern roof, it was located at TL04204945 and was opened in 1868. Initially it utilized the facilities of its predecessor (TL0449.1/1A) but, following the construction of the avoiding line in 1894, a coal stage and turntable were provided in the shed yard.

The shed was re-roofed in 1951 ...
Bedford (BR)^{TL0449.2/1B}
A flat roof with a brick screen was installed by the Midland Region. The depot was closed to steam in August 1963 and subsequently saw brief use as a diesel depot. The building was still standing in 1995.

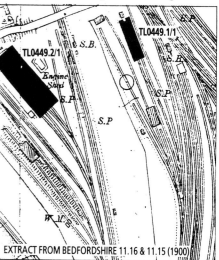

EXTRACT FROM BEDFORDSHIRE 11.16 & 11.15 (1900)

Site TL0548.1; On the north side of the line, at the west end of Bedford St.Johns Station.
Bedford St.Johns (Bedford)^{TL0548.1/1A}
A brick built 2TS through road shed with a slated gable style roof, it was located at TL05124882 and was opened by the Bedford Railway on November 17th, 1846. A turntable was not required as locomotives turned on the adjacent triangle, and water was taken at the station. The line was worked by the L&NWR from the outset and was absorbed by them in 1879. The depot was closed by the LMS on January 1st, 1924 and was subsequently demolished.

Bedford's 1886 MR shed (TL0449.2/1B) on view, late in 1956; the former northlight roof had been replaced in 1951/2. It does not require a sharp eye to detect ex-SR Class D 4-4-0 No.31577 in the yard, laying over after railtour duty. This loco along with No.31075 were by now the two last Class D's in service.

The MR had an earlier 2TS depot (TL0449.1/1A) and this was sited just out of picture to the right and adjacent to the overbridge arches. A small portion of that building still stood in 1997 as did the remains of the 4TS building, lying derelict over thirty years after closure to steam.

Author's Collection

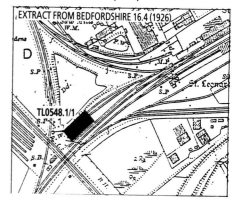

EXTRACT FROM BEDFORDSHIRE 16.4 (1926)

TL0548.1/1

ESSEX

TL5438 Saffron Walden
TL8130 Halstead
TL6030 Thaxted
TL7622 Braintree
TL8619 Kelvedon
TL8215 Witham
TL7007 Chelmsford
TL7107 Chelmsford
TL5503 Ongar
TL4601 Epping
TQ8097 Woodham Ferrers
TQ9699 Southminster
TQ4295 Loughton
TQ6194 Shenfield
TQ5993 Brentwood
TQ7493 Wickford
TQ5188 Romford
TQ5389 Gidea Park
TQ5686 Upminster
TQ8785 Southend on Sea
TQ8886 Southend Victoria
TQ8885 Southend on Sea
TQ9385 Shoeburyness
TQ6475 Tilbury
TL9926 Colchester
TL9123 Marks Tey
TM0816 Brightlingsea
TM2521 Walton on Naze
TM1715 Clacton
TM2432 Parkeston Quay
TM2532 Harwich
TM2531 Dovercourt Bay
TL8507 Maldon

For convenience CHINGFORD, GOODMAYES and ILFORD depots have been included in the GREATER LONDON section.

BRAINTREE

Site TL7622.1; In the goods yard on the north side of the line, east of Braintree Station.
Braintree (GER)[TL7622.1/1A]
A timber built 1TS through road shed it was located at TL76412284 and was opened on August 15th, 1848. Details of the facilities are not known, but a turntable was installed at the station in 1869. The building was destroyed in a gale on December 16th, 1909.

Replaced on the same site by ...
Braintree (GER)[TL7622.1/1B]
A brick built 1TS through road shed with a shallow tiled gable style roof it was opened on December 21st, 1911. The facilities included a coal stage and water tank. The depot was closed by BR in November 1959 and was subsequently demolished.

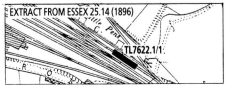

EXTRACT FROM ESSEX 25.14 (1896)
TL7622.1/1

BRENTWOOD

Site TQ5993.1; On the north side of Brentwood & Warley Station.
Brentwood (ECR)[TQ5993.1/F1]
Some form of facility, including a turntable probably located at TQ59489304, was opened here by the Eastern Counties Railway on July 1st, 1840. It was closed in 1872.

Replaced by ...
Brentwood (GER)[TQ5993.1/1A]
A timber built 2TS dead ended shed, it was located at TQ59429304 and was opened in 1872. The facilities included a turntable. By 1894 it was considered to be too small and was demolished.

Replaced on the same site by ...
Brentwood (GER)[TQ5993.1/1B]
A brick built 3TS dead ended shed with a wooden gable and slated pitched roof, it was opened in 1894. The facilities included a coal stage, water tank and a turntable which was removed in 1917. The depot was closed by BR in 1949*.

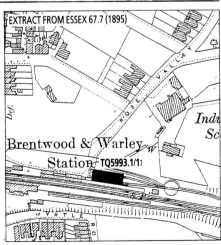

EXTRACT FROM ESSEX 67.7 (1895)

Brentwood & Warley Station TQ5993.1/1

*Following closure a small petrol shunter was stabled in the yard until its withdrawal in September 1956.

CLACTON

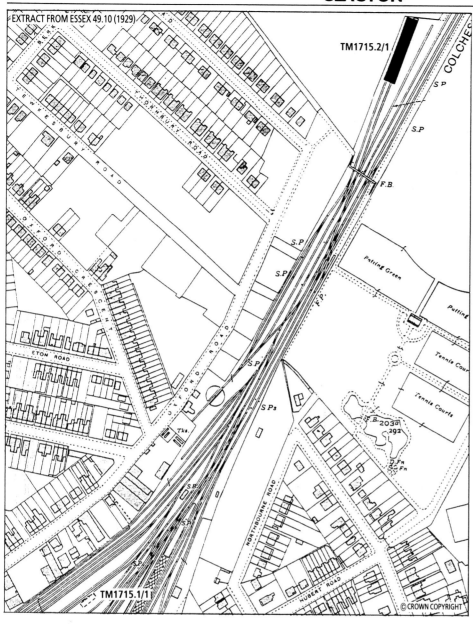

EXTRACT FROM ESSEX 49.10 (1929)

TM1715.2/1

TM1715.1/1

© CROWN COPYRIGHT

Site TM1715.1; On the west side of Clacton Station.
Clacton (Clacton)^{TM1715.1/1A} TM1715.1/1A
A timber built 1TS through road shed with a slated gable style roof, located at TM17621545 and opened by the Clacton-on-Sea Railway on July 4th, 1882. The facilities included a turntable and coal stage.

The building was modified ...
Clacton (GER)^{TM1715.1/1B} TM1715.1/1B
At some stage the shed was altered to a through road structure and water tanks were installed in 1914. The shed was destroyed by a storm in 1927.

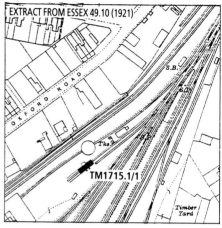

EXTRACT FROM ESSEX 49.10 (1921)

TM1715.1/1

Replaced by ...
Site TM1715.2; On the west side of the line, north of Clacton Station.
Clacton (LNER)^{TM1715.2/1A} TM1715.2/1A
A timber built 2TS dead ended shed with a gable style roof, located at TM17901595 and opened in 1928. The facilities included a 60ft turntable, coal stage and water tank. The building was closed to steam by BR on April 13th, 1959 and converted for use as an emu depot*

Replaced, for steam locomotives, by ...
Clacton (BR)^{TM1715.2/2A} TM1715.2/2A
A temporary shed was built in the shed yard by the Eastern Region. Despite the relatively recent construction date no further details are known except that it was dispensed with in 1961.

*The building was lengthened at its southern end by a corrugated asbestos extension with a corrugated asbestos gable style roof (TM1715.2/1B)

CHELMSFORD

Site TL7007.0; In the vicinity of Chelmsford Station.
Chelmsford (ECR)^{TL7007.0/F1} TL7007.0/F1
A locomotive was stabled here by the Eastern Counties Railway from March 7th, 1843. No more details are known.

Site TL7007.1; On the south side of the line, at the east end of Chelmsford Station.
Chelmsford (GER)^{TL7007.1/F1} TL7007.1/F1
A servicing area consisting of a siding and coke/coal stage, located at TL70770719, was opened in 1867. It was closed on November 27th, 1883.

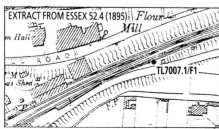

EXTRACT FROM ESSEX 52.4 (1895)

TL7007.1/F1

Replaced by ...
Site TL7107.1; In the goods yard on the north side of the line, east of Chelmsford Station.
Chelmsford (GER)^{TL7107.1/F1} TL7107.1/F1
A servicing area consisting of coal stage, water tank, pit and sidings was opened on November 27th, 1883. It was located at TL71350748 and was closed by BR in 1961.

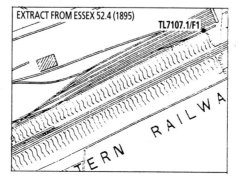

EXTRACT FROM ESSEX 52.4 (1895)

TL7107.1/F1

GIDEA PARK

Site TQ5389.1; On the north side of the line, east of Gidea Park Station.
Gidea Park (LNER)^{TQ5389.1/F1} TQ5389.1/F1
A servicing point consisting of a water column and engine pit it was located at TQ53188950. It was opened prior to 1932* and probably lasted into BR days.

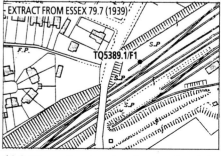

EXTRACT FROM ESSEX 79.7 (1939)

TQ5389.1/F1

*A facility may have been in existence prior to this, but no specific details are known.

COLCHESTER

Site TL9926.1; At the west end of Colchester Station.

Colchester (ECR)[TL9926.1/1A]

A shed was opened here by the Eastern Counties Railway on March 7th, 1843. No further details are known.

Site TL9926.2; On the north side of the line, east of Colchester Station.

Colchester (EUR)[TL9926.2/1A]

A 1TS shed, it was opened by the Eastern Union Railway in 1846, but did not last for long being destroyed by a fire on January 25th, 1850. The precise location is not known but it is assumed to have been that of its antecedents at TL99512638.

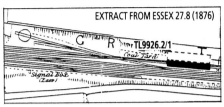

EXTRACT FROM ESSEX 27.8 (1876)

Replaced on the same site by ...

Colchester (EUR)[TL9926.2/1B]

A dead ended 1TS shed, it was opened by the Eastern Union Railway in 1850. The facilities included a turntable and coal stage.

The building was extended ...

Colchester (EUR)[TL9926.2/1C]

Some sort of extension was built during the period 1869-77. The shed was closed in 1890.

Replaced on the same site by ...

Colchester (GER)[TL9926.2/1D]

A brick built 3TS shed with one through road and a slated northlight pattern roof, it was opened in 1890.

The shed was re-roofed.

Colchester (LNER)[TL9926.2/1E]

During improvements completed in 1936 the depot was rebuilt with LNER-style *blockhouse* gables and slated roof and a small mechanical coaler was installed. The shed was closed by BR on November 2nd, 1959.

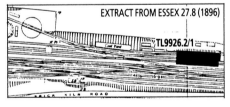

EXTRACT FROM ESSEX 27.8 (1896)

KELVEDON

Site TL8619.1; On the north side of the line, at the west end of Kelvedon Low Level Station.

Kelvedon (GER)[TL8619.1/1A]

A concrete built 1TS dead ended shed with a corrugated iron gable style roof, it was located at TL86401936 and was opened on October 1st, 1904. The facilities included a water tank and coal stage sited outside of the shed entrance. The shed was closed by BR on May 5th, 1951.

EXTRACT FROM ESSEX N36.13 (1920)

BRIGHTLINGSEA

Site TM0816.1; On the west side of Brightlingsea Station.

Brightlingsea (W&BR)[TM0816.1/F1]

A servicing area consisting of a coal stage and water tank was opened on April 18th, 1866 by the Wivenhoe & Brightlingsea Railway. The line was later absorbed by the GE in 1893. The precise location is not known but is assumed to have been in the general area of the shed (TM0816.1/1A) which subsequently replaced it in 1901.

Replaced by ...

Brightlingsea (GE)[TM0816.1/1A]

A brick built 1TS dead ended shed with a northlight pattern roof, it was located at TM08231662 and was opened in 1901. The facilities included a coal stage and water column sited on the shed road. The depot was closed by the LNER in June 1939 but it was not demolished immediately, lasting in a semi-derelict state until at least 1960. The site has since been cleared.

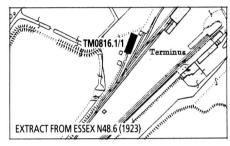

EXTRACT FROM ESSEX N48.6 (1923)

EPPING

Site TL4601.1; On the west side of Epping Station.

Epping (GER)[TL4601.1/F1]

Some sort of locomotive facility was in use here from at least 1865. No further details are known.

Replaced by ...

Epping (GER)[TL4601.1/1A]

A brick built 2TS dead ended shed with a slated northlight pattern roof, it was located at TL46110154 and was opened in 1893. The facilities included a 50ft turntable and water column.

The shed was rebuilt in 1949 ...

Epping (LTE)[TL4601.1/1B]

The building was reconstructed with a brick screen and new roof by London Transport. The depot was closed on November 18th, 1957.

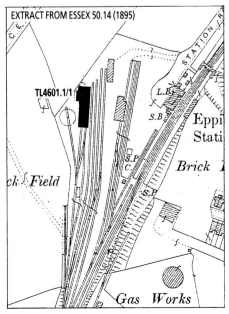

EXTRACT FROM ESSEX 50.14 (1895)

HARWICH

Site TM2532.1; On the east side of the line, at the south end of Harwich Town Station.

Harwich Town (ECR)[TM2532.1/F1]

A servicing area consisting of a 42ft turntable, located at TM25973227, and a coal stage was opened by the Eastern Counties Railway on August 15th, 1854. It is not known when the facility was closed but it was still being utilized in LNER days.

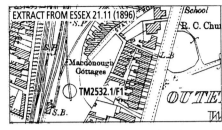

EXTRACT FROM ESSEX 21.11 (1896)

Site TM2531.1; On the south side of the line, at the west end of Dovercourt Bay Station.

Dovercourt Bay (ECR)[TM2531.1/1A]

A timber built 1TS through road shed, it was located at TM25473174 and was opened by the Eastern Counties Railway on August 15th, 1854. The shed was closed by the GER in March 1883.

EXTRACT FROM ESSEX 21.11 (1874)

Replaced by ...
Site TM2432.1; On the east side of the line, at the south end of Parkeston Station.

Parkeston Quay (GER)[TM2432.1/1A]

A brick built 4TS dead ended shed with a slated twin gable style roof incorporating a large water tank, it was located at TM24173252 and was opened in March 1883. Other facilities included a 50ft turntable and a coal stage.

The shed was re-roofed in 1950 ...

Parkeston Quay (BR)[TM2432.1/1B]

The gable ends and roof were replaced with corrugated asbestos sheeting by the Eastern Region. The shed was closed to steam in January 1960 and was partially demolished.

A brick built 1TS through road shed with a gable style roof was added by the LNER in 1947 to the east wall of the main building (TM2432.1/1) at TM24183253. This was utilized as a small diesel depot (TM2432.1/2A).

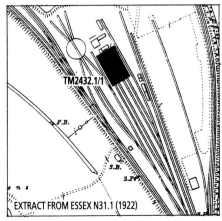

EXTRACT FROM ESSEX N31.1 (1922)

The depot was totally closed in February 1967 and subsequently demolished.

HALSTEAD

Site TL8130.1; On the east side of the line, south of Halstead Station.

Halstead (CV&HR)^{TL8130.1/1A}
A timber built 1TS dead ended shed, it was located at TL81243037 and was opened by the Colne Valley & Halstead Railway on June 16th, 1860. The shed was closed in c1903 and demolished to facilitate the re-modelling of the yard.

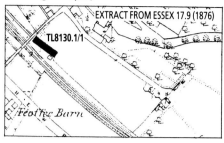

EXTRACT FROM ESSEX 17.9 (1876)

Replaced by ...

Halstead (CV&HR)^{TL8130.1/2A}
A corrugated iron 2TS dead ended shed, it was located at TL81333031 and was opened by the Colne Valley & Halstead Railway in c1903. The depot took over from Haverhill (TL6744.1/1A) as the works for the line. The shed was closed by the LNER in January 1924.

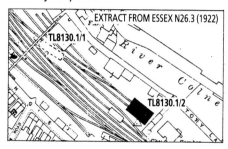

EXTRACT FROM ESSEX N26.3 (1922)

UPMINSTER

Site TQ5686.1; On the north side of the line, at the east end of Upminster Station.

Upminster (LT&SR)^{TQ5686.1/1A}
A brick built 2TS through road shed with a slated gable style roof, it was located at TQ56408689 and was opened by the London Tilbury & Southend Railway in 1893. The facilities included a water tank, turntable and coal stage. The shed was closed by the LMS in 1931 and demolished to facilitate track widening.

Replaced by ...

Upminster (LMS)^{TQ5686.1/2A}
A brick built 1TS through road shed with a slated gable style roof, it was located closer to the station at TQ56318689 and was opened in 1931. The facilities included a covered coal stage and water tank. The shed was closed by BR on September 17th, 1956 and subsequently demolished.

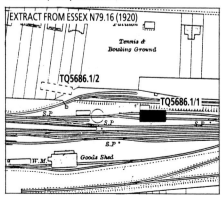

EXTRACT FROM ESSEX N79.16 (1920)

ONGAR

Site TL5503.1; On the north side of Ongar Station.

Ongar (GER)^{TL5503.1/1A}
A brick built 1TS through road shed, with a slated gable style roof, it was located at TL55050350 and was opened on April 24th, 1865. The facilities included a 40ft turntable, coal stage and water tank. The shed was closed by the LNER in c1944 and demolished.

A servicing point was then established ...

Ongar LNER^{TL5503.1/F1}
Locomotives were then stabled and serviced on the shed site. The depot was officially closed by BR on September 25th, 1949 but saw further use until the end of steam on the branch in 1957.

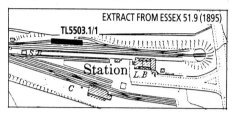

EXTRACT FROM ESSEX 51.9 (1895)

MALDON EAST

Site TL8507.1; On the east side of the line, at the south end of Maldon East Station.

Maldon East (ECR)^{TL8507.1/1A}
A brick built 2TS dead ended shed with a large brick screen incorporating a water tank, and single pitched roof, it was located at TL85460738 and was opened by the Eastern Counties Railway on August 15th, 1848. The facilities also included a coal stage and turntable. The shed was closed by BR on November 2nd, 1959 and was let for private use, not being demolished until 1995.

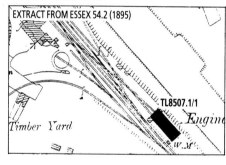

EXTRACT FROM ESSEX 54.2 (1895)

MARKS TEY

Site TL9123.1; In the fork of the Sudbury and Witham lines, at the west end of Marks Tey Station.

Marks Tey (CSVS&HR)^{TL9123.1/1}
A 1TS dead ended shed, it was located at TL91572392 and was opened by the Colchester, Stour Valley, Sudbury & Halstead Railway on July 2nd, 1849. Details of the facilities are not available. The line was worked by the Eastern Union Railway and the shed was closed in 1865. The building was not demolished, initially becoming incorporated in a small gasworks and later seeing use, until at least 1963, as a private dwelling.

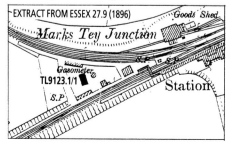

EXTRACT FROM ESSEX 27.9 (1896)

SHOEBURYNESS

Site TQ9385.1; On the north side of Shoeburyness Station.

Shoeburyness (LT&SR)^{TQ9385.1/1A}
A brick built 2TS through road shed with a slated gable style roof, it was located at TQ93968511 and was opened by the London Tilbury & Southend Railway on February 1st, 1884. The facilities included a 42ft turntable coal stage and water tank.

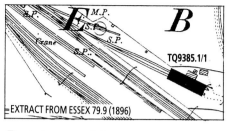

EXTRACT FROM ESSEX 79.9 (1896)

The shed was extended ...

Shoeburyness (LT&SR)^{TQ9385.1/1B}
The building was doubled in length in 1896, becoming a dead ended shed.

Adjoined by ...

Shoeburyness (LT&SR)^{TQ9385.1/2A}
A timber built 1TS dead ended shed with a pitched corrugated iron roof, it was constructed in 1898 and sited adjacently to the south side of the depot (TQ9385.1/1) at TQ93968510.

It was rebuilt ...

Shoeburyness (LMS)^{TQ9385.1/2B}
A corrugated iron 2TS dead ended shed with a corrugated iron gable style roof, it was built in 1933.

It was rebuilt again ...

Shoeburyness (BR)^{TQ9385.1/2C}
The shed was re-roofed in corrugated iron by the London Midland Region in 1955.

The depot was closed by BR on June 18th, 1962 and replaced by ....

Shoeburyness (BR)^{TQ9385.1/F1}
The shed buildings were demolished and a servicing area consisting of a new coal stage and water columns established around the turntable at TQ93858519. It went out of use in the mid-60s.

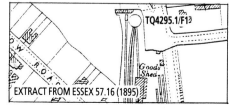

EXTRACT FROM TQ9385 (1962) © CROWN COPYRIGHT

LOUGHTON

Site TQ4295.1; At the north end of the goods yard, on the west side of Loughton Station.

Loughton (GER)^{TQ4295.1/F1}
A servicing area consisting of a turntable, located at TQ42219578, coal stage and siding was established here. The opening date is not known but it went out of use in about 1883.

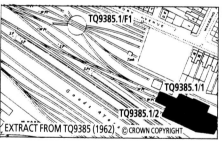

EXTRACT FROM ESSEX 57.16 (1895)

SOUTHEND ON SEA

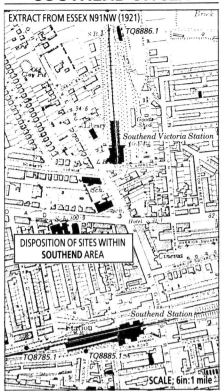

EXTRACT FROM ESSEX N91NW (1921):

DISPOSITION OF SITES WITHIN SOUTHEND AREA

Southend Victoria Station

Southend Station

SCALE; 6in:1 mile

Site TQ8885.1; On the south side of Southend Station.

Southend on Sea (LT&SR)^{TQ8885.1/1A}
A 2TS through road shed with a pitched roof, it was located at TQ88068548 and was opened by the London Tilbury & Southend Railway on March 1st,1856. The facilities included a turntable and coal stage. The shed was closed in 1884 and demolished.

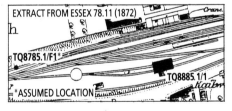

EXTRACT FROM ESSEX 78.11 (1872)

TQ8785.1/F1*

TQ8885.1/1

*ASSUMED LOCATION

Replaced by ...
Site TQ8785.1; On the north side of the line, at the west end of Southend Station.

Southend on Sea (LT&SR)^{TQ8785.1/F1}
A servicing area consisting of a coal stage and probably located at TQ87908547 was established in 1884. The depot was closed by BR on June 18th, 1962.

Site TQ8886.1; On the east side of the line, at the north end of Southend Victoria Station.

Southend Victoria (GER)^{TQ8886.1/1A}
A brick built 2TS through road shed with a slated gable style roof, it was located at TQ88138636 and was opened on October 1st, 1889. The facilities included a water tank, coal stage (later replaced by a small mechanical coaler) and 50ft turntable.

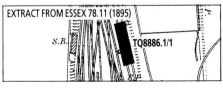

EXTRACT FROM ESSEX 78.11 (1895)

TQ8886.1/1

At some stage it was rebuilt ...
Southend Victoria (BR)^{TQ8886.1/1B}
The shed entrance, gable ends and roof were rebuilt, probably by the Eastern Region and at some time prior to 1955. The shed was closed by BR in 1957.

TILBURY

Site TQ6475.1; In the triangle of lines, north of Tilbury Station.

Tilbury (LT&SR)^{TQ6475.1/1A}
A 2TS dead ended shed with a gable style pitched roof, it was located at TQ64397560 and was opened by the London Tilbury & Southend Railway on April 13th, 1854. The facilities included a turntable, coal stage and water tank. The shed was closed in 1908 and saw further use as a store until it was demolished in the 1940s.

Replaced by ...
Tilbury (LT&SR)^{TQ6475.1/2A}
A corrugated iron 4TS through road shed with a corrugated iron twin gable style roof, it was located at TQ64447579 and was opened in 1912. The facilities included the turntable of its predecessor (TQ6475.1/1) and a small coaling plant installed later by the LMS. By BR days the building was totally decrepit.

It was rebuilt in 1956 ...
Tilbury (BR)^{TQ6475.1/2B}
The building was totally re-clad in corrugated asbestos by the Eastern Region. The shed was closed on June 18th, 1962 and was subsequently demolished.

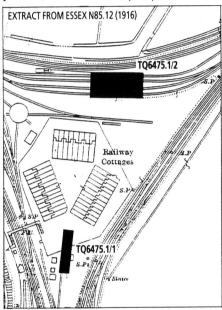

EXTRACT FROM ESSEX N85.12 (1916)

TQ6475.1/2

Railway Cottages

TQ6475.1/1

ROMFORD

Site TQ5188.1; On the south side of the line, west of Romford Station.

Romford (GER)^{TQ5188.1/F1}
A servicing area consisting of a pit, water column and coaling stage, it was located at TQ51028829. The opening and closure dates are not known, but it did last until BR days.

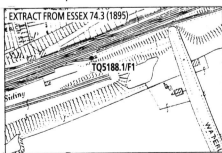

EXTRACT FROM ESSEX 74.3 (1895)

TQ5188.1/F1

An engine shed may have been in existence at Romford Factory (at TQ535896), but no details are available.

SHENFIELD

Site TQ6194.1; On the east side of the line, at the south end of Shenfield & Hutton Junction Station.

Shenfield (GER)^{TQ6194.1/F1}
A servicing area consisting of a turntable and siding, it was located at TQ61319481. No further details are known.

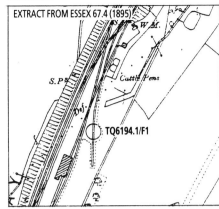

EXTRACT FROM ESSEX 67.4 (1895)

TQ6194.1/F1

SOUTHMINSTER

Site TQ9699.1; On the east side of Southminster Station.

Southminster (GER)^{TQ9699.1/1A}
A brick built 2TS through road shed with a slated gable style roof, it was located at TQ96229955 and was opened on June 1st, 1889. The facilities included a 50ft turntable, water column and coal stage. The building was roofless by BR days with locomotives being serviced in the shed yard. The depot was closed by BR in c1956.

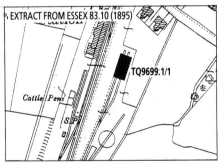

EXTRACT FROM ESSEX 83.10 (1895)

TQ9699.1/1

Cattle Pens

THAXTED

Site TL6030.1; At the end of the line, at the north end of Thaxted Station.

Thaxted (E&TR)^{TL6030.1/1A}
A brick built 1TS dead ended shed with a slated gable style roof, it was located at TL60493009 and was opened by the Elsenham & Thaxted Railway on February 1st, 1913. The facilities included a water tank. The line was worked by the GER from the outset and the shed was closed by BR on September 13th, 1952. The building was not demolished and was still standing, in private use, in 1996.

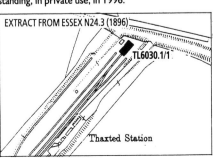

EXTRACT FROM ESSEX N24.3 (1896)

TL6030.1/1

Thaxted Station

SAFFRON WALDEN

Site TL5438.1; On the south side of the line, east of Saffron Walden Station.
Saffron Walden (Saffron Walden)[TL5438.1/1A]
A brick built 1TS through road shed with timber gables and a slated pitched roof, it was located at TL54163804 and was opened by the Saffron Walden Railway on October 22nd, 1866. The facilities included a water tank, coal stage sited outside of the shed entrance and a 40ft turntable at the rear. The line was worked by the GER and absorbed by them on January 1st, 1877. The shed was closed by BR in July 1958.

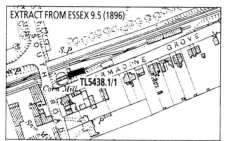
EXTRACT FROM ESSEX 9.5 (1896)
TL5438.1/1

WITHAM

Site TL8215.1; In the fork of the Braintree and Colchester lines, at the north end of Witham Station.
Witham (GER)[TL8215.1/F1]
A servicing area consisting of a 42ft turntable, located at TL82241546, and a coal stage. It was in place prior to 1875 and an enlarged turntable was on the site in BR days. The precise opening and closure dates are not known.

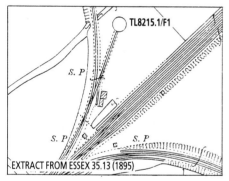
TL8215.1/F1
EXTRACT FROM ESSEX 35.13 (1895)

WOODHAM FERRERS

Site TQ8097.1; On the south side of Woodham Ferrers Station.
Woodham Ferrers* (GER)[TQ8097.1/F1]
A servicing area consisting of a turntable, located at TQ80369777, coal stage and engine pit, it was opened on June 1st, 1889. It fell out of use at some time prior to 1911.

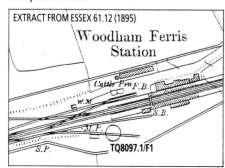
EXTRACT FROM ESSEX 61.12 (1895)
Woodham Ferris Station
TQ8097.1/F1

The location was originally known as Woodham Ferris.

WALTON ON NAZE

Site TM2521.1; On the north side of Walton on Naze Station.
Walton on Naze (THR)[TM2521.1/1A]
A brick built 1TS dead ended shed with a slated gable style roof, it was located at TM25102145 and was opened by the Tendring Hundred Railway on May 17th, 1867. The facilities included a 45ft turntable, water tank and coal stage. The line was worked by the GER and absorbed by them on July 1st, 1883.

The shed was re-roofed ...
Walton on Naze (BR)[TM2521.1/1B]
The gable ends and roof were rebuilt, probably by BR. The shed was closed in June 1963.

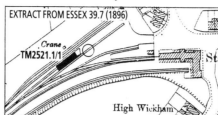
EXTRACT FROM ESSEX 39.7 (1896)
Crane
TM2521.1/1
High Wickham

Situated by the original branch terminus station **Braintree**'s 1TS shed (TL7622.1/1B) is seen on April 16th, 1949 with ex-LNER Class F5 2-4-2T No.67192 and ex-LNER Class J69 0-6-0T No.(6)8629 in residence. This building had been provided in December 1911 - to replace an 1848 shed (TL7622.1/1A) which had been blown down in a gale in December 1909 - and was itself closed around the end of 1959.   *WA Camwell*

The GER's 1893 2TS northlight shed (TL4601.1/1A) at **Epping** was somewhat in need of repair when the LTE took over the line in 1949 to provide an extension to the Central Line tube services for passengers. Goods traffic, however, was to remain in the hands of BR and, after some bargaining no doubt, BR got the LTE to repair Epping Shed. The results (as TL4601.1/1B) are seen here in August 1953 with ex-LNER Class C12 4-4-2T No.67363 of Stratford Shed in residence. In the next month this loco would be transferred away from this Essex backwater to Annesley shed.   *Author's Collection*

WICKFORD

Site TQ7493.1; On the west side of Wickford Station.
Wickford (GER)[TQ7493.1/F1]
A servicing area consisting of a turntable, located at TQ74479369, coal stage, water tank and engine pit. It opened on January 1st, 1889 and was closed by BR in 1954.

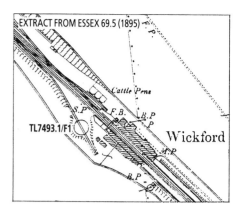
EXTRACT FROM ESSEX 69.5 (1895)
TL7493.1/F1
Cattle Pens
Wickford

NORFOLK

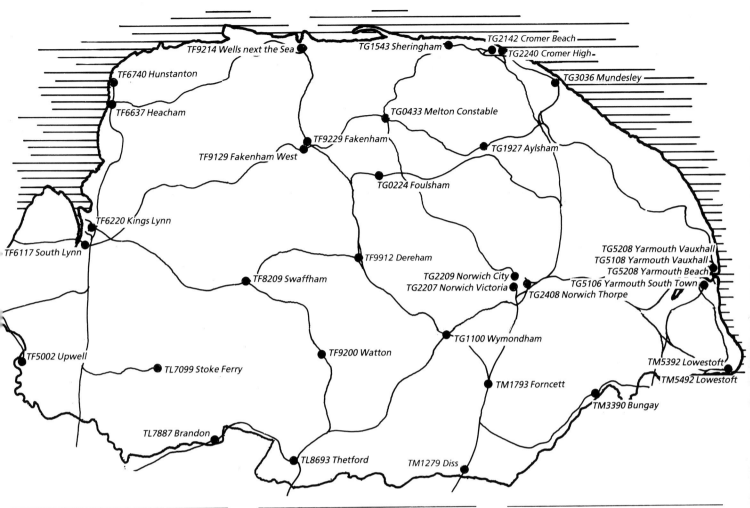

TG2142 Cromer Beach
TG1543 Sheringham
TG2240 Cromer High
TF9214 Wells next the Sea
TG3036 Mundesley
TF6740 Hunstanton
TF6637 Heacham
TG0433 Melton Constable
TF9229 Fakenham
TG1927 Aylsham
TF9129 Fakenham West
TG0224 Foulsham
TF6220 Kings Lynn
TF6117 South Lynn
TF9912 Dereham
TG5208 Yarmouth Vauxhall
TG5108 Yarmouth Vauxhall
TG5208 Yarmouth Beach
TG2209 Norwich City
TG2207 Norwich Victoria
TG5106 Yarmouth South Town
TF8209 Swaffham
TG2408 Norwich Thorpe
TF5002 Upwell
TG1100 Wymondham
TF9200 Watton
TM5392 Lowestoft
TL7099 Stoke Ferry
TM5492 Lowestoft
TM1793 Forncett
TM3390 Bungay
TL7887 Brandon
TL8693 Thetford
TM1279 Diss

AYLSHAM

Site TG1927.1; In the vicinity of Aylsham (M&GNR) Station.

Aylsham (M&GNR)^{TG1927.1/F1}
A servicing area consisting of a turntable and coal stage, it was opened in 1899. No further details are known.

BRANDON

Site TL7887.1; On the north side of the line, at the east end of Brandon Station.

Brandon (Norfolk)^{TL7887.1/1A}
A brick built 6TS through road shed, probably with three slated gable style roofs, it was located at TL78528729 and was opened by the Norfolk Railway on July 29th, 1845. The facilities included a water tank. The line was absorbed by the Eastern Counties Railway on May 8th, 1848 and the shed was closed in 1850. It was not demolished immediately, being utilized for other purposes until at least 1912.

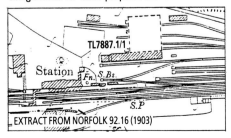

TL7887.1/1
Station Fn. S.Bs.
S.P
EXTRACT FROM NORFOLK 92.16 (1903)

DEREHAM

Site TF9912.1; In the triangle of lines, at the south end of Dereham Station.

Dereham (Norfolk)^{TF9912.1/1A}
A timber built 2TS dead ended shed with a slated gable style roof, located at TF99371289 and opened by the Norfolk Railway on December 7th, 1846. The facilities included a turntable. The line was absorbed by the Eastern Counties Railway in 1848. The building became life expired and was closed by the LNER in 1927.

Replaced, on the same site, by ...
Dereham (LNER)^{TF9912.1/1B}
A brick built 2TS dead ended shed with a slated gable style roof, it was opened in 1927. The depot was closed to steam by BR on September 19th, 1955 and the building was then utilized as a stabling point for dmus until total closure in 1969.

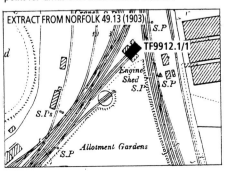

EXTRACT FROM NORFOLK 49.13 (1903)
TF9912.1/1
Engine Shed
S.P
Allotment Gardens

BUNGAY

Site TM3390.1; In the vicinity of Bungay Station.
Bungay (WVR)^{TM3390.1/1A}
Some form of facility, approximately located at TM332901, was opened here by the Waveney Valley Railway on November 2nd, 1860 and was closed on March 2nd, 1863. No further details are known.

FORNCETT

Site TM1793.1; On the east side of the line, north of Forncett Station.
Forncett (GER)^{TM1793.1/F1}
A servicing area consisting of a 44ft turntable, located at TM17359383, was opened on May 2nd, 1881 with an engine pit and siding being added in 1892. The depot was closed by the LNER in 1923.

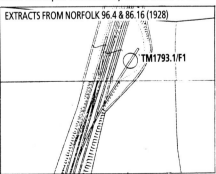

EXTRACTS FROM NORFOLK 96.4 & 86.16 (1928)
TM1793.1/F1

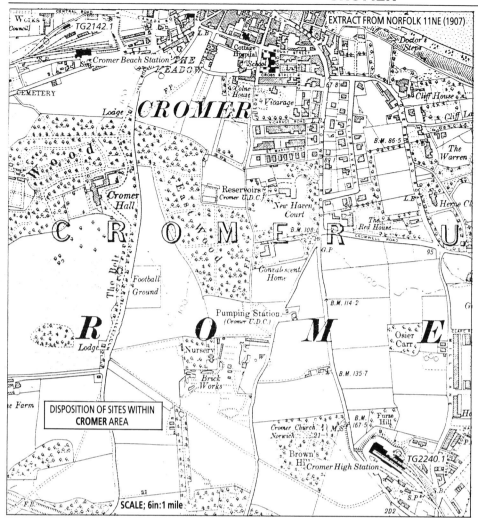

EXTRACT FROM NORFOLK 11NE (1907)

DISPOSITION OF SITES WITHIN
CROMER AREA

SCALE; 6in:1 mile

Site TG2142.1; On the north side of Cromer Beach Station

Cromer Beach (E&MR) ^{TG2142.1/1A}
A brick built 1TS dead ended shed with a slated gable style roof, located at TG21364212 and opened by the Eastern & Midlands Railway on June 16th, 1887. The facilities originally included a 47ft turntable, coal stage and water tank. The shed was closed by BR on March 2nd, 1959 but was not demolished immmediately, remaining standing until at least 1987.

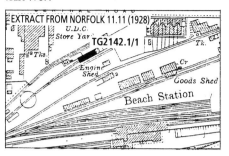

EXTRACT FROM NORFOLK 11.11 (1928)

Site TG2240.1; On the east side of Cromer High Station.

Cromer High (ENR) ^{TG2240.1/1A}
A brick built 1TS dead ended shed with a slated gable style roof, located at TG22364096 and opened by the East Norfolk Railway on March 26th, 1877. The facilities included a turntable. The line was worked by the GER and absorbed by them in 1881.

The shed was extended ...
Cromer High (GER) ^{TG2240.1/1B}
The building was doubled in length with a brick built extension incorporating a water tank in the roof. The shed was closed by BR on September 20th, 1954 and subsequently demolished.

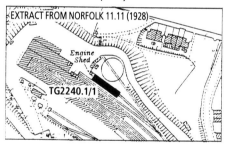

EXTRACT FROM NORFOLK 11.11 (1928)

MELTON CONSTABLE

Site TG0433.1; On the south side of Melton Constable Station.

Melton Constable (L&FR) ^{TG0433.1/1A}
A brick built 3TS dead ended shed with a slated pitched roof and timber gables, it was located at TG04233303 and was opened by the Lynn & Fakenham Railway on January 19th, 1882. The shed was adjacent to the works and had the benefit of all facilities. The line was absorbed by the Eastern & Midlands Railway on January 1st, 1883.

The shed was rebuilt ...
Melton Constable (BR) ^{TG0433.1/1B}
A brick built 3TS dead ended shed with a brick screen and louvre style roof, it was rebuilt by the Eastern Region in 1951. The shed was closed on March 2nd, 1959 but was not demolished, the buildings on the site forming an industrial estate. It was still standing in 1996, in use as a potato store.

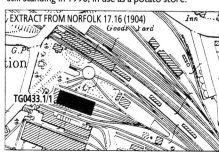

EXTRACT FROM NORFOLK 17.16 (1904)

SWAFFHAM

Site TF8209.1; On the south side of the line east of Swaffham Station.

Swaffham (L&DR) ^{TF8209.1/1A}
A timber built 2TS dead ended shed with a gable style roof, it was located at TF82130949 and was opened by the Lynn & Dereham Railway on August 10th, 1847. The facilities included a water tank, coal stage and, sited outside of the shed entrance, a 45ft turntable. At some stage, probably in LNER days, the shed was demolished.

A servicing point was then established ...
Swaffham (LNER) ^{TF8209.1/F1}
A facility consisting of the water tank, coal stage and an engine pit located at TF82140951. It was closed by BR on April 2nd, 1962.

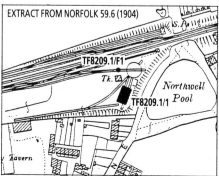

EXTRACT FROM NORFOLK 59.6 (1904)

STOKE FERRY

Site TL7099.1; On the north side of Stoke Ferry Station.

Stoke Ferry (D&SFR) ^{TL7099.1/1A}
A brick built 1TS through road shed, it was located at TL70629966 and was opened by the Downham & Stoke Ferry Railway on August 1st, 1882. The facilities included a coal stage and water tank. The depot was temporarily closed by the GER during World War I and totally closed by the LNER on September 20th, 1930. It was demolished in 1935.

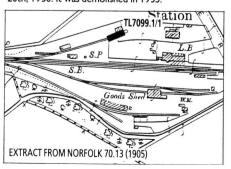

EXTRACT FROM NORFOLK 70.13 (1905)

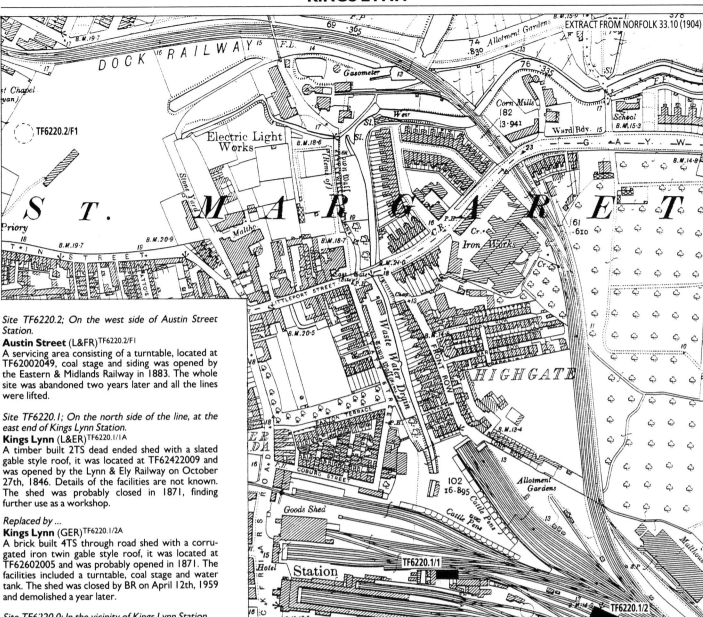

EXTRACT FROM NORFOLK 33.10 (1904)

Site TF6220.2; On the west side of Austin Street Station.

Austin Street (L&FR)^{TF6220.2/F1}
A servicing area consisting of a turntable, located at TF62002049, coal stage and siding was opened by the Eastern & Midlands Railway in 1883. The whole site was abandoned two years later and all the lines were lifted.

Site TF6220.1; On the north side of the line, at the east end of Kings Lynn Station.

Kings Lynn (L&ER)^{TF6220.1/1A}
A timber built 2TS dead ended shed with a slated gable style roof, it was located at TF62422009 and was opened by the Lynn & Ely Railway on October 27th, 1846. Details of the facilities are not known. The shed was probably closed in 1871, finding further use as a workshop.

Replaced by ...

Kings Lynn (GER)^{TF6220.1/2A}
A brick built 4TS through road shed with a corrugated iron twin gable style roof, it was located at TF62602005 and was probably opened in 1871. The facilities included a turntable, coal stage and water tank. The shed was closed by BR on April 12th, 1959 and demolished a year later.

Site TF6220.0; In the vicinity of Kings Lynn Station.

Kings Lynn (L&FR)^{TF6220.0/1A}
A 1TS shed, it was opened by the Lynn & Fakenham Railway on August 16th, 1879. No further details are known.

Site TG1543.1; On the south side of the line, west of Sheringham Station.

Sheringham (GER)^{TG1543.1/F1}
A servicing area consisting of an engine pit and siding, it was located at TG15314312 and was opened in 1906. The facility was closed by the LNER in 1923.

EXTRACT FROM NORFOLK 10.8 (1928)

Site TF6117.1; On the west side of the line, at the south end of South Lynn Station.

South Lynn (E&MR)^{TF6117.1/1A}
A timber built 2TS dead ended shed with a slated gable style roof, it was located at TF61791796 and was opened by the Eastern & Midlands Railway on January 1st, 1886. The facilities included a 47ft turntable, coal stage and water tank.

EXTRACT FROM NORFOLK 33.14 (1905)

The shed was enlarged ...

South Lynn (GER)^{TF6117.1/1B}
A duplicate shed was constructed alongside, making it a 4TS dead ended building. By 1957 it had become very dilapidated.

The shed was rebuilt ...

South Lynn (BR)^{TF6117.1/1C}
A corrugated asbestos 4TS dead ended shed with a twin corrugated asbestos gable style roof, it was opened by the Eastern Region in 1958 and closed by them on February 28th, 1959. It found further use as a NCL depot before being demolished in 1989.

FAKENHAM

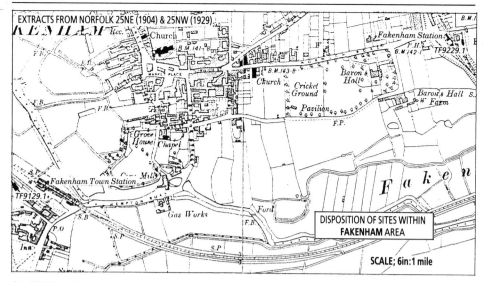

EXTRACTS FROM NORFOLK 25NE (1904) & 25NW (1929)

DISPOSITION OF SITES WITHIN FAKENHAM AREA

SCALE; 6in:1 mile

Site TF9229.1; On the east side of Fakenham Station.
Fakenham (ECR)[TF9229.1/1A]
A 1TS through road shed, it was located at TF92782978 and was opened by the Eastern Counties Railway on March 20th, 1849. The facilities included a turntable. The shed was closed in 1857.

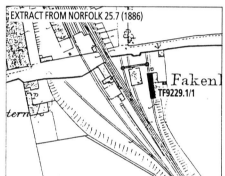

EXTRACT FROM NORFOLK 25.7 (1886)

TF9229.1/1

Site TF9129.1; On the west side of the line, at the north end of Fakenham Town Station.
Fakenham West (L&FR)[TF9129.1/1A]
A concrete block built 2TS dead ended shed with a twin dutch barn style roof in corrugated iron, it was located at TF91482933 and was opened by the Lynn & Fakenham Railway on March 27th, 1880. The facilities included a 45ft turntable. The depot was utilized for locomotive storage during winter months. The closure date is not known.

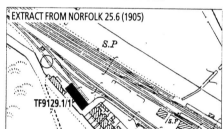

EXTRACT FROM NORFOLK 25.6 (1905)

TF9129.1/1

FOULSHAM

Site TG0224.1; On the north side of the line, east of Foulsham Station.
Foulsham (GER)[TG0224.1/F1]
A servicing area consisting of a siding, engine pit and water tank, it was probably located at TG02592428 and was opened in 1897. It was closed in 1917.

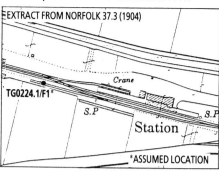

EXTRACT FROM NORFOLK 37.3 (1904)

TG0224.1/F1*

*ASSUMED LOCATION

HEACHAM

Site TF6637.1; On the east side of Heacham Station.
Heacham (GER)[TF6637.1/F1]
A servicing point consisting of a turntable, located at TF66923752, and siding. No further details are known.

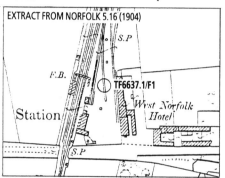

EXTRACT FROM NORFOLK 5.16 (1904)

TF6637.1/F1

LOWESTOFT

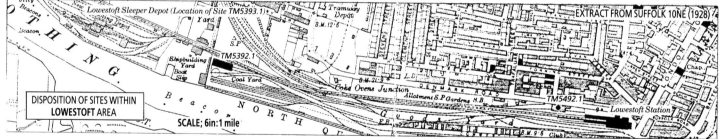

DISPOSITION OF SITES WITHIN LOWESTOFT AREA

SCALE; 6in:1 mile

EXTRACT FROM SUFFOLK 10NE (1928)

Site TM5492.1; On the north side of Lowestoft Station.
Lowestoft (Norfolk)[TM5492.1/1A]
A brick built 2TS shed, it was located at TM54599290 and was opened by the Norfolk Railway on July 1st, 1848. The facilities included a turntable. The line was absorbed by the Eastern Counties Railway in 1848 and the shed was closed in 1883, being regarded as too small for the locomotive allocation.

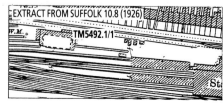

EXTRACT FROM SUFFOLK 10.8 (1926)

TM5492.1/1

Replaced by ...
Site TM5392.1; On the south side of the line, west of Lowestoft Station.
Lowestoft (GER)[TM5392.1/1A]
A brick built 4TS dead ended shed with a slated twin gable style roof, it was located at TM53619297 and was opened in 1883. The facilities included a water tank, turntable and coal stage.

The shed was re-roofed ...
Lowestoft (BR)[TM5392.1/1B]
The building was re-roofed in corrugated asbestos, probably during BR days. The shed was closed on July 7th, 1962 and served as a cattle quarantine station for some years before being demolished.

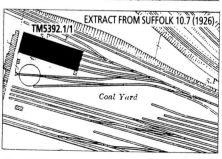

EXTRACT FROM SUFFOLK 10.7 (1926)

TM5392.1/1

Coal Yard

Site TM5393.1; In Lowestoft Sleeper Depot.
Lowestoft Sleeper Depot (GER)[TM5393.1/F1]
Some form of facility was in use to service the Departmental Locomotive from 1914. It went out of use in 1964. No further details are known.

DISPOSITION OF SITES WITHIN
NORWICH AREA

EXTRACT FROM NORFOLK 63SE (1905)

SCALE; 4.24in:1 mile

Site TG2209.1; On the east side of the line, at the north end of Norwich City Station.

Norwich City (L&FR)^{TG2209.1/1A}

A brick built 3TS dead ended shed with timber gables (later replaced with glass) and a slated pitched roof, it was located at TG22490948 and was opened by the Lynn & Fakenham Railway on December 2nd, 1882. The facilities included a 45ft turntable (replaced in 1931 with a 60ft unit), coal stage and water tank. The depot suffered from bomb damage in 1941.

The shed was rebuilt ...

Norwich City (LNER)^{TG2209.1/1B}

A corrugated iron 2TS dead ended shed with a flat corrugated iron roof, it was built in 1942. The depot was closed by BR on February 25th, 1959, the building being sold and re-erected at Weybourne on the *North Norfolk Railway*.

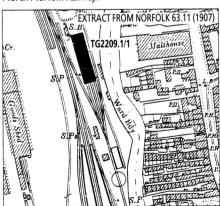

EXTRACT FROM NORFOLK 63.11 (1907)

Site TG2408.1; On the south side of Norwich Thorpe Station.

Norwich Thorpe (Y&NR)^{TG2408.1/1A}

A brick built 4TS through road shed with a brick screen and hipped roofs, one over three tracks and the other over one. It was located at TG24120808 and was opened by the Yarmouth & Norwich Railway on April 30th, 1844. Being sited adjacently to a loco works it possessed all facilities.

The shed was re-roofed ...

Norwich Thorpe (LNER)^{TG2408.1/1B}

Improvements to the facilities and shed were made in 1934, including the installation of a new flat roof. The shed was closed to steam by BR on April 2nd, 1962 and converted to a diesel depot. It was totally closed in the early 1990s and subsequently demolished.

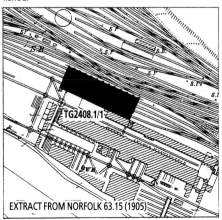

EXTRACT FROM NORFOLK 63.15 (1905)

Site TG2207.1; On the west side of Norwich Victoria Station.

Norwich Victoria (GER)^{TG2207.1/1A}

A 2TS through road shed, it was located at TG22830787, and its facilities included a turntable. No further details are known except that it was out of use by 1916.

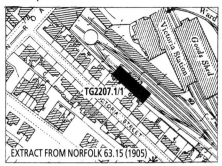

EXTRACT FROM NORFOLK 63.15 (1905)

WELLS NEXT THE SEA

Site TF9214.1; On the north side of Wells next the Sea Station.

Wells next the Sea (W&FR)^{TF9214.1/1A}

A brick built 2TS dead ended shed with wooden gables and a slated pitched roof, it was located at TF92014335 and was opened by the Wells & Fakenham Railway on December 1st, 1857. Unusually the depot also doubled as the goods department with one of the roads used intermittently for loco stabling. The facilities included a water tank, coal stage and turntable. The line was absorbed by the GER in 1862 and although the shed was officially closed by BR on September 15th, 1955 locomotives continued to be serviced until 1960.

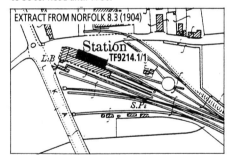

EXTRACT FROM NORFOLK 8.3 (1904)

WATTON

Site TF9200.1; On the west side of the line, at the south end of Watton Station.

Watton (T&WR) ^{TF9200.1/1A}

A 1TS dead ended shed, it was located at TF92300055 and was opened by the Thetford & Watton Railway in 1870. The facilities included a turntable. No further details are known other than it was closed in 1875 and remained standing, in private use, until at least 1974.

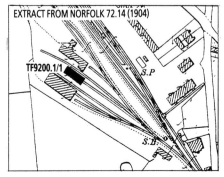

EXTRACT FROM NORFOLK 72.14 (1904)

HUNSTANTON

Site TF6740.1; At the north end of Hunstanton Station.
Hunstanton (L&HR)[TF6740.1/1A]
A 1TS shed, it was located at TF67174076 and was opened by the Lynn & Hunstanton Railway on October 3rd, 1862. Details of its construction are not known other than the roof was formed by an extension of the station canopy. The facilities included a 40ft turntable. The line was absorbed by the GER on July 1st, 1890 and the shed was closed by them in 1899.

Replaced by ...
Site TF6740.2; On the west side of the line, south of Hunstanton Station.
Hunstanton (GER)[TF6740.2/1A]
A brick built 2TS dead ended shed with a slated northlight pattern roof, it was located at TF67124035 and was opened in 1899. The facilities included a turntable, coal stage and water tank.

The shed was re-arranged in 1937 ...
Hunstanton (LNER)[TF6740.2/1B]
The building was converted to a through road shed and the roof was probably renewed at this time. The depot was closed by BR in November 1958.

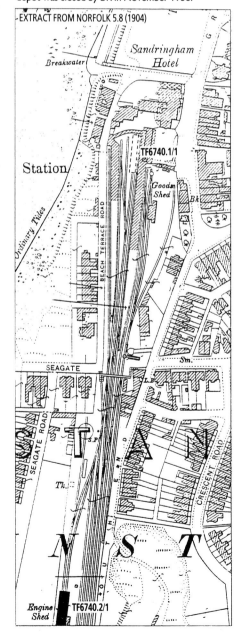

MUNDESLEY

Site TG3036.1; On the east side of the line, north of Mundesley Station.
Mundesley (N&SJR)[TG3036.1/1A]
A corrugated iron 2TS dead ended shed with a corrugated iron pitched roof, it was located at TG30953669 and was opened by the Norfolk & Suffolk Joint (GE/M&GN) line on June 20th, 1898. Details of the facilities are not known. The shed was closed by the LNER in 1928 and demolished a year later.

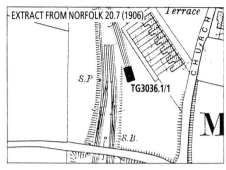

THETFORD

Site TL8693.1; In the vicinity of Thetford Station.
Thetford (T&WR)[TL8693.1/1A]
A 1TS shed, it was opened by the Thetford & Watton Railway on January 26th, 1869. The building may have stood until the station was rebuilt in 1890. No further details are known.

DISS

Site TM1279.1; In the vicinity of Diss Station.
Diss (EUR)[TM1279.1/F1]
A servicing area consisting of a siding, approximately located at TM128797, was opened here by the Eastern Union Railway in 1848 and closed in 1849. No further details are known.

WYMONDHAM

Site TG1100.1; In the fork of the lines at the west end of Wymondham Station.
Wymondham (GER)[TG1100.1/F1]
A servicing area consisting of a turntable, located at TG11250087, and a siding, it was opened on August 18th, 1847. The facility was closed to steam by BR in June 1958 and was subsequently used as a stabling point for a diesel shunter until 1974.

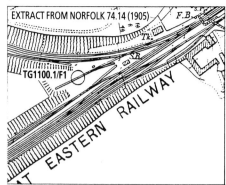

UPWELL

Site TF5002.1; On the north side of the line, at the west end of Upwell Tram Depot.
Upwell (GER)[TF5002.1/F1]
A servicing point consisting of a water tank and engine pit, it was located at TF50680254 and was opened on September 8th, 1884. It was closed by BR during July 1952.

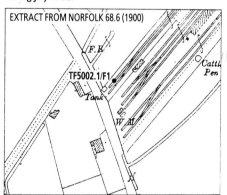

Super-power occupants for **Cromer Beach**'s small engine shed (TQ2142.1/1A). The depot had been opened by the Eastern & Midlands Railway in June 1887, to finally closed with the demise of the M&GNR in March 1959. Even so the building still stood, complete with internal pit and rails, until the early 1990s when it was removed to make way for housing.
J Edgington

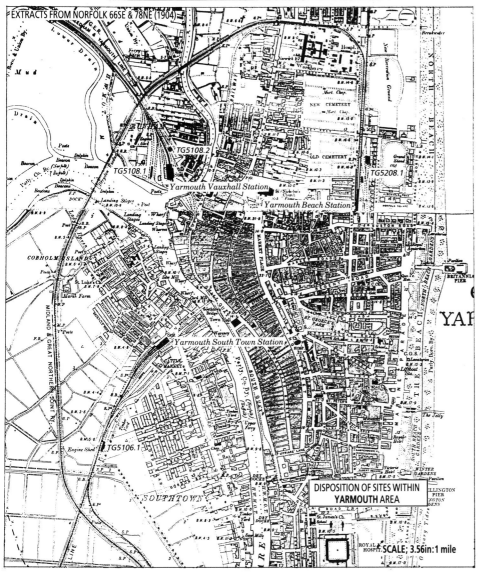

EXTRACTS FROM NORFOLK 66SE & 78NE (1904)

DISPOSITION OF SITES WITHIN YARMOUTH AREA

SCALE; 3.56in:1 mile

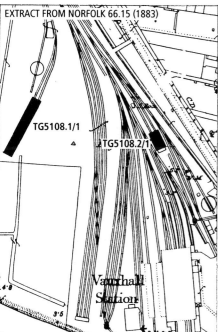

EXTRACT FROM NORFOLK 66.15 (1883)

The shed was temporarily re-roofed ...
South Town (BR)^{TG5106.1/1B}
By 1953 the roof had fallen into total disrepair and was removed. As a temporary measure one track was left exposed with the other being covered by the Eastern Region with a simple lightweight flat roof as was employed at Yarmouth Beach (TG5208.1/2B).

The shed was rebuilt in 1956 ...
South Town (BR)^{TG5106.1/1C}
The shed was reconstructed with new brick walls and an asbestos sheeted gable style roof. It was closed on November 2nd, 1959 and later demolished.

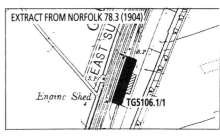

EXTRACT FROM NORFOLK 78.3 (1904)

Site TG5208.0; In the vicinity of Yarmouth Beach Station.

Yarmouth Beach (GtY&SLR)^{TL5208.0/1A}
A temporary shed was opened here by the Great Yarmouth & Stalham Light Railway on August 7th, 1877. It was closed on January 17th, 1880. No further details are known.

Site TG5208.1; On the east side of Yarmouth Beach Station.

Yarmouth Beach (Y&NNR)^{TG5208.1/1A}
A concrete block built 2TS dead ended shed with a dutch barn style corrugated iron roof, it was located at TG52880811 and was opened by the Yarmouth & North Norfolk Railway on January 17th, 1880. The facilities are not known. The shed was closed in 1903 and demolished two years later to accommodate station improvements.

Replaced by ...

Yarmouth Beach (M&GNR)^{TG5208.1/2A}
A concrete block built 4TS shed with two through roads and a twin dutch barn style corrugated iron roof, it was located further north from its predecessor (TG5208.1/1A) at TG52900820. It was opened by the Midland & Great Northern Joint Railway in 1903, having previously been a workshop and sheet factory. The facilities included a 46ft turntable, water tank and a coal stage later replaced by a small mechanical coal plant.

The shed was modified ...

Yarmouth Beach (BR)^{TG5208.1/2B}
A simple lightweight flat roof was installed by the Eastern Region, replacing the dutch barn style and at some stage the building was reduced to a 3TS depot. The shed was closed on March 2nd, 1959.

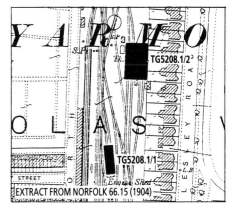

EXTRACT FROM NORFOLK 66.15 (1904)

Site TG5108.2; On the east side of the line, at the north end of Yarmouth Vauxhall Station.

Yarmouth (Y&NR)^{TG5108.2/1A}
A brick built 2TS dead ended shed, it was opened by the Yarmouth & Norwich Railway on April 30th, 1844 and was located at TG51950824. The facilities included a turntable. The shed was closed by the GER on March 12th, 1883 and demolished to accommodate station enlargements.

Replaced by ...
Site TG5108.1; On the west side of Yarmouth Vauxhall Station.

Vauxhall (GER)^{TG5108.1/1A}
A brick built 2TS dead ended shed with a slated gable style roof incorporating a water tank, it was located at TG51820825 and was opened on March 12th, 1883. The other facilities included a 50ft turntable and a coal stage. The shed was closed by BR on January 5th, 1959 and given over to private use. It was demolished in 1993.

Site TG5106.1; On the east side of the line, south of Yarmouth South Town Station.

South Town (Y&HR)^{TG5106.1/1A}
A brick built 2TS through road shed with a slated gable style roof, it was located at TG51700682 and was opened by the Yarmouth & Haddiscoe Railway on June 1st, 1859. The facilities included a 45ft turntable (latterly replaced) and water tank. The line was operated by the Eastern Counties Railway.

SUFFOLK

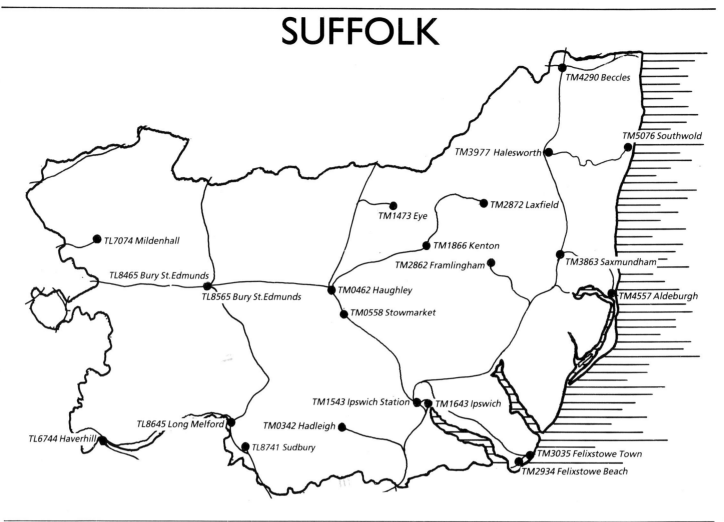

- TM4290 Beccles
- TM5076 Southwold
- TM3977 Halesworth
- TM2872 Laxfield
- TM1473 Eye
- TM1866 Kenton
- TM2862 Framlingham
- TM3863 Saxmundham
- TL7074 Mildenhall
- TL8465 Bury St.Edmunds
- TL8565 Bury St.Edmunds
- TM0462 Haughley
- TM4557 Aldeburgh
- TM0558 Stowmarket
- TM1543 Ipswich Station
- TM1643 Ipswich
- TL8645 Long Melford
- TM0342 Hadleigh
- TL6744 Haverhill
- TL8741 Sudbury
- TM3035 Felixstowe Town
- TM2934 Felixstowe Beach

BURY ST.EDMUNDS

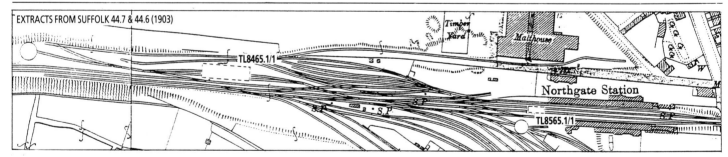

EXTRACTS FROM SUFFOLK 44.7 & 44.6 (1903)

TL8465.1/1

TL8565.1/1

Northgate Station

Site TL8565.1; At the west end of Bury St.Edmunds Station.

Bury St.Edmunds (I&BSt.ER)^{TL8565.1/1A}
A 1TS dead ended shed, it was located at TL85196519 and was opened by the Ipswich & Bury St.Edmunds Railway on November 30th, 1846. The facilities included a turntable sited outside of the shed entrance. The station was at this time a terminus and the shed occupied the end of the line. It was closed and demolished on April 1st, 1854 when the line was extended to Newmarket.

Replaced by ...
Site TL8565.1; On the north side of the line, west of Bury St.Edmunds Station.

Bury St.Edmunds (ECR)^{TL8465.1/1A}
A timber built 2TS shed with a slated gable style roof, it was located at TL84906521 and was opened on April 1st, 1854. The facilities included a turntable. The shed roof was destroyed in a storm in 1901 and by the following year was virtually totally derelict.

Replaced, on the same site, by ...
Bury St.Edmunds (GER)^{TL8465.1/1B}
A brick built 3TS through road shed with a slated northlight pattern roof, it was opened in 1904. The facilities included a new re-sited turntable and water column.

The shed was re-roofed ...
Bury St.Edmunds (BR)^{TL8465.1/1C}
A corrugated asbestos single pitched roof with timber gables was installed, probably by the Eastern Region, at some time prior to 1951. The shed was closed on January 5th, 1959 but continued to stable diesel locomotives until June 1959.

LONG MELFORD

Site TL8645.1; In the vicinity of Long Melford Station.

Long Melford (GER)^{TL8645.1/F1}
Some sort of facility was opened here on August 9th, 1865. No further details are known.

SAXMUNDHAM

Site TM3863.1; In the vicinity of Saxmundham Station.

Saxmundham (ESR)^{TM3863.1/F1}
Some sort of facility was opened here by the East Suffolk Railway on June 1st, 1859. No further details are known.

BECCLES

Site TM4290.1; On the east side of the line, south of Beccles Station.
Beccles (WVR)[TM4290.1/1A]
A 1TS shed, it was probably located at TM42689035 and was opened by the Waveney Valley Railway on March 2nd, 1863. The facilities included a water tank and, sited outside of the shed entrance, a 38ft turntable. It was closed by the GER in 1888.

Replaced by ...
Site TM4290.2; In the fork of the Bungay and Yarmouth lines, north of Beccles Station.
Beccles (GER)[TM4290.2/2A]
A brick built 2TS through road shed with a gable style roof, it was located at TM42629083 and was opened in 1888. The facilities included a 50ft turntable, coal stage and water tank. The shed was closed by the LNER in 1944 and given over to private use. It was still standing in 1995.

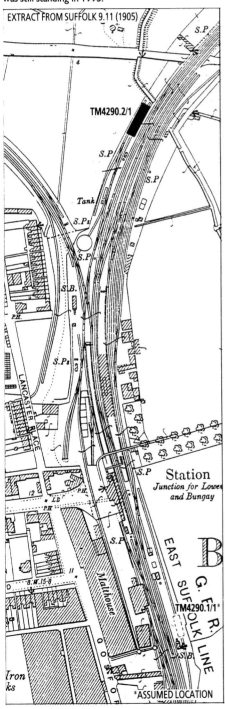
EXTRACT FROM SUFFOLK 9.11 (1905)
*ASSUMED LOCATION

ALDEBURGH

Site TM4557.1; On the east side of the line, at the north end of Aldeburgh Station.
Aldeburgh (ESR)[TM4557.1/1A]
A brick built 1TS through road shed with a tiled gable style roof, it was located at TM45955722 and was opened by the East Suffolk Railway on April 12th, 1860. The facilities included a water tower and coal stage. The shed was closed by BR in April 1955.

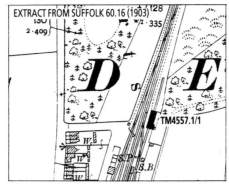
EXTRACT FROM SUFFOLK 60.16 (1903)

EYE

Site TM1473.1; On the west side of Eye Station.
Eye (M&ER)[TM1473.1/1A]
A brick built 1TS dead ended shed, it was located at TM14257384 and was opened by the Mellis & Eye Railway on April 2nd, 1867. The facilities included a water tank and coal stage. The line was absorbed by the GER in 1898 and the shed was closed by the LNER on February 2nd, 1931 and subsequently demolished.

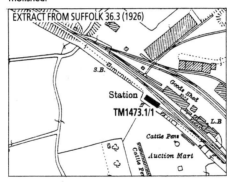
EXTRACT FROM SUFFOLK 36.3 (1926)

FRAMLINGHAM

Site TM2862.1; On the west side of the line, south of Framlingham Station.
Framlingham (ESR)[TM2862.1/1A]
A brick built 1TS dead ended shed with a slated gable style roof, it was located at TM28416274 and was opened by the East Suffolk Railway on June 1st, 1859. The facilities included a water tank and coal stage. The shed was closed by BR on November 3rd, 1952 and subsequently demolished.

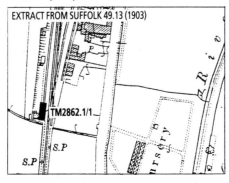
EXTRACT FROM SUFFOLK 49.13 (1903)

HAVERHILL

Site TL6744.1; On the west side of Haverhill South Station.
Haverhill (CV&HR)[TL6744.1/1A]
A corrugated iron 2TS dead ended shed with a corrugated iron gable style roof, it was located at TL67354496 and was opened by the Colne Valley & Halstead Railway on May 10th, 1863. The depot was also utilized as the works for the line until they were removed to Halstead (TL8130.1/2A) in 1905. The facilities included a water tank and a coal stage

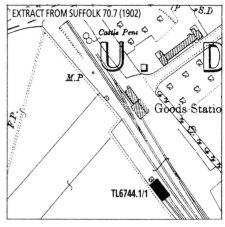
EXTRACT FROM SUFFOLK 70.7 (1902)

The shed was reduced in size ...
Haverhill (CV&HR)[TL6744.1/1B]
The depot was rebuilt as a corrugated iron 1TS dead ended shed with a corrugated iron gable style roof. It was opened in 1915 and closed by the LNER in January 1924.

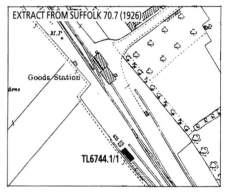
EXTRACT FROM SUFFOLK 70.7 (1926)

HADLEIGH

Site TM0342.1; On the east side of the line, at the south end of Hadleigh Station.
Hadleigh (EU&HR)[TM0342.1/1A]
A timber built 1TS through road shed with a slated pitched roof, it was located at TM03204210 and was opened by the Eastern Union & Hadleigh Railway on August 21st, 1847. The facilities included a coal stage. The shed was derelict by the time it was closed by the LNER in February 1932.

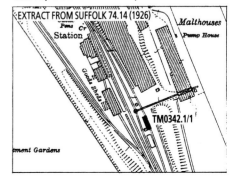
EXTRACT FROM SUFFOLK 74.14 (1926)

FELIXSTOWE

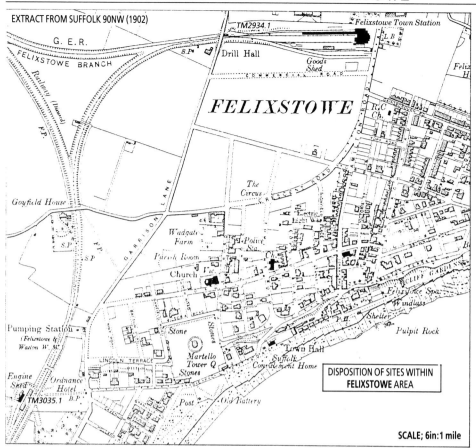

EXTRACT FROM SUFFOLK 90NW (1902)

DISPOSITION OF SITES WITHIN **FELIXSTOWE** AREA

SCALE; 6in:1 mile

Site TM3035.1; On the north side of the line, at the west end of Felixstowe Town Station.

Felixstowe Town (GER)TM3035.1/F1
A servicing area consisting of a turntable, located at TM30083516, engine pits and water columns, it was opened on July 1st, 1898. The facility was closed by BR in 1959.

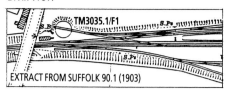

EXTRACT FROM SUFFOLK 90.1 (1903)

Site TM2934.1; On the west side of the line, north of Felixstowe Beach Station.

Felixstowe Beach* (FR&P)TM2934.1/1A
A brick built 2TS dead ended shed with a gable style roof, it was located at TM29433410 and was opened by the Felixstowe Railway & Pier Company on May 1st, 1877. The facilities included a coal stage and water tank. By 1938 the building had become derelict.

A servicing point was established ...
Felixstowe Beach (LNER)TM2934.1/F1
Locomotives made use of the sidings, engine pits, coal stage and water tank until closed by BR in c1950.

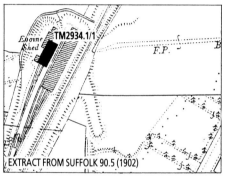

EXTRACT FROM SUFFOLK 90.5 (1902)

*The location was known as Felixstowe Town until July 1st, 1898.

STOWMARKET

Site TM0558.1; On the east side of the line, south of Stowmarket Station.
Stowmarket (GER)TM0558.1/F1
A stabling point consisting of an engine pit, located at TM05415855, coal stage and siding, it was opened in 1920. The facility was closed to steam by BR in 1960 and the site subsequently utilized as a diesel stabling point.

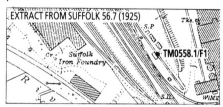

EXTRACT FROM SUFFOLK 56.7 (1925)

MILDENHALL

Site TL7074.1; On the south side of Mildenhall Station.
Mildenhall (GER)TL7074.1/F1
A servicing area consisting of a 50ft turntable, located at TL70867401, and siding it was opened on April 1st, 1885. The facility was closed in 1915, although locomotives continued to use the turntable as required until 1962.

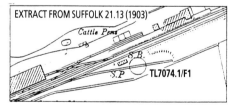

EXTRACT FROM SUFFOLK 21.13 (1903)

SUDBURY

Site TL8741.1; In the goods yard on the north side of Sudbury Station.
Sudbury (CSVS&HR)TL8741.1/1A
A brick built 1TS through road shed with a slated shallow pitched gable style roof, located at TL87584123 and opened by the Colchester, Stour Valley, Sudbury & Halstead Railway on July 2nd, 1849. The shed was demolished by BR in c1950.

A servicing point was then established ...
Sudbury (BR)TL8741.1/F1
Locomotives were stabled and serviced on the engine pit until the facility closed in c1959.

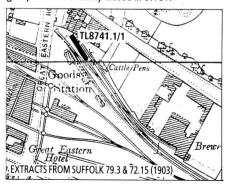

EXTRACTS FROM SUFFOLK 79.3 & 72.15 (1903)

HALESWORTH

Site TM3977.1; On the north side of the line, east of Halesworth Station.
Halesworth (Southwold)TM3977.1/1A
A 3ft gauge asbestos sheeting clad 1TS dead ended shed with a single pitched gable style roof, located at TM39317725 and opened by the Southwold Railway in 1914. The facilities included a water pump. The shed closed on April 12th, 1929.

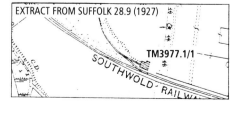

EXTRACT FROM SUFFOLK 28.9 (1927)

SOUTHWOLD

Site TM5076.1; At the end of the line, at the east end of Southwold Station.
Southwold (Southwold)TM5076.1/1A
A timber built 3ft gauge 1TS dead ended shed with a slated gable style roof, it was located at TM50487667 and was opened by the Southwold Railway on September 24th, 1879. The facilities included a water tank and coal stage. The shed was closed on April 12th, 1929.

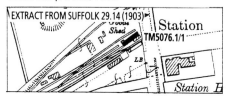

EXTRACT FROM SUFFOLK 29.14 (1903)

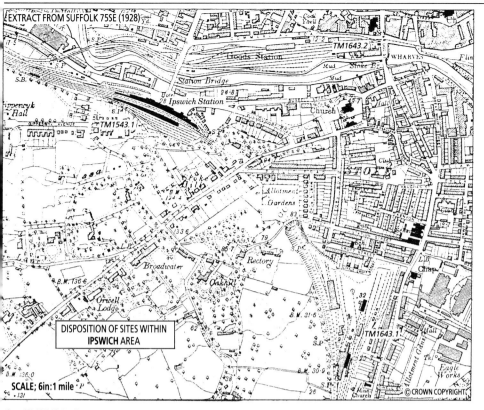

EXTRACT FROM SUFFOLK 75SE (1928)

DISPOSITION OF SITES WITHIN **IPSWICH AREA**

SCALE; 6in:1 mile

© CROWN COPYRIGHT

Site TM1543.1; On the south side of Ipswich (GER) Station.

Ipswich Station (GER)^TM1543.1/F1
A servicing area consisting of a 45ft turntable, located at TM15664374, coal stage, engine pit and sidings, it was opened in 1862. The facility was closed by BR in 1959 and a diesel stabling point established on the site.

EXTRACT FROM SUFFOLK 75.15 (1908)   Statio

YK ROAD   TM1543.1/F1

HAUGHLEY

Site TM0462.1; On the west side of Haughley Station.
Haughley (GER) ^TM0462.1/1A
A 1TS shed, it was probably located at TM04136233 and was opened on July 9th, 1849. The facilities included a turntable. The depot was closed in 1904.

Replaced by ...
Site TM0462.2; On the east side of Haughley (MSR) Station.
Haughley (MSR) ^TM0462.2/1A
A 1TS shed it was approximately located at TM042624 and was opened by the Mid-Suffolk Light Railway in 1904. Details of the facilities are not known. It only enjoyed a short existence, closing in 1905.

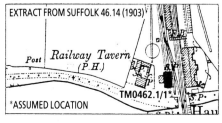

EXTRACT FROM SUFFOLK 46.14 (1903)

Post   *Railway Tavern* (P.H.)

TM0462.1/1*

*ASSUMED LOCATION

Site TM1643.2; On the south side of the dock line, at the east end of Commercial Road Goods Station.
Ipswich Docks (GER)^TM1643.2/F1
A servicing area consisting of a coal stage and water column, it was located at TM16194396 and was opened in 1863.

Replaced, on the same site, by ...
Ipswich Docks (GER)^TM1643.2/1A
A corrugated iron 1TS dead ended shed with a corrugated iron gable style roof, it was opened in 1891. The shed was closed by BR in c1954.

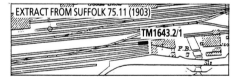

EXTRACT FROM SUFFOLK 75.11 (1903)

TM1643.2/1

LAXFIELD

Site TM2872.1; On the south side of the line, at the west end of Laxfield Station.
Laxfield (MSR)^TM2872.1/1A
A timber built 1TS dead ended shed with a gable style roof, it was located at TM28747236 and was opened by the Mid-Suffolk Light Railway on September 30th, 1904. The facilities included a water tank. The line was absorbed by the LNER on July 1st, 1924 and the shed was closed by BR on July 28th, 1952.

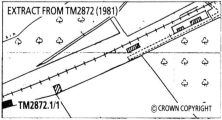

EXTRACT FROM TM2872 (1981)

TM2872.1/1   © CROWN COPYRIGHT

Please Note; The construction and dismantling dates of this line precludes its inclusion in a complete form in OS maps. Some, or all, of the buildings and track have been superimposed.

Site TM1643.1; In the fork of the Ipswich (EUR) Station and Ipswich (GER) Station lines, south of Ipswich (GER) Station.
Ipswich (EUR)^TM1643.1/1A
A brick built 2TS dead ended shed with a slated gable style roof, it was located at TM16314327 and was opened by the Eastern Union Railway on June 1st, 1846. The facilities included a turntable and water tank. The building was latterly used for boiler washouts and the LNER demolished it in c1939.

Ipswich (EUR)^TM1643.1/2A
A brick built 2TS through road shed with a slated gable style roof, it was located at TM16274312 and was opened by the Eastern Union Railway on June 1st, 1846. The building was adjoined by the locomotive works and they along with the running shed were apparently involved in a fire in 1878.

The shed was repaired in 1879...
Ipswich (GER)^TM1643.1/2B
The building was re-roofed in similar style and the walls were renovated.

The shed was rebuilt in 1954...
Ipswich (BR)^TM1643.1/2C
A concrete framed 4TS through road shed with a shallow pitched concrete and corrugated asbestos roof, it was completed by the Eastern Region in 1954. Major improvements were made including the installation of a mechanical coaling plant and covered inspection bay. The depot had been designed to easily facilitate dieselization and it was closed to steam shortly after on November 2nd, 1959. The shed was totally closed in 1968.

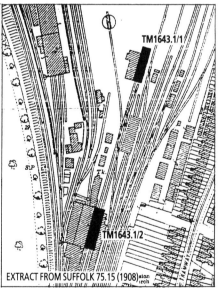

TM1643.1/1

TM1643.1/2

EXTRACT FROM SUFFOLK 75.15 (1908)

KENTON

Site TM1866.1; At the east end of Kenton Station.
Kenton (MSR)^TM1866.1/1A
A 1TS shed, it was approximately located at TM18856695 and was opened by the Mid-Suffolk Light Railway in 1904. Details of the facilities are not known. It was closed in 1912.

Replaced by ...
Site TM1866.2; At the west end of Kenton Station.
Kenton (MSR)^TM1866.2/1A
A 1TS shed, it was approximately located at TM18956699 and was opened by the Mid-Suffolk Light Railway in 1912. Details of the facilities are not known. It was closed in 1919.

CAMBRIDGESHIRE

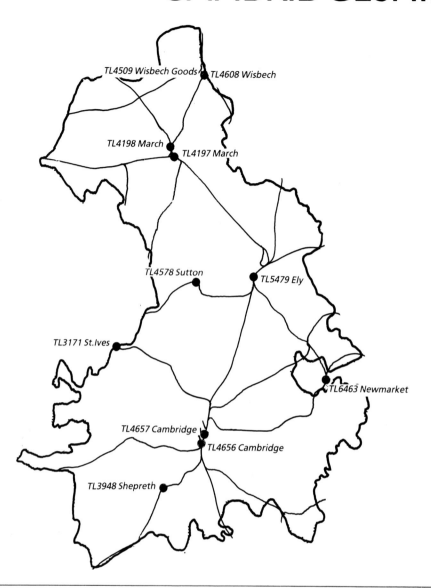

TL4509 Wisbech Goods ● ● TL4608 Wisbech

TL4198 March ● ● TL4197 March

TL4578 Sutton ● ● TL5479 Ely

TL3171 St.Ives ●

● TL6463 Newmarket

TL4657 Cambridge ●
● TL4656 Cambridge

TL3948 Shepreth ●

ELY

Site TL5479.1; On the east side of the line, south of Ely Station.
Ely (L&ER)$^{TL5479.1/1A}$
A ITS through road shed, it was located at TL54157904 and was opened by the Lynn & Ely Railway on October 26th, 1847. The facilities included a turntable. No further details are known except that it had been removed by 1866. .

. Replaced by ...
Ely (GER)$^{TL5479.1/2A}$
A corrugated iron ITS through road shed with a corrugated iron dutch barn style roof, it was located at TL54227917 and was opened in 1867. The facilities included a water tank, coal stage and the turntable of its predecessor (TL5479.1/1A). At some point it fell into total disrepair and was removed, probably by the LNER.

A servicing point was then established ...
Ely (LNER)$^{TL5479.1/F1}$
Engines stabled by the water tank at TL54227914. The facility was closed by BR in c1962. .

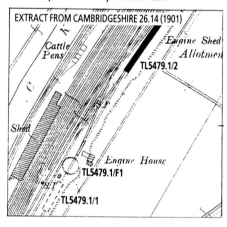

EXTRACT FROM CAMBRIDGESHIRE 26.14 (1901)

Cattle Pens

Engine Shed

Allotmen

TL5479.1/2

Shed

Engine House

TL5479.1/F1

TL5479.1/1

WISBECH

Site TL4509.1; On the east side of the line, south of Wisbech Terminus Station.
Wisbech (WStI&CJR)$^{TL4509.1/1A}$
A brick built 2TS dead ended shed, it is assumed to have been located at TL45920907 and was opened by the Wisbech, St.Ives & Cambridge Junction Railway on May 3rd, 1847. The facilities included a turntable. The line was worked by the Eastern Counties Railway and they closed the shed in 1868, possibly as the result of fire damage.

Replaced by ...
Site TL4509.2; On the west side of the line, south of Wisbech Terminus Station.
Wisbech Goods (GER)$^{TL4509.2/1A}$
A timber built 2TS dead ended shed, it was located at TL45870905 and was opened in 1868. The facilities included a water tank and coal stage. Initially the turntable of its predecessor (TL4509.1/1A) was utilized but later on a new 45ft unit was installed in the shed yard and the old one dispensed with. The shed was closed by the LNER in 1923.

Site TL4608.1; On the south side of Wisbech (GER) Station.
Wisbech (GER)$^{TL4608.1/1A}$
A brick built ITS dead ended shed with a slated gable style roof, it was located at TL46130893 and was opened on August 20th, 1883 for use by the Wisbech & Upwell Tramway. The facilities included a water tank and coal stage.

The shed was enlarged in 1895...
Wisbech (GER)$^{TL4608.1/1B}$
The shed was doubled in size by the addition of an identical brick built ITS dead ended shed along the north wall.

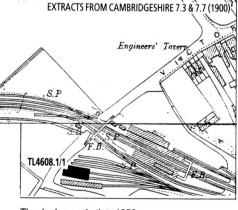

EXTRACTS FROM CAMBRIDGESHIRE 7.3 & 7.7 (1900)

TL4509.1/1*

TL4509.2/1

*ASSUMED LOCATION

Engineers' Tavern

S.P

TL4608.1/1

The shed was rebuilt in 1958 ...
Wisbech (BR)$^{TL4608.1/1C}$
Following the introduction of diesel shunters the northern portion of the building was demolished by the Eastern Region and the remaining ITS section refurbished. The shed was closed on May 23rd, 1966.

CAMBRIDGE

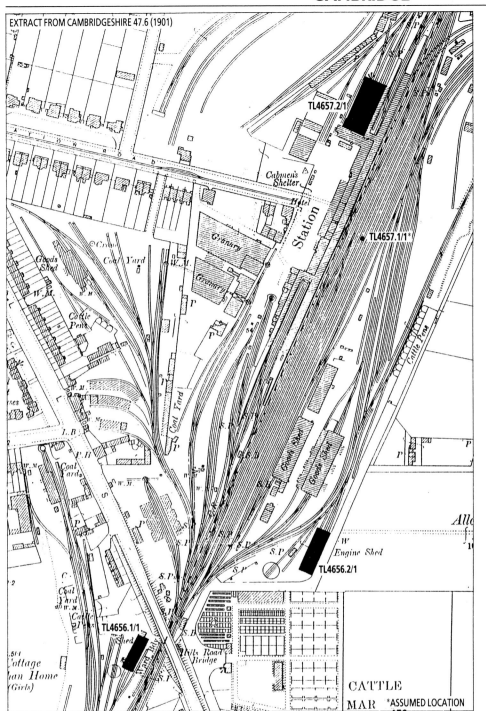

EXTRACT FROM CAMBRIDGESHIRE 47.6 (1901)

TL4657.2/1

TL4657.1/1*

TL4656.2/1

TL4656.1/1

*ASSUMED LOCATION

Site TL4657.1; On the east side of Cambridge Station.
Cambridge (ECR)[TL4657.1/1A]
A 2TS shed, it was approximately located at TL462571 and was opened by the Eastern Counties Railway on July 30th, 1845. The line was absorbed by the GER in 1854 and they closed the shed in 1865.

Site TL4657.2; On the west side of the line, at the north end of Cambridge Station.
Cambridge (ECR)[TL4657.2/1A]
A brick built 4TS dead ended shed probably with a slated twin gable style roof, it was located at TL46225738 and was opened by the Eastern Counties Railway in 1847. The facilities included a turntable and coke/coal stage.

The shed was enlarged ...
Cambridge (GER)[TL4657.2/1B]
A brick built 7TS dead ended shed with a slated northlight pattern roof, it was opened in 1913.

The shed was enlarged again ...
Cambridge (LNER)[TL4657.2/1C]
The shed was extended by 200ft and the roof was renewed. A mechanical coaling plant and new turntable were also installed at the same time in 1932. The shed was closed by BR on June 18th, 1962 and was subsequently demolished, the site being converted to a car park.

Site TL4656.2; On the east side of the line, at the south end of Cambridge Station.
Cambridge (GNR)[TL4656.2/1A]
A brick built 3TS dead ended shed with a tiled gable style roof, it was located at TL46185693 and was opened on July 15th, 1879 by the GER for the GNR. The facilities included a 45ft turntable, coal stage and water tank. The shed was closed by the LNER in 1924, thereafter being utilized as a wagon works until BR days. It was demolished in 1985.

Site TL4656.1; On the west side of the line, south of Cambridge Station.
Cambridge (B&CR)[TL4656.1/1A]
A brick built 2TS dead ended shed with a slated gable style roof, it was located at TL46015684 and was opened by the Bedford & Cambridge Railway on July 7th, 1862. The facilities included a turntable and water tank. Although the shed was closed by the LMS on December 2nd, 1935 locomotives unofficially continued to be serviced in the shed yard until 1951. The building was demolished in 1964.

ST.IVES

Site TL3171.1; In the vicinity of St.Ives Station.
St.Ives (GER)[TL3171.1/F1]
Some form of facility may have been in place here, approximately located at TL317711. It would have been dispensed with by the LNER in 1923.

SUTTON

Site TL4578.1; In the vicinity of Sutton (1st) Station.
Sutton (EH&SR)[TL4578.1/1A]
A 1TS shed was opened here by the Ely, Haddenham & Sutton Railway on April 16th, 1866. No further details are known.

NEWMARKET

Site TL6463.0; In the vicinity of Newmarket Station.
Newmarket (N&CR)[TL6463.0/1A]
Some sort of facility was opened here by the Newmarket & Chesterford Railway on January 3rd, 1848. No further details are known.

Site TL6463.1; On the east side of the line, south of Newmarket (1st) Station.
Newmarket (GER)[TL6463.1/1A]
A 1TS through road shed, it was located at TL64816305 and was opened in 1880. The facilities included a water tank and, sited outside of the shed entrance a 45ft turntable. The turntable was replaced with a 60ft unit and slightly resited by the LNER. The shed was closed in 1932.

A servicing point was then established ...
Newmarket (LNER)[TL6463.1/F1]
Locomotives utilized the water tank, engine pit and turntable, probably until BR days.

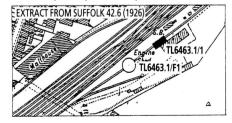

EXTRACT FROM SUFFOLK 42.6 (1926)

TL6463.1/1

TL6463.1/F1

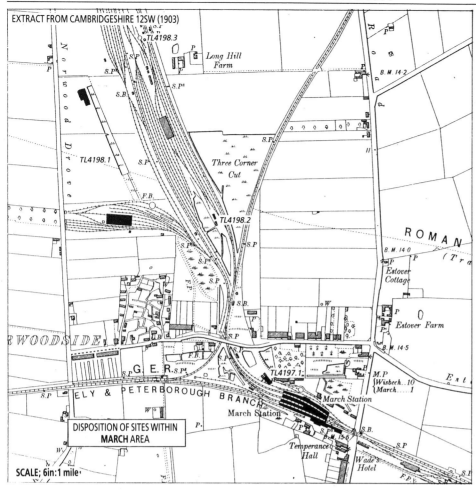

EXTRACT FROM CAMBRIDGESHIRE 12SW (1903)

DISPOSITION OF SITES WITHIN **MARCH** AREA

SCALE; 6in:1 mile

Site TL4197.1; In the fork of the Peterborough and Wisbech lines, west of March Station.

March (ECR)^{TL4197.1/1A}

A 1TS dead ended shed, it was located at TL41729796 and was opened by the Eastern Counties Railway in 1850. The facilities included a turntable, sited outside of the shed entrance, and a water tank. No further details are known other than it was closed in 1870.

Replaced, on the same site, by ...

March (GER)^{TL4197.1/1B}

A 3TS shed with one through road, it was opened in 1870. The facilities included a turntable, coal stage and water tank. No further details are known except that it was closed in 1884 and demolished to accommodate track realignments.

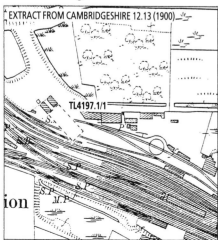

EXTRACT FROM CAMBRIDGESHIRE 12.13 (1900)

TL4197.1/1

Replaced by ...

Site TL4198.1; On the west side of Whitemoor Yard, north of March Station.

March (GER)^{TL4198.1/1A}

A brick built 6TS shed with two through roads and three slated gable style roofs, it was located at TL41279839 and was opened in 1884. The facilities included a water tank, running along the back end of the shed building and a simple coal stage.

Engine Shed

TL4198.1/1

EXTRACT FROM CAMBRIDGESHIRE 12.13 (1900)

Major alterations were carried out in 1925 ...

March (LNER)^{TL4198.1/2A}

A corrugated asbestos 4TS through road shed with a twin gable corrugated asbestos roof, it was constructed along the north side of the original depot (TL4198.1/1A) at TL41279841. At the same time a mechanical coaler was erected and a 70ft turntable installed in the yard.

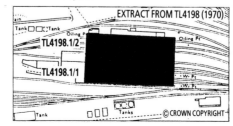

EXTRACT FROM TL4198 (1970)

TL4198.1/2

TL4198.1/1

© CROWN COPYRIGHT

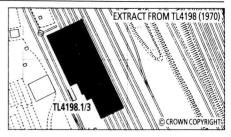

EXTRACT FROM TL4198 (1970)

TL4198.1/3

© CROWN COPYRIGHT

Whitemoor (LNER)^{TL4198.1/3A}

A brick built 5TS through road shed with a corrugated asbestos northlight pattern roof, it was located at TL41159870 and was opened in 1933. Although classified as a wash-out shed it was utilized for general locomotive servicing and shared the facilities of its neighbours (TL4198.1/1A & 2A).

The depot was closed to steam by BR in December 1963. The first shed (TL4198.1/1A) was utilized as it stood for diesel locomotives, but TL4198.1/2A was demolished and replaced with a purpose built diesel depot (TL4198.1/2B). Whitemoor (TL4198.1/3A) was used for wagon storage for a number of years.

Site TL4198.2; On the west side of the Wisbech line, north of March Station.

March (GNR)^{TL4198.2/1A}

A 2TS shed it is assumed to have been located at TL41559840 and was opened on April 1st, 1867. The building was erected by J.Jackson, the contractor constructing the GE/GN Joint line and taken over by the GNR. It was closed in 1882. No more details are known.

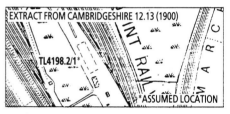

EXTRACT FROM CAMBRIDGESHIRE 12.13 (1900)

TL4198.2/1*

*ASSUMED LOCATION

Site TL4198.3; On the west side of the Wisbech line, in Whitemoor Yard.

Whitemoor Yard (GER)^{TL4198.3/F1}

A servicing area consisting of a turntable and siding, it was located at TL41319890. No further details are known.

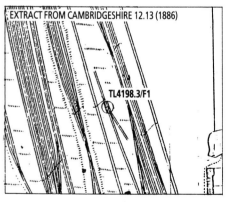

EXTRACT FROM CAMBRIDGESHIRE 12.13 (1886)

TL4198.3/F1

SHEPRETH

Site TL3948.1; In the vicinity of Shepreth Station.

Shepreth (R&HR)^{TL3948.1/1A}

A timber built shed was erected here and opened by the Royston & Hitchin Railway on August 3rd, 1851. The approximate location would have been TL392482. The building probably closed when the leasing GNR sub-leased the R&H to the Eastern Counties Railway from April 1st, 1852. No further details are known.

WORCESTERSHIRE

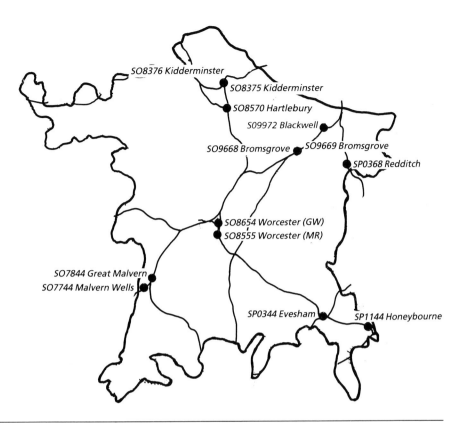

SO8376 Kidderminster
SO8375 Kidderminster
SO8570 Hartlebury
SO9972 Blackwell
SO9668 Bromsgrove   SO9669 Bromsgrove
SP0368 Redditch
SO8654 Worcester (GW)
SO8555 Worcester (MR)
SO7844 Great Malvern
SO7744 Malvern Wells
SP0344 Evesham
SP1144 Honeybourne

HONEYBOURNE

Site SP1144.1; On the north side of the line, at the west end of Honeybourne Station.

Honeybourne (OW&W)^{SP1144.1/1A}
A brick built ITS through road shed with a slated gable style roof, it was located at SP11414486 and was opened by the Oxford, Worcester & Wolverhampton Railway on June 4th, 1853. The facilities included a small coal stage sited outside of the shed entrance. The line was absorbed by the GWR in 1863 and the building was removed in 1907 to accommodate track widening.

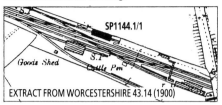

SP1144.1/1
Goods Shed
S.I
Cattle Pen
EXTRACT FROM WORCESTERSHIRE 43.14 (1900)

Replaced by ...
Honeybourne (GWR)^{SP1144.1/2A}
A brick built ITS shed with a slated gable style roof, it was located slightly north of its predecessor (SP1144.1/1A) at SP11424487. It is not clear if it was the same building but it seems more likely that the materials were re-used in the new shed to the same design as previously. The depot was destroyed by a fire and was closed on September 13th, 1911.

Replaced by ...
Honeybourne (GWR)^{SP1141.1/F1}
A servicing area consisting of a coal stage and siding, it was located at SP11354491. The facility was closed by BR in December 1965.

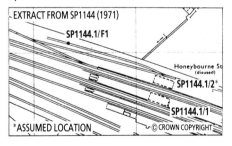

EXTRACT FROM SP1144 (1971)
SP1144.1/F1
Honeybourne St (disused)
SP1144.1/2*
SP1144.1/1
*ASSUMED LOCATION   © CROWN COPYRIGHT

REDDITCH

Site SP0368.1; On the west side of the line, north of Redditch Station.
Redditch (MR)^{SP0368.1/1A}
A brick built ITS dead ended shed with a slated gable style roof, it was located at SP03966813 and was opened in 1872. The facilities included a coal stage, water column and a 42ft turntable which was removed prior to 1902.

The shed was re-roofed in 1938 ...
Redditch (LMS)^{SP0368.1/1B}
The roof was replaced with a standard LMS single pitch style. The shed was closed by BR on June 1st, 1964.

EXTRACT FROM WORCESTERSHIRE 23.7 (1903)
SP0368.1/1
Engine Shed

MALVERN

Site SO7844.1; On the east side of the line, south of Great Malvern Station.
Great Malvern (T&MR)^{SO7844.1/1A}
A ITS dead ended shed, it was located at SO78114492 and was opened by the Tewkesbury & Malvern Railway on May 16th, 1864. Details of its construction and facilities are not known. Severe gales in 1867/68 caused major damage to the building.

The shed was repaired in 1868 ...
Great Malvern (T&MR)^{SO7844.1/1B}
The roof was replaced. The line was absorbed by the MR in 1877.

The shed was rebuilt in 1883 ...
Great Malvern (MR)^{SO7844.1/1C}
The building was re-constructed in timber.

The shed was extended in 1898 ...
Great Malvern (MR)^{SO7844.1/1D}
Some form of extension to its length was built in timber. By this time the facilities included a turntable and water tank. The depot was closed by the LMS on September 14th, 1931 but the water tank and turntable saw further use until at least 1940.

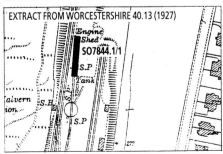

EXTRACT FROM WORCESTERSHIRE 40.13 (1927)
Engine Shed
SO7844.1/1
S.P
Tank
Malvern on
S.B
S.P

Site SO7744.1;. On the east side of the line, at the south end of Malvern Wells Station.
Malvern Wells (W&HR)^{SO7744.1/1A}
A brick built ITS dead ended shed with a slated gable style roof, it was located at SO77904405 and was opened by the Worcester & Hereford Railway on May 17th, 1860. The facilities included a 40ft turntable, sited outside of the shed entrance, and water tank. The shed was closed in 1901 and demolished.

Replaced, on the same site, by ...
Malvern Wells (GWR)^{SO7744.1/1B}
A brick built ITS dead ended shed with a slated gable style roof, it was opened on January 23rd, 1902. The facilities were those of its predecessor (SO7744.1/1A) although the turntable was removed sometime later in May 1913. The depot was closed to locomotives in July 1922 thereafter being utilized to stable an auto-trailer. It was still standing in the late 1930s.

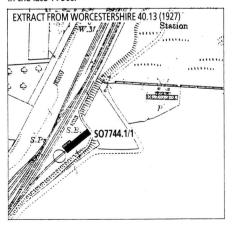

EXTRACT FROM WORCESTERSHIRE 40.13 (1927)
Station
W.M
SO7744.1/1
S.P   S.B

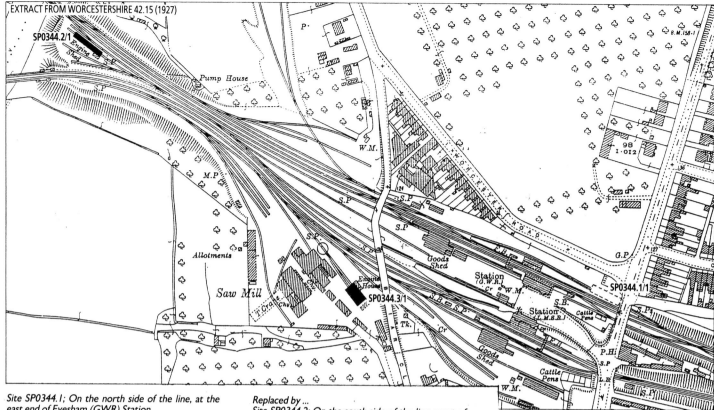

EXTRACT FROM WORCESTERSHIRE 42.15 (1927)

Site SP0344.1; On the north side of the line, at the east end of Evesham (GWR) Station.

Evesham (OW&W)^{SP0344.1/1A}
A timber built 1TS dead ended shed with a slated pitched roof, it was located at SP03684444 and abutted a railway bridge which formed an extension at the eastern end. Details of the facilities are not known. It was opened by the Oxford, Worcester & Wolverhampton Railway on January 1st, 1852. The line was absorbed by the GWR in 1863 and the shed was closed in 1901.

Replaced by ...
Site SP0344.2; On the south side of the line, west of Evesham (GWR) Station.
Evesham (GWR)^{SP0344.2/1A}
A brick built 1TS through road shed with a slated gable style roof, it was located at SP03254466 and was opened in 1901. The facilities included a water tank. The shed was closed by BR in June 1961 and demolished.

Site SP0344.3; On the south side of the line, at the west end of Evesham (MR) Station.
Evesham (MR)^{SP0344.3/1A}
A timber built 2TS dead ended shed, it was located at SP03534444 and was opened in 1871. The facilities included a 42ft turntable. The shed was closed by the LMS on September 14th, 1931.

A servicing point was then established ...
Evesham (LMS)^{SP0344.3/1F}
Locomotives were stabled and serviced in the shed yard. At some point the shed building was demolished and a new turntable installed on the shed site. Although the facility was officially closed by BR on May 7th, 1951 it saw further use until 1954.

BROMSGROVE

Site SO9669.1; On the east side of Bromsgrove Station.
Bromsgrove (B'ham & G) ^{SO9669.1/1A}
A brick built 1TS dead ended shed with a slated gable style roof, located at SO96846926 and opened by the Birmingham & Gloucester Railway on June 24th, 1840. The facilities included a water tank. The line was absorbed by the Midland Railway on May 7th, 1845.

The shed was enlarged ...
Bromsgrove (MR)^{SO9669.1/1B}
At some stage a brick built 2TS extension with one through road and a slated twin gable style roof was constructed along the northern wall of SO9669.1/1A. A turntable, which was removed in 1892, may have been provided at this time.

The shed was refurbished ...
Bromsgrove (BR)^{SO9669.1/1C}
The gable ends were rebuilt and it was probably re-roofed by the London Midland Region in c1951. The depot closed on September 27th, 1964 and remained standing in a derelict condition until demolition in the late 1980s.

EXTRACT FROM WORCESTERSHIRE 22.4 & 23.1 (1902)

Site SO9669.2; In the vicinity of Bromsgrove Station.
Bromsgrove (B'ham & G)^{SO9669.2/F1}
A banker engine siding was established here on June 24th, 1840 by the Birmingham & Gloucester Railway. No further details are known.

Site SO9668.1; On both sides of the line, south of Bromsgrove Station.
Bromsgrove South (MR) ^{SO9668.1/F1}
A servicing area consisting of a stand siding and coaling stage on the west side of the line at SO96586870 and a 46ft turntable on the east, it was opened in c1892. It was closed to steam by BR on September 27th, 1964 following track re-alignment at Bromsgrove Station which allowed diesel hauled passenger trains to ascend the Lickey Bank unassisted. Diesel locomotives for banking freight trains continued to utilize the siding for parking between duties.

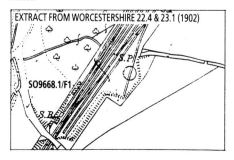

EXTRACT FROM WORCESTERSHIRE 22.4 & 23.1 (1902)

HARTLEBURY

Site SO8570.1; On the west side of the line, at the north end of Hartlebury Station.
Hartlebury (GWR)^{SO8570.1/1A}
A 1TS shed, approximately located at SO85007080, is believed to have existed here until c1880.

Replaced in 1880 by ...
Hartlebury (GWR)^{SO8570.1/F1}
A servicing area consisting of a turntable, water tank and siding was established on the site. The turntable was removed by 1925 and the facility was closed in 1932.

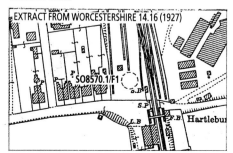

EXTRACT FROM WORCESTERSHIRE 14.16 (1927)

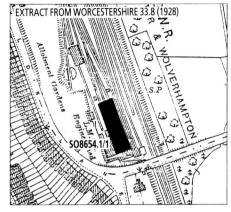

EXTRACT FROM WORCESTERSHIRE 33NE (1902)

SO8555.1

Sheet Sheds

Gas Works

Worcester Shrub Hill Station
(Location of Site SO8654.0)

Shrub Hill China Works

W O R

SPRING HILL

Cottage Homes

Site of Battle of Worcester

SO8654.1

DISPOSITION OF SITES WITHIN WORCESTER AREA

SCALE: 6in:1 mile

Site SO8654.1; On the west side of the line, south of Worcester Shrub Hill Station.
Worcester (MR)^SO8654.1/1A
A shed was opened here in 1870. It was probably a 3TS structure located at SO86095433. No further details are known.

The shed was rebuilt ...
Worcester (MR)^SO8654.1/1B
A timber built 3TS dead ended shed with a slated gable style roof, it was opened in 1894. The facilities included a coal stage, turntable and water tank. The depot was closed by the LMS on December 12th, 1932 and removed some years later.

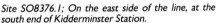

EXTRACT FROM WORCESTERSHIRE 33.8 (1928)

Allotment Gardens

N.R. & WOLVERHAMPTON

SO8654.1/1

Site SO8555.0; In the vicinity of Worcester Shrub Hill Station.
Worcester (OW&W)^SO8555.0/1A
A timber built 3TS shed, it was opened by the Oxford, Worcester & Wolverhampton Railway on October 5th, 1850. No further details are known.

Site SO8555.1; In the fork of the Hartlebury and Hereford lines, north of Worcester Shrub Hill Station.
Worcester (GWR)^SO8555.1/1A
A brick built 4TS through road shed with a slated gable style roof, it was located at SO85685555 and was known as the *goods engine depot*. The opening date is not known.

The shed was re-roofed ...
Worcester (GWR)^SO8555.1/1B
At some stage the roof was re-clad in corrugated sheeting.

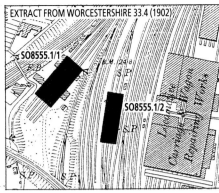

EXTRACT FROM WORCESTERSHIRE 33.4 (1902)

SO8555.1/1

SO8555.1/2

Adjoined by ...
Worcester (GWR)^SO8555.1/2A
A brick built 3TS through road shed with a slated gable style roof, it was located at SO85735552 and was known as the *passenger engine depot*. The opening date is not known.

The shed was re-roofed ...
Worcester (GWR)^SO8555.1/2B
At some stage the roof was re-clad in corrugated sheeting.

The facilities included a coal stage, water tank and turntable. The depot was closed to steam by BR in December 1965 with SO8555.1/2B being utilized as a diesel depot until c1985.

BLACKWELL

Site SO9972.1; In the vicinity of Blackwell Station.
Blackwell (B'ham & G)^SO9972.1/1A
A shed, probably 1TS and approximately located at SO994721 was opened here in 1842 by the Birmingham & Gloucester Railway. The facilities included a water column. No further details are known.

KIDDERMINSTER

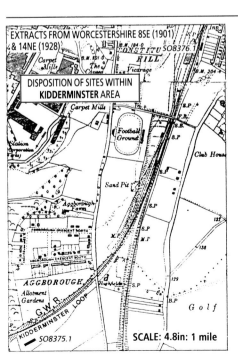

EXTRACTS FROM WORCESTERSHIRE 8SE (1901) & 14NE (1928)

SO8376.1

DISPOSITION OF SITES WITHIN KIDDERMINSTER AREA

Carpet Mills

Football Ground

Club House

Sand Pit

Aggborough Farm

AGGBOROUGH

Allotment Gardens

GWR

KIDDERMINSTER LOOP

Golf

SO8375.1

SCALE: 4.8in: 1 mile

Site SO8376.1; On the east side of the line, at the south end of Kidderminster Station.
Kidderminster (OW&W)^SO8376.1/1A
A timber built 1TS dead ended shed with a slated gable style roof, it was located at SO83837616 and was opened by the Oxford, Worcester & Wolverhampton Railway in September 1852. The facilities included a coal stage and 42ft turntable. The line was absorbed by the GWR in 1863.

The shed was modified in 1899 ...
Kidderminster (GWR)^SO8376.1/1B
The turntable was removed and the depot rebuilt as a through type. The shed was closed in February 1932 and subsequently demolished.

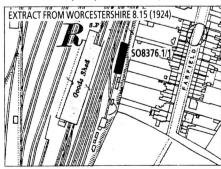

EXTRACT FROM WORCESTERSHIRE 8.15 (1924)

R

Goods Shed

FAIRFIELD

SO8376.1/1

Replaced by ...
Site SO8375.1; On the east side of the Severn Valley line, south of Kidderminster Station.
Kidderminster (GWR)^SO8375.1/1A
A corrugated iron 2TS dead ended shed with a corrugated iron gable style roof, it was located at SO83257512 and was opened in February 1932. The building was removed from Bassaleg (Brecon & Merthyr Railway) where it had served as an engine shed (ST2787.1/2A) between 1921 and 1929. The facilities included a ramped coal stage. The depot was closed by BR on August 10th, 1964 and demolished.

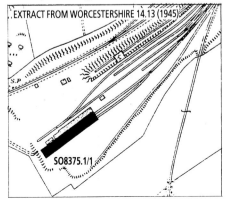

EXTRACT FROM WORCESTERSHIRE 14.13 (1945)

SO8375.1/1

HEREFORDSHIRE

SO3069 Kington

SO5059 Leominster

SO5058 Leominster

SO6554 Bromyard

SO2545 Clifford

HEREFORD

(See Enlargement)

SO7038 Ledbury

SO3928 Pontrilas

SO6024 Ross on Wye

PONTRILAS

Site SO3928.1; On the west side of the Hay branch about 0.5 miles north of Pontrilas Station.
Pontrilas (GVR)SO3928.1/1A
A 1TS through road shed, it was probably built in timber and was located at SO39912821. The depot was opened by the Golden Valley Railway on September 1st, 1881 and was destroyed by a fire in 1901.

Replaced, on the same site, by ...
Pontrilas (GWR)SO3928.1/1B
A timber built 1TS through road shed with a slated gable style roof, it was opened in 1901. The facilities included a water tank and coal stage. The depot was closed by BR on February 2nd, 1953 and removed, the site being returned to agricultural use..

EXTRACT FROM HEREFORDSHIRE 44.11 (1903)
SO3928.1/1

KINGTON

Site SO3069.1; On the north side of the line, west of Kington Station.
Kington (L&KR)SO3069.1/1A
A brick built 1TS dead ended shed with a slated gable style roof, it was located at SO30206999 and was opened by the Leominster & Kington Railway on August 2nd, 1857. The facilities included a coal stage sited outside of the shed entrance. The depot was closed by BR in February 1951 and removed.

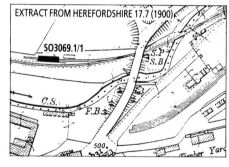

EXTRACT FROM HEREFORDSHIRE 17.7 (1900)
SO3069.1/1

BROMYARD

Site SO6554.1; On the north side of the line, at the west end of Bromyard Station.
Bromyard (WB&L)SO6554.1/1A
A timber built 1TS dead ended shed with a slated dual pitch roof, it was located at SO65685486 and was opened by the Worcester, Bromyard & Leominster Railway on October 22nd, 1877. Details of the facilities are not known. The shed was closed in September 1897 and demolished to accommodate an extension of the line through to Steens Bridge.

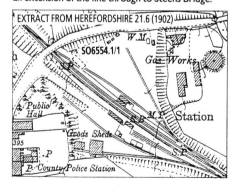

EXTRACT FROM HEREFORDSHIRE 21.6 (1902)
SO6554.1/1

ROSS ON WYE

Site SO6024.1; In the fork of the Gloucester and Lydbrook Junction lines, at the east end of Ross on Wye Station.
Ross on Wye (GWR)SO6024.1/1A
A stone built 1TS dead ended shed with a slated gable style roof, it was located at SO60862429 and was opened on June 1st, 1855. The facilities included a coal stage and, sited outside of the shed entrance, a turntable.

The shed was re-roofed ...
Ross on Wye (GWR)SO6024.1/1B
At some stage the roof was renewed and the turntable and coal stage removed. The depot was closed by BR in October 1963 and given over to private use. It was still standing in 1996 being utilized by an antiques business.

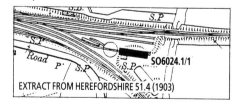

SO6024.1/1
EXTRACT FROM HEREFORDSHIRE 51.4 (1903)

CLIFFORD

Site SO2545.1; On the north side of Clifford Station.
Clifford (GV)SO2545.1/1A
A 1TS through road shed it was probably constructed in timber with a slated tiled roof. The depot was located at SO25204573 and was opened by the Golden Valley Railway on May 27th, 1889. The facilities included a water tank. It was closed by the GWR in 1897 and demolished. .

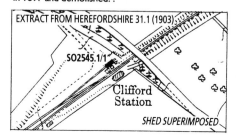

EXTRACT FROM HEREFORDSHIRE 31.1 (1903)
SO2545.1/1
Clifford Station
SHED SUPERIMPOSED

LEDBURY

Site SO7038.1; On the north side of Ledbury Station.
Ledbury (WMR)SO7038.1/F1
A servicing area consisting of a turntable, located at SO70943864, coal stage, water tank and engine pit, it was opened by the West Midland Railway on September 13th, 1861. The facility was closed by BR in July 1964.

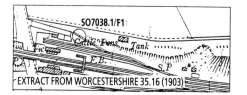

SO7038.1/F1
EXTRACT FROM WORCESTERSHIRE 35.16 (1903)

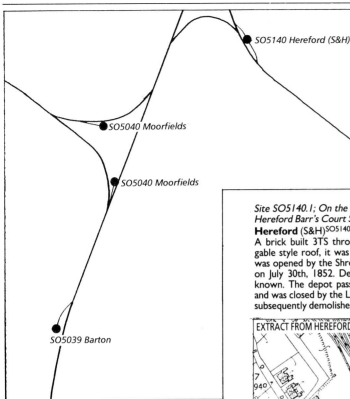

Site SO5040.1; On the west side of the line, north of Hereford Barton Station.

Hereford Moorfields (HH&B) SO5040.1/1A

A 1TS dead ended shed, located at SO50584043 and opened on October 24th, 1862 by the Hereford, Hay & Brecon Railway. No further details are known. The line was absorbed by the MR in 1876 and they closed the depot in 1894.

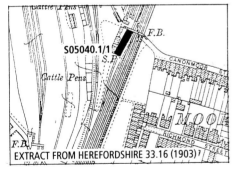

Replaced by ...
Site SO5040.2; In the fork of the Shrewsbury and Brecon lines, east of Moorfields Junction.

Hereford Moorfields (MR) SO5040.2/1A

A brick built 2TS dead ended shed with a slated gable style, located at SO50534067 and opened in 1894. The facilities included a 50ft turntable. The depot was closed by the LMS on December 10th, 1924 and later demolished.

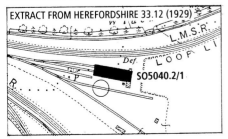

Site SO5140.1; On the east side of the line, north of Hereford Barr's Court Station.

Hereford (S&H) SO5140.1/1A

A brick built 3TS through road shed with a slated gable style roof, it was located at SO51154098 and was opened by the Shrewsbury & Hereford Railway on July 30th, 1852. Details of the facilities are not known. The depot passed to the L&NWR in 1867 and was closed by the LMS on July 4th, 1938 and was subsequently demolished.

Site SO5039.1; On the west side of the line, at the south end of Hereford Barton Station.

Hereford Barton (NA&H) SO5039.1/1A

A stone built 8TS shed with four through roads and a triple slated transverse pitched roof, it was located at SO50313984 and was opened by the Newport, Abergavenny & Hereford Railway on January 16th, 1854. The line was absorbed by the GWR in August 1869. The facilities included a ramped coal stage, water tank, turntable and repair shop.

The depot was improved in 1923 ...

Hereford Barton (GWR) SO5039.1/1B

The turntable was re-sited, the yard layout altered and coaling facilities improved. At some time after 1923 the shed was re-roofed in corrugated iron and it is reasonable to assume that it occurred during these improvements. The depot was closed by BR on November 2nd, 1964 and was subsequently demolished.

Site SO5140.2; On the east side of the line, at the south end of Hereford Barr's Court Station.

Hereford Barr's Court (HR&G) SO5140.2/1A

A stone built 2TS dead ended shed with a slated gable style roof, it was located at SO51684045 and was opened by the Hereford, Ross & Gloucester Railway in June 1855. Details of the facilities are not known. The depot was closed by the GWR in August 1869 and was subsequently utilized as a carriage shed until at least 1940 before being demolished.

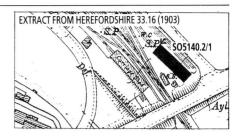

LEOMINSTER

Site SO5058.1; On the east side of the line, at the south end of Leominster Station.

Leominster (S&H) SO5058.1/1A

A brick built 2TS shed with one through road and a slated gable style roof, it was located at SO50255876 and was opened by the Shrewsbury & Hereford Railway on December 6th, 1853. The facilities included a coal stage, water column and 22ft turntable. The line was absorbed by the GWR/L&NWR in 1867 and the depot was closed by the GWR in April 1901 to accommodate station enlargements.

Replaced by ...
Site SO5059.1; On the east side of the line, north of Leominster Station.

Leominster (GWR) SO5059.1/1A

A brick built 2TS through road shed with a glazed northlight pattern roof, it was located at SO50125914 and was opened in October 1901. The facilities included a turntable, water column and coal stage with crane. The depot was closed by BR on April 2nd, 1962 and demolished.

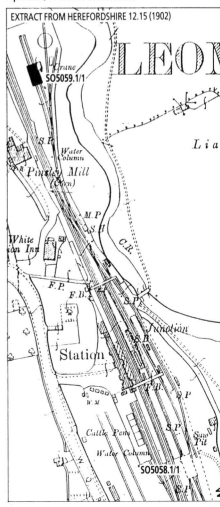

SHROPSHIRE

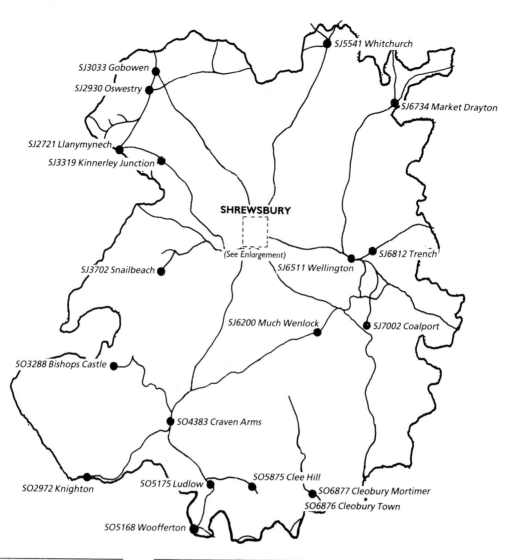

SJ5541 Whitchurch

SJ3033 Gobowen

SJ2930 Oswestry

SJ6734 Market Drayton

SJ2721 Llanymynech

SJ3319 Kinnerley Junction

SHREWSBURY

(See Enlargement)

SJ6812 Trench

SJ3702 Snailbeach

SJ6511 Wellington

SJ6200 Much Wenlock

SJ7002 Coalport

SO3288 Bishops Castle

SO4383 Craven Arms

SO5875 Clee Hill

SO2972 Knighton

SO5175 Ludlow

SO6877 Cleobury Mortimer

SO6876 Cleobury Town

SO5168 Woofferton

LLANYMYNECH

Site SJ2721.1; In the fork of the Shrewsbury and Oswestry lines, at the north end of Llanymynech Station.

Llanymynech (PS&NWR)[SJ2721.1/1A]
A timber built ITS through road shed with a gable style roof, it was located at SJ27162108 and was opened by the Potteries, Shrewsbury & North Wales Railway on August 13th, 1866. The facilities included a turntable, sited outside of the rear of the shed, and a water tank. The line was closed on December 21st, 1866 and re-opened in December 1868. The depot was closed when the line was totally abandoned on June 22nd, 1880* but remained standing for many years after.

EXTRACT FROM SHROPSHIRE 26.5 (1900)

SJ2721.1/1

* The line was re-opened on April 13th, 1911 as the Shropshire & Montgomeryshire Railway, not finally closing until March 20th, 1960.

LUDLOW

Site SO5175.1; On the east side of the line, north of Ludlow Station.

Ludlow (S&HR)[SO5175.1/1A]
A brick built ITS through road shed with a slated gable style roof, it was located at SO51287525 and was opened by the Shrewsbury & Hereford Railway in 1857. The facilities included a water tank and a turntable which was later removed. The line was absorbed by the GW/L&NWR in 1867.

The shed was extended ...
Ludlow (GW/L&NWR)[SO5175.1/1B]
At some stage a timber extension with a slated gable style roof was added at the northern end. The depot was closed by BR on December 29th, 1951. The building was let out for private use in 1976/7 and was still standing in 1995 as part of an industrial estate.

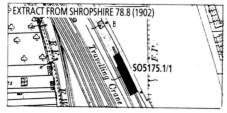

EXTRACT FROM SHROPSHIRE 78.8 (1902)

SO5175.1/1

MARKET DRAYTON

Site SJ6734.1; On the east side of the line, at the north end of Market Drayton Station.

Market Drayton (N&MDR)[SJ6734.1/1A]
A timber built ITS dead ended shed with a slated gable style roof, it was located at SJ67303489 and was opened by the Nantwich & Market Drayton Railway on October 20th, 1863. The facilities included a turntable. The line was absorbed by the GWR and in February 1870 they transferred use of the depot to the North Staffordshire Railway.

The shed was extended prior to 1877 ...
Market Drayton (NSR)[SJ6734.1/1B]
A timber extension with a slated gable style roof was added to the end of the building. The turntable was replaced with a 40ft unit by the GWR in 1889. The depot was closed by the LMS on December 8th, 1934 and demolished.

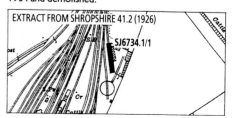

EXTRACT FROM SHROPSHIRE 41.2 (1926)

SJ6734.1/1

CRAVEN ARMS

Site SO4383.1; On the west side of the line, at the north end of Craven Arms & Stokesay Station.

Craven Arms (S&HR)^{SO4383.1/1A}
A 1TS shed, it was probably located at SO43108313 and was opened by the Shrewsbury & Hereford Railway in 1856. Further details of its construction and facilities are not known. The line was absorbed by the L&NWR in 1868 and the shed was closed in 1869.

Replaced, on the same site, by ...

Craven Arms (L&NWR)^{SO4383.1/1B}
A stone built 4TS dead ended shed with a twin slated hipped roof, it was opened in 1869. The facilities included a coal stage and 42ft turntable.

The shed was reduced to 3TS ...

Craven Arms (LMS)^{SO4383.1/1C}
One of the shed roads was removed in April 1937. The depot was closed by BR on May 22nd, 1964 and was later demolished.

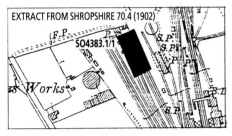

BISHOP'S CASTLE

Site SO3288.1; At the west end of Bishop's Castle Station.

Bishop's Castle (BCR)^{SO3288.1/1A}
A 1TS dead ended shed, it was located at SO32508866 and was opened by the Bishop's Castle Railway on October 24th, 1865. The facilities included a turntable. The depot, along with the line, was closed on April 20th, 1935 and demolished.

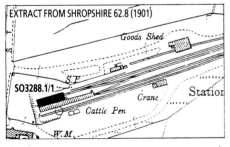

SNAILBEACH

Site SJ3702; At the Snailbeach Mine on the east side of the line, north of Snailbeach Station.

Snailbeach (SDR)^{SJ3702.1/1A}
A 2ft 4in gauge 2TS dead ended shed, it was located at SJ37440219 and was opened by the Snailbeach District Railway in 1874. No further details are known except that it was closed in 1946. The shed was still standing in 1973.

COALPORT

Site SJ7002.1; On the north side of the line, at the east end of Coalport Station.

Coalport (L&NWR)^{SJ7002.1/1A}
A brick built 2TS dead ended shed with a slated gable style roof, it was located at SJ70240214 and was opened on June 17th, 1861. The facilities included a water tank and a turntable which was later removed. The shed suffered from subsidence during 1924 and remedial work was carried out.

The shed was partially rebuilt in 1924 ...

Coalport (LMS)^{SJ7002.1/1B}
The building was reduced to a 1TS structure to accommodate strengthening of the end walls and the construction of a brick support. The depot was closed by BR on May 31st, 1952 and demolished.

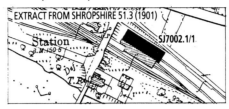

GOBOWEN

Site SJ3033.1; On the west side of the line, at the south end of Gobowen Station.

Gobowen (S&CR)^{SJ3033.1/1A}
A stone built 1TS dead ended shed with a slated gable style roof, it was located at SJ30423322 and was opened by the Shrewsbury & Chester Railway on December 23rd, 1848. The facilities included a water tank. The depot was closed by the GWR on December 4th, 1922 and demolished in January 1937.

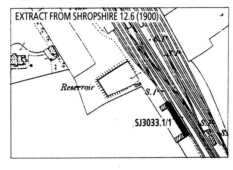

WOOFFERTON

Site SO5168.1; On the north side of the Tenbury Wells branch, north of Woofferton Station.

Woofferton (W&TW)^{SO5168.1/1A}
A brick built 1TS through road shed with a slated gable style roof incorporating a water tank, it was located at SO51676850 and was opened by the Woofferton & Tenbury Wells Railway on August 1st, 1861. The line was absorbed by the GW/L&NWR in January 1869 and the depot was closed in November 1896. It was not demolished immediately and was still standing in 1936.

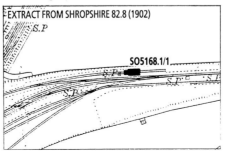

WELLINGTON

Site SJ6511.1; On the north side of Wellington Station.

Wellington (GWR)^{SJ6511.1/1A}
A brick built 3TS shed with one through road and a slated pitched roof with wood and brick gables, it had probably been converted from a goods shed and was located at SJ65251168. The depot was opened in 1876 and the facilities included a coal stage and a turntable which was removed during the 1930s. The shed was closed by BR on August 10th, 1964 and subsequently demolished.

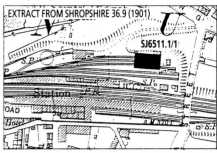

KINNERLEY JUNCTION

Site SJ3319.1; In the fork of the Melverley and Llanymynech lines, at the west end of Kinnerley Station.

Kinnerley Junction (S&MR)^{SJ3319.1/1A}
A timber built 2TS dead ended shed with a corrugated iron gable style roof, it was located at SJ33551983 and was opened by the Shropshire & Montgomeryshire Railway on April 13th, 1911. The facilities included a water tank. The line was taken over by the Government in September 1939 and was requisitioned by the War Department in 1941. The depot was closed on February 29th, 1960. The shed was still standing, in private use, in 1973.

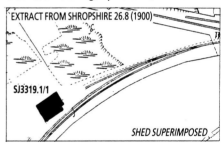

KNIGHTON

Site SO2972.1; On the north side of the line, east of Knighton Station.

Knighton (Knighton)^{SO2972.1/1A}
A stone built 1TS through road shed with a slated hipped roof, it was located at SO29437241 and was opened by the Knighton Railway in 1870. The line was worked from the outset by the L&NWR and the depot was closed by BR on January 1st, 1962 and later demolished.

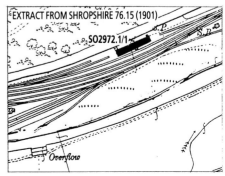

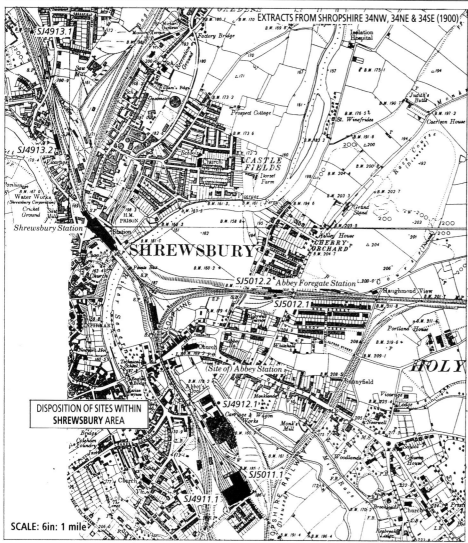

EXTRACTS FROM SHROPSHIRE 34NW, 34NE & 34SE (1900)

DISPOSITION OF SITES WITHIN
SHREWSBURY AREA

SCALE: 6in: 1 mile

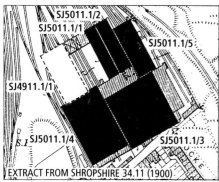

EXTRACT FROM SHROPSHIRE 34.11 (1900)

Site SJ4911.1 & SJ5011.1; On the east side of the Hereford line, south of Shrewsbury Station.

Coleham (S&HR) SJ5011.1/1A
A brick built 3TS dead ended shed with a slated hipped roof, located at SJ50011195 and opened by the Shrewsbury & Hereford Railway on April 1st, 1852. It was probably closed as an engine shed in 1855/56 and converted to a locomotive works.

The GWR took over the building in 1865 and converted it to a carriage works, removing the centre track.

It was re-instated as an engine shed ...
Coleham (GWR) SJ5011.1/1B
The centre track was relaid and the building re-opened as an engine shed following the construction of the roundhouse (SJ5011.1/3A) in 1883.

Adjoined by ...
Coleham (S&HR) SJ5011.1/2A
A brick built 2TS shed with a slated hipped roof, it was built along the eastern wall of SJ5011.1/1A at SJ50021195 and was opened by the Shrewsbury & Hereford Railway in 1856. It was closed by the GWR in 1865 and converted to a carriage works.

It was re-instated as an engine shed ...
Coleham (GWR) SJ5011.1/2B
The building re-opened as an engine repair shop in 1883 and was later used for stabling locomotives.

Coleham (S&HR) SJ4911.1/1A
A 4TS dead ended shed, located at SJ49971193 and opened by the Shrewsbury & Hereford Railway in 1856. It is not certain whether it was initially used as a locomotive works or as a running shed but by 1865, when it was taken over by the L&NWR they were utilizing it as an engine shed. At the same time a coaling shed was erected in the shed yard.

Replaced, in 1877, by ...
Coleham (L&NWR) SJ5011.1/4A
A brick built 10TS dead ended shed with a north-light pattern roof, it was sited slightly south of its predecessor (SJ4911.1/1A) at SJ50001186.

The shed was reduced in size ...
Coleham (LMS) SJ5011.1/4B
One of the tracks was removed, reducing it to a 9TS building. At some stage a turntable was installed on the western side of the shed.

Coleham (GWR) SJ5011.1/3A
A brick built 1RH shed with a northlight pattern roof, it was opened in 1883 and adjoined the later L&NWR shed (SJ5011.1/4A) along its eastern wall at SJ50041190. An unusual feature, for the GWR, was the provision of a single road along the western wall. The facilities included a coal stage.

The shed was re-roofed ...
Coleham (GWR) SJ5011.1/3B
It was re-roofed in 1938.

Coleham (GWR) SJ5011.1/5A
A corrugated iron sheeted 3TS dead ended shed with a corrugated iron gable style roof, it adjoined SJ5011.2/1A along its eastern wall at SJ50041195 and opened in 1932.

The depot was closed to steam by BR on November 6th, 1967 and utilized for diesel locomotive servicing for a few years until demolition commenced in 1972.

EXTRACT FROM SHROPSHIRE 34.11 (1900)

Site SJ4912.1; On the west side of the line, south of Shrewsbury Abbey Station.

Abbey (PS&NWR) SJ4912.1/1A
A 2TS dead ended shed, probably constructed in timber, located at SJ49961224 and opened by the Potteries, Shrewsbury & North Wales Railway on August 13th, 1866. The facilities included the use of a turntable which was sited in the adjacent Midland Railway C&W Company works. The shed, along with the line, closed on June 22nd, 1880 and the building was utilized for the next ten years as a store for the company's four locomotives until it was demolished in c1891.

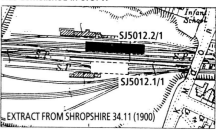

EXTRACT FROM SHROPSHIRE 34.11 (1900)

Site SJ5012.1; On the south side of Shrewsbury Abbey Foregate Station.

Abbey Foregate (S&BR) SJ5012.1/1A
A timber built 3TS shed with timber gables, located at SJ50211266 and opened by the Shrewsbury & Birmingham Railway on June 1st, 1849. Details of the facilities are not known. The line was absorbed by the GWR on September 1st, 1854 and the depot closed in 1865 with the locomotives transferring to Coton Hill North (SJ4913.1/1A). The building was demolished in c 1883

Site SJ5012.2; On the north side of Shrewsbury Abbey Foregate Station.

Abbey Foregate (SUR) SJ5012.2/1A
A 2TS through road shed located at SJ50211268 and opened by the Shropshire Union Railway on June 1st, 1849. Details of the facilities are not known. The line had been leased by the L&NWR from July 2nd, 1849 and the shed closed in 1877 upon the opening of Coleham shed (SJ5011.1/1A).

The building was converted into a wagon works and was utilized as such until the early 1900s when it was demolished.

Continued ...

SHREWSBURY cont ...

Site SJ4913.1; On the east side of the Chester line, north of Shrewsbury Station.
Coton Hill North (GWR)^{SJ4913.1/1A}

A brick built 4TS through road shed with a slated pitched roof and glazed gables, it was located at SJ49201374 and opened in 1865. The facilities included a coal stage. The depot closed in 1883 following the opening of Coleham (SJ5011.1/3A) and was subsequently demolished, the site being utilized for sidings.

EXTRACT FROM SHROPSHIRE 34.6 (1900)

Site SJ4913.2; On the west side of the Chester line, north of Shrewsbury Station.
Coton Hill South (S&CR)^{SJ4913.2/1A}

A brick built 3TS dead ended shed with a slated hipped roof, located at SJ49301331 and opened by the Shrewsbury & Chester Railway on October 12th, 1848. The facilities included a turntable. The line was absorbed by the GWR on September 1st, 1854 and the depot closed in 1883. It was converted to goods use and was still standing in 1999, in private use.

MUCH WENLOCK

Site SJ6200.1; On the east side of the line, south of Much Wenlock Station.
Much Wenlock (MW&SJR)^{SJ6200.1/1A}

A brick built 1TS dead ended shed with a slated gable style roof incorporating a water tank at the rear, it was located at SJ62110007 and was opened by the Much Wenlock & Severn Junction Railway on February 1st, 1862. The depot was closed by BR on December 31st, 1951 and demolished.

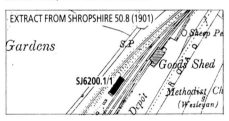

EXTRACT FROM SHROPSHIRE 50.8 (1901)

TRENCH

Site SJ6812.1; On the south side of the line, west of Trench Crossing Station.
Trench (L&NWR)^{SJ6812.1/1A}

A timber built 1TS dead ended shed with a corrugated iron dutch barn style roof, it was located at SJ68311258. The opening date is not known. The facilities included a water tank. The depot was closed by the LMS in 1943 and demolished.

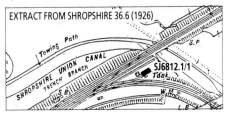

EXTRACT FROM SHROPSHIRE 36.6 (1926)

OSWESTRY

Site SJ2930.1; In the fork of the Gobowen and Whitchurch lines, north of Oswestry Station.
Oswestry (O&NR)^{SJ2930.1/1A}

A brick built 4TS dead ended shed with a twin slated hipped roof and brick screen, it was located at SJ29823033 and was opened by the Oswestry & Newtown Railway on May 1st, 1860. The facilities included a coal stage, water tank and turntable. The line was absorbed by the Cambrian Railway on July 25th, 1864.

The shed was enlarged ...
Oswestry (CamR)^{SJ2930.1/1B}

Prior to 1900 a brick built 2TS dead ended shed with a slated hipped roof was added to the east side of the shed.

The shed was re-roofed in 1949/50 ...
Oswestry (BR)^{SJ2930.1/1C}

The roof was rebuilt by the Western Region in a double and single gable style with corrugated sheeting. The depot was closed by BR on January 18th, 1965 and was still standing in 1995

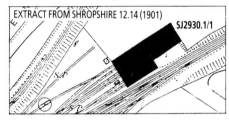

EXTRACT FROM SHROPSHIRE 12.14 (1901)

CLEE HILL

Site SO5875.1; On the south side of the Clee Hill branch a short distance east of the top of the incline.
Clee Hill (L&CH)^{SO5875.1/1A}

A timber built 1TS dead ended shed with a slated pitched roof, it was located at SO58937594 and was opened by the Ludlow & Clee Hill Railway in 1877. The facilities included a water tank. The line was vested jointly into the GW/L&NW in 1893.

The building was lengthened in 1902 ...
Clee Hill (GW/L&NW)^{SO5875.1/1B}

An additional 20ft, incorporating an internal coal stage, was added to the rear of the shed. The building was propped up with timber supports and this may have been done at this stage. The depot was closed by BR on November 14th, 1960 and removed.

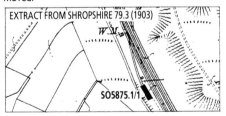

EXTRACT FROM SHROPSHIRE 79.3 (1903)

CLEOBURY MORTIMER

Site SO6876.1; On the east side of the line, at the north end of Cleobury Town Station.
Cleobury Town (CM&DP)^{SO6876.1/1A}

A timber built 1TS dead ended shed, it was located at SO68047698 and was taken over from the lines contractors by the Cleobury Mortimer & Ditton Priors Railway in 1908. It was equipped with a water tank but further details of its facilities are not known. The depot was closed in 1917 and pulled down.

Replaced by ...
Site SO6877.1; On the east side of the line, north of Cleobury Town Station.
Cleobury Mortimer (CM&DP)^{SO6877.1/1A}

A concrete block built 1TS dead ended shed with a shallow pitch concrete roof, it was located north of its predecessor (SO6877.1/1A) at SO68027727 and was opened by the Cleobury Mortimer & Ditton Priors Railway in 1917. The facilities included a coal stage, sited outside of the shed entrance, and a water tank at the station. The line was absorbed by the GWR on January 1st, 1922 and the depot was officially closed on September 26th, 1938 although the shed yard was utilized as a servicing area until 1965. The building was not demolished and despite being struck by lightning it was still standing, in a derelict condition, in 1989.

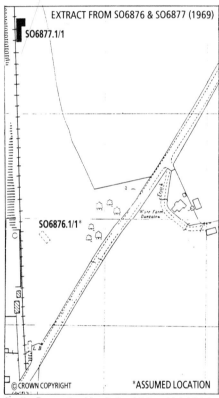

EXTRACT FROM SO6876 & SO6877 (1969)

Please Note; The construction and dismantling dates of this line precludes its inclusion in a complete form on OS maps. Some, or all, of the buildings and track have been superimposed.

WHITCHURCH

Site SJ5541.0; In the vicinity of Whitchurch Station.
Whitchurch (L&NWR)^{SJ5541.0/1A}

A 1TS shed, it was opened on October 1st, 1872 and closed in 1883. No further details are known.

Replaced by ...
Site SJ5541.1; On the east side of Whitchurch Station.
Whitchurch (L&NWR)^{SJ5541.1/1A}

A brick built 4TS dead ended shed with a slated northlight pattern roof, it was located at SJ55104150 and was opened in 1883. The facilities included a water tank and turntable. The depot was closed by BR in September 1957 and demolished.

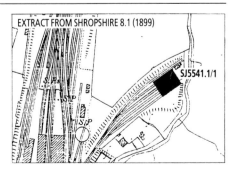

EXTRACT FROM SHROPSHIRE 8.1 (1899)

HUNTINGDON

SOMERSHAM

Site TL3677.1; On the west side of the line, south of Somersham Station.

Somersham (GER) TL3677.1/1A

A 2TS dead ended shed, located at TL36597772 was opened here prior to 1887. No further details are known except that it was closed by the LNER at some time after 1927.

EXTRACT FROM HUNTINGDONSHIRE 19.3 (1902)

TL3677.1/1

TL2885 Ramsey North
TL2884 Ramsey East
TL3677 Somersham
TL2371 Huntingdon   TL2471 Godmanchester

GODMANCHESTER

Site TL2471.1: On the north side of Godmanchester Station.

Godmanchester (E&HR) TL2471.1/1A

A 1TS shed was opened here by the Ely & Huntingdon Railway on August 17th, 1847. Details of the facilities are not known. It was approximately located at TL24497138 and was closed in May 1883.

HUNTINGDON EAST

Site TL2371.1; On the north side of the line, at the east end of Huntingdon East Station.

Huntingdon East (GER) TL2371.1/1A

A brick built 1TS dead ended shed with a slated gable style roof, it was located at TL23457152 and was opened in August 1885. The facilities included a 50ft turntable and coal stage. The depot was closed by BR in c1959 and was subsequently demolished.

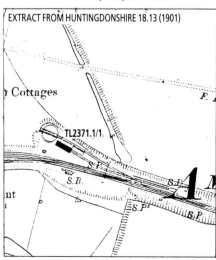

EXTRACT FROM HUNTINGDONSHIRE 18.13 (1901)

Cottages

TL2371.1/1

RAMSEY

EXTRACT FROM HUNTINGDONSHIRE 10SE (1900)

TL2885.1

Ramsey North Station

DISPOSITION OF SITES WITHIN **RAMSEY** AREA

THE FIELDS

Grammar School

Cricket Ground
Pavilion

Ramsey East Station
Westward Ho!

Goods Shed

SCALE; 6in:1 mile

TL2884.1

Site TL2884.1; On the west side of the line, south of Ramsey East Station.

Ramsey East (GER) TL2884.1/1A

A brick built 1TS dead ended shed, it was located at TL28568454 and was opened on September 16th, 1889. The facilities included a coal stage. The depot was closed by the LNER on September 22nd, 1930 and subsequently demolished.

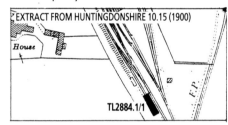

EXTRACT FROM HUNTINGDONSHIRE 10.15 (1900)

House

TL2884.1/1

Site TL2885.1; On the west side of Ramsey North Station.

Ramsey North (Ramsey) TL2885.1/1A

A corrugated iron 1TS through road shed, it was located at TL28248574 and was opened by the Ramsey Railway on July 22nd, 1863. The facilities probably included a coke/coal stage and water column. The line was initially worked on a seven year lease by the GNR but the Ramsey Railway was bought by the GER in 1870 and they renewed the lease to the GN with the shed passing into GER ownership. The depot ceased to be used by the GNR in 1885 but was not until 1897 that they asked the GER for permission to demolish it as it was life-expired.

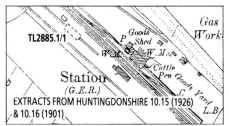

TL2885.1/1

Goods Shed

Station (G.E.R.)

Gas Works

Cattle Pen Goods Yard

EXTRACTS FROM HUNTINGDONSHIRE 10.15 (1926) & 10.16 (1901)

WARWICKSHIRE

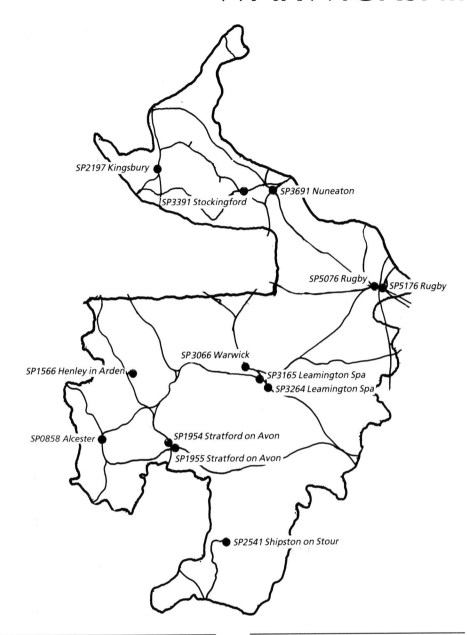

HENLEY IN ARDEN

Site SP1566.1; On the east side of Henley in Arden (B&HIAR) Station.

Henley in Arden (B&HIAR)[SP1566.1/1A]
A brick built 1TS dead ended shed with a slated gable style roof incorporating a water tank, it was located at SP15326654 and was opened by the Birmingham & Henley in Arden Railway on June 6th, 1894. The facilities also included a coal stage. The line was absorbed by the GWR on July 1st, 1900 and they closed the shed on July 1st, 1908 following the opening of the Bearley branch and new Henley in Arden station. The building was incorporated in the goods yard and was later given over to industrial use, not being demolished until the 1970s.

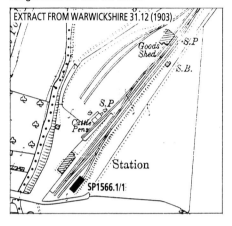

EXTRACT FROM WARWICKSHIRE 31.12 (1903)

SP1566.1/1

STOCKINGFORD

Site SP3391.0; In the vicinity of Stockingford Station.

Stockingford (MR)[SP3391.0/F1]
Some form of facility consisting of a siding and water tank was opened here on November 1st, 1864. A turntable was added in 1873. The depot was closed in 1903.

Replaced by ...
Site SP3391.1; On the south side of Stockingford Station.

Stockingford (MR)[SP3391.1/1A]
A timber built 3TS dead ended shed with a slated gable style roof, it was located at SP33319174 and was opened in 1903. The facilities included a water tank, coal stage and 60ft turntable. Although the depot was officially closed by the LMS on November 7th, 1932 locomotives continued to be serviced in the shed yard. The building itself was utilized as a store depot for locomotive coal until 1958. It was subsequently demolished.

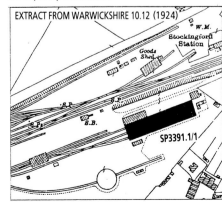

EXTRACT FROM WARWICKSHIRE 10.12 (1924)

SP3391.1/1

KINGSBURY

Site SP2197.1; On the east side of Kingsbury Junction.

Kingsbury (MR)[SP2197.1/F1]
A servicing area consisting of a water tank and siding it was located at SP21869707. The opening date is not known but it was utilized until March 6th, 1967 when Saltley shed closed to steam.

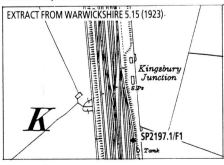

EXTRACT FROM WARWICKSHIRE 5.15 (1923)

SP2197.1/F1

SHIPSTON ON STOUR

Site SP2541.1; On the west side of the line, at the north end of Shipston on Stour Station.

Shipston on Stour (GWR)[SP2541.1/1A]
A brick built 1TS dead ended shed with a slated gable style roof, it was located at SP25744122 and was opened on July 1st, 1889. There were no facilities provided. The depot ceased to be used by the GWR in November 1916 and was handed over for military use. It was restored back to its owners in November 1918 and was eventually dispensed with in October 1923. The building was then utilized as a garage and was still standing, in use as a workshop, in 1991.

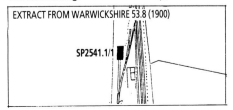

EXTRACT FROM WARWICKSHIRE 53.8 (1900)

SP2541.1/1

WARWICK & LEAMINGTON SPA

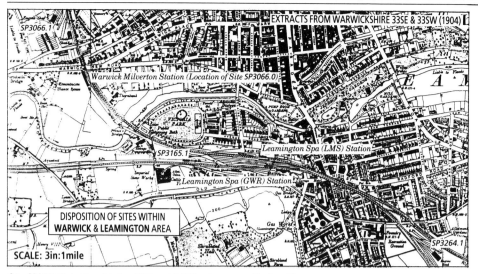

EXTRACTS FROM WARWICKSHIRE 33SE & 33SW (1904)

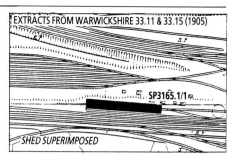

EXTRACTS FROM WARWICKSHIRE 33.11 & 33.15 (1905)

SHED SUPERIMPOSED

Site SP3066.0; *In the vicinity of Warwick Milverton Station.*

Warwick (L&B)^{SP3066.0/1A}
A shed was opened here by the London & Birmingham Railway on December 9th, 1844. It was closed in 1881. No further details are known.

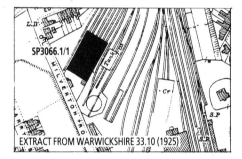

EXTRACT FROM WARWICKSHIRE 33.10 (1925)

Replaced by ...
Site SP3066.1; *On the west side of the line, north of Warwick Milverton Station.*
Warwick (L&NWR)^{SP3066.1/1A}
A brick built 6TS dead ended shed with a glazed northlight pattern roof, it was located at SP30406608 and was opened in 1881. The facilities included a coal stage, with water tank over, and a turntable. The depot was closed by BR on November 17th, 1958 and was demolished

Site SP3165.1; *On the north side of the line, west of Leamington Spa (GWR) Station.*
Leamington Spa (GWR)^{SP3165.1/1A}
A timber built 1TS dead ended shed with a slated gable style roof, it was located at SP31206529 and was opened in c1855. The facilities included a water tank, coal stage and a 41ft 10in turntable installed in 1881. The building was destroyed by a fire on March 10th, 1902.

A servicing point was then established ...
Leamington Spa (GWR)^{SP3165.1/F1}
A temporary servicing area incorporating the shed site and existing facilities was utilized until September 1906.

Replaced by ...
Site SP3264.1; *On the east side of the line, south of Leamington Spa (GWR) Station.*
Leamington Spa (GWR)^{SP3264.1/1A}
A brick built 4TS dead ended shed with a slated twin gable style roof, it was located at SP32636479 and was opened in September 1906. The facilities included a ramped coaling stage, water tower and turntable. The depot was closed by BR on June 14th, 1965 and demolished, the site being utilized as an industrial estate.

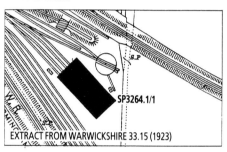

EXTRACT FROM WARWICKSHIRE 33.15 (1923)

RUGBY

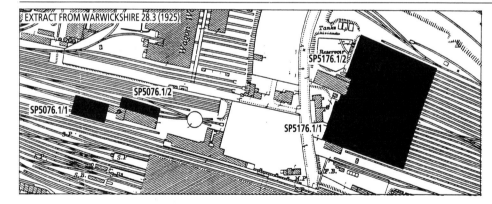

EXTRACT FROM WARWICKSHIRE 28.3 (1925)

Site SP5175.0; *In the vicinity of Rugby Station.*
Rugby (L&B)^{SP5175.0/4A}
A shed ".... for 3 locomotives" was opened here on April 9th, 1838 by the London & Birmingham Railway. No further details are known.

Rugby (L&B)^{SP5175.0/1A}
A shed was opened here by the London & Birmingham Railway in 1847. No further details are known. It was closed in 1852

Rugby (L&NWR)^{SP5175.0/2A}
A 3TS shed was opened here in 1851 for use of the *Northern Division.* No further details are known. It was closed in 1876.

Rugby (L&NWR)^{SP5175.0/3A}
A shed was opened here in 1852 for use of the *Southern Division.* No further details are known. It was closed in 1876.

Site SP5176.1; *On the north side of Rugby Station.*
Rugby No.1 (L&NWR)^{SP5176.1/1A}
A brick built 12TS dead ended shed with a northlight pattern roof, it was located at SP51217603 and was opened in 1876. The facilities included a coal stage, water tank, 40ft turntable and large repair shop.

It was rebuilt in 1955 ...
Rugby No.1 (BR)^{SP5176.1/1B}
The building was reduced in length and a new roof constructed in corrugated sheeting installed. It was closed to steam by BR on May 25th, 1965 and found further use for a short while as a stabling point for dmus and diesel shunters. It was later demolished.

Adjoined by ...
Rugby No.2 (L&NWR)^{SP5176.1/2A}
A brick built 12TS shed with one through road and a northlight pattern roof, it was located at SP51247608 and was opened in 1886. It was constructed adjacently to the north side of No.1 shed (SP5176.1/1A) and shared the facilities. It was closed by BR in 1960 and demolished.

Site SP5076.1; *On the north side of the line, at the west end of Rugby Station.*
Rugby (MCR)^{SP5076.1/1A}
A 4TS shed with one through road, it was located at SP50947605 and was opened by the Midland Counties Railway on July 1st, 1840.

Rugby (MCR)^{SP5076.1/2A}
A 2TS through road shed, it was located at SP50997605 and was opened by the Midland Counties Railway on July 1st, 1840.

The facilities included a turntable installed in 1876. No further details are known. The depot was closed by the LMS in 1923, locomotives transferring to the adjacent ex-L&NWR shed (SP5176.1/1A & 2A).

SCALE; 6in:1 mile

ALCESTER

Site SP0858.1; On the east side of the line, north of Alcester Station.
Alcester (Alcester)SP0858.1/1A
A brick built 1TS through road shed with a slated gable style roof, it was located at SP08335809 and was opened by the Alcester Railway on September 4th, 1876. The facilities included a water tank and coal stage. The depot was temporarily closed by the GWR in February 1917 as a wartime measure and re-opened in August 1923. Although it was then officially closed on October 27th, 1939 it was utilized for servicing locomotives until the closure of the Bearley branch by BR on March 1st, 1951. The shed was later demolished.

Site SP1955.1; On the east side of the line, at the south end of Stratford upon Avon (GW) Station.
Stratford upon Avon (OW&WR)SP1955.1/1A
A timber built 1TS through road shed with a slated gable style roof, it was located at SP19495505 and was opened by the Oxford, Worcester & Wolverhampton Railway in July 1859. The facilities included a coal stage. The depot was closed by the GWR in October 1910 and demolished.

Replaced by ...
Site SP1955.2; On the east side of the line, north of Stratford upon Avon (GW) Station.
Stratford upon Avon (GWR)SP1955.2/1A
A brick built 2TS dead ended shed with a slated gable style roof, it was located at SP19555555 and was opened in October 1910. The facilities included a ramped coal stage and water tower. The depot was closed by BR on September 10th, 1962 and demolished.

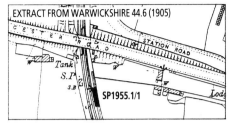

Site SP1954.1; On the south side of Stratford upon Avon (E&WJR) Station.
Stratford upon Avon (E&WJR)SP1954.1/1A
A timber built 2TS dead ended shed with a gable style roof, it was located at SP19905401 and was opened by the East & West Junction Railway on July 1st, 1873. The depot was utilized as the works for the line and as such the facilities included a fitting shop, 42ft turntable, coal stage and water tank. The water tank and coal stage were both upgraded by 1901.

It was enlarged in 1908 ...
Stratford upon Avon (E&WJR)SP1954.1/2A
A timber built 2TS dead ended shed with a corrugated iron twin dutch barn style roof was built adjoining the (rebuilt in brick) southern wall of the first shed (SP1954.1/1A). At the same time the turntable was re-sited and replaced with a 52ft unit. The line became part of the Stratford upon Avon and Midland Junction Railway on August 1st, 1908

The shed was rebuilt in 1934 ...
Stratford upon Avon (LMS)SP1954.1/2B
The roofs were removed and replaced with a corrugated asbestos twin gable style roof. The depot was closed by BR on July 22nd, 1957 and was subsequently demolished.

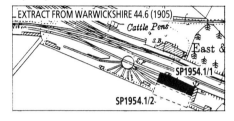

NUNEATON

Site SP3692.0; In the vicinity of Nuneaton Station.
Nuneaton (L&NWR)SP3692.0/1A
A 1TS shed was opened here on July 13th, 1847. No further details are known. The depot was closed in 1878.

Replaced by ...
Site SP3691.1; In the fork of the Coventry and Rugby lines, south of Nuneaton Station.
Nuneaton (L&NWR)SP3691.1/1A
A brick built 4TS shed with a glazed northlight pattern roof, it was located at SP36909167 and was opened in 1878. The facilities included a 42ft turntable and coal stage.

The shed was enlarged in 1888 ...
Nuneaton (L&NWR)SP3691.1/1B
The building was doubled in size to an 8TS shed.

The shed was enlarged again in 1897 ...
Nuneaton (L&NWR)SP3691.1/1C
The building was extended by 90ft at the rear. At the same time a larger coal stage, incorporating a water tank, was installed and the turntable was enlarged to 50ft and re-sited.

The shed was re-roofed in c1952 ...
Nuneaton (BR)SP3691.1/1D
An LMS-style louvre pitched roof with brick screen was installed by the London Midland Region shortly after nationalization. The depot was closed on June 6th, 1966 and subsequently demolished.

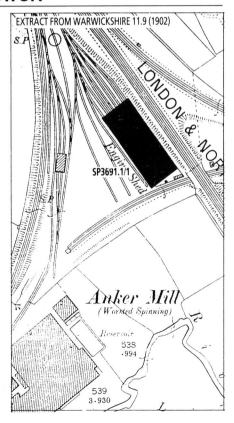

NORTHAMPTONSHIRE

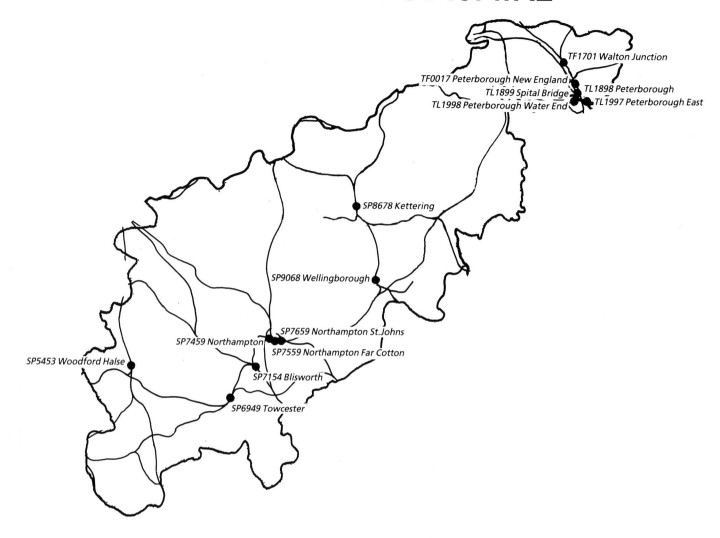

TF1701 Walton Junction

TF0017 Peterborough New England
TL1899 Spital Bridge
TL1998 Peterborough Water End

TL1898 Peterborough
TL1997 Peterborough East

SP8678 Kettering

SP9068 Wellingborough

SP7659 Northampton St.Johns
SP7459 Northampton
SP7559 Northampton Far Cotton

SP5453 Woodford Halse

SP7154 Blisworth

SP6949 Towcester

One of the fascinations of the hobby of studying engine sheds is that you never know when a surprise will turn up. Imagine then the comment caused when the building pictured here was "rediscovered" in 1995. **Northampton Far Cotton** shed (SP7559.1/2A) was erected as long ago as 1855 to replace a London & Birmingham structure (SP7559.1/1A) that had been blown down some three years earlier.

The L&NWR extended Far Cotton in 1870 and they closed it in October 1881 upon the opening of the 10TS shed (SP7459.1/1A) to the west. Following this Far Cotton was employed for many years as a carriage shed before passing to the Civil Engineers department in whose hands it (tenuously) still survived into 1998, some 143 years on and no less than 117 years after it last hosted locomotives!

B Matthews Collection

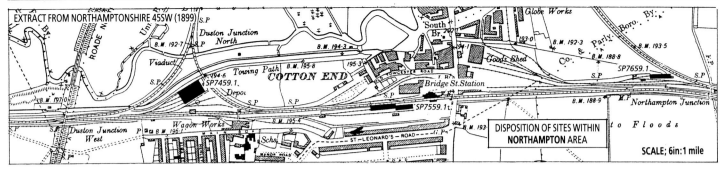

EXTRACT FROM NORTHAMPTONSHIRE 45SW (1899)

DISPOSITION OF SITES WITHIN **NORTHAMPTON** AREA

SCALE; 6in:1 mile

Site SP7559.1; On the south side of the line, at the west end of Bridge Street Station.

Northampton Far Cotton (L&B)SP7559.1/1A

A 2TS shed, probably built in timber, it was located at SP75325952 and was opened by the London & Birmingham Railway in c1850. No further details are known except that it was blown down in 1852.

Replaced, on the same site, by ....

Northampton Far Cotton (L&NWR)SP7559.1/1B

A brick built 2TS shed with a slated gable style roof, it was opened in 1855. No further details are known.

It was extended in 1871 ...

Northampton Far Cotton (L&NWR)SP7559.1/2A

A brick built 3TS shed with a slated gable style roof was added at the western end. It was located at SP75325952 and was closed in 1881. No further details are known. The building was then utilized as a carriage shed and later on it was passed to a BR engineering department. It was still standing in 1996.

EXTRACT FROM NORTHAMPTONSHIRE 45.9 (1925)

Replaced by ...
Site SP7459.1; In the fork of the Northampton Castle and Blisworth lines, west of Northampton Bridge Street Station.

Northampton (L&NWR)SP7459.1/1A

A brick built 10TS dead ended shed with a northlight pattern roof, it was located at SP74735956 and was opened in 1881. The facilities included a 42ft turntable, water tank and coal stage.

The shed was re-roofed in 1949 ...

Northampton (BR)SP7459.1/1B

An LMS-style louvre roof with brick screen was installed by the London Midland Region. The depot was closed on September 27th, 1965 and subsequently demolished.

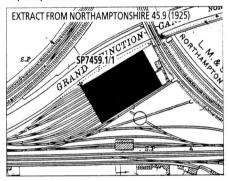

EXTRACT FROM NORTHAMPTONSHIRE 45.9 (1925)

Site SP7659.1; On the north side of the line, east of Northampton Bridge Street Station.

Northampton St.Johns (MR)SP7659.1/1A

A shed was opened here on October 1st, 1866 and closed in 1873. No further details are known.

Replaced by ...

Northampton St.Johns (MR)SP7659.1/2A

A brick built 2TS dead ended shed with a slated gable style roof, it was sited near to its predecessor (SP7659.1/1A) at SP76055960 and was opened in 1873. The facilities included a water column. The depot was closed by the LMS on October 1st, 1924. The building was not demolished, being utilized by various railway departments. It was still standing in 1996.

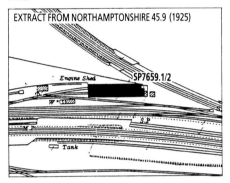

EXTRACT FROM NORTHAMPTONSHIRE 45.9 (1925)

KETTERING

Site SP8678.0; In the vicinity of Kettering Station.

Kettering (MR)SP8678.0/1A

A 1TS shed, it was opened in 1866. The facilities included a turntable. No further details are known. The depot was closed in 1876.

Replaced by ....
Site SP8678.1; On the east side of the line at the north end of Kettering Station.

Kettering (MR)SP8678.1/1A

A brick built 4TS dead ended shed with a slated twin gable roof, it was located at SP86407808 and was opened in 1876. The facilities included a turntable, re-sited in 1896, water tank and ramped coal stage. The depot was closed by BR on June 14th, 1965 and was subsequently demolished.

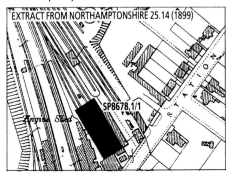

EXTRACT FROM NORTHAMPTONSHIRE 25.14 (1899)

BLISWORTH

Site SP7154.1; In the fork of the Towcester and Rugby lines, north of Blisworth Station.

Blisworth (N&BJR)SP7154.1/1A

A corrugated iron 1TS dead ended shed with a corrugated iron gable style roof, it was located at SP71835475 and was opened by the Northampton & Banbury Junction Railway in 1882. The facilities included a turntable over which access was gained to the shed. The line became part of the Stratford upon Avon & Midland Junction Railway on April 29th, 1910. Although the depot was officially closed by the LMS on August 10th, 1929 locomotives continued to be serviced in the shed yard until BR days. The building itself was dismantled immediately after closure and re-erected as a goods shed at Towcester Station.

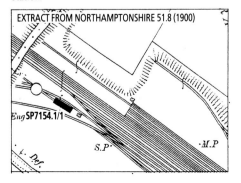

EXTRACT FROM NORTHAMPTONSHIRE 51.8 (1900)

WALTON JUNCTION

Site TF1701.1; In the vicinity of Walton Junction.

Walton Junction (GNR)TF1701.1/1A

A temporary shed it was probably erected in timber by the contractors Messrs Peto & Betts and was opened on October 17th, 1848. It was closed in 1850 upon the opening of Peterborough Station shed (TL1898.1/1A) and was removed to Boston yard in 1851 where it found further use as a carriage shed.

Site TF0017.1; On the east side of the line, north of Peterborough North Station.

New England (GNR)^{TF0017.1/1A}

A brick built 6TS through road shed with a corrugated iron-clad twin gable roof, it was located at TF00701794 and was opened in 1852. Being sited adjacently to a locomotive works the depot enjoyed the use of all facilities including a coal stage, water tank and 40ft turntable.

The shed was enlarged ...

New England (GNR)^{TF0017.1/1B}

In 1854 the shed was extended at each end by 45ft.

The shed was enlarged again in 1866...

New England (GNR)^{TF0017.1/1C}

The adjacent 3TS tender/paint shop was taken over and at the same time it, and the original shed (TF0017.1/1B) were extended to form a 9TS through road shed measuring some 305ft in length.

The shed was rebuilt ...

New England (BR)^{TF0017.1/1D}

The building was reconstructed by the Eastern Region in 1952 with brick and concrete with a corrugated asbestos northlight pattern roof.

Adjoined by ...

New England (GN)^{TF0017.1/2A}

A brick built 6TS dead ended shed with a twin gable style roof, it was located at TF00691797 and was opened in 1901. The building was originally utilized as a spare engine/paint shop within the works complex and was converted to locomotive use.

The shed was rebuilt ...

New England (BR)^{TF0017.1/2B}

The building was reconstructed by the Eastern Region in 1952 in brick and concrete with a twin corrugated asbestos pitched roof and brick screen

The depot was closed to steam by BR in January 1965 and totally on September 30th, 1968. The buildings were demolished during 1969 and the site was redeveloped.

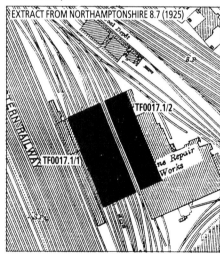

EXTRACT FROM NORTHAMPTONSHIRE 8.7 (1925)

EXTRACTS FROM NORTHAMPTONSHIRE 8NE & 8SE (1900)

DISPOSITION OF SITES WITHIN
PETERBOROUGH AREA

SCALE: 3in:1mile

Site TL1997.1; On the north side of the line, at the east end of Peterborough East Station.

Peterborough East (ECR)^{TL1997.1/1A}

A brick built 3TS dead ended shed with a slated gable style roof, it was located at TL19579795 and was opened by the Eastern Counties Railway on December 10th, 1846.

Adjoined on the north side by ...

Peterborough East (MCR)^{TL1997.1/2A}

A brick built 3TS dead ended shed with a slated gable style roof, it was located at TL19579797 and was opened by the Midland Counties Railway on March 20th, 1848.

The two buildings formed a single depot, the ex-MCR shed (TL1997.1/2A) was vacated by the Midland Railway upon the opening of Spital Bridge (TL1889.1/1A) in 1872 and the Great Eastern Railway assumed total control of the shed. The facilities included a turntable, water tank, two coke/coal stages and engine repair shops. The depot was closed by the LNER on April 30th, 1939 but locomotives continued to use the facilities with a new turntable and ash pit being installed as late as 1960. The buildings remain standing in private use having been given 'listed' status.

Peterborough East (L&BR)^{TL1997.1/3A}

A timber built 2TS dead ended shed, it was located at TL19539794 and was opened by the London & Birmingham Railway on May 31st, 1845. The facilities included a water tank, coke/coal stage and turntable. The line was incorporated into the L&NWR on January 1st, 1846. It was closed in September 1885.

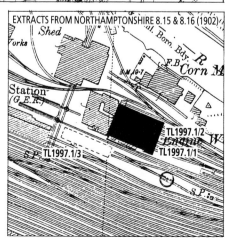

EXTRACTS FROM NORTHAMPTONSHIRE 8.15 & 8.16 (1902)

Continued ...

Replaced by ...
Site TL1998.1; In the fork of the Peterborough North and Seaton lines, west of Peterborough East Station.

Water End* (L&NWR)^{TL1998.1/1A}
A brick built 6TS dead ended shed with a glazed and tiled northlight pattern roof, it was located at TL19889813 and was opened in September 1885. The facilities included a coal stage with water tank over, and a 42ft turntable.

The shed was re-roofed in c1931
Water End (LMS)^{TL1998.1/1B}
The building was re-roofed shortly before it was closed by the LMS on February 8th, 1932. Locomotives continued to utilize the shed yard for servicing until BR days. The building itself was not demolished immediately but was given over to rolling stock storage and later was in use as a store. The shed was finally demolished in 1965 and the site became part of the Nene Valley Railway.

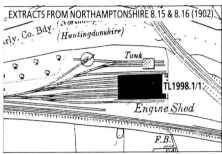

EXTRACTS FROM NORTHAMPTONSHIRE 8.15 & 8.16 (1902)

*The depot was also known as Woodstone.

Site TL1899.1; On the west side of the line, north of Peterborough North Station.
Spital Bridge (MR)^{TL1899.1/1A}
A brick built 1RH shed with a triple pitched roof, it was located at TL18449918 and was opened in 1872. The facilities included a coal stage, water tower and repair shop. The depot was closed by BR on February 1st, 1960 and was subsequently demolished.

EXTRACT FROM NORTHAMPTONSHIRE 8.11 (1926)

Site TL1898.1; On the east side of Peterborough North Station.
Peterborough Station (GNR)^{TL1898.1/1A}
A brick built 8TS dead ended shed with a twin slated gable style roof, it was located at TL18689895 and was opened on August 7th, 1850. The facilities included a coal stage with water tank, 40ft turntable and an engine repair shop. When the depot was closed is not clear, it was officially dispensed with in c1904 but the yard at least remained in use as a servicing area until and including BR days. The building itself could have been utilized as a rolling stock store depot at some stage, but was eventually demolished in 1963.

EXTRACT FROM NORTHAMPTONSHIRE 8.11 (1926)

TOWCESTER

Site SP6949.1; On the west side of Towcester Station.
Towcester (N&BJR)^{SP6949.1/1A}
A timber built 1TS dead ended shed with a gable style roof, it was located at SP69024944 and was opened by the Northampton & Banbury Junction Railway in 1873. The facilities included a coal stage.

The shed was modified ...
Towcester (N&BJR)^{SP6949.1/1B}
The building was reduced in length in c1884 and the depot was closed in 1900 and demolished.

Replaced by ...
Site SP6949.2; On the east side of the line, at the south end of Towcester Station..
Towcester (N&BJR)^{SP6949.2/F1}
A servicing area consisting of a turntable, located at SP69014933, coal stage and siding was opened by the Northampton & Banbury Junction Railway in 1900. The facility was closed by the LMS in 1930.

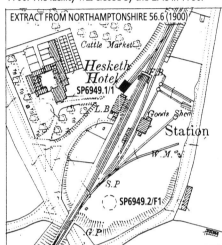

EXTRACT FROM NORTHAMPTONSHIRE 56.6 (1900)

WELLINGBOROUGH

Site SP9068.1; On the east side of the line, north of Wellingborough Station.
Wellingborough No.1 (MR)^{SP9068.1/1A}
A brick built square 1RH shed with a triple pitched roof, it was located at SP90476873 and was opened in 1868. The facilities included a coal shed, later converted to an engine shed (SP9068.1/3A), water tank and fitting shop.

The shed was renovated in c1932 ...
Wellingborough (LMS)^{SP9068.1/1B}
The shed roof was reconditioned and the internal turntable was increased in size to 60ft. The building was demolished by BR in July 1964.

Wellingborough No.2 (MR)^{SP9068.1/2A}
A brick built square 1RH shed with a triple pitched roof, it was located at the south end of the site at SP90416855 and was opened in 1872. The original coal shed was replaced by a double coal stage in 1881.

Wellingborough (LMS)^{SP9068.1/3A}
A brick built 2TS through road shed with a twin gable style roof, it was unusually tapered in planform and was located at SP90436866. It was constructed in 1868 as the original coal shed and was utilized as such until 1881 when the new coal shed (qv) came into use. It was re-opened in 1935 as an engine shed for the Beyer-Garratt locomotives and thereafter as additional accommodation for other engines.

The depot was closed to steam by BR on June 13th, 1966 and a 2TS diesel depot (SP9068.1/4A) established at the north end of the site at SP90486881. No.2 shed was still standing in 1993, in private use.

WOODFORD HALSE

Site SP5453.1; On the east side of the line, north of Woodford & Hinton Station.
Woodford Halse (GCR)^{SP5453.1/1A}
A brick built 6TS dead ended shed with a northlight pattern roof, it was located at SP54265343 and was opened in 1897. The facilities included a water tank, ramped coal stage and turntable.

At some stage it was re-roofed ...
Woodford Halse (BR)^{SP5453.1/1B}
The shed was rebuilt with an LMS-style louvre roof with brick screen by the Eastern Region. The depot was closed on June 14th, 1965 and was subsequently demolished.

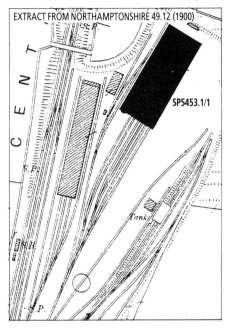

EXTRACT FROM NORTHAMPTONSHIRE 49.12 (1900)

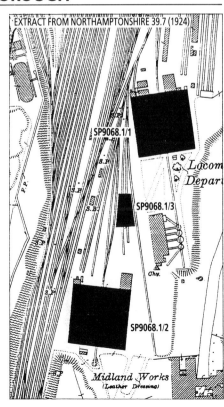

EXTRACT FROM NORTHAMPTONSHIRE 39.7 (1924)

WEST MIDLANDS

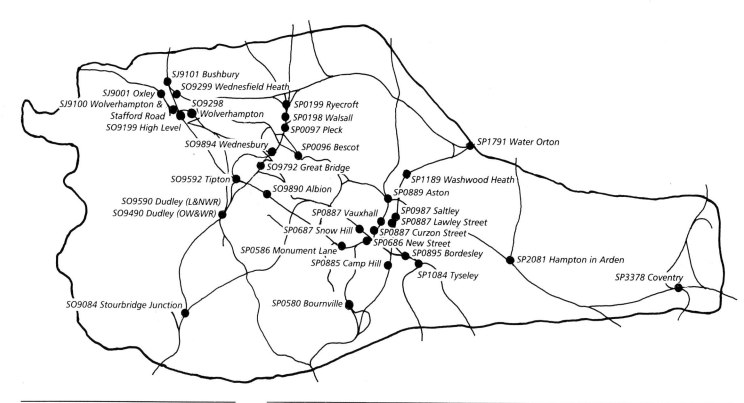

- SJ9101 Bushbury
- SO9299 Wednesfield Heath
- SJ9001 Oxley
- SJ9100 Wolverhampton & Stafford Road
- SO9298 Wolverhampton
- SO9199 High Level
- SP0199 Ryecroft
- SP0198 Walsall
- SP0097 Pleck
- SO9894 Wednesbury
- SP0096 Bescot
- SO9792 Great Bridge
- SP1791 Water Orton
- SO9592 Tipton
- SO9890 Albion
- SP1189 Washwood Heath
- SO9590 Dudley (L&NWR)
- SP0889 Aston
- SO9490 Dudley (OW&WR)
- SP0887 Vauxhall
- SP0987 Saltley
- SP0887 Lawley Street
- SP0687 Snow Hill
- SP0887 Curzon Street
- SP0586 Monument Lane
- SP0686 New Street
- SP0895 Bordesley
- SP0885 Camp Hill
- SP1084 Tyseley
- SP2081 Hampton in Arden
- SP3378 Coventry
- SO9084 Stourbridge Junction
- SP0580 Bournville

MONUMENT LANE

Site SP0586.0; In the vicinity of Edgbaston Station*
Edgbaston (BW&SVR) SP0586.0/1A
A 1TS shed was opened here by the Birmingham, Wolverhampton & Stour Valley Railway. No further details are known other than it was closed on November 14th, 1854

*Renamed as Monument Lane in 1874.

Site SP0586.1; On the south side of the line, east of Monument Lane Station.
Monument Lane (L&NWR) SP0586.1/1A
A brick built 3TS through road shed, it was located at SP05848685 and was opened in November 1858. For a number of years one of the tracks was utilized by the carriage department. The building was demolished in 1932 to facilitate track improvements in the shed yard.

Monument Lane (L&NWR) SP0586.1/2A
A brick built 6TS dead ended shed with a slated twin gable style roof, it was located at SP05738683 and was opened in 1884. The facilities included a 42ft turntable and coal stage. The depot was closed by BR on February 12th, 1962 and demolished. In 1986 the site was utilized as part of the National Indoor Arena.

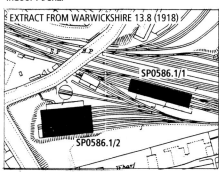

EXTRACT FROM WARWICKSHIRE 13.8 (1918)
SP0586.1/1
SP0586.1/2

SALTLEY

Site SP0987.1; On the east side of the line, south of Saltley Station.
Saltley No.1 (MR) SP0987.1/1A
A brick built 1RH shed with a slated triple pitched roof, it was located at SP09348768 and was opened in 1868. The facilities included a water tank and coal stage. A fitting shop was added in 1877.

The shed was re-roofed ...
Saltley No.1 (BR) SP0987.1/1B
The building was re-roofed in concrete by the London Midland Region in 1948.

Adjoined by ...
Saltley No.2 (MR) SP0987.1/2A
A brick built 1RH shed with a slated triple pitched roof, it was built along the western wall of SP0987.1/1A and was located at SP09288769. The building opened in 1876.

The shed was re-roofed ...
Saltley No.2 (BR) SP0987.1/2B
The building was re-roofed in concrete by the London Midland Region in 1948.

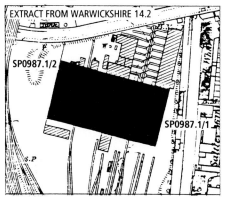

EXTRACT FROM WARWICKSHIRE 14.2
SP0987.1/2
SP0987.1/1

Adjoined by ...
Saltley No.3 (MR) SP0987.1/3A
A brick built 1RH shed with a slated triple pitched roof, it was built along the southern wall of SP0987.1/1A and was located at SP09338762. The building opened in 1900.

The shed was re-roofed ...
Saltley No.3 (BR) SP0987.1/3B
The building was re-roofed in glass and steel by the London Midland Region in 1951.

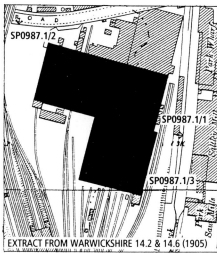

EXTRACT FROM WARWICKSHIRE 14.2 & 14.6 (1905)
SP0987.1/2
SP0987.1/1
SP0987.1/3

During its existence the turntables in each of the buildings were enlarged at various times and the coal stage was improved. The depot was closed to steam on March 6th, 1967 and all but the westernmost wall of No.2 shed demolished. A 3TS diesel depot (SP0987.1/4A) was built in the shed yard at SP09238757 and was still operational in 1999.

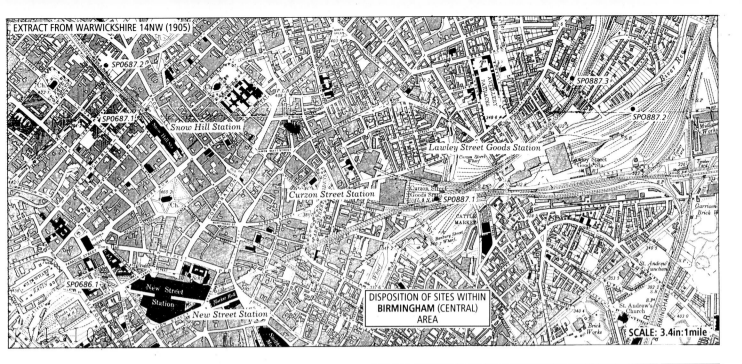

EXTRACT FROM WARWICKSHIRE 14NW (1905)

DISPOSITION OF SITES WITHIN
BIRMINGHAM (CENTRAL)
AREA

SCALE: 3.4in:1mile

VAUXHALL

Site SP0887.3; On the west side of Vauxhall (GJR) Temporary Station.
Vauxhall (GJR) SP0887.3/1A
A 2TS shed, probably built in timber, it was sited adjacently to the goods shed and was probably located at SP08648753. It was opened prior to 1840 by the Grand Junction Railway. No further details are known.

The shed was enlarged ...
Vauxhall (L&NWR) SP0887.3/2A
A timber shed, it was transferred from Camden and installed here in 1855. No further details are known.

The shed was enlarged again ...
Vauxhall (L&NWR) SP0887.3/3A
Further enlargements were carried out in 1858. The depot was closed in 1882 and demolished.

EXTRACT FROM WARWICKSHIRE 14.2, 14.5 & 14.6

SP0887.3/1&2*

*ASSUMED LOCATION

CURZON STREET

Site SP0887.1; On the south side of the line, at the east end of Birmingham Curzon Street Station.
Curzon Street (L&BR) SP0887.1/1A
A brick built 1RH shed incorporating a water tank surmounting the shed entrance, it was located at SP08078705 and was opened by the London & Birmingham Railway on April 9th, 1838. The facilities also included a coke store which was situated beneath the shed and was served by a short 18in gauge tramway from the adjacent canal. The depot was closed in 1859 and demolished to accommodate track widening into New Street Station.

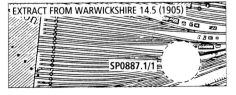

EXTRACT FROM WARWICKSHIRE 14.5 (1905)

SP0887.1/1

LAWLEY STREET

Site SP0887.2; In Lawley Street Goods Yard.
Lawley Street (B&DJR) SP0887.2/1A
A brick built 2TS through road shed with a pitched roof, it was located at SP08718727 and was opened by the Birmingham & Derby Junction Railway on February 10th, 1842. Details of the facilities are not known. The depot was closed by the Midland Railway in 1855 and demolished after 1875.

Replaced by ...
Lawley Street (MR) SP0887.2/2A
A brick built 1RH shed with a conical roof, it was located at SP08898739 and was opened in 1855. The facilities included a repair shop, coal stage and an additional turntable was added in the yard. The depot was closed in 1877 and demolished in c1900.

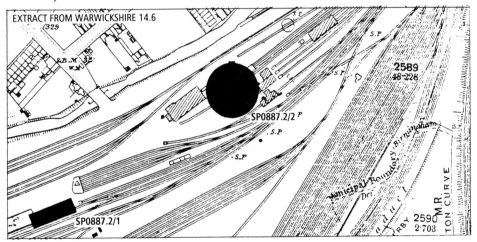

EXTRACT FROM WARWICKSHIRE 14.6

SP0887.2/2

SP0887.2/1

SNOW HILL

Site SP0687.1; On the west side of the line, at the north end of Birmingham Snow Hill Station.
Snow Hill (GWR) SP0687.1/F1
A servicing area consisting of a turntable, located at SP06858736, and sidings was opened here, probably in 1869. The facility was closed in c1909 to accommodate station enlargements.

EXTRACT FROM WARWICKSHIRE 14.5 (1902)

SP0687.1/F1

Replaced by ...
Site SP0687.2; On the east side of the line, at the north end of Birmingham Snow Hill Station.
Snow Hill (GWR) SP0687.2/F1
A servicing area consisting of a turntable, located at SP06728760 and sidings was opened here in 1909. It was dispensed with by BR in the mid-60s.

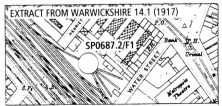

EXTRACT FROM WARWICKSHIRE 14.1 (1917)

SP0687.2/F1

NEW STREET

Site SP0686.1; On the south side of the Wolverhampton line, at the west end of Birmingham New Street Station.

New Street (L&NWR) SP0686.1/F1
A servicing facility consisting of a turntable, located at SP06728668 came into use in 1854.

The facility was improved ...
New Street (L&NWR) SP0686.1/F2
Stalls and engine pits were added around the turntable in about 1880. The facility was dispensed with by BR in c1962 when the station was rebuilt. A power signal box was built on part of the site and a stabling area for electric locomotives established on the remainder.

EXTRACT FROM WARWICKSHIRE 14.5 (1905)
SP0686.1/1

GREAT BRIDGE

Site SO9792.1; On the east side of the line, at the south end of Great Bridge (L&NWR) Station.

Great Bridge (L&NWR) SO9792.1/1A
A 1TS dead ended building was located at SO97649270 and it is believed to have been used as an engine shed. No further details are known other than it was demolished some time after 1919.

Replaced, on the same site, by ...
Great Bridge (L&NWR) SO9792.1/F1
A servicing area was then established for coaling and ash removal. The opening date for this is not known but the facility lasted until it was closed by BR in 1965.

EXTRACT FROM STAFFORDSHIRE 68.15 (1919)
SO9792.1/1

TIPTON

Site SO9592.1; In the goods yard, on the south side of line, at the east end of Tipton Station.

Tipton (L&NWR) SO9592.1/1A
A brick and timber built 1TS dead ended shed with a slated gable style roof incorporating a water tank, it was located at SO95649247 and was opened in 1885. The construction was unusual in that a retaining wall formed one side of the shed and the other was built on top of an existing wall. There were no other facilities. The depot was closed by BR in c1956 and demolished although the two walls which formed part of the shed building were still *in situ* in 1995.

EXTRACT FROM STAFFORDSHIRE 67.8 (1904)
SO9592.1/1

TYSELEY

Site SP1084.1; On the south side of the line at the west end of Tyseley Station.

Tyseley (GWR) SP1084.1/1A
A brick built 2RH shed with a slated six-pitched roof, it was located at SP10658405 and was opened in June 1908. It had the benefit of all facilities including a repair shop which was demolished by BR and a purpose built diesel depot (SP1084.1/2A) constructed on the site. The remainder of the depot was closed to steam by BR on November 7th, 1966 and was subsequently demolished. The *Birmingham Railway Museum* was established here with the coal stage being developed as the main building and the shed floor and turntables forming an open air site.

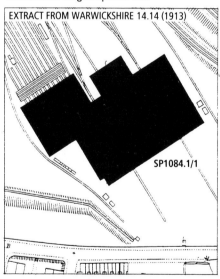
EXTRACT FROM WARWICKSHIRE 14.14 (1913)
SP1084.1/1

ASTON

Site SP0889.1; In the fork of the Stechford and Birmingham New Street lines, south of Aston Station.

Aston (L&NWR) SP0889.1/1A
A brick built 12TS shed with one through road and a northlight pattern roof, it was located at SP08978925 and was opened in 1883. The facilities included a 42ft turntable, coal stage and water tank. These were improved by the LMS in 1935 through the provision of a 60ft turntable, coal and ash plant and a new water tank.

The shed was re-roofed ...
Aston (LMS) SP0889.1/1B
A louvre-style roof with brick screen was installed in 1944. The depot was closed by BR on October 11th, 1965 and was subsequently demolished.

EXTRACT FROM WARWICKSHIRE 8.14 (1902)
SP0889.1/1

BESCOT

Site SP0096.1; On the west side of the line, at the north end of Bescot Station.

Bescot (L&NWR) SP0096.1/1A
A brick built 8TS dead ended shed with a northlight pattern roof, it was located at SP00509618 and was opened in 1892. The facilities included a 42ft turntable, coal stage and water tank.

The shed was re-roofed ...
Bescot (BR) SP0096.1/1B
An LMS-style louvre roof with brick screen was installed in c1950 by the London Midland Region. The depot was closed on March 28th, 1966 and a new purpose built diesel depot (SP0096.1/2A) was constructed in the shed yard at SP00629608. The original building (SP0096.1/1B) was not demolished but found further use for rolling stock storage and was still standing in 1996.

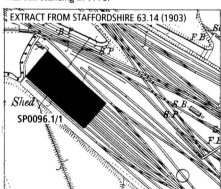
EXTRACT FROM STAFFORDSHIRE 63.14 (1903)
SP0096.1/1

WEDNESFIELD HEATH

Site SO9299.1; In the vicinity of Wednesfield Heath Station.

Wednesfield Heath (GJR) SO9299.1/1A
A shed *"for 2 or 3 engines"* was opened here, approximately located at SO9266999, by the Grand Junction Railway on July 4th, 1837. No further details are known.

BOURNVILLE

Site SP0580.1; On the west side of the line, south of Bournville Station.

Bournville (MR) SP0580.1/1A
A brick built 1RH shed with a slated triple pitched roof, it was located at SP05108073 and was opened in 1895. The facilities included a ramped coal stage and water tank. The depot was closed by BR on February 14th, 1960 and was subsequently demolished.

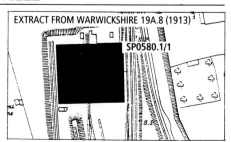
EXTRACT FROM WARWICKSHIRE 19A.8 (1913)
SP0580.1/1

COVENTRY

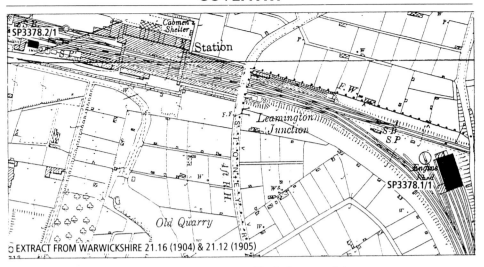

Site SP3378.0; In the vicinity of Coventry Station.
Coventry (L&BR) SP3378.0/1A

A 1TS shed was opened here by the London & Birmingham Railway on April 9th, 1838. No further details are known. The line became part of the L&NWR on January 1st, 1846 and the shed was closed in 1866.

Replaced by ...
Site SP3378.1; In the fork of the Warwick and Rugby lines, east of Coventry Station
Coventry (L&NWR) SP3378.1/1A

A brick built 2TS dead ended shed with a slated gable style roof and arched entrances, it was located at SP33497809 and was opened in 1866.

The shed was enlarged in 1897 ...
Coventry (L&NWR) SP3378.1/1B

A brick built 2TS dead ended shed with a slated gable style roof was added and the entrances rebuilt with a single lintel. The facilities included a 42ft turntable and water column.

The shed was re-roofed ...
Coventry (BR) SP3378.1/1C

The shed was rebuilt in 1957 by the London Midland Region with a corrugated steel transverse multi-pitched roof and screen. The depot was closed shortly afterwards on November 17th, 1958. It was used for a short while as a store for condemned locomotives until it was demolished to make way for a power signal box.

Site SP3378.2; On the south side of the line, at the west end of Coventry Station.
Coventry (MR) SP3378.2/1A

A brick built 1TS dead ended shed with a slated gable style roof incorporating a water tower, it was located at SP33087821 and was opened on September 1st, 1865. The facilities also included a coal stage. The depot was closed in 1904 but was not demolished until 1959.

HAMPTON IN ARDEN

Site SP2081.1; In the fork of the Birmingham and Derby lines, at the north end of Hampton Junction Station.

Hampton in Arden (B&DJR) SP2081.1/1A

A shed, probably 2TS, was opened here by the Birmingham & Derby Junction Railway on August 12th, 1839 and closed shortly afterwards on February 10th, 1840. It was a locomotive shop for the railway and it is assumed that it was converted to the goods shed which was located at SP20198178. The building was leased for private use and was still standing in 1954, as part of a saw mill.

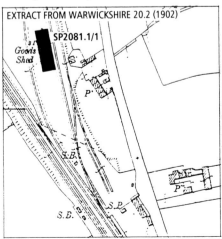

BORDESLEY

Site SP0985.0; In the vicinity of Small Heath & Sparkbrook Station.
Birmingham (GWR) SP0985.0/1A

A temporary shed was opened here on October 1st, 1852. It could have occupied the site of, or was located nearby, its replacement. Details of the facilities are not known. The depot was closed in 1855.

Replaced by ...
Site SP0985.1; On the south side of the line, west of Small Heath & Sparkbrook Station.
Bordesley Junction (GWR) SP0985.1/1A

A brick built 4TS through road shed with a slated gable style roof and glazed gable ends, it was located at SP09328529 and was opened in 1855. The facilities included a coal stage and 45ft turntable. The depot was closed upon the opening of Tyseley shed (SP1084.1/1A) in June 1908 and subsequently demolished.

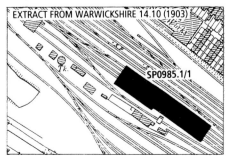

WATER ORTON

Site SP1791.1; On the north side of the line, west of Water Orton Station.
Water Orton (MR) SP1791.1/F1

A servicing area consisting of two sidings, engine pits and a water tank, it was located at SP17049126. The opening date is not known but it was probably installed by the MR. The facility was closed by BR on March 6th, 1967. All lines have since been lifted.

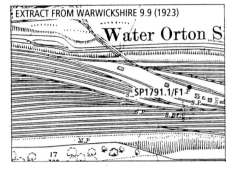

CAMP HILL

Site SP0885.1; In Camp Hill Goods Station.
Camp Hill (B'ham & G) SP0885.1/F1

A stabling point was established here, possibly as early as 1841 when the station was given over to goods use following the extension of the line through to Curzon Street. No further details are known of its early history but by LMS days locomotives stabled within the goods shed at SP08278550 during weekends. The Goods Station was closed on February 7th, 1966.

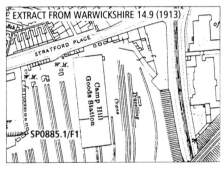

WASHWOOD HEATH

Site SP1189.1; On the north side of the line, west of Bromford Bridge Station.
Washwood Heath (LMS) SP1189.1/F1

A servicing area consisting of a turntable, located at SP11238963, water tank and siding. It was probably opened some time after 1927 and was primarily designed to accommodate Beyer-Garratt locomotives which were difficult to service at Saltley shed. Although the facility was closed by BR after the withdrawal of the last of this class of engines on February 18th, 1958, other locomotives continued to utilize it for some years later.

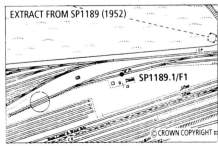

DUDLEY

Site SO9590.1; On the east side of the line, at the south end of Dudley Station.
Dudley (L&NWR) SO9590.1/1A
A brick built 2TS dead ended shed, it was located at SO95059067 and was opened in 1865. Due to the constrained nature of the site one of the roads was considerably shorter than the other to accommodate the turntable. Details of other facilities are not known. The depot was closed by the LMS in 1941 and was subsequently demolished.

Site SO9490.1; On the west side of the Wolverhampton line, at the north end of Dudley Station.
Dudley (OW&WR) SO9490.1/1A
A timber built 1TS dead ended shed with a slated gable style roof, it was located at SO94989097 and was opened by the Oxford, Worcester and Wolverhampton Railway on November 16th, 1852. The facilities included a turntable. The depot was closed in c1870 and the building dismantled and re-utilized as a grain store.*

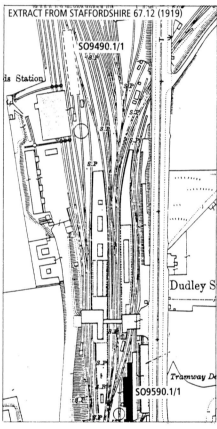

EXTRACT FROM STAFFORDSHIRE 67.12 (1919)
SO9490.1/1
SO9590.1/1

It could well have been re-sited in the goods station at SO94959085, in which case it would have survived until at least 1964.

ALBION

Site SO9890.1; On the north side of Albion Station.
Albion (L&NWR) SO9890.1/F1
A stabling point consisting of a siding, but with no facilities, it was located at SO98479097. The opening date is not known, but it was closed by BR in 1960. No further details are available.

EXTRACT FROM STAFFORDSHIRE 68.9 (1919)
SO9890.1/F1

WALSALL

Site SP0198.0; In the vicinity of Walsall Station.
Walsall (SSR) SP0198.0/1A
A shed was opened here by the South Staffs Railway on November 1st, 1847. The line was absorbed by the L&NWR on February 1st, 1861 and the shed was closed by them in 1878. No further details are known.

Replaced by ...
Site SP0199.1; In the fork of the Cannock and Lichfield lines, north of Walsall Station.
Ryecroft (L&NWR) SP0199.1/1A
A brick built 12TS dead ended shed with a northlight pattern roof, it was located at SP01579975 and was opened in 1878. The facilities included a coal stage, with water tank over, and a turntable. By BR days the building was virtually roofless.

The shed was rebuilt ...
Ryecroft (BR) SP0199.1/1B
The building was reduced to a 10TS structure and a new transverse pitched roof with brick screen was installed by the London Midland Region. The shed was closed to steam on June 9th, 1958 and was utilized as a dmu depot until the mid-1960s when it was totally closed and subsequently demolished.

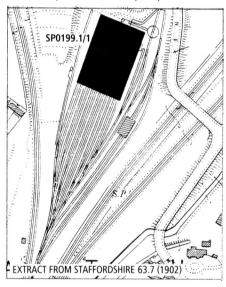

SP0199.1/1
EXTRACT FROM STAFFORDSHIRE 63.7 (1902)

Site SP0097.1; On the east side of the line, south of Walsall Station.
Pleck (MR) SP0097.1/1A
A brick built 3TS shed with one through road and a corrugated iron gable style roof, it was located at SP00569748 and was opened in 1880. The facilities included a water tank, coal stage and 50ft turntable. The depot was closed by the LMS on September 2nd, 1925 and given over to rolling stock storage. It survived until the mid-1970s at least but has since been demolished.

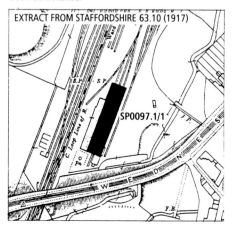

EXTRACT FROM STAFFORDSHIRE 63.10 (1917)
SP0097.1/1

STOURBRIDGE JUNCTION

Site SO9084.1; On the west side of the Wolverhampton line, north of Stourbridge Junction Station.
Stourbridge Junction (GWR) SO9084.1/1A
A brick built 4TS dead ended shed with a slated gable style roof, it was located at SO90618478 and was opened in 1870. The facilities included a coal stage, water tank and 45ft turntable. The shed was officially closed on February 8th, 1926 following the opening of the adjacent roundhouse shed (SO9084.1/2A) but found further use as a depot for steamcars and, later on, diesel railcars. In 1944 it re-opened as a steam shed.

At some stage it was re-roofed ...
Stourbridge Junction (GWR) SO9084.1/1B
The building was re-roofed, possibly in 1944.

Stourbridge Junction (GWR) SO9084.1/2A
A brick built 1RH shed with a slated triple pitched roof, it was located nearby at SO90558492 and was opened on February 8th, 1926. It had the benefit of all major facilities.

The depot was closed by BR on July 11th, 1966 and was subsequently demolished. The site is now occupied by housing.

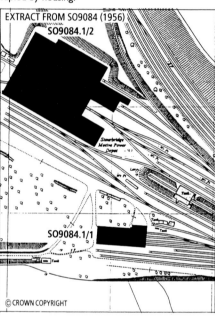

EXTRACT FROM SO9084 (1956)
SO9084.1/2
SO9084.1/1

WEDNESBURY

Site SO9894.1; On the north side of Wednesbury (L&NWR) Station.
Wednesbury (L&NWR) SO9894.1/F1
A servicing area consisting of a siding and water tank, it was located at SO98699460. The opening date is not known but it was probably installed by the L&NWR. The facility was officially closed by the LMS in 1939 as a wartime measure but saw further use until the end of steam in the area in c1967.

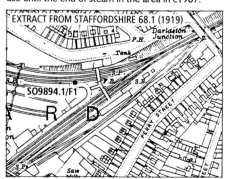

EXTRACT FROM STAFFORDSHIRE 68.1 (1919)
SO9894.1/F1

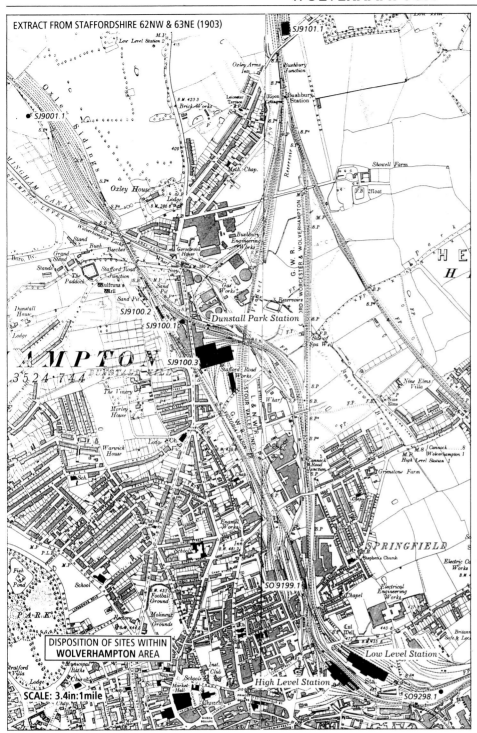

EXTRACT FROM STAFFORDSHIRE 62NW & 63NE (1903)

DISPOSITION OF SITES WITHIN
WOLVERHAMPTON AREA

SCALE: 3.4in:1mile

*Site SJ9101.1; On the east side of the line, at Bush-
bury Junction, north of Wolverhampton High Level
Station.*
Bushbury (L&NWR) SJ9101.1/1A
A 4TS shed "for 12 locomotives", it was located at
SJ91690146 and was opened in 1859. No further
details are known. The shed was closed in 1883.

Replaced, on the same site, by ...
Bushbury (L&NWR) SJ9101.1/1B
A brick built 8TS dead ended shed with a northlight
pattern roof, it was opened in 1883.

The facilities included a 42ft turntable, later enlarged to 70ft, and coal stage with water tank over.

The shed was re-roofed ...
Bushbury (BR) SJ9101.1/1C
The shed was rebuilt in 1958 by the London Midland Region with an SR-style corrugated asbestos
multi-pitched roof. The depot was closed on April
12th, 1965 and was subsequently demolished.

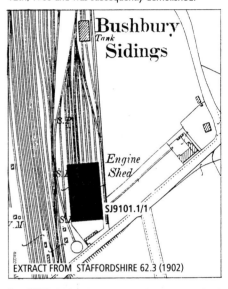

EXTRACT FROM STAFFORDSHIRE 62.3 (1902)

*Site SJ9001.1; On the west side of the line, north of
Dunstall Park Station.*
Oxley (GWR) SJ9001.1/1A
A brick built 2RH shed with three slated pitched
roofs, it was located at SJ90600105 and was
opened on July 1st, 1907. The facilities included a
ramped coal stage, with water tank over, and a
lifting shop. The depot was closed by BR on March
6th, 1967 and demolished to be replaced by sidings.

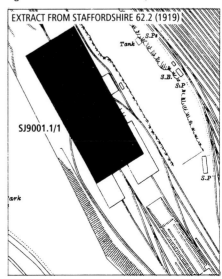

EXTRACT FROM STAFFORDSHIRE 62.2 (1919)

*Site SO9199.1; On the east side of the line, north of
Wolverhampton (L&NWR) Station.*
High Level (L&NWR) SO9199.1/1A
A timber built shed with a slated roof was opened
here at some time prior to 1852. It was probably
located at SO91819925 and was closed in 1859,
following the opening of Bushbury shed
(SJ9101.1/1A). The building was taken over by the
carriage department and, following its incorpora-
tion into later and larger rolling stock sheds, it is
believed to have survived until the 1960s before
being demolished.

EXTRACT FROM STAFFORDSHIRE 62.7 (1902)

Continued ...

Site SJ9100.3; On the south side of Dunstall Park Station.

Stafford Road (GWR) SJ9100.3/1A

A brick built 3TS dead ended shed, it was located at SJ91370018 and was opened on November 14th, 1854.

It was enlarged in 1865 ...

Stafford Road (GWR) SJ9100.3/1B

The building was increased to a 4TS dead ended shed and was utilized as a tender shop from 1869. The building reverted back to locomotive use in 1932.

The shed was re-roofed ...

Stafford Road (GWR) SJ9100.3/1C

The shed was installed with a corrugated iron gable style roof in 1932.

Stafford Road No.1 (GWR) SJ9100.3/2A

A brick built 1RH shed with a slated multi-pitched roof, it was located at SJ91400013 and was opened in 1860.

The shed was re-roofed ...

Stafford Road No.1 (GWR) SJ9100.3/2B

At some stage, possibly in 1932, it was re-roofed in corrugated iron.

Adjoined by ...

Stafford Road No.2 (GWR) SJ9100.3/4A

A brick built 1RH with a slated multi-pitched roof, it was located at SJ91430015 and was opened in 1874.

The shed was re-roofed ...

Stafford Road No.2 (GWR) SJ9100.3/4B

At some stage, possibly in 1932, it was re-roofed in corrugated iron. The building fell into disrepair and it ceased to be used as an engine shed in about 1948. Locomotives stabled on the shed roads until the depot closed.

Adjoined by ...

Stafford Road No.3 (GWR) SJ9100.3/5A

A brick built 1RH shed with a slated multi-pitched roof, it was located at SJ91480016 and opened in 1875.

The shed was re-roofed ...

Stafford Road No.3 (GWR) SJ9100.3/5B

At some stage, possibly in 1932, it was re-roofed in corrugated iron. It ceased to be used for locomotive purposes and was utilized as a tank repair shop until the building became totally dilapidated and was dispensed with in 1948. Locomotives stabled on the shed roads until the depot closed.

Stafford Road No.4* (GWR) SJ9100.3/3A

A 2TS shed it was located at SJ91380017 and was opened in 1865.

The shed was re-roofed ...

Stafford Road No.4* (GWR) SJ9100.3/3B

The building was re-roofed with a corrugated iron gable style roof in 1932.

*The building was originally known as "The Arcade"

Stafford Road No.5 (GWR) SJ9100.3/6A

A 4TS dead ended shed, it was located at SJ91500005 and opened in 1882. Access to the building could only be gained via some roads from No.3 (SJ9100.3/5A) shed. The building was utilized as a road motor transport depot from 1932.

The facilities improved steadily from 1854, culminating in an elevated coal stage and outside turntable being installed in 1932. The depot was closed by BR on September 9th, 1963 and the site was cleared.

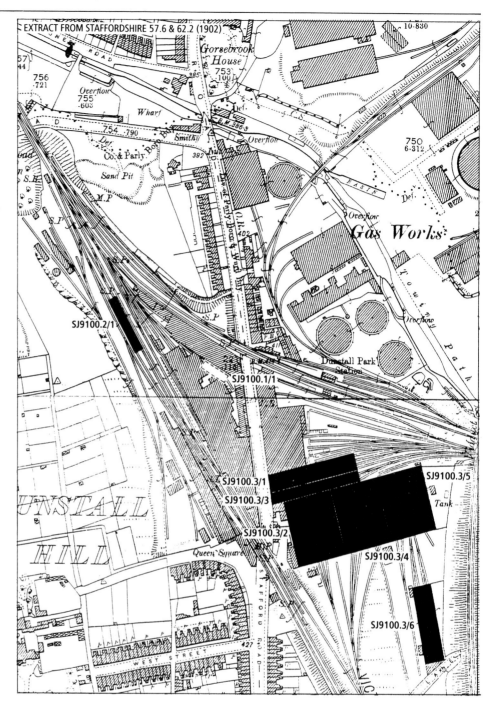

EXTRACT FROM STAFFORDSHIRE 57.6 & 62.2 (1902)

Site SJ9100.1; In the fork of the Victoria Basin and Wolverhampton (GWR) Station lines, west of Dunstall Park Station.

Wolverhampton (S&BR) SJ9100.1/1A

A 2TS dead ended shed, it was probably built in timber with a gable style slated roof. It was located at SJ91290028 and was opened by the Shrewsbury & Birmingham Railway on November 12th, 1849. Details of the facilities are not known. The depot was closed in November 1854, the site being absorbed into Wolverhampton Works.

Replaced by ...
Site SJ9100.2; On the west side of the Victoria Basin line, west of Dunstall Park Station.

Wolverhampton (GWR) SJ9100.2/1A

A brick built 2TS through road shed with a gable style slated roof, it was located at SJ91210031 and was opened in November 1854. The facilities included a coal stage, water tank and 20ft turntable. The depot was closed in c1881 and the building was utilized within Wolverhampton Works.

Site SO9298.1; On the north side of the Birmingham line, at the east end of Wolverhampton (GWR) Station.

Wolverhampton (OW&WR) SO9298.1/1A

A 3TS dead ended shed, it was probably built in timber with a gable style slated roof. It was located at SO92389883 and was opened by the Oxford, Worcester & Wolverhampton Railway in 1854. The facilities included a small coal stage and 30ft turntable. The line was absorbed by the GWR in 1863 and they closed the depot in 1872.

EXTRACT FROM STAFFORDSHIRE 62.7 (1902)

MONMOUTH

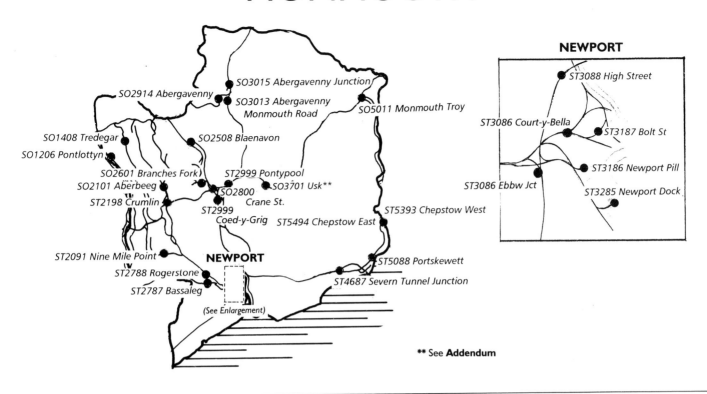

SO3015 Abergavenny Junction
SO2914 Abergavenny
SO3013 Abergavenny Monmouth Road
SO5011 Monmouth Troy
SO1408 Tredegar
SO2508 Blaenavon
SO1206 Pontlottyn
SO2601 Branches Fork
ST2999 Pontypool
SO2101 Aberbeeg
SO3701 Usk**
ST2198 Crumlin
SO2800 Crane St.
ST2999 Coed-y-Grig
ST5393 Chepstow West
ST5494 Chepstow East
ST2091 Nine Mile Point
ST2788 Rogerstone
NEWPORT
ST2787 Bassaleg
(See Enlargement)
ST5088 Portskewett
ST4687 Severn Tunnel Junction

NEWPORT

ST3088 High Street
ST3086 Court-y-Bella
ST3187 Bolt St
ST3186 Newport Pill
ST3086 Ebbw Jct
ST3285 Newport Dock

** See **Addendum**

SEVERN TUNNEL JUNCTION

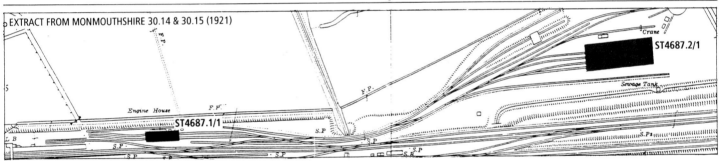

EXTRACT FROM MONMOUTHSHIRE 30.14 & 30.15 (1921)

ST4687.2/1

ST4687.1/1

Site ST4687.1; On the north side of the line, at the east end of Severn Tunnel Junction Station.
Severn Tunnel Junction (GWR) ST4687.1/1A
A corrugated iron 2TS through road shed with a corrugated iron northlight pattern roof, it was located at ST46408758 and was opened in December 1886. The facilities included a 45ft 3in turntable and coal stage with water tank over. It was closed to steam locomotives upon the opening of ST4687.2/1 in December 1907 but was retained as a steam-car shed until June 20th, 1927. It was subsequently demolished.

Replaced by ...
Site ST4687.2; On the north side of the line, east of Severn Tunnel Junction Station.
Severn Tunnel Junction (GWR) ST4687.2/1A
A brick built 4TS through road shed with a slated twin gable roof, it was located at ST46858765 and was opened in 1907. The facilities included a ramped coal stage with water tank over and a turntable.

It was enlarged in 1931...
Severn Tunnel Junction (GWR) ST4687.2/1B
An additional 2TS bay, of similar construction, was added along the southern wall. The depot was closed by BR in October 1965 and the building leased out for motor vehicle storage. The shed was later demolished.

PONTLOTTYN

Site SO1206.1; On the east side of the line, at the south end of Pontlottyn (Rhymney) Station.
Pontlottyn (B&MR) SO1206.1/1A
A 1TS dead ended shed*, probably built in stone with a slated gable style roof, it was located at SO12130616 and was opened by the Brecon & Merthyr Railway in 1865. The facilities included a 30ft turntable. The depot was closed by the GWR on January 25th, 1925 and demolished.

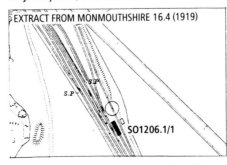

EXTRACT FROM MONMOUTHSHIRE 16.4 (1919)

SO1206.1/1

The shed may have been extended in 1916 following the closure of Fleur-de-Lis (ST1596.1/1).

BRANCHES FORK

Site SO2601.1; On the north side of the Pontnewynydd Junction to Branches Fork Junction line, east of Branches Fork Junction.
Branches Fork (GWR) SO2601.1/1A
A brick built 1TS dead ended shed with a slated gable style roof, it was located at SO26800166 and was opened in 1892. The facilities included a water tank. The depot was closed by BR on October 20th, 1951.

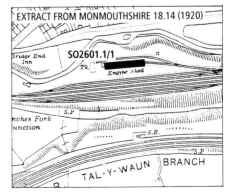

EXTRACT FROM MONMOUTHSHIRE 18.14 (1920)

SO2601.1/1

TAL-Y-WAUN BRANCH

Site SO2101.1; On the east side of the line, south of Aberbeeg Junction Station.

Aberbeeg (MR&C) SO2101.1/1A

A stone built 1TS through road shed with a gable style slated roof incorporating a water tank, it was located at SO21050163 and was opened by the Monmouthshire Railway & Canal Company in 1858. The facilities also included a coal stage sited outside of the shed entrance. The line was worked by the GWR from 1875 and the depot closed by them on April 7th, 1919. The building was subsequently demolished and the site was utilized with sidings.

Replaced by ...
Site SO2101.2; On the west side of the line, south of Aberbeeg Junction.

Aberbeeg (GWR) SO2101.2/1A

A brick built 4TS dead ended shed with a twin gable style slated roof, it was located at SO21000110 and was opened on April 7th, 1919. The facilities included a ramped coal stage and water tank. The depot was closed by BR in December 1964 and was still standing in 1997, in use as a foundry.

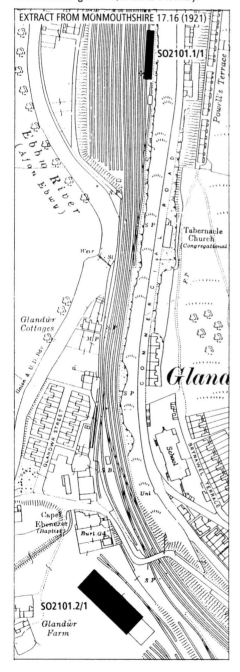

EXTRACT FROM MONMOUTHSHIRE 17.16 (1921)

SO2101.1/1

SO2101.2/1

Site SO3015.0; In the vicinity of Abergavenny Junction.

Abergavenny Junction (MT&AR) SO3015.0/1A

A 1TS shed, it was opened by the Merthyr, Tredegar & Abergavenny Railway on September 29th, 1862 and was approximately located at SO309158. The line was absorbed by the L&NWR on October 1st, 1862 and the depot was closed in 1867. No further details are known.

Replaced by ...
Site SO2914.1; On the west side of the line, south of Abergavenny Brecon Road Station.

Abergavenny (L&NWR) SO2914.1/1A

A stone built 4TS dead ended shed with a slated and glazed northlight pattern roof, it was located at SO29091415 and was opened in 1867.

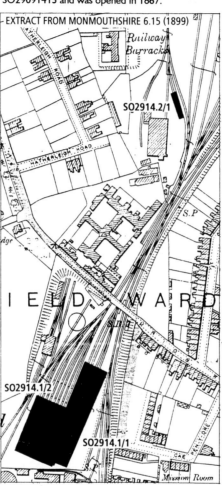

EXTRACT FROM MONMOUTHSHIRE 6.15 (1899)

SO2914.2/1

SO2914.1/2

SO2914.1/1

The building was extended ...
Abergavenny (L&NWR) SO2914.1/1B
The shed was lengthened by some 130ft in 1897.

Adjoined by ...
Abergavenny (L&NWR) SO2914.1/2A
A stone built 8TS dead ended shed with a slated and glazed northlight pattern roof, it eventually adjoined the first building along its western wall, being located at SO29071416. The actual opening date of this building is not known other than it was in existence by 1880.

The building was modified ...
Abergavenny (LMS) SO2914.1/2B
The roof was cut back in 1935 to cover just the two easternmost tracks.

The facilities included a 42ft turntable, resited in 1899, and a coal stage with water tank over. The depot was downgraded to a stabling point by BR on November 22nd, 1954 and totally closed on January 4th, 1958. It was subsequently demolished.

Site SO2914.2; On the west side of the line, at the south end of Abergavenny Brecon Road Station.

Engineers Department (L&NWR) SO2914.2/1A

A timber built 1TS dead ended shed with a slated gable style roof, it was located at SO29211446. The opening date and details of the facilities are not known. The depot, which housed the Engineers Saloon and its permanently-coupled locomotive, was closed upon its withdrawal in 1921. The building was still standing in 1996.

Site SO3013.1; On the east side of the line, south of Monmouth Road Station.

Monmouth Road (NA&HR) SO3013.1/1A

A stone built 1TS through road shed with a slated gable style roof, it was located at SO30581329 and was opened by the Newport, Abergavenny & Hereford Railway on December 6th, 1853. The facilities included a coal stage and water tank. The line was absorbed by the GWR in 1869 and the depot was closed on July 2nd, 1932.

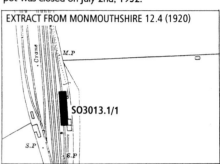

EXTRACT FROM MONMOUTHSHIRE 12.4 (1920)

SO3013.1/1

BASSALEG

Site ST2787.1; On the north side of the line, at the west end of Bassaleg Station.
Bassaleg (RT) ST2787.1/1A

A shed was opened here by the Rumney Tramroad. It is assumed to have occupied the same site as its replacement, being located at ST27618724. No further details are known.

Replaced, probably on the same site, by ...
Bassaleg (B&MR) ST2787.1/1B

A stone built 2TS through road shed with a slated hipped roof, it was opened by the Brecon & Merthyr Railway in 1875. The facilities included a water tank.

Bassaleg (B&MR) ST2787.1/2A

A corrugated iron 2TS dead ended shed with a gable style corrugated iron roof, it was sited at the east end of the shed yard at ST27678721 and was opened in 1921.

The depot was closed by the GWR on March 31st, 1929 with the latter shed, ST2787.1/2A, being dismantled and re-erected at Kidderminster (as SO8375.1/1A).

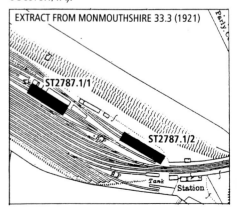

EXTRACT FROM MONMOUTHSHIRE 33.3 (1921)

ST2787.1/1

ST2787.1/2

PONTYPOOL

Site ST2999.1; On the east side of the line, at the north end of Panteg Station.
Coed-y-Grig (Monmouthshire) ST2999.1/1A
A 2 track semi-roundhouse shed, it was located at ST29479902 and was opened by the Monmouthshire Railway on July 1st, 1852. The facilities included a 40ft turntable. No further details are known except that it was closed in c1865 and subsequently demolished.

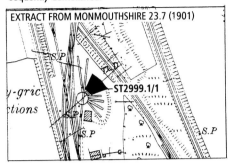

EXTRACT FROM MONMOUTHSHIRE 23.7 (1901)

Replaced by ...
Site ST2999.2; On the east side of the Panteg line, south of Pontypool Road Station.
Pontypool Road (GWR*) ST2999.2/1A
A stone built 8TS shed, probably dead ended, with a slated twin hipped roof, it was located at ST29469965 and probably opened in 1869.

Adjoined by ...
Pontypool Road (GWR) ST2999.2/2A
A brick built 1RH shed with a slated single pitched roof and glazed gable, it was constructed at the north end of ST2999.2/1A and located at ST29500971. The two buildings were linked by one track passing through the two sheds.

The facilities included a ramped coaling stage and water tank. The depot was closed by BR in May 1965 and later demolished.

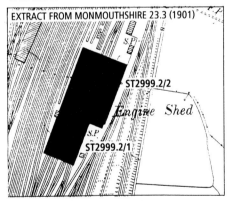

EXTRACT FROM MONMOUTHSHIRE 23.3 (1901)

*It may possibly be of Monmouthshire Railway origin.

Site SO2800.1; On the east side of the line, at the south end of Crane Street Station.
Crane Street (Monmouthshire) SO2800.1/1A
A 1TS dead ended shed, it was located at SO28110076 and was opened by the Monmouthshire Railway on October 2nd, 1854. The facilities included a coal stage and 25ft turntable. The line was worked by the GWR from 1875 and they closed the depot in 1879. It was demolished and the station expanded over the site.

EXTRACT FROM MONMOUTHSHIRE 23.3 (1901)

BLAENAVON

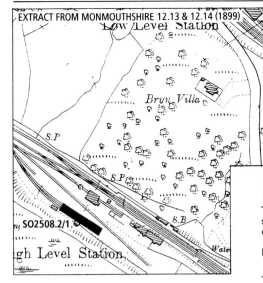

EXTRACT FROM MONMOUTHSHIRE 12.13 & 12.14 (1899)

Site SO2508.1; On the north side of the line, east of Blaenavon (Low Level) Station.
Blaenavon (GWR) SO2508.1/1A
A timber built shed with a slated gable style roof, it was located at SO25450845 and was opened in 1878. The facilities included a water tower and coal stage. The depot was closed on February 1st, 1912 and was subsequently demolished.

Site SO2508.2; On the south side of Blaenavon (High Level) Station.
Blaenavon (L&NWR) SO2508.2/1A
A stone built 2TS dead ended shed with a slated northlight pattern roof, it was located at SO25450845 and was opened in June 1881.

CHEPSTOW

Site ST5494.1; On the north side of the line in the vicinity of Wye Valley Junction.
Chepstow East (SWR) ST5494.1/1A
A temporary shed was opened here on September 10th, 1851 by the South Wales Railway. It was approximately located at ST545944 and was closed when the bridge over the River Wye was opened on July 19th, 1852. No further details are known.

Site ST5393.1; On the east side of the line, south of Chepstow Station.
Chepstow West (SWR) ST5393.1/1A
A timber built 2TS shed with a slated gable style roof was opened here on June 18th, 1850 by the South Wales Railway. It was approximately located at ST536935 and was closed in August 1854. The building was removed to Neyland and re-erected as SM9605.1/1A.

CRUMLIN

Site ST2198.1; In the vicinity of Crumlin Junction.
Crumlin (NA&HR) ST2198.1/1A
A temporary shed was opened here on August 20th, 1855 by the Newport, Abergavenny & Hereford (Taff Vale Extension) Railway. It was approximately located at ST216987 and was closed on June 1st, 1857.

MONMOUTH

Site SO5011.1; In the vicinity of Monmouth Troy Station.
Monmouth Troy (GWR) SO5011.1/1A
A shed, approximately located at SO509118, was opened here in 1857. No further details are known.

The shed was enlarged ...
Blaenavon (L&NWR) SO2508.2/1B
The shed was extended in 1889 to accommodate six engines. The facilities included a coal stage. The depot was closed by the LMS on 5th September, 1942 but remained standing until the 1960s before being demolished.

ROGERSTONE

Site ST2788.1; In Rogerstone Sidings.
Rogerstone (GWR) ST2788.1/F1
Some form of facility, approximately located at ST271880, was opened here. No further details are known.

PORTSKEWETT

Site ST5088.1; On the south side of the line, at the west end of Portskewett Station.
Portskewett (B&SWUR) ST5088.1/1A
A 1TS dead ended shed, it was located at ST50518819 and was opened by the Bristol & South Wales Union Railway in January 1864. No further details are known except that it was closed by the GWR upon the opening of the Severn Tunnel in December 1886.

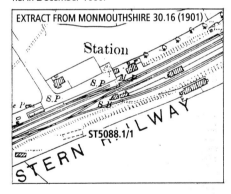

EXTRACT FROM MONMOUTHSHIRE 30.16 (1901)

NINE MILE POINT

Site ST2091.1; In the vicinity of Nine Mile Point Station.
Nine Mile Point (Sirhowy) ST2091.1/1A
A 1TS dead ended shed, it was located at ST20409106 and was opened by the Sirhowy Railway in 1863. The depot was closed in 1873 and subsequently demolished.

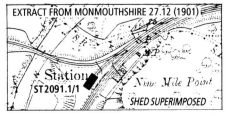

EXTRACT FROM MONMOUTHSHIRE 27.12 (1901)

Site ST3086.2; In the vicinity of Court-y-Bella Junction.
Court-y-Bella (Monmouthshire) ST3086.2/1A
A temporary shed was opened here by the Monmouthshire Railway in 1851 and closed in April 1854.

Replaced by ...
Site ST3187.1; On the north side of the Pillbank Branch, east of Pillbank Junction.
Bolt Street (Monmouthshire) ST3187.1/1A
A brick built 4TS through road shed with a slated gable style roof, it was located at ST31618709.

Connected by traverser to ...
Bolt Street (Monmouthshire) ST3187.1/2A
A brick built 6TS dead ended shed with a slated multi-pitched gable style roof, it was located at ST31618706 and was only accessed by means of the traverser.

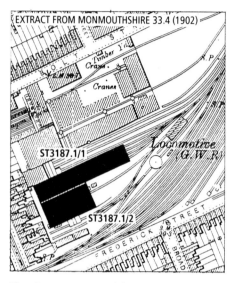

EXTRACT FROM MONMOUTHSHIRE 33.4 (1902)
ST3187.1/1
ST3187.1/2

The depot was opened by the Monmouthshire Railway in April 1854 and, being sited adjacent to the works possessed all facilities. It was closed in August 1918 and demolished.

Replaced by ...
Dock Street (GWR) ST3187.1/1B
A brick built 4TS dead ended shed with a twin gable style slated pitched roof, it occupied the same site as ST3187.1/1A and was opened in February 1920. The facilities included a 65ft turntable and a ramped coal stage with water tank over. The depot only enjoyed a short existence, being closed on March 31st, 1929. It was converted to a wagon works and was still standing in 1997, in industrial use.

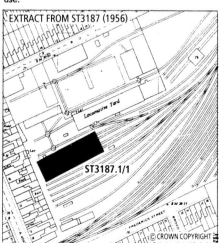

EXTRACT FROM ST3187 (1956)
ST3187.1/1

Site ST3285.1; At the end of a short spur between Alexandra and South Docks, on the Monmouthshire Branch.
Newport Dock (Alexandra Dock) ST3285.1/1A
A brick built 2TS through road shed with a slated gable style roof, it was located at ST32108539 and was opened by the Alexandra (Newport & South Wales) Dock & Railway Company in April 1875. Details of the facilities are not known. Access to the depot was made inconvenient by the construction of the South Dock in 1893 and it was closed in 1898. The building was not demolished but was absorbed as part of the adjacent workshops buildings and was still standing and in use in 1997.

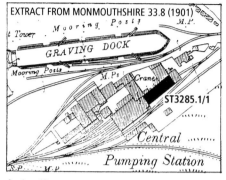

EXTRACT FROM MONMOUTHSHIRE 33.8 (1901)
ST3285.1/1

Replaced by ...
Site ST3186.1; On the east side of the Monmouthshire branch, at the north end of Alexandra Dock.
Newport Pill (Alexandra Dock) ST3186.1/1A
A brick built 2TS dead ended shed with a northlight pattern roof, it was located at ST31288619 and was opened by the Alexandra (Newport & South Wales) Dock & Railway Company in 1898. The facilities included a coal stage with water tank over. The depot was closed by BR on June 17th, 1965 but was utilized for stabling diesel shunters for a short while after. It has since been demolished.

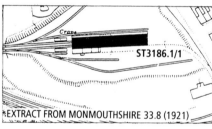

EXTRACT FROM MONMOUTHSHIRE 33.8 (1921)
ST3186.1/1

Site ST3088.1; On the west side of the line, at the south end of Newport High Street Station.
High Street (SWR) ST3088.1/1A
A stone built 4TS dead ended shed with a slated gable style roof, it was located at ST30658811 and was opened by the South Wales Railway in August 1854. The facilities, which were improved in 1879, included a 45ft turntable and coal stage with water tank over. The depot was closed by the GWR on July 17th, 1915 and demolished in 1916.

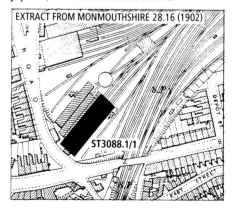

EXTRACT FROM MONMOUTHSHIRE 28.16 (1902)
ST3088.1/1

Replaced by ...
Site ST3086.1; On the west side of Ebbw Junction, about 1 mile south of Newport High Street Station.
Ebbw Junction (GWR) ST3086.1/1A
A brick built 2RH shed with a multi-pitched slated gable style roof, it was located at ST30058616 and was opened in July 1915. It possessed all facilities including a large repair shop. The depot was closed by BR in October 1965 and was subsequently demolished.

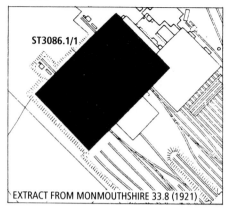

ST3086.1/1
EXTRACT FROM MONMOUTHSHIRE 33.8 (1921)

TREDEGAR

Site SO1408.2; On the west side of the line, south of Tredegar Station.
Tredegar (Sirhowy) SO1408.2/1A
A 3TS dead ended shed, it was located at SO14510811 and was opened here by the Sirhowy Railway in 1863. It was closed in 1886 and subsequently demolished. No further details are known.

Replaced by ...
Site SO1408.1; On the west side of Tredegar Station.
Tredegar (L&NWR) SO1408.1/1A
A brick built 4TS dead ended shed with a slated northlight pattern roof, it was located at SO14470829 and was opened in 1886. The facilities included a coal stage with water tank over.

The shed was damaged by fire ...
Tredegar (L&NWR) SO1408.1/1B
At some stage the rear end of the building was destroyed by a fire and a timber wall erected, shortening the length of the depot by 50ft. By the time that the shed was closed by BR on June 11th, 1960 the front end had been removed. It was not demolished immediately but remained standing in a derelict condition until the mid 1970s at least.

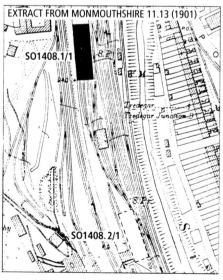

EXTRACT FROM MONMOUTHSHIRE 11.13 (1901)
SO1408.1/1
SO1408.2/1

SOUTH WALES

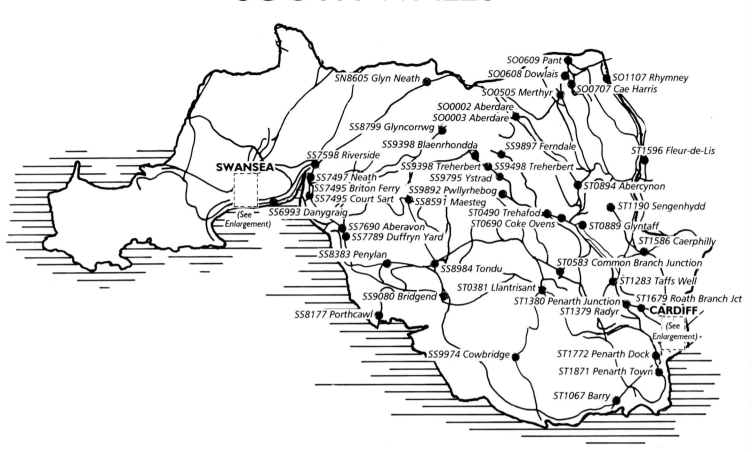

- SN8605 Glyn Neath
- SO0609 Pant
- SO0608 Dowlais
- SO0505 Merthyr
- SO1107 Rhymney
- SO0707 Cae Harris
- SO0002 Aberdare
- SO0003 Aberdare
- SS8799 Glyncorrwg
- SS9398 Blaenrhondda
- SS9897 Ferndale
- ST1596 Fleur-de-Lis
- SS7598 Riverside
- SS9398 Treherbert
- SS9498 Treherbert
- ST0894 Abercynon
- SS7497 Neath
- SS9795 Ystrad
- SS7495 Briton Ferry
- SS9892 Pwllyrhebog
- ST1190 Sengenhydd
- SS7495 Court Sart
- SS8591 Maesteg
- ST0490 Trehafod
- ST0889 Glyntaff
- SS6993 Danygraig
- ST0690 Coke Ovens
- ST1586 Caerphilly
- *(See Enlargement)*
- SS7690 Aberavon
- SS7789 Duffryn Yard
- SS8383 Penylan
- ST0583 Common Branch Junction
- SS8984 Tondu
- ST1283 Taffs Well
- ST0381 Llantrisant
- ST1679 Roath Branch Jct
- SS9080 Bridgend
- ST1380 Penarth Junction
- ST1379 Radyr
- **CARDIFF**
- SS8177 Porthcawl
- *(See Enlargement)*
- SS9974 Cowbridge
- ST1772 Penarth Dock
- ST1871 Penarth Town
- ST1067 Barry
- **SWANSEA**

SWANSEA

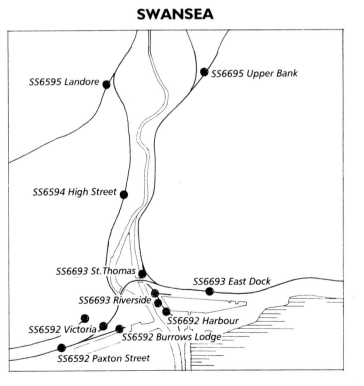

- SS6595 Landore
- SS6695 Upper Bank
- SS6594 High Street
- SS6693 St.Thomas
- SS6693 East Dock
- SS6693 Riverside
- SS6592 Victoria
- SS6692 Harbour
- SS6592 Burrows Lodge
- SS6592 Paxton Street

CARDIFF

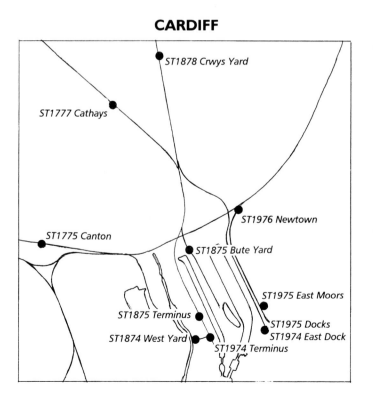

- ST1878 Crwys Yard
- ST1777 Cathays
- ST1976 Newtown
- ST1775 Canton
- ST1875 Bute Yard
- ST1975 East Moors
- ST1875 Terminus
- ST1975 Docks
- ST1874 West Yard
- ST1974 East Dock
- ST1974 Terminus

Site SO0002.1; On the west side of the line, north of Aberdare (Taff Vale) Station.
Aberdare (Aberdare) SO0002.1/1A
A timber built 1TS dead ended shed with a slated gable style pitched roof, it was located at SO00440269 and was opened by the Aberdare Railway in 1846.

Site SO0002.2; On the east side of the line, north of Aberdare (Taff Vale) Station.
Aberdare (Aberdare) SO0002.1/2A
A timber built 1TS dead ended shed with a slated gable style pitched roof, it was located at SO00450269 and was opened by the Aberdare Railway in 1846.

These two sheds were considered as one depot and details of the facilities are not known. By 1853 they had become totally derelict and were closed and demolished.

Site SO0002.3; In the Aberdare (GWR/VNRJ) Station yard.
Aberdare (VNR) SO0002.3/1A
Locomotives were stabled under the station roof at SO00440281 by the Vale of Neath Railway. The opening date and details of the facilities are not known. The practice ceased upon the opening of SO0002.3/2A in 1864.

Replaced by ...
Aberdare (GWR/VNRJ) SO0002.3/2A
A 2TS dead ended shed, probably built in timber with a slated gable style pitched roof, it was located at SO00400284 and was opened by the GWR/Vale of Neath Railway Joint in 1864. The facilities included a 35ft turntable. The depot was closed in 1872.

Site SO0002.4; On the north side of Aberdare (GWR) Station.
Aberdare (GWR) SO0002.4/1A
A stone built 4TS dead ended shed with a slated gable style pitched roof, it was located at SO00470288 and was opened in 1867. The facilities included a 45ft turntable, water tank and coal stage.

It was enlarged in 1874 ...
Aberdare (GWR) SO0002.4/2A
A stone built 4TS dead ended shed with a slated gable style pitched roof, it was located at SO00470289 and was constructed along the northern wall of SO0002.4/1A. The depot was closed on November 11th, 1907 and subsequently demolished although parts of the walls were still *in situ* in 1997.

Replaced by ...
Site SO0003.1; On the east side of the line, north of Aberdare (GWR) Station.
Aberdare (GWR) SO0003.1/1A
A brick built 1RH shed with a slated gable style multi-pitched roof, it was located at SO00230320 and was opened on November 11th, 1907. The facilities included a coal stage with water tank over and a repair shop. The depot was closed by BR on March 1st, 1965 and was subsequently demolished.

Site SO0002.5; On the east side of Aberdare (TVR) Station.
Aberdare (TVR) SO0002.5/1A
A stone built 2TS dead ended shed with a slated gable style pitched roof, it was located at SO00530259.

Aberdare (TVR) SO0002.5/2A
A stone built 2TS through road shed with a slated gable style pitched roof, it was sited at the south end of the shed yard and was located at SO00570244.

The facilities included a coal stage, water tank and turntable. The depot was closed by the GWR on December 5th, 1927.

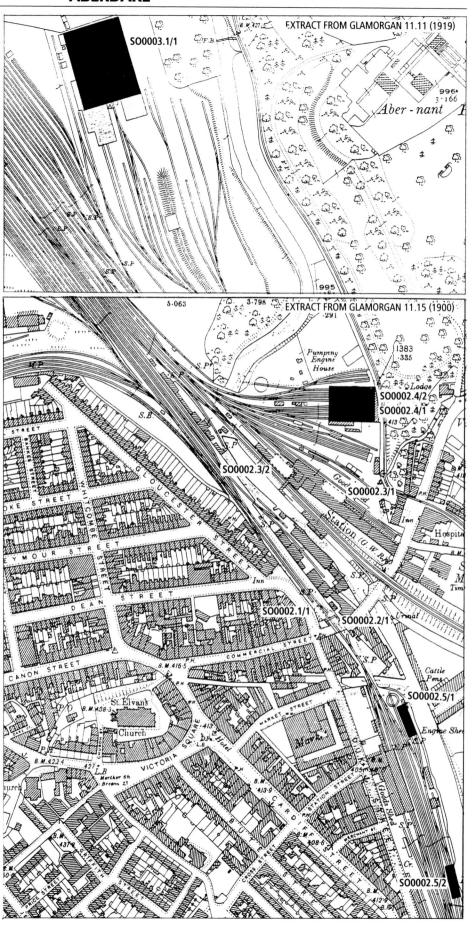

EXTRACT FROM GLAMORGAN 11.11 (1919)

EXTRACT FROM GLAMORGAN 11.15 (1900)

ABERAVON

Site SS7690.1; In the fork of the Maesteg and Duffryn lines, at the north end of Aberavon Station.

Aberavon (R&SBR) SS7690.1/1A

A timber built 2TS through road shed with a slated gable style pitched roof, it was located at SS76739034 and was opened by the Rhonddda & Swansea Bay Railway in November 1885. The facilities included a water tank. The building was demolished at some time prior to 1921.

It was extended ...

Aberavon (R&SBR) SS7690.1/2A

A stone built 2TS through road shed with a slated northlight pattern roof was added to the northern end of the depot in 1889. At the same time the facilities were improved by the addition of a coal stage and crane. The depot was closed by the GWR on November 20th, 1922.

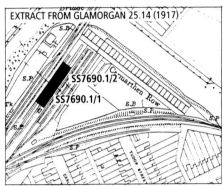

EXTRACT FROM GLAMORGAN 25.14 (1917)

ABERCYNON

Site ST0894.1; On the east side of the line, at the north end of Abercynon Station.

Abercynon (TVR) ST0894.1/1A

A stone built 1TS dead ended shed with a slated gable style pitched roof, it was located at ST08259477 and was opened by the Taff Vale Railway in 1853. Details of the facilities are not known. The depot was closed by the GWR in 1928.

Replaced by ...

Abercynon (GWR) ST0894.1/2A

A brick and corrugated asbestos built 2TS dead ended shed with a metal sheeted gable style pitched roof, it was sited adjacently to its predecessor (ST0894.1/1A), being located at ST08259474. The facilities included a ramped coal stage with water tank over. The depot was closed by BR on November 2nd, 1964 and the building was let out for private use. It was still standing in 1996, being utilized as a foundry.

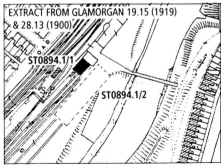

EXTRACT FROM GLAMORGAN 19.15 (1919) & 28.13 (1900)

CAERPHILLY

Site ST1586.1; In the vicinity of Caerphilly Station.

Caerphilly (Rhymney) ST1586.1/F1

Some sort of facility, approximately located at ST159865, was established here by the Rhymney Railway. No further details are known.

BRIDGEND

Site SS9080.1; On the east side of the line, north of Bridgend Station.

Bridgend (L&OR) SS9080.1/1A

A stone built 1TS dead ended shed with a slated gable style pitched roof, it was located at SS90558047 and was opened by the Lynfi & Ogmore Railway in 1866. The facilities included a water tank. The depot was closed by BR on April 17th, 1950 and was subsequently demolished.

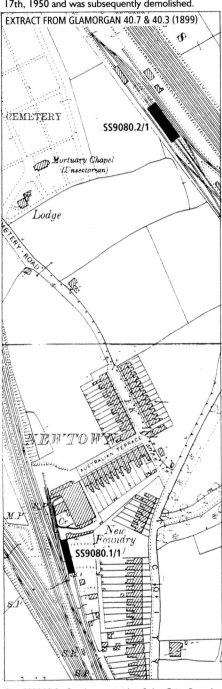

EXTRACT FROM GLAMORGAN 40.7 & 40.3 (1899)

Site SS9080.2; On the west side of the Coity Branch, south of Coity Junction.

Coity Junction (Barry) SS9080.2/1A

A brick built 2TS through road shed with a slated northlight pattern roof, it was located at SS90658087 and was opened by the Barry Railway on December 1st, 1897. The facilities included a water tank. Although the depot was officially closed in 1906 it remained partially in use for the light servicing of locomotives for a few years afterwards. The building itself was utilized as a goods shed and warehouse, not being demolished until BR days.

BARRY

Site ST1167.1; On the east side of the line, north of Barry Station.

Barry Docks (Barry) ST1167.1/1A

A contractors shed was taken over by the Barry Railway in December 1888. No further details are known except that it was approximately located at ST111676 on the site of Barry Works and was closed in 1890.

Replaced by ...

Site ST1067.1; On the east side of Barry Station.

Barry (Barry) ST1067.1/1A

A brick built 6TS through road shed with a slated northlight pattern roof, it was located at ST10776718 and was opened in 1890. The facilities included a coal stage, water columns and turntable (later removed).

It was re-roofed ...

Barry (GWR) ST1067.1/1B

At some stage it was rebuilt with a corrugated northlight pattern roof set at a higher level than previous to increase headroom. The depot was closed by BR in September 1964 and converted to a wagon works. It was still standing in 1997.

Site ST1067.2; In the fork of the Barry Island and Bridgend lines, at the south end of Barry Station.

Barry Railmotor Shed (GWR) ST1067.2/1A

A 3TS dead ended shed, it was located at ST10646702 and was opened in 1905. No further details are known except that it was closed in 1914 and demolished.

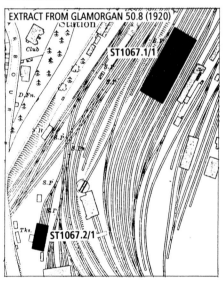

EXTRACT FROM GLAMORGAN 50.8 (1920)

PANT

Site SO0609.1; On the east side of the Dowlais line, south of Pant Station.

Pant (B&MR) SO0609.1/1A

A 1TS dead ended shed, probably built in timber, it was located at SO06040949 and was opened by the Brecon & Merthyr Railway on May 1st, 1863. Details of the facilities are not known. Following a fire which destroyed the building on August 8th, 1887 an agreement was made with the L&NWR to lease Ivor Junction shed (SO0608.1/1) and the depot was closed.

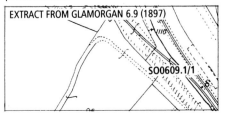

EXTRACT FROM GLAMORGAN 6.9 (1897)

DOWLAIS

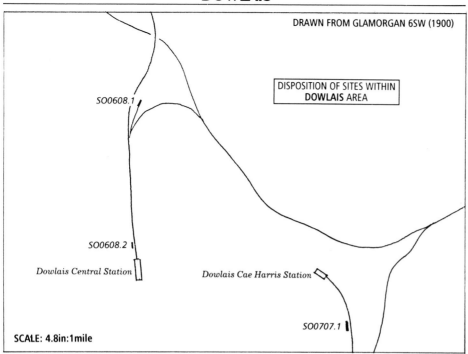

DRAWN FROM GLAMORGAN 6SW (1900)

DISPOSITION OF SITES WITHIN
DOWLAIS AREA

SO0608.1

SO0608.2

Dowlais Central Station

Dowlais Cae Harris Station

SO0707.1

SCALE: 4.8in:1mile

Site SO0608.1; In the fork of the Pant and Dowlais High Street lines, north of Dowlais Central Station.
Ivor Junction (L&NWR) SO0608.1/1A
A 1TS dead ended shed, probably built in brick with a slated gable style pitched roof, it was located at SO06580860 and was opened in 1871. The facilities included a turntable. The depot was closed by the L&NWR upon the opening of High Street Station but was taken over by the Brecon & Merthyr Railway in 1887 following the destruction of their shed at Pant (SO0609.1/1). The shed was closed in 1898 and subsequently demolished.

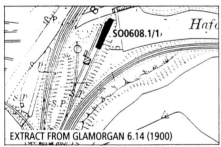

EXTRACT FROM GLAMORGAN 6.14 (1900)

Replaced by ...
Site SO0608.2; On the west side of Dowlais Central Station.
Dowlais Central (B&MR) SO0608.2/1A
A corrugated iron 1TS dead ended shed with a gable style pitched corrugated iron roof, it was located at SO06520803 and was opened by the Brecon & Merthyr Railway in 1898. There were no additional facilities. The building was destroyed by a blizzard on March 27th, 1916.

Replaced, on the same site, by ...
Dowlais Central (B&MR) SO0608.2/1B
A brick built 1TS dead ended shed with a slated gable style pitched roof, it was opened in 1916. The depot was closed by BR in December 1964 and was subsequently demolished.

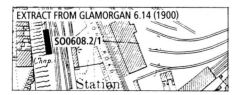

EXTRACT FROM GLAMORGAN 6.14 (1900)

Site SO0707.1; On the west side of the line, at the south end of Cae Harris Station.
Cae Harris (GWR/Rhymney) SO0707.1/1A
A stone built 3TS shed with one through road and a slated gable style pitched roof, it was located at SO07410769 and was opened in 1876. The facilities included a water tank, coal stage and turntable. The depot was closed by BR in December 1964 but was retained to stable diesel locomotives until the mid-1970s when it was subsequently demolished.

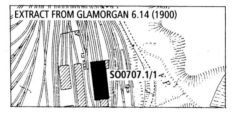

EXTRACT FROM GLAMORGAN 6.14 (1900)

COMMON BRANCH JCT

Site ST0583.1; In the fork of the Llantrisant and Ely Valley lines at Common Branch Junction.
Common Branch Junction (TVR) ST0583.1/1A
A 2TS dead ended shed, probably built in stone with a gable style slated pitched roof, it was located at ST05858377 and was opened by the Taff Vale Railway in June 1870. Details of the facilities are not known. The depot was closed in 1904 but continued to be utilized for locomotive servicing until c1915. The building was demolished at some stage prior to 1919.

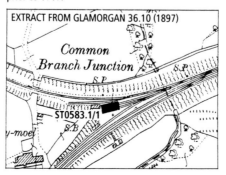

EXTRACT FROM GLAMORGAN 36.10 (1897)

Common Branch Junction

ST0583.1/1

BLAENRHONDDA

Site SS9398.1; On the east side of the line, south of Blaenrhondda Station.
Blaenrhondda (R&SBR) SS9398.1/1A
A 1TS dead ended shed, it was probably built in timber with a slated gable style pitched roof and is assumed to have been located at SS93299871. Details of the facilities are not known. The depot was probably of a temporary nature as it was opened by the Rhondda & Swansea Bay Railway in 1891 and closed in 1894.

Replaced, on the same site, by ...
Blaenrhondda (R&SBR) SS9398.1/1B
A corrugated iron 1TS dead ended shed with a timber and felt gable style pitched roof, it was opened in 1894. The building was blown down on December 27th, 1914.

Replaced, on the same site, by ...
Blaenrhondda (R&SBR) SS9398.1/1C
A 1TS dead ended shed, it was probably constructed in the same way as its predecessor (SS9398.1/1B) and was in use by 1915. The depot was closed by the GWR in August 1922.

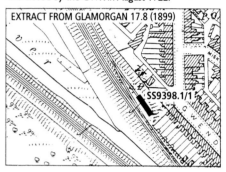

EXTRACT FROM GLAMORGAN 17.8 (1899)

SS9398.1/1

GLYN NEATH

Site SN8605.1; On the north side of the line, at the east end of Glyn Neath Station.
Glyn Neath (GWR) SN8605.1/1A
A brick built 1TS through road shed with a water tank, mounted on cast iron columns, forming the roof. It was located at SN86810557 and was opened in 1879.

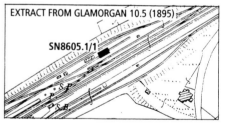

EXTRACT FROM GLAMORGAN 10.5 (1895)

SN8605.1/1

The shed was extended ...
Glyn Neath (GWR) SN8605.1/2A
A brick built 1TS through road shed with a gable style corrugated asbestos pitched roof and measuring 80ft was added at the eastern end. It was located at SN86830558 and was completed in 1937. At the same time improvements were made to the coaling arrangements. The depot was closed by BR on October 5th, 1964 and was subsequently demolished.

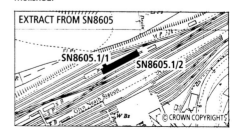

EXTRACT FROM SN8605

SN8605.1/1   SN8605.1/2

© CROWN COPYRIGHT

NEATH

Site SS7497.0; In the vicinity of Neath (VNR) Station.
Neath (VNR) SS7497.0/1A
From 1854 the Vale of Neath Railway stabled locomotives under bridges in the area. No further details are known except that the practice ceased upon the opening of SS7497.1/1A in 1862.

Replaced by ...
Neath (VNR) SS7497.1/1A
A stone built 2TS shed with one through road and a slated gable style roof, it was joined at its southern end to a 2TS building which was either additional shed accommodation or a repair depot. The depot was located at SS74979724 and was opened by the Vale of Neath Railway in 1862. The line was worked by the GWR from 1865 and they closed the depot in 1876. The shed was subsequently demolished.

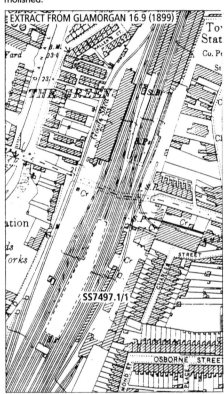

Replaced by ...
Site SS7495.1; On the west side of the line, south of Neath General Station.
Court Sart (GWR) SS7495.1/1A
A brick built 2RH shed with a slated gable style triple pitched roof, it was located at SS74009572 and was opened in 1876. The facilities included a ramped coal stage with water tank over. The depot was closed by BR in June 1965 and was subsequently demolished.

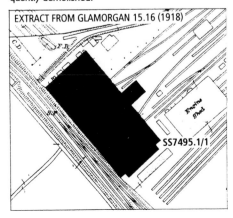

EXTRACT FROM GLAMORGAN 15.16 (1918)

SS7495.1/1

EXTRACT FROM GLAMORGAN 16.9 (1899)

SS7598.1/1

Site SS7598.1; On the west side of the line, north of Neath Riverside Station.
Riverside (N&B) SS7598.1/1A
A 1TS dead ended shed it was probably built in timber and was located at SS75239822 and was opened by the Neath & Brecon Railway on October 2nd, 1864. The facilities included a 35ft turntable, water tank and coal stage. At some stage it was demolished and by 1921 a carriage shed occupied the site.

There may have been some sort of enlargement to the shed (as SS7598.1/1B) which would have been completed by 1899. No specific details are known.

Riverside (N&B) SS7598.1/2A
A corrugated iron 4TS dead ended shed with a corrugated iron northlight pattern roof, it adjoined the north side of SS7598.1/1A and was located at SS75229823. The building was probably brought into use in c1902 but by 1939 it was extremely dilapidated and although due for demolition the outbreak of WW2 postponed this until 1946.

Replaced, on the same site, by ...
Riverside (GWR) SS7598.1/2B
A brick built 2TS dead ended shed with a corrugated asbestos gable style pitched roof, it was opened in 1946. The depot was closed by BR in June 1964 and was still standing in 1997.

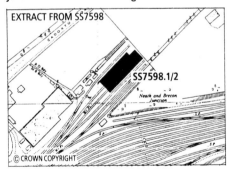

EXTRACT FROM SS7598

SS7598.1/2

© CROWN COPYRIGHT

MAESTEG

Site SS8591.1; On the south side of the line, at the east end of Maesteg (Castle Road) Station.
Maesteg (LVR) SS8591.1/1A
A stone built 1TS dead ended shed with a slated gable style pitched roof, it was located at SS85339142 and was opened by the Lynvi Valley Railway in August 1861. The facilities included a 23ft 6in turntable. The depot was closed in October 1887 and demolished in August 1905.

EXTRACT FROM GLAMORGAN 26.9 (1895)

SS8591.1/1

COWBRIDGE

Site SS9974.1; On the west side of the line, at the north end of Cowbridge (1st) Station.
Cowbridge (Cowbridge) SS9974.1/1A
A 2TS dead ended shed, probably built in timber, it was located at SS99947458 and was opened by the Cowbridge Railway on September 18th, 1865. The facilities included a water tank and 35ft turntable sited outside of the shed entrance. The line was worked by the Taff Vale Railway and they closed the depot in 1886. It was subsequently demolished.

Replaced by ...
Site SS9974.2; On the east side of the line, at the north end of Cowbridge (1st) Station.
Cowbridge (TVR) SS9974.2/1A
A stone built 2TS dead ended shed with a slated gable style roof, it was located at SS99967459 and was opened by the Taff Vale Railway in 1886. The facilities included a coal stage and water tank. The depot was closed by the GWR on March 8th, 1924.

EXTRACT FROM GLAMORGAN 45.3 (1899)

SS9974.1/1
SS9974.2/1

GLYNTAFF

Site ST0889.1; On the north side of Glyntaff Halt.
Glyntaff (ADR) ST0889.1/1A
A stone built 1TS dead ended shed with a slated gable style pitched roof, it was located at ST08468958 and was opened by the Alexandra (Newport & South Wales) Dock Railway Co. on September 1st, 1904. It was built to house a steam car but became an engine shed proper upon its withdrawal in 1917. The depot was closed in September 1922 and demolished.

Glyntaff (ADR) ST0889.1/2A
A stone built 1TS dead ended shed with a slated gable style pitched roof, it was located at ST08338963 and was opened in April 1905. Details of the facilities are not known. The depot, which was also built to house a steam car only, was closed in 1911 and the building was converted into a goods shed.

Site ST0889.2; On the south side of the line, at the east end of Glyntaff Halt.
Glyntaff Railmotor Shed (ADR) ST0889.2/1A
A 1TS dead ended shed, it was located at ST08438956. No further details are known.

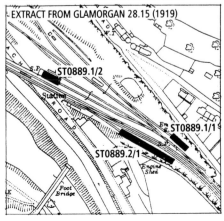

EXTRACT FROM GLAMORGAN 28.15 (1919)

ST0889.1/2
ST0889.1/1
ST0889.2/1

MERTHYR

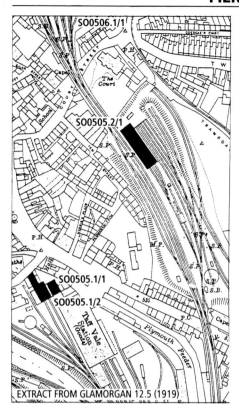

EXTRACT FROM GLAMORGAN 12.5 (1919)

Site SO0505.1; On the west side of Merthyr (Taff Vale) Station.

Merthyr (TVR)^{SO0505.1/1A}

A stone built 2TS dead ended shed with a slated pitched roof, it was located at SO05030568 and was opened by the Taff Vale Railway on April 12th, 1841. Details of the facilities are not known. The depot was closed in January 1846 and the building was converted to a goods shed.

Replaced by ...
Merthyr (TVR)^{SO0505.1/2A}

A stone built 2TS dead ended shed with a slated gable style pitched roof, it was located at SO05020568 and was opened by the Taff Vale Railway in January 1846. The facilities included a coal stage, water tank, turntable and small repair shop. The depot was closed by the GWR on September 1st, 1923.

Site SO0506.1; In the vicinity of Merthyr (VNR) Station.

Merthyr (VNR)^{SO0506.1/1A}

Locomotives were stabled under the station roof at approximately SO050060 by the Vale of Neath Railway. The opening date and details of the facilities are not known. The practice ceased upon the opening of SO0505.2/1A in 1853.

Replaced by ...
Site SO0505.2; On the east side of the line, south of Merthyr (VNR) Station.
Merthyr (VNR)^{SO0505.2/1A}

A 2TS dead ended shed, probably constructed in timber with a slated pitched roof, it was located at SO05120581 and was opened by the Vale of Neath Railway in 1853. The facilities included a turntable. The depot was closed by the GWR in 1877 and demolished.

Replaced, on the same site, by ...
Merthyr (GWR)^{SO0505.2/1B}

A brick built 3TS dead ended shed, probably with a slated gable style pitched roof, it was opened in 1877. The facilities included a coal stage and turntable.

The depot was improved in 1931 ...
Merthyr (GWR)^{SO0505.2/1C}

The shed building was lengthened by 45ft and the yard layout improved with a larger coal stage being installed and a new 55ft turntable being re-sited adjacent to the shed building. The depot was closed by BR on November 2nd, 1964 and the building was let out for industrial use. It was still standing in 1987.

GLYNCORRWG

Site SS8799.1; On the north side of the line, east of Glyncorrwg Station.
Glyncorrwg (SWMR)^{SS8799.1/1A}

A stone built 1TS dead ended shed with a slated gable style pitched roof, it was located at SS87569926 and was opened by the South Wales Mineral Railway in March 1863. The facilities included a water tank. The depot was closed in 1908 but was retained for the stabling and servicing of engines until c1965. The building was subsequently demolished.

EXTRACT FROM GLAMORGAN 17.6 (1899)

PORTHCAWL

Site SS8177.1; On the east side of the line, north of Porthcawl Station.
Porthcawl (LVR)^{SS8177.1/F1}

A servicing area consisting of a siding and engine pit, it was located at SS81927728 and was opened by the Llynvi Valley Railway in 1861. No further details are known.

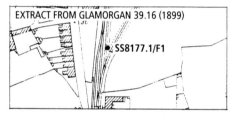

EXTRACT FROM GLAMORGAN 39.16 (1899)

FERNDALE

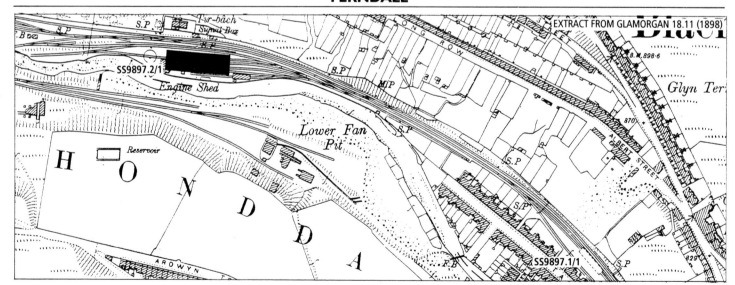

EXTRACT FROM GLAMORGAN 18.11 (1898)

Site SS9897.1; On the west side of the line, at the north end of Ferndale Station.
Ferndale (TVR)^{SS9897.1/1A}

A 1TS dead ended shed, probably built in timber with a slated gable style pitched roof, it was located at SS98979740 and was opened by the Taff Vale Railway in 1866. The facilities included a coal stage, water tank and turntable. The depot was closed in 1884.

Replaced by ...
Site SS9897.2; On the west side of the line, north of Ferndale Station.
Ferndale (TVR)^{SS9897.2/1A}

A stone built 4TS shed with one through road, it was located at SS98589760 and was opened by the Taff Vale Railway in 1884. The facilities included a coal stage, water tank and turntable.

The shed was reduced in c1935 ...
Ferndale (GWR)^{SS9897.2/1B}

The building was removed from the two northernmost tracks leaving a 2TS dead ended shed with a slated pitched roof and boarded gables. The depot was closed by BR in September 1964 and was subsequently demolished.

PWLLYRHEBOG

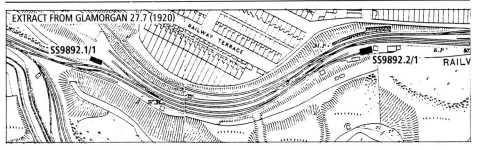

EXTRACT FROM GLAMORGAN 27.7 (1920)

SS9892.1/1

SS9892.2/1

Site SS9892.1; On the north side of the line, west of the top of the Pwllyrhebog Incline.

Pwllyrhebog (TVR) SS9892.1/1A

A 1TS dead ended shed, probably built in timber, it was located at SS98389279 and was opened by the Taff Vale Railway in 1863. No further details are known except that it was closed in 1884.

Replaced by ...

Site SS9892.2; On the south side of the line, at the top of the Pwllyrhebog Incline.

Pwllyrhebog (TVR) SS9892.2/1A

A corrugated iron 1TS dead ended shed with a corrugated iron gable style pitched roof, it was located at SS98649275 and was opened in 1884. The facilities included a water tank. The depot was closed by BR in July 1951 and was subsequently demolished.

PONTYPRIDD

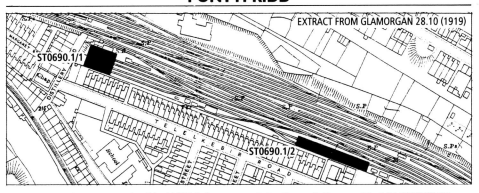

EXTRACT FROM GLAMORGAN 28.10 (1919)

ST0690.1/1

ST0690.1/2

Site ST0690.1; On the west side of the Taff Vale line, north of Pontypridd Station.

Coke Ovens (TVR) ST0690.1/1A

A brick built 4TS dead ended shed with a slated northlight pattern roof, it was located at ST06039064 and was opened by the Taff Vale Railway in 1896. The facilities included a coal stage and water tank. The depot was closed by the GWR on December 31st, 1933.

Coke Ovens Railmotor Shed (TVR) ST0690.1/2A

A 2TS shed with one through road, it was sited at the east end of the yard and was located at ST06279056. It was opened in 1905 and closed by the GWR in 1927, finding further use as a carriage shed.

DANYGRAIG

Site SS6993.1; On the south side of the R&SBR line, east of Danygraig Station.

Danygraig (R&SBR) SS6993.1/1A

A stone built 4TS shed with two through roads and a northlight pattern roof, it was located at SS69389319 and was opened by the Rhondda & Swansea Bay Railway in 1896. The running shed occupied the northern part of a larger building which also incorporated a repair shop and carriage and wagon works. The facilities also included a ramped coaling stage and water tank. The depot was closed to steam by BR on January 4th, 1960 and totally in March 1964. The building was not demolished but leased out for industrial use and was still standing in 1995.

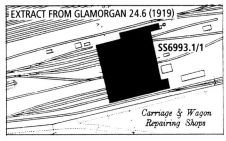

EXTRACT FROM GLAMORGAN 24.6 (1919)

SS6993.1/1

Carriage & Wagon Repairing Shops

PENYLAN

Site SS8383.1; On the east side of Waterhall Junction.

Penylan (C&PR) SS8383.1/1A

A 2TS shed was opened here by the Cefn & Pyle Railway in c1876. It is assumed to have been located at SS83188315. The line was absorbed by the Port Talbot Railway in January 1897 and no further details are known except that it was closed in May 1908*.

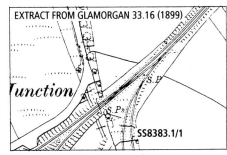

EXTRACT FROM GLAMORGAN 33.16 (1899)

Junction

SS8383.1/1

*The map shown above does not show any buildings on the site and it could be assumed that the shed was demolished at some stage and a stabling point (SS8383.1/F1) was established here, being utilized until the closure date.

TONDU

Site SS8984.2; On the east side of the Tondu North Loop, north of Tondu Station.

Tondu (L&OR) SS8984.2/1A

A 1TS dead ended shed, it was located at SS89588459 and was opened by the Llynvi & Ogmore Railway in 1868. No further details are known except that the depot was closed by the GWR in 1889 and demolished, the site being utilized for additional running lines.

Site SS8984.1; In the triangle of lines at the north end of Tondu Station.

Tondu (Ogmore Valley) SS8984.1/1A

A 1TS dead ended shed, it was located at SS89558465 and was opened by the Ogmore Valley Railway in August 1865. The building adjoined the main repair shops of the line. The Ogmore Valley amalgamated with the Llynvi Valley Railway in 1866 to form the Llynvi & Ogmore Railway. The depot was closed by the GWR in 1889 and demolished.

Replaced by ...

Tondu (GWR) SS8984.1/2A

A brick built 1RH shed with a northlight pattern roof, it was located at SS89558456 and was opened in 1889. The facilities included a ramped coal stage with water tank over.

The shed was re-roofed ...

Tondu (BR) SS8984.1/2B

The roof was reclad in corrugated asbestos sheeting by the Western Region in 1953. The depot was closed in February 1964 and demolished.

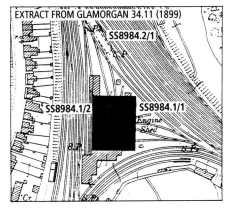

EXTRACT FROM GLAMORGAN 34.11 (1899)

SS8984.2/1

SS8984.1/2

SS8984.1/1

Engine Shed

RHYMNEY

Site SO1107.1; On the west side of the line, at the south end of Rhymney Station.

Rhymney (Rhymney) SO1107.1/1A

A stone built 3TS dead ended shed with a slated gable style pitched roof, it was located at SO11100740 and was opened by the Rhymney Railway in 1864. The facilities included a turntable and coal stage.

The shed was re-roofed ...

Rhymney (GWR) SO1107.1/1B

At some stage the shed was re-roofed. The depot was closed by BR in March 1965 and was subsequently demolished.

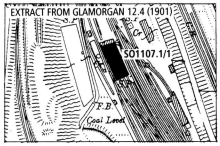

EXTRACT FROM GLAMORGAN 12.4 (1901)

SO1107.1/1

F.B.

Coal Level

TREHAFOD

Site ST0490.1; On the south side of the line, east of Trehafod Station.

Trehafod (Barry) ST0490.1/1A

A stone built 3TS through road shed with a slated northlight pattern roof, it was located at ST04989091 and was opened by the Barry Railway in 1890. The facilities included a coal stage and water column. The depot was closed by the GWR on October 15th, 1925 and was subsequently demolished.

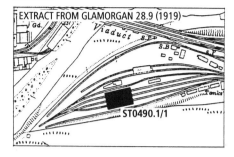

EXTRACT FROM GLAMORGAN 28.9 (1919)

ST0490.1/1

BRITON FERRY

Site SS7495.2; On the west side of the SWMR line, north of Briton Ferry Station.

Briton Ferry (SWMR) SS7495.2/1A

A 1TS shed, probably built in timber, it was located at SS74139503 and was opened by the South Wales Mineral Railway in June 1861. No further details are known except that it was very dilapidated by the time it was closed in 1877.

Replaced by ...
Site SS7495.3; On the east side of the SWMR line, north of Briton Ferry Station.

Briton Ferry (SWMR) SS7495.3/1A

A 1TS dead ended shed, probably built in timber, it was located at SS74149502 and was opened in 1877. Details of the facilities are not known. The line was absorbed by the GWR in 1908 and the engines were transferred to Neath Court Sart shed (SS7495.1/1) in June 1910, leaving the depot in use as a stabling point only until c1923. Demolition was authorized in 1927.

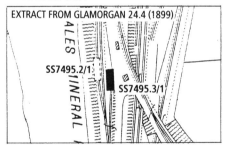

EXTRACT FROM GLAMORGAN 24.4 (1899)

SS7495.2/1

SS7495.3/1

FLEUR-DE-LIS

Site ST1596.1; On the west side of the line, south of Fleur-de-Lis Station.

Fleur-de-Lis (B&MR) ST1596.1/1A

A 1TS dead ended shed, it was located at ST15559618 and was opened by the Brecon & Merthyr Railway in 1890. No further details are known except that it was closed in 1916 and demolished.

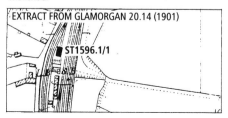

EXTRACT FROM GLAMORGAN 20.14 (1901)

ST1596.1/1

TREHERBERT

Site SS9398.1; On the west side of the line, at the south end of Treherbert Station.

Treherbert (TVR) SS9398.1/1A

A stone built 7 track semi-roundhouse with a slated continuous pitched roof, it was located at SS93899809 and was opened by the Taff Vale Railway in 1866. The facilities included a water tank, coal stage and turntable. The depot was closed by GWR in June 1931 and demolished.

Replaced by ...
Site SS9498.1; On the east side of the line, at the south end of Treherbert Station.

Treherbert (GWR) SS9498.1/1A

A brick and asbestos built 4TS dead ended shed with a twin steel sheeted gable style pitched roof, it was located at SS94019815 and was opened in June 1931. The facilities included a turntable and coal stage with water tank over. The depot was closed by BR on March 1st, 1965 and was subsequently demolished.

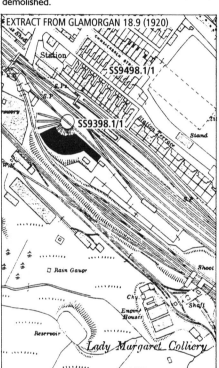

EXTRACT FROM GLAMORGAN 18.9 (1920)

SS9498.1/1

SS9398.1/1

PORT TALBOT

Site SS7789.1; On the south side of Duffryn Junction.

Duffryn Yard (PTR) SS7789.1/1A

A brick built 5TS dead ended shed with a slated northlight pattern roof, it was located at SS77808960 and was opened by the Port Talbot Railway in 1896. (Although the building was large enough to accommodate six tracks only five were used). The facilities included a turntable, coal stage and water tank.

The shed was rebuilt in 1931 ...
Duffryn Yard (GWR) SS7789.1/1B

The shed was re-roofed and the sixth track brought into use. At the same time the yard was re-modelled with the turntable being re-sited and enlarged, and the coal stage was rebuilt and improved. The depot was closed by BR on March 2nd, 1964 and subsequently demolished.

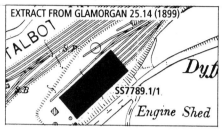

EXTRACT FROM GLAMORGAN 25.14 (1899)

SS7789.1/1

YSTRAD

Site SS9795.1; On the south side of the line, at the east end of Ystrad Station.

Ystrad (TVR) SS9795.1/F1

A servicing area consisting of a turntable, located at SS97439523, and an engine pit, it was opened by the Taff Vale Railway at some time after 1875. It only enjoyed a brief existence, being removed in 1883.

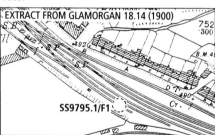

EXTRACT FROM GLAMORGAN 18.14 (1900)

SS9795.1/F1

Nothing epitomises more the spectacle of *"South Wales on a Sunday"* than this view of the yard at **Newport Ebbw Junction** shed (ST3086.1/1A) in June 1949. Row upon row of locomotives greeted railway enthusiasts at almost every depot and made it a number-collectors paradise.

The large double-turntable shed at Ebbw Junction was opened by the GWR in July 1915 to replace the life-expired 4TS SWR building (ST3088.1/1A) sited adjacently to Newport High Street Station. The steady decline in South Wales coal traffic took away the need for so many locomotives and the change to diesel power brought about the demise of the depot in October 1965.

J Edgington

LLANTRISANT

Site ST0381.1; On the east side of the Ely Valley branch, north of Llantrisant Station.

Llantrisant (EVR) ST0381.1/1A

A stone built 2TS dead ended shed with a slated gable style pitched roof, it was located at ST03248179 and was opened by the Ely Valley Railway in August 1860. The facilities included a coal stage, water tank and 45ft turntable. The line was worked by the GWR and leased to them in 1861. The depot was closed by the GWR in October 1900 and demolished.

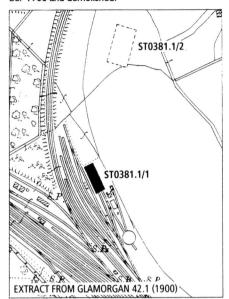

EXTRACT FROM GLAMORGAN 42.1 (1900)

Replaced by ...

Llantrisant (GWR) ST0381.1/2A

A stone built 3TS through road shed with a slated northlight pattern roof, it was sited a short distance north of its predecessor (ST0381.1/1) and was located at ST03268191. It was opened in October 1900 and the facilities included a ramped coaling stage with water tank over and a turntable. The depot was closed by BR in October 1964 and demolished.

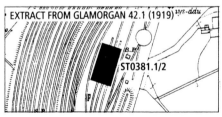

EXTRACT FROM GLAMORGAN 42.1 (1919) *n/s-ddu*

ROATH BRANCH JUNCTION

Site ST1679.1; On the south side of the Roath Docks branch, east of Roath Branch Junction.

Roath Branch Junction* (TVR) ST1679.1/1A

A stone built 1TS dead ended shed with a slated gable style pitched roof, it was located at ST16277912 and was opened by the Taff Vale Railway in 1901. The facilities included a coal stage and water tank. The depot was closed by the GWR on May 8th, 1923 and was subsequently demolished.

EXTRACT FROM GLAMORGAN 43.6 (1920)

*It was also known as Roath Line Junction.

PENARTH

Site ST1772.1; On the east side of Penarth Dock Station.

Penarth Dock (TVR) ST1772.1/1A

A stone built 3TS dead ended shed with a slated gable style pitched roof, it was located at ST17617252 and was opened by the Taff Vale Railway in 1887. The facilities included a coal stage and water tank. The depot was closed as a running shed by the GWR on February 13th, 1929 when it was subsequently taken over by the Docks Traffic Department.

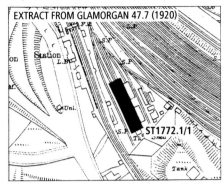

EXTRACT FROM GLAMORGAN 47.7 (1920)

Site ST1871.1; On the east side of the line, south of Penarth Town Station.

Penarth Town (CP&BJR) ST1871.1/1A

A 1TS shed, probably built in timber, it was located at ST18467116 and was opened by the Cardiff, Penarth & Barry Junction Railway in 1873. The facilities included a turntable sited outside of the shed entrance. The depot was closed in 1888 and demolished.

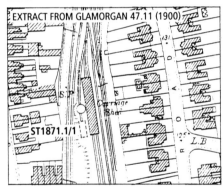

EXTRACT FROM GLAMORGAN 47.11 (1900)

SENGHENYDD

Site ST1190.1; On the east side of Senghenydd Station.

Senghenydd (Rhymney) ST1190.1/1A

A stone built 2TS dead ended shed with a slated gable style pitched roof, it was located at ST11419096 and was opened by the Rhymney Railway in 1894. The facilities included a coal stage and water tank. The depot was closed by the GWR on May 23rd, 1931 and was subsequently demolished.

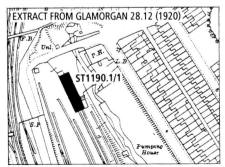

EXTRACT FROM GLAMORGAN 28.12 (1920)

RADYR

Site ST1380.1; On the south side of the line, at the east end of Penarth Junction Station.

Penarth Junction (TVR) ST1380.1/1A

A timber built 2TS dead ended shed with a slated gable style pitched roof, it was located at ST13508038 and was opened by the Taff Vale Railway in 1865. The facilities included a coal stage and 45ft turntable. The depot was closed by the GWR on March 29th, 1931.

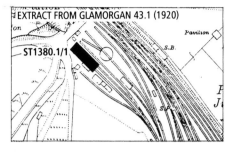

EXTRACT FROM GLAMORGAN 43.1 (1920)

Replaced by ...

Site ST1379.1; On the south side of the line, east of Penarth Junction Station.

Radyr (GWR) ST1379.1/1A

A brick and asbestos built 4TS dead ended shed with a twin steel sheeted gable style pitched roof, it was located at ST13907981 and was opened on September 29th, 1931. The facilities included a ramped coal stage with water tank over and a 65ft turntable. The depot was closed by BR on July 26th, 1965 and was subsequently utilized for a short while for stabling diesels. The building was still standing in 1995.

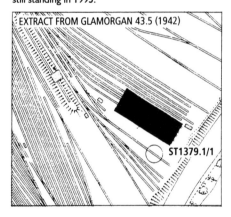

EXTRACT FROM GLAMORGAN 43.5 (1942)

TAFFS WELL

Site ST1283.1; On the east side of the line, at the south end of Taffs Well Station.

Taffs Well * (Rhymney) ST1283.1/1A

A brick built 1TS dead ended shed with a slated gable style pitched roof, it was located at ST12548314 and was opened by the Rhymney Railway on February 25th, 1858. The facilities included a coal stage. The depot was closed by the GWR in September 1922 and the building was leased out for private use. It was still standing in 1996.

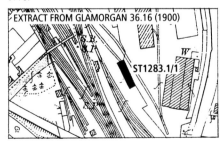

EXTRACT FROM GLAMORGAN 36.16 (1900)

*It was also known as Walnut Tree Junction

Site SS6693.1; On the south side of the line, west of East Dock Station.

Riverside (VNR) SS6693.1/1A

A 1TS dead ended shed, probably built in stone with a slated pitched roof, it was located at SS66319315 and was opened by the Vale of Neath Railway in 1863. The facilities included a water tank and 20ft turntable sited outside of the shed entrance. The depot was closed in 1881 and demolished.

Replaced by ...

Site SS6592.1; On the east side of Victoria Station.

Burrows Lodge (P&M) SS6592.1/1A

A timber built 1TS dead ended shed with a slated gable style pitched roof, it was located at SS65919266 and was opened by Powesland & Mason in 1881. There were no facilities. The company was taken over by the GWR on January 1st, 1924 and although they officially closed the depot on April 20th, 1924 it remained in use for locomotive stabling and servicing until c1938.

Site SS6693.2; On the south side of the line, adjacent to the north end of Prince of Wales Dock and east of East Dock Station.

Riverside (Westlake) SS6693.2/1A

A 1TS shed it was located at SS66389306 and was incorporated in a larger fitters and stores building. No further details are known except that it was opened by William Westlake, a contractor, in January 1886 and closed in March 1894 following the opening of his second shed (SS6693.4/1A). The building was demolished, partially to accommodate the construction of Riverside (Rhondda & Swansea Bay Railway) Station.

Replaced by ..

Riverside (Rowland) SS6693.2/1B

A 3TS dead ended shed it occupied part of the original site of its predecessor (SS6693.2./1A) and was opened by Christopher Rowland, a contractor, in May 1905. No further details of its construction or facilities are known. The shed was leased to Powesland & Mason in 1910, following the death of Mr Rowland and this lease was taken up by the GWR in 1922. The depot was closed on April 20th, 1924 and demolished.

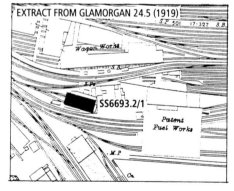

EXTRACT FROM GLAMORGAN 24.5 (1919)

Riverside (R&SBR) SS6693.2/2A

A 1TS dead ended shed, it was located at SS66559302 and was opened by the Rhondda & Swansea Bay Railway in December 1894. The facilities included a 45ft turntable sited outside of the shed entrance. No further details are known except that it was closed in 1898 and was subsequently demolished.

Site SS6693.4; On the south side of the line, adjacent to the east bank of the River Tawe and at the north end of the dock area.

Riverside (Westlake) SS6693.4/1A

A 1TS shed, it was located at SS66369306 and was incorporated in a larger building. No further details are known except that it was opened by William Westlake in March 1894 and closed by him upon the surrender of his lease on February 22nd, 1900. The building was subsequently demolished.

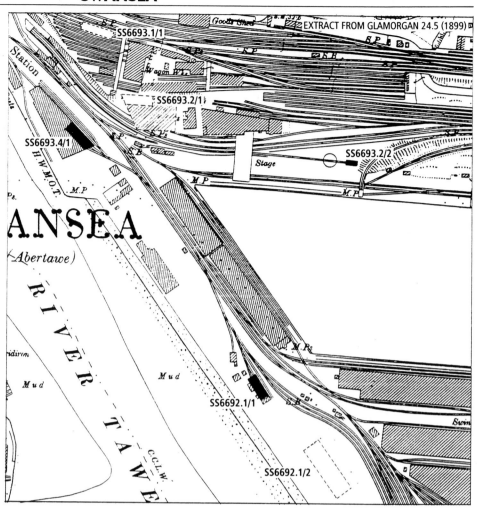

EXTRACT FROM GLAMORGAN 24.5 (1899)

Site SS6693.3; On the north side of the line, at the east end of East Dock Station.

East Dock (GWR) SS6693.3/1A

A brick built 3TS dead ended shed with a slated gable style pitched roof, it was located at SS66979313 and was opened in 1893. The facilities included a ramped coal stage and water tank. The depot was closed by BR in June 1964.

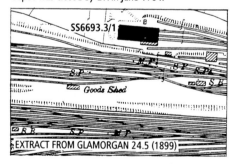

EXTRACT FROM GLAMORGAN 24.5 (1899)

Site SS6692.1; On the south side of the line, adjacent to the east bank of the River Tawe and at the south end of the dock area.

Riverside (Rowland) SS6692.1/1A

A 1TS dead ended shed, it was located at SS66479283 and was opened by Christopher Rowland, a contractor, on August 1st, 1891. No further details are known.

It was enlarged ...

Riverside (Rowland) SS6692.1/1B

At some stage the shed was doubled in size to a 2TS building. The depot was taken over by the Swansea Harbour Trust upon expiry of the original lease on May 29th, 1905 and it was closed in 1912.

Replaced by ...

Harbour (SHT) SS6692.1/2A

A corrugated iron 3TS through road shed with a corrugated iron gable style pitched roof, it was sited slightly south of its predecessor (SS6692.1/1) at SS66549276. It was opened by the Swansea Harbour Trust in 1912 and the facilities included a water tank. The depot was closed by the GWR on June 2nd, 1930 and although it was subsequently demolished the site was utilized for temporary stabling and servicing of locomotives until c1952.

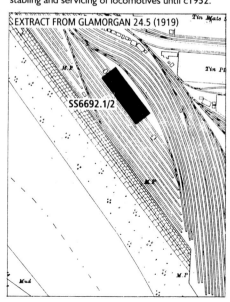

EXTRACT FROM GLAMORGAN 24.5 (1919)

Continued ...

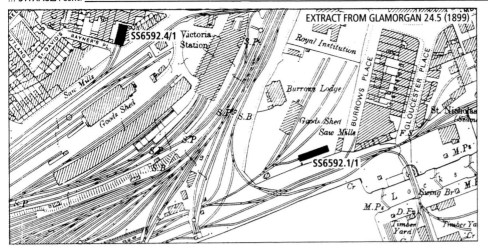

EXTRACT FROM GLAMORGAN 24.5 (1899)

SS6592.4/1 Victoria Station

SS6592.1/1

Landore (GWR) SS6595.1/2A
A brick built 4TS dead ended shed with a slated gable style pitched roof, it was sited further south in the shed yard at SS65849521 and was opened in 1932. The facilities were improved and re-sited at the same time.

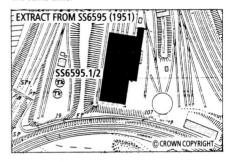

EXTRACT FROM SS6595 (1951)

SS6595.1/2

© CROWN COPYRIGHT

The depot was closed to steam by BR on June 11th, 1961 and a purpose built diesel depot (SS6595.1/3A) established on the site in 1963.

Site SS6693.5; On the west side of St. Thomas's Station.
St. Thomas's (SVR) SS6693.5/1A
A 2TS dead ended shed with a slated gable style roof, it was located at SS66179332 and was opened by the Swansea Vale Railway on February 21st, 1860. The line was leased to the MR on July 1st, 1874 and absorbed by them on August 11th, 1876. No further details are known except that it was closed by the MR in 1893.

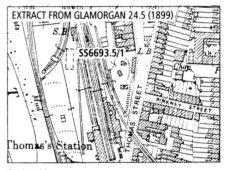

EXTRACT FROM GLAMORGAN 24.5 (1899)

SS6693.5/1

Thomas's Station

Replaced by ...
Site SS6695.1; On the north side of the line, east of Upper Bank Station.
Upper Bank (MR) SS6695.1/1A
A brick built 2TS dead ended shed with a slated gable style pitched roof, it was located at SS66969550 and was opened in 1893. The facilities included a ramped coal stage, 42ft turntable and water tank. The depot was closed by BR on February 4th, 1963 and was subsequently demolished.

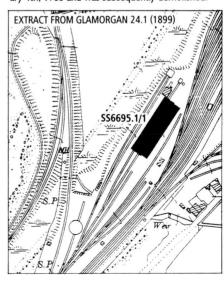

EXTRACT FROM GLAMORGAN 24.1 (1899)

SS6695.1/1

Site SS6592.4; On the north side of the line, at Rayners Place.
Swansea (Oystermouth) SS6592.4/1A
A 2TS dead ended shed, it was located at SS65719276 and was opened by the Oystermouth Railway on August 16th, 1877. The facilities included a water tank, incorporated in the shed roof. Coaling was effected from wagons but there was no turntable. The line became part of the Swansea & Mumbles Railway on March 31st, 1879 and the depot was closed on March 2nd, 1929.

Site SS6592.2; In the vicinity of Victoria Station.
Victoria (Llanelly) SS6592.2/1A
A shed, approximately located at SS657927, was opened here by the Llanelly Railway on December 14th, 1867. The line was worked by the L&NWR from January 1st, 1873. No further details are known.

The shed was enlarged ....
Victoria (L&NWR) SS6592.2/1B
Some sort of extension was provided in 1873. The depot closed on January 6th, 1882.

Replaced by ...
Site SS6592.3; On the south side of the line, west of Victoria Station.
Paxton Street (L&NWR) SS6592.3/1A
A brick built 6TS dead ended shed with a slated and glazed northlight pattern roof, it was located at SS65259234 and was opened on January 6th, 1882. The facilities included a coal stage with water tank over and a 42ft turntable, enlarged to 60ft in 1920. The depot was closed by BR on August 31st, 1959 and subsequently demolished.

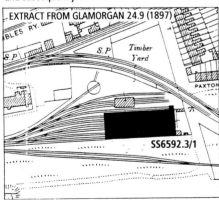

EXTRACT FROM GLAMORGAN 24.9 (1897)

SS6592.3/1

Site SS6594.1; On the west side of the line, north of High Street Station.
High Street (SWR) SS6594.1/1A
A stone built 2TS dead ended shed with a gable style slated pitched roof, it was located at SS65929418 and was opened by the South Wales Railway on June 18th, 1850. The facilities included a water tank, coal stage and 40ft turntable.

The shed was extended ...
High Street (SWR) SS6594.1/1B
The building was increased in length at its northern end by 50ft in 1854.

The shed was extended again ...
High Street (SWR) SS6594.1/1C
The building was increased in length at its northern end by a further 60ft in 1856. The line was absorbed by the GWR in 1862.

The shed was extended again ...
High Street (GWR) SS6594.1/1D
The building was increased to its final length of 360ft by 1870. The depot was closed in 1874 and the building was converted to a goods shed and remained standing, in industrial use, until the early 1990s.

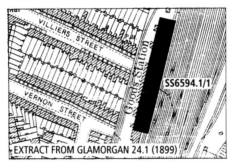

SS6594.1/1

EXTRACT FROM GLAMORGAN 24.1 (1899)

Replaced by ...
Site SS6595.1; In the fork of the Llanelly and High Street lines, at the south end of Landore Junction Station.
Landore (GWR) SS6595.1/1A
A stone built 4TS dead ended shed with a slated gable style pitched roof, it was located at SS65829529 and was opened in 1874. The facilities included a coal stage with water tank over and a turntable.

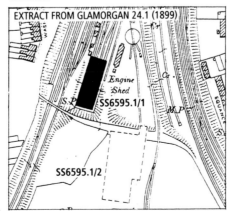

EXTRACT FROM GLAMORGAN 24.1 (1899)

Engine Shed
SS6595.1/1

SS6595.1/2

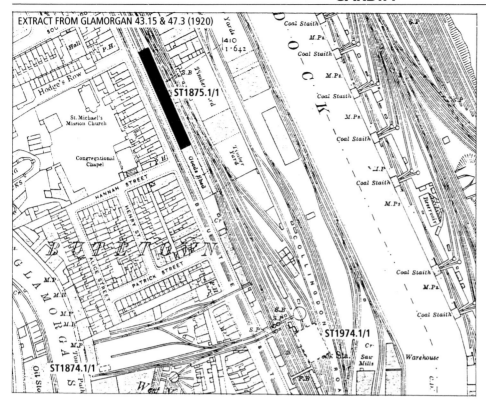

EXTRACT FROM GLAMORGAN 43.15 & 47.3 (1920)

Site ST1874.1; In West Yard Works, on the west side of the Bute West Dock line.
West Yard (TVR)^{ST1874.1/1A}

A 1TS dead ended shed, it was located at ST18907486 and was opened by the Taff Vale Railway on October 9th, 1840. No further details are known except that it was closed in 1845 and converted to a carriage shed.

Replaced by ...
Site ST1875.1; On the west side of the Bute West Dock line.
Terminus (TVR)^{ST1875.1/1A}

A timber built 2TS through road shed with a slated gable style pitched roof, it was located at ST18967511 and was opened by the Taff Vale Railway in 1845. Details of the facilities are not known.

The shed was enlarged ....
Terminus (TVR)^{ST1875.1/1B}

A stone built 165ft extension was added to the southern end of the shed in 1847.

The shed was enlarged again....
Terminus (TVR)^{ST1875.1/1C}

A stone built 97ft extension was added to the southern end of the shed in 1849.

The original portion was rebuilt ....
Terminus (TVR)^{ST1875.1/1D}

The timber walls were rebuilt in stone in 1853. Despite all the extensions to accommodation the depot still proved to be too small and it was closed in 1857. The building was not demolished but was converted to a goods shed.

Replaced by ...
Site ST1974.1; On the east side of the Bute West Dock line.
Terminus (TVR)^{ST1974.1/1A}

A stone built 6TS through road shed with a gable style slated triple pitched roof, it was located at ST19107488 and was opened by the Taff Vale Railway in 1857. The facilities included a coal stage and turntable. The depot was closed in 1884 and demolished to accommodate the building of Cardiff Docks Station in 1885.

Replaced by ...
Site ST1777.1; On the west side of the line, north of Queen Street Station.
Cathays (TVR)^{ST1777.1/1A}

A stone built 10TS dead ended shed with a twin gable style slated and glazed pitched roof, it was located at ST17967751 and was opened by the Taff Vale Railway in 1884. The facilities included a coal stage, water tank, turntable and repair shop. The depot was improved by the GWR in 1929.

The shed was modified in 1938...
Cathays (GWR)^{ST1777.1/1B}

The eastern bay was cut back to leave open sidings and all the roofing was replaced with corrugated sheeting. The depot was partially given over to dmus by BR in 1959 and was closed to steam in 1961. The shed was totally closed in November 1964 and subsequently demolished.

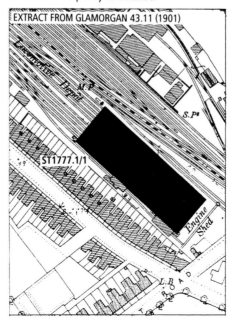

EXTRACT FROM GLAMORGAN 43.11 (1901)

Site ST1976.1; On the east side of the Bute East Dock line, south of Roath Station.
Newtown (SWR)^{ST1976.1/1A}

A 1TS dead ended shed, it was located at ST19467630 and was opened by the South Wales Railway in 1858. The line was absorbed by the GWR in 1862. Details of its construction and facilities are not known.

The shed was enlarged ...
Newtown (GWR)^{ST1976.1/1B}

The depot was doubled in size to a 2TS shed in 1872 and it was closed in June 1882.

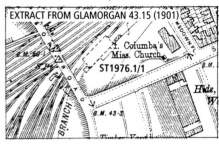

EXTRACT FROM GLAMORGAN 43.15 (1901)

Replaced by ...
Site ST1775.1; On the south side of the line, west of Cardiff General Station.
Canton (GWR)^{ST1775.1/1A}

A brick built 6TS dead ended shed with a slated northlight pattern roof, it was located at ST17187593 and was opened in 1882.

Adjoined, on the western wall, by ...
Canton (GWR)^{ST1775.1/1A}

A brick built 1RH shed with a slated multi-pitched gable style roof, it was located at ST17117591 and was opened in 1897.

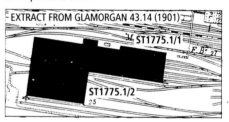

EXTRACT FROM GLAMORGAN 43.14 (1901)

The depot possessed all facilities including a repair shop. Improvements were made to the shed yard layout in 1925 and 1931. It was closed to steam by BR on September 10th, 1962 and a purpose built diesel depot (ST1775.1/2B) erected on the site of the roundhouse (ST1775.1/2A). The 6TS shed (ST1775.1/1A) was converted to diesel servicing and was still in use in 1997.

Site ST1878.1; On the east side of the Caerphilly line, north of Queen Street Station.
Crwys Yard (Rhymney)^{ST1878.1/1A}

A brick and corrugated iron 1TS through road shed, with a corrugated iron gable style pitched roof, it was located at ST18597809 and was opened by the Rhymney Railway in 1900. The facilities included a covered coal stage built alongside the east side of the shed. The depot was closed by the GWR in 1925 and was subsequently demolished.

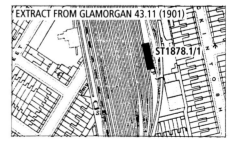

EXTRACT FROM GLAMORGAN 43.11 (1901)

Continued ...

Site ST1875.2; On the east side of the TVR East Branch, south of Queen Street Station.

Bute Yard *(MBT)* ST1875.2/1A

A stone built 2TS dead ended shed with a slated hipped roof, it was located at ST18917590 and was opened by the Marquis of Bute Trustees in 1862. There were no facilities. The depot was closed in 1881 and the building was utilized as a wagon shop in the adjacent works.

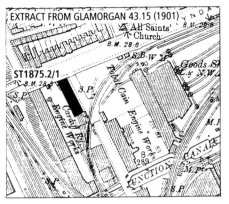

EXTRACT FROM GLAMORGAN 43.15 (1901)

It was also known as Tyndall Street.

Replaced by ...
Site ST1975.2; Near the terminus and on the east side of the East Bute Dock Branch.

East Moors *(MBT)* ST1975.2/1A

A brick built 6TS through road shed with a triple slated pitched roof and wooden gables, it was located at ST19797523 and was opened by the Marquis of Bute Trustees in 1881. Details of the facilities are not known. The line became part of the Bute Dock Company system in 1887, the Cardiff Railway in 1897 and was finally absorbed by the GWR in September 1922. The depot was closed on March 8th, 1926 and subsequently demolished.

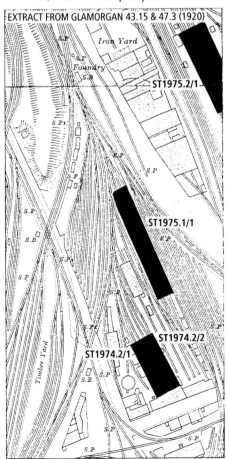

EXTRACT FROM GLAMORGAN 43.15 & 47.3 (1920)

Site ST1974.2 & ST1975.1; Near the terminus and on the west side of the East Bute Dock Branch.

Cardiff Docks *(Rhymney)* ST1975.1/1A

A stone built 4TS shed with three through roads and a gable style slated pitched roof, it was located at ST19727508 and was opened by the Rhymney Railway in September 1857. The facilities included a water tank, coal stage and 40ft turntable.

The shed was extended ...
Cardiff Docks *(Rhymney)* ST1975.1/1B
The building was lengthened in 1873.

Cardiff Docks *(Rhymney)* ST1974.2/1A

A stone built 3TS dead ended shed with a slated gable style pitched roof, it was located at ST19737496 and was opened in 1901. The building was formerly the Fitting Shop of the adjacent works.

Adjoined by ...
Cardiff Docks *(Rhymney)* ST1974.2/2A

A stone built 3TS dead ended shed with a slated gable style pitched roof, it was located at ST19747496 and was opened in 1901. The building was formerly the Carriage Shop of the adjacent works.

The depot was closed by the GWR on January 19th, 1931 and the two former works buildings (ST1974.2/1 and ST1974.2/2) were demolished immediately whilst the original shed (ST1975.1/1) was retained until the replacement shed, East Dock (ST1974.2/3) was brought into use later in the year.

Replaced by ...
East Dock *(GWR)* ST1974.2/3A

A brick and corrugated asbestos built 8TS dead ended shed with a multi-pitched corrugated asbestos gable style roof, it was mainly constructed on the site of ST1974.2/1&2 and was located at ST19757496. It opened in 1931 and the facilities included a ramped coal stage with water tank over and a turntable. By 1962 the shed had been run down ready for closure, but with the decision taken to utilize Canton (ST1775.1/1&2) as a diesel depot it received the whole of Canton's steam allocation and became the last steam depot in the area until it was closed by BR on August 2nd, 1965. It was subsequently demolished.

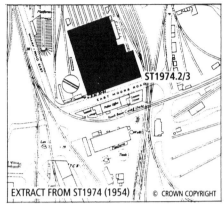

EXTRACT FROM ST1974 (1954)   © CROWN COPYRIGHT

The **East Moors** 6TS shed (ST1975.2/1A) of the Marquis of Bute Railways - later Cardiff Railway - origins was rarely photographed. This brick and timber structure was opened in 1881 to replace the 1862 MofBR shed (ST1875.2/1A) at Tyndall Street. East Moors closed in March 1926 as part of a GWR rationalization scheme and is shown here some four years prior to closure.   *Author's Collection*

Taff Vale Railway sheds in Cardiff numbered four between the years of 1845 and 1884, when the building seen here was opened. The picture was taken in October 1954, some seventeen years after the original ten covered roads had been halved. The many tank engines seen were handling the copious Valleys passenger traffic, which within a few years would pass into the care of dmus. **Cardiff Cathays** depot (ST1777.1/1B) closed to steam in 1961 and hosted diesels for a further three years before final closure and demolition.   *W Potter*

CARMARTHENSHIRE

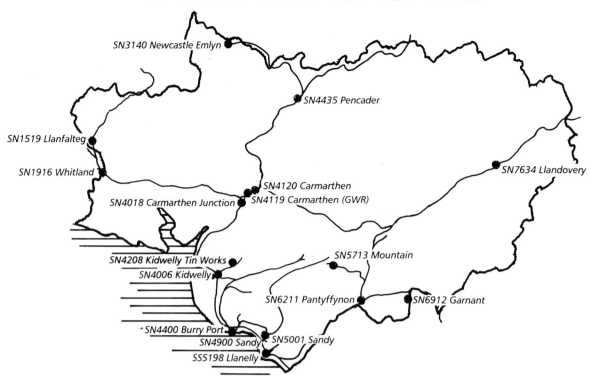

SN3140 Newcastle Emlyn

SN4435 Pencader

SN1519 Llanfalteg

SN1916 Whitland

SN7634 Llandovery

SN4120 Carmarthen
SN4119 Carmarthen (GWR)
SN4018 Carmarthen Junction

SN5713 Mountain

SN4208 Kidwelly Tin Works

SN4006 Kidwelly

SN6211 Pantyffynon

SN6912 Garnant

SN4400 Burry Port
SN4900 Sandy
SS5198 Llanelly

SN5001 Sandy

LLANDOVERY

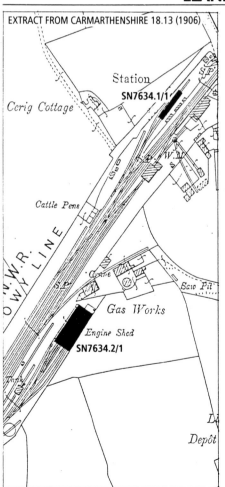

EXTRACT FROM CARMARTHENSHIRE 18.13 (1906)

Station
SN7634.1/1

Cerig Cottage

Cattle Pens

G.W.R. LINE

TOWY LINE

Gas Works

Engine Shed
SN7634.2/1

Scic Pit

Depôt

Site SN7634.1; On the west side of Llandovery Station.

Llandovery (Vale of Towy) SN7634.1/1A
A timber built 1TS through road shed with a slated gable style pitched roof, it was located at SN76293452 and was opened by the Vale of Towy Railway on April 1st, 1858. The facilities included a water tank. The line was worked by the Llanelly Railway & Dock Company, leased to the GWR on January 1st, 1873 and absorbed by them in 1889. The depot was closed on February 11th, 1935 and the locomotives were transferred to the LMS shed (SN7634.2/1).

Site SN7634.2; On the east side of the line, south of Llandovery Station.

Llandovery (L&NWR) SN7634.2/1A
A timber built 3TS dead ended shed, it was located at SN76183431 and was opened on October 8th, 1868. The building had been removed from Llandrindod Wells where it had been a temporary engine shed (SO0661.1/1A). Details of the facilities are not known. The building had become unserviceable by 1900.

Replaced by ...

Llandovery (L&NWR) SN7634.2/1B
A brick built 4TS dead ended shed with a slated northlight pattern roof, it was sited slightly east of the previous building at SN76203431 and was opened in 1901. The facilities included a ramped coal stage with water tank over and a 42ft turntable.

The shed was reduced in size ...

Llandovery (LMS) SN7634.2/1C
In c1937 two of the tracks were abandoned and the pits filled in. The depot was closed by BR on August 10th, 1964 and was subsequently demolished.

GARNANT

Site SN6912.1; On the west side of the line, south of Garnant Station.

Garnant (Llanelly) SN6912.1/1A
A stone built 2TS dead ended shed with a slated gable style pitched roof, it was located at SN69611275 and was opened by the Llanelly Railway in March 1840.

The building was modified ...

Garnant (Llanelly) SN6912.1/1B
In January 1905 it was reduced to a 1TS building and a timber extension with a slated gable style pitched roof was added at the southern end. The facilities included a water tank. The depot was closed by the GWR on March 9th, 1931 and was subsequently demolished.

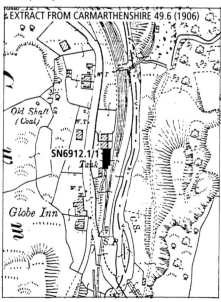

EXTRACT FROM CARMARTHENSHIRE 49.6 (1906)

Old Shaft
(Coal)

SN6912.1/1

Tank

Globe Inn

CARMARTHEN

Site SN4120.1; On the west side of the line, north of Carmarthen Town Station.

Carmarthen (C&CR) SN4120.1/1A

A timber built 1TS dead ended shed with a slated gable style pitched roof, it was located at SN41902035 and was opened by the Carmarthen & Cardigan Railway on September 3rd, 1860. The facilities included a 24ft 5in turntable. The depot was closed on December 31st, 1860, re-opened on September 12th, 1861 and was finally closed in 1872. The building was not demolished and survived until the 1930s at least.

Replaced by ...

Carmarthen (C&CR) SN4120.1/2A

A corrugated iron built 2TS dead ended shed with a slated gable style pitched roof, it was sited slightly north of its predecessor at SN41932037. The facilities included a coal stage, water tank and the 24ft 5in turntable. The line was absorbed by the GWR on July 1st, 1881 and they handed the shed over to the L&NWR in April, 1897, transferring all the GWR locomotives to Carmarthen Junction (SN4018.1/1).

The shed was re-roofed ...

Carmarthen (L&NWR) SN4120.1/2B

A timber northlight pattern roof was installed, probably shortly after taking over the shed in 1897. The depot was closed by the LMS on July 4th, 1938.

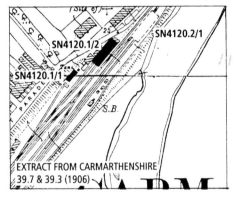

EXTRACT FROM CARMARTHENSHIRE 39.7 & 39.3 (1906)

Site SN4120.2; On the east side of the line, north of Carmarthen Town Station.

Carmarthen (CW&CJR) SN4120.2/1A

A timber built 2TS dead ended shed, with a slated gable style twin pitched roof, it was located at SN41962038 and was opened by the Central Wales & Carmarthen Junction Railway in 1875. Details of the facilities are not known. The line was absorbed by the L&NWR and by 1897 the building had become virtually derelict. With the opportunity available to acquire the vacated GWR shed (SN4120.1/2), located on the other side of the line, the depot was closed and the stock transferred to the new premises. The building was subsequently destroyed in a gale.

Site SN4018.1; On the west side of the line, at the north end of Carmarthen Junction Station.

Carmarthen Junction (SWR) SN4018.1/1A

A shed was erected here by the South Wales Railway and opened in April 1852. It is assumed to have been located at SN40891878 and lasted for only a brief period of time, being destroyed in a storm in August of the same year. No further details are known.

Replaced, on the same site, by ...

Carmarthen Junction (SWR) SN4018.1/1B

A timber built 3TS shed with one through road and a slated gable style pitched roof, it was opened by the South Wales Railway on October 11th, 1852. The facilities included a coal stage and 42ft turntable. The line was absorbed by the GWR in 1862 and the depot was closed on February 11th, 1907 and demolished in August 1909.

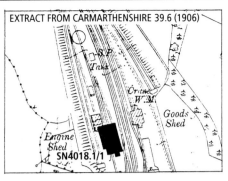

EXTRACT FROM CARMARTHENSHIRE 39.6 (1906)

Replaced by ...

Site SN4119.1; On the east side of Carmarthen Town Station.

Carmarthen Town (GWR) SN4119.1/1A

A brick built 6TS dead ended shed with a triple pitched slated gable style roof, it was located at SN41251958 and was opened on February 11th, 1907. The shed possessed all facilities including a repair shop. The depot was closed by BR on April 13th, 1964 and was subsequently demolished.

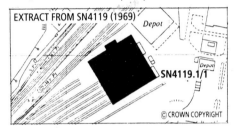

EXTRACT FROM SN4119 (1969)

© CROWN COPYRIGHT

KIDWELLY

Site SN4006.1; In the fork of the Llanelly line and the Tin Plate Works Branch, east of Kidwelly Station.

Kidwelly (GVR) SN4006.1/1A

A 1TS dead ended shed, it was located at SN40510619 and was opened by the Gwendraeth Valley Railway in 1871. The line was worked by the Burry Port & Gwendraeth Valley Railway from 1892 onwards. No further details are known except that at some stage it was taken over by the Kidwelly Tinplate Company and closed in 1904.

EXTRACT FROM CARMARTHENSHIRE 53.6 (1906)

Replaced by ...

Site SN4208.1; In Kidwelly Tinplate Works.

Kidwelly Tinplate Works (GVR) SN4208.1/1A

A brick built 1TS dead ended shed with a slated gable style pitched roof, it was located at SN42200800 and was opened by the Gwendraeth Valley Railway in 1905. The building had been the original works engine shed and it was subsequently taken over by the GWR in 1921. No further details are known except that it was closed in June 1923.

EXTRACT FROM CARMARTHENSHIRE 53.3 (1914)

BURRY PORT

Site SN4400.1; On the south side of Pembrey Station.

Burry Port (BP&GR) SN4400.1/1A

A timber built 3TS shed with two through roads and a triple pitched gable style slated roof, it was located at SN44680061 and was opened by the Burry Port & Gwendraeth Railway in 1875. The facilities included a coal stage. The depot was closed by BR on February 24th, 1962 and was subsequently demolished.

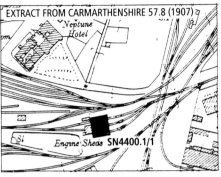

EXTRACT FROM CARMARTHENSHIRE 57.8 (1907)

PANTYFFYNON

Site SN6211.1; On the west side of the Garnant line, north of Pantyffynon Station.

Pantyffynon (GWR) SN6211.1/1A

A brick and corrugated asbestos built 4TS dead ended shed with a corrugated asbestos gable style pitched roof, it was located at SN62521125 and was opened in March 1931. The facilities included a ramped coal stage with tank over and a turntable. The depot was closed by BR in August 1964 and was subsequently demolished.

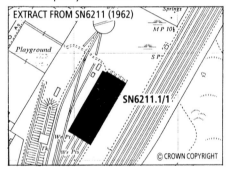

EXTRACT FROM SN6211 (1962)

© CROWN COPYRIGHT

NEWCASTLE EMLYN

Site SN3140.1; On the north side of the line, east of Newcastle Emlyn Station.

Newcastle Emlyn (GWR) SN3140.1/1A

A corrugated iron 1TS through road shed with a corrugated iron dutch barn roof, it was located at SN31564055 and was opened on July 1st, 1895. The facilities included a turntable sited outside of the shed entrance. The depot was closed by BR on September 15th, 1952 and was subsequently demolished.

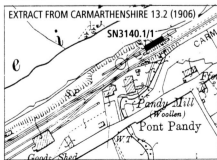

EXTRACT FROM CARMARTHENSHIRE 13.2 (1906)

LLANELLY

Site SS5198.0; In the vicinity of Llanelly Docks.
Llanelly Dock (LR&DC) SS5198.0/1A
A shed was opened here by the Llanelly Railway & Dock Company on June 1st, 1839. No further details are known.

Replaced by ...
Site SS5198.1; On the south side of the Llanelly Dock line, west of Llandilo Junction.
Llanelly Dock (LR&DC) SS5198.1/1A
A stone built 2TS dead ended shed with a slated gable style pitched roof, it was located at SS51379865 and was opened in c1840 by the Llanelly Railway & Dock Company. The facilities included a water tank and coal stage. The line was leased to the GWR on January 1st, 1873.

The shed was extended ...
Llanelly Dock (GWR) SS5198.1/1B
The building was extended to 190ft in 1875. The depot was closed on March 30th, 1925 and subsequently demolished.

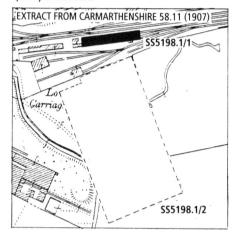

Replaced by ...
Llanelly (GWR) SS5198.2/1A
A brick built 2RH shed with a multi-pitched gable style slated roof, it was sited slightly south of its predecessor at SS51389857 and was opened on March 30th, 1925. The depot possessed all facilities, including a repair shop. The shed was closed by BR on September 14th, 1965 and was subsequently demolished.

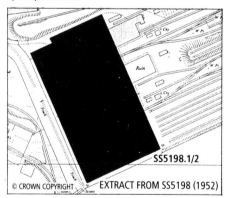

EXTRACT FROM SS5198 (1952)

WHITLAND

Site SN1916.1; On the south side of Whitland Station.
Whitland (P&TR) SN1916.1/1A
A 1TS through road shed, it was located at SN19841645 and was opened by the Pembroke & Tenby Railway in July 1863. The line was absorbed by the GWR in 1897. No further details are known.

Replaced, on the same site, by ...
Whitland (GWR) SN1916.1/1B
A corrugated iron 1TS through road shed with a corrugated iron dutch barn roof, it was opened in 1901. The building had originally been the first engine shed at Letterston (as SM9529.1/1A) and the facilities included a turntable, located outside of the shed entrance, and a coal stage.

The shed was rebuilt ...
Whitland (GWR) SN1916.1/1C
At some stage, possibly just prior to nationalization, the shed was reconstructed with new corrugated sheeting on the walls and a corrugated iron gable style pitched roof. The turntable was probably removed at the same time. The depot was closed by BR on September 9th, 1963 and was subsequently demolished.

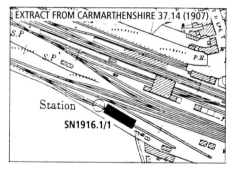

PENCADER

Site SN4435.1; On the west side of the line, south of Pencader Station.
Pencader (M&MR) SN4435.1/1A
A corrugated iron 1TS through road shed with a corrugated iron gable style pitched roof, it was located at SN44403593 and was opened by the Manchester & Milford Railway on January 1st, 1866. The line was absorbed by the GWR in 1896.

The shed was enlarged ...
Pencader (GWR) SN4435.1/1B
At some stage the building was increased to a 2TS through road shed. The depot closed on March 2nd, 1918 and was subsequently demolished.

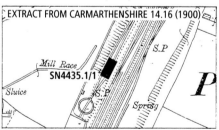

SANDY

Site SN5001.1; On the west side of the Cross Hands branch, adjacent to Castle Colliery.
Sandy (L&MMR) SN5001.1/1A
A 1TS dead ended shed, probably built in brick with a slated gable style pitched roof, it was located at SN50020104 and was opened by the Llanelly & Mynydd Mawr Railway in January 1883. Details of the facilities are not known. The shed became too small and although the depot was closed in c1913 it was utilized for the storing of locomotives awaiting repair and was not demolished until 1922.

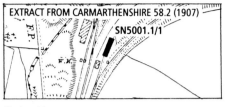

Replaced by ...
Site SN4900.1; On the east side of the Cross Hands branch, at Sandy Junction.
Sandy, Pwll (L&MMR) SN4900.1/1A
A brick built 2TS dead ended shed with a slated gable style pitched roof, it was located at SN49890053 and was opened in c1913. Details of the facilities are not known. The depot was closed by the GWR in July 1946 and was subsequently demolished.

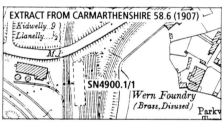

MOUNTAIN

Site SN5713.1; On the west side of the Mountain Branch, adjacent to Gors-goch Colliery.
Mountain* (Llanelly) SN5713.1/1A
A timber built 1TS dead ended shed with a slated gable style pitched roof, it was located at SN57221319 and was opened by the Llanelly Railway on May 6th, 1841. The facilities included a water tank. By 1904 the building had become totally derelict and the depot was officially closed on July 5th.

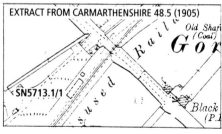

*It was also known as Tirydail.

LLANFALTEG

Site SN1519.1; On the east side of the line, at the south end of Llanfalteg Station.
Llanfalteg (W&TVR) SN1519.1/1A
A stone built 1TS dead ended shed with a slated gable style pitched roof, it was located at SN16551987 and was opened by the Whitland & Taff Vale Railway in April 1873. The facilities included a coal stage.

The shed was extended ...
Llanfalteg (W&TVR) SN1519.1/1B
The building was lengthened in 1876. The line became part of the Whitland & Cardigan Railway in 1877 and the depot was closed on September 1st, 1886. The shed remained standing and was handed over to the Civil Engineering Department in July 1904, surviving until at least 1936. It was subsequently demolished.

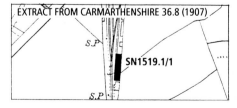

CARDIGANSHIRE

ABERYSTWYTH

Site SN5881.1; On the west side of the line, at the south end of Aberystwyth Station.

Aberystwyth (A&WCR) SN5881.1/1A

A brick built 2TS through road shed with a slated gable style pitched roof, it was located at SN58738131 and was opened by the Aberystwyth & Welsh Coast Railway in May 1864. The facilities included a water tank, coal stage and 40ft turntable. The line was absorbed by the Cambrian Railway on July 5th, 1865.

The shed was extended ...

Aberystwyth (Cambrian) SN5881.1/1B

The building was probably extended in 1867.

The shed was rebuilt in 1938 ...

Aberystwyth (GWR) SN5881.1/1C

A new brick built 2TS through road shed with a slated gable style pitched roof was built on the same site. By this time yard improvements had been made to the coal stage and the turntable had been upgraded to 55ft and re-sited. The depot was closed to standard gauge steam locomotives by BR on April 10th, 1965.

The shed was re-gauged ...

Aberystwyth (BR) SN5881.1/1D

In 1965 the building was adapted to house the former Vale of Rheidol 1ft 11.5in gauge locomotives and was still in use in 1999.

Site SN5881.2; On the north side of the line, at the west end of Aberystwyth (VofR) Station.

Aberystwyth (VofR) SN5881.2/1A

A 1ft 11.5in gauge corrugated iron 1TS dead ended shed with a corrugated iron gable style pitched roof, it was located at SN58438127 and was opened by the Vale of Rheidol Railway in July 1902 The facilities included a water tank and coal stage.

Aberystwyth (VofR) SN5881.2/2A

A 1ft 11.5in gauge corrugated iron 1TS dead ended shed with a corrugated iron gable style pitched roof, it was sited adjacently to the north side of SN5881.2/1A at SN58428128 and was opened by the Vale of Rheidol Railway in July 1902.

The sheds were amalgamated ...

Aberystwyth (VofR) SN5881.2/3A

At some stage the two sheds were joined together to form one building. The depot was closed by BR in 1965 and the locomotives were transferred to the former standard gauge building (SN5881.1/1). The shed was demolished and the site cleared.

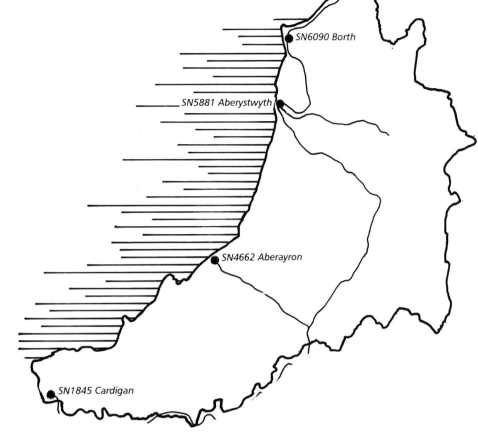

SN6090 Borth

SN5881 Aberystwyth

SN4662 Aberayron

SN1845 Cardigan

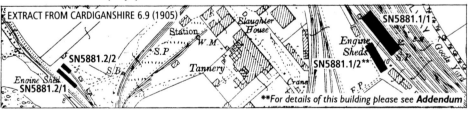

EXTRACT FROM CARDIGANSHIRE 6.9 (1905)

SN5881.2/2

SN5881.1/1

SN5881.1/2**

Engine Sheds

Engine Shed

SN5881.2/1

Station

Slaughter House

Tannery

**For details of this building please see Addendum

ABERAYRON

Site SN4662.1; On the east side of the line, south of Aberayron Station.

Aberayron (LA&NQLR) SN4662.1/1A

A 1TS dead ended shed, it was located at SN46166213 and was opened by the Lampeter, Aberayron and New Quay Light Railway on April 10th, 1911. The line was worked by the GWR and absorbed by them on January 1st, 1923. The building was destroyed in a fire in 1925.

Replaced, on the same site, by ...

Aberayron (GWR) SN4662.1/1B

A corrugated iron 1TS dead ended shed with a corrugated iron gable style pitched roof, it was opened in 1926. The building had originally been the engine shed at Wrexham Central (as SJ3350.1/1A) and the facilities included a coal stage. The depot was closed by BR on April 30th, 1962 and was subsequently demolished.

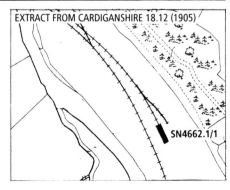

EXTRACT FROM CARDIGANSHIRE 18.12 (1905)

SN4662.1/1

Please Note: The construction and dismantling dates of this line precludes its inclusion in a complete form in OS maps. Some, or all, of the buildings and track have been superimposed.

BORTH

Site SN6090.1; In the vicinity of Borth Station.

Borth (A&WCR) SN6090.1/1A

A temporary shed, approximately located at SN609901, was opened here by the Aberystwyth & Welsh Coast Railway on July 1st, 1863. The line was worked by Savin, a contractor, and the depot was closed in May 1864. No further details are known.

CARDIGAN

Site SN1845.1; On the north side of Cardigan Station.

Cardigan (C&WR) SN1845.1/1A

A brick built 1TS through road shed with a slated gable style pitched roof, it was located at SN18084586 and was opened by the Cardigan & Whitland Railway on September 1st, 1886. The facilities included a turntable, sited outside of the shed entrance, and a water tank. The line was absorbed by the GWR and the depot was closed by BR on September 16th, 1962 and subsequently demolished.

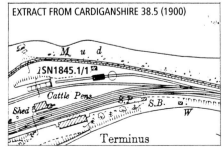

EXTRACT FROM CARDIGANSHIRE 38.5 (1900)

SN1845.1/1

Mud

Cattle Pens

Shed

Terminus

MONTGOMERYSHIRE

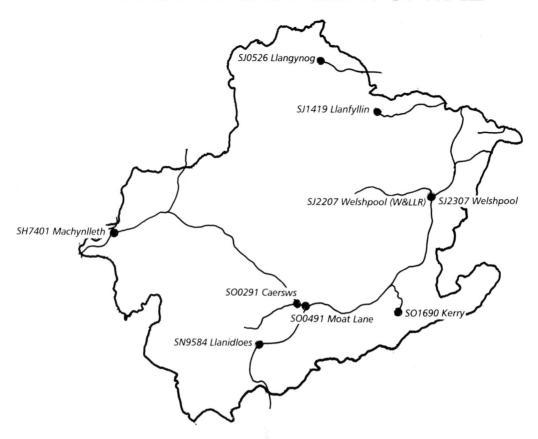

SJ0526 Llangynog

SJ1419 Llanfyllin

SJ2207 Welshpool (W&LLR)   SJ2307 Welshpool

SH7401 Machynlleth

SO0291 Caersws

SO0491 Moat Lane   SO1690 Kerry

SN9584 Llanidloes

MOAT LANE

Site SO0491.1; In the fork of the Llanidloes and Machynlleth lines, west of Moat Lane Junction Station.
Moat Lane (L&NR)SO0491.1/1A
A timber built 2TS dead ended shed with a twin slated gable style roof, it was located at SO04279108 and was opened by the Llanidloes & Newtown Railway in 1859. The facilities included a water column and, added sometime after opening, a turntable. The line was absorbed by the Cambrian Railway on July 25th, 1864. By 1956 the fabric of the building was in a derelict condition.

The shed was rebuilt...
Moat Lane (BR)SO0491.1/1B
The depot was reconstructed in corrugated iron with a corrugated iron gable style single pitched roof by the Western Region in 1957. The depot was closed on December 31st, 1962 and was let out for private use. It was still standing in 1999.

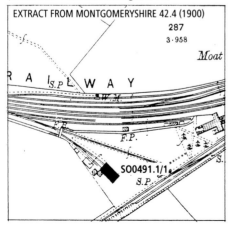

EXTRACT FROM MONTGOMERYSHIRE 42.4 (1900)
287
3·958
Moat
RAILWAY
SO0491.1/1

MACHYNLLETH

Site SH7401.1; On the east side of the line, north of Machynlleth Station.
Machynlleth (N&MR)SH7401.1/1A
A stone built 3TS shed with two through roads and a slated gable style pitched roof, it was located at SH74650145 and was opened by the Newtown & Machynlleth Railway on January 3rd, 1863. The facilities included a turntable, coal stage and water tank. The line was absorbed by the Cambrian Railway on July 25th, 1864.

Adjoined by ...
Machynlleth (Cambrian)SH7401.1/2A
A stone built 2TS through road shed with a slated gable style roof it was attached to the northern end of SH7401.1/1A and was located at SH74670148. The opening date of this building is not known, but it is assumed to have been a later addition by the Cambrian Railway.

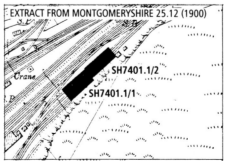

EXTRACT FROM MONTGOMERYSHIRE 25.12 (1900)
Crane
SH7401.1/2
SH7401.1/1

The depot was closed to steam by BR on December 5th, 1966 and was given over to servicing dmus. By 1996 SH7401.1/1A had been demolished but the remainder was still in use in 1999 for servicing Sprinters.

WELSHPOOL

Site SJ2307.1; On the east side of the line, at the north end of Welshpool Station.
Welshpool (O&NR)SJ2307.1/1A
A 2TS dead ended shed, it was probably built in timber with a slated gable style roof and was located at SJ23100741. It was opened by the Oswestry & Newtown Railway on August 14th, 1860 and the facilities included a water tank and turntable. The line was absorbed by the Cambrian Railway on July 25th, 1864 and the building was demolished by the GWR in c1935.

A servicing point was then established ...
Welshpool (GWR)SJ2307.1/F1
Locomotives stabled on the shed road and utilized the facilities until it was closed by BR in 1954.

Site SJ2207.1; On the east side of the line at the north end of Welshpool (W&LLR) Station.
Welshpool (W&LLR)SJ2207.1/1A
A 2ft 6in gauge corrugated iron 1TS dead ended shed with a corrugated iron gable style pitched roof, it was located at SJ22930736 and was opened by the Welshpool & Llanfair Light Railway on March 9th, 1903. The facilities included a water column. The depot was closed by BR on November 5th, 1956 and the building was let out for private use. It has since been demolished.

EXTRACT FROM MONTGOMERYSHIRE 23.8 (1900)
Camp
Bowling Green
Pavilion
Tumulus
Pavilion
SJ2307.1/1
SJ2207.1/1

LLANIDLOES

Site SN9584.1; On the east side of the line, at the north end of Llanidloes (L&NR) Station.

Llanidloes (L&NR) ^{SN9584.1/1A}

A 1TS dead ended shed, it was located at SN95958479 and was opened by the Llanidloes & Newtown Railway on April 30th, 1859. Details of its construction and facilities are not known. The line was absorbed by the Cambrian Railway on July 25th, 1864 and the depot was probably closed in the same year. It was not demolished immediately but found further use as a store.

Replaced by ...
Site SN9584.2; On the east side of the line, at the north end of Llanidloes (Mid Wales) Station.

Llanidloes (Cambrian) ^{SN9584.2/2A}

A brick built 2TS dead ended shed with a slated gable style pitched roof, it was located at SN95828449 and was opened by the Cambrian Railway in 1864. The facilities included a coal stage and use of the adjacent turntable. The depot was closed in December 1962 and was subsequently demolished.

Llanidloes (Mid Wales) ^{SN9584.2/1A}

A brick built 1TS dead ended shed with a slated gable style pitched roof, it was located at SN95838454 and was opened by the Mid Wales Railway on September 1st, 1864. The facilities included a 41ft turntable sited outside of the shed entrance. The line was absorbed by the Cambrian Railway on June 24th, 1904 and the depot was probably closed in the same year. It was later demolished.

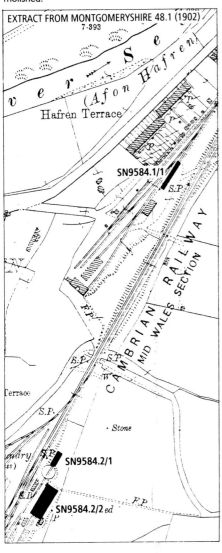

CAERSWS

Site SO0291.1; On the north side of Caersws (Van Railway) Station.

Caersws (Van) ^{SO0291.1/1A}

A brick built 1TS dead ended shed with a slated gable style pitched roof, it was located at SO02839181 and was opened by the Van Railway on August 14th, 1871. Details of the facilities are not known. The shed was closed in 1893, re-opened by the Cambrian Railway on August 1st, 1896 and although it officially finally closed in 1922 it had not been used for locomotive purposes since 1910. The building was utilized as an engineering workshop and still stood in 1999.

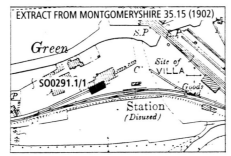

LLANGYNOG

Site SJ0526.1; On the south side of the line, at the west end of Llangynog Station.

Llangynog (Tanat Valley) ^{SJ0526.1/1A}

A corrugated iron 1TS dead ended shed with a gable style pitched roof, it was located at SJ05352623 and was opened by the Tanat Valley Light Railway on January 5th, 1904. The facilities included a coal stage with water tank over. Although it was closed in 1909 and demolished, the site was used as a stabling point until 1922 with the facilities being utilized until closure of the line on July 1st, 1952.

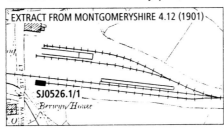

Please Note; The construction and dismantling dates of this line precludes its inclusion in a complete form in OS maps. Some, or all, of the buildings and track have been superimposed.

KERRY

Site SO1690.1; On the north side of the line, at the east end of Kerry Station.

Kerry (O&NR) ^{SO1690.1/1A}

A corrugated iron 1TS dead ended shed, with a gable style slated pitched roof, it was located at SO16429043 and was opened by the Oswestry & Newtown Railway on March 2nd, 1863. The facilities included a water tank. The line was absorbed by the Cambrian Railway on July 25th, 1864 and although the depot was closed by the GWR on February 9th, 1931 it was still utilized, as a stabling point, probably until the line was closed by BR on May 1st, 1956. The building was still standing in 1998.

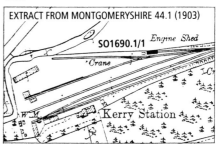

LLANFYLLIN

Site SJ1419.1; On the south side of the line, at the east end of Llanfyllin Station.

Llanfyllin (O&NR) ^{SJ1419.1/1A}

A corrugated iron 1TS dead ended shed with a slated gable style pitched roof, it was located at SJ14801912 and was opened by the Oswestry & Newtown Railway on April 10th, 1863. The facilities included a water tank, coal stage and turntable sited outside of the shed entrance. The depot was closed by BR on September 27th, 1952 and was subsequently demolished.

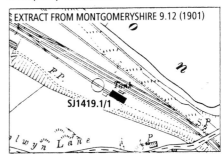

Van Railway operations were centred on **Caersws** where was sited the line's only shed (SO0291.1/1A) which opened in August 1871 and is seen here in 1948. The railway passed to the Cambrian which closed the depot in 1893, only to re-open it three years later. Final closure came in 1922 but the building still stood in 1998, in use as a store.
H Garrett Collection

PEMBROKESHIRE

SM9438 Goodwick

SM9529 Letterston

SN0729 Rosebush

SM9006 Milford Haven

SM9605 Neyland

SM9703 Pembroke Dock

SN1200 Tenby

LETTERSTON

Site SM9529.1; On the south side of Letterston Station.

Letterston (NP&FR)^{SM9529.1/1A}
A corrugated iron 2TS dead ended shed with a corrugated iron dutch barn style roof, it was located at SM95372966 and was opened by the North Pembrokeshire & Fishguard Railway in 1894. Details of the facilities are not known. The building was originally the contractors engine shed and it was converted to a carriage shed upon the opening of SM9529.1/2A in the following year. On October 3rd, 1901 it was dismantled and re-erected at Whitland for use as the engine shed (SN1916.1/1B) there.

Replaced by ...

Letterston (GWR)^{SM9529.1/2A}
A timber built 1TS dead ended shed with a slated gable style pitched roof, it was located slightly east of its predecessor (SM9529.1/1A) at SM95442964. It was opened on March 14th, 1895 and the facilities included a coal stage. The depot was closed in 1906.

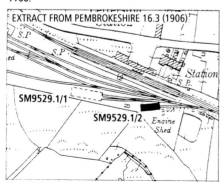

EXTRACT FROM PEMBROKESHIRE 16.3 (1906)

SM9529.1/1

SM9529.1/2

PEMBROKE DOCK

Site SM9703.1; On the south side of the line, east of Pembroke Dock Station.

Pembroke Dock (P&TR)^{SM9703.1/1A}
A stone built 2TS dead ended shed with a slated gable style roof, it was located at SM97370348 and was opened by the Pembroke & Tenby Railway on July 30th, 1863. The facilities, which were improved in c1900, included a coal stage, water column and turntable. The line was absorbed by the GWR in 1897.

The shed was extended ...

Pembroke Dock (GWR)^{SM9703.1/1B}
A 30ft corrugated asbestos extension with a corrugated asbestos pitched roof was added at the rear of the shed in 1932. The depot was closed by BR on September 9th, 1963 and was subsequently demolished.

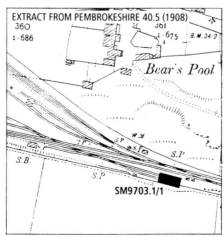

EXTRACT FROM PEMBROKESHIRE 40.5 (1908)

Bear's Pool

SM9703.1/1

NEYLAND

Site SM9605.1; At the north end of Neyland Station.
Neyland (SWR)^{SM9605.1/1A}
A timber built 2TS shed with one through road and a slated gable style pitched roof, it was located at SM96670511 and was opened by the South Wales Railway on April 15th, 1856. The building had been removed from Chepstow West where it had served as an engine shed (as ST5393.1/1A).

Adjoined by ...
Neyland (SWR)^{SM9605.1/2A}
A timber built 1TS through road shed it was attached to the north end of SM9605.1/1A and was located at SM96680514. It is not known whether it was built at the same time or was a later extension. The facilities included a coal stage, water tank and a 55ft turntable. The line was absorbed by the GWR in 1862 and modification to the yard layout, including upgrading of the turntable to 65ft, was carried out in 1932. The depot was closed by BR on September 9th, 1963 and was subsequently demolished.

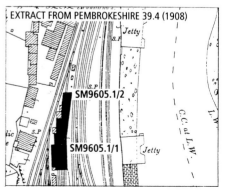

EXTRACT FROM PEMBROKESHIRE 39.4 (1908)

SM9605.1/2

SM9605.1/1

ROSEBUSH

Site SN0729.1; On the east side of the Quarry branch, north of Rosebush Station.

Rosebush Quarry (NR&MR) SN0729.1/1A

A stone built ITS dead ended shed with a slated gable style pitched roof, it was located at SN07712997 and was opened by the Narberth Road & Maenclochog Railway on September 19th, 1876. Details of the facilities are not known. The depot was closed on December 31st, 1882 and re-opened by the North Pembrokeshire & Fishguard Railway on March 14th, 1895. It was probably closed upon the amalgamation of the NP&FR and GWR in 1898. The building was subsequently abandoned.

Site SN0729.2; On the west side of Rosebush Station.

Rosebush Station (NR&MR) SN0729.2/1A

A stone built ITS dead ended shed with a slated gable style pitched roof, it was located at SN07482942 and was opened by the Narberth Road & Maenclochog Railway on September 19th, 1876. Details of the facilities are not known. The depot was closed on December 31st, 1882 and re-opened by the North Pembrokeshire & Fishguard Railway on March 14th, 1895. Following the opening of Letterston (SM9529.1/2A) in the same year the shed was then utilized as a stabling point. The NP&FR and the GWR amalgamated in 1898 and the depot was closed in c1912 and demolished.

EXTRACT FROM PEMBROKESHIRE 17.4 & 18.1 (1907)

SN0729.1/1

SN0729.2/1

Rosebush

TENBY

Site SN1200.1; On the west side of Tenby Station.

Tenby (P&TR) SN1200.1/1A

A timber built ITS dead ended shed with a slated gable style pitched roof, it was located at SN12840064.

Tenby (P&TR) SN1200.1/2A

A timber built ITS dead ended shed with a slated gable style pitched roof, it was located at SN12850068.

The depot was opened by the Pembroke & Tenby Railway on July 30th, 1863 and as it formed part of the main repairing and engine shops of the line all facilities were available. The GWR absorbed the P&TR in 1897 and the two sheds were dispensed with in 1907, with SN1200.1/2A being demolished immediately.

Replaced by ...

Tenby (GWR) SN1200.1/3A

A timber built 2TS dead ended shed with a slated gable style pitched roof, it was located at SN12830069 and was opened in 1907. The building had originally been the engine repair shop of the P&TR works until locomotive repairs were transferred to Carmarthen Junction shed (SN4018.1/1B) in the same year. The depot was closed on September 12th, 1932.

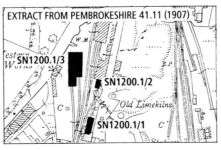

EXTRACT FROM PEMBROKESHIRE 41.11 (1907)

SN1200.1/3

SN1200.1/2

SN1200.1/1

MILFORD HAVEN

Site SM9006.1; On the west side of the Docks line, at the south end of Milford Haven Station.

Milford Haven (Milford) SM9006.1/1A

A timber built ITS dead ended shed with a gable style slated pitched roof, it was located at SM90030620 and was opened by the Milford Railway on August 1st, 1863. Details of the facilities are not known. The line was worked by the GWR and the depot was closed in December 1890.

Replaced by ...

Site SM9006.2; On the east side of the line, north of Milford Haven Station.

Milford Haven (Milford) SM9006.2/1A

A brick built ITS dead ended shed with a slated gable style pitched roof, it was located at SM90110642 and was opened in December 1890. The facilities included a water tank. The line was absorbed by the GWR in 1896 and the depot was closed by BR in December 1962. The building was later demolished.

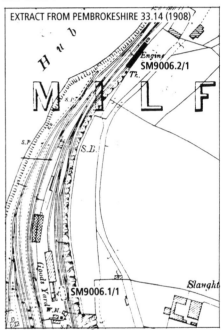

EXTRACT FROM PEMBROKESHIRE 33.14 (1908)

SM9006.2/1

SM9006.1/1

FISHGUARD

Site SM9438.1; On the west side of the line, south of Goodwick Station.

Goodwick (GWR) SM9438.1/1A

A brick built 2TS dead ended shed with a slated gable style pitched roof, it was located at SM94373805 and was opened on August 30th, 1906. The facilities included a ramped coal stage with a water tank over and a turntable. The depot was closed by BR on September 9th, 1963 and was subsequently demolished.

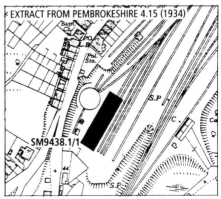

EXTRACT FROM PEMBROKESHIRE 4.15 (1934)

SM9438.1/1

BRECKNOCK

SO0528 Brecon
SO1127 Talyllyn Junction
SO1223 Talybont on Usk
SN7709 Gurnos

BRECON

Site SO0528.1; On the south side of the line, east of Brecon Joint Station.
Brecon (B&MR) SO0528.1/1A
A brick built 2TS through road shed with a slated pitched roof and timber gables, it was located at SO05282806 and was opened by the Brecon & Merthyr Railway on May 1st, 1863. The facilities included a coal stage and a water tank. The depot was closed by BR on December 31st, 1962 and was subsequently demolished.

Brecon (MWR) SO0528.1/2A
A brick built 1TS through road shed with a slated gable style pitched roof, it was located at SO05352804 and was opened by the Mid Wales Railway on August 23rd, 1864. The building was made redundant by the GWR in 1922 and it was demolished in c1934.

Site SO0528.0; In the vicinity of Brecon Mount Street Station.
Brecon (N&BR) SO0528.0/1A
A shed was opened here by the Neath & Brecon Railway on June 3rd, 1867 and closed in 1875. No further details are known.

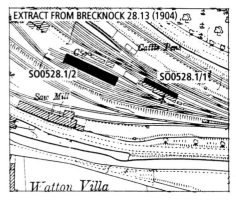

EXTRACT FROM BRECKNOCK 28.13 (1904)
SO0528.1/2
SO0528.1/1
Watton Villa

GURNOS

Site SN7709.0; In the vicinity of Gurnos Junction.
Gurnos (MR) SN7709.0/1A
A timber built 1TS shed was opened here by the Midland Railway in 1865 and closed in 1900. No further details are known.

Replaced by ...
Site SN7709.1; In the fork of the Brynamman and Ynyscedwyn lines at Gurnos Junction.
Gurnos (MR) SN7709.1/1A
A brick built 2TS dead ended shed with a slated gable style pitched roof, it was located at SN77420950 and was opened in 1900. The facilities included a water tower and coal stage. The depot was closed by BR on April 2nd, 1962 and was subsequently demolished.

EXTRACT FROM BRECKNOCK 43.14 (1904)
Gurnos
SN7709.1/1
Aubrey Arms (P.H.)

TALYLLYN JUNCTION

Site SO1127.1; In the triangle of lines at the east end of Talyllyn Junction Station.
Talyllyn Junction (B&MR) SO1127.1/1A
A stone built 2TS through road shed with a slated gable style pitched roof, it was located at SO11062723 and was opened by the Brecon & Merthyr Railway in May 1863. The facilities included a water column. The depot was closed in 1869 and converted to an engine and wagon repair shop.

It was rebuilt ...
Talyllyn Junction (B&MR) SO1127.1/1B
At some stage it was reconstructed in timber as a 3TS dead ended building and was re-opened as an engine shed. By 1903 it had been converted to a carriage shed.

Adjoined by ...
Talyllyn Junction (B&MR) SO1127.1/2A
A dead ended timber built 1TS lean-to shed was added along the southern wall of SO1127.1/1B in c1903. It was located at SO11062721 and was closed by the GWR in October 1922.

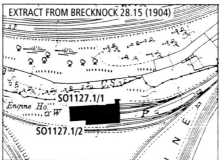

EXTRACT FROM BRECKNOCK 28.15 (1904)
Engine Ho.
SO1127.1/1
SO1127.1/2

TALYBONT ON USK

Site SO1223.1; On the east side of the line, at the north end of Talybont on Usk Station.
Talybont on Usk (B&MR) SO1223.1/1A
A stone built 1TS dead ended shed with a slated gable style pitched roof, it was located at SO12012315 and was opened by the Brecon & Merthyr Railway in 1863. There were no facilities. The depot was closed in 1900 and converted to a goods shed, surviving until the 1960s before being demolished.

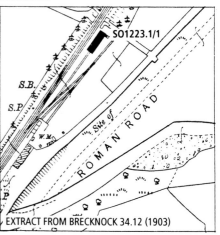

SO1223.1/1
S.B.
S.P.
W.M.
ROMAN ROAD
Site of
EXTRACT FROM BRECKNOCK 34.12 (1903)

RADNORSHIRE

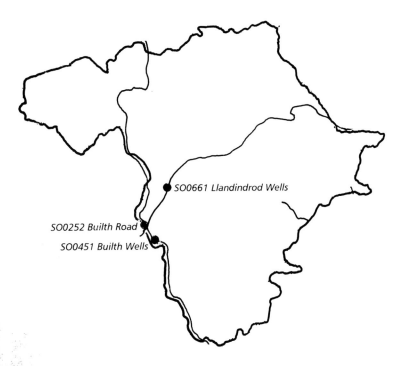

SO0661 Llandindrod Wells

SO0252 Builth Road
SO0451 Builth Wells

BUILTH ROAD

Site SO0252.1; On the west side of the line, south of Builth Road (L&NWR) Station.

Builth Road (L&NWR) SO0252.1/1A

A timber built 1TS dead ended shed with a slated gable style pitched roof, it was located at SO02405290 and was opened in 1870. The facilities included a 42ft turntable. The depot was closed by BR on December 31st, 1962 and was subsequently demolished.

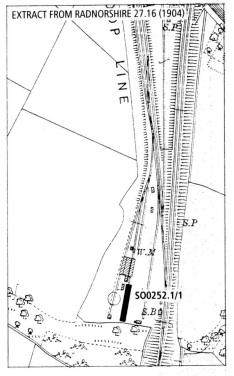

BUILTH WELLS

Site SO0451.1; On the south side of the line, at the east end of Builth Wells Station.

Builth Wells (MWR) SO0451.1/1A

A brick and corrugated iron built 1TS through road shed with a corrugated iron gable style pitched roof, it was located at SO04455160 and was opened by the Mid Wales Railway on September 1st, 1864. The facilities included a turntable and a coal stage. The depot was closed by BR on September 14th, 1957 and was subsequently demolished.

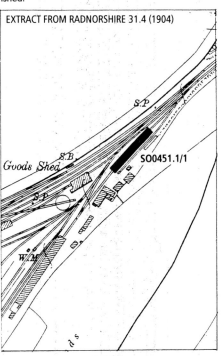

LLANDRINDOD WELLS

Site SO0661.1; In the vicinity of Llandrindod Wells Station.

Llandrindod Wells (L&NWR) SO0661.1/1A

A temporary timber built 3TS shed, approximately located at SO060615, was opened here on October 10th, 1865. The facilities included a coal stage. The depot was closed in 1868 and the building was removed to Llandovery and re-erected as SN7634.2/1A.

MERIONETHSHIRE

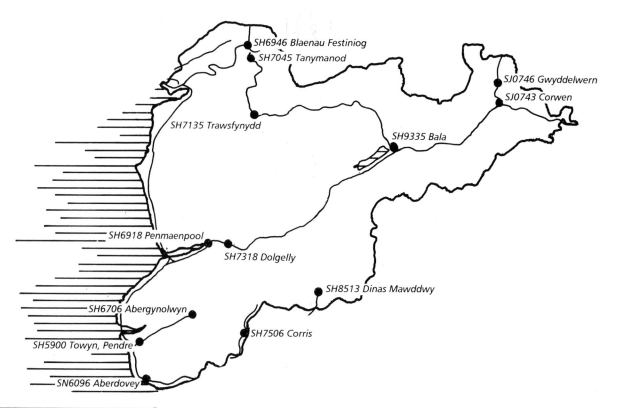

SH6946 Blaenau Festiniog
SH7045 Tanymanod
SJ0746 Gwyddelwern
SJ0743 Corwen
SH7135 Trawsfynydd
SH9335 Bala
SH6918 Penmaenpool
SH7318 Dolgelly
SH8513 Dinas Mawddwy
SH6706 Abergynolwyn
SH7506 Corris
SH5900 Towyn, Pendre
SN6096 Aberdovey

BLAENAU FESTINIOG

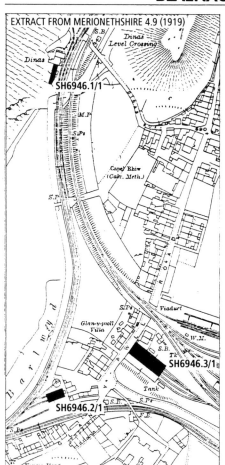

EXTRACT FROM MERIONETHSHIRE 4.9 (1919)

SH6946.1/1

SH6946.3/1

SH6946.2/1

Site SH6946.1; On the west side of the Oakley Quarries branch, north of Dinas Junction.
Dinas (FR) SH6946.1/1A
A 1ft 11.5in gauge stone built 1TS dead ended shed it was located at SH69394640 and was opened by the Festiniog Railway in November 1863. Details of the facilities are not known. Following the construction of a new loop from Dinas Junction and the abandonment of the original line the depot was closed in 1900.

Replaced by ...
Site SH6946.2; In the fork of the lines at Dinas Junction.
Glanypwll (FR) SH6946.2/1A
A 1ft 11.5in gauge 2TS dead ended shed, it was located at SH69394640 and was opened by the Festiniog Railway in 1900. The facilities included a turntable. The depot was utilized until the line closed on August 1st, 1946 and it was later let out for use as a sawmill. At some stage following the re-opening of the line in 1955 the depot was rebuilt in concrete blocks with a corrugated sheeting gable style pitched roof and it was re-instated for railway use as a permanent way depot.

Site SH6946.3; On the south side of the line, at the west end of Blaenau Festiniog (L&NWR) Station.
Blaenau Festiniog (L&NWR) SH6946.3/1A
A stone built 2TS dead ended shed with a slated hipped roof, it was located at SH69474613 and was opened in 1881. It was part of a four road building with the northern 2-road bay utilized for carriages and the remainder for locomotives. The facilities included a water tank and, sited in the goods yard, a turntable. The depot was closed by the LMS on September 14th, 1931 and the building was totally used for carriage storage. It was subsequently demolished.

DINAS MAWDDWY

Site SH8513.1; On the west side of the line, at the south end of Dinas Mawddwy Station.
Dinas Mawddwy (Mawddwy) SH8513.1/1A
A 1TS through road shed, it was located at SH85921381 and was opened by the Mawddwy Railway on October 1st, 1867. Details of the construction and facilities are not known. The depot was closed on April 8th, 1908 and was re-opened by the Cambrian Railway on July 29th, 1911.

The shed was rebuilt in 1911...
Dinas Mawddwy (Cambrian) SH8513.1/1B
A corrugated iron 1TS dead ended shed with a slated gable style pitched roof, but of much reduced length was built on the same site by the Cambrian Railway. The depot was closed by the GWR on January 1st, 1931 and was let out for private use. It was still standing in 1997, in use as a weaving shed.

EXTRACT FROM MERIONETHSHIRE 38.12 (1901)

SH8513.1/1

GWYDDELWERN

Site SJ0746.1; In the vicinity of Gwyddelwern Station.
Gwyddelwern (DG&CR) SJ0746.1/1A
A temporary shed was opened here by the Denbigh, Ruthin & Corwen Railway in March 1863. The line was worked by the Vale of Clwyd Railway and the depot was approximately located at SJ073466. It was closed on October 6th, 1864.

TRAWSFYNYDD

Site SH7135.1; On the south side of the line, at the east end of Trawsfynydd Station.

Trawsfynydd (B&FR) SH7135.1/1A

A brick built 1TS through road shed with a slated lean-to roof, it was attached to the goods shed and was located at SH71473595. It was opened by the Bala & Festiniog Railway on November 1st, 1882 and the facilities included a water tank. The depot was closed by BR in January 1961 and let out for private use. The goods and engine sheds were still standing in 1999, in use as a store.

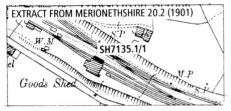

CORRIS

Site SH7506.1; On the west side of the line, south of Corris.

Maespoeth (Corris) SH7506.1/1A

A 2ft 3in gauge stone built 1TS dead ended shed with a slated gable style pitched roof, it was located at SH75290681 and was opened by the Corris Railway in 1879. The building also housed the engine repair shop and the facilities also included a water tank. The depot was closed by BR in July 1st, 1948 and remained standing until the line was taken over for preservation and the shed was re-opened.

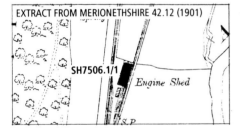

DOLGELLY

Site SH7318.1; On the south side of the line, at the east end of Dolgelly Station.

Dolgelly (B&DR) SH7318.1/F1

A servicing area consisting of a turntable, located at SH73021801, and siding was opened here by the Bala & Dolgelly Railway on August 4th, 1868. The line was absorbed by the GWR in 1877. No further details are known.

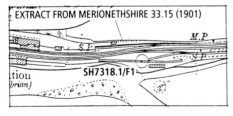

ABERDOVEY

Site SN6096.1; In the vicinity of Aberdovey Station.

Aberdovey (A&WCR) SN6096.1/1A

A temporary shed, approximately located at SN604961, was opened here by the Aberystwyth & Welsh Coast Railway on October 24th, 1863. The line was worked by Savin, a contractor and it was taken over by the Cambrian Railway on July 5th, 1865. The depot was closed on April 14th, 1867. No further details are known.

TOWYN

Site SH5900.1; On the east side of Pendre Station.

Pendre (Talyllyn) SH5900.1/1A

A 2ft 3in gauge stone built 1TS dead ended shed with a slated gable style pitched roof, it was located at SH59100085 and opened by the Talyllyn Railway on October 1st, 1866. The shed formed part of the engine repair works and other facilities included a water tank. The depot was still operational in 1999.

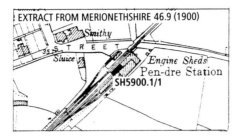

ABERGYNOLWYN

Site SH6706.1; On the south side of the line, east of Abergynolwyn Station.

Abergynolwyn (Talyllyn) SH6706.1/1A

A 2ft 3in gauge timber built 1TS shed, it was located at SH67600660 and was opened by the Talyllyn Railway in 1865. The facilities included a water tank. The depot was closed in 1866, probably upon the opening of Pendre shed (SH5900.1/1A) on October 1st. The building was reduced in size and utilized as a platelayers hut, surviving until c1939 when it was either demolished or collapsed.

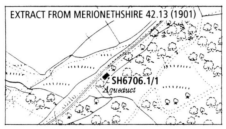

CORWEN

Site SJ0743.1; On the north side of the line, west of Corwen Station.

Corwen (L&C/DR&CR) SJ0743.1/1A

A stone built 2TS through road shed with a slated gable style pitched roof, it was located at SJ07034336 and was opened by the Llangollen & Corwen/Denbigh, Ruthin & Corwen Railway on May 8th, 1865. The facilities included a water tank, coal stage and 45ft turntable. The Denbigh, Ruthin & Corwen Railway was absorbed by the L&NWR on July 15th, 1867 and the Llangollen & Corwen Railway by the GWR in 1896. The GWR vacated the shed in April 1927 and the depot was closed by the LMS on August 6th, 1928.

A servicing point was then established ...

Corwen (LMS) SJ0743.1/F1

The turntable and a siding was utilized for servicing locomotives. The date when the facility was dispensed with is not known.

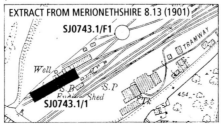

PENMAENPOOL

Site SH6918.1; On the south side of the line, west of Penmaenpool Station.

Penmaenpool (A&WCR) SH6918.1/1A

A timber built 2TS dead ended shed with a slated gable style pitched roof, it was located at SH69201836 and was opened by the Aberystwyth & Welsh Coast Railway on June 1st, 1869. The facilities included a coal stage and water tank.

At some stage the shed was rebuilt ...

Penmaenpool (GWR) SH6918.1/1B

The building was re-clad in corrugated sheeting by the GWR. The depot was closed by BR on January 18th, 1965 and subsequently demolished.

TANYMANOD

Site SH7045.1; On the east side of the line, south of Blaenau Festiniog.

Tanymanod (B&FR) SH7045.1/1A

A brick built 1TS dead ended shed with a slated gable style pitched roof, it was located at SH70634529 and was opened by the Bala & Festiniog Railway on September 10th, 1883. The facilities included a water tank and 45ft turntable. The depot was closed by the GWR in 1906.

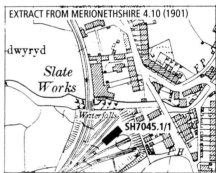

BALA

Site SH9335.1; On the east side of the line, south of Bala Station.

Bala (B&FR) SH9335.1/1A

A brick built 1TS dead ended shed with a slated pitched roof surmounted by a water tank, it was located at SH93143592 and was opened by the Bala & Festiniog Railway on November 1st, 1882. The facilities also included a coal stage. The depot was closed by BR on January 18th, 1965 and was subsequently demolished.

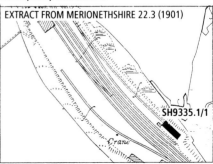

CARNARVONSHIRE

SH7881 Llandudno

SH5771 Bangor

SH4863 Carnarvon

SH4760 Pant

SH4758 Dinas Junction

SH5859 Llanberis

SH7956 Bettws-y-Coed

SH4852 Nantlle

SH5639 Portmadoc

SH5838 Portmadoc Boston Lodge

SH3835 Pwllheli

PWLLHELI

Site SH3835.1; On the north side of the line, at the east end of Pwllheli (1st) Station.

Pwllheli (Cambrian) SH3835.1/1A

A 1TS dead ended shed, possibly built in timber with a slated gable style pitched roof, it was located at SH38373541 and was opened by the Cambrian Railway on October 10th, 1867. Details of the facilities are not known. The depot was closed in 1907 to make way for the extension of the line into the town.

Replaced by ...

Site SH3835.2; On the south side of Pwllheli (1st) Station.

Pwllheli (Cambrian) SH3835.2/1A

A corrugated iron 1TS dead ended shed with a slated gable style pitched roof, it was located at SH38223543 and was opened by the Cambrian Railway in 1907. Details of the facilities are not known. This building had originally been sited to the east of the first depot (SH3835.1/1) and was in use as a carriage shed prior to relocation. By 1955 the depot was very dilapidated and was demolished by BR.

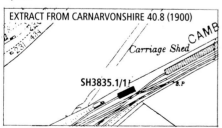

EXTRACT FROM CARNARVONSHIRE 40.8 (1900)

Carriage Shed CAMB

SH3835.1/1

Replaced by ...

Pwllheli (BR) SH3835.2/2A

A brick and glazed built 2TS dead ended shed with a corrugated asbestos gable style pitched roof, it was sited slightly to the south of SH5835.2/1 at SH38263525. The shed was opened by the Western Region in 1958 and the facilities included a coal stage, water columns and turntable. The depot was closed in 1966 and let out for private use. It was still standing, utilized as a coal depot, in 1999.

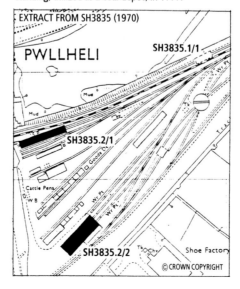

EXTRACT FROM SH3835 (1970)

PWLLHELI

SH3835.1/1

SH3835.2/1

SH3835.2/2

© CROWN COPYRIGHT

CAERNARVON

Site SH4863.0; In the vicinity of Caernarvon Station.

Caernarvon (B&CR) SH4863.0/1A

A shed, approximately located at SH482633, was opened here by the Bangor & Caernarvon Railway on July 1st, 1875. The line was worked by the Chester & Holyhead Railway, leased to it in 1854 and then leased to the L&NWR in 1867. The depot was closed in c1875.

Replaced by ...

Site SH4863.1; On the west side of the line, north of Caernarvon Station.

Caernarvon (L&NWR) SH4863.1/1A

A brick built 2TS dead ended shed with a slated gable style pitched roof, it was located at SH48256340 and was opened in c1875. The facilities included a coal stage, water tank and turntable.

The shed was re-roofed ...

Caernarvon (L&NWR) SH4863.1/1B

At some stage it was rebuilt with a northlight pattern roof. The depot was closed by the LMS on September 14th, 1931 and remained standing in a derelict condition for a number of years before being demolished.

EXTRACT FROM CARNARVONSHIRE 15.4 (1918)

SH4863.1/1

BANGOR

Site SH5771.0; In the vicinity of Bangor Station.
Bangor (C&HR) ^{SH5771.0/1A}
A shed, approximately located at SH575716, was opened here by the Chester & Holyhead Railway on May 1st, 1848. The line was absorbed by the L&NWR on January 1st, 1859 and the depot was closed in 1859. No further details are known.

Replaced by ...
Bangor (L&NWR) ^{SH5771.0/2A}
A shed was opened here by the L&NWR in 1859 and closed in 1884. No further details are known.

Replaced by ...
Site SH5771.1; On the south side of Bangor Station.
Bangor (L&NWR) ^{SH5771.1/1A}
A brick built 6TS dead ended shed with a northlight pattern roof, it was located at SH57567157 and was opened in 1884. The facilities included a coal stage with water tank over and a turntable.

The shed was rebuilt ...
Bangor (BR) ^{SH5771.1/1B}
In 1957 a new roof was installed by the London Midland Region and the length of the shed reduced. The depot closed on June 14th, 1965 and the building was let out for private use. It was still standing in 1999.

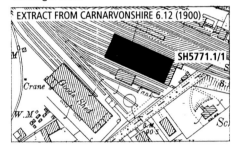

EXTRACT FROM CARNARVONSHIRE 6.12 (1900)
SH5771.1/1

PANT

Site SH4760.1; In the vicinity of Pant (Caernarvon) Station.
Pant (L&NWR) ^{SH4760.1/F1}
A facility consisting of a turntable and siding, probably located at SH47686075 and opened in 1867. No further details are known other than it closed on July 5th, 1870 following the extension of the line to Caernarvon Town Station.

EXTRACT FROM CARNARVONSHIRE 15.8 (1900)
• SH4760.1/F1*

*ASSUMED LOCATION

NANTLLE

Site SH4852.1; At the east end of Nantlle Station.
Nantlle (L&NWR) ^{SH4852.1/F1}
A servicing area consisting of a turntable, located at SH48805294 and siding. No further details are known.

SH4852.1/F1

EXTRACT FROM CARNARVONSHIRE 20.12 & 21.9 (1900)

LLANBERIS

Site SH5859.1; On the east side of the line, at the south end of Llanberis (L&NWR) Station.
Llanberis (L&NWR) ^{SH5859.1/1A}
A stone built 1TS dead ended shed with a slated hipped roof, it was located at SH58145999 and was opened on July 1st, 1869. The facilities included a water tank and turntable. The depot was closed by the LMS on September 22nd, 1930 and was later demolished.

Site SH5859.2; On the west side of the line, at the south end of Llanberis (SMR) Station.
Llanberis (SMR) ^{SH5859.2/1A}
A 2ft 7.5in gauge 2TS dead ended shed, it was located at SH58185969 and was opened by the Snowdon Mountain Railway on April 6th, 1896.

The shed was rebuilt ...
Llanberis (SMR) ^{SH5859.2/1B}
A timber built 3TS dead ended shed with a slated gable style pitched roof was erected on the same site at some time after 1900. The facilities included a water tank and coal stage. The depot was still operational in 1999.

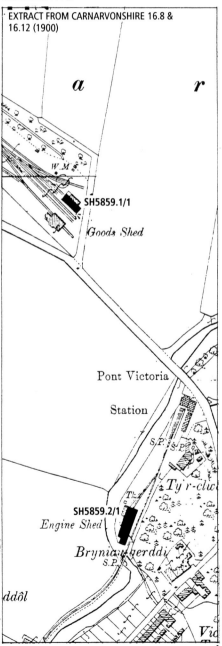

EXTRACT FROM CARNARVONSHIRE 16.8 & 16.12 (1900)

SH5859.1/1

SH5859.2/1

DINAS JUNCTION

Site SH4758.1; On the west side of the line, south of Dinas Junction Station.
Dinas Junction (NWNGR) ^{SH4758.1/1A}
A 1ft 11.5in gauge timber built 2TS dead ended shed with a gable style pitched roof, it was located at SH47615841 and was opened by the North Wales Narrow Gauge Railway on May 21st, 1877. The facilities included a water tank. The line was absorbed by the Welsh Highland Railway in 1922 and leased to the Festiniog Railway on July 1st, 1934. The depot was closed, along with the line, on July 1st, 1937 and was subsequently demolished.

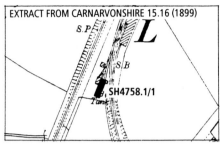

EXTRACT FROM CARNARVONSHIRE 15.16 (1899)
SH4758.1/1

BETTWS-Y-COED

Site SH7956.1; On the west side of the line, north of Bettws-y-Coed Station.
Bettws-y-Coed (L&NWR) ^{SH7956.1/1A}
A stone built 1TS through road shed with a slated gable style roof, it was located at SH79565681 and was opened on April 6th, 1868. The facilities included a water tank. The depot was closed in 1900 and was not demolished immediately, surviving until at least 1932, possibly in goods use.

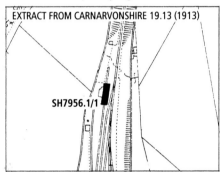

EXTRACT FROM CARNARVONSHIRE 19.13 (1913)
SH7956.1/1

LLANDUDNO

Site SH7881.1; On the west side of the line, south of Llandudno Station.
Llandudno (L&NWR) ^{SH7881.1/F1}
A servicing area consisting of a turntable, located at SH78048163, coal stage and water tank was opened here. No further details are known.

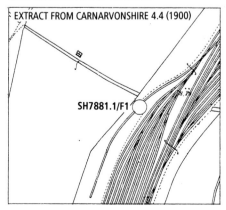

EXTRACT FROM CARNARVONSHIRE 4.4 (1900)
SH7881.1/F1

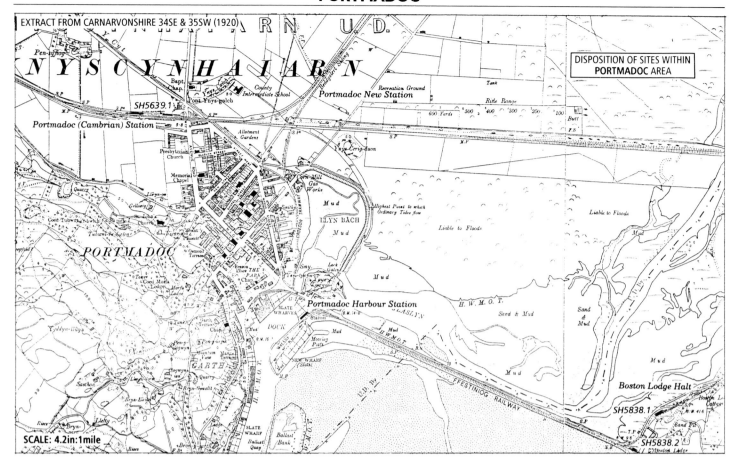

EXTRACT FROM CARNARVONSHIRE 34SE & 35SW (1920)

DISPOSITION OF SITES WITHIN **PORTMADOC** AREA

SCALE: 4.2in:1mile

Site SH5639.1; On the north side of the line, at the west end of Portmadoc Station.

Portmadoc (Cambrian) SH5639.1/1A

A corrugated iron ITS through road shed with a slated gable style pitched roof, it was located at SH56453921 and was opened by the Cambrian Railway on October 10th, 1867. Details of the facilities are not known. The depot was closed in 1907.

Replaced, on the same site, by ...

Portmadoc (Cambrian) SH5639.1/1B

A brick built 2TS dead ended shed with a slated gable style pitched roof, it was opened by the Cambrian Railway in 1907. The facilities included a water tank. The depot was closed by BR in August 1963 and was subsequently demolished.

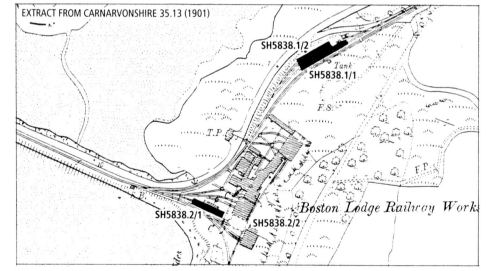

EXTRACT FROM CARNARVONSHIRE 35.13 (1901)

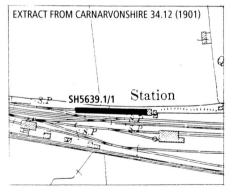

EXTRACT FROM CARNARVONSHIRE 34.12 (1901)

Station

Site SH5838.1; On the west side of the line at the south end of Boston Lodge Halt.

Boston Lodge (Festiniog) SH5838.1/1A

A 1ft 11.5in gauge stone built 2TS shed with one through road and a slated gable style pitched roof, it was located at SH58553898 and was opened by the Festiniog Railway in 1863.

The shed was enlarged ...

Boston Lodge (Festiniog) SH5838.1/1B

The building was extended at its eastern end in 1892.

Adjoined by ...

Boston Lodge (Festiniog) SH5838.1/2A

A 1ft 11.5in gauge timber built ITS dead ended shed with a slated gable style roof was built alongside the northern wall of SH5838.1/1. It was located at SH58553899 and was opened in 1887.

The facilities included a water tank and 22ft turntable. The depot was closed on August 1st, 1946. Upon re-opening of the line in 1955 the buildings were utilized for carriage storage.

Replaced by ...

Site SH5838.2; In Boston Lodge Works.

Boston Lodge (Festiniog) SH5838.2/1A

A 1ft 11.5in gauge stone built ITS dead ended shed with a slated gable style pitched roof, it was located at SH58443885 and was opened in 1956. The building had originally been utilized as the works Paint Shop. Details of the facilities are not known. The depot was closed in 1988 and demolished.

Replaced by ...

Boston Lodge (Festiniog) SH5838.2/2A

A 1ft 11.5in gauge corrugated steel 3TS dead ended shed with a gable style corrugated steel pitched roof, it was located at SH58473883 and was opened in c1988. The depot was still operational in 1999.

FLINT

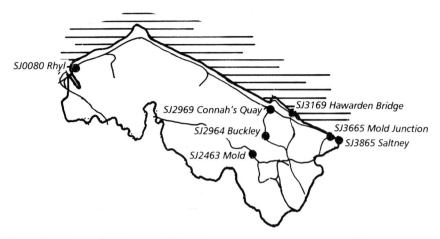

MOLD

Site SJ2463.1; On the east side of the line, at the south end of Mold Station.
Mold (Mold) SJ2463.1/1A
A 2TS through road shed, it was located at SJ24126385 and was opened by the Mold Railway on August 14th, 1849. Details of the facilities are not known. The line was worked by the L&NWR and they closed the depot in 1890. It was not demolished immediately, being utilized as a grain warehouse for some years.

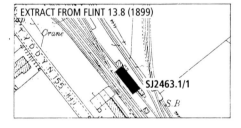

EXTRACT FROM FLINT 13.8 (1899)
SJ2463.1/1

BUCKLEY

Site SJ2964.1; In the fork of the lines at the south end of Buckley Station.
Buckley (WM&CQR) SJ2964.1/1A
A 1TS dead ended shed, it was located at SJ29026427 and was opened by the Wrexham, Mold & Connah's Quay Railway in 1896. Details of the facilities are not known other than a turntable was available some 500 yards north of the depot. It was closed in June 1919 and was subsequently demolished.

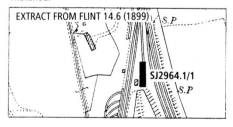

EXTRACT FROM FLINT 14.6 (1899)
SJ2964.1/1

HAWARDEN BRIDGE

Site SJ3169.1; In the vicinity of Hawarden Bridge Station.
Hawarden Bridge (MS&LR) SJ3169.1/1A
Some sort of facility, approximately located at SJ311695 was opened here on August 3rd, 1889 and closed by the GCR in 1920. No further details are known.

MOLD JUNCTION

Site SJ3665.1; On the south side of Saltney Ferry Station.
Mold Junction (L&NWR) SJ3665.1/1A
A brick built 8TS dead ended shed with a northlight pattern roof, it was located at SJ36846514 and was opened on October 1st, 1890. The facilities included a coal stage with water tank over and a 42ft turntable. The yard layout was altered by the LMS and modification included an improved coal plant and a larger 60ft turntable.

The shed was re-roofed ...
Mold Junction (BR) SJ3665.1/1B
An LMS-style louvre roof with brick screen was installed by the London Midland Region in 1948. The depot was closed on April 18th, 1966 and was let out for private use. The building was still standing in 1997.

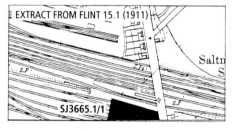

EXTRACT FROM FLINT 15.1 (1911)
SJ3665.1/1

CONNAH'S QUAY

Site SJ2969.1; On the east side of the Buckley line, south of Connah's Quay Station.
Connah's Quay (WM&CQR) SJ2969.1/1A
A 1TS dead ended shed, it was located at SJ29346948 and was opened by the Wrexham, Mold & Connah's Quay Railway in 1875. The facilities included a water column. The depot was closed in June 1919 and it was subsequently demolished.

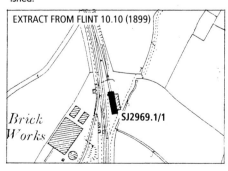

EXTRACT FROM FLINT 10.10 (1899)
Brick Works
SJ2969.1/1

RHYL

Site SJ0080.1; On the west side of the line, south of Rhyl Station.
Rhyl (VofCR) SJ0080.1/1A
A shed was opened here by the Vale of Clwyd Railway on October 5th, 1858. It was probably 1TS and was located at SJ00668096. The line was absorbed by the L&NWR on July 15th, 1867 and the depot was closed in 1870. No further details are known.

Replaced, on the same site, by ...
Rhyl (L&NWR) SJ0080.1/1B
A brick built 3TS dead ended shed with a slated gable style roof, it was opened in 1870. The facilities included a water column and a turntable, sited at the station.

The shed was enlarged ...
Rhyl (L&NWR) SJ0080.1/1C
The building was extended to double its length in c1900. At the same time the turntable was re-sited in the shed yard.

The shed was re-roofed ...
Rhyl (LMS) SJ0080.1/1D
In 1938 an LMS-style louvre roof with a brick screen was installed, and the turntable was replaced with a 60ft unit. The depot was closed by BR on February 11th, 1963 and was subsequently utilized as a pw depot. It was later demolished.

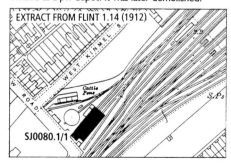

EXTRACT FROM FLINT 1.14 (1912)
SJ0080.1/1

SALTNEY

Site SJ3865.1; In Saltney Works.
Saltney (NWMR) SJ3865.1/1A
A 1TS shed, it was approximately located at SJ386650 and was opened by the North Wales Mineral Railway on November 4th, 1846. The depot was closed in 1854 after the line was amalgamated with the GWR and the works were altered to carriage and wagon repairs only. No further details are known.

DENBIGH

SH8579 Colwyn
SH7977 Llandudno Junction
SJ0567 Denbigh
SH7962 Llanrwst
SJ1258 Ruthin
SJ2953 Brymbo
SJ2952 Vron
SJ3350 Wrexham Central
SJ2037 Glynceiriog
SJ3154 Ffrwd Junction
SJ3153 Summerhill
SJ3351 Rhosddu
SJ3250 Croes Newydd
SJ2943 Ruabon
SJ2742 Pontcysyllte
SJ2837 Chirk

SUMMERHILL

Site SJ3153.1; On the north side of the Wheatsheaf branch, at the east end of Westminster Colliery tunnel.

Summerhill (NWMR) SJ3153.1/1A
A stone built 1TS dead ended shed with a slated gable style pitched roof, it was located at SJ31155344 and was built by the Shrewsbury & Chester Railway for the North Wales Mineral Railway in 1847. There were no facilities. The depot was closed in September 1902 and demolished in November 1904.

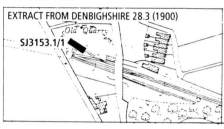

EXTRACT FROM DENBIGHSHIRE 28.3 (1900)
SJ3153.1/1

RUABON

Site SJ2943.1; On the north side of the line, at the west end of Ruabon Station.

Ruabon (S&CR) SJ2943.1/1A
A 1TS shed, it was located at SJ29984379 and was opened by the Shrewsbury & Chester Railway on November 4th, 1846. The facilities included a 35ft turntable. The line was absorbed by the GWR in 1854 and the depot was closed in the same year. Although the building was demolished the facilities may have remained in use until the opening of the Corwen line in 1865.

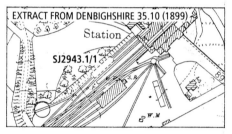

EXTRACT FROM DENBIGHSHIRE 35.10 (1899)
Station
SJ2943.1/1

TREVOR

Site SJ2742.1; On the east side of the line, at the end of the Pontcysyllte branch.

Pontcysyllte (L&NWR/SUR) SJ2742.1/1A
A stone built 2TS shed with one through road and a slated gable style pitched roof, it was located at SJ27244248 and was opened by the L&NWR/Shropshire Union Railway in 1863. The building was unusual in that the engine shed occupied one half and a boarded over canal, in which the goods department was housed, the other. The facilities included a coal stage and water tank. The line was leased to the GWR on February 12th, 1896 and the depot was closed in September 1902.

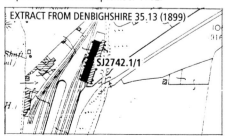

EXTRACT FROM DENBIGHSHIRE 35.13 (1899)
SJ2742.1/1

BRYMBO

Site SJ2953.1; On the west side of the line, north of Brymbo (GWR) Station.

Brymbo (NWMR) SJ2953.1/1A
A 2TS dead ended shed, it was located at SJ29615377 and was opened by the North Wales Mineral Railway in November 1847. The facilities included a water tank. The line was worked by the Shrewsbury & Chester Railway and the depot was closed in 1872.

Replaced, on the same site, by ...
Brymbo (GWR) SJ2953.1/1B
A stone built 1TS dead ended shed with a slated gable style pitched roof, it opened in 1872. The depot was closed in September 1902 and subsequently demolished.

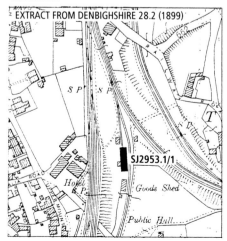

EXTRACT FROM DENBIGHSHIRE 28.2 (1899)
SJ2953.1/1

GLYNCEIRIOG

Site SJ2037.1; On the north side of Glynceiriog Station.

Glynceiriog (GVT) SJ2037.1/1A
A 2ft 4.5in gauge timber built 1TS dead ended shed with a slated gable style pitched roof, it was located at SJ20293782 and was opened by the Glyn Valley Tramway in June 1888. The facilities included a turntable, sited outside of the shed entrance. Although the depot was closed, along with the line, on July 6th, 1935 it found further use and was still standing in 1993.

EXTRACT FROM DENBIGHSHIRE 39.10 (1900)
SJ2037.1/1

VRON

Site SJ2952.1; On the west side of the line, at the end of the Vron branch.

Vron (WM&CQR) SJ2952.1/1A
A 1TS dead ended shed, it was located at SJ29345235 and was opened by the Wrexham, Mold & Connah's Quay Railway in c1905. The depot was probably closed in 1940, at the same time as the line. There are no further details.

EXTRACT FROM DENBIGHSHIRE 28.6 (1900)
SJ2952.1/1

WREXHAM

Site SJ3350.0; In the vicinity of Wrexham Central Station.
Wrexham (WM&CQR) SJ3350.0/1A
A 2TS shed was opened here by the Wrexham, Mold & Connah's Quay Railway on January 1st, 1866. The line became part of the GCR in 1901 and the building was destroyed in a storm in 1910. No further details are known*.

Replaced by ...
Site SJ3351.1; On the west side of the line, north of Wrexham General Station.
Rhosddu (GCR) SJ3351.1/1A
A brick built 6TS dead ended shed with a transverse multi-pitched roof, it was located at SJ33005161 and was opened in 1912. The facilities included a water tank and ramped coal stage.

The shed was modified ...
Rhosddu (BR) SJ3351.1/1B
At some stage the building was reduced in length by the London Midland Region. The depot was closed on January 4th, 1960 and was subsequently demolished.

*This shed may have previously occupied the same site as Rhosddu (SJ3351.1/1A).

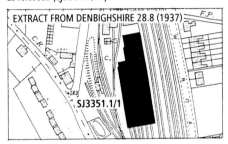
EXTRACT FROM DENBIGHSHIRE 28.8 (1937)
SJ3351.1/1

Site SJ3350.1; On the south side of the line, at the west end of Wrexham Central Station.
Wrexham Central (W&ER) SJ3350.1/1A
A corrugated iron 1TS dead ended shed with a slated gable style pitched roof, it was located at SJ33155032 and was opened by the Wrexham & Ellesmere Railway on November 2nd, 1895. The facilities included a water tank and turntable. The line was worked by the Cambrian Railway and the depot was closed by the GWR in September 1925. The building was dismantled and re-erected at Aberayron (as SN4662.1/1B).

EXTRACT FROM DENBIGHSHIRE 28.8 (1909)
SJ3350.1/1

Site SJ3250.1; In the triangle of lines at Croes Newydd Junction.
Croes Newydd (GWR) SJ3250.1/1A
A brick built 1RH shed with a slated northlight pattern roof, it was located at SJ32705013 and was opened in 1902. The facilities included a coal stage, with water tank over, and a repair shop.

The shed was re-roofed ...
Croes Newydd (GWR) SJ3250.1/1B
The roof was renewed in 1924 and the depot was closed by BR on June 5th, 1967.

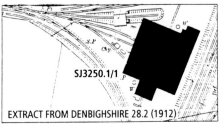
SJ3250.1/1
EXTRACT FROM DENBIGHSHIRE 28.2 (1912)

LLANDUDNO JUNCTION

Site SH7977.1; On the south side of Llandudno Junction Station.
Llandudno Junction (StGHC) SH7977.1/1A
A shed was opened here by the St.George's Harbour Company on October 1st, 1858. It is assumed to have been a 2TS building and may possibly have been located at SH79497776. The line was leased to the L&NWR in 1862 and absorbed by them on July 28th, 1873. The depot closed in 1880.

Replaced by ...
Llandudno Junction (L&NWR) SH7977.1/2A
A brick built 4TS dead ended shed with a northlight pattern roof, it was sited south of its predecessor (SH7977.1/1) at SH79557755. The depot opened in 1880 and the facilities included a coal stage, water pump and turntable.

The shed was enlarged ...
Llandudno Junction (L&NWR) SH7977.1/2B
In 1899 the building was increased to 320ft in length and made into a through road shed.

The shed was re-roofed ...
Llandudno Junction (BR) SH7977.1/2C
An LMS-style louvre roof with brick screen was installed by the London Midland Region in 1957. The depot closed on October 3rd, 1966 and was later demolished.

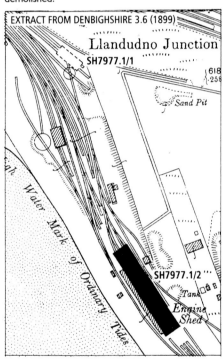
EXTRACT FROM DENBIGHSHIRE 3.6 (1899)
Llandudno Junction
SH7977.1/1
Sand Pit
Water Mark of Ordinary Tides
SH7977.1/2
Tank
Engine Shed

CHIRK

Site SJ2837.1; On the west side of the line, at the north end of Chirk Station.
Chirk (GVT) SJ2837.1/1A
A 2ft 4.5in gauge 1TS through road shed, it was located at SJ28413791 and was opened by the Glyn Valley Tramway in June 1888. The facilities included a turntable sited outside of the shed entrance. The depot was closed, along with the line, on July 6th, 1935.

SJ2837.1/1
EXTRACT FROM DENBIGHSHIRE 40.10 (1899)

DENBIGH

Site SJ0566.1; In the vicinity of Denbigh Station.
Denbigh (VofCR) SJ0566.1/1A
A shed, approximately located at SJ057666, was opened here by the Vale of Clwyd Railway in 1864. The line was absorbed by the L&NWR on July 15th, 1867 and the depot was closed in 1870. No further details are known.

Replaced by ...
Site SJ0567.1; On the east side of the line, north of Denbigh Station.
Denbigh (L&NWR) SJ0567.1/1A
A brick built 2TS dead ended shed with a slated gable style pitched roof, it was located at SJ05896707 and was opened in 1870. The facilities included a coal stage, water tank and 42ft turntable.

The shed was re-roofed ...
Denbigh (LMS) SJ0567.1/1B
A louvre style roof with brick screen was installed in 1947. The depot was closed by BR on September 19th, 1955 and the building was let for private use. It was still standing in 1996.

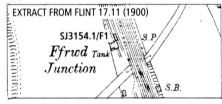
EXTRACT FROM DENBIGHSHIRE 13.4 (1899)
SJ0567.1/1

FFRWD JUNCTION

Site SJ3154.1; On the west side of Ffrwd Junction.
Ffrwd Junction (WM&CQR) SJ3154.1/F1
A servicing area consisting of a water tank and siding, it was located at SJ31375472 and was opened by the Wrexham, Mold & Connah's Quay Railway on January 1st, 1866. No further details are known.

EXTRACT FROM FLINT 17.11 (1900)
SJ3154.1/F1
Ffrwd Tank Junction

RUTHIN

Site SJ1258.1; In the vicinity of Ruthin Station.
Ruthin (DR&CR) SJ1258.1/1A
A shed, approximately located at SJ126585, was opened here by the Denbigh, Ruthin & Corwen Railway in 1866. The line was worked by the Vale of Clwyd Railway and it was absorbed by the L&NWR on July 15th, 1867. No further details are known.

LLANRWST

Site SH7962.1; In the vicinity of Llanrwst Station.
Llanrwst (C&LR) SH7962.1/1A
A 1TS shed, approximately located at SH795623, was opened here by the Conway & Llanrwst Railway in September 1867. The facilities included a water tank. The depot was closed in 1881 and was subsequently demolished.

COLWYN

Site SH8579.1; In the vicinity of Colwyn Station.
Colwyn (L&NWR) SH8579.1/1A
A 1TS shed, approximately located at SH853790, was opened here in 1848 and closed in 1880. No further details are known.

ANGLESEY

SH4392 Amlwch

SH2383 Holyhead, Soldiers Point

SH2481 Holyhead

SH5211 Llanfair

HOLYHEAD

Site SH2481.1; On the west side of the line, south of Holyhead Station.
Holyhead (C&HR) ^{SH2481.1/1A}
A 4TS through road shed, it was located at SH24878182 and was opened by the Chester & Holyhead Railway on August 1st, 1848. The facilities included a repair shop. The depot was closed in 1861 and the building was converted to a wagon works, surviving until at least 1967 before being demolished.

Replaced by ...
Site SH2481.2; On the east side of the line, south of Holyhead Station.
Holyhead (L&NWR) ^{SH2481.2/1A}
A stone built 4TS through road shed with a twin gable style slated pitched roof, it was located at SH24928187 and was opened in 1861. The facilities included a coal stage, water column and a 40ft turntable (Later re-sited and enlarged to 45ft).

The shed was re-roofed ...
Holyhead (BR) ^{SH2481.2/1B}
An LMS-style louvre roof with brick screen was installed by the London Midland Region in 1950. The depot was closed to steam on December 5th, 1966 and continued to service diesel locomotives until c1990. It was subsequently demolished.

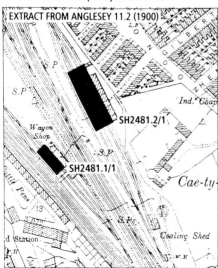

EXTRACT FROM ANGLESEY 11.2 (1900)

SH2481.2/1

SH2481.1/1

Site SH2383.1; On the south side of the line at Soldier's Point.
Soldier's Point (HB) ^{SH2383.1/1A}
A stone built 2TS dead ended shed with a slated gable style pitched roof, it was located at SH23528357. The depot was built by the Holyhead Breakwater Tramway and the facilities included a water tank. The line was originally connected to the national network but at some time prior to 1900 the spur was removed. During L&NWR and LMS days contractors locomotives were utilized intermittently as the need arose. The depot was effectively closed to steam by BR in 1966 when the diesel service locomotive ED6 was allocated here. The building was still standing in 1996, in use as a maintenance workshop.

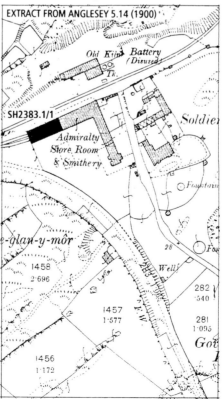

EXTRACT FROM ANGLESEY 5.14 (1900)

SH2383.1/1

AMLWCH

Site SH4392.0; In the vicinity of Amlwch Station.
Amlwch (ACR) ^{SH4392.0/1A}
A 1TS shed was opened here by the Anglesey Central Railway on June 3rd, 1867. The line was worked by a contractor until it was taken over by the L&NWR in 1868. It was absorbed by them on July 1st, 1876 and the depot was closed in 1878. No further details are known.

Replaced by ...
Site SH4392.1; On the north side of the line, west of Amlwch Station.
Amlwch (L&NWR) ^{SH4392.1/1A}
A stone built 1TS through road shed with a slated gable style roof, it was located at SH43909272 and was opened in 1878. There were no facilities. The depot was closed by the LMS on September 14th, 1931 and was subsequently demolished.

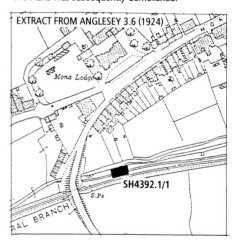

EXTRACT FROM ANGLESEY 3.6 (1924)

SH4392.1/1

LLANFAIR

Site SH5211.1; In the vicinity of Llanfair Station.
Llanfair (C&HR) ^{SH5211.1/1A}
A temporary shed, approximately located at SH526116, was opened here by the Chester & Holyhead Railway on August 1st, 1848. It was made redundant upon the opening of the Britannia Tubular Bridge on March 18th, 1850 and was removed in 1851. No further details are known.

This marvellous human and locomotive portrait from around 1867 gives the only known glimpse of the Midland Railway's shed (TL1929.3/1A) at **Hitchin** in its original guise, with the ornate brickwork typical of the period.

On December 11th, 1891 the building would largely be destroyed in a storm, with subsequent rebuilding in a more restrained style of brickwork (as TL1923.3/1B). Nevertheless the rebuilt structure continued to stand into the 1980s, latterly utilized by National Carriers.   *Author's Collection*

(See Page 106)

When the Great Northern Railway started running services to **Cambridge** its engines were housed at the Great Eastern shed (TL4657.2/1A). However, after some years and under the terms of an agreement somewhat biased in favour of the GNR, the GE provided its "guest" with a shed of its own (TL4656.2/1A), sited at the south eastern corner of the goods yard.

That 3TS building is seen here on August 8th, 1939, some 15 years after closure to locomotives and re-use as a wagon works. That duty finally ceased and the building was removed in 1985.

WA Camwell

(See Page 141)

A 2TS Midland Railway shed (SP0344.3/1A) was put up at **Evesham** in 1871. Despite the fact that the building is said to have survived until 1951 photographic evidence has, so far, been very sparse. Hence the inclusion of this picture dating from around 1905, which was doubtlessly taken to display the considerable damage done to MR 0-6-0 No.700 in an accident. What is more interesting, though is that the picture also offers a rare glimpse of Evesham's wooden MR engine shed.

Author's Collection

(See Page 144)

Eccentricity abounded in the Welsh border railways. This included the Potteries, Shrewsbury & North Western Railway which, at its western end, made junction with the Cambrian at **Llanymynech** where a 1TS shed (SJ2721.1/1A) was provided.

The PS&NWR opened in 1866 and closed in 1880. In 1911 it was revived as the Shropshire & Montgomeryshire Railway but the shed at Llanymynech was never re-opened. It is partly seen here, on the left, during the period of dormancy.

Author's Collection

(See Page 148)

With the re-opening of the PS&NW in 1911 as the Shropshire & Montgomeryshire Railway, the new company provided itself with a locomotive operating base at **Kinnerley Junction**, comprising of the 2TS shed (SJ3319.1/1A) seen here, with the famous 2-2-2 *Gazelle* outside, the date is just prior to opening.

The S&MR passed to the War Department in 1939 and closed in 1960. In 1999 much of the rebuilt shed still stood, utilized as a store house.

Ian Allan Library

(See Page 149)

Four railways served Shrewsbury in the earliest days, each company erecting its own locomotive shed. Not surprisingly these early buildings rarely appear in photographs, but we are indeed fortunate that a portrait of ex-S&HR 2-2-2 No.219 shows, in the background, the 3TS Shrewsbury & Birmingham Railway shed (SO5012.1.1A) at **Abbey Foregate**. The date is around 1860, eleven years after opening and five years before closure and demolition. However, the office building just visible in the background stood into the 1970s.

Author's Collection

(See Page 150)

Delightfully eccentric, the Bishop's Castle Railway was intended to run from the Shrewsbury & Hereford line near Craven Arms to the Oswetry & Newtown, near Montgomery. The closest that it got to the latter was **Bishop's Castle** itself and even then this involved a reversal in the middle of Lydham Heath! The idiosyncrasy continued in that the BCR was specifically excluded from the Grouping, so after unsuccessfully trying to get the mighty GWR to buy it, the BCR finally closed in 1935.

A small engine shed (SO3288.1/1A) at Bishop's Castle sufficed for all the line's history and this is seen here in May 1932. The authors have long pondered upon the purpose of the signal beside the shed - further idiosyncrasy perhaps or, when operated, a sign that a passenger might be waiting for that superb bus? *HC Casserley*

(See Page 149)

The Cleobury Mortimer & Ditton Priors Railway opened in 1908 and, initially, use was made of the engine shed (SO6876.1/1A) at **Cleobury Town** put up by the contractor who built the line. This somewhat ramshackle building, with attendant water tank and coal stage, is here depicted about 1909, some eight years before replacement by a concrete building (SO6877.1/1A) sited to the left of the picture.

The second shed closed in 1938 but was "visited" by locomotives until the 1965 closure of the line. Even so, the abandoned and decrepit, remains of the concrete shed were still to be seen in 1999. *Author's Collection*

(See Page 151)

The head of the valley town of **Merthyr** had four engine sheds over the years; A Vale of Neath Railway building (SO0505.2/1A) giving way to one of GWR origins (SO0505.2/1B), and two Taff Vale Railway Sheds (SO0505.1/1A & 1/2A), the second serving from 1846 to 1923. Fortunately, it was not immediately dispensed with so, when in 1931, the GWR shed underwent major alterations *(as SO0505.2/1C)*, some of its stud of locomotives were housed for a few months at the re-opened TVR shed.

We are indeed fortunate that a picture was taken during that brief period of resurrection as, soon after, the TVR building underwent a demolition process that lasted for several years. *Allan Sommerfield*

(See Page 176)

With its origins in the Oystermouth Railway, the Swansea & Mumbles Railway was worked by steam locomotives between 1877 and 1929, when electric tramcars took over. The steam engines were kept in the rather rudimentary **Swansea (S&MR)** shed (SS6592.4/1A) seen here, in a picture dating from a year or two before closure.   *Author's Collection*

(See Page 181)

As a railhead for the years between 1868 and 1879, **Bettws-y-Coed** was provided with an engine shed (SH7956.1/1A) which did not close, in fact, until 1900. After that the building stood until around 1934, but its attendant water tank and siding were still utilized for servicing locomotives for a further period of years. The elusive shed is seen here, on the right, on June 3rd, 1932.   *HC Casserley*

(See Page 197)

Opened by the Wrexham, Mold & Connah's Quay Company in 1875 the engine shed (SJ2969.1/1A) at **Connah's Quay** served until 1919, after which its site was utilized for occasional servicing. The site of the shed, with its former pit, is shown here at an unknown date, but it is evident from the cinders between the rails beside the water column that locomotives regularly stood here.

A Brown, cty John Hooper

(See Page 199)

INDEX

APPENDIX

Throughout this volume the more well known railway companies are identified merely by initials that are not expanded upon in the text. In order to assist those readers not totally familiar with these a short list is reproduced below;

GCR; *Great Central Railway*
GER; *Great Eastern Railway*
GNR; *Great Northern Railway*
GWR; *Great Western Railway*
L&NWR; *London & North Western Railway*
L&SWR or LSWR; *London & South Western Railway*
LB&SCR; *London, Brighton & South Coast Railway*
LC&DR; *London, Chatham & Dover Railway*
LMS; *London Midland & Scottish Railway*
LNER; *London & North Eastern Railway*
LT; *London Transport*
LT&SR; *London Tilbury & Southend Railway*
Met; *Metropolitan Railway*
MR; *Midland Railway*
NSR; *North Staffordshire Railway*
SECR or SE&CR; *South Eastern & Chatham Railway*
SER; *South Eastern Railway*
SR; *Southern Railway*
TVR; *Taff Vale Railway*

The importance of the railway crossroads of Peterborough was exemplified by the fact that over the years it sported no less than eight engine sheds! Two of these were of London & Birmingham/ L&NWR origin with the former's 2TS shed at Peterborough East (TL1997.1/3A) opening in May 1845. This edifice sufficed until growing traffic decreed the need for a larger shed (TL1998.1/1A) which was finally put up at a site sometimes known as **Peterborough Water End**.

The standard Webb northlight pattern building is seen here in 1950 (as TL1998.1/1B) some 18 years after closure and another fifteen before the building was finally demolished. Today the *Nene Valley Railway* intends to open its International Museum of Locomotives on the same site so, with luck, Water End will one day host an engine shed again.

H Garrett Collection

ADDENDA

CORNWALL

P.10 **Bude** (SS2105.1/1A). *Steam locomotive servicing ceased in January 1965.*

P.10 **Delabole** (SX0783.1/1A). *It closed in 1897*

P.11 **Falmouth** (SX8132.1/F1). *The steam servicing area closed in March, 1962.*

P.11 **Launceston** (SX3384.1/1A). *The depot closed on March 1952 and the turntable closed in June 1963.*

P.11 **Liskeard** (SX2463.1/1A). *The servicing facility closed in April, 1918.*

P.11 **Looe** (SX2553.1/1A). *Closed in April 1917.*

P.13 **Padstow** (SW9275.1/F2). *The facility closed in January 1967.*

P.14 **Truro** (SW8144.2/1A). *The depot may have closed to steam in March 1962.*

SOMERSET

P.20 **Bridgwater North** (ST3037.2/1A). *The shed closed in 1922 and the turntable and servicing area ceased to be utilized in October 1954.*

P.22 **Glastonbury** (ST4838.1/1A). *The temporary facility closed in August 1859.*

P.22 **Highbridge** (ST3246.1/1A). *Locomotive servicing continued until March 1966.*

P.26 **Wells Priory Road** (ST5445.2/1B). *The depot closed in October 1947.*

DEVON

P.32 **Exeter Queen Street** (SX9293.1/F1). *Servicing ceased in March 1931.*

P.33 **Ilfracombe**. *The first shed (SS5146.1/1A) was closed in July 1928 and the second (SS5146.2/1A) in September 1964.*

P.34 **Meldon Quarry** (SX5692.1/1B). *It was closed to steam in October 1966.*

P.34 **Moretonhampstead** (SX7585.1/1A). *Servicing locomotives ceased in February 1959.*

P.36 **Sidmouth** (SY1288.1/1B). *The turntable was closed in 1932 and the shed in 1938.*

HAMPSHIRE

P.51 **Brockenhurst** (SU3001.1/F1). *The servicing area closed in December 1965.*

P.52 **Fratton** (SU6500.1/1B). *The shed was totally closed in October 1966.*

P.52 **Redbridge Sleeper Depot** (SU3713.1/1A). *The shed was closed in March 1967.*

P.54 **Southampton New Docks**. *Both of the facilities (SU4011.1/F1 & SU3912.1/F1) closed in July 1967.*

GREATER LONDON

P.83 **Richmond** (TQ1875.2/F1). *The facility was closed in March 1936.*

P.87 **Clapham Junction** (TQ2775.1/1A). *The shed was opened in 1860.*

P.91 **Marylebone Goods** (TQ2782.3/1A). *The shed was closed in 1914.*

P.92 **Ranelagh Road** (TQ2581.2/F1). *It was opened in 1908 and was closed to steam in January 1966.*

P.94 **Addiscombe** (TQ3366.1/F1). *The turntable was resited in 1899 and the facility was closed in July 1926.*

P.97 **Holloway Carriage Sidings** (TQ3085.1/F1). *The servicing area was closed between 1913 and 1947.*

P.98 **Fenchurch Street Station** (TQ3380.2/F1). *The facility was opened in 1858 and closed at some point between 1916 and 1932.*

P.98 **Plaistow** (TQ3983.2/1A). *The shed was totally closed in June 1962.*

P.99 **Canning Town** (TQ3981.1/F1). *It was opened prior to 1894 and closed in February 1957.*

P.99 **Devonshire Street Goods** (TQ3582.1/F1). *The facility was closed in January 1957.*

P.100 **Stratford Dept Shed** (TQ3884.2/3A). *It was probably opened in 1930.*

P.101 **Holborn Viaduct** (TQ3181.1/F1). *The shed was closed in July 1939.*

P.102 **Chingford**. *Both the facilities (TQ3994.1/F1 & TQ3994.2/F1) were closed in November 1960.*

Additional Depots ...

BLACKHEATH

Site TQ3975.1; On the north side of the line, west of Blackheath Station.

Blackheath (SE&CR) TQ3975.1/F1

A servicing area consisting of sidings, it was approximately located at TQ39207599 and was opened in 1901. The facility was dispensed with by the SR in June 1926.

MAZE HILL

Site TQ3977.1; In the vicinity of Maze Hill Station.

Maze Hill (SE&CR) TQ3977.1/F1

A servicing area consisting of sidings, it was approximately located at TQ39207790 and was opened in 1901. The facility was dispensed with by the SR in June 1926.

PLUMSTEAD

Site TQ4578.1; On the north side of the line, east of Plumstead Station.

Plumstead (SE&CR) TQ4578.1/F1

A servicing area consisting of sidings, it was approximately located at TQ45107890 and was opened in 1901. The facility was dispensed with by the SR in June 1926.

RIPPLE LANE

Site TQ4783.1; On the south side of the line, west of Dagenham Dock Station.

Ripple Lane (BR) TQ4783.1/F1

A servicing area consisting of a turntable, located at TQ47278391and siding, it was opened by the Eastern Region in 1958. The facility was dispensed with in May 1968.

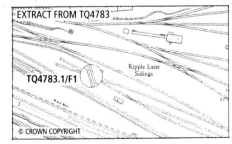

EXTRACT FROM TQ4783

TQ4783.1/F1

Ripple Lane Sidings

© CROWN COPYRIGHT

HERTFORDSHIRE

P.104 **Buntingford** (TL3628.1/F1). *A turntable existed until 1890.*

P.106 **Watford** (TQ1197.1/1A). *The depot was extended to two roads in 1862 (as TQ1197.1/1B).*

OXFORDSHIRE

P.108 **Banbury** (SP4640.2/F1). *The servicing point may have closed to steam in October 1956.*

GLOUCESTERSHIRE

P.110 **Ashchurch** (SO9203.1/1A). *The facility was closed by the LMS in 1933.*

P.110 **Brimscombe** (SO8702.1/1B). *Locomotive servicing continued until March 1965.*

P.111 **Chalford** (SO9002.1/1A). *The shed closed in January 1916 and it was utilized as a servicing area from that date.*

P.112 **Nailsworth** (SO8400.1/F1). *The servicing facility probably closed in December 1957.*

P.114 **Gloucester (MR)** (SO8318.2/1A). *The roundhouse closed in April 1894.*

P.116 **Moreton in Marsh** (SP2032.1/F1). *The facility was closed in 1916.*

P.116 **Tetbury** (ST8993.1/1A). *The shed closed to steam in February 1966.*

BUCKINGHAMSHIRE

P.120 **Wolverton Works** (SP8141.4/1A). *The shed was closed to steam in February 1966.*

BEDFORDSHIRE

P.122 **Bedford** (TL0449.2/1B). *Steam locomotives were serviced at the shed until August 1965.*

ESSEX

P.124 **Clacton** (TL1715.2/2A). *The facilities included a turntable and the depot was closed in January 1961.*

P.126 **Loughton** (TQ4295.1/F1). *The facility was opened at some time prior to 1872 and the turntable was closed by BR in September 1949.*

P.127 **Romford** (TQ5188.1/F1). *The facility was opened in 1839 and was closed by BR in March 1960.*

P.127 **Shenfield** (TQ6194.1/F1). *The facility was opened in 1887 and was closed by BR at some time after 1956.*

P.127 **Southminster** (TQ9699.1/1A). *The shed was closed in September 1956.*

P.128 **Witham** (TL8215.1/F1). *The facility was opened in 1848. The turntable was closed by BR in 1958 and the servicing area was totally closed in September 1962.*

NORFOLK

P.129 **Forncett** (TM1793.1/F1). *The turntable remained open until 1932.*

P.131 **South Lynn** (TF6117.1/1B). *The duplicate shed building was constructed in 1895 and locomotive servicing continued until May 1961.*

P.132 **Fakenham West** (TF9129.1/1A). *The shed was closed in July 1893 and the turntable in December 1936.*

P.132 **Heacham** (TF6637.1/F1). *The turntable was opened in 1866 and closed at some time after 1939.*

SUFFOLK

P.136 **Long Melford** (TL8645.1/F1). *The facility included a turntable which was closed at some point between 1932 and 1967.*

P.138 **Felixstowe Beach** (TM2934.1/1A). *The shed was closed by the LNER in February 1937.*

P.139 **Ipswich Docks** (TM1643.2/1A). *The shed was closed in January 1955.*

P.138 **Sudbury** (TM8741.1/1A). *The shed was closed by BR in July 1956 and the servicing area (TM8741.1/F1) in October 1959.*

CAMBRIDGESHIRE

P.140 **Ely**. *The first shed (TL5479.1/1A) closed in November 1866 and its successor (TL5479.1/2A) before August 1954. The servicing point (TL5479.1/F1) was closed by BR in June 1962.*

P.141 **Cambridge (GNR)** (TL4656.2/1A). *The shed yard was utilized for locomotive servicing until January 1931.*

P.141 **St.Ives** (TL3171.1/F1). *The facility opened in 1870.*

SHROPSHIRE

P.151 **Trench** (SJ6812.1/1A). *The shed was opened at some point between 1881 and 1926 and may have officially lasted until closed by BR in November 1950.*

HUNTINGDON

P.152 **Huntingdon East** (TL2371.1/1A). *The locomotives were serviced at a turntable and siding from 1885 until the shed opened in 1903. The depot was closed by BR in June 1959.*

WARWICKSHIRE

P.154 **Rugby.** *The 2-road MCR shed (SP5076.1/2A) was closed by the MR in April 1909 and the 4-road MCR depot (SP5076.1/1A) in December 1922.*

*There were BR stabling points at **Arley Colliery**, **Birch Coppice Colliery** and a 1TS shed at **Haunchwood Colliery**.*

NORTHAMPTONSHIRE

P.157 **Blisworth** (SP7154.1/1A). *Servicing continued until November 1955.*
P.159 **Peterborough Station** (TL1898.1/1A). *The servicing of locomotives ceased in January 1965.*

WEST MIDLANDS

P.161 **Snow Hill.** *The first facility, SP0687.1/F1, was opened in 1852 and closed in 1911. The second servicing area, SP0687.2/F1, closed in 1960.*
P.164 **Albion** (SO9890.1/F1). *Opened prior to 1935.*

MONMOUTHSHIRE

P.169 **Monmouth Troy** (SO5011.1/1A). *The shed closed between May 1874 and August 1876.*
P.169 **Pontypool Road** (ST2999.2/1A). *The building was opened in 1879.*

Additional Depot ...

USK

Site ST3701.1; On the south side of Usk Station.
Usk (GWR) ST3701.1/1A

A 1TS through road shed, it was located at ST37540124 and was opened in 1856. Details of the facilities are not known. It was closed and demolished at some point between 1881 and 1899.

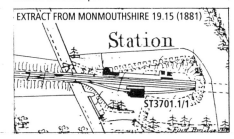

EXTRACT FROM MONMOUTHSHIRE 19.15 (1881)

SOUTH WALES

P.173 **Caerphilly.** *A facility was established in the works, east of the station, in 1901, and consisted of a turntable at the west end of the site and a locomotive siding at the east. This may have been ST1586.1/F1 or an additional servicing area, or a replacement.*
P.173 **Coity Junction** (SS9080.2/1A). *Servicing ceased in 1922.*
P.175 **Neath.** *The Swansea & Neath Railway opened a shed here in 1851(SS7497.0/2A). It was closed in 1881. No further details are known.*
P.176 **Glyncorrwg** (SS8799.1/1A). *The servicing of steam locomotives ceased in June 1965.*
P.183 **Cardiff East Dock** (ST1974.2/3A). *The shed closed in March 1958 and re-opened in September 1962.*

*The Neath & Brecon Railway Works at **Machen** may have been used as an engine shed until August 1922.*

CARDIGANSHIRE

Additional Depot ...

ABERYSTWYTH

Site SN5881.1; On the west side of the line, at the south end of Aberystwyth Station.
Aberystwyth (M&MR) SN5881.1/2A

A corrugated iron 1TS dead ended shed with a corrugated iron dutch barn roof it was located at SN58738128 and was opened by the Manchester & Milford Railway. Details of the facilities and opening date are not known but it was utilized by the GWR as a repair shop in 1923, closing in 1925. The building was demolished to facilitate construction of the ramped coal stage.

(For map extract please refer to P.187)

The fear of the Lord is the beginning of knowledge; fools despise wisdom and instruction. **Proverbs 1.7**

Bangor saw three engine sheds over the years, the first two dating from 1848 (SH5771.0/1A) and 1859 (SH5771.0/2A). The last, a 6TS structure was opened by the L&NWR in 1884.
The northlight pattern depot was re-roofed and shortened in 1957/8 and is seen here in its final state (as SH5771.1/1B) in May 1961. The shed closed in June 1964 but, being virtually a new building, it survived in industrial use until at least 1998. *WT Stubbs Collection*

UPDATE

As additional information comes to hand it will be published in

RAILWAY ·WORLD·

The new details will be printed in the same format as this publication and, in order to keep this volume up to date, readers are invited to cut out or photocopy the appropriate section and paste it on to this and subsequent pages;